W9-BCS-412
science

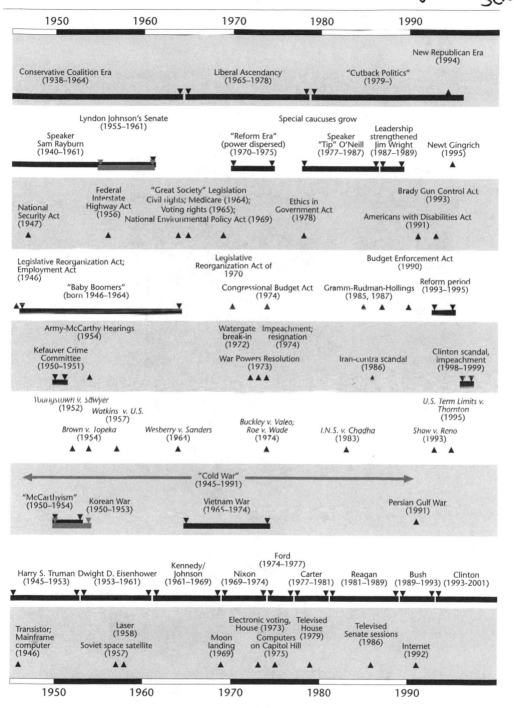

1950   1960   1970   1980   1990

New Republican Era
(1994)

Conservative Coalition Era
(1938–1964)

Liberal Ascendancy
(1965–1978)

"Cutback Politics"
(1979–)

Lyndon Johnson's Senate
(1955–1961)

Special caucuses grow

Leadership
strengthened
Jim Wright
(1987–1989)

Speaker
Sam Rayburn
(1940–1961)

"Reform Era"
(power dispersed)
(1970–1975)

Speaker
"Tip" O'Neill
(1977–1987)

Newt Gingrich
(1995)

Federal
Interstate
Highway Act
(1956)

"Great Society" Legislation
Civil rights; Medicare (1964);
Voting rights (1965);
National Environmental Policy Act (1969)

Ethics in
Government Act
(1978)

Brady Gun Control Act
(1993)

National
Security Act
(1947)

Americans with Disabilities Act
(1991)

Legislative Reorganization Act;
Employment Act
(1946)

Legislative
Reorganization Act of
1970

Budget Enforcement Act
(1990)

"Baby Boomers"
(born 1946–1964)

Congressional Budget Act
(1974)

Gramm-Rudman-Hollings
(1985, 1987)

Reform period
(1993–1995)

Army-McCarthy Hearings
(1954)

Watergate
break-in
(1972)

Impeachment;
resignation
(1974)

Kefauver Crime
Committee
(1950–1951)

War Powers Resolution
(1973)

Iran-contra scandal
(1986)

Clinton scandal,
impeachment
(1998–1999)

Youngstown v. Sawyer
(1952)

Watkins v. U.S.
(1957)

U.S. Term Limits v.
Thornton
(1995)

Brown v. Topeka
(1954)

Wesberry v. Sanders
(1964)

Buckley v. Valeo;
Roe v. Wade
(1974)

I.N.S. v. Chadha
(1983)

Shaw v. Reno
(1993)

"Cold War"
(1945–1991)

"McCarthyism"
(1950–1954)

Korean War
(1950–1953)

Vietnam War
(1965–1974)

Persian Gulf War
(1991)

Ford
(1974–1977)

Kennedy/
Johnson
(1961–1969)

Harry S. Truman
(1945–1953)

Dwight D. Eisenhower
(1953–1961)

Nixon
(1969–1974)

Carter
(1977–1981)

Reagan
(1981–1989)

Bush
(1989–1993)

Clinton
(1993-2001)

Transistor;
Mainframe
computer
(1946)

Laser
(1958)

Soviet space satellite
(1957)

Electronic voting,
House (1973)

Televised
House
(1979)

Televised
Senate sessions
(1986)

Moon
landing
(1969)

Computers
on Capitol Hill
(1975)

Internet
(1992)

1950   1960   1970   1980   1990

Classic moment in congressional politics. Lyndon B. Johnson, the persuasive Senate majority leader (1955–1961), gives "The Treatment" to a hapless Sen. Theodore Francis Green, D-R.I.

Congress
and Its Members

Seventh Edition

Roger H. Davidson
University of Maryland

Walter J. Oleszek
Congressional Research Service

CQ PRESS

A Division of Congressional Quarterly Inc.
Washington, D.C.

CQ Press
A Division of Congressional Quarterly Inc.
1414 22nd Street, N.W.
Washington, D.C. 20037

(202) 822-1475; (800) 638-1710

http://books.cq.com

Copyright © 2000 Congressional Quarterly Inc.

All rights reserved. No part of this publication may be reproduced or transmitted in any form or by any means, electronic or mechanical, including photocopy, recording, or any information storage and retrieval system, without permission in writing from the publisher.

Printed in the United States of America

Photo credits: Agence France-Presse, 380 (bottom); AP/Wide World, 162 (top); Architect of the Capitol, 226; Congressional Quarterly file photo, 42 (bottom), 126 (middle); Scott J. Ferrell, Congressional Quarterly, 162 (middle), 196 (top), 354 (bottom); Douglas Graham, Congressional Quarterly, 162 (bottom), 284 (top and middle), 334 (top left), 354 (top), 380 (top); R. Michael Jenkins, Congressional Quarterly, 196 (bottom), 310 (top), 334 (bottom); Deborah Kalb, Congressional Quarterly, 42 (top); Dave Kaplan, Congressional Quarterly, 126 (top); Library of Congress, 12; *New York Times,* frontispiece, 126 (bottom), 406; Reuters, 2 (bottom), 88 (top and bottom), 284 (bottom), 310 (bottom), 334 (top right and middle); *U.S. News & World Report,* 256; *Washington Post,* 2 (top).

Acknowledgments: Letter to Sen. William S. Cohen (p. 210) reprinted by permission of Senator Cohen. Figure 11-2 reprinted from *The Politics of Presidential Appointments* by G. Calvin Mackenzie, © 1981, with the permission of The Free Press, a division of Simon & Schuster.

Cover design: Debra Naylor

Library of Congress Cataloging-in-Publication Data

Davidson, Roger H.
    Congress and its members / Roger H. Davidson, Walter J. Oleszek.—
    7th ed.
      p.   cm.
    Includes bibliographical references and index.
    ISBN 1-56802-519-X. — ISBN 1-56802-433-9 (pbk.)
      1. United States. Congress. 2. Legislators—United States.
I. Oleszek, Walter J.   II. Title.
JK1021.D38   1999
328.73—dc21   99-36620

For Nancy; Douglas, Victoria, Elizabeth, and Thomas;
Chris, Theo, and Emily
R.H.D.

For Janet, Mark, and Eric
W.J.O.

Contents

Part 3   A Deliberative Assembly of One Nation   161

6   Leaders and Parties in Congress   163

7   Committees: Workshops of Congress   197

8   Congressional Rules and Procedures   227

9   Decision Making in Congress   257

Part 4 Policy Making and Change in the Two Congresses 283

Preface

As authors of the seventh edition of a book that first appeared in 1981, we are perforce believers in the maxim that in politics six months is a long time and four years practically a lifetime. Recent events surely bear out this wisdom.

Exhibit A is President Bill Clinton's roller-coaster ride with Congress and the American people. Clinton's legislative record in his first two years (1993–1994) was the most successful of any president since Lyndon B. Johnson in the 1960s. In 1995, after the Republicans captured Congress, it was the least successful in the modern era. The following year, as the Republican "revolution" wore out its welcome with the public, Clinton's fortunes rebounded. In mid-1997 President Clinton enjoyed job ratings twice as high as those of Congress. In 1998 the scandal surrounding the president's relationship with Monica Lewinsky dominated the political news and ended with Clinton's impeachment by the House and subsequent acquittal by the Senate. Although many commentators pronounced the end of the Clinton presidency—either before or after the impeachment—the president continued to dominate the agenda in the face of divided Republicans and to exert presidential prerogatives over foreign policymaking.

Exhibit B is the GOP majority in Congress. The Republicans' stunning, unexpected victory in 1994 won them, and their leader Newt Gingrich, control of the House after a forty-year exile in the minority. At the same time, the party recaptured control of the Senate after a lapse of eight years. The House leadership's aggressive "Contract with America" dominated their early policy agenda, though it ran into opposition from the Senate and the White House. Defying presidential vetoes, Republicans were blamed for shutting down the federal government twice during the winter of 1995–1996. From that time on their troubles mounted, and they barely escaped losing the House in the November 1998 elections. Pursuing impeachment seemed a winning issue for the GOP, but the effort not only failed to oust the president but portrayed the party as obsessed with bringing him down. Although much of their overall agenda has taken hold—even the president agreed to a balanced budget and welfare reform and conceded that "the era of big government is over"—the Republicans' assaults on specific government programs drew a mixed reception. Their House leaders were hampered by narrow majorities and internal feuding.

The fluctuating fortunes of President Clinton and the congressional Republicans remind us of the pervasive pluralism of our political system, with its diversity of viewpoints and interests. What the president and the GOP saw

as their mandates soon bumped against the Founders' intricate "auxiliary precautions" for preventing majorities from winning quick or total victories. Not the least of the system's qualities is what we call the "two Congresses" dilemma: Congress is a conduit for localized interests and concerns as well as a maker of national policy.

In this edition we discuss new developments and fresh research findings regarding nearly every aspect of Congress. The growing strength of partisanship and party leadership—perhaps the biggest Capitol Hill "story"—has now gained serious attention from analysts. We record changes in the committee system, floor procedures, and the Capitol Hill "establishment." Congress's shifting relationships with President Clinton illustrate the centrality of the White House–Capitol Hill connection and raise once again fundamental questions about the results of unified versus divided party control.

The continuing centrality of fiscal issues, even in a period of federal surpluses, dictates detailed coverage of the budget and domestic policy making. We have tried to avoid the arcane terminology of budget process specialists, preferring instead to emphasize how budget practices reflect and in turn frame political conflicts. In examining foreign and national security policies, we stress the effects upon Congress of the post–cold war world—for example, the altered international agenda and a downsized military establishment. Finally, we consider the ambivalent relationship between Congress and the American people, whose views in the 1990s veered from skepticism and distrust to acceptance, if not affection.

Amid all these legal, political, and institutional changes, there are underlying constants in Congress's character and behavior. Most important is the dual nature of Congress as a collection of career-minded politicians and a forum for shaping and refining national policy. We employ the "two Congresses" theme to explain the details of congressional life as well as the scholarly findings about legislators' behavior. Colorful personalities and practical examples illustrate the enduring topics essential for understanding Capitol Hill. We strive to describe recent events and trends precisely and perceptively; more than that, we try to place these developments in the broader historical and conceptual frameworks necessary for understanding how Congress and its members function.

For *fin de siècle* congressional scholars, these are the best of times and the worst of times. On the one hand, we have witnessed an era of astonishing change on Capitol Hill—dramatic shifts in congressional membership, partisan control, structural and procedural arrangements, and policy agenda. Once again Congress proves itself as an engine of national policy making. Yet, at the same time, opinion makers and the general public profess extreme distrust of Congress and other governmental institutions. In our judgment, and that of most careful observers, this cynicism far outruns the institution's actual defects and shortcomings—a paradox that is manifested in our new edition of *Congress and Its Members*.

This edition, like its predecessors, is addressed to general readers seeking an introduction to the modern Congress as well as to college or university students taking courses on the legislative process or national policy making. We have tried to provide our readers with the most accurate, timely, and readable information possible, along with the most important and thoughtful interpretations from scholars and practitioners alike. Although wrapped around our core theme and a number of subthemes, the book's chapters are long on analysis. For this we do not apologize. Lawmaking is a complicated business that demands special skills; those who would understand it must encounter its details and nuances. At the same time, we trust we have conveyed something of the energy and excitement of the place. After all, our journalist friends are right: Capitol Hill is the best "beat" in town.

Anyone who has prepared seven editions of a book has incurred more debts to friends and fellow scholars than could ever be recounted. Authors are primarily indebted to their readers, in this case the students and teachers at the hundreds of colleges and universities here and abroad where our book has been adopted. For this edition we were guided by the commentaries of three outstanding young scholars: Scott Adler of the University of Colorado, Richard Forgette of Miami University of Ohio, and a third, anonymous reviewer.

We acknowledge our colleagues at the Congressional Research Service: Mildred Amer, Stanley Bach, Richard Beth, Joe Cantor, Royce Crocker, Paul E. Dwyer, Louis Fisher, Gary Galemore, David Huckabee, Frederick Kaiser, Robert Keith, Johnny H. Killian, Ronald Moe, John S. Pontius, Sula P. Richardson, Richard Sachs, and Judy Schneider.

Our friends at CQ Press deserve special appreciation. Brenda Carter, director of the college division, patiently encouraged us at every step. Ann Davies, managing editor of textbooks and reference, proved once again the exceptional quality of CQ's editorial work. Barbara de Boinville and Carolyn Goldinger provided skilled and probing editorial assistance. Gwenda Larsen coordinated the entire effort and kept us to our deadlines. Talia Greenberg gave invaluable advice on photo research. Deborah Ismond fashioned fresh graphics throughout the book and implemented our concept of congressional time lines.

Our deep appreciation for our families, for their love and support, cannot be adequately expressed in words. As a measure of our affection, this edition is dedicated to them.

Roger H. Davidson, Santa Barbara
Walter J. Oleszek, Washington, D.C.
July 1999

Congress
and Its Members

Part 1

In Search of the Two Congresses

Citizen McCarthy and the "two Congresses." Carolyn McCarthy, a Democrat, prepares to greet voters and hand out leaflets to commuters at a Long Island Railroad station during her successful 1996 House campaign. As a second-termer (below), she and thirty other women representatives call upon House leaders to allow floor debate on gun-safety legislation.

1

The Two Congresses

Carolyn McCarthy waited on the platform as commuter trains pulled into the Mineola, Long Island, station on the afternoon following election day 1996. As photographers jostled for position, she greeted and thanked homebound commuters for electing her as Long Island's first-ever woman member of Congress. "Carolyn! Carolyn!" a woman shouted at McCarthy and, giving a thumbs-up sign, added, "Remember us!"[1]

Not that McCarthy or her constituents are likely to forget each other. On this very rail line, three years earlier, a gunman opened fire and killed six people, including her husband, and wounded nineteen others, including her son. (The family's home is in nearby Mineola.) The Long Island Railroad massacre transformed McCarthy into an advocate of gun control. "I chose to try to make something good come out of a horrible situation," she explained. "Most of the time, that's how an activist starts."[2] When her representative, first-termer Daniel Frisa, voted in 1996 to repeal the ban on assault weapons—a law she had lobbied for—she was so outraged that she decided to run against him.

One problem: McCarthy, like Representative Frisa, was a registered Republican. The powerful GOP organization in Nassau County spurned her candidacy. The Democrats, however, wooed her. They saw in McCarthy a chance to gain one of the seats they needed to recapture the House. Soon she was summoned to the nation's capital to meet with Democratic leader Richard A. Gephardt, D-Mo. When she told him, "Look, I'm a Republican," he was not deterred.

Thus McCarthy decided to plunge into big-time politics as a Democrat. By election day she had raised nearly $1.1 million and had spent almost all of it— half in the frantic three weeks before the balloting. She got minimal financial support from her newfound party, but its allies had plenty of resources. The AFL-CIO's $25 million nationwide barrage of attack ads in 1996 aroused GOP ire, but equally potent was the $10 million it poured into key local campaigns, headed by paid coordinators. In the Fourth District, union members contacted 2,000 union households in a "labor to neighbor" program; "all told, labor . . . distributed more than 130,000 pro-McCarthy pieces of literature and made more than 150,000 phone calls on her behalf."[3]

McCarthy had to overcome charges—voiced by her opponent and harbored by many voters—that she was just a one-issue candidate. In response, she and her allies aggressively attacked not only Representative Frisa's vote on gun control but his whole record—in Gephardt's sarcastic words, his "robot votes for the Gingrich program." In the end the Republicans retained control

of Congress. But McCarthy's sweeping triumph by 35,000 votes—57 percent of the total—was one of the biggest election night stories.

Two years later McCarthy was no longer simply a "media star." She was an incumbent defending her seat against an aggressive opponent in a fiercely competitive district. That meant she could raise the campaign funds she needed (some $800,000)—even though the state's big Democratic money (nearly $10 million) flowed into Rep. Charles Schumer's successful Senate race against Alfonse D'Amato, the Republican incumbent. It also meant that McCarthy had a record to defend. She stressed her work on gun control and teacher training and her success in snagging federal funds for a local water project. But some of her votes had alienated constituents. Conservatives were furious when she opposed a ban on late-term abortions. Liberals who resented her vote to begin the inquiry on the impeachment of President Clinton had to be reassured (by a personal message played in automated phone calls to every registered Democrat) that, yes, the president supported her reelection. Though her campaign was obscured by the Schumer–D'Amato food fight, McCarthy nonetheless prevailed by a narrow 52–47 percent margin.

McCarthy's career illustrates the themes in this book. First is the partisanship that infuses so much of today's politics—in electoral campaigns, especially in swing districts, in many statewide races, and nationally in battles over control of Congress. National political organizations, issues, and resources shape local campaigns and the way they are waged. Party organizations fueled McCarthy's decision to enter politics and her ability (and that of her opponents) to wage costly campaigns. Yet congressional politics is also rooted in local affairs—beginning in this case with a community tragedy but ever present in McCarthy's bonds with her constituents.

The Dual Nature of Congress

The contests in New York's Fourth District thus underscore the dual nature of Congress. Like all members of Congress, McCarthy inhabits two very different but closely linked worlds. On Capitol Hill she was a green, albeit highly visible, newcomer forced to master not only a new environment but a wholly new career. At the same time her constituents, whose votes brought her rare national renown, watched and judged her performance, just as they did her predecessor's. The Fourth remains a competitive district; Republican Party organizers will continue to target her. After the 1998 ballots were counted, however, the Democratic county chairman vowed, "My commitment to Carolyn McCarthy is that she will never win by such a close margin, ever again."[4] And because she resides in the nation's premier media market, her mistakes as well as her triumphs are covered in merciless detail. McCarthy's career highlights integral aspects of our national legislature—Congress as a lawmaking institution and as an assembly of local representatives. The question is how can these disparate elements be reconciled?

The answer is that there are really two Congresses. One is the Congress of textbooks, of "how a bill becomes a law." It is Congress acting as a collegial

body, performing constitutional duties and debating legislative issues. And it is an intriguing subject. To tourists and C-SPAN viewers no less than to veteran analysts, Capitol Hill is a fascinating arena where converge many of the forces of American political life—ambitious politicians, Cabinet members, lowly bureaucrats, and lobbyists both powerful and weak. The issues they voice on Capitol Hill, to invoke a time-worn sentiment, affect the well-being of us all.

This Congress is more than a collection of its members at any given time. It is a mature institution with a complex network of rules, structures, and traditions. These norms mark the boundaries of the legislative playing field and define the rules by which the game is played. Individual members generally must accept Congress on its own terms and conform to its established ways of doing things. Paradoxically, the institution at once both resists change and constantly invites change.

There is also a second Congress, which we glimpsed in New York's Fourth District, that is every bit as important as the Congress of the textbooks. This is the representative assemblage of 540 individuals (100 senators, 435 representatives, four delegates, and one resident commissioner). It comprises men and women of diverse ages, backgrounds, and routes to office. The electoral fortunes of its members depend less upon what Congress produces as an institution than upon the support and goodwill of voters hundreds or thousands of miles away. Journalist Richard Rovere once compared members of Congress with tribal leaders whose chief concern while in Washington was what was going on around the council fires back home. This analogy may be an exaggeration, but it contains an important truth: not all congressional activity takes place in Capitol Hill chambers or committee rooms.

The two Congresses are in some ways widely separated. The tight-knit, complex world of Capitol Hill is a long way from New York's Fourth District, in perspective and outlook as well as in miles. Moreover, the two Congresses are analytically distinct. Studies suggest that public officials and citizens view the twin functions of elected assemblies—lawmaking and representing—as separate, definable tasks.

Yet these two Congresses are closely bound together. What affects one sooner or later affects the other. McCarthy has fashioned her own representational style. The images she projects back home reflect what she achieves, or hopes to achieve, on Capitol Hill. In 1996 she was a party-switching independent, an amateur propelled by personal tragedy into public life; three years later she was a leader of the Democrats' gun control forces. Thus far the voters have endorsed her, but who knows what they will decide in the future?

The Historical Basis

The dual character of Congress is rooted in history. Congress's mandate to write the nation's laws is found in Article I of the Constitution, which details the powers of government as set forth by the Founders in 1787. It was no accident that the Constitution's drafters devoted the first article to the legislature nor that

here were enumerated most of the government's powers. Familiar with the British Parliament's prolonged struggles with the Crown, the Constitution's authors assumed the legislature would be the chief policy-making body and the bulwark against arbitrary executives. ("In republican government, the legislative authority necessarily predominates," observed James Madison in *The Federalist Papers*.)[5] Although in the ensuing years initiative shifted many times between the legislative and executive branches, the U.S. Congress remains virtually the only national assembly in the world that drafts in detail the laws it passes, rather than simply ratifying measures prepared by the government in power.

As a representative body, Congress must respond to the insistent demands of voters and constituents. Although not specifically spelled out in the Constitution, these duties inevitably flow from constitutional provisions for electing representatives and senators.

The House of Representatives is, and was intended to be, the most representative element of our government. Representatives are elected directly by the people for two-year terms to ensure that they do not stray too far from popular opinion. As Madison explained, the House should have "an immediate dependence on, and an intimate sympathy with, the people."[6] For most members of the House, this two-year cycle means nonstop campaigning, visiting, looking after constituents, and errand running. For a few the job is simpler than for others; yet no elected official is totally immune to electoral defeat.

The Senate originally was intended to be one step removed from popular voting to temper the House's popular passions: state legislatures selected senators. But the Founders ultimately were overruled. In 1913 the people were assured of a voice with the ratification of the Seventeenth Amendment, which provided for direct election of senators. Although elected for six-year terms, senators must stay in close touch with the electorate. Like their House colleagues, senators typically regard themselves as servants of their constituents; most have transformed their office staffs into veritable cottage industries for generating publicity and handling constituents' inquiries.

Thus the Constitution and subsequent historical developments affirm Congress's dual functions of lawmaker and representative assembly. Although the roles are tightly bound together, they nonetheless impose separate duties and functions.

Legislators' Tasks

This dualism between institutional and individual duties surfaces in legislators' daily activities and roles. As Speaker Sam Rayburn, D-Texas, once remarked: "A congressman has two constituencies—he has his constituents at home, and his colleagues here in the House. To serve his constituents at home, he must also serve his colleagues here in the House."[7]

Like most of us, senators and representatives suffer from a lack of time to accomplish what is expected of them. No problem vexes members more than that of juggling constituency and legislative tasks. Despite scheduled recesses

for constituency business (called "district work periods" by the House, "non-legislative periods" by the Senate), the pull of constituency business is relentless. The average representative spends 120 days a year in the home constituency, the average senator 80 days.[8] Even in Washington, legislative and constituency demands clash constantly. According to one study, less than 40 percent of a representative's Washington time is allotted to lawmaking duties on the floor of the House or in committee.[9]

Members of Congress, when asked to describe the functions they should perform in office, stress the twin roles of legislator and representative. Naturally, legislators vary in how they balance these roles, not to mention what time and resources they devote to them. With their longer terms, senators can display a more cyclical attention span, stressing voter outreach and fence mending during the year or so before reelection but focusing on legislative activities at other times. Yet senatorial contests normally are more competitive than House races, and many senators now run flat out for reelection all the time—like most of their House colleagues.[10]

Legislators often must choose between the demands of these two roles. A congressionally sponsored survey asked members about how they actually spent their time and what they would like to do ideally as a member of Congress. By a wide margin the senators and representatives said they would devote extra time to lawmaking and other Capitol Hill duties rather than to constituency demands.[11]

Congress's dual nature—the unresolved dichotomy between its lawmaking and representative functions—is dictated by the Constitution, validated by historical experience, and reinforced by the inclinations of voters and legislators alike. Yet Congress is literally one body, not two. The same members who shape bills in committee and vote on the floor must rush to catch planes back to their districts, where they are plunged into a different world, one of local problems and personalities. And the same candidates who must sell themselves at shopping center rallies must, in Washington, focus on baffling issues such as budget numbers or military weapons systems. The unique character of Congress arises directly from its dual role as a representative assembly and a lawmaking body.

Popular Images

The notion of the two Congresses also conforms with the perceptions of the average person. Opinion studies reveal that citizens view the Congress in Washington through lenses different from those through which they see their individual senators and representatives. Congress as an institution is seen primarily as a lawmaking body. It is judged mainly on the basis of citizens' overall attitudes about politics, policies, and the state of the union. Do people like the way things are going, or do they not? Are they optimistic or pessimistic about the nation's future? Do they subscribe to Mark Twain's cynical view that Congress is a "distinctly native criminal class"?

By contrast, citizens view their own legislators as agents of local interests. They measure these legislators by such yardsticks as service to the district, communication with constituents, and "home style"—that is, the way the officeholder deals with the home folks. In judging their senators or representative, voters are likely to ponder questions such as these: Do I trust the legislator? Does the legislator communicate well with the state (or district) by answering mail promptly and offering timely help to constituents? Does the legislator listen to the state (or district) and its concerns?[12]

The public's divergent expectations of Congress and its members often send conflicting signals to senators and representatives. Congress as a whole is judged by policies and results, however vaguely these are perceived by voters. Individual legislators are more apt to be elected, and returned to office, because of personal qualities and constituent service. To many legislators, this incongruity dictates a strategy of opening as much space as possible between themselves and "those other politicians" back in Washington—including their party's leaders. Carolyn McCarthy, remember, initially sold herself as a distant outsider battling an entrenched insider.

Back to Burke

On November 3, 1774, in Bristol, England, the British statesman and philosopher Edmund Burke set forth for his constituents the dual character of a national legislature. The constituent-oriented parliament, or Congress, he described as

a Congress of ambassadors from different and hostile interests, which interests each must maintain, as an agent and advocate, against other agents and advocates.

The parliament of substantive lawmaking he portrayed in different terms:

a deliberative assembly of one nation, with one interest, that of the whole—where not local purposes, not local prejudices, ought to guide, but the general good, resulting from the general reason of the whole.[13]

Burke himself preferred the second concept and did not hesitate to let his voters know it; he would give local opinion a hearing, but his judgment and conscience would prevail in all cases. "Your faithful friend, your devoted servant, I shall be to the end of my life," he declared; "flatterer you do not wish for."[14]

Burke's Bristol speech is an enduring statement of the dilemma confronting members of representative assemblies. Burke was an inspired lawmaker. (He even sympathized with the cause of the American colonists.) But, as we might say today, he suffered from an inept "home style." His candor earned him no thanks from his constituents, who turned him out of office at the first opportunity.

Burke's dilemma applies equally on this side of the Atlantic. From colonial times to the present, this country's voters have tended to prefer their lawmakers to be delegates, who listen carefully to constituents and follow their guidance. During an encounter in Borger, Texas, an irate Baptist minister shouted at then-representative Bill Sarpalius, D-Texas, "We didn't send you to Washington to make intelligent decisions. We sent you to represent us."[15] Sarpalius lost that argument: he was defeated in 1994. The authors of the Constitution expected such intimate bonds between voters and lawmakers (at least in the House), indeed ensuring them by providing frequent elections.

But that is by no means the whole story. We still extol Burke's idea that legislators are trustees of the nation's common good. In a 1995 decision Supreme Court justice John Paul Stevens noted that, once elected, members of Congress become "servants of the people of the United States. They are not merely delegates appointed by separate, sovereign states; they occupy offices that are integral and essential components of a single national Government."[16]

Nor must we assume that legislators always engage in self-interested bidding for local constituents' votes. Politicians are (like the rest of us) self-interested, and winning elections is the prerequisite for achieving long-range political goals. And, as we will see, politicians harbor a range of ultimate goals, the most prominent of which is promoting what they view as the public interest. It is perfectly reasonable, therefore, to assume that elected officials "make an honest effort to achieve good public policy."[17]

Burke posed the tension between the two Congresses so vividly that we have adopted his language to describe the conceptual distinction that forms the crux of this book. From Burke, we have also drawn the titles for Part 2, "A Congress of Ambassadors," and Part 3, "A Deliberative Assembly of One Nation." Every legislator sooner or later must come to terms with Burke's dichotomous Congress; as citizens and voters you will have to form your own answers.

Divergent Views of Congress

Congress has been the subject of a bewildering array of books, monographs, and articles. Many of its features make Congress a favorite object of scholarly scrutiny. It is open and accessible. Its work can be measured by statistical indicators (floor votes, for example) that permit elaborate comparative analyses. And Congress is, above all, a fascinating place—the very best site from which to view the varied actors in the American political drama. Many of these same features attract journalists and interpretive reporters to Congress.

Writers of an interpretive book on the U.S. Congress thus can draw on many sources, an embarrassment of riches. Studies of Congress constitute a vast body of political literature. This is a mixed blessing because we have to integrate this information into something resembling a coherent whole. Moreover, much of the writing is highly specialized, technical, or theoretical; we have tried to put such material into perspective, make it understandable to interested nonspecialists, and use illustrative examples wherever possible.

A gaping chasm exists between this rich literature and the caricature of Congress often prevalent in our popular culture. Pundits and humorists from Mark Twain and Will Rogers to Jay Leno and David Letterman have found Congress an inexhaustible source of raw material. The other branches of government have nothing quite like the cartoon image of lawmakers as corrupt, pompous windbags. Citizens tend to share this disdain toward the legislative branch—especially at moments of furor over, say, congressional pay raises or ethics scandals or the rank partisanship surrounding the House's impeachment of President Clinton.

The views of Congress conveyed in the media are scarcely more flattering than those of the public. Journalistic hit-and-run specialists, especially news magazines, editorial writers, and talk show hosts, perpetuate a cartoonish stereotype: an irresponsible and somewhat sleazy gang resembling Woodrow Wilson's caustic description of the House as "a disintegrated mass of jarring elements."[18] Legislators in their home states or districts often contribute to Congress's poor image by portraying themselves as escapees from the funny farm on Capitol Hill. As Richard F. Fenno Jr. puts it, they "run for Congress by running against Congress."[19]

Citizens' ambivalence toward the popular branch of government—which, by the way, goes back to the beginnings of the Republic—tells us something of the milieu in which public policy is made. To comprehend how the two Congresses function—both the institution and individual members—we must move beyond popular stereotypes and examine the complex realities. This book is intended to fill in the details left unexamined in popular accounts. We believe we know our subject well enough to appreciate Congress's foibles and understand why it works the way it does. Yet we try to maintain a professional—yes, scholarly—distance from it.

According to an old saying, two things should never be viewed up close: making sausage and making laws. Despite this warning, we urge readers to take a good look and form their own opinions about Congress's effectiveness. Some may recoil from what they discover. Numerous flaws can be identified in members' personal or public behavior, in their priorities (incentive structures), and in their lawmaking practices. But careful observers also will discover much behavior in Congress that is purposeful and principled, many policies that are reasonable and workable. We invite students and colleagues to examine with us what Congress has done thus far and consider what prospects lie ahead.

"Uncle Joe." Speaker Joseph G. Cannon (1903–1911), a Republican stalwart from Illinois, ruled the House until a coalition of Democrats and Progressive Republicans curtailed his powers in the historic revolt of 1910.

2

Evolution of the Modern Congress

The first Congress met in New York City, the seat of government, in the spring of 1789. Business was delayed until a majority of members arrived to make a quorum. On April 1 the thirtieth of the fifty-nine elected representatives reached New York; Frederick A. C. Muhlenberg of Pennsylvania promptly was chosen Speaker of the House. Five days later the Senate achieved its quorum, although its presiding officer, Vice President John Adams, did not arrive for another two weeks.

New York City was then a bustling port on the southern tip of Manhattan Island. Congress met in Federal Hall at the corner of Broad and Wall Streets. The House occupied a large chamber on the first floor and the Senate a more intimate chamber upstairs. The new chief executive, George Washington, was still en route from his home at Mount Vernon, his trip having turned into a triumphal procession with crowds and celebrations at every stop. To most of his countrymen, Washington—austere, dignified, the epitome of propriety—embodied a government that was otherwise little more than a plan on paper.

The two houses of Congress, headstrong even then, did not wait for Washington's arrival. The House began debating tariffs, a perennially popular legislative topic. Upstairs in the Senate, Vice President Adams, a brilliant but self-important man, needled his colleagues to decide upon proper titles for addressing the president and himself. Adams was dubbed "His Rotundity" by a colleague who thought the whole discussion absurd.

On inaugural day, April 30, Adams was still worrying about how to address the president. The issue was discarded when the representatives, led by Speaker Muhlenberg, burst into the Senate chamber and seated themselves. Meanwhile, a special committee was dispatched to escort Washington to the chamber for the ceremony. The swearing-in was conducted on an outside balcony in front of thousands of assembled citizens. The nervous Washington haltingly read his speech. Then everyone adjourned to St. Paul's Chapel for a special prayer service. Thus the U.S. Congress became part of a functioning government.[1]

Antecedents of Congress

The legislative branch of the new government was untried and unknown, groping for procedures and precedents. And yet it grew out of a rich history of development—stretching back more than five hundred years in Great Britain,

13

no less than a century and a half in North America. If the architects of the Constitution of 1787 were unsure how well their new design would work, they had firm ideas about what they intended.

The English Heritage

From the time of the English king Edward the Confessor in the eleventh century, the central problem of political theory and practice was the relationship of the Crown to its subjects. Out of prolonged struggles, a strong, representative parliament emerged that rivaled and eventually eclipsed the power of the Crown. The evolution of representative institutions on a national scale began in medieval Europe. Monarchs gained power over large territories where inhabitants were divided into social groupings—among them the nobility, clergy, landed gentry, and town officials. The monarchs brought together leaders of these groupings, or estates of the realm, not to create representative government but to fill the royal coffers. As Charles A. Beard and John Lewis observed, "Even the most despotic medieval monarch could not tax and exploit his subjects without limits; as a matter of expediency, he had also to consider ways and means."[2]

These groups —parliaments, they came to be called—evolved over the centuries into the representative assemblies we know today. Four distinct stages of their development have been identified. At first the parliaments, representing the various estates, met to vote taxes for the royal treasury, engaging in very little discussion. Next, these tax-voting bodies evolved into lawmaking bodies that presented the king with grievances for redress. Third, by a gradual process that culminated in the revolutions of the seventeenth and eighteenth centuries, parliaments wrested lawmaking and tax-voting power from the king, turning themselves into truly sovereign bodies. In the nineteenth century, finally, parliamentary representation extended beyond the older privileged groups to embrace the masses, eventually every man and woman.[3]

By the time the New World colonies were founded in the 1600s, the struggle for parliamentary rights was well advanced into the third stage, at least in England. Bloody conflicts, culminating in the beheading of Charles I in 1649 and the dethroning of James II in 1688 (the "Glorious Revolution"), established parliamentary influence over the Crown. Out of such struggles flowed a remarkable body of political and philosophic writings. By the eighteenth century, works by James Harrington (1611–1677), John Locke (1632–1704), and others were the common heritage of educated people—including the leaders of the American Revolution.

The Colonial Experience

This tradition of representative government migrated to the New World. As early as 1619 the thousand or so Virginia colonists elected twenty-two delegates, or burgesses, to a General Assembly. In 1630 the Massachusetts Bay Company established itself as the governing body for the Bay Colony, subject

to annual elections. The other colonies, some of them virtually self-governing, followed suit.

Representative government took firm root in the colonies. The broad expanse of ocean shielding America fostered self-reliance and autonomy on the part of colonial assemblies. Claiming prerogatives similar to those of the British House of Commons, these assemblies exercised the full range of law-making powers—levying taxes, issuing money, and providing for colonial defense. Legislation could be vetoed by colonial governors (appointed by the Crown in the eight royal colonies), but the governors, cut off from the home government and depending on local assemblies for revenues and even for their own salaries, usually preferred to reach agreement with the locals. Royal vetoes could emanate from London, but these took time and were infrequent.[4]

Other elements nourished the tree of liberty. Many of the colonists were free spirits, dissidents set on resisting all authority, especially that of the Crown. Readily available land, harsh frontier life, and—by the eighteenth century—a robust economy fed the colonists' self-confidence. The town meeting form of government in New England and the separatists' church assemblies helped cultivate habits of self-government. Newspapers, unfettered by royal licenses or government taxes, stimulated lively exchanges of opinions.

When Britain decided in the 1760s to tighten its rein upon the American colonies, the restraint was met, not surprisingly, with stubborn opposition. Did not the colonists enjoy the same rights as Englishmen? Were not the colonial assemblies the legitimate governments, deriving their authority from popular elections? As parliamentary enactments grew increasingly unpopular, along with the governors who tried to enforce them, the locally based colonial legislatures took up the cause of their constituents.

The colonists especially resented the Stamp Act of 1765 (later repealed) and the import duties imposed in 1767. From these inflated customs receipts the home government began paying the salaries of royal governors and other officials, thus freeing those officials from the grasp of colonial assemblies. The crisis worsened in the winter of 1773–1774, when a group of colonists staged a revolt, the now famous Boston Tea Party, to protest the Tea Act. In retaliation, the House of Commons closed the port of Boston and passed a series of "Intolerable Acts," further tightening royal control.

National representative assemblies in America were born on September 5, 1774, when the First Continental Congress convened in Philadelphia. Every colony except Georgia sent delegates, a varied group that included peaceable loyalists, moderates like John Dickinson, and firebrands like Samuel Adams and Paul Revere. Gradually anti-British sentiment congealed, and the Congress passed a series of declarations and resolutions (each colony casting one vote) amounting to a declaration of war against the mother country.[5] After the Congress adjourned on October 22, King George III declared that the colonies were "now in a state of rebellion; blows must decide whether they are to be subject to this country or independent."[6]

If the First Continental Congress gave colonists a taste of collective decision making, the Second Continental Congress proclaimed their independence from Britain. When this body convened on May 10, 1775, many still thought war might be avoided. A petition to King George asking for "happy and permanent reconciliation" was even approved. The British responded by proclaiming a state of rebellion and launching efforts to crush it. Sentiment in the colonies swung increasingly toward independence, and by the middle of 1776 the Congress was debating Thomas Jefferson's draft resolution that "these United Colonies are, and of right ought to be, free and independent states."[7]

The two Continental Congresses gave birth to national politics in this country. Riding the wave of patriotism unleashed by the British indignities of 1773–1774, the Congresses succeeded in pushing the sentiments of leaders and the general public toward confrontation and away from accommodation with the mother country. They did so by defining issues one by one and by reaching compromises acceptable to both moderates and radicals—no small accomplishment. Shared legislative experience, in other words, moved the delegates to the threshold of independence. Their achievement was all the more remarkable in light of what historian Jack Rakove describes as the "peculiar status" of the Continental Congress, "an extra-legal body whose authority would obviously depend on its ability to maintain a broad range of support."[8]

More than five years of bloody conflict ensued before the colonies won their independence. Meanwhile, the colonies hastened to form new governments and draft constitutions. Unlike the English constitution, these charters were written documents. All included some sort of bill of rights and all paid tribute to the doctrine of separating powers among legislative, executive, and judicial branches of government. Equal branches of government were not created, however. Nearly all the constitutions gave the bulk of powers to their legislatures. Earlier conflicts with the Crown and the royal governors had instilled in the colonists a fear of executive authority. "In actual operation," a historian wrote, "these first state constitutions produced what was tantamount to legislative omnipotence."[9]

The national government was likewise, as James Sterling Young puts it, "born with a legislative body and no head."[10] Strictly speaking, no national executive existed between 1776 and 1789—the years of the Revolutionary War and the Articles of Confederation (adopted in 1781). On its own, the Congress struggled to wage war against the world's most powerful nation, enlist diplomatic allies, and manage internal affairs. As the war progressed and legislative direction proved unwieldy, the Congress tended to delegate authority to its own committees and to permanent (executive) agencies. Strictly military affairs were placed in the hands of a designated leader: George Washington, who at the war's end returned his commission to Congress in a public ceremony. Considering the obstacles it faced, congressional government was by no means a failure. Yet the mounting inability of all-powerful legislative bodies, state and national, to deal with postwar problems spurred demands for change.

At the state level, Massachusetts and New York rewrote their constitutions, adding provisions for potentially strong executives. At the national level, the Confederation's frailty led many to advocate a more "energetic" government—one with enough authority to implement laws, control currency, levy taxes, dispose of war debts, and, if necessary, put down rebellion. Legislative prerogatives, it was argued, should be counterbalanced with a vigorous, independent executive.

In this spirit, delegates from the states convened in Philadelphia on May 25, 1787, intending to strengthen the Articles of Confederation. Instead, they drew up an entirely new governmental charter.

Congress in the Constitution

The structure and powers of Congress formed the very core of the Constitutional Convention's deliberations. On these questions, the fifty-five delegates at the Philadelphia convention were divided, and more than three months passed before they completed their work. A tripartite governmental system was outlined, with Congress named first in the Constitution. The plan, agreed upon and signed September 17, 1787, was a bundle of compromises. Nationalist and states' rights interests, large states and small ones, northern states and southern had to be placated. The result was a singular blend of national and federal features based on republican principles of representation and limited government. The Constitution served the nationalists' goal of an energetic central government that could function independently of the states. It also conceded the states' rights principle of limited powers shared by the various branches.

Powers of Congress

The federal government's powers are shared by three branches: legislative, executive, and judicial. Although considered one of the Constitution's most innovative features, "separation of powers" arose naturally from English and colonial experience, which argued for dispersing governmental functions. It was advocated by philosophers Harrington, Locke, and the baron de Montesquieu. Many Americans regarded as a mistake the failure of the Articles of Confederation to separate these functions.

Legislators are accorded latitude in performing their duties. To prevent intimidation, they cannot be arrested during sessions or while traveling to and from sessions (except for treason, felony, or breach of the peace). In speech and debate, "they shall not be questioned in any other place" (Article I, Section 6). They have unfettered authority to organize the chambers as they see fit.

Despite their worries over all-powerful legislatures, the Founders laid down an expansive mandate for the new Congress. Mindful of the achievements of New World assemblies, not to mention the British Parliament's agelong struggles with the Crown, they naturally viewed the legislature as the chief repository of governmental powers. Locke had observed that "the leg-

islative is not only the supreme power, but is sacred and unalterable in the hands where the community have placed it."[11] Locke's doctrine found expression in Article I, Section 8, which enumerates Congress's breathtaking array of powers. Here virtually the entire scope of governmental authority as the eighteenth-century Founders understood it is spelled out. No one reading this portion of the Constitution can fail to be impressed with the Founders' vision of a vigorous legislature as the engine of an energetic government.

Raising and spending money for governmental purposes lies at the heart of Congress's prerogatives. The "power of the purse" was the lever by which parliaments historically gained bargaining advantages over kings and queens. The Constitution's authors, well aware of this, gave Congress full power of the purse. There are two components of this power: taxing and spending.

Financing the government is carried out under a broad mandate in Article I, Section 8: "The Congress shall have power to lay and collect taxes, duties, imposts and excises, to pay the debts and provide for the common defense and general welfare of the United States." Although this wording covered almost all known forms of taxing, there were limitations: taxes had to be uniform throughout the country; duties were prohibited on goods traveling between states; and "capitation . . . or other direct" taxes were prohibited, unless levied according to population (Article I, Section 9). This last provision proved troublesome, especially when the Supreme Court held in 1895 (*Pollock v. Farmers' Loan and Trust Co.*) that it applied to taxes on incomes. To overcome this confusion, the Sixteenth Amendment, ratified eighteen years later, explicitly conferred the power to levy income taxes.

Congressional power over government spending is no less sweeping than revenue power. Congress is to provide for the "common defense and general welfare" of the country (Article I, Section 8). Furthermore, "No money shall be drawn from the Treasury, but in consequence of appropriations made by law" (Article I, Section 9). This provision is one of the legislature's most potent weapons in overseeing the executive branch.

Although the three branches presumably are coequal, the legislature takes the lead in formulating the structure and duties of the other two. The Constitution mentions executive departments and officers, but it does not specify their structure or duties, aside from those of the president. Thus the design of the executive branch, including cabinet departments and other agencies, is spelled out in laws passed by Congress and signed by the president. The judiciary, too, is largely a creation of statutes. It consists of a Supreme Court and "such inferior courts as the Congress may from time to time ordain and establish" (Article III, Section 1). Although the courts' jurisdiction is delineated, the Supreme Court's appellate jurisdiction is subject to "such exceptions" and "such regulations as the Congress shall make" (Article III, Section 2).

Congress possesses potentially broad powers to promote the nation's economic well-being and political security. It has the power to regulate interstate and foreign commerce—which it has used to regulate not only trade but also

transportation, communications, and such disparate subjects as labor practices, civil rights, and crime. This power is not unlimited and historically has been legally and politically contentious (see Chapter 13). Congress may also coin money, incur debts, establish post offices, build post roads, issue patents and copyrights, provide for a militia, and call forth the militia to repel invasions or suppress rebellions.

Congress is a full partner in foreign relations with its power to declare war, ratify treaties, raise and support armies, provide and maintain a navy, and make rules governing the military forces. Finally, Congress is vested with the power "to make all laws which shall be necessary and proper for carrying into execution the foregoing powers" (Article I, Section 8). This "elastic clause," probably added to give Congress the means to implement its enumerated powers, has provoked far-reaching debates over the scope and reach of governmental activity.

Limits on Legislative Power

Congress's enumerated powers—those "herein granted"—are not boundless. The very act of listing the powers was intended to limit government, for by implication those powers that are not listed are prohibited. The Tenth Amendment reserves to the states or to the people all those powers neither explicitly delegated nor prohibited by the Constitution. This guarantee is a rallying point for those who take exception to particular federal policies or who wish broadly to curtail federal powers.

Eight specific limitations on Congress's powers are noted in Article I, Section 9. The most important bans are against bills of attainder, which pronounce a particular individual guilty of a crime without trial or conviction and impose a sentence, and ex post facto laws, which make an action a crime after it has been committed or otherwise alter the legal consequences of some past action. Bills of attainder and ex post facto laws are traditional tools of authoritarian regimes. Congress's enumerated powers are also limited in matters such as the slave trade, taxation, appropriations, and titles of nobility.

The original Constitution contained no bill of rights or list of guarantees for citizens or states. Pressed by opponents during the ratification debate, supporters of the Constitution promised early enactment of amendments to remedy this omission. The resulting ten amendments, drawn up by the first Congress and ratified December 15, 1791, are a basic charter of liberties that limits the reach of government. The First Amendment prohibits Congress from establishing a national religion, preventing the free exercise of religion, or abridging the freedoms of speech, press, peaceable assembly, and petition. Other amendments secure the rights of personal property and fair trial and prohibit arbitrary arrest, questioning, or punishment.

Rights not enumerated in the Bill of Rights are not necessarily denied. In fact, subsequent amendments, legislative enactments, and judicial rulings have enlarged citizens' rights to include the rights of citizenship, of privacy, of vot-

ing, and of "equal protection of the laws." Initially, the Bill of Rights was held to limit only the national government, but the Fourteenth Amendment, ratified in 1868, prohibits states from impairing citizens' "privileges and immunities," depriving them of life, liberty, or property without "due process of law," and denying anyone "equal protection of the laws." At first, courts held that these clauses mainly covered economic rights. Beginning in 1925 (*Gitlow v. New York*), however, the Supreme Court began to incorporate Bill of Rights guarantees under the "due process" clause. Today almost every portion of the Bill of Rights applies to the states as well as to the federal government.

Separate Branches, Shared Powers

The Constitution not only delineates Congress's powers but also distinguishes them from those of the other two branches. For all practical purposes, senators and representatives, while in office, are prohibited from serving in other federal posts; those who serve in such posts are in turn forbidden from serving in Congress (Article I, Section 6). This restriction forecloses any form of parliamentary government, in which leading members of the dominant parliamentary party or coalition form a cabinet to direct the ministries and other executive agencies.

Legislative Interdependence. Because the branches are separated, some people presume that the powers they exert should also be isolated, like so many bottles of inert chemicals on a shelf. In practice, however, governmental powers are interwoven, even if the branches are separate. James Madison explained that the Constitution created not a system of separate institutions performing separate functions but separate institutions that share functions so that "these departments be so far connected and blended as to give each a constitutional control over the others."[12]

Congress cannot act alone, even in lawmaking. Although the Constitution vests Congress with "all legislative powers," these powers cannot be exercised without involvement by the president and even by the courts. This same interdependency applies to executive and judicial powers. The president is a key figure in lawmaking. According to Article II, the president can convene one or both houses of Congress in special session. Although unable to introduce legislation directly, the president "shall from time to time give to the Congress information on the state of the Union, and recommend to their consideration such measures as he shall judge necessary and expedient." The president also has the power to veto congressional enactments. After a bill or resolution has passed both houses of Congress and been delivered to the White House, the president must sign it or return it within ten days (excluding Sundays). Overruling a presidential veto requires a two-thirds vote in each house.

Carrying out laws is the duty of the president, who is enjoined by the Constitution to take care that laws are faithfully executed. As head of the executive branch, the president has the power to appoint "officers of the United States," with the Senate's advice and consent. Although Congress sets up the

executive departments and agencies, outlining their missions by statute, chief executives and their appointees manage the character and pace of executive activity.

In diplomacy and national defense, traditional domains of royal prerogative, the Constitution apportions powers between the executive and legislative branches. Following tradition, presidents are given wide discretion in such matters: they appoint ambassadors and other envoys, they negotiate treaties, and they command the country's armed forces.

Here, too, functions are intermeshed. Like other high-ranking presidential appointees, ambassadors and envoys must be approved by the Senate. Treaties do not become the law of the land until they are ratified by the Senate. Although the president may dispatch troops, only Congress has the power of formally declaring war. Reacting to the Vietnam War, Congress in 1973 passed the War Powers Resolution, a pointed reminder to presidents of congressional war-making powers.

Historically, presidents and Congresses (and courts) have reached accommodations in order to exercise the powers they share. As Justice Joseph Story once wrote, the authors of the Constitution sought to "prove that rigid adherence to [separation of powers] in all cases would be subversive to the efficiency of government and result in the destruction of the public liberties." Justice Robert Jackson wisely noted in 1952 that "while the Constitution diffuses power the better to secure liberty, it also contemplates that practice will integrate the dispersed powers into a workable government."[13] (See box, p. 22.)

Impeachment. In extreme cases Congress has power to impeach and remove the president, the vice president, and other "civil officers of the United States" for treason, bribery, or "other high crimes and misdemeanors." The British parliament had fashioned this power to curb despotic monarchs; but by the time it was written into our Constitution, parliament—which by then reigned supreme—had no need of it. The House of Representatives has the sole authority to draw up and adopt (by majority vote) articles of impeachment, which are charges that the individual has engaged in one of the named forms of misconduct. The Senate is the final judge of whether to convict on any of the articles of impeachment. A two-thirds majority is required to remove the individual from office or to remove and bar the individual from any future "offices of public trust."

Three attributes of impeachment fix it within the separation-of-powers framework. First, it is exclusively the domain of Congress. (Even though the chief justice presides over Senate trials of the president, his rulings may be overturned by majority vote.) The two chambers have freedom to chart their own procedures in reaching their decisions. The Supreme Court flatly refused to review the Senate's procedures when a former federal judge, Walter L. Nixon Jr. (no relation of President Richard Nixon), objected that, although he had been convicted by the full Senate, the evidence in his case had been taken by a committee rather than the full Senate.[14]

Constitutional Anomaly: The Independent Counsel Law

The Ethics in Government Act of 1978 was a post-Watergate enactment under whose Title VI the Justice Department could appoint independent counsels (ICs) to investigate charges of wrongdoing within the executive branch. To ensure the ICs' independence, the authors of the law created a hybrid entity. Although nominally appointed by the attorney general, ICs were picked by a three-judge panel that was in turn named by the chief justice. ICs could be fired, but no attorney general ever dared to do so: after all, it was President Nixon's removal of a Watergate prosecutor that led to the enactment of the law.

Did this strange hybrid amount to a legislative (or judicial) invasion of executive prerogatives? This was the question considered by the Supreme Court in *Morrison v. Olson*, 487 U.S. 654 (1988). Invoking a series of tests for breaches of the separation of powers doctrine, Justice William Rehnquist, writing for a 7–1 majority, concluded that ICs were permissible. The law was not "an attempt by Congress to increase its own powers at the expense of the executive branch." It did not represent any "judicial usurpation of properly executive functions" or "impermissibly undermine" executive powers. Finally, it did not disrupt the proper balance between the branches by "preventing the executive branch from accomplishing its constitutional assigned functions." These tests added up to a rough, Madisonian measure of what is required by separation of powers. "We have never held," Rehnquist claimed, "that the Constitution requires that the three branches of Government 'operate with absolute independence.'"

The Court's lone dissenter, Justice Antonin Scalia, followed a more formalistic reading of the Constitution. The executive power given the president under Article II embraces the conduct of criminal prosecutions, including investigations to decide whether to prosecute. Because the law deprived the president of exclusive control over exercising that power, Scalia held that it should be voided:

> A system of separate and coordinate powers necessarily involves an acceptance of exclusive power that can theoretically be abused. . . . The checks against any Branch's abuse of its exclusive powers are twofold: First, retaliation by one of the other Branch's use of its exclusive powers: Congress, for example, can impeach an executive who willfully fails to enforce the laws. . . . Second, and ultimately, there is the political check that the people will replace those in the political branches . . . who are guilty of abuse.

Long before the ICs were invented, Scalia noted, political pressures had led to the naming of special prosecutors—for example, in the Teapot Dome (1924) and Watergate (1973) scandals.

Even worse, Scalia mused, what if the selecting judges were "politically partisan, as judges have been known to be"? What if they named "a prosecutor antagonistic to the administration, or even to the particular individual who has been selected for this special treatment"? If executive officers and judges were afraid or unwilling to ensure that accepted investigatory standards were followed, "there would be no one accountable to the public to whom the blame could be assigned." These very defects surfaced in Kenneth W. Starr's prolonged probe of President Clinton, resulting in grave breaches in the doctrine of separation of powers and raising questions about the wisdom, if not the underlying logic, of the Court's 1988 ruling. Congress allowed the law to lapse in 1999.

Second, as a legislative proceeding impeachment is essentially political in character. The structure may appear judicial—the House a grand jury, the Senate a trial court—but lawmakers decide whether and how to proceed, which evidence to consider, and even what constitutes an impeachable offense. Treason is defined by the Constitution, and bribery by statute. Toward the end of the Philadelphia convention, however, the Virginia statesman George Mason complained that simply to bar those two misdeeds "[would] not reach many great and dangerous offenses," including "attempts to subvert the Constitution." After rejecting as too vague or subjective such terms as "corruption," "maladministration," and "neglect of duty," the phrase "high crimes and misdemeanors" was added.[15] Although open to interpretation, these are usually defined as (in Alexander Hamilton's words) "abuse or violation of some public trust"—on-the-job offenses against the state, the political order, or the society at large.[16] This means they can be either more or less than garden-variety criminal offenses. Both presidential impeachment trials (Andrew Johnson, 1868; Bill Clinton, 1998–1999) were fiercely partisan affairs, in which combatants disputed not only the facts but the appropriate grounds for impeachment.

Finally, impeachment is a blunt, unwieldy instrument for removing officials for the gravest of offenses. Congress has many lesser ways of reining in wayward officials, and in any event presidents and vice presidents serve limited terms. (Gouverneur Morris, among the wisest of the Framers of the Constitution, suggested that terms were short enough that impeachments would not be needed, but his view was swiftly overridden.) Still, although impeachments are often proposed, only fifteen Senate trials have taken place, and only seven individuals have been convicted. Significantly, the seven who were removed from office were all judges—who, unlike executive officers, enjoy open-ended terms of office.[17]

Judicial Review

The third of the separated branches, the judiciary, has assumed a leading role in interpreting laws and determining their constitutionality. Whether the Founders anticipated this function of "judicial review" is open to question. Perhaps they expected each branch to reach its own judgments on constitutional questions, especially those pertaining to its own powers. This reading of the Founders' intent is the doctrine of "coordinate construction."

Whatever the original intent, Chief Justice John Marshall soon preempted the other two branches with his Court's unanimous assertion of judicial review in *Marbury v. Madison* (1803). Judicial review involves both interpretation and judgment. First, "it is emphatically the province and duty of the judicial department to say what the law is." Second, the Supreme Court has the duty of weighing laws against the Constitution, the "supreme law of the land," and invalidating those that are inconsistent—in the *Marbury* case a minor provision of the Judiciary Act of 1789.[18] Yet Congress, not the Court, remained the primary forum for weighty constitutional debates throughout the nineteenth cen-

tury. Until the Civil War only one other law, the Missouri Compromise, had been declared unconstitutional by the Court (*Dred Scott v. Sandford*, 1857). Since the Civil War, however, the Court has been more aggressive in interpreting and judging congressional handiwork.

For the record, the Supreme Court has invalidated 143 congressional statutes, in whole or in part, from *Marbury* in 1803 through mid-1999.[19] This count does not include lower court holdings that have not been reviewed by the Supreme Court. Nor does it cover laws whose validity has been impaired because a similar law was struck down. For example, in the 1983 case of *Immigration and Naturalization Service v. Chadha*, the Court invalidated many forms of the so-called legislative veto, which authorized administrators or agencies to take certain actions subject to congressional approval or veto. Although only one law was at issue, more than 120 other laws containing one or more such provisions were called into question by the ruling (see Chapter 11).

Does this mean the Supreme Court has the last word in "saying what the law is"? By no means. Its interpretations of laws may be questioned and reversed. If the congressional sponsors or supporters of a law disagree with the judges' readings of the text, they may clarify or modify the language in subsequent enactments. A study of the 1967–1990 period found that 121 of the Court's interpretive decisions had been overridden, an average of ten per Congress. The author of the study concluded that "congressional committees in fact carefully monitor Supreme Court decisions" and that Congress was apt to override decisions of a closely divided Court favoring conservative interpretations, decisions that rely on the law's plain meaning, and decisions that clash with positions taken by federal, state, and local governments.[20]

Nor is the Court the sole arbiter of what is or is not constitutional. Courts routinely accept customs and practices developed by the other two branches. Likewise, they usually decline to decide sensitive "political questions" in the province of Congress and the executive. When courts strike down an enactment, Congress may turn around and enact statutes that meet the courts' objections or achieve the same goal by different means.

Congress sometimes reacts to judicial holdings by trying to impede, modify, reverse, or simply ignore them. The *Dred Scott* decision helped bring about the Civil War; Reconstruction laws and constitutional amendments after the war explicitly nullified the Court's holding. Two years after the landmark decision *Miranda v. Arizona* (1966)—which requires that criminal suspects be read their rights before being questioned—Congress passed a law making it easier for federal prosecutors to sidestep the rule when a suspect confesses willingly. Although the Justice Department declined to enforce the 1968 law, it has recently been unearthed to challenge the Miranda ruling. And despite *Chadha*, legislative veto provisions continue to be enacted; political prudence usually impels administrators to honor such provisions.

The courts play a leading but not exclusive role in interpreting laws and the regulations emanating from them. When Congress passes a law, the policy-

making process has just begun. Courts and administrative agencies then assume the task of refining the policy, but they do so under Congress's watchful eye. "What is 'final' at one stage of our political development," Louis Fisher observes, "may be reopened at some later date, leading to revisions, fresh interpretations, and reversals of Court doctrines. Through this process of interaction among the branches, all three institutions are able to expose weaknesses, hold excesses in check, and gradually forge a consensus on constitutional issues."[21]

Bicameralism

Although we talk about "the Congress" as if it were a single entity, Congress is divided internally into two very different, virtually autonomous chambers. Following the pattern initiated by Parliament and imitated by most of the states, the Constitution outlines a bicameral legislature. If tradition recommended the two-house formula, the politics of the early Republic commanded it. Large states preferred the "nationalist" principle of popularly based representation, but the smaller states insisted on a "federal" principle also ensuring representation by states.

The first branch—as the House was termed by Madison and Gouverneur Morris, among others—rests on the nationalist idea that the legislature should answer to people rather than to states. As George Mason put it, the House "was to be the grand depository of the democratic principles of the government."[22] Many years later the Supreme Court ruled (in *Wesberry v. Sanders,* 1964) that these principles demanded that congressional districts within each state be essentially equal in population.

In contrast, the Senate embodied the federal idea: each state would have two seats, the occupants to be chosen by the state legislatures rather than by popular vote. The Senate would serve to curb the excesses of popular government. "The use of the Senate," explained Madison, "is to consist in its proceeding with more coolness, with more system, and with more wisdom, than the popular branch."[23]

Historical evolution overran the Founders' intentions. In most cases, to be sure, senators tended to voice dominant economic interests and shun the general public. British commentator Lord Bryce once remarked that the Senate seemed to care more for its "collective self-esteem" than it did for public opinion.[24] Yet state legislators frequently "instructed" their senators how to vote on vital issues. In some states legislative elections turned into statewide "canvasses" focusing on senatorial candidates. Such was the famous 1858 Illinois contest between Sen. Stephen A. Douglas and challenger Abraham Lincoln. The Democrats captured the legislature and sent Douglas back to Washington, but Lincoln's eloquent arguments against extending slavery to the territories west of the Mississippi River vaulted him into national prominence.

Direct election of senators came with the Seventeenth Amendment, ratified in 1913. A byproduct of the Progressive movement, the new arrangement was designed to broaden citizens' participation and blunt the power of shad-

owy special interests, such as party bosses and business trusts. Thus the Senate became directly subject to popular will.

Bicameralism is the most obvious organizational feature of the U.S. Congress. Each chamber has a distinct process for considering legislation. According to the Constitution, each house determines its own rules, keeps a journal of its proceedings, and serves as final judge of its members' elections and qualifications. In addition, the Constitution assigns unique duties to each of the two chambers. The Senate ratifies treaties and approves presidential appointments. The House must originate all revenue measures; by tradition, it also originates appropriations bills. In impeachments, the House prepares and tries the case, and the Senate serves as the court.

The two houses jealously guard their prerogatives and resist intrusions by "the other body." Despite claims that one or the other chamber is more important—for instance, that the Senate has more prestige or that the House pays more attention to legislative details—the two houses staunchly defend their equal places. On Capitol Hill there is no "upper" or "lower" chamber.

Institutional Evolution

Written constitutions, even those as farsighted as the 1787 one, go only a short way in explaining how real-life governmental institutions work. On many questions such documents are inevitably silent or ambiguous; issues that lie between the lines must be resolved in the course of later events.

In adapting to demands far removed from those of eighteenth-century America, Congress has evolved dramatically. Many of these changes can be subsumed under the term *institutionalization*—the process whereby structures and procedures take shape and become regularized. Rather than being unformed and unpredictable, the institution becomes structured and routinized, following established traditions and widely held expectations about how it should perform. Institutionalization has shaped the two Congresses—Congress as deliberative body and Congress as individual representatives.

The Size of Congress

Looking at the government of 1789 through modern lenses, one is struck by the relatively small circles of people involved. The House of Representatives, that "impetuous council," was composed of sixty-five members—when all of them showed up. The aristocratic Senate boasted only twenty-six members, two from each of the thirteen original states.

Article I, Section 2, of the Constitution sets forth the method of apportioning House members—a decennial census. When the first census was taken in 1790, the nation's population was fewer than four million—smaller than that of an average state today. (See Table 2-1 to follow the historical growth of the House.) There were thirty-two senators in 1800, sixty-two in 1850, and ninety in 1900. Since 1912 only the states of Alaska and Hawaii have been added, and the House has stabilized at 435 members.

Table 2-1   Growth in Size of House and Its Constituents, 1790–1990
Censuses and Projections

Year of census	Congress	Population base[a] (1,000s)	Number of states	Number of representatives[b]	Population per House district
—	1st–2d	—	13	65	30,000[c]
1790	3d–7th	3,616	15	105	34,438
1800	8th–12th	4,880	16	141	34,609
1810	13th–17th	6,584	17	181	36,377
1820	18th–22d	8,972	24	213	42,124
1830	23d–27th	11,931	24	240	49,712
1840	28th–32d	15,908	26	223	71,338
1850	33d–37th	21,767	31	234	93,020
1860	38th–42d	29,550	34	241	122,614
1870	43d–47th	38,116	37	292	130,533
1880	48th–52d	49,371	38	325	151,912
1890	53d–57th	61,909	44	356	173,901
1900	58th–62d	74,563	45	386	193,167
1910	63d–66th	91,604	46	435	210,583
1920[d]	67th–72d	105,711	48	435	243,013
1930	73d–77th	122,093	48	435	280,675
1940	78th–82d	131,006	48	435	301,164
1950	83d–87th	149,895	48	435	334,587
1960	88th–92d	178,559	50	435	410,481
1970	93d–97th	201,721	50	435	463,726
1980	98th–102d	226,546	50	435	520,795
1990	103d–107th	248,143	50	435	570,444
2000 (est.)	108th–112th	276,000	50	435	634,483
2050 (est.)	133d–137th	392,000	50	435	901,149

Sources: U.S. Department of Commerce, Bureau of the Census, *Historical Statistics of the United States, Colonial Times to 1970,* Pt. 2 (Washington, D.C.: U.S. Government Printing Office, 1975, 1084). Recent figures from U.S. Bureau of the Census, *Statistical Abstract of the United States: 1998,* 118th ed. (Washington, D.C.: U.S. Government Printing Office, 1998), 9 (Tables 3, 4).

[a] Population figures used for House districting purposes exclude people living in the District of Columbia, U.S. territories, and foreign countries. Historically, the populations of outlying areas, the number of Indians not taxed, and (prior to 1870) two-fifths of the slave population also were excluded.

[b] Actual number of representatives apportioned at the beginning of the decade.

[c] The minimum ratio of population to representatives stated in Article 1, Section 2, of the Constitution.

[d] No apportionment was made after the census of 1920.

In addition to its 435 full-fledged members, the House has one resident commissioner and four delegates. Their posts are created by statute. Puerto Rico in 1900 was granted the right to elect a commissioner. More recently, nonvoting delegates were approved for the District of Columbia (1971), Guam (1972), the Virgin Islands (1972), and American Samoa (1980). These individuals enjoy most but not all of the privileges of regular House members: they have offices and staffs; they hold seats and vote in committees.

The size of the House is set by law and could, of course, be changed. Suggestions to enlarge the House are made periodically—especially by representatives from states losing seats after a census. More seriously, some worry that congressional constituencies are too populous to permit meaningful communication between citizens and their representatives.[25] The framers contemplated House districts of no more than 30,000 people— huge by 1789 standards. Following that guideline would now require a House of some 9,000 members. Modest enlargement would only marginally alleviate the problem. And most observers concur with Speaker Sam Rayburn, who served in Congress from 1913 to 1961, that the House is already at or above its optimum size for legislating.

Size profoundly affects an organization's work. Growth compelled the House to develop strong leaders, to rely heavily on its committees, to impose strict limits on floor debate, and to devise elaborate ways of channeling the flow of floor business. It is no accident that strong leaders emerged during the House's periods of rapid growth. After the initial growth spurt in the first two decades of the Republic, vigorous leadership appeared in the person of Henry Clay, whose speakerships (1811–1814, 1815–1820, and 1823–1825) demonstrated the potentialities of that office. Similarly, post–Civil War growth was accompanied by an era of forceful Speakers that lasted from the 1870s until 1910. Size is not the only impetus for strong leadership, but it tends to centralize procedural control.

In the smaller and more intimate Senate, vigorous leadership has been the exception rather than the rule. The relative informality of Senate procedures, not to mention the long-cherished right of unlimited debate, testifies to looser reins of leadership. Compared with the House's complex rules and voluminous precedents, the Senate's rules are brief and simple. Informal negotiations among senators interested in a given measure prevail, and debate typically is governed by unanimous consent agreements—agreed-upon ways of proceeding, brokered by the parties' floor leaders. Although too large for its members to draw their chairs around the fireplace on a chilly winter morning—as they did in the early years—the Senate today retains a clubby atmosphere that the House lacks.

The congressional establishment itself has changed in scale, with staffs added gradually. In 1891 a grand total of 142 clerks, 62 for the House and 80 for the Senate, were on hand to serve members of Congress. Many senators and all representatives handled their own correspondence; keeping records and counting votes were the duties of committee clerks. After the turn of this

century, House and Senate members, their clerks, and their committees moved into two ornate office buildings, one for each house. Today the legislative branch embraces some 24,000 staff members. Housed in nearly a dozen Capitol Hill buildings, they include experts in virtually every area of government policy and constitute a distinct Washington subculture.

The Legislative Workload

During the Republic's early days, the government at Washington was "at a distance and out of sight."[26] Lawmaking was a part-time occupation. As President John F. Kennedy was fond of remarking, the Clays, Calhouns, and Websters of the nineteenth century could afford to devote a whole generation or more to debating and refining the few great controversies at hand. Rep. Joseph W. Martin, R-Mass., who entered the House in 1925 and went on to become Speaker (1947–1949, 1953–1955), described the leisurely atmosphere of earlier days and the workload changes during his service:

> From one end of a session to another Congress would scarcely have three or four issues of consequence besides appropriations bills. And the issues themselves were fundamentally simpler than those that surge in upon us today in such a torrent that the individual member cannot analyze all of them adequately before he is compelled to vote. In my early years in Congress the main issues were few enough so that almost any conscientious member could with application make himself a quasi-expert at least. In the complexity and volume of today's legislation, however, most members have to trust somebody else's word or the recommendation of a committee. Nowadays bills, which thirty years ago would have been thrashed out for hours or days, go through in ten minutes.[27]

The most pressing issue considered by the Foreign Affairs Committee during one session, Martin related, was a $20,000 authorization for an international poultry show in Tulsa.

Even in the 1950s the legislative schedule was quite manageable, as indicated in the following summary of a representative's day offered by former Speaker Rayburn:

> The average member will come down to the office around eight or eightthirty. He spends his time with visitors until around ten o'clock, then he goes to a committee meeting, and when the committee adjourns he comes to the House of Representatives, or should, and stays around the House chamber and listens.[28]

Needless to say, the days of a single morning committee meeting and time to witness an entire afternoon's floor proceedings have gone the way of the manual typewriter. Conflicting committee sessions, snatches of floor deliberation, and repeated roll calls are now the order of the day.

Table 2-2   Measures Introduced and Enacted, Selected Congresses, 1789–1999

Years	Congress	Measures introduced			Measures enacted		
		Total	Bills	Joint resolutions	Total	Public	Private
1789–1791	1st	144	144	—	118	108	10
1803–1805	8th	217	217	—	111	93	18
1819–1821	16th	480	480	—	208	117	91
1835–1837	24th	1,107	1,055	52	459	144	315
1851–1853	32d	1,167	1,011	156	306	137	169
1867–1869	40th	3,723	3,003	720	765	354	411
1883–1885	48th	11,443	10,961	482	969	284	685
1899–1901	56th	20,893	20,409	484	1,942	443	1,499
1915–1917	64th	30,052	29,438	614	684	458	226
1931–1933	72d	21,382	20,501	881	843	516	327
1947–1949	80th	10,797	10,108	689	1,363	906	458
1963–1965	88th	17,480	16,079	1,401	1,026	666	360
1979–1981	96th	12,583	11,722	861	736	613	123
1989–1991	101st	12,555	11,247	1,308	387	385	2
1997–1999	105th	9,143	7,532	200	404	394	10

Sources: U.S. Department of Commerce, Bureau of the Census, *Historical Statistics of the United States: Colonial Times to 1970*, Part 2 (Washington, D.C.: U.S. Government Printing Office, 1975), 1081–1082; Bureau of the Census, *Statistical Abstract of the United States, 1980* (Washington, D.C.: U.S. Government Printing Office, 1980), 509; Rozanne M. Barry, *Bills Introduced and Laws Enacted: Selected Legislative Statistics, 1947–1994* (Washington, D.C.: Congressional Research Service, 1995); *Congressional Record* 145, 106th Cong., 1st sess., Jan. 19, 1999, D29.

Note: Measures introduced and enacted exclude simple and concurrent resolutions.

Congress's workload—once limited in scope, small in volume, and simple in content—has burgeoned since 1789. Recent downturns in the number of measures introduced and enacted, reflect not so much slackened activity as an altered agenda: for example, the tendency to enact lengthy "megabills" on basic matters and to spend more time overseeing the executive branch (see Table 2-2). The number of hours Congress is in session also has increased (see Figure 2-1). By most measures—hours in session, committee meetings, floor votes—the congressional workload has just about doubled since the 1950s.

Legislative business has expanded in scope and complexity as well as in sheer volume. Today's Congress grapples with many issues that once were left to state or local agencies or were considered entirely outside the purview of governmental activity. Moreover, legislation tends to be more complex than it

Figure 2-1 Hours in Session, House of Representatives, Selected Congresses, 1955–1999

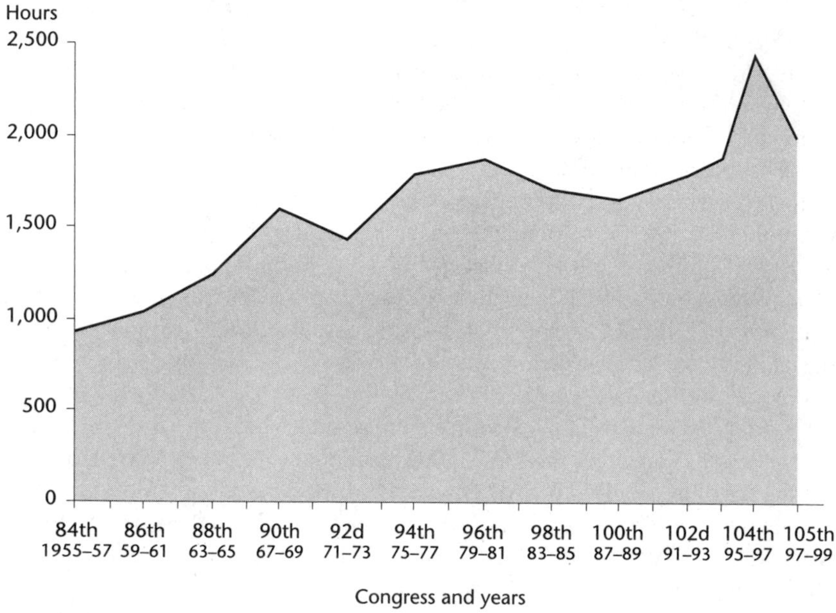

Sources: Norman J. Ornstein, Thomas E. Mann, and Michael J. Malbin, *Vital Statistics on Congress, 1997–1998* (Washington, D.C.: Congressional Quarterly, 1998), 160–161. Figures for the 105th Congress are from *Congressional Record* 145, 106th Cong., 1st sess., Jan. 19, 1999, D29.

used to be. The average public bill of the late 1940s was two and a half pages long; by the mid-1990s it ran to more than nineteen pages.[29]

For most of its history Congress was a part-time institution. Well into the twentieth century Congress remained in session for only nine of every twenty-four months, the members spending the rest of their time at home attending to private business. In recent decades legislative business has kept the House and Senate almost perpetually in session—punctuated by constituency work periods. During the average two-year Congress the Senate is in session nearly 300 eight-hour days; the more efficient House gets by on somewhat less time.[30] The average senator or representative works an eleven-hour day when Congress is in session.[31]

Structures and Procedures

A mature institution is marked not only by the professionalism of its members but also by the number and complexity of its structures and procedures. By that measure today's House and Senate are mature institutions indeed.

No trait illustrates Congress's institutional growth more dramatically than the division of labor through the committee system. Although fashioned gradually and seemingly inexorably, the committee system rests on precedents drawn from the British House of Commons, the colonial assemblies, and the Continental Congresses.[32] The first House standing committee (Elections) was created in 1789, but legislative business in both houses tended to be handled by temporary committees or on the floor. By the third decade of the nineteenth century, however, the standing committee system was well established.

The creation and, occasionally, abolition of committees parallel important historical events and shifting perceptions of public problems.[33] As novel policy problems arose, new committees were added. The House, for example, established Commerce and Manufactures in 1795, Public Lands in 1805, Freedmen's Affairs in 1866, Roads in 1913, Science and Astronautics in 1958, Standards of Official Conduct in 1967, and Small Business in 1975. Numerous committees have existed at one time or another—as many as sixty-one in the House and seventy-four in the Senate.

Today the Senate has sixteen standing committees and the House has nineteen (see Chapter 7, Table 7-2). The Senate also has four select, or special, committees; the House has two. These committees are only the tip of the iceberg, however. House committees now have nearly ninety subcommittees, whereas Senate committees have nearly seventy subcommittees. Four joint House–Senate committees have been retained. This adds up to some 200 work groups, plus an abundance of task forces, party committees, voting blocs, informal caucuses, and the like.

The number of formal and informal leaders in Congress has grown as a function of proliferating work groups. Every committee and subcommittee has a chairman and a ranking minority member. The formal party leaders help organize the two chambers, assign members to committees, schedule business, and devise parliamentary strategy. Supplementing formal leadership posts in Congress are a host of informal leaders who represent factions, regions, economic interests, or issue positions. Thus formal leaders are now obliged to adopt what Barbara Sinclair calls a "strategy of inclusion"—that is, "drawing into the leadership's orbit and including in leadership efforts as many [partisans] as possible."[34] The result is ever more complex networks of give-and-take relationships in which less informed members seek cues from better informed colleagues, issue by issue (see Chapter 9). Today's Congress, in other words, abounds in leaders of every stripe.

In the early days, proceedings at the Capitol were disorderly, especially in the crowded, noisy, and badly ventilated chambers. "Debate has been rough and tumble, no holds barred, bruising, taunting, raucous, sometimes brutal," one historian related. "The floor of the House has been no place for the timid or the craven."[35] Before the Civil War, duels between quarreling legislators were not uncommon. One celebrated incident occurred in 1856, when Rep. Preston Brooks, a southern Democrat, coldly stalked Sen. Charles Sumner, a

Republican from Massachusetts, and beat him senseless with a cane on the Senate floor for his views on slavery in the new territories.

As Congress matured, decorum by and large replaced chaos, and stricter rules of order came to govern the proceedings. Today there are formidable rules and precedents as well as numerous informal norms and traditions. Altering the rules is not a casual matter. (The House adopts its rules anew with each new Congress; as a continuing body the Senate has ongoing rules.) Most rules changes result from concerted effort by the leadership, party caucuses, or the respective rules committees. When major rules changes or committee realignments are considered, select committees may be established to make recommendations. Since World War II more than ten formal reorganization committees or study commissions have been created, the most recent in 1997.

In short, Congress is no longer an informal institution. It bristles with norms and traditions, rules and procedures, committees and subcommittees. The modern Congress, in other words, is highly institutionalized. How different from the first Congress, personified by fussy John Adams worrying about what forms of address to use! The institutional complexity of today's Congress enables it to cope with a staggering workload while for the most part containing personal conflict. Institutional complexity, however, carries its own costs—in rigidity and the cumbersome administrative apparatus needed to keep the system afloat.

Despite institutional inertia the Senate and House repeatedly shift and adapt their ways of doing things—partly in response to changes in public and workload demands, partly in reaction to altered partisan or factional alignments, partly to accommodate ongoing shifts in membership. Just as physical anthropologists believe the earth's history is marked by periods of intense, even cataclysmic change—"punctuated equilibrium"—so historians of Congress have identified several eras of extensive institutional change. "Reconstitutive change" is what Elaine K. Swift calls these instances of "rapid, marked, and enduring shift[s] in the fundamental dimensions of the institution."[36] During one such period (1809–1829), Swift argues, the Senate was transformed from an elitist, insulated "American House of Lords" into an active, powerful institution whose debates stirred the public and attracted the most talented politicians of the time. Another such period was the Progressive Era (roughly the first two decades of the twentieth century), when House leaders were toppled and the Senate became an elective body. Arguably, the so-called reform era of the 1960s and 1970s qualifies as a third time of wide-ranging change, ushering in a period of heightened partisanship.

Not all institutional changes are so concentrated. Incremental changes of one kind or another are always unfolding: for example, the House in 1999 streamlined and codified its rules, and hardly anyone noticed. In a detailed examination of changes in committee jurisdictions, David C. King showed that periodic, large-scale jurisdictional "reform acts" were mainly compilations of gradually accumulated precedents created as novel bills were introduced.[37]

Evolution of the Legislator's Job

What is it like to be a member of Congress? The legislator's job, like the institution of Congress, has evolved since 1789. During the early Congresses being a senator or representative was a part-time occupation. Few members regarded congressional service as a career, and from most accounts the rewards were slim. Since then the lawmakers' exposure to constituents' demands, their career expectations, and their factional loyalties have changed dramatically. Electoral units, too, have grown very large. Congressional constituencies— states and districts—are among the most populous electoral units in the world. The mean congressional district now numbers more than half a million people, the average state more than five million.

Constituency Demands

Constituency demands on legislators are many: they must make personal appearances in the district or state, communicate through newsletters and electronic media, explain stands on legislative issues, assist constituents with problems ("constituency casework"), and correspond with constituents. American legislators have always been expected to remain close to their voters. From the very first, representatives reported to their constituents through circular letters, communications passed around throughout their districts.[38]

In an era of limited government, however, there was little constituent errand running. "It was a pretty nice job that a member of Congress had in those days," recalled Rep. Robert Ramspeck, D-Ga., describing the Washington of 1911, when he came to take a staff job:

> At that time the government affected the people directly in only a minor way. . . . It was an entirely different job from the job we have to do today. It was primarily a legislative job, as the Constitution intended it to be.[39]

In those days a member's mail was confined mainly to awarding rural mail routes, arranging for Spanish War pensions, sending out free seed, and only occasionally explaining legislation. At most, a single clerk was required to handle correspondence. Members from one-party areas often did little personal constituency work. It was said that Democratic Speaker John Nance Garner, who was elected to the House in 1913 and ended his career as vice president (1933–1941), "for thirty years did not canvass his [south Texas] district and franked no speeches home."[40] His major constituency outreach consisted of barbecues given at his home in Uvalde, Texas.

This unhurried pace has long since vanished. Reflecting on his forty years on Capitol Hill, Representative Martin remarked on the dramatic upsurge of constituent awareness

> Today the federal government is far more complex, as is every phase of national life. People have to turn to their Representative for aid. I used to think

ten letters a day was a big batch; now I get several hundred a day. In earlier
times, constituents didn't know their Congressman's views. With better communications, their knowledge has increased along with their expectations of
what he must know.[41]

Even Martin, who left the House in 1967, would be astonished at the volume of constituency work now handled by House and Senate offices. Not only
are constituents more numerous than ever before; they are better educated,
served by faster communication and transportation, and mobilized by lobby organizations. Public opinion surveys show that voters expect legislators to dispense federal services and to communicate frequently with the home folks. Even
though the crasser forms of pork barrel politics have come under attack, there
is little reason to suppose that constituents' demands will ebb in the future.

The Congressional Career

During its early years Congress was an institution composed of transients.
The nation's capital was an unsightly place; its culture was provincial, and its
summers humid and mosquito ridden. Members remained in Washington
only a few months, spending their unpleasant sojourns in boardinghouses.
"While there were a few for whom the Hill was more than a way station in the
pursuit of a career," James Sterling Young observes, "affiliation with the congressional community tended to be brief."[42]

The early Congresses failed to command the loyalty needed to keep members in office. Congressional service was regarded more as odious duty than as
rewarding work. "My dear friend," wrote a North Carolina representative to his
constituents in 1796, "there is nothing in this service, exclusive of the confidence and gratitude of my constituents, worth the sacrifice. . . . Having se-
cured this, I could freely give place to any fellow citizen, that others too might
obtain the consolation due to faithful service."[43] Of the ninety-four senators
who served between 1789 and 1801, thirty-three resigned before completing
their terms, only six to take other federal posts.[44] In the House almost 6 percent of all early-nineteenth-century members resigned during each Congress.
"Citizen legislators," not professional politicians, characterized that era.

Careerism mounted as the nineteenth century ended. As late as the 1870s
more than half the House members at any given time were freshmen, and the
mean length of service for members was barely two terms. By the end of the
century, however, the proportion of newcomers had fallen to 30 percent, and
average House tenure reached three terms, or six years. About the same time,
senators' mean term of service topped six years, or one full term.[45] Today the
average senator has served 13.2 years (slightly more than two terms), the average representative 9.8 years (nearly five terms)—this in spite of impressive electoral turnover in the 1990s. Table 2-3 shows changes since 1789 in the percentages of new and veteran members and the mean number of terms claimed
by incumbents.

Table 2-3 Length of Service in House and Senate, 1789–1999

| | Congress | | | |
| | 1st–56th | 57th–103d | 104th–105th | 106th |
Terms	(1789–1901)	(1901–1995)	(1995–1999)	(1999–2001)
	House			
One (up to 2 years)	44.0%	23.3%	18.2%	9.2%
Two to six (3–12 years)	53.4	49.7	51.9	61.4
Seven or more (12+ years)	2.6	27.0	30.0	29.4
Mean number of terms[a]	2.1	4.8	5.0	5.3
	Senate			
One (up to 6 years)	65.6%	45.6%	33.5%	36.0%
Two (7–12 years)	23.4	22.4	27.5	31.0
Three or more (12+ years)	11.0	32.0	39.0	33.0
Mean number of terms[a]	1.5	2.2	2.4	2.6

Source: Adapted from David C. Huckabee, *Length of Service for Representatives and Senators: 1st–103d Congresses,* Congressional Research Service Report, No. 95-426GOV, March 27, 1995. Authors' calculations for the 104th through 106th Congresses.

[a] Figures are derived from the total number of terms claimed by members whether or not those terms have been served out. For example, members in their initial year of service are counted as having one full term, and so on. Thus the figures cannot be equated precisely with years of service.

Rising careerism had a number of causes. For one thing, proliferating one-party states and districts following the Civil War, and especially after the partisan realignment of 1896, made possible repeated reelection of a dominant party's candidates: Democrats in the core cities and the South, Republicans in the Midwest and the rural Northeast. Militant state and local party organizations dominated the recruitment process and tended to select party careerists to fill safe seats.[46] About the turn of the century, however, electoral reforms—for example, direct primaries and the so-called Australian ballot (a uniform, secret, government-printed ballot)—blunted party control at the polling booth and encouraged candidates to appeal directly to their followers.

At the same time the power of the legislative branch, epitomized in Woodrow Wilson's phrase "congressional government," made federal service ever more attractive and rewarding.[47] The government's subsequent growth enhanced the excitement and glamour of the national political scene, especially compared with state or local politics. Moreover, the physical environment of the nation's capital eventually improved. As Representative Martin related:

> The installation of air conditioning in the 1930s did more, I believe, than cool the Capitol: it prolonged the session. The members were no longer in

such a hurry to flee Washington in July. The southerners especially had no place else to go that was half as comfortable.[48]

The rise of careerism, aided by turn-of-the-century political warfare between Progressives and the "Old Guard" (mainly within the dominant Republican Party), established the seniority "rule" to reward lengthy service. As long as senior members were scarce, they dominated their chambers and relied more on party loyalty than seniority in naming committees or chairmen. With careerists more numerous, greater respect had to be paid to seniority in distributing favored committee posts.

Seniority triumphed in both chambers at about the same time. In the Senate there was no decisive event; indeed, seniority was largely unchallenged after 1877.[49] In the House strong post–Civil War Speakers, struggling to control the unruly chamber, sometimes ignored seniority to appoint loyal lieutenants to major committees. But in 1910, when Speaker Joseph G. Cannon passed over senior members for assignments and behaved arbitrarily in other ways, the House revolted, divesting the Speaker of committee assignment power. With the Speaker's clout diminished, David Brady relates, "seniority came to be the most important criterion for committee assignments and chairmanships, and committees rather than parties became the major policy actors."[50]

Adherence to seniority fostered career patterns within the two houses. New members found themselves at the bottom of internal career ladders that they could ascend only through continued service. In recent decades seniority barriers have been lowered somewhat: party and committee reforms of the 1970s multiplied the number of career ladders, and since then both parties have occasionally departed from strict seniority in selecting committee chairmen and ranking minority members. Extended service, however, remains a prerequisite for top party and committee posts.

Parties and Factions

Political parties had no place in the constitutional blueprint, which was deliberately fashioned to divide and dilute factional interests. With the unveiling of Treasury Secretary Alexander Hamilton's financial program in 1790, however, a genuine partisan spirit infused Capitol Hill. The Federalists, with Hamilton as their intellectual leader, espoused "energetic government" to deal forcefully with national problems. The rival Republicans, who looked to Thomas Jefferson and James Madison for leadership, rallied opponents of Federalist policies and championed local autonomy, weaker national government, and programs favoring lower class or debtor interests.

When war broke out in Europe between revolutionary France and a coalition of old regimes, the Federalists sided with the dependable (and commercially profitable) British, while the Republicans tended to admire "French principles." As early as 1794 Sen. John Taylor of Virginia could write:

> The existence of two parties in Congress is apparent. The fact is disclosed almost upon every important question. Whether the subject be foreign or domestic—relative to war or peace—navigation or commerce—the magnetism of opposite views draws them wide as the poles asunder.[51]

In this country Speakers have always been political officers, and so they quickly came to reflect partisan divisions in wielding their powers. The other partisan institution in those early days was the congressional nominating caucus that selected a faction's presidential candidates. Not all members professed clear-cut partisan or factional affiliations, however. During the "Era of Good Feeling" (roughly 1815–1825), party voting was the exception rather than the rule. With the conspicuous exception of the nominating caucuses, no formal party apparatus existed. Between the quadrennial caucuses, Young explains, "the party had no officers, even of figurehead importance, for the guidance or management of legislative processes."[52] The nominating caucus collapsed after 1824, and the Jacksonians laid the foundation for something approaching a stable party system based on grassroots support.

Parties flourished in the years following the Civil War. Regional conflicts, along with economic upheavals produced by rapid industrialization, nurtured partisan differences. The Civil War and World War I mark the boundaries of the era of strongest partisanship on Capitol Hill and in the country at large. At the grassroots level the parties were divided along class, occupational, and regional lines to a degree unimaginable today; grassroots party organizations were massive and militant by American standards. Strong Speakers ruled the House, and a coterie of statewide party "bosses" dominated the Senate.

After World War I the parties declined, but by no means did they wither away. After 1910 party caucuses or committees assumed responsibility for assigning members to committees and sometimes even for formulating policy. Today the parties' formal apparatus is extensive. There are policy committees, campaign committees, research committees, elaborate whip systems, and countless task forces. Nearly 200 staff aides are employed by party leaders and perhaps an equal number by assorted party committees.[53] Party-oriented voting bloc groups (such as the Conservative Democratic Forum or the Republicans' Tuesday Lunch Bunch), "class clubs" (such as the Republican Freshman Class or the Democratic First Term Class), and social groups complement and reinforce partisan ties.

Despite the repeatedly proclaimed "death" of traditional political parties, partisanship and factionalism are very much alive on Capitol Hill. The first thing a visitor to the House or Senate chamber notices is that the seats or desks are divided along partisan lines—Democrats to the left facing the dais, Republicans to the right. Seating arrangements betoken the parties' role in organizing the legislative branch. By means of party mechanisms, leaders are selected, committee assignments made, and floor debates scheduled. Parties also supply members with voting cues. Indeed, recent Congresses have seen modern-day peaks of party-line voting (see Chapter 9).

Partisanship has been underscored by events of the 1990s. Despite the American public's professed antipathy toward partisanship (and toward the two major parties in particular), recent elections have had distinctly partisan effects. One outgrowth of robust partisanship is the advent of congressional party "platforms" designed to attract voters and validate the party's bid for power. The House Republicans' conservative manifesto, the 1994 "Contract with America," though by no means the first such document, was shrewdly put together, aggressively marketed, and employed as the party's agenda during their first few months in power.[54] Five years later, the Clinton impeachment became a pitched battle along partisan lines, dividing not only lawmakers but also their constituents. With gaping policy differences and bitter personal battles, Capitol Hill political alignments are more rigid, and appeals to partisan loyalty more shrill, than at any time in nearly a century.

Conclusion

At its birth the U.S. Congress was an unstructured body. Although the Founders well understood the guiding principles of representative assemblies, they could not have foreseen exactly what sort of institution they had created. They wrote into the Constitution the powers of the legislature as they understood them and left the details to future generations. During its rich and eventful history, Congress has developed into a mature organization with highly articulated structures, procedures, routines, and traditions. In a word, it became institutionalized.

This fact must be taken into account by anyone who seeks to understand Congress. Capitol Hill newcomers—even those who vow to shake things up—confront not an undeveloped, pliable institution but an established, traditional one that largely must be accepted on its own terms. This institutionalism has a number of important consequences, some good and some bad.

Institutionalization enables Congress to cope with its contemporary workload. Division of labor, primarily through standing committees, permits the two houses to process a wide variety of issues at the same time. In tandem with staff resources, this specialization allows Congress to compete with the executive branch in assembling information and applying expertise to given problems. Division of labor also serves the personal and political diversity of Congress. At the same time, careerism encourages legislators to develop skills and expertise in specific issues. Procedures and traditions can contain conflict and channel the political energies that converge upon the lawmaking process.

The danger of institutionalization is organizational rigidity. Institutions that are too brittle can frustrate policy making, especially in periods of rapid social or political change. Structures that are too complex can tie people in knots, producing delays and confusion. Such organizational tie-ups often produce agitation for reform. Even with its size and complexity, the contemporary Congress continues to adapt and change. Most recently, the institutional changes after the Republicans won majority status in 1994 show vividly that Congress's evolution has by no means run its full course.

Part 2

A Congress of
Ambassadors

*Rep. Cynthia A. McKinney, D-Ga., mingles
with voters (top). She was elected twice from
the Eleventh District, which as a Georgia
House member she helped to create. Outside the
Supreme Court, which in 1995 voided her old
district lines, she vows to fight on. Tailoring her
message for a biracial constituency, she
retained her seat in the next two elections.*

3

Going for It:
Recruitment Roulette

The Senate is convening on the first day of the 106th Congress. Waiting expectantly for their names to be called is a group that includes a veterinarian, a shoe salesman, an investment banker, a frozen-food company executive, and even a political science professor. They come from places like Hughes, Arkansas; Ignacio, Colorado; Brooklyn, New York; Searchlight, Nevada, and Baltimore, Maryland. The sergeant at arms calls them forward alphabetically in groups of four. Colleagues from their states escort them to the front of the Senate chamber, where the vice president, the Senate's constitutionally designated presiding officer, administers the oath of office. Newly elected or reelected, the senators are now officially members of "the world's greatest deliberative body," as the Senate likes to call itself. Over in the House chamber, 440 elected or reelected members have just been sworn in as well.

How did these people get to Congress? There is no single answer to that question. In the broadest sense all incumbent legislators are products of *recruitment,* the social and political process through which people achieve leadership posts. Social analysts agree that recruitment is a key to the effective functioning of all institutions, including legislatures. The first great book about politics, Plato's *Republic,* addressed the question of finding and enlisting the ablest individuals to lead their community. Conservatives, following Plato, believe that societies should be ruled by the most talented people—in John Adams's phrase, the "rich and the wise and the well-born." Marxists believe recruitment reflects a society's class structure, with the most privileged people landing in the ranks of leadership. Contemporary political scientists, regardless of ideology, eagerly chart the paths individuals travel to posts in Congress and other institutions of government.

Any recruitment process has both formal and informal elements. In the case of Congress, formal elements include the constitutional framework and state and federal laws governing nominations and elections. Equally important are informal, often unwritten, "rules of the game." Some people are more ambitious than others for elective office; skills and attributes make some aspirants more "eligible" than others; and certain preferences persuade citizens to vote for some aspirants and against others. Taken together, such elements make up a screening process in which some individuals succeed. Like roulette, recruitment is a mix of rules, probabilities, and chance. The recruitment process and its "biases," both overt and hidden, affect the day-to day operation of the House and Senate, not to mention the quality of representation and decision making.

Formal Rules of the Game

The constitutional qualifications for holding congressional office are few and simple, though quite specific. The three are *age* (twenty-five years of age for the House, thirty for the Senate); *citizenship* (seven years for the House, nine years for the Senate); and *residency* in the state from which the office-holder is elected. Thus the constitutional gateways to congressional office-holding are fairly wide.

These qualifications cannot be augmented by the states (or by Congress, for that matter) without altering the Constitution itself, as the Supreme Court ruled in a 1995 case involving term limits.[1] By the early 1990s twenty-three states had adopted restrictions on the number of terms their members of Congress could serve. The state of Arkansas, whose law the Court reviewed, argued that its scheme did not create an additional "qualification" for holding office but had been written as a ballot-access measure within the state's power to regulate the "times, places, and manner of holding elections" (Article I, Section 4). Speaking for the Court, Justice John Paul Stevens spurned this subterfuge as "an indirect attempt to accomplish what the Constitution prohibits Arkansas from accomplishing directly." (State laws limiting the terms of state or local officials were unaffected by the ruling.) A proposed constitutional amendment on the subject has thus far fallen short of the needed two-thirds vote in Congress.

As the term limits controversy showed, even the three simple requirements for holding congressional office can arouse controversy. The authors of the Constitution considered but eventually rejected several other proposed qualifications, such as property ownership and even term limits (a popular idea then as now). If we are to trust comments made by the Framers (especially by the authors of *the Federalist*), reelection of senators and representatives was left unrestricted because (1) the Framers did not wish to limit electors' choices; (2) they regarded the reelection option as a powerful incentive for faithful service by incumbent officeholders; and (3) they valued the contributions that experienced lawmakers could bring to legislative deliberations. Opposing term limits during the House's 1997 debate on the issue, Rep. Barney Frank, D-Mass., caustically remarked, "We must be the only profession in the world where an indication that your employers are satisfied with your work is taken as an indication that something is wrong."[2]

The residency requirement, because of America's localist tradition, has traditionally been stricter in practice than the Constitution prescribes. Voters tend to shun "carpetbaggers" and favor candidates with longstanding ties to their states or districts. Attack ads for Sen. Sam Brownback, R-Kan., branded his 1996 general election foe, Jill Docking, as "Too Liberal for Kansas," partly because she was "born and raised in Massachusetts." (To underscore the point, the ad flashed pictures of such Bay State notables as Democratic senator Edward Kennedy and former governor Michael Dukakis.)[3]

Yet Americans' high geographical mobility yields a sizable "carpetbagger caucus" on Capitol Hill. In the 106th Congress (1999–2001), about a third of the members of both chambers were born outside the states they represented. Especially in fast-growing areas shrewd candidates thus can overcome objections to their outsider status. Sen. John McCain, R-Ariz., a career navy officer, combat hero, and six-year prisoner of war in North Vietnam, beat three established politicians for a congressional nomination barely a year after he settled in Arizona. He stifled carpetbagging charges by explaining that as a navy officer and the son of one, he had never been able to put down roots: "The longest place I ever lived was Hanoi."

Senate Apportionment

The Senate was intended to add stability, wisdom, and forbearance to the actions of the popularly elected House. Thus the Founders stipulated that two senators for each state be chosen by the respective state legislatures, not by the voters themselves. This distinction between the two houses was eroded by the Seventeenth Amendment, which, in 1913, provided for the direct popular election of senators. Because states vary wildly in population, the Senate is the one legislative body in the nation where "one person, one vote" emphatically does not apply.

Yet Senate apportionment is not entirely a dead letter. Disparities in state population have widened. After the first census in 1790, the spread of House seats between the most populous state (Virginia) and the least populous ones was 10 to 1. Today the spread between California and the least populous states is 52 to 1. Representatives of the most populous states complain that they are shortchanged in the federal bargain: compared with lightly populated states, they contribute more revenue and receive fewer benefits. Writes Sen. Daniel Patrick Moynihan, D-N.Y., "Sometime in the next century the United States is going to have to address the question of apportionment in the Senate."[4]

Today's senators tend to approach their tasks from a generalist's or nationwide perspective because their constituencies usually are large and diverse. When senators were selected indirectly and states were less populous, the Senate tended to be a collection of promoters for dominant regional interests such as cotton, railroads, or tobacco. Today, however, most states boast highly developed economies and reasonably competitive politics. Statewide electorates display ethnic, racial, and social diversity; many are microcosms of the whole nation. Senate seats are, in fact, more competitive than House seats—a state of affairs that would surely have confounded the Framers. So, although the Senate is malapportioned by design, it is not *necessarily* unrepresentative.

House Apportionment

The 435 House seats are apportioned among the states by population. This apportionment process excludes the four delegates (Guam, the District of Columbia, Virgin Islands, and Samoa) and one resident commissioner (Puerto

Rico); they speak for populations ranging from 70,000 (American Samoa) to 3.8 million (Puerto Rico).

To allocate House seats among the states, a census of population is taken every ten years by the Commerce Department's Bureau of the Census. These census figures also govern the allocation of legislative seats within the states. Moreover, the federal government uses population numbers and other census data (numbers of poor, city dwellers, ethnic groups, and so forth) to distribute funds to states and other entities; private researchers and business firms also rely upon these data.

Once the population figures from the decennial census are gathered, apportionment is derived by a mathematical formula called the method of equal proportions.[5] The idea is that proportional differences in the number of persons per representative for any pair of states should be kept to a minimum. The first fifty seats are fixed because the Constitution allots to each state at least one representative. The question then becomes: which state deserves the fifty-first seat, the fifty-second, and so forth? The mathematical formula yields a priority value for each seat, up to any desired number.

As the nation's population shifts, states gain or lose congressional representation. This outcome is especially true today, when the (presumably) fixed size of the House means that one state's gain is another's loss. For several decades older industrial and farm states of the Northeast and Midwest have lost ground to fast-growing states of the South and West—the declining Rust Belt versus the booming Sun Belt.

The 1990 census showed what a difference ten years can make: one inner-city Detroit district fell 134,000 persons below the national average of 570,000 people per district, while districts in California, Florida, and Texas overflowed with new residents. The resulting reapportionment shifted nineteen seats among the states. Winners were California (seven new seats); Florida (four); Texas (three); Arizona, Georgia, North Carolina, Virginia, and Washington (one each). Losers were New York (down three); Illinois, Michigan, Ohio, and Pennsylvania (down two each); Kansas, Kentucky, Louisiana, Massachusetts, Montana, and New Jersey (down one each). Figure 3-1 shows the 1990 allocation along with projected gains and losses from the 2000 census.

The decennial census is described as an "actual enumeration" (Article I, Section 2). But counting such a large and diverse population—there are 60,000 census tracts, each with some 1,700 dwellings—is logistically and methodologically daunting. Even when the direct count for the most recent decennial census (April 1, 1990) was supplemented with surveys and statistical adjustments, certain hard-to-contact groupings—transients, the homeless, renters, immigrants (legal or otherwise), and lower socioeconomic groups generally—eluded census takers and were undercounted.

Because population figures determine seats and affect power, nearly everything concerning the apportionment and districting process is controversial. Representatives from urban and border areas, where the hard-to count are

Figure 3-1 House Apportionment after the 1990 and 2000 Censuses

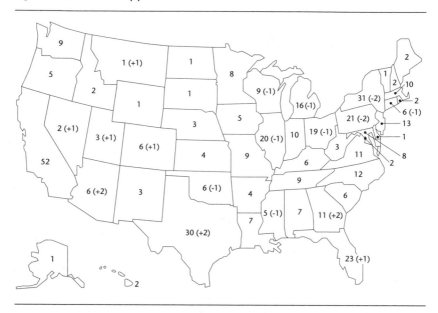

Source: David C. Huckabee, *House Apportionment Following the 2000 Census: Preliminary Projections,* Congressional Research Service Report, No. 98-135GOV, Dec. 31, 1998.

Note: Numbers in parentheses show projected gains and losses after 2000 census.

concentrated, successfully demanded a recount of the 1990 census. They hoped to minimize their losses of legislative seats and federal dollars. The Census Bureau's revised estimate, utilizing statistical projections, found that the original count missed more than 5 million residents, or 2.1 percent of the total. (The General Accounting Office placed the undercount at 9.7 million, or 3.9 percent.) Hispanics were undercounted (by as much as 5.2 percent), as were Native Americans (5 percent), blacks (4.8 percent), and Asians-Pacific Islanders (3.1 percent). If the revised estimate had been used to reapportion seats, Arizona and California could have gained seats at the expense of Oklahoma and Wisconsin. But the Republican secretary of commerce opted for the original figures amid cries from Capitol Hill Democrats that both counts had been politically biased. Ultimately, the Supreme Court upheld his decision. The grounds were that Congress had delegated to the secretary virtually unlimited discretion over conducting the census and that the Bureau's efforts had been "extraordinary" and, in the main, successful.[6]

The issue of statistical sampling became the pivot for partisan and regional conflict over the 2000 census. Census Bureau statisticians, backed by the Clinton administration, proposed counting only 90 percent of the people in 2000 and using statistical sampling and surveys to determine the rest. But Republi-

can leaders, led by House Speakers Newt Gingrich of Georgia and his successor, J. Dennis Hastert of Illinois, stoutly resisted sampling as "ripe for political manipulation." GOP strategists feared that higher counts of Democratically inclined groups would adversely affect the party in census-driven redistricting for elections in 2002 and beyond. (Many leaders in fast-growing, GOP-leaning states, like Texas and Florida, however, tended to support sampling because they figured it would benefit them in census-based federal aid formulas.)

The Republican House created a new subcommittee to track the census and sued in federal court to prevent the Census Bureau from implementing its sampling plan. The Supreme Court's ruling, on a 5–4 vote, did little to resolve the controversy. Rather than clarifying the Constitution's mandate for an "actual enumeration," the Court relied on the federal statute, which required an actual count for congressional apportionment but allowed alternative methods for other purposes. The Clinton administration chose to take the Court at its word: the 2000 census would try to count directly for House apportionment but would use sampling and surveys for other counts. Everyone, including the states, could choose whichever set of numbers suited them.

Because of population disparities between the states, reapportionment does not yield precisely equal districts. (Congressional districts cannot cross state lines.) Montana, reduced to a single House seat after the 1990 census, became the nation's largest single district, with 822,000 people. Its neighbor, Wyoming, with fewer than half a million people, was the least populated district.

Districting in the House

Once congressional seats are apportioned, those states with more than one seat must create districts. Each district is represented by a single member: a 1967 statute prohibits at-large or multimember elections in states with more than one seat. Districts must be nearly equal in population within states—a standard rigorously enforced by the courts—and they must not dilute representation of racial minorities, an outgrowth of amendments to the Voting Rights Act of 1965.

Redistricting is a fiercely political process upon which hinges the fortunes of the Republican and Democratic Parties, not to mention other intensely interested people—state legislators, governors, incumbent House members, lobbyists, and leaders of racial and ethnic causes. In the redistricting wars no weapons are left untouched. Consider the two parties' weapons in the redistricting cycle in the early 1990s. Democrats, who had dominated the statehouses for decades, controlled both chambers in thirty-one states after the 1990 elections. Republicans controlled both chambers in only five states; in thirteen states legislative chambers were divided between the two parties; in several—California and Illinois, for example—Republican governors could check the power of Democratic legislatures. If these political actors become deadlocked on redistricting, or if they fail to observe legal guidelines, judges may step in to finish the job—sometimes conferring victory on parties that lost out earlier in the political fracas.

Both parties thus engaged in "forum shopping," seeking the friendliest court to aid them in the remapping process. During President George Bush's administration, Republicans could rely on the Justice Department and a cooperative federal bench fortified by a decade of GOP appointments. Judicial partisanship was apparent in Alabama and Illinois, where Republican-appointed judges imposed Republican plans in opposition to Democratic majorities in both legislative chambers. (State courts should be preferred over federal courts in drawing up redistricting plans, the Supreme Court has ruled.)[7]

Districting for elections from 2002 through 2010 will hinge on how the contending parties utilize the same array of national and state resources. The Republicans entered the battle far stronger than a decade earlier: since 1992 they have won a net gain of fifty-seven House and eight Senate seats, not to mention ten governorships and hundreds of state seats. In 1999 GOP governors served in thirty-one states, including eight of the ten most populous ones. In fifteen states Republicans controlled the governorship and both legislative chambers. (Democrats had such control in eleven states, with divided government in the remaining twenty-four.) But Republican fortunes were clouded by emerging demographics—mainly the swelling ranks of Hispanic and African American voters who tended (as in 1998) to favor Democrats. So the GOP grappled with the Clinton administration over control of census taking. The 2000 elections would further determine who commanded the heights in the reapportionment and redistricting wars.

Because congressional seats are political prizes, districting is an instrument of partisan, factional, or even personal advantage. Two historical anomalies of districting are *malapportionment* and *gerrymandering*.

Malapportionment

Before 1964 districts of grossly unequal populations often existed side by side. Within a single state, districts varied by as much as eight to one. Rural regions tended to dominate growing urban areas in the state legislatures, where population disparities were even greater than among congressional districts. Sometimes malapportionment resulted from explicit actions; more often legislators simply failed to redistrict, letting population movements and demographic trends do the job for them. This failure to act was called the "silent gerrymander."

Preferring a posture of judicial restraint, the courts were slow to venture into the political thicket of districting. By the 1960s, however, the problem of unequal representation cried out for resolution. Although metropolitan areas had expanded in population and political clout, their representation still lagged in state legislatures and in Congress. Meanwhile, a new spirit of judicial activism had taken hold. In 1961 a group of Tennessee city-dwellers challenged the state's legislative districting, unaltered since 1901. In 1962 the Supreme Court held that federal courts had a right to review legislative districting under the Fourteenth Amendment's equal protection clause (*Baker v. Carr*). Two years later the Court was ready to strike down state districting

schemes that failed to meet standards of equality (*Reynolds v. Sims*, 1964). Chief Justice Earl Warren declared that state legislative seats, even under bicameral arrangements, must be apportioned "substantially on population."

That same year the principle of "one person, one vote" was extended to the U.S. House of Representatives. An Atlantan who served in the Georgia senate, James P. Wesberry Jr., charged that the state's congressional districting violated equal protection of the laws, and the Supreme Court upheld his challenge (*Wesberry v. Sanders*, 1964). The decision was based on Article I, Section 2, of the Constitution, which directs that representatives be apportioned among the states according to their respective numbers and that they be chosen by the people of the several states. This language, argued Justice Hugo Black, means that "as nearly as is practicable, one [person's] vote in a congressional election is to be worth as much as another's."

How much equality of population is "practicable" within the states? The Supreme Court has adopted rigid mathematical equality as the underlying standard. In a 1983 case (*Karcher v. Daggett*), a 5–4 majority voided a New Jersey plan in which districts varied by no more than one-seventh of 1 percent. "Adopting any standard other than population equality would subtly erode the Constitution's ideal of equal representation," wrote Justice William J. Brennan for the majority. This doctrine guarantees the federal courts an active role in redistricting. The dissenting judges, speaking through Justice Byron R. White, contended that the majority opinion would ensure "extensive intrusion of the judiciary into legislative business." They also maintained it was an "unreasonable insistence on an unattainable perfection" that would encourage gerrymandering by making mathematics more important than geographic or political boundaries. The Court invited states to defend districting plans that deviated from equality—for example, plans intended to make districts compact, follow municipal boundaries, preserve the cores of prior districts, or avoid contests between incumbent representatives. Yet such considerations had been summarily rejected in a 1969 Missouri case (*Kirkpatrick v. Preisler*).

Population equality thus is achieved at the expense of other goals. To achieve strict parity in numbers of residents, district makers must often violate political divisions, crossing city and county lines. It is not easy to follow economic, social, or geographic boundaries. The congressional district, therefore, tends to be an artificial creation with little relationship to real communities of interest—economic or geographic or political. "The main casualty of the tortuous redistricting process now under way," remarked journalist Alan Ehrenhalt in 1992, "is the erosion of geographical community—of place—as the basis of political representation."[8] The congressional district's isolation from other natural or political boundaries forces candidates to forge their own unique factions and alliances. It also aids candidates (incumbents especially) who have ways of reaching voters beyond relying on costly commercial communications media.

Traditional Gerrymandering

"All districting is gerrymandering" in the sense that single-member districts with a winner-take-all feature normally favor the majority party. The term *gerrymander* is usually reserved, however, for conscious line drawing to maximize seats for one's party or voting group. The gerrymander takes its name from Gov. Elbridge Gerry of Massachusetts, who in 1811 created a peculiar salamander-shaped district north of Boston to benefit his Democratic Party. Gerrymandering is used not only to provide partisan advantage but also to protect incumbents, boost state legislators' political ambitions, punish political enemies, and help or hinder racial or ethnic groups.

Congressional reapportionment laws from the mid-nineteenth to the early twentieth century usually required that districts be equal in population and contiguous in territory. A 1911 law specifying "contiguous and compact territory" lapsed, however, and has not been replaced, despite attempts to enact congressional districting standards. For most of its history, Congress has regarded gerrymandering as part of the spoils of partisan warfare.

Two gerrymandering techniques are *cracking* and *packing*. Cracking a district splits an area of partisan strength among two or more districts, thus diluting that party's voting leverage. Packing a district draws the lines to contain as many of one party's voters as possible, thus rendering the district "safe"— either to make your own party's representatives more secure or to confine your opponents' seats. Whatever the motivation, packed districts "waste" votes because the party wins with far more votes than it needs. For example, the racial and ethnic gerrymanders of the 1990s crowded Democratic voters into so-called majority-minority districts, in turn concentrating white voters in suburban Republican districts.

Partisan Gerrymandering. The most common form of gerrymandering, partisan districting, has occurred in states in which one political party clearly controls the process. A classic example was the 1981 California districting, masterminded by the late Democratic representative Phillip Burton. Burton's plan crushed several incumbent Republicans, bolstered threatened Democrats, and created districts for friendly state legislators. A GOP lawmaker called it the "mine-shaft plan": Democrats could say, "I got mine," and Republicans could say, "I got the shaft."[9] The plan netted five Democratic seats in 1982, surviving court challenges and a statewide referendum.

Such clear partisan gain from districting is relatively rare, and in any event the net effects tend to wash out in the nation as a whole. In the 1990's redistricting cycle, "neither party benefited in a major way nationwide," according to John Swain, Stephen Borelli, and Brian Reed.[10] Their measures recorded a Republican "advantage" of four districts in less than 1 percent of all House districts. (They did, however, note a decline in truly competitive districts for the decade.) "Partisan gerrymandering is, to say the least, an inexact science," Bruce Cain and David Butler caution. "In an era in which party loyalty has

been steadily declining, it is hard to predict whether a change in district composition will lead to a change in electoral outcome."[11]

The feasibility of partisan gerrymanders seems to depend on whether a state gains seats, loses seats, or retains the same number.[12] Where seats are added by reapportionment, a dominant party (like the California Democrats of the 1980s) can enlarge its delegation by shifting voters from safe-incumbent districts to new districts. If the state's apportionment is unchanged, partisan stability in districting is the norm because gerrymandering offers limited advantages. In states losing seats, partisan gerrymandering opportunities are also constrained. Such situations are so disruptive and threatening that the result is like a game of musical chairs, with incumbents of both parties fighting to save their seats.

On the issue of partisan gerrymandering the Supreme Court (like Congress) has chosen to look the other way. In a 1986 case involving Indiana state legislative districts, a Court majority held that gerrymandering was a justiciable issue (*Davis v. Bandemer*).[13] If the gerrymandering were substantial, long-standing, and truly harmful to the political minority, it could violate the Constitution's equal protection clause. At the same time, the Court's majority was not convinced the Indiana gerrymander met those tests. Although the Court invited legal challenges to partisan districting schemes, it has never confronted the problem of measuring inequities. And by 1999 the Court was ready explicitly to embrace a state's right to engage in "constitutional political gerrymandering"—whatever that might mean (*Hunt v. Cromartie*).[14]

Pro-incumbent Gerrymandering. Bipartisan or "sweetheart" gerrymanders are those with lines drawn to protect incumbents. Any gains or losses in the number of seats are shared by the two parties. These gerrymanders are commonly byproducts of divided party control—within the legislature or between the legislature and the governor. Such was the case in Ohio, which lost two House seats as a result of the 1990 census. The southern Ohio district of Republican representative Clarence E. Miller was obliterated in the state's new plan. After failing to win nomination in an adjacent district, Miller sued the state, contending that bipartisan gerrymandering violated the equal protection clause and that electoral districts should be politically neutral. In 1996 a three-judge federal panel rejected this argument, declaring that districting is a political process and legislators are entitled to draw up plans that protect incumbents. The Supreme Court upheld the decision without comment.[15]

Partisan advantage and incumbent advantage sometimes compete in districting. Naturally, safe districts are preferred by incumbents, but by furnishing outsized victories they squander the majority party's votes. More competitive or marginal districts (those won by, say, less than 55 percent of the votes) are tougher for a party to capture and hold, but they hold the promise of yielding legislative seats with a modest number of voters (that is, a minimal winning coalition).

By yielding more safe districts than competitive districts, gerrymandering has been blamed for contributing to the rising success of incumbents after the

late 1960s. The evidence, however, does not point in that direction. Incumbents are reelected just as frequently in unredistricted areas as in redistricted ones. Compared with other advantages of incumbency, districting seems to play a secondary role. Yet incumbents still seek and gain specific benefits from districting—for example, retention of familiar voters or exclusion of potential challengers.[16] Moreover, districting can affect the representation of political minorities, including racial and ethnic groupings.

Racial Gerrymandering

Another form of gerrymandering is intended to promote the election of racial minorities. The Voting Rights Act, enacted in 1965 to ensure the right of blacks to vote in elections, is credited with virtually eliminating voting discrimination. Coverage of language minorities was added in 1975. Amendments added in 1982 barred election laws having the intent or effect of reducing minority voting power (Section 2). States (mainly southern) that historically discriminated against minorities are required (under Section 5 of the act) to "preclear" changes in election rules with federal authorities to ensure that the changes do not have the purpose or effect of "denying or abridging the right to vote on account of race or color."

Under cover of the 1982 provisions, states not only were restrained from diluting ("cracking") minority votes, but were encouraged to "pack" districts to elect minority officeholders (majority-minority districts). Some commentators claimed that the act mandated or implied quotas for minority representation, even in the face of a proviso denying that the act "establishes a right to have members of a protected class elected in numbers equal to their proportion in the population." In a 1986 decision the Supreme Court enunciated tests to determine whether a minority's representation had been compromised. Is the group large enough and located in a compact enough area to elect a representative if grouped into a single district? Is the group politically cohesive? Is there evidence of racially polarized voting by the majority against candidates of that group?[17]

Faced with redistricting after the 1990 census, a number of states set about creating majority-minority black or Latino districts. States targeted as past offenders by the Voting Rights Act had additional prodding from the Bush administration's Justice Department. Its expansive reading of Section 5 of the act dictated *maximizing* the number of majority-minority districts (an interpretation ultimately rejected by the Supreme Court). It was not lost on Republican Party strategists that confining minority (mostly Democratic) voters into safe (mainly urban) districts would strengthen the GOP in outlying suburban areas. (A few Republicans objected that the strategy violated the party's stand against racial quotas of any kind.)[18] Democrats were paralyzed by internal divisions: traditional liberals could hardly argue against boosting the ranks of minority officeholders, even though racial gerrymandering threatened some longtime white incumbents and in a few areas pitted African American and Latino groups against one another.

The 1990s thus saw the creation of fifteen new African American districts, thirteen of them in the South (for a total of thirty-two nationwide, seventeen of them in the South) and nine new Latino districts (totaling twenty). Many of these were artfully contrived to concentrate minority voters, making Governor Gerry's 1811 creation look innocent by comparison. The Illinois Fourth District was drawn in a horseshoe shape to elect a Latino member. North Carolina's narrow Twelfth District (later twice redrawn) linked African American neighborhoods along 160 miles of Interstate 85 from Durham to Charlotte (see Figure 3-2). "I love the district," one candidate quipped, "because I can drive down I-85 with both car doors open and hit every person in the district."[19]

Minority officeholders and groups supporting them viewed racially gerrymandered districts as "the political equivalent to the ethnically homogeneous neighborhood," in the words of University of Pennsylvania law professor Lani Guinier. "They are a safe haven for members of that group, a bit of turf that one ethnic grouping controls, a place where their voice is pre-eminent."[20] But categorizing voters by race and ethnicity troubled critics. It created majority-minority enclaves while further "bleaching" nonminority districts. "Racial districting is a vision of America deeply at odds with that upon which the civil rights revolution was built," warned Abigail M. Thernstrom, a leading opponent. "Race-based districting has been unprincipled, unnecessary—and (to top it off) a gross distortion of the law."[21] In Justice O'Connor's words, racial districting conveys "the belief . . . that individuals should be judged by the color of their skin."[22]

Others wondered whether racial gerrymandering was really the most efficient way to advance minorities' interests. Concentrating minorities in their own districts, of course, wastes their votes by producing outsized electoral majorities for the winning candidates. In doing so, minority voters, along with whatever leverage they have, are drained from areas surrounding the new districts. Even if the number of minority officeholders rises, "the number of white legislators who have any political need to respond to minority concerns goes down as their minority constituents are peeled off to form the new black and Hispanic districts."[23] A better strategy for maximizing the political influence of minorities might be to maintain substantial minorities, say 40 percent or so, in the largest number of districts (termed "influence districts") in order to keep officeholders responsive to minority needs.[24]

Racial redistricting in the 1990s contributed to the Democratic Party's meltdown in the South. Political scientist Charles S. Bullock noted that "all districts held by Democrats in 1991 in which redistricting reduced the black percentage by more than 10 points have now fallen to the Republicans."[25] The GOP captured four of these districts in 1992, two more in 1994, and another in 1996; in 1998 it held these gains. Bullock summarized the impact of racial gerrymandering in the South:

After 1994, Republicans received handsome rewards while black Democrats were becoming an increasing numerical force within the minority party. The

Figure 3-2   Gerrymandering in the 1990s: North Carolina's First and Twelfth Districts

After the 1990 census (1992)

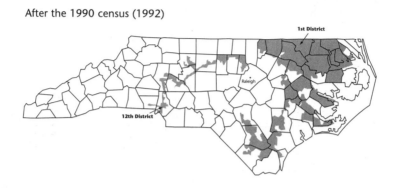

Two remaps later, after federal court decisions (1998)

Sources: Congressional Districts in the 1990s: A Portrait of America (Washington, D.C.: Congressional Quarterly, 1993), 548; *Congressional Staff Directory* 1999.

Note: North Carolina's First and Twelfth Districts were drawn to give the state its first black representatives in ninety-three years. Elected in 1992, the two representatives were reelected in 1994 and 1996.

replacement of moderate white Democrats with conservative Republicans, even with the addition of a few African American legislative seats, bodes ill for the ability of African American legislators to find the allies they need to achieve their policy goals.[26]

Political scientist David Lublin describes what he calls a "paradox of representation": majority-minority districts have fostered more minority lawmakers but have led to a more conservative House and reduced minorities' ability to influence legislative outcomes.[27]

The Court Enters the Quagmire

Since the 1960s the Supreme Court has repeatedly ruled against districts drawn deliberately to disadvantage a racial or ethnic group. In 1960 the Court declared unconstitutional the "obscene, 28-sided" boundaries of Tuskegee, Alabama, that disfranchised blacks by excluding them from the city (*Gomillion v. Lightfoot*).[28] Courts upheld the Voting Rights Act of 1965 and its later amendments, which, as we have seen, forbid districting that dilutes the voting power of racial or language minorities. But would districting aimed at multiplying minority officeholders pass constitutional muster?

Confronting Majority-Minority Districts. In a 1993 case, *Shaw v Reno*, the Court drew the line at the two oddly shaped North Carolina congressional districts mentioned earlier in this chapter, the First and Twelfth. White citizens contended that such blatant gerrymandering violated their right to equal protection under the law by diluting their votes. Although conceding that race-conscious districting might be permissible, the Court's narrow 5–4 majority was clearly shocked at the bizarre boundaries of the Twelfth District. Ironically, the majority opinion was written by the same Justice O'Connor who in 1987 had warned the judiciary against the slippery slope of gerrymandering standards. Here, O'Connor and her colleagues questioned "districting so highly irregular that, on its face, it rationally cannot be understood as anything other than an effort to segregat[e] voters . . . on the basis of race."[29]

In remanding the case to lower courts for further adjudication, the Court's majority suggested that districting (presumably even if race conscious) would be defensible if it followed "traditional . . . principles such as compactness, contiguity, and respect for political subdivisions." Yet, as dissenting justice John Paul Stevens pointed out, "there is no independent constitutional requirement of compactness or contiguity." Nor can one discern historical consensus about such principles: neat district lines have been thwarted not only by politics but also by judicial insistence upon mathematical equality of districts.

The very vagueness of *Shaw v. Reno* provoked a string of fresh legal challenges against race-conscious districts. Many of the fifty-two African American or Latino majority districts were open to challenge on the ground that they were created solely for racial separation that "lacks sufficient justification." In the next five years federal courts ruled on districting plans in several states—

most notably, California, Florida, Georgia, Louisiana, North Carolina (twice), and Texas.

In *Miller v. Johnson* (1995), the Supreme Court took a giant step along the path it began in *Shaw* by rejecting two Georgia districts drawn with race as the "predominant factor."[30] Justice Anthony Kennedy, writing for a 5–4 majority, began by correcting the implication in *Shaw* that "bizarre shape" itself was the key feature of impermissible districting. A district's shape taken alone is not decisive; however, it may offer one piece of persuasive evidence that "a state redistricting plan, on its face, has no rational explanation save as an effort to separate voters on the basis of race." To challenge a districting scheme as violating the equal protection clause, a plaintiff must prove that "race was the predominant factor motivating the legislature's decision to place a significant number of voters within or without a particular district." To prove racial predominance, it must be shown that "the legislature subordinated [to racial considerations] traditional race-neutral districting principles, including but not limited to compactness, contiguity, respect for political subdivisions of communities defined by actual shared interests." The fact that a state was simply complying with Justice Department pressure was not a compelling argument: the Court's majority found that the department's maximization policy—requiring states to create majority-minority districts wherever possible—not only exceeded Congress's intent in the Voting Rights Act but forced states to engage in "presumptively unconstitutional race-based districting."

The Court's minority, speaking through Justice Ruth Bader Ginsburg, noted that "legislative districting is a highly political business" and that "apportionment schemes, by their very nature, assemble people in groups." Historically, ethnic groupings have often sought and gained recognition through their own voting districts. "Until now, no constitutional infirmity has been seen in districting Irish or Italian voters together, for example." Why, she asked, shouldn't African Americans be accorded the same right? "Special circumstances justify vigilant judicial inspection to protect minority voters—circumstances that do not apply to majority voters."

By the decade's end several states had drawn new district maps in response to the Court's ruling in *Miller*. Affected majority-minority districts were in Texas (two of thirteen redrawn districts), Georgia (two), North Carolina (two), and Florida, Louisiana, and Virginia (one each). North Carolina's shoestring Twelfth District remained under a legal cloud after two remappings. Virtually all the minority members running in their new districts in 1996 and 1998 were victorious, some with widened margins. (The incumbent in Louisiana's Fourth District retired rather than run for reelection in an unfriendly area, and he was replaced by a white.) Foes of racial gerrymandering seized on the results as vindication. "The idea that minorities have to have a super-majority of black voters to win in their districts, that's history now," declared the lawyer who had challenged the Georgia districts. Black officeholders credited their success to incumbency, which they argued was made possi-

ble by racial gerrymandering. As explained by Democratic representative Cynthia A. McKinney, the feisty and flamboyant Georgian who fought fiercely to retain her old district and then to win her new one: "representing the old Eleventh District allowed me to run and win the new Fourth District without having to change my views, my gold tennis shoes, my braids, or having to auction off my principles to the highest bidder."[31]

Ultimately, answering the question of whether southern blacks can win in "bleached" districts must await future elections, with larger numbers of nonincumbents in such districts. In post-1995 elections Representative McKinney and other redistricted blacks have won by combining overwhelming black support with about 30 percent of the white vote. For the future, Charles Bullock expresses cautious optimism:

> The historic disparity in black and white registration and turnout used to justify the elevation of race above traditional districting concerns . . . has waned. Black registration rates are approaching those for whites and in the former majority-black districts may even exceed white registration rates. Black turnout still generally lags white voting rates, but the gaps are often not what they used to be. White advantages in participation rates can be offset by the greater willingness of whites to vote for black candidates than for black voters to cross over to white candidates.[37]

In the South and non-South alike, the winner-take-all system naturally impedes minorities—whether they be racial, ethnic, or partisan. Of the thirty-seven black candidates elected to the House in 1996, for example, only seven won in districts where fewer than 40 percent of the people were black.[33] Two of those were the redrawn Georgia districts. The future of black political power, and that of other minorities, depends upon candidates who can cross racial barriers.[34]

More to Come. Race-conscious districting will be contested well beyond the 2000 census. On the one hand, the courts can be expected to protect minority voting power from being diluted—in Justice Kennedy's words, "eradicating invidious discrimination from the electoral process." Moreover, states must not violate the Fourteenth Amendment's equal protection clause by drawing irregularly shaped districts based solely or primarily upon racial or ethnic considerations.

On the other hand, majority-minority districts can be valid if they are properly drafted by the states to serve compelling state governmental interests and adhere to what the Court regards as "traditional principles"—such as equality, compactness, contiguity, and respect for local political boundaries or communities of interest. The plan California drew after the 1990 census, while being conscious of race, was upheld by the Court as a fair, thoughtful application of desirable districting standards.[35]

Indeed, the guideposts erected in a 1999 Supreme Court holding give the states "very significant breathing room" in the post-2000 round of redistrict-

ing. The case (*Hunt v. Cromartie*) involved the much litigated North Carolina Twelfth District, whose black population had been whittled from 57 to 47 percent after two remappings. A group of white voters had persuaded a lower court that the newly remapped district was still racially gerrymandered. The state, for its part, argued that it simply wanted to create a district of loyal Democrats, many of whom happened to be black. Although not deciding between these arguments, the Court sent the matter back to the lower court panel with instructions to weigh the state's claims. In his decision for the Court, Justice Clarence Thomas declared:

> A jurisdiction may engage in constitutional political gerrymandering, even if it so happens that the most loyal Democrats happen to be black Democrats and even if the state were conscious of that fact. Evidence that blacks constitute even a supermajority in one Congressional district while amounting to less than a plurality in a neighboring district will not, by itself, suffice to prove that a jurisdiction was motivated by race in drawing its district lines when the evidence also shows a high correlation between race and party preference.[36]

All nine judges agreed with the decision, but the four consistent dissenters in earlier racial gerrymandering cases declined to sign Justice Thomas's opinion. In an opinion written by Justice Stevens, they held that the evidence of race-based districting in this instance was weak.

From this contentious and evolving controversy, we can draw the following conclusions. First, the Supreme Court, like many Americans, is distressed by legal distinctions (district lines, in this instance) based solely or primarily on race, and it will strictly scrutinize such arrangements case by case. Second, the justices are sharply divided about the proper response to the question of racial gerrymandering: every case in which districting plans were overruled turned on a 5–4 vote. Finally, in relying on "traditional race-neutral districting principles," the Court is on very shaky ground. Equality among districts aside, these so-called standards, such as compactness, contiguity, and respect for natural community boundaries, have not been consistently honored in the past. Indeed, the Court's own insistence on rigorous equality (districts must be nearly equal in population within states) has made some of these standards (especially respect for local communities) virtually impossible to achieve.

The Court's plunge into these choppy waters ensures that districting, as a leading formal element in the House recruitment process, will command avid attention from lawyers, politicians, and scholars. "The Court has not yet spoken a final word," warned Justice Ginsburg, who deplored as "unwarranted" the expansion of the judicial role.[37]

The "Matthew Effect"

Gerrymandering underscores a basic recruitment effect of our single-member district representation. If districts are equally competitive, the party winning the most votes captures a disproportionately large share of legislative

seats. This phenomenon is the "Matthew effect," named for a biblical aphorism (Matthew 13:12): "For whosoever hath, to him shall be given, and he shall have more abundance; but whosoever hath not, from him shall be taken away even that he hath."

Political analysts and critics of gerrymandering point to the *votes-seats gap*—that is, the discrepancy between a party's votes and the seats it receives. Yet many factors distort the ratio of seats to votes. In winner-take-all contests, winners receive a "bonus," while losers receive nothing, no matter how close the outcome. In theory a party could capture all the seats by winning every contest by a bare majority, a highly improbable outcome. Generally, though, the larger the margin of votes garnered by the majority party, the larger the excess of seats over votes.

During their decades of dominance, the Democrats reaped this advantage. Their share of U.S. House seats exceeded their share of the popular vote in all but three elections between 1942 and 1994; their average "bonus" of seats was 5.8 percent. In this century Democrats won 50.2 percent of all votes cast in House contests and Republicans won 45.5 percent. (The remainder went to other candidates.) Since 1994 the tables have turned, though just barely. That year the Republicans captured 53 percent of House seats with 52.4 percent of the two-party vote; in 1996 they won 52 percent of the seats with 50.2 percent of the two-party vote (only 300,000 votes, or 0.3 percent, ahead of Democrats). In 1998 their share of the two-party vote was the same as their seats: 51 percent.[38] Since the first widespread popular voting for senators began in 1914, Democratic candidates have captured 49 percent of the votes and Republicans 46 percent (other candidates account for 5 percent). In a majority of the elections—but not all—the winning party garnered a slight bonus of Senate seats beyond its share of the vote. In 1998 the Democrats won eighteen of the thirty-four contested seats (53 percent) with only 50.7 percent of the popular vote—the same share of votes that two years earlier netted the Republicans twenty-one of the thirty-four seats (62 percent) up for election.

Some seats are uncontested. In an average election year, fifty or more lucky representatives, and sometimes a senator or two, face no major-party opponents. In 1998 there were no less than ninety-three such House seats—twenty of twenty-three seats in Florida alone—though none in the Senate. General election ballots are cast in some of these districts but not in many others. Either way, nationwide vote tallies are distorted. One can only speculate on the party margins had real contests taken place.

Equally serious problems confront efforts to calculate a normal or equitable party share of state or district votes. How many Republicans or Democrats are there in a given area? Party registration figures are unreliable. Not all states have them, many voters register as independents, and voters sometimes register with a party other than their own (for example, to take part in a dominant party's primaries in a one-party area). American voters are notoriously fickle about party labels, and they are becoming more so. In any given election

a third or more of them split their tickets between the parties. Past voting records are decent guides to party affiliation (the architects of gerrymanders use them), but they are by no means infallible.

Another complication: the turnout of voters on election day varies widely among districts. Competitive or economically affluent areas tend to record higher voter totals than do one-party or economically deprived areas. In 1998, for example, more than 200,000 votes were cast in California's Tenth Congressional District (in San Francisco's East Bay), where Democrat Ellen O. Tauscher bested Republican Charles Ball in a lively contest. Meanwhile, in a south-central Los Angeles district (the Thirty-third), which is 84 percent Latino, Democrat Lucille Roybal-Allard won 87 percent of the mere 45,000 ballots cast. Raw vote totals, even within a single state, conceal vast demographic variations.

One thing is certain: the use of single-member districts with winner-take-all voting is one of the most fundamental rules of the recruitment game. This principle affects the shape and character not only of electoral constituencies but also of House and Senate membership.

Becoming a Candidate

Not all who are eligible for Congress run. Candidates who meet the legal qualifications must weigh a variety of considerations—some personal and emotional, others practical and rational. Candidacy decisions are often the pivotal moments in the entire recruitment process, although students of politics have only recently given them the attention they deserve. "The decision to run obviously structures everything else that goes on in the primary process," writes Sandy Maisel. "Who runs, who does not run, how many candidates run. These questions set the stage for the campaigns themselves."[39]

Called or Chosen?

In their heyday in this country—roughly from the time of Andrew Jackson in the 1830s to the decline of big-city machines in the 1960s—party organizations customarily enlisted and sponsored candidates. Then, as local party organizations withered, the initiative passed to the candidates themselves: self-starters who pulled their own bandwagons. "The skills that work in American politics at this point in history," writes Alan Ehrenhalt, "are those of entrepreneurship. At all levels of the political system, from local boards and councils up to and including the presidency, it is unusual for parties to nominate people. People nominate themselves."[40]

Although candidates now launch their own careers, most rely also on nationalized networks of party committees and allied interest groups. At the heart of these networks are the two major parties' House and Senate campaign committees, which have become increasingly aggressive in all phases of congressional elections.[41] They seek out and encourage promising candidates at the local level, sometimes even intervening to help ensure their nomination.

Once nominated, candidates receive assistance in nearly every phase of the campaign, from financing to finding seasoned campaign managers to digging up dirt on opponents. Filing deadlines must be met, backers lined up, and financing sought. Candidates are free to keep their national party at arm's length, but few nonincumbents can turn their backs on party sponsorship. Most would-be officeholders seek advancement within the two major parties, which boast not only the "brand loyalties" of a majority of voters but impressive financial and logistical resources as well.

During the recruiting season—beginning in early 1999 for the 2000 contests—the two major parties' leaders and campaign committee staffs "reach out across the country in search of political talent. Like college football coaching staffs in hot pursuit of high-school prospects, they are . . . putting together the lineups of the future."[42] Prospects can expect calls from presidents, former presidents, governors, high-profile financial backers, and other notables. Rep. Steny H. Hoyer, D-Md., the Democrats' lead recruiter (his counterpart is Rep. Anne M. Northrup, R-Ky.), also used a coaching analogy:

> If we find top-tier candidates, we really go after them pretty hard. It's like a basketball coach or a football coach. When you're recruiting, you don't want to offend the player but you want them to know you think they would be a great success.[43]

Not all recruiting takes place on the road. Because open seats—newly created districts or those in which incumbents have died or retired—are less secure, party leaders strive also to discourage their incumbent colleagues from retiring.

The most celebrated party recruitment mechanism was GOPAC, founded in 1979 to "fund a 'farm team' of Republican candidates at the state level who would then be available to run for higher office."[44] When then-representative Newt Gingrich took over GOPAC in the mid-1980s, he transformed it into a machine for building a Republican majority in the House. (As long as aspirants for local and state offices were targeted, GOPAC could circumvent federal contribution limits, but its use of tax-exempt organizations to fund its projects brought Gingrich a House reprimand in 1997.) At the heart of GOPAC was a research shop that developed and packaged conservative issue messages, based on extensive surveys, focus groups, and workshops. "Republican state legislators across the country," a close ally of Gingrich relates, "in drives back and forth across their states have been listening to Newt's tapes for nearly a decade. They have become whips, leaders, committee chairmen, and even speakers."[45] GOPAC's methods paid off when many of its farm team recruits reached Capitol Hill in the 1990s. Its methods have been widely imitated.

In light of citizens' apparent coolness toward the two major parties, it's reasonable to assume that independents and minor party candidates will increasingly enter congressional contests and that a few of them will win. In fact,

some twenty-five parties appeared on ballots in 1998. Very few such candidates have been elected in recent decades: one independent, Vermont's Rep. Bernard Sanders, now serves in Congress. Even when they fail, however, third-party contenders can affect election results. In a 1997 special election in northern New Mexico's Third District, where Democrats hold a 2–1 registration edge, the environmentalist Green Party—a rising force in the state—drew 17 percent of the votes, enabling the Republican candidate to eke out a victory. (The following year a new contender, Tom Udall, co-opted the Greens and recaptured the seat for the Democrats.) For the time being, however, would-be officeholders seek advancement within the two major parties, which boast not only the "brand loyalties" of a majority of voters, but impressive financial and logistical resources as well.

Nonparty groups also can help launch congressional candidates. The leading small-business lobby, the National Federation of Independent Business, was a major contributor to the GOP cause in 1994, after which federation members included four senators and thirty-three representatives (all Republicans). In the 1995–1996 cycle the NFIB began to pick potential candidates from its own membership, train them, and help them run for office. "We're trying to develop a farm team for down the road," explained the organization's national political director, "so we can work in more of a proactive instead of a reactive way," fielding rather than just endorsing candidates who support the small-business agenda.[46] Other organizations with strong grassroots networks now pursue the same course.

Amateurs and Pros

How do would-be candidates, whether self-starters or handpicked by party leaders, make up their minds to run? The answer depends on whether the individual is an amateur or a strategic politician.

Amateurs are by definition candidates without previous political experience. Despite their liabilities—inexperience and low name recognition (celebrities are an exception)—many amateurs run for Congress, and a few of them manage to win. Some amateurs are serious political strategists whose behavior resembles that of experienced politicians. Others run to bring a specific issue before the public; they are less interested in winning than in advancing a cause. But most are what David Canon calls "hopeless amateurs"—people with little or no chance of winning.[47] A long-shot bid is their only way of becoming a candidate: they run because "it was something they knew they were going to do sometime and for whatever reasons [it] appeared to be the right time."[48] "I think his chances have gone from absolutely out of the question to extremely remote," explained the wife of one hopeless contender. "But he's learning a lot, and I think he has enjoyed it."[49]

Strategic politicians, unlike amateurs, painstakingly weigh the pros and cons of launching a campaign. Do the rewards exceed the drawbacks of the office, especially compared with what I am doing now? What are the chances of

success, and what will it cost to succeed? If there is an incumbent, what are his or her weaknesses? What are my strengths and weaknesses in campaigning, voter appeal, and fund raising? What local or national trends will boost, or lower, my chances?

The circle of people pondering these questions—the challenger pool—is large or small, depending on the office and the circumstances.[50] Any number of elected officials—especially state legislators (many of whom face retirement from state term limits), county officers, mayors, city council members, even governors—are weighing a race for Congress. If they are entrenched, they may wait for an opening.

Of all the inducements to launch a candidacy, the likelihood of winning stands at the top. A seat that is clearly winnable seldom lacks for candidates eager to capture it. Open seats especially attract contenders. Given the looseness of party ties, races lacking an incumbent candidate are more likely to be competitive and to shift in party control than those with an incumbent. Party strategies thus pinpoint those races.

In most House and Senate contests, however, incumbents will be running, and most of them will be reelected. As Gary C. Jacobson writes, "Nearly everything pertaining to candidates and campaigns for Congress is profoundly influenced by whether the candidate is an incumbent, challenging an incumbent, or pursuing an open seat."[51] With only slightly less force, the same could be said of the Senate.

Anyone contemplating a congressional race would do well to study Table 3-1 with care. Since World War II, on average, 92 percent of all incumbent representatives and 78 percent of incumbent senators running for reelection have been returned to office. Higher than normal casualty rates occur periodically: for example, the post–World War II generational shift (1946–1948), a midterm recession (1958), Barry Goldwater's failed candidacy (1964), the Watergate burglary fallout (1974), and a combination of generational shift and conservative realignment (1978–1980). During the early 1990s, political unrest, Capitol Hill scandals, an economic recession (in 1992), and voter anger at those in charge (the Democrats and President Clinton in 1994) conspired to produce the largest turnover in two generations. But 1996 and 1998 were very good years for incumbents. Historically, incumbents' reelection rates have always been robust, whereas voluntary turnover declined in the late nineteenth century and has remained low ever since (see Figures 3-3 and 3-4).

Nowadays defeating a House incumbent is an uphill struggle, short of a major scandal or misstep. This is a relatively recent phenomenon. Although incumbents have been fattening their margins of victory for some time, through the 1970s they were just as vulnerable to defeat as they had been earlier. That is, incumbents were, on average, winning by wider margins, when they did win, but they were just as likely to lose any given election as before.[52] By the 1980s, however, incumbents had erected imposing barriers against defeat by amassing campaign war chests and aggressively exploiting perquisites.

Table 3-1 The Advantage of Incumbency in the House and Senate, 1946–1998

Year	House					Senate				
	Seeking reelection	No opponent	Defeated Primary	Defeated General	Percent reelected	Seeking reelection	No opponent	Defeated Primary	Defeated General	Percent reelected
1946	398	81	18	52	82.4	30	1	6	7	56.7
1948	400	83	15	68	79.2	25	5	2	8	60.0
1950	400	99	6	32	90.5	32	3	5	5	68.8
1952	389	93	9	26	91.0	31	3	2	9	64.5
1954	407	86	6	22	93.0	32	6	2	6	75.0
1956	411	73	6	16	94.6	29	5	0	4	86.2
1958	396	94	3	37	89.9	28	1	0	10	64.3
1960	405	78	5	25	92.6	29	3	0	1	96.6
1962	402	58	12	22	91.5	35	1	1	5	82.9
1964	397	42	8	45	86.6	33	1	1	4	84.8
1966	411	56	8	41	88.0	32	3	3	1	87.5
1968	409	46	4	9	96.8	28	2	4	4	71.4
1970	401	59	10	12	94.5	31	0	1	6	77.4
1972	390	54	12	13	93.6	27	0	2	5	74.0
1974	391	59	8	40	87.7	27	2	2	2	85.2
1976	384	52	3	13	95.8	25	2	0	9	64.0
1978	382	69	5	19	93.7	25	1	3	7	60.0

(Table continues on next page)

Table 3-1 The Advantage of Incumbency in the House and Senate, 1946–1998 (*continued*)

| | House | | | | | Senate | | | | |
Year	Seeking reelection	No opponent	Defeated Primary	Defeated General	Percent reelected	Seeking reelection	No opponent	Defeated Primary	Defeated General	Percent reelected
1980	398	53	6	31	90.7	29	1	4	9	55.2
1982	396	53	18	29	90.6	30	0	0	2	93.3
1984	410	60	13	17	95.1	29	1	0	3	89.7
1986	393	71	12	6	98.0	28	0	0	6	75.0
1988	410	79	11	6	98.3	27	0	0	4	85.2
1990	406	74	10	15	96.3	32	5	0	1	96.8
1992	350	17	19	24	87.7	28	0	1	3	85.7
1994	389	38	14	34	90.2	26	0	0	2	92.3
1996	384	14	2	21	94.0	20	0	1	1	90.0
1998	401	93	1	6	98.3	29	0	0	3	89.7
Fifty-two-year average	396.5	63.1	7.0	26.0	91.8	28.7	1.3	1.6	4.7	78.2

Sources: *Congressional Quarterly Weekly Report*, April 5, 1980, 908; Nov. 8, 1980, 3302, 3320–3321; July 31, 1982, 1870; Nov. 6, 1982, 2781; Nov. 10, 1984, 2897, 2901; Nov. 12, 1988, 3264, 3270; Nov. 10, 1990, 3796–3805 Nov. 7, 1992, 3557–3564, 3570–3576; Nov. 12, 1994, 329ff; Feb. 15, 1997, 447–455; Nov. 7, 1998, 3027–3035.

Note: Percent reelected includes both primary and general election defeats.

Figure 3-3   House Reelection and Turnover Rates, 1790–1998

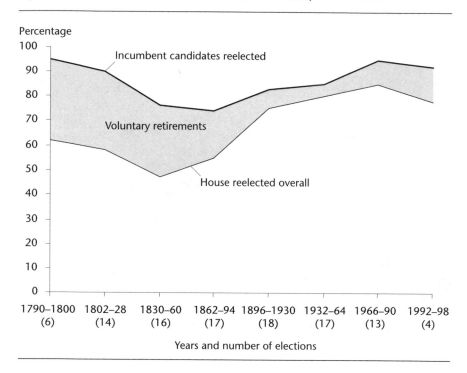

Percentage

1790–1800 1802–28 1830–60 1862–94 1896–1930 1932–64 1966–90 1992–98
   (6)   (14)   (16)   (17)   (18)   (17)   (13)   (4)

Years and number of elections

Sources: Calculated by the authors from David C. Huckabee, *Reelection Rates of House Incumbents, 1790–1988,* Congressional Research Service Report, No. 89-173, March 16, 1989, and from Table 3-1. Authors' figures are used for the 1990s.

Therefore, competition for their House seats dropped to exceedingly low levels. Incumbent advantage fell perceptibly in the early 1990s. The anti-incumbent atmosphere emboldened many strategically minded nonincumbents to try for House or Senate seats; even so, turnover resulted less from electoral defeats than from retirements (some of them involuntary, to be sure). In those years of upheaval from 1990 to 1994, 194 members retired and 112 were defeated for reelection.[53]

Senate races tend to be closer, and so challengers—often well known and amply financed—have a better chance of unseating incumbents than do challengers for House seats. Indeed, in the past two decades Senate contests have become somewhat more competitive overall than have House races. This competitiveness is mainly a byproduct of the South's dramatic shift from a Democratic to a Republican bastion—a statewide development that spread into House districts only in the 1990s. In nonsouthern states, however, Senate contests are less competitive than formerly. Four of five incumbents win the contests they enter; the proportion of "marginal" elections (candidates winning by

Figure 3-4   Senate Reelection and Turnover Rates, 1790–1998

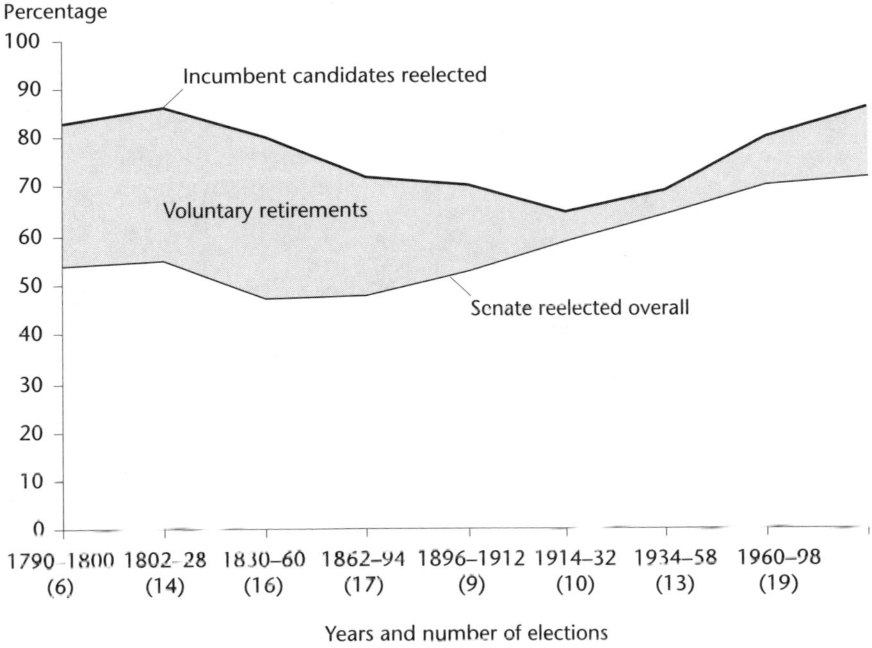

Percentage

Years and number of elections

Sources Calculated by the authors from David C. Huckabee, *Reelection Rates of Senate Incumbents, 1790–1988*, Congressional Research Service Report, No. 90-250, May 15, 1990, and from Table 3-1. Authors' figures are used for the 1990s.

less than 60 percent) has dropped. Winning candidates receive more than 60 percent of the vote in almost half of nonsouthern Senate elections.[54]

Why are incumbents so formidable? Political scientists have launched a veritable cottage industry to answer this question. It is no secret that incumbents have built-in methods of promoting support—through speeches, press coverage, newsletters, staff assistance, and constituent service. The average House member enjoys perquisites valued at nearly two million dollars in a two-year term; senators, with six-year terms, have resources between $10 million and $18 million.

Everyone concedes the value of incumbents' perquisites, but scholars differ sharply on exactly how they affect electoral success. One view is that incumbents exploit their resources to ensure reelection, seizing upon their ability to assist constituents in dealing with the bureaucracy to build electoral credit. Others counter that legislators simply are responding to constituents' demands and technological advances in communications. Still others question whether incumbents' resources are directly translatable into votes. However

these questions are resolved (we discuss them further in Chapters 4 and 5), incumbents spend much of their time and effort forging links with their voters, and these links typically hold fast on election day.[55]

As Jacobson observes, *"The incumbent's most effective electoral strategy is to discourage serious opposition."*[56] On average, some sixty representatives and one senator in each electoral cycle face no opponents at all. Impressive victory margins are beneficial; any drop may invite opponents the next time around. That is why wise incumbents try to sustain wide electoral margins, show unbroken strength, keep up constituency ties, and build giant war chests of funds. If these tactics fail, there is always the option of retiring more or less gracefully.

Finding the Quality Challengers

The quality of challengers and the vigor of their campaigns are critical factors in many battles for congressional seats.[57] Often the races turn on bids that are not made. During their decades of dominance on Capitol Hill, Democrats tended to field experienced candidates; the minority Republicans often fell short of matching them—even when a Republican occupied the White House. The upheavals of the 1990s brought out many challengers and forced many incumbents into retirement; but even then not a few incumbents coasted to victory because they had stockpiled enough goodwill and campaign resources to frighten off opponents.

The parties' successes at the polls in November hinge on their efforts during the recruitment season. The Republicans' recruiting bonanza for the 1994 and 1996 contests was no mystery: given citizens' anger and President Clinton's unpopularity, strategic politicians throughout the country could see that Democrats were vulnerable and that joining the GOP ticket offered them unusually good odds for advancement. Democrats, for their part, felt the foul political winds and decided to get out of the gale: fourteen of the party's senators and fifty representatives declined to run in those two elections, while scores of potential candidates declined to enter the races. Two senators and five representatives even switched to the GOP. As a result, the Democratic Party fielded a relatively weak team of challengers in 1996: only 22.1 percent of their candidates had previous experience in elective office. This number was below the party's average mix of such candidates (25.3 percent in postwar elections) and far short of what would be needed to make sizable inroads (35.7 percent in years of big Democratic gains).[58]

By the time the 1996 balloting occurred, citizens' anger had cooled, President Clinton's stock had rebounded, and it was the Republicans—blamed for shutting down the federal government in the winter of 1996 (see Chapter 13)—who struggled to cut their losses. But Democratic challengers were too weak to recapture the House: they netted an eight-seat gain, whereas eighteen seats were needed for a majority. Although twelve of the experienced challengers bested GOP incumbents, too few of the "amateurs" were successful.

(One exception was Long Island Democrat Carolyn McCarthy, discussed in Chapter 1.) The Democrats' failure to recapture the House can be attributed in part to their tepid recruitment season some months earlier. As for the Republicans, their majority status attracted strategically minded politicians and enabled them to recruit more experienced candidates than their opposition. In politics, nothing succeeds like success.

The playing field again shifted in 1998. Both parties recruited zealously. But with Clinton's reelection and the party's gains in the House, Democrats were able to nail down quality candidates early—before the White House sex scandal broke. The party also showed a willingness to seek out contenders in swing districts who did not fit the party's profile—who were, for example, conservative or anti-abortion.[59] By November these candidates were well positioned to ride the wave of anti-impeachment sentiment, and the party gained five more House seats—still short of a majority. The GOP also fielded strong contenders, although conservative groups vetoed some centrist prospects who might have held certain swing districts like California's Twenty-second (Santa Barbara). The run-up to 1999–2000 saw another fierce recruiting season, as both parties sought lineups that could win them House and Senate majorities.

When they beat the bushes for "quality challengers," what do party recruiters look for? Broadly speaking, quality challengers are people who are attractive to voters and skilled in presenting themselves as candidates. Attractiveness typically means having gained experience in public office, which implies visibility among, and credibility with, the voters. Alternatively, fame or notoriety may overcome lack of prior background or experience. Attributes in clude physical appearance and personality, a talent for organizing or motivating others, and the ability to raise enough money for an effective campaign.

All too often candidates of such caliber prefer to remain in the bushes. The road to public office can be arduous and costly, and the odds are often long, especially against a dominant party or an entrenched incumbent. Therefore, quality challengers may not surface. Needless to say, low-quality challengers raise less money and are less successful than the handful of blue-ribbon contenders. The dynamic works in Senate as well as House elections. "The quality of Senate challengers varies, and the higher the quality of a challenger the more votes he or she receives and the more likely the challenger is to defeat an incumbent."[60]

Most successful candidates are seasoned politicians long before they run for Congress. Grassroots organizations and movements are a breeding ground for a number of candidates—for example, environmental activists in the 1970s and religious conservatives in the 1990s. More often, elective offices are the springboards: mayors, district attorneys, or state legislators for the House, and for the Senate officeholders who have already faced a statewide electorate—governors, lieutenant governors, and attorneys general. House members, especially from smaller states, are also strategically positioned: no less than forty-six senators in the 106th Congress had moved over from the House.

Amateurs with highly visible nonpolitical careers may be nicely positioned to move into politics. Astronauts, war heroes, entertainers, and athletes are in big demand as candidates. Local or statewide television personalities also make attractive contenders. Although Minneapolis news anchor Rod Grams had never run for public office, he commissioned a poll to assess his chances as a House candidate and found that 92 percent of the voters in Minnesota's Sixth District already knew him.[61] Such high name recognition helped carry him to victory in the 1992 GOP primary and the general election (where he defeated a five-term incumbent) and to the Senate two years later. At least half a dozen members won initial visibility as television personalities. Only occasionally do other nonpolitical careers have such visibility. First elected to the Senate in 1988, Democrat Herb Kohl was familiar throughout Wisconsin from his family's food stores long before he wrote an $18.5 million check in 1985 to keep the Milwaukee Bucks basketball team from moving elsewhere—not a bad advertisement for a would-be senator.

The Personal Equation

Personal attributes also determine who is urged to run, and who decides to run, for Congress. Stamina, background, personal style, and physical appearance determine whether someone has "the right stuff" for campaigning. Ambition and a keen desire for public life and congressional perquisites lead people to become candidates and help them to succeed.[62]

Many potential candidates—no one knows how many—disqualify themselves because they are physically or emotionally unprepared for the rigors of campaigning. Not everyone has the capacity to hit the road nonstop, meet new people, attend meetings, sell themselves, ask for money, and endure verbal abuse—all the while appearing to enjoy it. "People who do not like to knock on strangers' doors or who find it tedious to repeat the same 30-second introduction thousands of times," explains Ehrenhalt, "are at a severe disadvantage in running for office."[63]

Other candidates reject campaigns because of the cost to their personal lives, incomes, and families. From the number of successful politicians who complain about such sacrifices, however, one can only conclude that many misjudge the costs before taking the plunge. Many simply indulge in self-delusion. Sandy Maisel, a political scientist who wrote candidly of his unsuccessful congressional primary campaign, described politicians' "incredible ability to delude themselves about their own chances. If I could honestly think that a young, liberal Jewish college professor from Buffalo could win a primary and then beat a popular incumbent in Downeast Maine, any level of delusion is possible."[64]

Nominating Politics

Nominating procedures, set forth in state laws and conditioned by party customs, help to shape the potential pool of candidates. Historically, they have

spread to ever wider circles of participants—a development that has diminished party leaders' power and thrust more initiative upon the candidates themselves. In most states the *direct primary* is the formal mechanism for nominating congressional candidates. Some Republican Parties in southern states use conventions, and several states combine conventions with primaries. But direct primaries are the ticket to nomination for the vast majority of members of Congress.

Despite the prevalence of primaries, state and district party organizations are not without leverage in nominations. To be sure, party organizations play no active part in the primary process in the majority of states.[65] But in nine states, parties have conventions that influence candidates' access to the primary ballot—for example, by conferring preprimary endorsements. In eight others, party organizations informally influence the process, through endorsements or other actions that can boost favored candidates. One such state is Illinois, where the following tale of party influence took place. Freshman representative John Grotberg, from the rock-ribbed Republican Fourteenth District, fell seriously ill early in 1986, then awoke from a five-week coma too late to withdraw from the primary. So in late May party leaders, lacking a candidate, convened to name a replacement. Because of deep divisions within some counties, the convention's choice was someone who had been appointed five years earlier to fill a vacant state legislative seat from the district's least populous county. Some disgruntled candidates grumbled at the outcome and threatened to bolt the party.[66] But after winning a close race in 1986, the new representative consolidated his district support and proved his worth on Capitol Hill. Twelve years later, another sudden resignation lifted the representative, J Dennis Hastert, to the House speakership.

Who should be permitted to vote in a party's primary? The states have adopted varying answers. The *closed primary*, found in twenty-six states, requires voters to declare party affiliation to vote on their parties' nominees. This affiliation is considered permanent until the voter takes steps to change it. Party leaders naturally prefer strict rules of participation that reward party loyalty, discourage outsider candidates, and maximize the leaders' influence over the outcome. Therefore, states with strong party traditions typically have closed primaries. In the *open primary*, conducted in twenty states, voters can vote in the primary of either party (but not in both) simply by requesting the party's ballot at the polling place. Alaska, California, Louisiana, and Washington use the *blanket, or nonpartisan, primary* (politicians call it the "jungle primary"). In these states a single multiparty ballot permits voters to cross party lines to vote for one candidate for each office; the top vote getter from each party advances to the general election. Louisiana employs a variation under which all candidates run on one ballot. If a candidate receives a majority, he or she is elected; if no one gains a majority, the top two vote getters, regardless of party, move on to the general election.

Not all primaries are competitive races. In the 1982–1990 period, nearly 70 percent of representatives and 60 percent of senators faced no challenge at

all for renomination. The 1994–1996 period saw similar figures. Only twelve incumbents faced closely contested primaries; only 30 percent had any contests at all.[67]

Contests usually occur in both parties if the House or Senate seat is open and within the challenging party if the seat is deemed competitive. The level of competition depends on the party's prospects in the general election. "If a district party is without an incumbent, and has a fighting chance in November," Harvey L. Schantz writes, "there is a strong possibility of a public contest for the U.S. House nomination."[68] In one-party areas the dominant party's nomination is "tantamount to" election. Within that party, open seats are virtually certain to be contested, and in some states runoff primaries are held when no one receives a majority. Contests also are likely in two-party competitive areas.

The direct primary was one of the reforms adopted early in the twentieth century to overcome corrupt, boss-dominated conventions. Certainly, it has permitted more participation in selecting candidates. Yet primaries normally attract a narrower segment of voters than do general elections (except in some one-party states, where primaries dictate the outcomes). Less publicized than general elections, primaries tend to attract voters who are somewhat older, wealthier, better educated, more politically aware, and more ideologically committed than the electorate as a whole.[69]

Primaries also have hampered the political parties by encouraging would-be officeholders to appeal directly to the public and construct support networks apart from party leaders. Of course, leaders still strive to influence who enters their primaries and who wins them. In recent years local and national Republican leaders pushed two controversial House freshmen into retirement, coaxed a former member to succeed one of them (with the promise of a committee chairmanship), and worked to quash primary challenges to several incumbents. GOP leaders, however, have sometimes been rebuffed when their moderate choices suffer defeat in primaries to candidates with right-wing appeal.

In Texas in 1996 Victor Morales, a former high school civics teacher who campaigned from a pick-up truck, upset Democratic representative John Bryant, the establishment's choice to take on Republican senator Phil Gramm. Morales won the Senate primary, Bryant explained, because "a lot of people very much love the idea of a guy [doing well] who's not connected in any way to an organized effort."[70] (Morales lost his face-off with Gramm.) In a bizarre case of nomination politics, Virginia's senior senator, John Warner, defied state party leaders yet won the party primary in 1996. Warner had angered his state's ultraconservative GOP leadership two years earlier by opposing their Senate candidate, right-wing hero Lt. Col. Oliver North. It is doubtful that the party's convention would have renominated Warner. But Virginia law allows incumbents to choose their nominating vehicle, and Warner shunned the convention in favor of an open primary. With support from moderates and some Democrats, Warner won the primary and eventually reelection.

primaries are a costly way of choosing candidates: unless candi-
with overwhelming advantages (such as incumbency), they must
lly the same kind of campaign in the primary that they must repeat later in the general election.

The Money Factor

"Money is the mother's milk of politics," declared California's legendary
boss, Jess Unruh. Money is not everything in politics, to be sure, but many
candidates falter for lack of it, and many others squander valuable time and
energy struggling to get it. Money attracts backers (who in turn give more
money), it can frighten away rivals, and it can augment or lessen the gap between incumbents and challengers. Every candidate, writes Paul S. Herrnson,
wages not one but two campaigns—a campaign for resources that precedes,
and underwrites, the more visible campaign for votes.[71]

Campaigns in the United States are very costly. In the 1997–1998 electoral
cycle, congressional candidates raised $665 million and spent most of it. The
average Senate race now costs $3.5 million. House contests average $533,000;
twenty-five years ago (when modern record keeping began) no House candidate spent that much.[72] Competitive races run much higher: in 1998 ninety-
four House contenders spent in excess of $1 million (three-quarters of them
won). Even controlling for inflation, expenditures for congressional campaigns
more than doubled between 1974 and 1998. And beyond what candidates
spend, interest groups of all stripes throw untold millions of dollars into independent efforts aimed at changing election outcomes.

No mystery surrounds these skyrocketing costs. Inflation, population
growth, and new campaign technologies—media ads, polling, and consultants
of all kinds—account for much of the increase. Moreover, long-term changes
in the campaign process itself have escalated costs. In old-style campaigns,
candidates were nominated by party insiders in a caucus or convention; at the
general election stage, candidates could call upon the party's legions of volunteers to mobilize loyal voters and to canvass precincts. Contrast that process
with modern campaigns in which candidates are nominated by winning a primary election and then must face general election voters who can be reached
most effectively through direct mail, phone banks, or electronic media. Campaign services once provided by well-oiled parties must now be purchased on
the open market. That is why today's costs of reaching voters are so high.

Campaign price tags also depend on the level of competition and other
characteristics of the electoral unit. "Candidates for open seats tend to raise
and spend the most money because when neither candidate enjoys the benefits of incumbency, both parties normally field strong candidates, and the election is usually close."[73] Costs in competitive races can be astronomical. New
York's 1998 Senate slugfest between Republican incumbent Alfonse M. D'Amato
and Democratic representative Charles E. Schumer cost $40.3 million—that
year's most expensive race.

A district's demography also affects campaign costs. One study showed that suburban districts have the most expensive campaigns and urban districts the least expensive, with rural districts somewhere in between.[74] In the suburbs partisan loyalties are notoriously weak and contests volatile. Lacking stable party organizations, candidates must advertise through paid media. In rural districts wide open spaces keep costs high: candidates must travel farther and advertise in many small media markets to get their messages across. In cities candidates shun media contests because of the huge cost and wasted effort of televising to adjoining districts. Here, too, party organizations are strongest. The cheapest victory in 1998 was in New York's Sixth District (Queens), where incumbent Gregory W. Meeks, who was unopposed, spent less than $40,000.

The Haves and Have Nots

Although incumbents need less money than do challengers, they receive more—a double-barreled financial advantage (see Figure 3-5). Because they are better known and have government-subsidized ways of communicating with constituents, incumbents usually can communicate their message less expensively than challengers can. Incumbents tend to attract more money than challengers do because contributors see them as better "investments." As Jacobson points out, "Incumbents can raise whatever they think they need. They are very likely to win, and even when they lose, it is almost always in a close contest."[75]

Many incumbents, in fact, finish their campaigns with a surplus: after the 1997–1998 electoral cycle, the average returning House member had about a quarter-million dollars on hand. This money can be hoarded for future races, dispensed to needier candidates, or used to buy constituency goodwill through outreach projects or charitable donations.

The incumbency advantage in fund raising, especially in House contests, is bipartisan. From the mid-1970s through 1994, the advantage worked to the benefit of Democrats, who had more incumbents than Republicans had. This advantage has now shifted toward Republican incumbents. As a party the GOP has consistently been more effective at raising funds than have the Democrats; as a congressional majority party it harvests a bounty from lobby groups, eager as always to back winners in order to gain access to the policy-making process. As long as Democrats threaten to recapture majority status, however, they will gather funds from groups eager to bet on their prospects.

Shaking the Money Tree

Raising money preoccupies all candidates. Incumbents need it to scare off opponents, challengers need it to gain visibility, and contenders for open seats need it to gain an edge. Fund raising is time consuming, odious, and demeaning. "I'd rather wrestle a gorilla than ask anybody for another fifty cents," grumbled John Glenn, D-Ohio, as he departed in 1998 after twenty-four years in the Senate.[76]

Figure 3-5   Average Campaign Expenditures for Incumbents, Challengers, and Open-Seat Candidates, House and Senate (1972–1998)

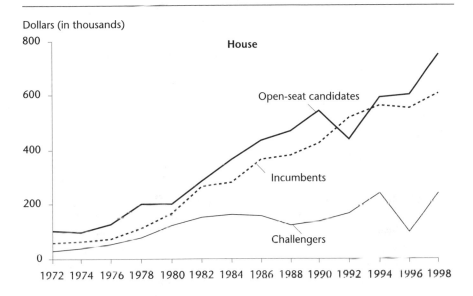

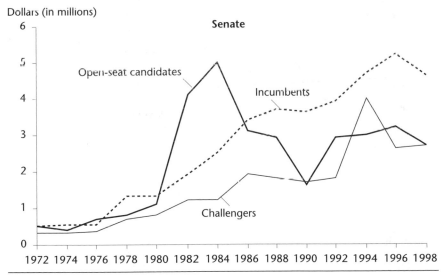

Sources: Congressional Research Service reports by Joseph E. Cantor, *Cost of Congressional Elections, 1972–1982: Statistics on Total Average Campaign Spending,* Aug. 6, 1984; Joseph E. Cantor and David Huckabee, *House Campaign Expenditures, Receipts and Sources of Funds: 1980–1992,* June 1993, 20; *Senate Campaign Expenditures, Receipts and Sources of Funds: 1980–1992,* May 19, 1993, 20; Norman J. Ornstein, Thomas E. Mann, and Michael J. Malbin, *Vital Statistics on Congress, 1997–1998* (Washington, D.C.: Congressional Quarterly, 1998), 81–85; Federal Election Commission, "1998 Congressional Activity Declines," news release, Dec. 29, 1998.

Funding sources fall into several categories: donations from individuals (including those from candidates and their families), from party committees, and from political action committees (PACs). Major sources are summarized in Table 3-2.

Individuals. More than half the money raised by House candidates comes from individuals. (The percentage is greater for Senate candidates.) Individuals may lawfully contribute up to $1,000 per candidate for primaries and $1,000 per candidate in the general elections, totaling no more than $5,000 in any given year. Primary, runoff, and general contests are regarded as separate elections. Individuals may contribute up to $20,000 a year to a political party, and they may spend an unlimited amount independently to promote parties, causes, or candidates. Expenditures greater than $250 must be reported, and the individual must declare that the money was not spent in collusion with the candidate. (Individuals may give up to $1,000 for a candidate and $2,000 for a party in volunteer expenses—housing, food, personal travel—without reporting it.) Many individual donations are solicited by interest groups, which seek to magnify their influence by collecting and then forwarding these personal checks to the designated candidates, a practice known as *bundling.*

There are no restrictions on how much congressional candidates may contribute to their own cause. (Donations and loans from family members also are unrestricted.) In the 1997–1998 cycle, Senate contenders contributed or lent more than 10 percent of their campaign funds; House candidates provided 6 percent.

In long-shot races a candidate's ability to shoulder the financial burden may attract support from party or group leaders. In other cases heavy spending by the candidate may help pad a front-runner's margin of victory or boost an underdog's chances of winning. Sen. John D. Rockefeller IV, D-W.Va., spent about $10 million of his fortune to win his Senate seat in 1984—more than $27 for every vote he received. But the costliest votes were probably those snagged by venture capitalist Christopher Gabrieli, who spent $5.2 million in his 1998 bid for the Democratic nomination in the Boston-area Eighth District (a seat being vacated by Joseph Kennedy, whose uncle, John F. Kennedy, had also held it). Gabrieli ran sixth in the primary with only 5,740 votes (6.8 percent)—$904 per vote!

Federal law requires strict accounting by candidates and political committees. All contributions of $50 or more must be recorded; donors of more than $100 must be identified. Accounting of funds must be made by a single committee for each candidate, and receipts and expenditures must be reported regularly.

Party Committees. National, congressional, and state party campaign committees may contribute $5,000 apiece to each House candidate at each stage of the electoral process—primary, runoff, and general election. The national and senatorial committees can give a combined total of $17,500 to each Senate candidate in an election cycle, whereas state committees can give $5,000.

Table 3-2 House and Senate Campaign Contributions by Source, 1984–1998 (in thousands of dollars)

Contribution	1984	1986	1988	1990	1992	1994	1996	1998
				House Elections				
Average total	$ 249	$ 289	$ 306	$ 319	$ 389	$ 451	$ 528	$ 533
Percentage from								
Individuals	47%	48%	46%	44%	47%	49%	52%	53%
PACs	36	35	40	40	36	34	25	32
Parties [a]	7	4	4	3	5	5	5	5
Candidates [b]	6	6	5	6	9	8	10	6
Miscellaneous [c]	5	6	5	7	3	4	8	4
				Senate Elections				
Average total	$2,319	$3,068	$3,021	$2,851	$3,017	$4,167	$3,558	$3,486
Percentage from								
Individuals	61%	60%	59%	61%	58%	54%	59%	62%
PACs	18	21	22	21	21	15	16	15
Parties [a]	6	9	9	7	13	8	9	4
Candidates [b]	10	6	5	5	5	19	8	11
Miscellaneous [c]	4	4	5	6	3	4	5	8

Sources: Data for 1984–1996 are derived from Federal Election Commission reports and reported in Norman J. Ornstein, Thomas E. Mann, and Michael J. Malbin, Vital Statistics on Congress, 1997–1998 (Washington, D.C.: Congressional Quarterly, 1998), 97–104. Figures for 1998 are from Federal Election Commission, "1998 Congressional Financial Activity Declines," news release, Dec. 29, 1998.

Note: Figures include all major party candidates on the general election ballot. Total dollar amounts are adjusted receipts (total receipts minus transfers among affiliated committees plus party coordinated expenditures) Percentages may not add to 100 because of rounding.

[a] Includes direct contributions and coordinated expenditures

[b] Candidates' contributions plus unrepaid loans.

[c] Interest on campaign receipts, refunds and rebates on services, and so forth.

Inflation has shrunk the buying power of these sums: party funds do not begin to cover the costs of campaigns today. Party contributions in 1998 amounted to an average of 5 percent of the total receipts in House races and 4 percent in Senate races—mostly in the form of coordinated expenditures rather than direct contributions.

Political parties are also permitted to make *coordinated expenditures,* funds a party pays for services (polling, producing ads, or buying media time) requested by a candidate who has a say in how they are spent. For Senate races, party committees may spend two cents (adjusted for inflation) for every person of voting age. In 1998 these figures ranged from $130,200 (in Alaska) to just over $3 million (in California). For House races, committees may spend no more than $32,550 in coordinated funds. (This amount is doubled for states with only one House seat.) Coordinated funds are used in general elections but not in primaries.

Political parties won an even greater stake in candidate funding by a controversial Supreme Court ruling in 1996 (*Colorado Republican Federal Campaign Committee v. Federal Election Commission*). A Court majority found that parties could make *independent expenditures* on behalf of those same candidates. These are defined as expenditures, usually for television ads, that expressly call for the election or defeat of a particular candidate but that are made without any coordination or cooperation with the candidate's own campaign organization. In the 1995–1996 cycle, the two major parties spent over $34 million on their own to advance their candidates' causes.[77] In the same decision the Court upheld the federal election statute's provisions limiting the amount political parties can spend on their candidates in a coordinated fashion. But even this limit seemed likely to evaporate, as subsequent federal court rulings interpreted such party activity as protected free speech.

Since its rebuilding effort after the post-Watergate electoral disaster of 1974, the Republican Party has had spectacular success in raising money—much of it from modest contributions solicited through targeted mailings and phone banks. In the 1997–1998 cycle, Republican committees raised $385 million, compared with $243 million for their Democratic counterparts.[78] Especially in Senate contests, the parties can pump in huge sums of money by means of cooperative arrangements among state committees and the several national committees.

Over and above money generated according to legally prescribed limits is *soft money*: individual, corporate, or union gifts to party entities that can be used for grassroots party-building activities but not for individual campaigns (see Figure 3-6). The parties' soft-money spending—the bulk of which supports their national organizations—exceeds their contributions to congressional candidates. But activities fueled by soft money, such as generic advertisements, voter registration, and get-out-the-vote drives, indirectly help all the parties' candidates. In the wake of the Clinton impeachment scandal, for example, the House Republicans' campaign committee launched "Operation

Figure 3-6   National Party Fund Raising, 1991–1998

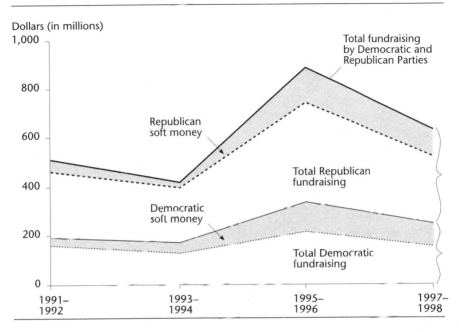

Source: Federal Election Commission, "Political Party Fundraising Continues to Climb," news release, Jan. 26, 1999.

Note: Figures are overall party receipts through ten days following the election. Federal, or "hard" money, can be used to fund individual candidates' campaigns. Nonfederal ("soft") money may be used for a variety of partisan activities—staffing, voter registration, generic ads, including "issue ads" that are often indistinguishable from candidate ads.

Breakout," a campaign budgeted at $10 million and designed to expand the party's expected gain in seats in 1998.[79] The scheme was judged a fiasco: although its TV ads reinforced the feelings of loyalists, they signaled to others that the GOP was simply the "impeachment party."

Funding patterns affect candidates' strategies and, on occasion, electoral outcomes. The Republican Party's fund-raising edge, some have argued, has helped to swell victories in good years and to minimize losses in bad years.[80] For a number of years, however, incumbents' funding advantages enabled Democrats to offset the GOP's national fund-raising superiority. With so many incumbents, House Democrats were able in the 1980s to fend off Republican assaults and even to add slightly to their ranks. But after their 1994 triumphs, the Republicans' basic fund-raising superiority was augmented by the inevitable windfalls of incumbency. In the 1997–1998 cycle, Republican representatives raised an average of $770,000, compared with Democrats' $652,000.[81]

Interest Groups. Under existing law corporations, federal contractors, and labor unions may not contribute funds directly to candidates. But such groups may indulge in *independent spending* for or against candidates but without the candidates' cooperation or consent. Corporations, labor unions, and membership organizations may recommend to their stockholders, personnel, or members the election or defeat of a candidate. Unions and corporations also may pay for "nonpartisan" voter registration or participation drives directed at their members, stockholders, or employees. Such group expenditures are unlimited, although amounts over $2,000 must be reported to the Federal Election Commission.

Independent expenditures from all sources amounted to nearly $21 million in 1995–1996. Barely half the funds (55 percent) wound up favoring candidates; the rest went to negative campaigns. The most talked-about group activity in the 1995–1996 cycle was organized labor's high-profile campaign of advertisements and voter mobilization on behalf of Democratic candidates in targeted districts. Business groups responded with similar ads. Whatever the outcome of that rivalry, Republicans benefited most from independent spending: nearly three-quarters of the funds directed at GOP candidates were for positive efforts; where Democratic candidates were concerned, seven of every eight independent dollars were aimed at defeating them.

PACs. Corporations, labor unions, and membership groups may also underwrite administrative or fund-raising costs of *political action committees.* For some years PACs have been the preferred method of channeling corporate or union energies into campaign war chests. Corporate executives contribute to PACs with such names as the Good Government Fund; most unions have PACs, the best known of which is the AFL-CIO's Committee on Political Education (COPE). Ostensibly, such groups are voluntary; however, it does not take a confirmed cynic to assume that subtle coercion and social pressure help draw money into the coffers.

Other kinds of groups are embraced by existing finance laws. Multicandidate committees may give no more than $5,000 per election to a candidate. These committees must have more than fifty members and must support five or more candidates. Such committees also may contribute up to $15,000 per year to a political party.

Political action committees are thriving, in part because the finance law encourages them. At the end of 1974 there were 608 PACs; by 1998 there were more than 3,700. All types of PACs grew in numbers, but corporate PACs grew most of all—from 89 in 1974 to 1,565 in 1998. The growth of PACs has changed the way campaigns are run. Candidates are forced to make the rounds of PACs to beg for funds. Incumbents attract PAC support by finding a lucrative committee assignment and compiling a good voting "report card." Nonincumbents gain support by knocking on doors, filling out forms, and undergoing interviews.[82]

PACs also have grown in financial clout. In 1972 they contributed $8.5 million to House and Senate candidates; in 1998 their contribution was $134

million. PAC donations are more significant in House races than in Senate races. In 1997–1998 PAC donations accounted for 32 percent of House campaign receipts but only 15 percent of Senate campaign receipts.

More than most interested parties, PACs favor incumbents and shun all but the most promising nonincumbents. Incumbents seeking reelection receive, on average, six times the PAC donations than their challengers receive. Increasing numbers are using their fund-raising prowess to start leadership PACs. These PACs trade on the name of their sponsor but are separate from the sponsor's own war chest. They are normally used to contribute to other candidates' campaigns as a way of gaining a party majority and earning their colleagues' gratitude. Consider the experience of Speaker Hastert's Keep Our Majority PAC. As a respected insider, Hastert collected a respectable $130,000 for his PAC during 1997–1998. In the first two months of 1999, after Hastert was catapulted to the Speakership, $350,000 poured into the fund.[83] In political vernacular this is called "catching the late train."

Pressure comes from both directions, of course. PAC officers complain that they are dogged by incumbents, many of whom do not need the contributions, and that members of Congress keep mental accounts of contributors. "I've had congressmen open up the door and look down a list to see if we have contributed," one of them said. "And I've had them say, 'Well, I like your organization but you haven't given me a contribution.' "[84]

PAC money follows those in power. Even before their 1994 victories, Republican leaders stepped up their efforts to win groups, especially business PACs, that had traditionally favored incumbent Democrats. Once in power, leaders made it clear they expected business PACs to fall in line. As one GOP operative noted, "We won't issue any threats, but we know who our friends are, and that matters." In a highly publicized incident, involving a 1997 special election in New York's Thirteenth District (Staten Island), what was termed "heavy-duty arm-twisting" persuaded the National Association of Home Builders to pull back an endorsement and a planned donation from their Build PAC for the Democratic candidate who had helped the industry while in the state legislature.[85]

After the GOP takeover, PAC giving flowed to the victors. "The shift in PACs from the Democrats to the Republicans was dramatic and almost overnight," noted Larry Makinson of the Center for Responsive Politics, a nonprofit reform group. "When the Republicans took over all these chairmanships and subcommittees, they reaped a whirlwind of money."[86] By the 1997–1998 cycle, thirteen of the seventeen major corporations on the House GOP's "Watch List" had increased the proportion of funds they gave to Republicans. In fact, many PACs hedged their bets in 1996 and 1998. With GOP control of the Senate never in doubt, Republican candidates gleaned a majority of the PAC contributions; but PAC strategists, unsure who would control the House, split their money fairly evenly between the two parties' candidates. Democrats still received the bulk of PAC money from labor and from groups like the As-

sociation of Trial Lawyers of America (determined to stave off GOP efforts to restrict lawsuits against business).

Candidate Funding: A Regulated Industry?

Financial inequalities—between incumbents and nonincumbents and between wealthy and poor donors—inevitably lead to demands for legal ways of monitoring or even controlling campaign finance. Laws have been passed not only to "clean up" campaigns but also to shift political influence from those who rely on financial contributions to those who depend on other resources. Several techniques have been employed. The primary ones thus far have been disclosure of campaign contributions and expenditures, limits on campaign contributions and expenditures, and (in presidential races) public financing of campaigns.

Reacting to campaign scandals of the early 1970s, Congress decided to erect regulatory standards for financing federal election campaigns. On October 15, 1974, President Gerald Ford signed into law a broad-gauged campaign finance law, the Federal Election Campaign Act Amendments of 1974.

The Supreme Court, ruling on a challenge to the law, held that Congress may limit *contributions* to congressional candidates but that it may not limit *expenditures* by candidates themselves, their campaign committees, or individuals or organizations independent of the candidate (*Buckley v. Valeo,* 1976). The reasoning was that, as a form of free expression protected by the First Amendment, spending to influence elections cannot be constrained. To end the confusion and meet the Court's constitutional objections, Congress quickly passed a revised act that aimed at reconciling the Court's rulings with the original congressional intent.

The *Buckley* decision, experience has shown, undercut Congress's intentions and ultimately rendered the law unworkable. The Court's reasoning has been criticized as muddled at best or wrongheaded at worst. First, it is stretching the First Amendment to treat the spending of money in federal campaigns as pure, protected speech. More logically, such spending might be treated as, say, economic activity—which of course may be regulated. "In fact," writes lawyer-novelist Scott Turow, "given *Buckley*'s rationale, I've never figured out why outright vote-buying isn't also protected by the First Amendment."[87] Second, with no enforceable restrictions on campaign spending, politicians and interested groups are free to exploit creative ways of maximizing their financial leverage, in the process stripping the law of the one fig leaf the Court sanctioned: contribution limits. The free-for-all system that resulted, critics charge, has replaced the principle of "one person–one vote" with a "regime of one dollar–one vote," which "distorts the fundamental principle of political equality underlying the First Amendment itself."[88]

Major features of the amended Federal Election Campaign Act, for what they are worth, include limits on individual contributions, limits on party and nonparty group contributions, and controls on campaign spending. The regu-

latory agency is a six-member, bipartisan Federal Election Commission, appointed by the president and confirmed by the Senate. The commission may issue regulations and advisory opinions, conduct investigations, and prosecute violations of the law. Most importantly, the FEC compiles and disseminates campaign finance data from the reports it receives. Indeed, disclosure of the sources and uses of campaign money is the one aspect of current regulations that everyone agrees is a success.

The 1976 act has failed utterly to reduce inequalities between incumbents and challengers. The changes may even have helped incumbents and made it harder for challengers to raise the money they need to win.[89] Campaign financing laws also have failed to limit the influence of "big money" in politics. Big money is alive and well in American elections, although now it flows through more issue and candidate groups than in the past. Moreover, many of the best-funded PACs depend on large numbers of mail-solicited donations rather than on a few from "fat cats." Finally, the "reforms" have blurred the distinction between interest groups and political parties. Labor unions, business and industry associations, consumer and environmental organizations, ideological movements, and a host of special-issue groups have invaded the electoral arena as never before. By boosting and even recruiting candidates—and hindering others—they hope to win favorable treatment for their causes on Capitol Hill.

Campaign finance laws are so loosely drawn that money pours freely into congressional elections. Parties and PACs use tax-exempt foundations to take donations in excess of legal limits. Creative accounting and "independent spending" on behalf of candidates are used to skirt legal limits on what PACs can give directly to candidates. Bankers and other moneyed people can lend money or extend credit to candidates under permissive rules. And money is moving underground, thwarting federal enforcement and disclosure efforts. "You can do just about anything, as long as you take care," said one party official.[90]

In campaign financing debates, where you stand depends on where your money comes from. Reformist groups and lobbies that rely on nonmonetary resources, claiming to speak for the public interest, condemn various practices as "loopholes" and demand sweeping changes. Most political leaders, skilled at digging for dollars, hail current untrammeled fund raising as "the American way" and decry limits on such activities. One approach, endorsed by conservatives, would abolish all limits on contributions to candidates and parties, relying solely upon electronic filing and reporting through the Internet.

Some liberal critics advocate public funding of Senate and House campaigns. As for presidential campaigns, the 1974 act included an optional public financing scheme that was intended to provide sufficient resources for candidates who agreed to use it—as most of them have done. But that has not stopped candidates and parties from raising money over and above the public funds, in violation of both the spirit and the letter of the law. In any event, Congress declined to extend public financing to its own elections. The public

funding option, moreover, runs afoul of public antipathy and concerns about the federal budget deficit.

Perhaps the most promising way to level the playing field, at least for incumbents and challengers, would be to provide the latter with subsidized mailings and free radio and TV time. This latter option, predictably, is fiercely opposed by broadcasters—a potent lobby because politicians crave the exposure their outlets provide. An early version of the bipartisan reform bill authored by Senators John McCain, R-Ariz., and Russell D. Feingold, D-Wis., offered thirty minutes of free television time to candidates who voluntarily agreed to spending caps. When the National Association of Broadcasters howled in protest, the idea was dropped to salvage the rest of the legislation.[91]

Change is resisted by those who thrive under existing rules. Democrats and Republicans both tout campaign funding reform, but both parties want it on terms favorable to them. In the past Democrats preferred overall spending limits, whereas Republicans opposed them, given their party's superior fundraising capabilities. The GOP sought to limit PAC contributions, which Democrats fought in order to keep PAC money flowing. But now that the Republicans are in power and on the receiving end of the PACs' largesse, their ardor for reform has cooled. Independent spending will remain uncontrolled as long as the Supreme Court sees fit to equate political spending with free expression. Some popular reform plans—those that would abolish PACs altogether, for example—are plainly unconstitutional. But it was protests from a wide range of groups with PACs—from the National Education Association to the International Association of Firefighters—that led McCain and Feingold to strip a ban on PAC contributions from their bill.

As eventually pared down, the McCain-Feingold bill would have banned unregulated soft money contributions to national parties and differentiated between ads that advocate issues and those that support candidates. Even so, the bill was opposed by Republican leaders, especially Speaker Gingrich and Senate majority leader Trent Lott, R-Miss. A similar House bill, sponsored by Reps. Christopher Shays, R-Conn., and Martin T. Meehan, D-Mass., would have eliminated soft money donations and issue ads. Overcoming obstacles raised by GOP leaders, a coalition of Democrats and reform-minded Republicans managed to pass the Shays-Meehan bill, 252–179; the measure was killed, however, by a Senate filibuster.

The campaign finance issue is by no means dead, but opposition from interests across the political spectrum makes thoroughgoing reform unlikely. And although reform commands public support, it is not a salient issue—a fact not lost on those who benefit from the current state of affairs. The Court's notion that spending money is protected speech is another huge obstacle. That interpretation has many critics, but who wants to campaign publicly for a narrower reading of the First Amendment?

Although conceding the need for further controls, most political scientists are skeptical about the benefits of many of the proposed changes in campaign

financing. Overall spending limits must be approached cautiously. Challengers need to be able to spend money to offset incumbents' advantages, and because they start from behind they get more value for every dollar they spend. As for PAC contributions, they are easily stigmatized, but they are nonetheless a lawful way for interested groups to give money—gifts that at least are recorded and scrutinized. Independent campaign activities of individuals or groups are forms of free expression that should be accorded wide elbowroom. Even the supposed loopholes in the law—soft money and bundling, for example—could be viewed as useful techniques for, respectively, underwriting party activities and articulating interest group views. Finally, there is what journalist Chuck Alston calls the "whack a mole" problem. In the arcade game "the mole pops up in one hole, and you whack him down. But then he pops up somewhere else. Similarly, campaign spending, whenever it is suppressed in one form, always pops up elsewhere."[92] That fate will confound any reform that is adopted.

Conclusion

In this chapter we have considered the "rules of the game" that narrow the potential field of congressional contenders. Think of these as a series of gates, each narrower than the one before. First are the constitutional qualifications for holding office. Then there are complex rules of apportionment and districting. Beyond these are nominating procedures (usually, though not always, primaries) and financial requirements. These gates cut down sharply the number of persons who are likely to become real contenders.

Most important, individuals must make up their own minds about running for the House or Senate. As we have seen, such choices embrace a range of considerations—many personal and emotional but all based on some estimate of the likely benefits and costs of their candidacy. This winnowing process presents voters with a limited choice on election day: two, rarely more, preselected candidates. From this restricted circle senators and representatives are chosen—as we explain in the next chapter.

High noon in the Golden State. Democratic senator Dianne Feinstein (top) faces then-representative Michael Huffington in California's 1994 Senate contest, history's costliest congressional race. The two spar before TV host Larry King (bottom) in a nationally televised debate. Feinstein won with a 2 percent margin of the almost eight million votes cast.

4

Making It:
The Electoral Game

The television spot opened and closed with photographs of California Senate candidates Dianne Feinstein, the Democratic incumbent, and Michael Huffington, a Republican representative making a bid for her Senate seat. But most of the thirty-second Huffington ad—entitled "Can You Tell?"—was just messages flashed on the screen and read by an announcer.

"Both Dianne Feinstein and Michael Huffington are worth at least $50 million," the ad began. "But Feinstein's taken more than $6 million from special interest PACs [political action committees]. Huffington won't take a penny." The numbers were flashed on a split screen, a red top half for Feinstein and a blue bottom half for Huffington. "Feinstein takes her $133,000 Senate salary. Huffington gives his to charity. Feinstein bills the government for travel. Huffington pays his own way. Feinstein uses a taxpayer-paid chauffeur to get to work. Huffington drives himself." The spot ended with a question: "Can you tell which one is the career politician?"[1]

The spot had two goals: to deflect criticism of Huffington's wealth and to show him as a down-to-earth independent pitted against a perk-laden incumbent. This ad—simple, straightforward, trivial, pulling viewers toward an obvious conclusion—was a model of its genre and was judged the best in Huffington's lavish but losing campaign.

The Feinstein-Huffington contest, the costliest congressional race in history, was fought the new-fashioned way: through a television blitz underwritten by truckloads of money. With fourteen major media markets, seventy-five major commercial stations, and more than 17 million television sets, California can be spanned only by video. Cheaper traditional methods simply will not reach this megastate of 32 million people. In the words of campaign consultant Robert Shrum: "A political rally in California consists of three people around a television set."[2]

Campaign Strategies

Campaigns are volatile mixtures of personal contacts, fund raising, speech making, advertising, and symbolic appeals. As acts of communication, campaigns are designed to convey messages to potential voters. The goal is to win over a plurality of those who cast ballots on election day.

Asking the Right Questions

Candidates, whether incumbents or challengers, strive to set the basic tone or thrust of their campaign. Their overall approach determines the allo-

cation of money, time, and personnel. In mapping out a successful strategy, candidates ask themselves: What sort of constituency do I have? Are my name, face, and career familiar to voters, or am I relatively unknown? What resources—money, group support, volunteers—am I likely to attract? What leaders and groups are pivotal to a winning campaign? What issues or moods are uppermost in the minds of potential voters? What are the easiest and cheapest means of reaching voters with my message? When should my campaign begin and how should it be paced? And what are my chances for victory? The answers to such questions define the campaign strategy.

The constituency dictates campaign plans. For statewide campaigns, Senate candidates must appeal to diverse economic and social groups, scattered over wide areas and typically partitioned into multiple media markets. In fast-growing states, Senate incumbents must introduce themselves to hordes of new voters who have arrived in the intervening six years. Few Senate candidates can know their states as intimately as House candidates know their districts. Most House districts are narrower entities than states, often paralleling no natural geographic, community, media market, or political divisions. They have fewer automatic forums or media outlets for candidates, not to mention fewer ready-made partisan organizations.[3] Would-be representatives are very much "on their own" to piece together a network of supporters.

Because incumbents are usually tough to beat, the presence or absence of an incumbent colors the entire electoral undertaking. Also important is the partisan distribution within the electorate, although split-ticket voting can throw off predictions. Candidates whose party dominates a given area stress party loyalty, underscore long standing partisan values (called "valence issues"), and sponsor get-out-the-vote drives—because high voter turnout usually aids their cause. Minority-party campaigns strive to highlight personalities, obscure partisan differences, and exploit factional splits within the majority party, perhaps by means of issues capable of prying voters away from their majority-party home ("wedge issues").

The perceptions and attitudes of voters are also major ingredients in campaign planning. Through sample surveys, focus groups, or informal "pulse taking," strategists try to detect what is on voters' minds and what, if anything, they know or think about the candidate. What is the candidate's "name recognition" level? If the candidate is well known, what "profile"—positive or negative—is conjured up by his or her name? Well-known candidates try to capitalize on their visibility; the lesser known run ads that repeat their names over and over again. Candidates with a reputation for openness and friendliness highlight those qualities in ads; those who are less outgoing stress experience and competence, at the same time displaying photos or film clips reminding voters that they, too, are human. Candidates who have made tough, unpopular decisions are touted as persons of courage. And so it goes.

As popular moods change, so do the self-images candidates seek to project. In crises, voters prefer experience, competence, and reassurance; in the wake of scandals, they prize honesty and openness. Candidates' appearances,

speeches, advertising, and appeals are designed to exploit such voter preferences. Not a few Democratic legislators who years before gained office by championing government activism found themselves in the 1990s advocating balanced budgets and lower taxes. By the same token, conservatives elected in 1992 and 1994 vowing to slash government spending discovered, once they were in office, that constituents still rely on government services and assistance. In the early 1990s challengers sold themselves as "outsiders" (even when they were political veterans); incumbents of both parties countered by portraying themselves as independent-minded apostles of change. By the decade's end political experience was back in fashion: the Capitol dome and its marble halls reappeared in campaign ads.

Choosing a Theme

A candidate's strategy usually is distilled into a single theme or message that is repeated on radio, TV, and billboards and in campaign literature. Strategists use these themes to *frame* the campaign—that is, to pose the election's core issue in such a way that voters respond favorably to their candidate or negatively to the opponent. "There's only three or four plots," explained Carter Eskew, a Democratic consultant. Plots for incumbents are Representative X is different from the rest; X can deliver; X stands with you. And the perennial plot for challengers is XX years are long enough; it's time for a change.[4]

Incumbents normally tout their experience and remind voters of past service. In his successful 1996 reelection bid, Sen. Joseph R. Biden Jr., D-Del., ran ads that simply displayed a seemingly endless list of laws he had helped enact during his four terms. The ad concluded with Biden's picture and the line: "Before they tell you what they'll do, make them show you what they've done." Two years later Sen. Christopher S. Bond, R-Mo., aired commercials with the tag line: "So much experience. So much he's done."[5]

Incumbency can be hazardous, however. Given citizens' suspicions about the honesty or effectiveness of elected officials, public service can turn into a liability. Aggressive challengers seize upon incumbents' flaws or weaknesses. Incumbents may be accused of laziness, inattention to local needs, or simply "Potomac fever." Age, failing health, inattentiveness to duties, or scandals— personal or official—normally are fair game. One of the most inspired anti-incumbent campaigns was waged by Des Moines plastic surgeon Greg Ganske in 1994 to oust veteran representative Neal Smith, D-Iowa, an Appropriations subcommittee chair. At the suggestion of Newt Gingrich, R-Ga., Ganske bought a rusty beige 1958 DeSoto—made the year Smith first went to Congress—and drove it around the district. A sign on its roof proclaimed, " '58 Nealmobile—WHY is it still running?" Ganske then pressed home his point: "What do 36-year career politicians always do? They blame each other, spend more money, and then raise your taxes."[6]

An extensive public record, moreover, gives enterprising opponents many potential openings to exploit. Votes or positions may be highlighted, and sometimes twisted, to discredit the officeholder. Incumbents may be shackled

to unpopular issues, such as nuclear waste dumps or hikes in Medicare premiums. Or they may commit errors that come back to haunt them. Rep. Michael Pappas, R-N.J., in a flashy display on the House floor in July 1998, sang a musical tribute to the nation's best-known independent counsel: "Twinkle, twinkle, Kenneth Starr, now we see how brave you are." That fall Democrat Rush Holt, the Princeton physicist who challenged Pappas, replayed the incident over and over in a TV ad (called "Little Starr") aimed at pegging Pappas as too conservative for his district. "Mike Pappas votes against working families. But sang a nursery rhyme to Ken Starr. Congressman Mike Pappas. Out of tune. Out of touch." The ad helped Holt to unseat Pappas.[7]

Officeholders are open to attacks linking them, accurately or not, to unpopular issues or personalities on the national scene. As their poll numbers fell, the GOP House and Speaker Gingrich were tempting targets for Democratic challengers. Numerous TV ads morphed the local member's image into that of Gingrich. In central Massachusetts's Third Congressional District, Democrat Jim McGovern coined a winning slogan in his bid to oust sophomore representative Peter I. Blute. "If you wouldn't vote for Newt, why would you ever vote for Blute?" In New Jersey the campaign logo of successful Democratic challenger Bill Pascrell Jr. showed freshman representative Bill Martini as a puppet on strings held by the Speaker. "When Newt Gingrich pulls, Bill Martini's hand goes up to vote every time," the mailers proclaimed. Voters bought the sales pitch: "Cut Martini's strings on November 5!"

To avoid being dragged down by unpopular features of politics in the nation's capital, incumbents strive to run away from the "Washington crowd." Democrats in the early 1990s scrambled to duck the anti-Washington blasts. One theme in television advertisements was, "He votes for what he believes in, not just the party" (Sen. Jeff Bingaman, D-N.M.). Another was, "He hasn't let Washington change him" (Sen. Herb Kohl, D-Wis.).[8] Both of these candidates managed to evade the anti-incumbent tide. Two years later many Republicans ran from the unpopular record of their 104th Congress. An ad for Sen. Mitch McConnell, R-Ky., boasted that he helped save the school lunch program— and sometimes "goes against what his party is advocating."[9]

Campaign Resources

Campaigns require resources to play out the strategy that has been devised. The cleverest strategy in the world is of no avail without the wherewithal to bring its message to voters. The type of state or district, incumbency status, candidate visibility, and party margin matter little if the candidate lacks two essential resources: money and campaign organization.

Allocating Resources

The importance of money in campaigns cannot be overemphasized. Virtually any kind of campaign can be mounted with enough money. Old-fashioned cut-rate alternatives, such as door-to-door canvassing or use of volunteer organizations, are still available, although they eat up time and re-

sources that might be used to reach larger numbers of voters. Candidates with tough contests in both primary and general elections face an especially vexing dilemma: should they ration their outflow of funds and risk losing the primary, or should they wage an expensive primary campaign and risk running out of money later on?

Especially useful is "early money"—funds on hand at the outset of the campaign, or even earlier. EMILY's List (Early Money Is Like Yeast), a group begun in 1985, was formed on this premise. EMILY's List collects ("bundles") checks for Democratic women candidates who support abortion rights. In 1998 the group disbursed $7.5 million to two dozen candidates, on top of money spent on voter projects of its own or in tandem with Democratic campaign committees.[10] Incumbents stockpile funds to scare off challengers; lackluster fund raising tells would-be challengers that they could mount a credible race. Challengers and open-seat candidates raise money to gain visibility, win credibility, and get a head start over other contenders. (For one open-seat candidate's fund-raising efforts, see Table 4-2, p. 97.) "Failure to raise enough money creates a vicious spiral," explains political analyst Thomas B. Edsall. "Some donors become reluctant to invest their cash, and then state and national parties are less likely to target their unlimited 'soft money' for party building and get out the vote drives in those races."[11]

"Late blitz money" also can turn the tide, although it is rare that money alone makes the difference. The final weeks of a campaign are tough because both sides are trying to reach undecided voters. "You've got to move that 10 or 15 percent, many of whom are not paying much attention," a Democratic consultant explained. "Unfortunately, the way to do that is with negative or comparative ads."[12] Late in the game opponents frantically attack and—despite the scant time—counterattack.

Incumbents raise more money and also spend more on their campaigns than challengers do (see Figure 4-1). Because incumbents are better known than challengers, their spending often has strategic purposes. *Preemptive spending* involves constant fund raising, which, along with surpluses from previous campaigns, can dissuade serious opponents. "If you look like a 900-pound gorilla, people won't want to take you on," remarked a GOP campaign aide.[13]

If a strong, well-financed challenger surfaces, incumbents can *spend reactively* to stave off defeat. The 1990s found incumbents spending more than ever to counter challengers (who were better financed than usual). In 1998 House incumbents spent more than $600,000 on average defending their seats—more than five times what their challengers spent.[14]

New incumbents tend to invest heavily in preemptive and reactive spending because they are more likely than longtime veterans to face vigorous challenges. More senior members raise and spend less than junior members, especially in the early campaign stages (before July of an election year). Incumbents who are sure-fire vote getters over the long haul—with five or more terms—may establish such commanding positions that they rarely have serious challenges.

Figure 4-1   Average House Campaign Expenditures by Incumbency and
Party, 1978–1998

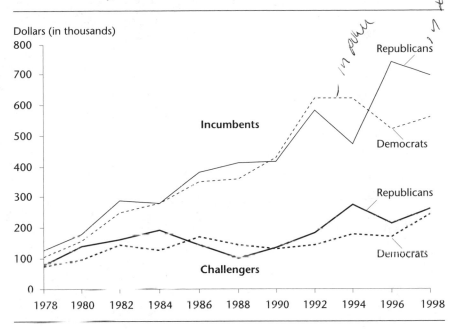

Sources: Norman J. Ornstein, Thomas E. Mann, and Michael J. Malbin, *Vital Statistics on Congress, 1997–1998* (Washington, D.C.: Congressional Quarterly, 1998), 81–82; Federal Election Commission, "FEC Reports on Congressional Fundraising for 1997–98," news release, April 28, 1999, 14 15.

Sometimes established incumbents deliberately overspend for reasons that lie beyond the race at hand. A decisive victory can establish a claim to higher office. Representatives may cast their eye on the Senate; senators may hope to be presidential contenders. Others strive to impress colleagues or interest groups with their electoral prowess. They may bid for freedom to concentrate on Capitol Hill business or other pursuits. Or they may distribute unused funds to needy colleagues in return for future support, perhaps in a leadership contest.

Incumbents' overspending is motivated, finally, by their sense of uncertainty and risk, which has grown in recent years. "Because of uncertainty," Gary C. Jacobson explains, "members tend to exaggerate electoral threats and overreact to them. They are inspired by worst-case scenarios—what would they have to do to win if everything went wrong?—rather than objective probabilities."[15]

Challengers, for their part, spend all the money they can raise to make their names and faces known to voters. And, because normally they start far behind, their campaigning dollars tend to be more cost effective than those of incumbents. As Jacobson has demonstrated, the more a challenger spends, the

Table 4-1 Where the Campaign Dollars Go: Percentage of Funds
Spent by Incumbents and Challengers (1992)

Spending categories	House candidates		Senate candidates	
	Incumbents	Challengers	Incumbents	Challengers
Advertising/media expenses	27%	36%	41%	45%
Office expenses	25	23	25	24
Fund-raising expenses	15	9	21	19
Campaigning/voter contact	20	26	8	9
Polling	4	3	3	2
Constituent gifts/entertainment	2	—a	—a	—a
Donations	5	—a	1	—a
Other	3	2	1	1

Source: Computed by the authors from data reported in Dwight Morris and Murielle E. Gamache, *Gold-Plated Politics: The 1992 Congressional Elections* (Washington, D.C.: Congressional Quarterly, 1994), 18–29. The database was compiled from Federal Election Commission reports by the *Los Angeles Times*'s Washington Bureau staff.

Note: Figures include percentages of all expenditures by candidates in the 1992 elections. For House candidates this covers a two-year cycle (1991–1992); for Senate candidates there is a six-year cycle (1987–1992). Percentages may not equal 100 because of rounding.

a Spending is less than 1 percent.

more votes he or she is likely to attract.[16] Recent elections (remember Carolyn McCarthy, discussed in Chapter 1) demonstrated once again the ability of well-financed challengers to defeat incumbents.

Spending Campaign Funds

As exercises in communication, campaigns are driven, and their budgets shaped, by the need to reach the largest number of voters at the lowest cost. Because campaigns differ from one another, spending patterns vary widely between the House and the Senate, among congressional districts and states, and between incumbents and challengers.

As a rule, statewide Senate races are mass media contests with messages conveyed mainly through radio and television. Costs are especially high in huge states, such as California, Florida, New York, and Texas—whose numerous media markets must be tapped to broadcast the candidate's message to huge, diverse, and mobile populations. Table 4-1 reports campaign spending of the two chambers over a typical electoral cycle. Senate candidates spent far more on media advertising and fund raising than did their House counterparts, but they spent only half as much on traditional means of voter contact.

Despite its astronomic costs, television advertising is popular because candidates find it cost effective, and they believe it works. They are probably right. Political scientist Thomas Patterson estimated that by the 1980s it cost only about one-half cent to get to a single television viewer, compared with one

and a half cents to reach a newspaper reader and twenty-five cents to reach a direct-mail recipient.[17]

Not all states feature such high-tech campaigns. Residents in smaller states usually expect personal appearances by the candidates at festivals, parades, or annual county fairs. Politicians are supposed to show up. "If you ain't seen at the county fair, you're preached about on Sunday," remarked an Oklahoma politician as he led his party's Senate candidate around the hog and sheep barns in Ada, Oklahoma.[18] In small states, first-name relationships are often valued. Of Vermont's voters, political scientist Garrison Nelson remarks, "They want to know you." Independent representative Bernard Sanders's bumper stickers there simply say, "Bernie."[19] In Bristol, on Rhode Island's coast, the Fourth of July parade—the oldest in the country—is "the first and perhaps biggest event of the campaign season."[20] Candidates are expected. By town decree, only public officials may march in the parade; nonofficeholders must work the crowd from the sidelines.

House races rely on the mass media less than Senate races do, but House candidates spend more on direct campaigning, voter contact, and organization, which includes salaries, office supplies, printing, travel, and professional fees. In four House races examined by *National Journal,* a majority of the funds went to organization, but spending for advertising (newspaper ads and radio and TV commercials) ranged widely from 13 to 36 percent, depending on whether the electoral district could be covered efficiently by television. It could be in Oregon's Fifth Congressional District. There the winner spent the bulk of his advertising budget on television because local stations reached most of the district's voters. In New Jersey's Ninth Congressional District, however, spending for TV coverage was inefficient. The district is in the New York City media market, which includes millions of people not eligible to vote in the Ninth. There the winning candidate spent 86 percent of his media budget on radio, which is less expensive and allows candidates to target their messages more precisely.[21]

The character of candidates and their party organizations also affects the media mix and budgeting. Confident incumbents can channel their money into newspaper ads or phone banks that target their messages to activists, partisans, and supporters. Lesser-known candidates must turn to broad-scale media, such as television or outdoor advertising, to promote name recognition.[22] (These differences are reflected in Table 4-1.) Both House and Senate challengers spend more on media and less on traditional campaigning than do incumbents. And, although challengers theoretically need more money to get their messages across, they spend less in fund raising than incumbents do.

Incumbents also spend more on constituent gifts and entertainment and donations to others. Campaign funds have been barred from "personal use" since 1989, and in 1995 the Federal Election Commission (FEC) tightened its definition of permissible uses—though the issue remains a thorny one. The FEC still allows gifts of "nominal value" to constituents. Spending reports from members' campaigns and their related PACs disclose a surprising array of ac-

Table 4-2   See How He Ran: Candidate Brian Baird's Time Budget,
July–October 1998

Activity	Hours/ minutes spent[1]	Percentage of time
Fund-raising call time	397:30	32%
Other fund raising	36:00	3
Meeting with individuals, groups, politicians	146:00	12
Public events	96:00	8
Meeting with media	31:00	2
Voter contact	89:15	7
Meeting with staff	58:45	5
Travel	203:15	16
Personal time	201:30	16
Total hours	1,259:15	100[2]
Hours per day	10:12	

Source: Baird for Congress Campaign, 1998. Reported in James A. Thurber and Carolyn Long, "Baird's Battle for Congress," in *The Battle for Congress,* ed. James A. Thurber (in press).

[1] Excludes the three days of campaigning in November: 33 hours, 15 minutes, mostly in voter contact.

[2] Percentages do not add exactly to 100 because of rounding.

tivities, such as buying flowers, leasing cars, organizing athletic teams, sponsoring contests and prizes, purchasing tickets to sporting events, and subsidizing travel and entertainment. In 1994 Rep. Steve Largent, R-Okla., a Hall of Fame football player, spent more than $2,500 in campaign funds to buy footballs for young constituents, and Rep. John D. Dingell, D-Mich., used $1,655 of his campaign money to pay for miscellaneous gifts.[23]

Organizing the Campaign

Implementing the campaign strategy is the job of the candidates and their organizations. Waging a campaign is not for the fainthearted. Take the case of psychology professor Brian Baird, a Democrat who won Washington's Third District seat in 1998. Having lost to the incumbent by a mere 887 votes two years earlier, Baird vowed to run full tilt the second time, when the incumbent bowed out to run for the Senate. His campaign schedule is summarized in Table 4-2. Baird spent nearly all his waking hours on the campaign during the peak campaign months (July through October)—more than ten hours a day for 123 days. By far the largest chunk of time—more than one-third—was spent raising the $1.3 million he needed to win the open seat. Most of those hours he sat in a tiny room he called his "bunker," wearing a headset and phoning potential contributors. Many of his meetings with individuals, groups,

or other politicians were also related to fund raising. Travel ate up many valuable hours, although the Third District (Olympia and southwest Washington) is about average in size. His days of hard campaigning are by no means over: his swing district will continue to be targeted by both parties.

In the past, contenders depended upon the local party apparatus to mobilize voters, and in some places they still do. But today few local party organizations have the personnel or the funds to carry out effective campaigns. Hired campaign consultants, augmented by citizen or interest group activists, have largely replaced the old local party pros and volunteers. Some populist campaigns make a point of mobilizing cadres of volunteers: workers from labor, women's, environmental, and seniors' groups, for example, contributed to the 1996 reelection victory of Sen. Paul Wellstone, D-Minn., and the successful challenge of Rep. Jim McGovern, D-Mass.[24]

Tammy Baldwin's winning run in 1998 for an open seat in Wisconsin's Second District (Madison) was boosted by some 3,000 volunteers, 1,700 of them University of Wisconsin students. Most of these helpers did a literature drop or two, or worked the phones for an evening. But some—thirty-five during the general election race—worked full time. Much of the volunteer effort targeted Madison's 40,000 UW students, notoriously indifferent voters who make up 10 percent of the district's potential electorate. Baldwin found their weekly field meetings "rejuvenating":

> I would go to these meetings just to listen to the discussion and to get fired up. Joe [the field consultant] would be on the speaker phone in the middle of the room barking out questions. "OK, how many building and floor captains do we have in the dorms?" Someone would answer, "We have 87 of the 150 positions." "How many more can we get by next week?" he would ask. . . . Everyone was energized by these meetings. In many ways our campaign was an old-fashioned, person-to-person effort. It really came together in the last week of the campaign.[25]

The volunteer effort paid off. Baldwin topped 70 percent of the vote in the six wards with the highest concentration of UW students.

As long as they can pay the price, candidates today can procure campaign services from political consulting firms. Some companies offer a wide array of services; others specialize in survey research, direct-mail appeals, phone banks, advertising, purchase of media time, coordination of volunteer efforts, fund raising, or financial management and accounting. Despite the hype they often receive, consultants rarely turn a campaign around. At best they can make the most of a candidate's resources and help combat opponents' attacks. They cannot compensate for an unskilled or lazy candidate or for a candidate's staff that does not follow through on details.

Enjoying greater resources, incumbents are more likely to have experienced, professional managers. Edie Goldenberg and Michael Traugott explain that incumbents' campaigns

tend to be managed by people who are experienced and earn their living by doing this kind of work. Overall, their campaign staffs are relatively large, heterogeneous teams possessing a wide variety of skills necessary to cope with a campaign environment that is becoming more complex, broader in scope, and increasingly reliant upon technology.[26]

Experienced aides on the office payroll help build support throughout the legislator's term of office. As one scholar described the process:

> The incumbent's staff, in short, allows him to attract and retain the nucleus of his personal political organization. . . . The incumbent fields a publicly paid team of experienced veterans to do a task they have succeeded in before, perhaps many times before, and which differs very little from their everyday jobs.[27]

Congressional aides are supposed to refrain from reelection activities during their official hours of work, but in practice the distinction is hard to draw. The normal duties of a member's office staff—especially constituent errand running and outreach—have inescapable electoral consequences.

Reliance upon professional firms raises its own set of problems. Not all firms are scrupulous in adhering to professional or ethical standards. One example is opposition research, the purpose of which is "to get the skinny on the client's opponents and, if all goes well, expose them as hypocrites, liars, thieves, or just plain unsavory characters."[28] Most campaigns invest in opposition research; some of them go too far, straying beyond the public record into private-eye snooping into personal matters. Another debatable form of campaigning is the "push poll." This is a survey instrument that features questions intended to change the opinion of the contacted voters. It divulges negative information about the opponent with the hope of pushing the voter away from him or her and pulling the voter toward the candidate paying for the polling.

Campaign Techniques

Campaigns are designed to convey the candidate's message to people who will support the candidate and vote in the election. Campaigns are not necessarily directed at all voters; often narrower groups are targeted, mainly those groups most likely to vote for the candidate. Indeed, campaign techniques are distinguished by the breadth and kind of audiences they reach.

The Ground War: "Pressing the Flesh" and Other Forms of Close Contact

Direct appeals to voters through personal appearances by the candidate—at shopping centers, factory gates, or even door-to-door—are part of every campaign. In his first Senate campaign in 1948, Lyndon B. Johnson swooped out of the sky in a helicopter to visit small Texas towns, grandly pitching his Stetson from the chopper for a bold entrance. (An aide was assigned to retrieve the hat for use at the next stop.)[29] Other candidates, preferring to stay closer

to the ground, stage walking tours or other events to attract attention. Few elected officials get by without doing a great deal of what is inelegantly called "pressing the flesh." Jim Bunning, R-Ky., a Hall of Fame baseball pitcher and six-term representative who won a Senate seat in 1998, conceded he had "learned to enjoy" glad-handing as a part of campaigning. "You don't get elected six times without doing this," said Bunning as he and his family briskly worked the crowd at the 118th Fancy Farm Picnic, the traditional kickoff for Kentucky's fall campaigns. "You have to get used to this."[30]

Personal contact is a potent campaign technique, especially in House districts and in small states. (Nearly a quarter of the citizens questioned in national surveys claim to have met their incumbent representatives personally.) One-on-one campaigning, however, is physically and emotionally challenging, and the payoff is often elusive. "The hardest doorbell for a candidate to ring is the first one," campaign specialist Ron Faucheux recalls of his canvassing days. "Canvassing takes an enormous amount of time and a serious commitment."[31] At best, he cautions, canvassers reach only about 30 percent of an area's voters: only about 60 percent of the people will be home, and the person who comes to the door may represent only half the household's eligible voters. To reach more voters per visit, candidates seek out shopping malls, organized groups, fairs, or rallies. Leafleting or targeted mailings reach even more voters.

In populous states, candidates have little time to spend with voters. They are too busy making fund-raising calls, appearing on radio or TV talk shows, or meeting with newspaper editorial boards. There is, however, at least one compelling reason to do a little carefully staged personal campaigning: the hope that local reporters or TV cameras will cover the appearance. Consider New Jersey's hard-fought Senate 1996 race between two representatives, Republican Richard A. Zimmer and Democrat Robert G. Torricelli, the winner. Although a compact state, New Jersey lies between two of the nation's biggest and costliest media markets. So the candidates made a point of "showing up every day somewhere for an hour or so—an elementary school, a welfare office, a police shooting range—in hopes of getting a little free air time and some newspaper ink."[32]

In certain strong party areas, voter contact is the job of ward, precinct, and block captains. Some candidates still dispense "walking around money" to encourage precinct captains to get out the vote and provide small financial rewards for voting. Few neighborhoods today boast tight party organizations. Candidates and their advisers must recruit workers—whether volunteers or professionals—to make sure constituents are registered, distribute campaign leaflets, produce crowds at rallies, and muster voters on election day. Campaign workers operate sophisticated telephone banks in central headquarters and trudge door-to-door to drum up support.

The Air War: Media and Other Mass Appeals

Candidates can often bypass face-to-face voter appeals by running advertisements and making televised appearances. Especially in statewide elections,

media efforts may be the only way for candidates to get their messages to the mass of voters. Television is the "broadest spectrum" medium and also the most effective; but it is crowded with ads, most of them nonpolitical. More than 750,000 political commercials bombarded viewers in the top seventy-five television markets over the 1996 election season. Even so, those ads accounted for only 1.3 percent of all the TV ads aired during that time period (April through October).[33]

Media efforts are distinguished by the degree to which their preparation and distribution are controlled by the candidate. Paradoxically, some of the most effective appeals—news coverage and endorsements, for example—are determined by persons other than the candidate. Journalists' interviews can raise unwanted or hostile questions, so many politicians seek out the friendlier environments of talk shows hosted by nonjournalists. Even more congenial are appeals bought and paid for by the candidate—newsletters, media ads, and direct mail—but these are less credible because they are seen as promotional material.

Yet campaign coverage by the news media is sketchy, especially for House races.[34] Therefore, most candidates are left to their own devices in reaching voters. Herein lies a major difference between House and Senate races: the former are covered less than the latter by the news media. Although Senate contenders draw wider publicity, they have less control over its content than do House candidates.

Positive Advertising. Most campaign themes call for promotions that evoke positive responses from citizens. Such ads introduce the candidates to voters, underscore their personal and public qualities, and tell of their accomplishments. Running in California's Twenty-second District (Santa Barbara, San Luis Obispo) following her husband's sudden death, Lois Capps introduced herself, stressed her local ties, and associated herself with popular issues:

> CAPPS: For thirty-three years I've lived and raised my family here. My husband, Walter, had the honor of representing you, and now I'm running to finish his term. As a teacher and a mother, I'll make improving our schools a top priority. I'll use my experience as a nurse to fight for health care that protects seniors and the right to choose our own doctor, and I'll support tax reform and tax relief for working families.
>
> ANNOUNCER: The experience of a lifetime makes Lois Capps the qualified choice for Congress.[35]

Between January and November 1998, Capps ran and outpolled her opponents in four separate contests—the special election and subsequent runoff for the partial term and then the primary and general election for a full term. Ads like hers present candidates in warm, human terms to which citizens can relate. Democrat Dennis Moore, a 1998 challenger in Kansas' Third District (northeast; Kansas City suburbs) had a superb résumé, but it was his talent as an amateur singer and guitar player that enabled him to connect with voters

on a personal level. Moore had to be coaxed into making a hokey TV spot entitled "Guitar Lessons." After mentioning a style of music (country, rock, blues), he would play a short tune and then apply it to an issue. Example: "Rock: We need to make Social Security solid as a rock."[36] Moore captured the seat with a 10,000-vote margin.

If skillfully done, TV ads can be artful as well as effective in bringing home the candidates' themes. A case in point was the series of brilliant, funny—and inexpensive—television ads that helped a little-known Wisconsin state legislator, Russell Feingold, win the Democratic primary over better-known and better-financed rivals and then to defeat a two-term incumbent senator.[37] As his opponents battered each other with negative ads, Feingold ran clever, personal spots describing himself as the "underdog candidate." One showed Elvis, alive and endorsing Feingold. Another showed Feingold walking through his modest home, opening up a closet and saying, "No skeletons." In another he posted his three key pledges on his garage door. Although outspent in both the primary and the general election, Feingold became one of five successful challengers in the 1992 Senate races.

Some media appeals are coordinated with field operations. Trolling for the student vote in Madison, Wisconsin, candidate Tammy Baldwin ran what her staff called the "Bucky" ad (for the UW mascot "Bucky Badger"). It ran on MTV and shows like *Ally McBeal*. The ad said that "there is one candidate who understands our issues" and ended with a pitch to get out and vote, with phone number and Baldwin's Web site. Every time the ad ran, all the headquarters phone lines would light up.[38]

Two researchers have compared Senate incumbent and challenger "videostyles," defined as "the presentation of self through political advertising."[39] Incumbents tend to use longer commercials, rely more heavily on testimonials, stress more positive themes, dress more formally, use other people's narrations more often, and emphasize competence. Challengers are more likely to use negative arguments, dress casually, show the candidate head-on, use their own voice in narration, and stress the themes of trustworthiness and closeness to the voters.

Attack Ads. Different from positive ads are those known as *contrast* ads, which separate the candidate from the opponent, and *negative* ads, which attack the opponent's behavior or views. The line between contrast ads and negative ads is not always clear. Dennis Moore's gun control spot was a contrast ad. The message was delivered by a seedy looking gunman prowling outside a school playground, and the "this could happen here" theme was played off against the incumbent's votes and positions on gun control. The ad was a hit with women in focus groups, but the wary campaign managers decided to use it at the very end of the campaign and only during nonprime hours.[40] Ads slide into negativism when they mainly attack the opponent. Some ads morph the opponent into negative images (Newt Gingrich or Bill Clinton have been frequent choices) or show the opponent's nose lengthening, like Pinocchio's, as "lies" are told. New York's 1998 Senate candidates, incumbent Alfonse M. D'Amato, a Republican, and Rep. Charles E. Schumer, a Democrat, attacked

each other for votes cast in the 1970s when they were, respectively, a town supervisor and a state assemblyman.[41]

In many races, voters' opinions are tracked throughout the campaign, and damaging opposition tactics are countered at once. More than one politician has been defeated by hesitating to counter opponents' thrusts. A prime example was Democrat Michael Dukakis's 1988 presidential campaign; his tardiness in responding to negative ads was widely blamed for the magnitude of his defeat by George Bush. "Mike Dukakis taught everybody a lesson," said an advertising producer for Senator Feinstein. "You can't let anything go. You've got to react."[42] Technology now enables reactive ads to be produced and distributed in a few hours; they can be sent by satellite to television stations on the campaign trail. Numerous attack and response ads may be produced in the course of a hard-fought campaign.

When attacked by negative advertising, candidates and their advisers are hard pressed to "stay positive." Negative ads have become an ugly byproduct of modern campaigning because politicians believe they work. Recent experiments by two noted communications researchers tend to confirm this intuition. Negative ads, the scholars found, do lift voters' information levels, even if the information conveyed is distorted or trivial. Neither positive nor negative ads have much effect on partisans: ads tend to reinforce previously held views and only slightly raise (or lower) their predisposition to vote. But negative ads work powerfully on citizens who have little information to begin with and on those with little or no party allegiance—a growing proportion of the electorate.[43] Far beyond specific campaigns, negative appeals also have a corrosive effect on civic life, provoking citizens' antipathy toward politicians and political institutions.

Distortions and Dirty Tricks. Like other forms of product promotion, political campaigns often stretch or distort the truth to make their point. Sometimes the disinformation is so blatant that the term *dirty tricks* applies. This includes not only misinformation but using doctored photographs or faking "news reports" or "news headlines." An especially sinister tactic is blaming an opponent for bad events over which the person had no control. Such was Nebraska representative Jon Christensen's attack upon popular Lincoln mayor Mike Johanns in a 1998 GOP gubernatorial primary. Referring to two Lincoln public-access cable shows, a Christensen flyer asked: "Would you allow your children to watch obscene television? Mike Johanns would." Johanns, by law, had no control over the cable outlet's programming. The mailing prompted denunciations from the local news media, the Republican senator, and two House members. The incident not only cost Christensen the election; it probably ended his political career as well.[44]

Some have proposed tighter controls on campaign advertising—for example, requiring candidates to appear in all ads that talk about their opponents or requiring them to state their approval of a broadcast ad. No jurisdictions, as far as we are aware, have been so bold as Minnesota, which passed a law that set criminal penalties for candidates who knowingly made demonstrably false claims in the course of their campaigns. An unsuccessful 1994 House con-

tender was indicted for allegedly false accusations made against his opponent in a television spot. A state court dismissed the case, holding that Minnesota's law violated the First Amendment's guarantee of free speech. Two years later a Republican House member from Oregon was indicted (and later convicted) on charges that he had misrepresented his military service in state voter guides, which are official documents—after party leaders had already shoved him into retirement over this and other questions raised about his past record.[45]

Formal or legal remedies against campaign misrepresentations are very unlikely to work because they raise thorny constitutional questions, not to mention the specter of excessive regulation and litigation. Instead, we surely are better off trusting that "the give-and-take of campaign thrust-and-parry and the activity of a free and skeptical press create a balance" between contenders.[46]

The Parallel Campaigns

Freshman Republican representative Greg Ganske of Iowa was surprised by a commercial that popped up on his television screen in Des Moines a few weeks before the 1996 balloting. It was "like manna from heaven," for it "extolled his record on issues like reducing the deficit, while attacking an advertising campaign sponsored by the AFL-CIO saying that [he] supported cuts in Medicare and education spending."[47] Ganske said he had neither paid for the ad nor had any hand in producing it, and there is no reason to doubt him. The ad—and many like it during the campaign—was the work of a coalition of business groups. Similar coalitions mounted parallel campaigns for liberal contenders.

Indeed, the big story about recent congressional campaigns is the soaring activity of groups not formally affiliated with the candidates or the parties. Campaigns no longer resemble boxing matches between two combatants; they are more like mud wrestling contests where anyone can take part.

Groups interested in congressional election outcomes have every reason to mount their own campaigns. Direct contributions by individuals to candidates have little impact: the legal limit of $10,000 ($5,000 for the primary, $5,000 for the general election) is a tiny drop in the bucket (see Chapter 3). But groups can indulge in unlimited "independent spending" for or against candidates, as long as it is reported to the Federal Election Commission and not coordinated with the candidates' own fund raising. Better yet is "issue advocacy," messages aimed at influencing voters' choices without explicitly advocating the election or defeat of specific candidates. Although such efforts are clearly designed to affect federal elections—most are indistinguishable from candidate advertising—the courts have rebuffed the FEC's attempts to limit them, citing the First Amendment. Because these latter efforts are not reported, it is difficult to estimate the extent of this activity, let alone the people and entities that carry it out.

Right-wing groups such as the Christian Coalition, the National Rifle Association, and the small-business lobby helped propel the Republicans' stunning takeover of Congress in 1994. Liberals, relegated to secondary status on Capitol Hill, mobilized to retake Congress; in 1996 and 1998 they made gains

but fell short of victory. Widely publicized activities by labor and environmental organizations were effective, but they also prodded pro-GOP groups to dig deeper into their pockets for late ad blitzes.

Today, interest group involvement in congressional elections resembles an arms race. Hundreds of organizations engage in congressional campaigning, most of them in league with one of four major power centers.[48] The power center that helped Representative Ganske is called the "Coalition." Spearheaded by the U.S. Chamber of Commerce, it embraces a wide spectrum of business groups such as the National Federation of Independent Business, which has 600,000 members from small companies. Besides mobilizing these members, the NFIB in 1996 contributed $1 million in cash or broadcast time and circulated 200,000 brochures.[49] A second association is the Wednesday Group, a loose-knit collection of staff representatives from ideologically conservative groups—those opposed to taxes, gun control, and abortion and those favoring term limits, prayer in schools, and home schooling. The highly visible Christian Coalition claimed to have distributed 67 million profamily "voter guides" late in the 1996 campaign cycle.[50]

On the left side of the spectrum, the AFL-CIO, the umbrella organization for seventy-seven labor unions, spent $35 million in targeted districts in the 1995–1996 cycle. About two-thirds of the money went for media programs, and the rest for grassroots organizing drives. Two years later, most labor money poured into ground-war efforts. "Magically, we have learned that when we talk to union members on the phone or face to face in the workplace and get them information, they vote—and they vote for the candidates and positions we have endorsed," explained the AFL-CIO's political chief.[51] The liberal equivalent of the Wednesday Group is the Progressive Network, described as "a progressive political coffee klatch where we exchange information, gossip, hearsay and innuendo."[52] An alliance of environmental, feminist, gay, and lesbian organizations, its influential members include the Sierra Club and the National Abortion and Reproductive Rights Action League (NARAL).

Many of the new players in the electoral game are little known, even to seasoned political observers. One example is Triad Management Services, a for-profit consulting firm that advises conservative donors on which candidates and PACs to support. Triad also finds people willing to donate to nonprofit groups with names like Citizens for Reform or Citizens for the Republic Education Fund, which then turn around and hire Triad to produce ads and buy media time. These entities have the appearance of paper organizations aimed at laundering money for campaign purposes. As a major broker, Triad "played the role of an orchestra leader," said Bill Hogan of the Center for Public Integrity, a nonprofit research group. "They had an ocean of money, and where it comes from and where it goes doesn't have to be disclosed. . . . It's secret money, and the level of it is worse today than during Watergate."[53] It is but one more manifestation of the "whack a mole" phenomenon described in Chapter 3. Campaigns parallel to, but formally independent of, the efforts of candidates and their parties are popping up everywhere.

Figure 4-2   Turnout in Presidential and House Elections, 1932–1998

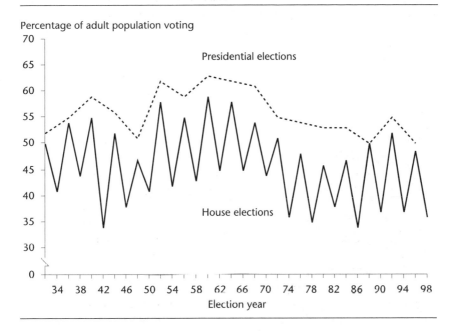

Percentage of adult population voting

Presidential elections

House elections

Election year

Sources: U.S. Bureau of the Census, *Statistical Abstract of the United States 1982–1983,* 103d ed. (Washington, D.C.: U.S. Government Printing Office, 1982), Table 801; U.S. Bureau of the Census, *Statistical Abstract of the United States 1989,* 109th ed. (Washington, D.C.: U.S. Government Printing Office, 1989), Table 433; Norman J. Ornstein, Thomas F. Mann, and Michael J. Malbin, *Vital Statistics on Congress, 1997–1998* (Washington, D.C.: Congressional Quarterly, 1998), 51; and "Overstated Turnout Woes," *Campaigns & Elections,* February 1999, 9.

Who Votes?

Although Congress is supposed to be the people's branch of government, fewer than half of voting-age citizens take part in House elections in presidential years, and fewer than 40 percent vote in off years. As Figure 4-2 indicates, voting participation in national elections has declined since 1960. About 72.5 million citizens cast ballots in the 1998 midterm elections, but they represented only 36.1 percent of the voting-age population. This number was more than ten percentage points below midterm elections of the 1962–1970 period and about fourteen percentage points behind the 1996 presidential-year turnout. Indeed, it was the lowest turnout since 1942, when millions of Americans were abroad fighting World War II.

Political analysts disagree over the reasons for the embarrassingly low voting levels in the United States, the lowest among all the Western democracies. Four explanations have been suggested. One is *demographic.* Today's expanded electorate, it is noted, embraces segments of the populace with traditionally low voting rates (young voters, African Americans, and Latinos). Young peo-

ple (ages eighteen through twenty-nine) are the least likely to vote of all age groups. Yet other trends ought to raise turnout: the single factor most closely linked with political engagement of virtually all kinds—education level—has been on the rise among the population.[54]

A second explanation stresses *barriers to voting*. Our citizens, unlike their European counterparts, must initiate the registration process; they are asked to vote far more often than people in parliamentary regimes; and election days are not holidays. Yet over the past generation states have lowered many barriers to registering and voting. Some states permit ballots to be submitted over a period of time; Oregon citizens may vote by telephone. Nationally, a law was passed in 1993 that linked voter registration to motor vehicle registration— the so-called motor voter law. By the 1998 elections, registration of eligible voters had risen about 3.8 percent nationwide, but that did not substantially raise voting levels, especially among the young and the poor, who were the targets of the measure. "Motor Voter is a howling success as a registration tool," remarked Kentucky's chief election officer, "but turnout is still a dog."[55]

A third explanation is *citizen disaffection:* the poor quality of candidates and campaigns supposedly has dissuaded people from voting. And, fourth, citizens may be *rationally abstaining from voting* in favor of other forms of political participation, including membership in political groups and activism on issues. Especially when so many congressional races are a foregone conclusion, citizens may seek more meaningful participation elsewhere. Or they may simply prefer to spend their time doing something else. One study of the 1996 elections discovered that one in five people who registered but did not vote said they were too busy or could not take time off from work. In sorting out explanations for the puzzle of nonvoting, then, "all of the above" seems the best answer we can give at the moment.[56]

Voting is the broadest and most accessible form of political involvement, but it is still biased in favor of people at the higher rungs of the social and generational ladders—those who are more mature, more affluent, better educated, more in touch with political events. Eight of ten people whose annual incomes exceed $50,000 vote in a typical election. This is twice the voting rate of the poor, defined as people with incomes of less than $15,000. Moreover, this gap has been widening over the past decade or so: in 1994 poor people accounted for nearly 20 percent of the voting-age population but only 7.7 percent of voters.[57]

Voting turnout is significant in part because alternative forms of political participation are even more sharply biased. For example, giving money— which the Supreme Court equates with free speech—is mainly an elite activity. In the sample Sidney Verba and his colleagues examined, 35 percent of all political money flowed from the 4 percent of people making more than $125,000 a year. Poor people, who were 19 percent of the sample, made only 2 percent of political donations.[58]

Turnout varies according to whether the election is held in a presidential or a midterm year (even in presidential years the congressional vote typically lags behind the presidential vote by about 5 percent). Midterm races often lack

the intense publicity and stimulus to vote provided by presidential contests. Since the 1930s, turnout in midterm congressional elections has averaged about 12 percent below that of the preceding presidential election. Midterm electorates include proportionately more people who are interested in politics and, incidentally, who are more affluent and better educated.[59] Turnout also varies by region. Fewer than 20 percent of the voters turn out in certain one-party areas; in competitive states turnout well above 50 percent is common.

How Voters Decide

What induces voters to cast their ballots for one candidate and not another? Long-standing neglect of this question (in favor of studying presidential elections) has been reversed by more frequent commercial surveys (including exit polls) and, since 1978, by the biennial National Election Study (NES) conducted by the University of Michigan's Center for Political Studies. These surveys have greatly expanded our understanding of voters' behavior in congressional contests.

When American voters enter the polling booth, they typically do not carry much ideological or even issue-specific baggage. In other words, they do not usually make detailed calculations about which party controls Congress, which party ought to control Congress, or which party favors what policies. As a general rule, voters reach their decisions on the basis of three considerations: party loyalties, candidates' assessments, and overall judgments about the state of the nation—government, its economy, and its most pressing issues. The relative strength of these forces varies over time and among specific races.

Party Loyalties

Political analysts traditionally have found party identification the single most powerful factor in determining voters' choices. In his exhaustive study of House elections between 1920 and 1964, Milton C. Cummings Jr. weighed the effect of party strength in a given constituency, "presidential tides," third parties, special local factors, and individual candidate appeals.[60] Party was far more powerful than candidate appeals in determining outcomes, although incumbency exerted an independent effect. Charles O. Jones's work yielded similar results: House incumbents had the advantage, but party affiliation was a key to election results.[61] When the incumbent was not running (that is, had died, retired, or been defeated in the primary), the incumbent's party still prevailed in three-quarters of the cases.

The 1998 elections found the electorate divided roughly in thirds among Democrats (32 percent), Republicans (30 percent), and independents (35 percent).[62] Many who claim to be independents are in fact "closet partisans" who lean toward one party or the other. Adding these people to the ranks of the two parties gives the Democrats a slight edge (47–42 percent), with about 11 percent true independents. These preferences, as measured by indexes of party identification, have remained relatively stable over the past several elections, despite short-term fluctuations. The Democrats received a measurable, though short-lived, bonus in party identification immediately after Bill Clinton's

Figure 4-3 Political Party Identification of the Electorate, 1952–1998

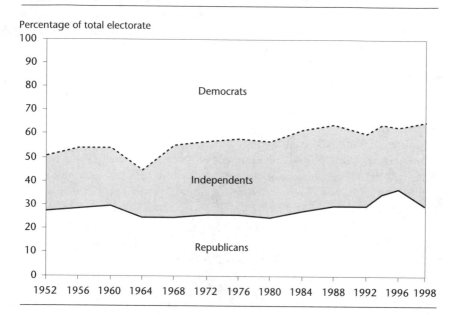

Percentage of total electorate

Sources: American National Election Study, Center for Political Studies, University of Michigan; and Kenneth Dautrich and Jennifer Dineen, "Stability in Vote Choice Characterizes the 1996 American Voter," *Public Perspective* 8 (Dec./Jan. 1997): 55; Everett Carll Ladd et al., *America at the Polls 1998* (Storrs, Conn.: Roper Center, 1999), 60–63.

Note: Democrats and Republicans include respondents expressing strong or weak identification. Independents include "true" independents and those leaning toward one party or the other. Apolitical respondents have been removed from the sample.

victories in 1992 and 1996—a temporary "bounce" from media reports of the election results (see Figure 4-3). The GOP reaped similar short-term dividends from Ronald Reagan's triumph in 1980 and the takeover of Congress in 1994.

Party affiliation remains the most powerful single correlate of voting in congressional elections. In 1998, nine of every ten Democrats and Republicans voted for their parties' candidates. Independents split their votes pretty evenly.[63]

Party Decline and Surge. Growing numbers of citizens consider themselves independents. Of those who continue to profess partisan leanings, fewer regard themselves as strong partisans. Because of weakened partisan identification, a larger proportion of congressional voters are potential party "defectors."

The erosion of partisanship among the American electorate in the past three decades can be traced to a variety of factors. In their heyday the party organizations supplied voters with political information and cues, a range of personal services, and even entertainment—benefits now furnished elsewhere in society. During the recent congressional campaigns, fewer than one in five voting-age citizens reported having been contacted by a political party worker.[64] Candidates today are obliged to, and are able to, bypass party organizations in taking their messages to voters. Elected officials have taxpayer-provided re-

sources for reaching constituents; all candidates can use electronic media or mass mailings to reach their audiences directly. Finally, in an era of blurred party lines, partisan voting cues simply convey less meaning. As Jacobson puts it, "The party label became less informative and thus less useful to voters as a shorthand cue for predicting what elected officials would do once in office. Information about individual candidates became more important."[65]

Voters may vote for a president of one party and congressional candidates of another. This *ticket splitting* has recently declined after rising for three decades. In 1956 only 9 percent of the voters (as indicated by a national sample survey) identified with one party but voted for House candidates of another party. But by the 1980s the number of defectors fluctuated between 20 percent and 30 percent of the electorate.[66] In surveys between 1952 and 1988 the number of voters who reported that they split their ticket between presidential and House candidates increased from 12 percent to 25 percent. Those who split their ballots between different parties' House and Senate candidates grew from 9 percent to 27 percent.[67] But in the past two presidential elections, ticket splitting (as reflected in exit polls) was back down to 9 percent—exactly the level of forty years earlier.

By the same token, the number of House districts voting for one party's presidential candidate and the other party's candidate for the House of Representatives rose even more dramatically, only to fall back in recent elections. In the twelve presidential elections from 1900 through 1944, only 11.3 percent of all House districts split their vote in this way; in the twelve elections from 1948 through 1990, nearly a third (30.7 percent) of districts fell into this category. Bill Clinton's victories in 1992 and 1996 were accompanied by split results in only about a quarter of all districts—the lowest such numbers since 1952.[68] Two of every ten House Republicans in the 106th Congress (1999–2001) represent districts that Clinton carried.

A look at the demographics of ticket splitting helps to clarify its sources. Many of the ticket splitters of the 1980s were so-called Reagan Democrats—voters who preferred the GOP's national tickets while backing Democrats in other races. Many of these voters were white southern conservatives who were making a slow but steady trek from their Democratic roots toward their new home with the Republicans. They were attracted to Republicans such as Dwight Eisenhower in the 1950s, Barry Goldwater in 1964, and Ronald Reagan and George Bush in the 1980s. Yet they continued to back Democrats in congressional and state races because the party put up conservative candidates and because it controlled legislative chambers and could deliver the most benefits to constituents. In 1984 Reagan carried 190 districts represented by Democrats in the House. Seventy-four of these split districts were in the South—slightly more than half of all that region's districts. By 1996, however, only fourteen southern districts (of nineteen nationwide) voted for Republican presidential nominee Bob Dole along with a Democratic House candidate.[69] Dole's relative weakness was partly at fault, but the main impetus for the decline of ticket splitting is the consolidation of GOP strength in the South. The

same phenomenon occurred to a lesser degree in the Northeast, where the popularity of the Democrats' national policies overflowed into local races.

Politicians once talked about "coattails"—how House and Senate candidates could be helped into office on the coattails of a popular presidential candidate of the same party. President Ronald Reagan, for example, boosted his party's congressional votes by 2 to 3 percent in 1980 and 4 to 5 percent in 1984. But President George Bush netted his party's congressional candidates only one percentage point; and the 1992 and 1996 elections saw little measurable pull from the presidential candidates.[70] Conversely, presidential candidates can gain from their party's local strength. In either case, spillovers from one contest to another are less frequent than they once were.

Divergent results in some recent elections remind us of the persistence of ticket splitting and the pull of candidate appeal and local versus national forces. Bush's 1988 presidential victory was accompanied by a two-seat loss of GOP House seats. Bill Clinton won a plurality of votes in 1992, while his party lost ten House seats; in 1996 he bested Dole by nearly 8 million votes, but his party gained only ten House seats.

Historically, partisan forces have operated rather differently in presidential years and midterm years. Until about 1960, presidential-year races displayed a high correlation between votes cast for president and votes cast for House members on a district-by-district basis. Since then the correlation has declined as ticket splitting has become more common.

Midterm Elections. What happens in midterm contests, when presidential candidates are not on the ballot? As already noted, the midterm electorate is both smaller than and different from the presidential-year electorate. Normally, midterm elections result in losses for the party that captured the White House two years earlier (see Table 4-3). In midterm elections during the twentieth century the presidential party has lost an average of thirty-two House seats and almost four Senate seats. In 1994 the Democrats lost a net of fifty-two seats in the House and eight in the Senate, a result that was certainly related to President Clinton's unpopularity at the time. The 1998 results were a surprise: the president's party gained five seats in the House and held its own in the Senate.

The "surge and decline" theory holds that shrinkage of the electorate in midterm years explains the normal falloff in the presidential party's votes. That is, a presidential surge, swollen by less motivated voters attracted by presidential campaigns, is followed two years later by a decline as these voters drop out of the electorate. But other studies suggest that midterm voters are no more or less partisan than those in presidential years and in fact share most of their demographic characteristics.[71]

As the link between presidential and congressional voting has loosened, other theories have been advanced to help explain midterm losses. First, midterm elections may serve in part as a referendum on the president's popularity and performance in office during the previous two years.[72] This is a plausible explanation and the only one that accounts for phenomena such as the Democrats' 1974 post-Watergate bonus of fifty-two representatives and four

Table 4-3   Midterm Fortunes of Presidential Parties, 1934–1998

Year	President	Seats gained or lost	
		House	Senate
1934	Roosevelt (D)	+9	+10
1938	Roosevelt (D)	−71	−6
1942	Roosevelt (D)	−55	−9
1946	Roosevelt-Truman (D)	−45	−12
1950	Truman (D)	−29	−6
1954	Eisenhower (R)	−18	−1
1958	Eisenhower (R)	−48	−13
1962	Kennedy (D)	−4	+3
1966	Johnson (D)	−47	−4
1970	Nixon (R)	−12	+2
1974	Nixon-Ford (R)	−48	−5
1978	Carter (D)	−15	−3
1982	Reagan (R)	−26	+1
1986	Reagan (R)	−5	−8
1990	Bush (R)	−8	−1
1994	Clinton (D)	−52	−8
1998	Clinton (D)	+5	0

Source: Compiled by the authors.

senators, their 1982 recession harvest of twenty-six House seats, and the Republicans' 1994 bonanza. Yet in other years the referendum aspect of midterm elections is harder to discern. In 1978 Alan Abramowitz concluded that "voters' evaluations of the performance of the Carter administration apparently had little or no bearing on how they cast their ballots for Senator or Representative."[73]

Second, economic conditions may explain the losses of the president's party in midterm elections. Votes shift toward the president's party when per capita income rises; they shift away from the president's party when income falls. Voters may hold the president's party responsible for their personal economic well-being ("pocketbook voting"). More likely, voters assess the president's party on the basis of their impression of the whole nation's economic health ("sociotropic voting").

What explains the singular results of the 1998 midterm elections, in which the president's party defied historical precedents? The tone was set by a generally satisfied public: even in the midst of the Clinton scandal and impeachment proceedings, voters expressed overall confidence—not only in the president, but in the high-flying U.S. economy. The two parties and their allied interest groups, therefore, focused on motivating their base voters: loyal supporters who could be counted on to vote for the party's nominees. Any shrinkage in their numbers can hurt their party, especially in close races. The GOP needed to reach economic and religious conservatives, older voters, white southerners, and anyone likely to be incensed by the president's behavior. The

Democrats needed to motivate the party's, and the president's, staunchest defenders: African Americans, women's organizations, union members, environmentalists, and liberals in general.

Most pundits (including the authors of this book) anticipated 1998 as a standout year for the GOP. On top of the dismal off-year record of presidential parties, the Clinton scandal should have led to a massive rejection of Democratic candidates. And surveys indicated that Republicans and anti-Clintonites would be more likely to vote than Democrats and Clinton supporters.[74] But by the time the lackluster 105th Congress adjourned in October, conservatives were dispirited: the president seemed to emerge the winner in last-minute budget deals, and by a margin of two to one the public continued to oppose impeaching him. To energize their conservative core, the House GOP launched "Operation Breakout," a $10-million advertising assault on Clinton. The pretested ads were beamed at thirty House districts, and for only a few days before the election.[75] But the ad campaign was widely reported in the press, a fact that solidified people's perception of Republicans as "the impeachment party." As two commentators concluded, "The Republicans' multimillion-dollar drive to turn the election into a referendum on President Clinton ran head-on into an electorate less interested in the Monica S. Lewinsky scandal than in maintaining the status quo of a healthy economy."[76]

"In any election," notes Curtis Gans, "the outcome is not determined by turnout, but by *who* turns out."[77] The 1998 off-year elections were no exception. Traditional Democrats—in particular, organized labor and African American leaders—mounted an aggressive ground war, a GOTV (get out the vote) campaign that paid off. Polling data indicated that voters from union households made up 23 percent of the 1998 electorate, up from just 14 percent in the GOP-victory year of 1994. Black voters moved from 9 percent to 11 percent of the electorate, Latino voters from 3 percent to 6 percent.[78] These citizens were propelled less by loyalty to Clinton than by fear that his enemies would bring him down, along with causes they believed in. Democrats also made gains among traditionally Republican demographic groups: middle-class and upscale voters and white males.

The Appeal of Candidates

After partisan loyalties, the appeal of given candidates is the strongest force in congressional voting. Not surprisingly, candidate appeal normally tilts toward incumbents. When voters abandon their party to vote for House or Senate candidates, they usually do so to vote for incumbents.

Over the past generation the incumbency factor has strengthened to the point that it rivals and often eclipses partisanship. Scholars estimate the incumbency advantage in House and Senate races at about 2 percent of the vote totals during the 1954–1960 period, after controlling for national trends and district partisanship. After 1960 this advantage grew to as much as 7 percent.[79] The proportion of marginal incumbents (those winning by less than 60 percent) fell by more than one-fourth. According to Jacobson, the proportion of marginal incumbents remained at this lower plateau (about 30 percent), dropping still fur-

ther for a period in the late 1980s.[80] But wider reelection margins did not prevent incumbents from losing office at traditional rates—except for the late 1980s and late 1990s, bonanza periods for incumbents (see Table 3-1). Indeed, Jacobson argues that the incumbency advantage boosted reelection prospects mainly for first-term incumbents. For other incumbents the advent of more candidate-centered politics has been a mixed blessing:

> A less reliably partisan electorate may make it easier for a representative to develop the kind of personal hold on a district that insulates him or her from external political forces. But a less partisan electorate is also more fickle; support from constituents is easier to lose as well as to win; an easy victory one year does not guarantee reelection next time.[81]

However one measures incumbency effects, it remains true that incumbency confers powerful advantages upon officeholders who work to build and maintain support and who shrewdly exploit the resources available to them.

Although its effects are more pronounced in House elections, "incumbency now serves . . . as an important alternate voting cue to party" in Senate contests.[82] Statewide contests can be quite lively, especially in those southern states that have developed vigorous two-party competition over the past generation; yet in nonsouthern states competition for Senate seats has actually declined since 1958. Although Senate seats are more hotly contested than House seats, "a substantial proportion of Senate races are low-key affairs that attract scant notice: media coverage is limited, spending by the challenger is relatively low, and the outcome is often a foregone conclusion."[83]

Incumbents are better known than their opponents. Even if voters cannot recall officeholders' names in an interview, they can identify and express opinions about them when the names are presented to them—as in the voting booth. In the first National Election Study survey, nearly all respondents were able to recognize and rate Senate and House incumbents running for reelection (96 percent and 93 percent, respectively). Senate challengers were recognized and rated by 86 percent of the respondents, House challengers by only 44 percent. Open-seat candidates fell somewhere between incumbents and challengers in visibility. Thus most voters can recognize and express views about congressional candidates, except for House challengers. These opinions exert a powerful effect on voting decisions. Indeed, in the eyes of some analysts they are the most potent influences on congressional voting.[84]

In evaluating candidates, voters normally favor incumbents over nonincumbents. Of voters' comments about incumbents in the NES survey, four of five were favorable. In contrast, only 57 percent of the comments about challengers were positive. Most of the comments centered on the candidates' job performance or personal characteristics; relatively few dealt with issues. Voters evaluated House incumbents largely on the basis of personal characteristics and noncontroversial activities such as casework and constituent outreach. Even on the issues, references to incumbents were overwhelmingly positive.

Only one voter in ten claimed to know how his or her representative had voted on a piece of legislation during the preceding two years, but more than two-thirds of those voters claimed to have agreed with their legislator's vote.

Incumbents' popularity depends in large part upon their success in shaping information that constituents receive about them and their performance—through advertising, credit claiming, and position taking.[85] Not surprisingly, high levels of contact are reported with House and Senate incumbents; the more contact voters have with their legislators, the more positive their evaluations are likely to be. In the initial NES survey, only 10 percent of all voters said they had no exposure of any kind to their representative; only 6 percent reported no exposure to their senator. Many constituents receive mail from their representatives or read about them in newspapers; almost a quarter have met the representative face to face. For senators, the major points of contact with voters are TV appearances or newspaper and magazine coverage.

The "visibility gap" between incumbents and challengers is wider in House races than in Senate races. Nine of every ten voters report some form of contact with their representative, but fewer than half that number have been exposed to challengers. Senate voters are more likely to be reached by both incumbent and challenger. Of those voters questioned in the first NES survey, 82 percent reported contact with nonincumbent Senate candidates in their state, compared with 94 percent reporting contact with incumbent senators. In open seats the gap is narrower. Candidates for seats with no incumbent are able to reach nearly three-quarters of their potential House voters and 90 percent of potential Senate voters.

These findings explain why senators are more vulnerable at the polls than are their House counterparts. First, surveys indicate that representatives are viewed more favorably than senators—probably because they are judged primarily on noncontroversial acts, such as personal contact or constituent service, while senators are more closely linked to divisive national issues. Second, Senate challengers are far more visible than House challengers. Senate contests are more widely reported by the media, and challengers can gain almost as much exposure as incumbents. Media coverage of House races is more fragmentary than that of Senate races, throwing more weight to incumbents' techniques of contacting voters. Third, senators cannot manipulate voter contacts as much as representatives do. Voters largely get their information about Senate races through organized media, which senators do not control. Representatives gain exposure through focused means—personal appearances, mailings, and newsletters—which they fashion to their own advantage. "Somewhat ironically," observes Michael Robinson, "powerful senators are less able to control their images than 'invisible' House members."[86] Finally, senatorial elections are more competitive than House elections. There are fewer one-party states than one-party congressional districts.

Although incumbency offers many advantages, such as name recognition and media coverage, one must not exaggerate their causes or extent, as so often happens in journalistic or reformist accounts. Jacobson surely captured

the normal state of affairs when he observed that "most incumbents face obscure, politically inexperienced opponents whose resources fall far short of what is necessary to mount a formidable campaign."[87]

Still, nonincumbents can and do win, with luck, timing, and attention to certain basic principles. Run for an open seat or against an incumbent whose support is slipping, or run in a year of voter restlessness. Be a credible, forceful candidate. Be prepared to spend money to erase the incumbent's visibility advantage. Blame the incumbent for the "mess in Washington." In some years (1992 and 1994, for example) this strategy works for many challengers. But even in years of political quiescence, like 1998, a handful of challengers will win by following these rules. That handful is usually enough to keep other incumbents on their guard.[88]

Issue Voting

According to conventional wisdom, issues and ideologies play a relatively minor role in voting, especially in congressional races. In their landmark 1962 study of House elections, Warren Miller and Donald Stokes found that voters knew next to nothing about the performance of either the parties or individual members of Congress.[89] Subsequent studies have done little to alter this judgment. Researchers have found that a large portion of those claiming to know House incumbents' stands on issues are wrong and that respondents resort mainly to guesswork when asked to place House or Senate candidates on a liberal–conservative scale.[90]

A slightly more optimistic picture emerged from later NES surveys. One-third of the respondents were able to name an issue they said was important to them in the House elections. Of those people, 40 percent preferred one of the candidates because of the issue they had cited. Yet 54 percent said the issue made no difference in their choice of candidates. Only 11 percent of the respondents, moreover, could remember how their representative had voted on any issue during the preceding two years; of those, 71 percent reported agreeing with the incumbent on that issue.[91]

As usual, we must distinguish between House and Senate voting. House incumbents and challengers can more easily sidestep divisive national issues and stress their personal qualities and district service. Senators, on the other hand, are more closely identified with issues. One study comparing incumbents' ratings by the Americans for Democratic Action with voters' self-classifications on a seven-point liberal–conservative scale found that ideology had "no discernible impact on evaluations of House candidates."[92] Contact was the prime influence on respondents' evaluations of House candidates; ideology and party identification were more important in evaluating Senate candidates. Another study, based on exit polls, found that "policy issues play an important role" in the Senate elections, where "policy effects are substantial and systematic."[93]

Given the subordinate role of issues in influencing voters' decisions, how are we to assess recent efforts by parties and other groups to develop and market nationwide "platforms" or themes for congressional campaigns? As early as

the 1970s, House Democrats and Republicans were drafting platforms—lists of goals or talking points to supply ammunition to candidates in the field, especially nonincumbents.[94] The most daring use of this device occurred in September 1994, when more than 300 GOP congressional candidates gathered on the steps of the U.S. Capitol's West Front to sign the Contract with America—a set of ten proposals that included a balanced-budget amendment, a presidential line-item veto, internal House reforms, term limits for members of Congress, and policy proposals on crime, welfare, business regulation, and tax cuts. The candidates pledged that, if a GOP majority were elected, they would put the measures to a House floor vote within the first hundred days of the new Congress. By signing what amounted to a national platform, the candidates seemingly defied the common assumption that issues do not win elections and the dictum of the late Thomas P. "Tip" O'Neill Jr. (Speaker, 1977–1987) that "all politics are local."

Flush with victory that November, Republican leaders were quick to claim a popular mandate to enact the Contract with America. However, what we know about issues in elections—and about the contract in particular—entitles us to be skeptical of its specific impact on voting choice. First, the contract was crafted to embrace themes that the party had been using over several previous elections and that seemed to resonate with voters. "To me, the Contract was just another campaign appeal, variations of which we heard every two years," remarked Illinois representative Ray LaHood, one of seven candidates who declined to sign it. Second, candidates' use of the contract in their campaigns varied widely. Some used it to underscore themes they had already been employing. Others rarely mentioned it. "I didn't use the Contract that much," reported a typical GOP candidate. "I made very limited reference to it and the voters didn't know much about it. . . . I did talk about things that were in the Contract, but that's not the same as using the Contract per se." Third, most voters claimed not to have heard about the contract. At best, no more than three in ten voters were acquainted with it. "Almost all the GOP candidates admitted that few voters, aside from a few 'C-SPAN groupies,' could recognize what the Contract was by election day."[95]

Whatever one's verdict on the effect of congressional platforms, issues figure prominently in candidates' and parties' appeals. Although the vast majority of voters may make up their minds on other grounds, at least some of them are attentive to issues, even basing their choices on a specific issue or cluster of issues. Issues matter at the margins, and not a few elections turn on those margins.

Voters' responses to political issues show up in the different patterns of choice displayed by demographic groups. Many Americans sort themselves out politically according to their sex, their income or social class, their race or ethnicity, their age, their region, even their habits of religious devotion. True, these differences are typically reflected in people's long-term party loyalties, but issues can exert an independent force. Consider the divisive issue of abortion. Although this issue cuts across party lines, the Democratic Party's generally pro-choice stance has cost it some support from its cadres of religious

conservatives—for example, southern white Evangelicals, ethnic Catholics, and devout blacks and Latinos. The Republican Party's record (strongly anti-abortion) has hurt its standing among middle- and upper-class women who might otherwise prefer the party's candidates. Abortion is an example of what politicians call "wedge issues"—those that have the power to move voters away from their normal party loyalties. For certain voters in certain elections, such issues can overpower long-standing party loyalties and, if they persist over time, even displace those party loyalties.

A demographic snapshot of the two parties' voters in the 1998 House elections, as gleaned from exit polls, appears in Table 4-4. Studying these numbers, one can discern the much-discussed "gender gap," which is the difference between the way men and women vote. In 1998 the gender gap amounted to 6 percent, which was a somewhat narrower margin than in recent years (perhaps a reaction to the president's affair with a White House intern). Gender gaps appear in virtually all recent contests. As pollster Celinda Lake remarked, "You'll get [a gender gap] in a race for dogcatcher in Montana, if it's a Republican against a Democrat."[96] The presence of a female candidate affects but does not remove the phenomenon. A study of U.S. Senate races for the years 1990–1994 showed that the gap invariably favored Democratic candidates; the margins were 8.6 percent (female Democrat versus male Republican), 5.4 percent (two male candidates), and 1.2 percent (male Democrat versus female Republican). The presence of a gap does not tell us what caused it: it could be that women moved toward one candidate, or that men moved toward the other, or some combination of the two. Researchers are hard at work pursuing this question, which involves the responses of men and women to political and social issues. Women may respond more positively than men to social equality issues such as government-sponsored health benefits, job training, child care, and welfare aid. Men are more attracted to issues such as military preparedness, tough anticrime laws, and restrictions on welfare recipients and immigrants.[97]

Examining Table 4-4 one can uncover a host of similar patterns. "There's a family gap, a generation gap, a gender gap," said GOP pollster Neil Newhouse of the fissures among the voting population. "They're all alive and well."[98] Many of the patterns are familiar: Republicans attract upper-income, conservative, well-educated voters who are not racial or ethnic minorities; Democrats draw in voters with opposite characteristics. Such loyalties are built on issues and themes adopted by parties and candidates over the years.

Regardless of what nationwide surveys may show, therefore, legislators and their advisers are highly sensitive to voters' expected reactions to stands on issues. Much energy is devoted to framing positions, communicating them (sometimes in deliberately obscure words), and assessing their effect. Moreover, every professional politician can relate instances when issues tipped an election one way or another. Frequently cited is the electoral influence of "single interest" groups. Some citizens vote according to a single issue they regard as paramount, such as gun control or abortion (pro or con). Even if small in numbers, these groups can decide close contests. That is why legislators dislike

Table 4-4   Demographic Groupings and Votes in the House, 1998, 1996, 1994

Demographic grouping	Percentage of vote					
	1998		1996		1994	
	Dem.	Rep.	Dem.	Rep.	Dem.	Rep.
Party identification						
Democrat	87	11	92	8	89	11
Republican	9	90	8	92	8	92
Independent	45	48	50	50	42	58
Ideology						
Liberal	81	16	89	11	82	18
Moderate	54	43	60	40	58	42
Conservative	17	80	23	77	20	80
Gender						
Men	45	52	49	51	43	57
Women	51	46	57	43	54	46
Race/ethnicity						
Whites	42	55	46	54	42	58
Blacks	88	11	86	14	92	8
Hispanics	59	35	75	25	60	40
Asians	54	42	44	56	55	45
Age						
18–29 years	48	48	55	45	51	49
30–44	49	49	50	50	47	53
45–59[a]	50	46	52	48	48	52
60+[b]	44	54	55	45	50	50
Education						
Less than high school	57	41	72	28	60	40
High school graduate	49	47	57	43	48	52
Some college	45	51	50	50	42	58
College graduate	44	53	48	52	50	50
Post graduate	52	45	—	—	56	42
Income[c]						
Less than $15,000	57	39	68	32	63	37
$15,000–$29,999	53	44	56	44	53	47
$30,000–$49,999	48	49	50	50	46	54
$50,000–$74,999	44	54	49	51	45	55
$75,000–$100,000	47	51	41	59	—	—
Over $100,000	44	53	41	59	—	—
Religion						
Protestant	37	60	42	58	40	60
Catholic	51	45	57	43	48	52
Other Christian	47	51	45	55	50	50

(Table continues on next page)

Table 4-4   (Continued)

Demographic grouping	Percentage of vote					
	1998		1996		1994	
	Dem.	Rep.	Dem.	Rep.	Dem.	Rep.
Jewish	78	21	79	21	78	22
None	65	32	69	31	63	37
Attend religious services						
Once a week per month	—	—	45	55	—	—
Less than once per month	—	—	60	40	—	—
Marital status						
Married	42	54	48	52	43	57
Not married	58	38	60	40	56	44
Young adults (18–29 years)						
Total	48	48	55	45	51	49
Women	53	44	62	38	58	52
Men	41	53	47	33	43	57
High school	42	50	54	46	55	45
College	45	51	51	49	51	49

Source: Surveys by *Los Angeles Times,* Nov. 5, 1996; Voter News Service, Nov. 8, 1994. The findings are reprinted in *Public Perspective* 10 (December/January 1999): 69–73.

Note: Percentages do not always add to 100 because of rounding and minor party candidate voting.

[a] For 1996 the age category was 45–64.
[b] For 1996 the age category was 65+.
[c] For 1996 the income categories are less than $20,000; $20,000–$39,999; $40,000–$59,999; $60,000–$74,999; $75,000–$100,000. For 1994 the highest income category was $50,000.

taking positions on issues that evoke extreme responses, issues that prompt certain voters to oppose them regardless of their record on other matters.

No matter how issues sway voters directly, they exert powerful indirect effects upon election outcomes. For one thing, issues motivate the voters who are opinion leaders, who can lend or withhold support far beyond their single vote. Issues are carefully monitored by organized interests, including political action committees, that are in a position to channel funds, publicity, or volunteer workers to the candidate's cause. Legislators devote time and attention to promoting issues and explaining them to attentive publics because it pays them to do so.

Portrait of a Congressional Voter

What portrait can we construct of voters in congressional elections? It is a rather complicated picture in which three elements—party, candidates, and issues—play varying roles. Despite weakening partisan ties, a large segment of the electorate seems to be adhering to a "standing decision" to vote for candi-

dates according to party affiliation. Factors relating to individual candidates are, however, of substantial and growing importance. Congressional candidates, especially incumbents, strive to fashion unique appeals based not on party loyalty but on "home style"—a mixture of personal style, voter contacts, and constituent service.[99]

Because of their superior resources for cultivating attractive home styles, incumbents have an edge at the polls. Through media exposure, Senate challengers can often overcome this advantage; lacking such outlets for their message, fewer House challengers can do so. In periods of citizen unrest, however, incumbency can be effectively countered. Finally, issues and ideologies motivate a core of dedicated voters and tilt the outcomes of at least some elections.

Election Outcomes

The process by which representatives and senators reach Capitol Hill is an essential aspect of the two Congresses notion. House and Senate contests are waged one by one on local turf. As Thomas Mann and Raymond Wolfinger conclude, "In deciding how to cast their ballots, most voters are influenced primarily by the choice of local candidates."[100] At the same time, these local contests are waged against a backdrop of national events and issues. Top-down trends in 1994 included economic malaise and uncertainty and the unpopularity of President Clinton and many of his policies. Two years later the overarching considerations were a buoyant economy and the unpopularity of what citizens judged as the excesses of the Republican Congresses—for example, its role in twice shutting down the federal government and pursuing their probe of President Clinton. The increasing involvement of national party committees and allied interest groups (labor unions for the Democrats, small business and the religious right for the Republicans) has brought national coordination to congressional campaigns. The result is that a mix of local and national forces converge on congressional elections to shape their conduct and their results.

Party Balance

Despite the much vaunted independence of candidates and voters, virtually all races are run with party labels. In 1998 some twenty-five parties appeared on ballots somewhere in the United States, including the Anti-Drug, New Union, Free Libertarian, Right to Life, Nuclear Freeze, and Socialist Workers parties. In terms of governance, however, only two parties really count: the Democrats or the Republicans have controlled Congress since 1855. (Appendix A lists the partisan majorities in the House and Senate since 1901.) Between 1896 and 1920 the two parties had approximately equal numbers of partisans in the electorate, but lower participation rates in Democratic areas tended to favor the Republicans. The GOP's relative position improved after 1920, when women received the vote. The New Deal realignment of the 1930s shifted the balance to the Democrats. After that the Democrats became virtually a perennial majority and the Republicans a permanent minority on Capitol Hill. In all that time the Republicans controlled both chambers simultaneously for

only four years (1947–1949, 1953–1955) and the Senate alone for only six years (1981–1987). Democratic sweeps in 1958, 1964, and 1974 padded Democratic majorities. Republicans eventually recovered from these setbacks, but Democratic dominance, especially in the House, was hard to overcome because incumbents learned how to exploit their reelection assets successfully.

In 1994, for the first time in forty years, the Republicans won control of both houses of Congress. Not one Republican incumbent was defeated, while thirty-four Democratic representatives and two senators lost their seats. In the two succeeding elections the parties fought to a virtual draw, with Democrats gaining ten (1996) and then five (1998) House seats, pulling to within seven seats of a majority.

Recent elections have confirmed historic shifts in the two parties' power bases. Historically, the Grand Old Party was dominant in the populous states of the Northeast and Midwest. "The Democracy," by contrast, owned the "solid South" from the Civil War era through the 1970s, as well as the large urban political machines. The tectonic plates of political alliances move slowly, sometimes producing results of earthquake proportions.

The 1994 earthquake underscored the Republicanization of the South. The GOP claimed a majority of the South's seats in the Senate and House for the first time in history, as nineteen House seats and four Senate seats moved into the party's fold. At the end of the decade the party's majority in that region remained secure: 82 of 140 House seats and 18 of 28 Senate seats.[101] The GOP is the party of choice for conservative white southerners and is unquestionably their philosophic home. Breaking the Democrats' historic stranglehold in the South—with its rapidly growing population—was the step that gave the Republicans their majorities on Capitol Hill. The most solid GOP region, however, is the Mountain West, where Democrats elect only 30 percent of the lawmakers.

Meanwhile, other changes altered the partisan landscape. New England and Mid-Atlantic states, historically Republican strongholds, began electing majorities of Democratic lawmakers as early as the 1960s. Democrats account for 13 of the region's 22 senators and 58 of the 96 representatives. They are now competitive in the Midwest, another historic GOP stronghold. And the Democrats capture a majority of seats in the Pacific states.

The result is that the two parties are closely competitive nationally, especially in races for the White House and the House of Representatives. Either party could plausibly capture those institutions. In the Senate the GOP has the edge, because of its advantage in the South and its dominance in the Mountain states, where modest populations yield proportionately more Senate seats than House seats.

Realignment or Dealignment?

Historically, political upheavals have shifted party control in the House or Senate with decisive results. Political scientists talk of "critical elections" or "critical periods," in which one party yields preeminence to another or major voting groups alter the shape of the parties' coalitions. The most recent such

watershed eras were the Civil War, the turbulent 1890s, the New Deal of the 1930s, and perhaps the unrest of the early 1990s. Each of these upheavals brought to Capitol Hill new lawmakers, new voting patterns, and new legislative priorities.[102]

For nearly fifty years political scientists have been on the lookout for a post–New Deal realignment; most have yet to spot one. Everett Carll Ladd likens this pursuit to Samuel Beckett's play *Waiting for Godot,* in which an anticipated character never appears. Meaningful changes can, however, take place even without an underlying party realignment. The Wilson-era Democratic dominance (1913–1919), the Johnson-era "Great Society" Congresses (1965–1967), the post-Watergate Democratic landslide (1974), the Reagan juggernaut (1981–1982), and the Republican "revolution" of 1994–1995 involved changes in partisan strength on Capitol Hill that for one reason or another went far beyond any underlying shifts in attitudes or voting habits within the electorate as a whole. Elected officeholders, like most political activists, tend to be more committed to ideology or policy than are most voters, even those of the officeholder's own party. Congress turned leftward in the 1960s and 1970s and rightward in the 1990s without any dramatic shifts in voters' attitudes.

Democratic dominance on Capitol Hill has coexisted in recent times with Republican successes in capturing the White House. With their victory in 1992, Democrats had won twenty straight House elections, capturing from 53 to 68 percent of the seats in each election; their control of the Senate during this period was marred only by six years of Republican control. Meanwhile, Republicans had won six of the ten presidential contests, several by landslides. (Only once, in 1964, did Democratic candidates win more than 50.1 percent of the popular vote.) Whether because of incumbents' strategies or voters' designs, GOP presidential successes had surprisingly little effect on party control of Congress. (Republican control of the Senate in the early 1980s was in part an exception to this rule, in part a product of unrelated factors.)

By the same token, when Democrats have managed to capture the White House they too have had scant impact on electoral results on Capitol Hill. Jimmy Carter's election in 1976 had a negligible effect on his party's congressional fortunes (a net gain of one seat in the House, none in the Senate). Bill Clinton's victory in the three-way 1992 race (Clinton, Bush, and independent Ross Perot) was accompanied by no Democratic Senate gains and a loss of ten House seats.

The Democrats' and Republicans' separate conquests have yielded long stretches of "divided government," or split partisan control of the two policymaking branches. Some analysts argue that voters deliberately split their ballots to maintain ideological balance between the two branches or to make sure that the two branches check one another. This theory imputes great cunning to the average voter: it is improbable that most voters would engage in such a logical exercise to ensure divided partisan control. Indeed, many voters are unaware which party controls the government, especially when party control is divided.[103] In recent elections voters have seemed to endorse the idea of divided government. Responding to fears about "gridlock" in Washington, a modest

majority by 1992 supported unified control. Four years later a plurality was inclined to vote for congressional Republicans as long as President Clinton was "the clear favorite" for reelection.[104] (The opposite outcome—a Republican president and a Democratic Congress—is equally possible, although we have already noted why the Senate may be more insulated from partisan swings.)

More plausible is the argument that voters, seeking different attributes in presidents and lawmakers, often find those attributes in candidates of different parties. Americans harbor inconsistent views about government, its benefits, and its burdens. Republican officeholders have purveyed a rhetoric of limited government ("no new taxes"), while Democrats in elective office have traditionally promoted government services that voters favor. Egged on by candidates' appeals, voters are encouraged to think they can have their cake and eat it too.[105] This account of voters' behavior provides a commonsense explanation for recent periods of divided government.

Turnover and Representation

Reelection rates should not be confused with turnover rates. Even in years when few members are turned out of office by the voters, many leave Capitol Hill voluntarily —to retire, to run for another office, or to follow other pursuits. In 1992 a combination of voluntary retirements and electoral defeats brought 110 new representatives (87 of whom returned in 1995)—the largest incoming class in two generations—and (eventually) 14 new senators. The 1994 contests added 86 new representatives and 11 new senators; the 1996 elections added 74 freshman representatives and 15 new senators. Even in 1998, a year of low turnover, 8 senators and 40 representatives were new to their jobs.

In other words, the natural process of membership change is ongoing. When the 106th Congress convened in January 1999, a majority of House members had been elected in the 1990s. High electoral turnovers in three successive elections made the chamber significantly younger and more junior than it was when the decade began. These elections followed an interlude of uncommonly low turnover (1984–1990) that brought only 162 newcomers to the House—an average of 9 percent per election, compared with a normal rate of 15 percent or more.

The Senate's membership has been altered to a lesser degree by recent elections. A majority of senators serving in the 106th Congress were elected in the 1990s; despite respectable turnovers in 1992 and 1994, the average age and seniority of senators remained fairly steady. A high number of retirements in 1996, however, represented a changing of the guard not unlike that already witnessed in the House.

For Congress to be a responsive institution, high turnover of members, whether by steady increments or by massive partisan realignments, may not be required. Even when few lawmakers are turned out of office, all of them are keenly aware of the threat of defeat. Most take steps to prevent that eventuality by heightened attentiveness to constituents' needs through personal visits, speeches, newsletters, and polls. But are voters' views accurately reflected by

the representatives they elect to Congress? This question is not easily answered. Popular control of policy makers is not the same thing as popular control of policies. Constituents' views are not precisely mirrored by legislators' voting behavior and the laws passed by the legislature.

Registering Voters' Views

What correlation exists between voters' attitudes and members' voting on issues? Miller and Stokes found that constituency attitudes correlated differently according to the kind of policy.[106] In foreign affairs a slight negative correlation existed between constituents' attitudes and legislators' votes; in social and economic welfare issues the correlation was moderate; in civil rights issues the correlation was very high. In other words, in at least one and possibly in two major policy areas the linkage was weak enough to cast some doubt on constituency control.

Political scientists explain the absence of strong linkages by noting how difficult it is to meet all the conditions needed for popular control of policies. Voters would have to identify the candidates' positions on issues, and they would have to vote by referring to those positions. Differences among candidates would have to be apparent, and winners would have to vote in accord with their preelection attitudes. These conditions are not always met. Candidates' stands are not always clear, and candidates do not invariably differentiate themselves on issues.

Political scientists John Sullivan and Robert O'Connor tried to test these conditions by submitting to all House candidates a questionnaire covering three issue areas—foreign affairs, civil rights, and domestic policies—and then following the successful candidates' voting records in the House.[107] Their findings suggest that elements of popular control are present. First, according to their inquiries, voters had meaningful choices among candidates. Second, winning candidates generally voted according to their preelection stands. Third, candidates were ideologically distinct, with Democrats invariably more liberal than Republicans. To these pieces of evidence we can add another: according to recent surveys, most congressional voters can rank their representative on a liberal–conservative scale, and most of these voters claim an affinity with their representative's ranking.[108] In other words, voters' attitudes and legislators' views are roughly parallel—even though they may diverge on numerous specific points.

After the Election Is Over

If ideological or attitudinal links between voters and their representatives are rough and variable, actual contacts between constituents and individual legislators are numerous and palpable. Individual legislators do not necessarily mirror their constituents, much less the nation as a whole, in terms of demographic characteristics. Yet much of their time and effort while in office are devoted to dealing with the "folks back home." Constituency politics are ever present in the daily lives of senators and representatives, and it is to this subject that we turn in the following chapter.

On the Hill, on the beach. California Republican Brian P. Bilbray's official photo (inset) gives little hint of his district style: an earnest door-to-door campaigner in a swing district and a former surfer from Imperial Beach, where he grew up.

5

Being There: Hill Styles
and Home Styles

As the Ohio River flood waters receded, Democratic representative Ted Strickland spent the Easter 1997 recess period visiting with constituents in his ravaged southeastern Ohio district. Already he had urged federal agencies and relief organizations to send help. The Federal Emergency Management Agency (FEMA) was handing out relief checks within a week; the Red Cross had more clothes than it could use. Now Strickland, in private life a teacher and a consulting psychologist, knew his constituents needed the personal touch. As he explained,

> Being there, as a member of Congress, has meaning for people. It's a way of saying your government cares about you. Your country cares. I've hugged a lot of people this month, and had a lot of strangers hug me. It's the way people are when you visit a funeral home.[1]

Electorally, Strickland was an at-risk incumbent: first elected in 1992, he was defeated in the GOP landslide in 1994 and reclaimed his seat two years later. But in Washington, D.C., Strickland had clout beyond his second-term status: his party controlled the executive branch but had lost the House and needed every seat it could get. Already he had goaded the Clinton administration into retaining an Energy Department uranium processing plant whose 2,500 jobs made it his district's largest employer. Asked what he would most like to accomplish in Congress, he cited his interest in children's health care and infrastructure improvements. But his main goal: "Being a scrapper, and fighting for every damn thing I can get for my district."

Local booster and Washington insider, Strickland personifies the "two Congresses." In this chapter we consider members of Congress and the two worlds in which they live and work: one on Capitol Hill and the other back home in their states or districts.

Hill Styles

Members of Congress, Richard F. Fenno Jr. reminds us, spend their lives "moving between two contexts, Washington and home, and between two activities, governing and campaigning."[2] The two contexts and the two activities are interwoven. How members govern is deeply affected by their campaign experience, especially that of the most recent election. In turn, their Capitol Hill activities affect all their subsequent contacts with people back home. Here we

examine what we call Hill styles. We consider who the lawmakers are, how they see their roles, and how they spend their time.

Who Are the Legislators?

The Constitution names only three criteria for individuals serving in Congress: age, citizenship, and residency. As we have seen, however, entrance requirements are really far more restrictive. It was Aristotle, after all, who first observed that elections are essentially oligarchic affairs that involve few active participants. By almost any measure, senators and representatives constitute an economic and social elite. They are well educated. They come from a small number of prestigious occupations. Many of them possess or amass material wealth. Forty percent of all senators are millionaires. The House is more middle class, economically speaking, yet more than sixty members are millionaires.[3] The pay of senators and representatives ($136,700 in 1999) puts them in the top 1 percent of the nation's wage earners. Yet expenses are high, especially for members who maintain a residence in Washington as well as one back home. A federal pay commission reported more than a decade ago that "most members of Congress find it difficult to live on their current salaries."[4] Most of them have outside sources of income, although several such income sources have been shut down—including gifts, travel, and honoraria (fees provided by interest groups for speeches or other appearances).

Occupation. Some humorist proposed that our government "of laws and not men" is really "of lawyers and not men." When the 106th Congress convened in January 1999, 230 members were lawyers. As Figure 5-1 indicates, lawyers typically outnumber other professions in both chambers, although their numbers have dwindled, and they are a majority only in the Senate.[5]

In the United States law and politics are closely linked. Many lawyers view forays into electoral politics as a form of professional advertising. The legal profession stresses personal skills, such as verbalization, advocacy, and negotiation, that are useful in gaining and holding public office. Important, too, is lawyers' monopoly over offices that serve as stepping-stones to Congress—especially elected law enforcement and judicial posts.[6] Unlike doctors, engineers, and most other high-status professionals, lawyers can move in and out of their jobs without jeopardizing their careers. (Fourteen medical practitioners, three nurses, three physicists, and four members of the clergy served in the 106th Congress.)

Business is the next most prevalent occupation. Historically, many business people have harbored antigovernment attitudes that have deterred them from entering public life. Corporate managers rarely come to Congress. Normally, they lack two qualities every would-be politician needs: visibility in their home communities and career mobility. Temporary leaves of absence can bump managers off the promotion ladder. Local proprietors (druggists, real estate brokers, and morticians, for example) are highly visible in their hometowns, but often they cannot afford to leave their businesses in the hands of others. Executives in service industries—publishing, broadcasting, technology,

Figure 5-1   Occupations of House Members in Twelve Selected Congresses

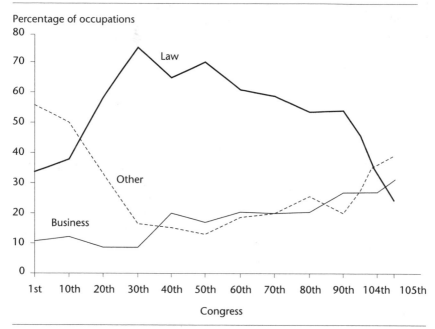

Percentage of occupations

Source: Roger H. Davidson, *The Role of the Congressman* (Indianapolis: Bobbs-Merrill, 1969), 38. Recent calculations by the authors from Norman J. Ornstein, Thomas E. Mann, and Michael J. Malbin, *Vital Statistics on Congress 1997–1998* (Washington, DC: Congressional Quarterly, 1998), 23.

Note: Because members may cite more than one occupation, percentages are of occupations rather than members.

and real estate, for example—are visible and mobile enough to make ideal candidates and increasingly are found in Congress. The Republicans' takeover from the Democrats as the majority party on Capitol Hill boosted the trend toward business backgrounds and away from law.

Other professions are represented in smaller numbers. Members of the "verbalizing professions"—teaching, journalism, and public service—also win seats in Congress. Nearly a hundred members of the 106th Congress spent part or all of their early careers in education; a couple dozen were in communications. As for prior public careers, the 106th Congress included fourteen state governors, a federal judge, a state supreme court justice, an ambassador, and 265 former state legislators.

Still other occupations are represented because they are uniquely visible. Historically, military heroes have been sought after, and following World War II a surge of returning veterans went to Congress. Among them were Reps. John F. Kennedy, Richard M. Nixon, and Gerald R. Ford. By the 1970s more

than seven of ten members were veterans. Today the proportion of veterans, especially those with combat experience, is dwindling: fewer than a third of the members of the 106th Congress had prior military service.

Today's media-centered campaigns have spawned a few celebrity legislators. Several astronauts, including former senator John Glenn, D-Ohio, have served. Former professional athletes serving in the 106th Congress included two Hall of Famers: Rep. Steve Largent, R-Okla., a wide receiver for the Seattle Seahawks, and Sen. Jim Bunning, R-Ky., who once pitched a perfect game for the Philadelphia Phillies.

Needless to say, many occupations are, and always have been, drastically underrepresented in Congress. Low-status occupations, including farm labor, service trades, manual and skilled labor, and domestic service, are rare on Capitol Hill. One blue-collar worker elected in recent years quit after one term in part because he was unhappy and self-conscious about his social status.

Education and Religion. By every measure, Congress is a highly educated body. All but a handful of members have college degrees; two-thirds have graduate degrees, which are required in the heavily represented professions such as law. There are numerous earned doctorates; three Rhodes scholars serve in the Senate and two in the House.

Although a few prestigious private universities are overrepresented, no schools hold the dominant position that Oxford and Cambridge do in British ruling circles. One reason is the lingering norm of localism in congressional recruitment; this means that local colleges and state universities have a large share of members. Of those members sitting in 1999, three-quarters of the representatives and two-thirds of the senators attended at least one in-state school

Virtually every member of the 106th Congress professed a formal religious affiliation, compared with about seven of ten Americans in surveys.[7] More than one-quarter of all House and Senate members are Roman Catholics, the largest single contingent. That number is slightly above the nationwide proportion of Catholics. Most other legislators are Protestants, either from mainline denominations—Methodists, Episcopalians, Presbyterians, and Baptists—or from evangelical groups. Jews, who make up 2.6 percent of the total U.S. population, accounted for 7 percent of the 106th Congress. Catholics, evangelical Protestants, and Jews have enlarged their share of Congress's membership, while mainline Protestants have declined in numbers. Another trend is that evangelicals, once mostly Democrats, now compose a sizable portion of the congressional GOP.

Sex and Sexual Orientation. Neither chamber accurately mirrors the nation in terms of sex or sexual identity. Congress historically has been a male bastion. Diversity has developed slowly.

Unable to vote until 1920, women have always been underrepresented in Congress. Beginning in 1916 with Jeannette Rankin, elected as a Republican from Montana, 199 women have been elected or appointed to Congress. At first, many gained office on the death of husbands who were representatives

or senators; some, like Margaret Chase Smith, R-Maine (House 1940–1949, Senate 1949–1970), enjoyed far more notable careers than did their husbands. As more women entered politics at all levels, they started to be elected on their own merits, often elevated from prior office. The old tradition of the "widow's mandate" has faded (although three recently elected representatives—including Sonny Bono's wife Mary, R-Calif.—replaced their husbands).[8]

Women now make up one-eighth of Congress's members, even though they account for more than half of the nation's population. In the 106th Congress a record number of women served—fifty-eight in the House (including two delegates) and nine in the Senate. Several of the newcomers won in open seats, taking advantage of retirements and redistricting.

The presence of sizable numbers of women has affected Capitol Hill in several ways. Aside from obvious details (installing a Senate women's restroom, opening the gymnasiums to both sexes), the influx of women has brought adjustments in political agendas and ways of doing things. Policy concerns once labeled "women's issues" now receive respectful hearing. For the first time, workplace and women's health issues—gender discrimination and "drive by" mastectomies, for example—had to be seriously addressed. Rep. Nita Lowey, D-N.Y., whose mother died of breast cancer, asked for $500 million for research on the disease. During debate over family leave policy, Sen. Patty Murray, D-Wash., talked about having to quit a secretarial job sixteen years earlier when she was pregnant with her first child. At a hearing on Social Security taxes for household help, Rep. Carrie P. Meek, D-Fla., a seventy-something granddaughter of slaves, brought her own vivid experiences to the proceedings. "I was once a domestic worker," she told her colleagues. "My mother was a domestic worker. All my sisters were domestic workers."[9] Referring to the women serving in the Senate, Senator Murray declared, "We've made it okay for men to talk about these [women's] issues, too."[10]

Gays and lesbians passed a milestone in 1998 when Tammy Baldwin, D-Wis., became the first lesbian representative whose sexual orientation was known before her initial election. The two gay men who also serve in the House (and two former representatives) revealed their sexuality or were "outed" after they had served for some time. Baldwin, who served six years in the state legislature, did not shy away from the issue. Her campaign slogan was "A different kind of candidate." Still, as Rep. Barney Frank, D-Mass., observed, the hardest part of running as a gay is "convincing voters that you will not disproportionately focus on that minority's issues."[11] That lesson applies to all candidates contending in districts where they are obviously in the minority—for example, blacks running in majority-white areas.

Race. African Americans, who make up 12 percent of the nation's population, account for 7 percent of Congress's members. In 1999 thirty-nine African Americans (including two delegates) served in the House. Indeed, in all U.S. history only 105 blacks have served in Congress, four of them in the Senate and the rest in the House. Half of these served during the Reconstruction era after the Civil War. All were Republicans, loyal to the party of Lincoln. No

blacks served in Congress from 1900 to 1928, when Rep. Oscar De Priest, a Republican, was elected from a heavily black district on Chicago's South Side. In the next twenty-five years only three more blacks entered Congress, but after the 1960s African American representation rose steadily. All but four of the twentieth-century black legislators have been Democrats. Only one black Republican served in the 106th Congress: Rep. J. C. Watts, whose southwest Oklahoma district is 7 percent black.

Other minorities are represented in smaller numbers. Latinos make up 10 percent of the population but less than 5 percent of the House membership (including two delegates); no Latinos serve in the Senate. Of the twenty Latino representatives, most are Mexican Americans, three are Cuban Americans, and three are of Puerto Rican descent. Asians and Pacific Islanders claim four representatives, two senators, and one delegate. Two Native Americans serve in the Senate: Ben Nighthorse Campbell, R-Colo., is part Northern Cheyenne, and Democrat Daniel K. Akaka, a native Hawaiian, represents his state.

Most minority members of the House represent "majority minority" districts, many of them created for this purpose after the 1990 census (see Chapter 3). The goal of boosting minority representation through redistricting succeeded: all but one of these districts elected minority lawmakers. Only a handful of African Americans and Latinos are now elected from areas with less than 50 percent minority population; the ranks of such members must grow if minorities are to gain anything approaching proportionate representation.

Age and Tenure. When the 106th Congress convened, the average age of representatives was fifty-three; for senators, it was fifty-eight.[12] Early in its history, Congress had younger members. House or Senate service was a part-time job, physically demanding but not especially exalted. Politicians stayed in Washington a few years and then moved on to other pursuits. After 1900, however, the seniority system and the political security of those from one-party areas—Democrats in the South, Republicans in the Midwest—led members to view congressional service as a long-term career. "Few die, and none retire," it was said. The average representative of the late 1990s had served eight years, or four House terms. The average senator had served nearly eleven years, or almost two full Senate terms.

Age and tenure levels fluctuate over time. Periods of relatively low turnover (the 1980s, for example) are punctuated by dramatic "changing of the guard" periods, as in the 1970s and the 1990s, involving both senior and junior members of Congress.[13] Electoral defeats play some role, but most members leave voluntarily. In the 1970s veterans were disgruntled by new norms of scheduling, constituency attentiveness, and fund raising; newer members were dismayed by the job's low financial rewards and high personal costs, especially those borne by their families. During the political upheavals of the early 1990s, older members wearied of the frantic pace and occasionally were dogged by scandal; younger members wanted to earn more money and see more of their families. When the 106th Congress assembled in 1999, a majority of representatives and senators had first arrived in the 1990s.

A certain balance between new blood and stable membership is un-doubtedly desirable for legislative bodies. The rapid turnover of the early 1990s heightened the generational conflict: most newly elected members had indulged in "Congress bashing" in their campaigns and wanted to shake up the institution, and not a few of them shunned the idea of making a career of pub-lic service. "They don't regard being defeated as the end of their life, just a change of jobs," Speaker Newt Gingrich, D-Ga., remarked of his young col-leagues. "That is very different than the sort of careerist view that had domi-nated for a long time."[14]

By the end of the decade, incumbency was no longer a dirty word, and turnover levels declined. Some of the firebrands who entered Congress promis-ing to get out after six years were having second thoughts. One of these was Rep. George Nethercutt, R-Wash., who in 1994 ousted Democratic Speaker Thomas S. Foley, a thirty-year veteran, with a promise that "six years is enough." Only four years later, Nethercutt admitted that experience had shown him that issues were so complicated that six years are "probably not enough."[15]

Representation. Must Congress demographically mirror the populace to be a representative institution? The question is hotly debated. Hannah Pitkin dis-tinguishes between two types of representation: *substantive* and *descriptive*.[16] To represent a category of people substantively, a legislator must consciously "act for" people and their interests, whether a member of that grouping or not. Leg-islators from farming districts can voice farmers' concerns even though they have never plowed a field; whites can champion equal opportunities for mi-norities. Few Asian Americans serve in Congress, but their proportion in a district affects a member's support of issues advocated by that group.[17] Con-versely, white representatives from districts that lost black voters in the gerry-mandering of the 1990s became more conservative and less supportive of policies preferred by African Americans.[18]

By and large, Congress is a body of local political pros for whom speak-ing for constituents comes naturally. Most members keep in touch with the home folks without even thinking about it. A majority of representatives in one survey agreed with the statement: "I seldom have to sound out my con-stituents because I think so much like them that I know how to react to almost any proposal."[19]

Yet descriptive, or symbolic, representation can be as important as sub-stantive representation. Symbolically, there is no real substitute for having a member of one's own grouping in a position of influence. When a member of an ethnic or racial minority goes to Congress, it is a badge of legitimacy for the entire grouping. Such legislators speak for people like them throughout the nation. Moreover, there can be tangible gains in the quality of representation. Studies tend to indicate that women members of Congress are more likely than men to introduce, sponsor, and press for bills of special concern to women and children.[20]

Nor is representation restrained by state or district boundaries. One mem-ber who suffers from epilepsy defends job rights for other sufferers of the dis-

Table 5-1   House Members' Views on the Jobs Expected of Them

Volunteered responses	Percentage[a]
Legislator	87
Constituency servant	79
Mentor/communicator	43
Representative	26
Politico	11
Overseer	9
Institutional broker	7
Office manager	6
Jack-of-all-trades	6
All other roles	4

Source: House Commission on Administrative Review, *Final Report*, 2 vols., H. Doc. 95-272, 95th Cong., 1st sess., Dec. 31, 1977, 2:874–875.

Note: N=146.

[a] Many members mentioned two or more jobs.

ease; another whose grandson was born prematurely champions funds for medical research into birth defects; a third, who fled the Nazis as a child in the 1940s, has sworn to perpetuate awareness of the Holocaust; members who are openly gay speak out for the rights of homosexuals. Such causes are close to members' hearts, even though they often pay scant political dividends and go largely unnoticed by the press and the public.

How Do Legislators Describe Their Jobs?

In the late 1970s the House Commission on Administrative Review asked 153 representatives to list "the major kinds of jobs, duties, or functions that you feel you are expected to perform as an individual member of Congress." This question elicited not so much the members' own priorities as their diverse perceptions of what colleagues, constituents, lobbyists, and others expect of them. The responses, summarized in Table 5-1, form a snapshot of members' views of their jobs. Although this survey has not been repeated, it remains a reasonably accurate representation of members' jobs as they see them.

Legislator. The rules, procedures, and traditions of the House and Senate impose many constraints on members' behavior. To be effective, new members must learn their way through the institutional maze. Legislators therefore stress the formal aspects of Capitol Hill duties and routines: legislative work, investigation, and committee specialization. Charles E. Schumer, D-N.Y., in elective office for more than half his life (he was elected to the state assembly at age twenty-three and served nine terms in the U.S. House), explained his commitment as a professional legislator during his successful 1998 campaign for the Senate:

> I love to legislate. Taking an idea—often not original with me—shaping it, molding it. Building a coalition of people who might not completely agree with it. Passing it and making the country a little bit of a better place. I love doing that.[21]

Most legislators pursue information and expertise on issues, not only because it is the way to shape public policy but also because it sways others in the chamber.

The legislator's role dovetails with that of representing constituents. Most members seek committee assignments that will serve the needs of their states or districts. One House member related how his interest in flood control and water resource development impelled him to ask for a seat on the committee responsible for those issues. "The interests of my district dictated my field of specialization," he explained, "but the decision to specialize in some legislative field is automatic for the member who wants to exercise any influence."[22]

Members soon learn the norms, or folkways, that expedite legislative bargaining and maximize productivity. Examining the post–World War II Senate, Donald Matthews identified six folkways governing behavior that were enforced in numerous informal ways. Senators should (1) serve an apprenticeship (exercising restraint and deference to elders in the early years); (2) concentrate on Senate work rather than on gaining publicity; (3) specialize in issues within their committees or affecting their home states; (4) act courteously to colleagues; (5) extend reciprocity to colleagues—that is, provide willing assistance with the expectation that it will be repaid in kind one day; and (6) loyally defend the Senate, "the greatest legislative and deliberative body in the world."[23]

In recent years certain Senate folkways have faded in importance. New senators now ignore the apprenticeship norm and participate immediately in most aspects of deliberation. Many senators, especially those with an eye on higher office, work tirelessly to attract national publicity and personal attention. Committee specialization, although still common, is less rigid than it once was: senators have many overlapping committee assignments and are expected to express views on a wide range of issues. The norms of courtesy and reciprocity are still invoked, but institutional loyalty wears thin in an era of harsh partisanship and cynicism about government.

The House relies more on formal channels of power than on informal norms. From interviews in the 1970s, however, Herbert Asher uncovered seven norms: (1) friendly relationships are desirable; (2) the important work of the House is done in committee; (3) procedural rules of the House are essential; (4) members should not personally criticize a colleague on the House floor; (5) members should be prepared to trade votes; (6) members should be specialists; and (7) freshmen should serve apprenticeships.[24]

Even this loose network of norms has come unraveled. New members, impatient to make their mark, plunge into the work of the House even before they learn their way around. Leadership comes earlier to members than it used

to. Specialization is still attractive—more so in the House than in the Senate—but many members branch out into unrelated issues. No longer are committees the sole forums for influencing legislation. Looser norms of floor participation and voting have expanded members' chances for shaping bills outside their own committees' jurisdictions. Many ideologically driven new members, like those elected in 1994, dismissed norms such as specialization, reciprocity, and compromise. Today's House (and Senate) remind political scientist Eric M. Uslaner of "day care centers in which colicky babies [get] their way by screaming at the top of their lungs."[25]

Legislation-minded members have reacted by declaring war on the decaying norms and rancorous outbursts that, for example, marked the conflict-ridden 104th Congress. Reassertions in the 105th and 106th Congresses of the need for cultivating civility and a spirit of compromise suggest that traditional institutional norms are not dead. Even in an era of high partisanship, reciprocity and compromise must be maintained if members' disparate goals are to be combined into legislation that can be passed.

Constituency Servant. Nearly eight of ten respondents in the 1977 House survey mentioned the role of constituency servant. The constituency servant attempts to give voice to citizens' concerns and solve their problems. This ombudsman role was cited by half the House members. Typically, the task is performed by legislators and their staffs as *casework*—individual cases triggered by constituent letters or visits. It is a chore that weighs heavily on members, even though most of them delegate it to staff aides. The philosophy of most legislators is expressed by one House member like this:

> Constituent work: that's something I feel very strongly about. The American people, with the growth of the bureaucracy, feel nobody cares. The only conduit a taxpayer has with the government is a congressional office.[26]

Sometimes members stress their constituency service to gain breathing room for legislative stands that stray from district norms. This strategy was successfully pursued by many of the seventy-four Democrats of the 1974 "Watergate class" and by many Republicans of the equally large "class of '94." Nearly half in each class had captured seats from the opposition party. Combining vigorous consistency service with some trimming of their earlier positions, many of them became entrenched in office, outliving the circumstances that initially brought them to Washington.

Constituency servants typically make sure their states or districts get their "fair share" of federal money and assistance. "It's a big pie down in Washington," Michael "Ozzie" Myers, then a Democratic representative from Pennsylvania, told FBI agents posing as aides of an Arab sheik during the so-called Abscam probe of influence peddling in the late 1970s:

> Each member's sent there to bring a piece of that pie back home. And if you go down there and you don't—you come back without milkin' it after a few terms . . . you don't go . . . back.[27]

The words are inelegant and the context sleazy, but they characterize members' traditional view of constituency advocacy, even if they rail against "pork" spending in other people's areas.

In recent years growing numbers of candidates have railed against this tradition of "bringing home the bacon." Philosophically committed to downsizing the federal establishment, they seek applause from constituents who oppose deficits, taxes, and federal bureaucrats. And because of modern-day budget constraints (see Chapter 13), there are fewer discretionary dollars to distribute to localities. Today's members are less likely to win earmarked funds for their constituents and more likely to seek nonfiscal benefits—for example, favorable regulatory rules or trade concessions for local industries.[28]

There is no reason, however, to think that pork has vanished from the congressional diet. Remaining government programs with highly visible local benefits—highway and mass transit grants, for example—are smothered with attention. Even in an era of lean budgets, pork barrel advocacy will survive: particularized benefits normally trump collective benefits. An Arkansas lobbyist tells the story of going to visit one of the state's Republican members who was known for his antipork speeches. "I know you're anti-pork," the lobbyist began, "but I have to tell you about our needs and how to position yourself." "What do you mean?" the congressman retorted. "As far as I can tell, it's not pork if it's for Arkansas."[29]

Mentor-Communicator and Representative. The mentor-communicator role is linked both to legislating and to constituency errand running. Most members who stress this role view it in connection with issues that must be debated and voted on. Another aspect of the mentor-communicator role is the act of keeping in touch with constituents by mail, by personal appearances, and by print and electronic media. Barber B. Conable Jr. conducted what he called a "dialogue of representation" by means of 254 newsletters to his Rochester, New York, constituents over his twenty distinguished years in the House (1965–1985). "Conable never campaigned," a local professor explained, "he just conducted seminars every other year" (actually, a majority of his newsletters went out during nonelection years).[30]

Closely allied is the role of the issue emissary ("representative"), articulated by a quarter of the House members. Constituents expect their representatives to understand and express their views in Washington. This role is the essence of elective office, both in theory and in practice, and incumbents take it very seriously indeed.

Other Roles. Some members pose as outsiders who adopt a maverick posture, but others act as Capitol Hill insiders. Some stress party leadership duties, others their social obligations, still others institutional brokerage— dealing with the executive branch, interest groups, and state and local governments. And, yes, a few members of Congress focus merely on campaigning and gaining reelection. One former member placed this goal in perspective: "All members of Congress have a primary interest in being reelected. Some members have no other interest."[31]

How Do Legislators Spend Their Time?

Few things are more precious to senators and representatives than time; the lack of it is their most frequent complaint about their jobs.[32] Allocating time requires exceedingly tough personal and political choices.

According to a 1993 congressional survey, members' daily priorities are roughly as follows: (1) meet on legislative issues with constituents, either at home or in Washington; (2) attend committee hearings, markups, and other committee meetings; (3) meet with government officials and lobbyists on legislative issues; (4) study pending legislation or talk about legislation with other members or staff; (5) work with informal caucus groups of colleagues; (6) attend floor debate or watch the debate on television; (7) complete nonlegislative work (casework) for constituents in Washington; (8) manage personal office operations and staffs; (9) raise funds for the next campaign, for others' campaigns, or for the political party; (10) work with party leaders to build legislative coalitions; (11) oversee how agencies are carrying out laws or policies; and (12) make appearances on legislation outside the state or district (see Table 5-2).[33] Staff members usually prepare daily schedules for members of Congress to refer to as they whirl through a busy day on Capitol Hill.

Scheduling is complicated by the large number of formal work groups—mainly committees and subcommittees, but also joint, party, and ad hoc panels. Despite downsizing in recent Congresses, the average senator sits on three full committees and seven subcommittees; representatives average two committees and three subcommittees (see Chapter 7).

With so many assignments, lawmakers are hard-pressed to control their crowded schedules. Committee quorums are difficult to achieve, and members' attentions are often focused elsewhere. All too often working sessions are composed of the chairman, perhaps one or two colleagues, and staff aides. Recent House rules tightening quorum requirements have only made scheduling problems worse.

Repeated floor votes, which lawmakers fear to miss, are another time-consuming duty. In a typical Congress as many as 1,000 recorded votes will be taken in the House chamber and perhaps 500 in the Senate. "We're like automatons," one senator complained. "We spend our time walking in tunnels to go to the floor to vote."[34]

Lawmakers' daily schedules in Washington are "long, fragmented, and unpredictable," according to a study based on time logs kept by senators' appointment secretaries.[35] "In Congress you are a total juggler," recalls former twelve-term representative Patricia Schroeder, D-Colo., now a trade association executive. "You have always got seventeen things pulling on your sleeve."[36] Members' schedules are splintered into so many tiny bits and pieces that effective pursuit of lawmaking, oversight, and constituent service is hampered. According to a management study of several senators' offices, an event occurs every five minutes, on average, to which the senator or the chief aide must respond personally.[37] Often members have scant notice that their pres-

Table 5-2 Activities of Members of Congress: Actual and Ideal
(in percentages)

Activity	Members actually spending time				Members preferring to spend more time
	Great deal	Moderate amount	A little	Almost none	
Representation					
Meet with citizens in state/district	68%	30%	1%	0%	17%
Meet in Washington with constituents	45	50	5	0	17
Manage office	6	45	39	10	13
Raise funds for next campaign, for others, for party	6	33	45	16	7
Lawmaking					
Attend committee hearings, markups, other meetings	48	46	6	0	43
Meet in Washington on legislative issues	37	56	6	0	31
Study, read, discuss pending legislation	25	56	17	2	78
Work with informal caucuses	8	43	36	13	25
Attend floor debate, follow it on television	7	37	44	12	59
Work with party leaders to build coalitions	6	33	43	18	42
Oversee how agencies are carrying out policies/programs	5	22	43	29	53
Give speeches about legislation outside state/district	5	23	49	23	16

Note: A total of 161 members of Congress (136 representatives, 25 senators) responded to this survey, conducted in early 1993 under the auspices of the Joint Committee on the Organization of Congress. This series of questions elicited responses from 152 to 155 members. U.S. Congress, Joint Committee on the Organization of Congress, *Organization of Congress, Final Report,* H. Rept. 103-413, 103d Congress, 1st sess., Dec. 1993, 2: 231–232, 275–287.

ence is required at a meeting or a hearing. Carefully developed schedules can be disrupted by changes in meeting hours, by unexpected events, or by sessions that run longer than expected.

Political scientists may pretend that Congress runs in harmony with members' needs, but the members know otherwise. In a 1987 survey of 114 House and Senate members, "inefficiency" was the thing that most surprised them about Congress (45 percent gave this response).[38] "[Congress] is a good job for someone with no family, no life of their own, no desire to do anything but get up, go to work, and live and die by their own press releases," quipped former representative (and star of TV's *Love Boat*) Fred Grandy, a Republican from Iowa, who left Congress in 1994. "It is a great job for deviant human beings."[39]

Nearly half the respondents in the 1987 survey agreed that they had "no personal time after work"; a third said they had "no time for family."[40] When they came to power in 1995, Republican leaders promised a "family friendly schedule," but the frantic pace of the 104th was anything but that. Subsequent Congresses took a more leisurely pace; House members and their families even held some weekend retreats to get to know one another better.

The dilemma legislators face in allocating their time is far more than a matter of scheduling. It is a case of conflicting role expectations. Look again at Table 5-2, where lawmakers' activities are arrayed to illustrate the tensions inherent in the two Congresses, from the representative Congress (at the top of the list) to the legislative Congress (at the bottom). More members want to devote extra time and effort to legislative duties than would choose to do so for constituency and political chores. According to the 1993 survey, an average of 43 percent of the members would like to spend more time on the eight "legislative" tasks, whereas on average only 14 percent of them would give more time to the four "representation" items. Eight of ten members would study more thoroughly the legislation they vote on; six of ten would follow floor debate more closely.[41] The two Congresses pull members in different directions. As a retiring House committee chairman remarked:

> One problem is that you're damned if you do and damned if you don't. If you do your work here, you're accused of neglecting your district. And if you spend too much time in your district, you're accused of neglecting your work here.[42]

The Shape of the Washington Career

Once a short-term activity (see Chapter 2), congressional service became a career. Accompanying this careerism, or longevity, is a discernible pattern of Washington activity: the longer members remain in office, the more they sponsor bills, deliver floor speeches, and offer amendments. Despite the democratizing reforms of the 1960s and 1970s, senior lawmakers continue to lead in all these categories. "The *apprenticeship norm* may or may not be dead, but *apprenticeship* is stronger than it has been in decades," John R. Hibbing concludes from his painstaking study of four cohorts of members who entered the House between 1957 and 1971.[43]

Long tenure also pulls members toward greater legislative specialization: members settle into their committee slots, cultivate expertise in a distinct policy field, and spend their time managing legislation and conducting oversight in that field. Seniority tends to confer legislative achievement; veterans usually enjoy more success than do freshmen in getting their bills passed.

The correlation between members' service and effectiveness reminds us of the indispensable role careerists play in the legislative process. As Hibbing observed:

> Senior members are the heart and soul of the legislative side of congressional service. . . . Relatively junior members can be given a subcommittee chairmanship, but it is not nearly so easy to give them an active, focused legislative agenda and the political savvy to enact it. Some things take time and experience, and successful participation in the legislative process appears to be one of those things.[44]

The wisdom of this statement has been amply borne out in the 1990s. The newcomers elected in these years brought with them zeal, energy, and fresh approaches. At the same time, many of them lacked patience, bargaining skills, institutional memory, and respect for the lawmaking process. Not a few of them demanded overnight reversals of long-standing policies and practices and vowed to retire voluntarily after a few terms. But after, say, six or twelve years in office, who is to say how ready these members will be to leave?

Looking Homeward

Not all of a representative's or a senator's duties lie in Washington, D.C. As we have stressed, legislators not only fashion policy for the nation's welfare; they also act as emissaries from their home states or districts.

What Is Representation?

Although found in virtually all political structures, representation most typifies democratic regimes dedicated to sharing power among citizens. In small communities decisions can be reached by face-to-face discussion, but in populous societies this sort of personalized consultation is impossible. Thus, according to traditional democratic theory, citizens can exert control by choosing "fiduciary agents" to act on their behalf, deliberating on legislation just as their principals, the voters, would do if they could be on hand themselves.[45] Pitkin puts it this way:

> The representative must act in such a way that, although he is independent, and his constituents are capable of action and judgment, no conflict arises between them. He must act in their interest, and this means he must not normally come into conflict with their wishes.[46]

The arrangement does not always work out precisely as democratic theory specifies. Unless it works fairly well most of the time, however, the system is defective.

Incumbent legislators give high priority to representation. As we have seen, four of five House members interviewed in 1977 saw themselves as constituency servants. Many were mentor-communicators, others issue spokespersons. In an earlier survey of eighty-seven members, the role most often expressed was called the tribune: the discoverer, reflector, or advocate of popular needs and wants.[47]

Although legislators agree on the importance of representation, they interpret it differently. One point of departure is Edmund Burke's dictum that legislators should voice the "general reason of the whole," rather than speak merely for "local purposes" and "local prejudices."[48] This conception of the legislator as *Burkean trustee* has always had its admirers. Speaking to a group of newly elected House members, Rep. Henry J. Hyde, R-Ill., voiced the Burkean ideal:

> If you are here simply as a tote board registering the current state of opinion in your district, you are not going to serve either your constituents or the Congress well. . . . You must take, at times, a national view, even if you risk the displeasure of your neighbors and friends back home. . . . If you don't know the principle, or the policy, for which you are willing to lose your office, then you are going to do damage here.[49]

Representative Hyde demonstrated his steadfastness to this principle as chairman of the Judiciary Committee that voted in 1998 to impeach President Clinton. Defying the weight of expert opinion, national opinion polls, and even some within his own party, he carried his committee's articles of impeachment to the full House, which adopted two of them, and then to the Senate, which rejected them.

Nearly every member can point to "conscience votes" cast on deeply felt issues. A few, like the late representative Mike Synar, compile a "contrarian" record, challenging voters to admire their independence if not their policies. Synar was an unabashed liberal Democrat from a state that now elects conservative Republicans. "I want to be a U.S. congressman from Oklahoma, not an Oklahoman congressman," Synar declared when he arrived in the capital.[50] If turned out of office by hostile sentiment (as Synar was in 1994), the Burkean can at least hope for history's vindication.

Electoral realities imperil the Burkean ideal. Burke himself was ousted from office for his candor. Modern electorates, motivated by self-interest and schooled in democratic norms, prefer *instructed delegates*—lawmakers who follow instructions rather than exercise independent judgments. In a recent survey 63 percent of those polled said they wanted members of Congress to "stick closely to American public opinion . . . including results of polls" when making legislative decisions. Only 34 percent thought members should "do what they think is best."[51]

Members have gotten the message. "I was elected to be an advocate for the people, for the interests, for the communities of our state. The businesses, et

cetera. The totality of our state. And that's what I've done here," explained former senator Alfonse M. D'Amato, R-N.Y.[52] Attention to the details of constituent advocacy won D'Amato the label "the pothole senator"—described by one of his friends as "taking care of things." Contrasting D'Amato with New York's scholarly and policy-immersed senior senator, Democrat Daniel Patrick Moynihan, political scientist Thomas E. Mann captured the conflict between the two roles: "Moynihan asks himself, 'What do we as a people need?' While D'Amato asks himself, 'What do my people want?' "[53]

In practice, legislators assume different representational styles according to the occasion. They ponder factors such as the nation's welfare, their personal convictions, and constituency opinions. "The weight assigned to each factor," writes Thomas Cavanagh, "varies according to the nature of the issue at hand, the availability of the information necessary for a decision, and the intensity of preference of the people concerned about the issue."[54]

Respondents in the 1977 House survey cited two categories of issues they reserved for personal conscience or discretion: issues of overwhelming national importance, such as foreign policy and national defense, and issues that entailed deep-seated convictions, such as abortion, gun control, or constitutional questions. In contrast, members said they deferred to districts on economic issues, such as public works, social needs, military projects, and farm programs. They give unqualified support to local needs because, as they see it, no other member is likely to do so.

Members of Congress are called upon to explain their choices to constituents—no matter how many or how few people truly care about the matter.[55] The anticipated need to explain oneself shapes a member's choices and in fact is part of the dilemma of choice. A cynical saying among lawmakers asserts that "a vote on anything [is] a wrong vote if you cannot explain it in a 30-second TV ad."[56] Votes to increase congressional pay and perquisites, for example, often fail simply because members fear having to explain their support to skeptical constituents.

What Are Constituencies?

No senator or representative is elected by, interacts with, or responds to all the people in a given state or district. The constituencies fixed in lawmakers' minds as they campaign or vote may be quite different from the boundaries found on maps. Fenno describes a "nest" of constituencies, ranging from the widest (geographic constituency) to the narrowest (personal constituency), which is made up of supporters, loyalists, and intimates.[57]

Geographic and Demographic Constituencies. The average House district in the 1990s exceeds 600,000 people, the average state nearly 5.5 million. These constituencies differ sharply from one another. More than half the people in Manhattan's Upper East Side (New York's Fourteenth Congressional District) have college degrees, compared with only 5 percent in south central Los Angeles (California's Thirty-third District). Average per capita income in these same two districts is, respectively, $41,000 and less than $7,000. You can buy

an average home for $23,200 in Rep. Carolyn Cheeks Kilpatrick's central Detroit district (Michigan's Fifteenth); in Rep. Henry A. Waxman's Beverly Hills district (California's Twenty-ninth), you would pay more than $500,000.[58] Such disparities among districts animate their representatives' outlooks.

There is also the political equivalent of microclimates. Democrat Nita Lowey's Eighteenth District of New York snakes southward from the upscale suburbs of Westchester County through a working-class sliver of the Bronx, jumps across Long Island Sound to an immigrant corridor in Flushing, and continues toward the tidy homes of southern Queens. Republican Mary Bono's sprawling southern California Forty-fourth District embraces smog-ridden suburbs east of Riverside, irrigated farmland of the Coachella Valley, and wealthy desert oases of Palm Springs and Palm Desert, where retired Hollywood stars reside. Even these geographical distinctions grossly simplify the complex and subtle mixtures of ethnic, economic, and social categories that make up these communities.

As a rule, demographics are linked to partisan differences in voting: some areas are traditionally "Democratic" and others traditionally "Republican." In general, Democratic-leaning areas are associated with the following demographic characteristics: dense population, blue-collar workers, ethnic groupings, African American or Latino concentrations, non-college educated residents, low-income families, and rental housing. Republican areas tend to display the opposite characteristics. Republicans held nearly three-quarters of the fifty "richest" House districts (measured by average per capita income) in the 105th Congress; Democrats claimed 80 percent of the fifty "poorest" districts.[59]

In a sense, partisan differences are constituency differences translated into issues. Members whose voting records deviate from their party's norm may simply represent areas with attributes associated with the opposition party. In the 1990s, for example, the "deviant" Republicans in the Senate included northeasterners James M. Jeffords of Vermont and John H. Chafee of Rhode Island. By the same token, the "maverick" Senate Democrats—for example, Louisiana's John B. Breaux and South Carolina's Ernest F. Hollings—were southerners whose states have shifted toward the Republicans.[60] Because such politicians are swimming against local or state currents, so to speak, their seats are vulnerable to challenge from the opposing party, when they retire if not before then.

Demographically, constituencies may be *homogeneous* or *heterogeneous*.[61] A few constituencies remain uniform and one-dimensional—mostly tobacco farmers or urban ghetto dwellers or small-town citizens. Because of increasing size, economic complexity, and educational levels, however, all constituencies, House as well as Senate, have become more heterogeneous than they used to be. The more heterogeneous a constituency, the more challenging is the representative's task.

Another attribute of constituencies is electoral balance, especially as manifested in the incumbent's reelection chances. Heterogeneous districts tend to be more competitive than uniform ones. Needless to say, incumbents prefer "safe" districts—those with a high proportion of groups sympathetic to their

partisan or ideological stance. Not only do safe districts favor reelection; they also imply that voters will be easier to please.[62]

Truly competitive districts are not the norm, especially in the House of Representatives. The number of competitive districts was generally low from the 1960s through the 1990 election, as evidenced by the high proportion of elections captured by wide margins (60 percent or more of the two-party vote).[63] The Senate picture is more clouded, but in the 1980s about half the contests were won by comfortable margins. Mid-1990s elections were unusually competitive, mainly because temporary conditions (retirements and scandals) put more seats into play. But, as Table 5-3 shows, competition plummeted in 1998: nearly three-quarters of all House contests, and two-thirds of the Senate ones, were won in a walk. Even so, Senate seats were more likely to be closely contested than House races.

Whatever the numbers show, few incumbents regard themselves as truly "safe." The threat of losing is very real. Most lawmakers have a close call at some time in their congressional careers, and a third of them eventually suffer defeat.[64] Incumbents worry not only about winning or losing but also about their margins of safety. Downturns in normal electoral support narrow the member's "breathing space" in the job and may invite challengers for future contests.[65]

Paradoxically, as members become more successful at winning reelection, they seem less willing to make decisions that could stir controversy. The increased heterogeneity of constituencies is partly to blame as more and more issues arouse conflicting pressures. Another factor is members' heavy reliance on campaign funds and support from interest groups. If legislators resist the groups' priorities, they may face adverse publicity, unwanted controversy, and antagonistic voting blocs in the next election.

Political and Personal Constituencies. As candidates or incumbents analyze their electoral units, three narrower "constituencies" can be discerned: *supporters* (the reelection constituency); *loyalists* (the primary constituency); and *intimates* (the personal constituency).[66] Supporters are expected to vote for them on election day, but, naturally, some do not. Candidates and their advisers repeatedly monitor these voters, reassessing precinct-level political demography—registration figures, survey data, and recent electoral trends. The more elections incumbents have survived, the more precisely they can identify supporters. Areas and groups with the biggest payoff are usually targeted.

Loyalists are the politician's staunchest supporters. They may be from preelectoral activities—civil rights or environmental causes, for example. They may be concentrated in religious or ethnic groups, or political or civic clubs. They may be friends and neighbors. They are willing volunteers who can be counted on to lend a hand in reelection campaigns.

Candidates dare not ignore these loyalists. A favorite story of the late House Speaker Thomas P. "Tip" O'Neill Jr. came from his first, losing, campaign for city council. A neighbor supposedly told him, "Tom, I'm going to vote for you even though you didn't ask me." "Mrs. O'Brien," replied a surprised O'Neill, "I've lived across the street from you for 18 years. I shovel your

Table 5-3   House and Senate Margins of Victory, 1974–1998

| Election year | Percentage of vote | | | | (N) |
	Under 55	55–59.9	60 plus	Unopposed	
			House		
1974	24%	16%	46%	14%	(435)
1976	17	14	56	12	(435)
1978	17	14	53	16	(435)
1980	18	14	60	8	(435)
1982	16	16	63	6	(435)
1984	12	13	61	14	(435)
1986	9	10	64	17	(435)
1988	6	9	67	18	(435)
1990	11	16	58	15	(435)
1992	20	18	58	3	(435)
1994	22	17	52	9	(435)
1996	22	18	57	3	(435)
1998	10	17	63	10	(435)
			Senate		
1974	41	18	35	6	(34)
1976	30	33	30	6	(33)
1978	24	33	36	6	(33)
1980	58	18	21	3	(34)
1982	30	27	43		(33)
1984	18	21	58	3	(33)
1986	38	15	47	—	(34)
1988	33	15	52	—	(33)
1990	26	11	49	14	(34)
1992	34	34	32	—	(35)
1994	32	34	34	—	(35)
1996	59	18	24	—	(34)
1998	29	9	62	—	(34)

Source: Congressional Quarterly Weekly Report and authors' calculations.

Note: Percentages may not add to 100 because of rounding.

walk in the winter. I cut your grass in the summer. I didn't think I had to ask you for your vote." To this the lady replied, "Tom, I want you to know something: people like to be asked."[67]

Even entrenched officeholders worry about keeping their core supporters energized. Rep. Gene Green, D-Texas, who had never won with less than 65 percent of the vote, took the advice of his wife (who was his campaign manager) and threw a 1998 election night party, even though he had no opponent. "You have to keep your base volunteer group knowing that you appreciate

them," he explained.[68] In Peoria, Illinois, Republican Ray LaHood had assembled a team that helped him win two solid victories. When he too found himself unopposed in 1998, he forged ahead with an aggressive campaign—not only to remind voters of his service but to help GOP gubernatorial and senatorial candidates. "Back in my district," LaHood said, "the volunteers I have built up over the last two campaigns will be working for others."

Loyalists are also a politician's defenders in times of adversity. "There's a big difference between the people who are for you and the people who are excitedly for you," an Iowa politician told Fenno, "between those who will vote if they feel like it and those for whom the only election is [your] election. You need as many of that group as you can get." An inadequate base of core support, the informant explained, spelled the downfall of two one-term Democratic senators elected from Iowa in the 1970s. One had a base that was a mile wide and an inch deep; the other's support was an inch wide and a mile deep.[69]

Intimates are close friends who supply political advice and emotional support. Nearly every candidate or incumbent knows a few of them. They may be members of the candidate's family, trusted staff members, political mentors, or individuals who shared decisive experiences early in the candidate's career. Fenno relates the following account of an informal gathering of intimates one Sunday afternoon in the home of a representative's chief district aide. Also present were the representative, a state assemblyman from the member's home county, and the district attorney of the same county.

> Between plays and at half-time, over beer and cheese, the four friends discussed every aspect of the congressman's campaign, listened to and commented on his taped radio spots, analyzed several newspaper reports, discussed local and national personalities, relived old political campaigns and hijinks, and discussed their respective political ambitions. Ostensibly they were watching the football game. Actually, the congressman was exchanging political advice, information, and perspectives with three of his oldest and closest political associates.[70]

The setting and the players differ from state to state and from district to district. Tip O'Neill's inner circle was the "boys" of Barry's Corner, a local clubhouse in Cambridge, Massachusetts, whose families O'Neill had known intimately for more than fifty years of political life. Such intimates play an indispensable role: they provide unvarnished advice on political matters and serve as sounding boards for ideas and strategies.

The danger is that intimates may give faulty advice or inaccurately assess the larger constituencies. Long-term incumbents run a special risk if their intimates lose touch with constituency shifts. Musing on Georgia Democrat Wyche Fowler's reelection defeat after one term in the Senate, an observer said,

> Fowler's team was (essentially) the same one as in 1986. In that year, this was a quality team matched with a quality candidate. But in 1992, they were not a quality team. And they did not produce a quality effort.[71]

Politicians confront the constant dilemma of deciding which advisers to trust; more than most of us, they pay a public price for those who let them down.

Home Styles

Legislators evolve distinctive ways of presenting or projecting themselves and their records to their constituents—what Fenno calls their home styles. These styles are manifested in the members' personal appearances, mailings, newsletters, press releases, telephone conversations, radio or television spots, and home pages on the Internet. We know little about how home styles arise, but they are linked to members' personalities, backgrounds, constituency features, and resources. The concept of home style shifts the focus of constituency linkage from *representation* to *presentation*. As Fenno states, "It is the style, not the issue content, that counts most in the reelection constituency."[72]

Presentation of Self. The core ingredient of a successful home style is trust—constituents' faith that legislators are what they claim to be and will do what they promise.[73] Winning voters' trust does not happen over night; it takes time. Three major ingredients of trust are *qualification,* the belief that legislators are capable of handling the job, a critical threshold that nonincumbents especially must cross; *identification,* the impression that legislators resemble their constituents, that they are part of the state or region, and *empathy,* the sense that legislators understand constituents' problems and care about them.

Given variations among legislators and constituencies, there are countless available home styles that effectively build the trust relationship. The legendary Speaker "Mr. Sam" Rayburn represented his East Texas district for nearly fifty years (1913–1961) as a plain dirt farmer. Once back in his hometown of Bonham, his drawl thickened; his tailored suits were exchanged for khakis, an old shirt, and slouch hat; and he traveled in a well-dented pickup truck, not in the Speaker's limousine he used in the capital. A biographer relates:

> If Rayburn ever chewed tobacco in Washington, a long-time aide could not recall it, but in Bonham he always seemed to have a plug in his cheek. He made certain always to spit in the fireplace at his home when constituents were visiting, so that if nothing else, they would take away the idea that Mr. Sam was just a plain fellow.[74]

Today's legislators are no less inventive in fashioning home styles. Congressman A employs a direct style rooted in face-to-face contacts with people in his primary constituency. He rarely mentions issues because most people in his district agree on them. Congressman B, a popular local athlete, uses the national defense issue to symbolize his oneness with a district supportive of military preparedness. Congresswoman C, articulate and personable, comes across as "everybody's sister." Congressman D displays himself as an issue-oriented and verbal activist, an outsider ill at ease with conventional politicians. Congressman E projects an image of "surfer-chic" in his coastal California district. And so on. The repertoire of home styles is limitless.

Voters are likely to remember style long after they forget issue pronouncements or voting records. Even so, legislators know full well that they must explain their decisions to others.[75]

Explaining Washington Activity. Explaining is an integral part of decision making. In home district forums, constituents expect members to be able to describe, interpret, and justify their actions. If they do not agree with the member's conclusions, they may at least respect the decision-making style:

> They don't know much about my votes. Most of what they know is what I tell them. They know more of what kind of a guy I am. It comes through in my letters: "You care about the little guy."[76]

Although few incumbents fear that a single vote can defeat them, all realize that voters' disenchantment with their total record can be fatal. For this reason, members stockpile reasons for virtually every position they take—often more than are really needed. Facing especially thorny choices—for example, on abortion policy or Medicare reform—they may find an independent stance to be the best defense. Inconsistency is not only mentally costly, but it can be politically costly as well. Thus politicians give pretty much the same account of themselves, no matter what group they are talking to (contrary to the popular belief that politicians talk out of both sides of their mouths).

Legislators' accounts of Congress to constituents rarely convey any of the chummy comfort they may enjoy as part of the institution. Often members defend their own voting record by belittling Congress—portraying themselves as knights-errant battling sinister forces and feckless colleagues.

Constituency Careers. Constituency ties evolve over the course of a senator's or representative's career. Constituency careers have at least two recognizable stages: *expansionism* and *protectionism.* In the first stage the member constructs a reelection constituency by solidifying the help of hard-core supporters and reaching out to attract added blocs of support. This aggressive expansionism—plus enterprising use of the perquisites of incumbency, such as the election-year avalanche of mail to constituents—accounts for the "sophomore surge," in which newcomers typically boost their margin in their first reelection bid.[77] In the second stage the member ceases to expand the base of support, content with protecting already won support. Once established, a successful style is rarely altered.

Certain developments, however, can lead to a change in a member's constituency style. One is a *contextual* change in the constituency: a population shift or redistricting that forces a member to cope with unfamiliar voters or territory. A second cause is a *strategic* reaction, as a fresh challenger or a novel issue threatens established voting patterns. Because coalitions may shift over time, members and their advisers scrutinize the results of the past election (and, whenever available, survey findings).

Finally, home styles may change with new *personal goals and ambitions.* A member may seek higher office or may lose touch with voters and reject the

reelection goal entirely. Growing responsibilities in Washington can divert attention from home state business, from family responsibilities, and, frankly, from amassing wealth. For Sen. William S. Cohen, R-Maine, the epiphany came with the death of his father and a heightened sense that time was passing, that "tomorrow is not promised to any of us":

> I really asked myself, is this what I want to do for the next six years? . . . Waiting to answer a senseless quorum call for no other reason than to have a quorum call? The endless back and forth and waste of time? The sense that rather than painting the broad landscape we're engaged in a pointillist approach—each little aspect of the dots?[78]

Cohen retired after eighteen years in the Senate. (Far from leaving public life, he became President Clinton's third secretary of defense.) His sentiments are echoed by many veteran legislators. Faced with new aspirations or shifting constituency demands, not a few members decide to retire. Others struggle ineffectively and are defeated. Still others rejuvenate their constituency base and survive.

Office of the Member, Inc.

Home style is more than a philosophy for weighing constituents' claims. It affects the way a member answers day-to-day questions: How much attention should I devote to state or district needs? How much time should I spend in the state or district? How should I maintain contact with my constituents? How should I deploy my staff aides to deal with constituents' concerns? One of the most vexing problems is how to balance demands for being in Washington with the need to be back home with constituents.

Road Tripping

During the nineteenth century legislators spent much of their time at home, traveling to Washington only when Congress was in session. After World War II, however, congressional sessions lengthened until they spanned virtually the entire year. Legislators began to set up permanent residence in the nation's capital, a practice that in earlier times would have struck citizens as arrogant. By the 1970s both houses had adopted parallel schedules of sessions punctuated with brief "district work periods" (House) or "nonlegislative periods" (Senate).

At the same time, the two houses authorized members to make more paid trips to states or districts. In the early 1960s senators and representatives were allowed three government-paid trips home each year. Today they are allowed as many trips home as they want, subject to the limits of their official expense allowances.

Currently fashionable home styles entail frequent commutes. "Not a single House freshman would admit to planning to move the family to D.C.," Susan B. Glasser of *Roll Call* reported following the 1994 elections.[79] Most made a point of traveling back to their home bases every week, renting rooms or even sleeping in their offices during weekdays.

Although travel has increased for all members, the more time consuming the trip home, the less often it is made. (Members from Alaska and Hawaii make about a dozen round trips a year—each requiring an elapsed twenty-four hours and spanning four or five time zones.)[80] When their families remain at home, members are more inclined to travel. They tend to avoid their districts during periods of congressional unpopularity, but they spend more time there during times of adverse economic conditions. As election day approaches, representatives stay close to their districts.[81]

Seniority is also a factor: senior members tend to make fewer trips to their districts than do junior members—perhaps reflecting junior members' greater attentiveness to their districts. Finally, members' decisions to retire voluntarily are usually accompanied by large drops in trips home. "There was no reason to go back," one member told Hibbing. "My engagement calendar used to be booked up for seven or eight months in advance; after I announced, no one seemed anxious to have me. I stayed in town and found out that Washington was not as bad as I had thought all those years."[82]

Constituency Casework

"All God's chillun got problems," exclaimed Billy Matthews, then a Democratic representative from Florida, as he brooded over mail from his constituents.[83] In the early days lawmakers lacked staff aides and wrote personally to executive agencies for help in such matters as pension or land claims and appointments to military academies. The Legislative Reorganization Act of 1946 provided de facto authority for hiring caseworkers, first in Senate offices and later in the House.

What are these "cases" all about? As respondents in a nationwide survey reported, the most frequent reason for contacting a member's office (16 percent of all cases) is to express views or obtain information on legislative issues. Requests for help in finding government jobs form the next largest category, followed by cases dealing with government services such as Social Security, veterans' benefits, or unemployment compensation. Military cases (exemptions from service, discharges, transfers) are numerous, as are tax, legal, and immigration problems. Constituents often ask for government publications: copies of legislative bills and reports, executive branch regulations, agricultural yearbooks, infant care booklets, and tourist information about the nation's capital. And there are requests for flags that have flown over the U.S. Capitol.

Most cases come to legislators' offices by letter, although phone calls, e-mails, faxes, or walk-ins at district or mobile offices are not uncommon. Occasionally, members themselves pick up cases from talking to constituents; many hold office hours in their districts for this purpose. When a constituent's request is received, it is usually acknowledged immediately by a letter that either fills the request or promises that an answer will be forthcoming.

If the request requires contacting a federal agency, caseworkers communicate by e-mail, phone, letter, or buckslip (a preprinted referral form).[84] Usually, the contact in the executive agency is a liaison officer, although some case-

workers prefer to deal directly with line officers or regional officials. Once the problem has been conveyed, it is a matter of time before a decision is reached and a reply forwarded to the congressional office. The reply is then sent along to the constituent, perhaps with a cover letter signed by the member. If the agency's reply is deemed faulty, the caseworker may challenge it and ask for reconsideration, and in some cases the member may be brought in to lend weight to the appeal.

Although not all members are eager to handle casework personally, they all concede that prompt and effective casework pays off at election time. This principle applies to senators no less than to representatives. "Many freshmen view their role differently than twenty-five years ago, when a senator was only a legislator," says Sen. Richard C. Shelby. "Now a senator is also a grantsman, an ombudsman, and a caseworker, and cannot ignore those other roles. When we are asked by our constituents to help, we can't say we don't have time because we are focusing on national and international issues."[85]

Keeping up with incoming communications is a priority for all congressional offices. During fiscal 1998, representatives received some 40 million pieces of mail, senators 35 million. Low-cost phone calls, faxes, and e-mail messages, often prompted by concerted group efforts, have boosted constituents' communications to unprecedented (and uncounted) levels. Now virtually all representatives and senators have Internet e-mail addresses; most of these members have home pages, some of them interactive. "With the new software programs today, 16,000 kids at a college can send me a letter with a push of a button," noted Rep. Sam Gejdenson, D-Conn., who reads his electronic mail every day. "I don't have the ability to go through all of that. As far as I'm concerned, the first people who deserve an answer are the people from my district."[86]

Casework loads vary from state to state and from district to district. Some House offices studied years ago by John R. Johannes handled no more than 5 or 10 cases a week, others nearly 500.[87] In both chambers senior legislators apparently receive proportionately more casework requests than do junior members.[88] Perhaps senior legislators are considered more powerful and better equipped to resolve constituents' problems; legislators themselves certainly cultivate this image in seeking reelection. Demographic variations among electorates can affect casework volume: some citizens simply are more likely than others to have contact with government agencies.

From all accounts, casework pays off in citizens' support for individual legislators. In the 1990 National Election Study survey, 17 percent of all adults reported that they or members of their families had requested help from their own representatives. Eighty-five percent of them said they were satisfied with the response they received; seven in ten felt the representative would be helpful if asked in the future.[89] "Casework is all profit," contends Morris P. Fiorina. If so, the profit statements may be written in disappearing ink: only 16 percent of all citizens in the 1990 survey could remember anything specific the representative had done for the people of the district while in office.[90] A sen-

sible middle-ground view holds that "service responsiveness has an electoral payoff for incumbents regardless of issue positions or other factors. Casework does not operate to supplant issue positions, however."[91]

Some criticize constituency casework as unfair or biased in practice. Citizens may not enjoy equal access to senators' or representatives' offices. Political supporters or cronies may get favored treatment at others' expense. Finally, administrative agencies may be pressured into giving special treatment to congressional requests, distorting the administration of laws. Fiascoes like the "Keating Five" scandal of the late 1980s have forced a rethinking of the limits of constituency service. Five senators had pressured regulators to go easy on Charles Keating, a savings and loan executive later convicted of reckless practices. Although the senators claimed to be concerned about a local firm and its jobs (Keating's enterprise straddled several states), their bullying of regulatory officers—which compounded eventual losses to the public—exceeded the bounds of legitimate constituency service.

Personal Staff

Legislators head sizable office enterprises that reflect their "two Congresses" responsibilities within the institution and toward their constituents (see box "Congressional Allowances"). In 1999 each House member was entitled to an annual staff allowance of $632,355. With this money members may hire no more than eighteen full-time and four part-time employees. The average House member's full-time staff numbers about fourteen. Representatives also are entitled to an annual office allowance, which in 1999 averaged about $200,000. This money is used for travel, telecommunications, district office rental, office equipment, stationery, and computer services. In addition, each member has a mail allowance, which averages $108,000 following a formula based on three annual mailings per district household.[92]

Senators' personal staffs range in size from thirteen to seventy-one; the average is about thirty-four full-time employees. Unlike the House, the Senate places no limits on the number of staff a senator may employ from their two personnel accounts: the administrative and clerical account (which varies according to a state's population) and the account for hiring legislative assistants. In 1999 the administrative and clerical allowance ranged from $1.2 million for senators representing fewer than 5 million people, the lowest of twenty-five population categories, to $2.2 million for each of California's senators. Regardless of population, each senator has an allowance of nearly $400,000 to hire legislative assistants. A senator's office expense account depends upon factors such as the state's population and its distance from Washington, D.C.; the amount varies from $127,000 to $470,000. Separate categories for mailing, stationery, local offices, and furniture can be shifted within the overall financial allotments.

Although levels of paid staffers have remained unchanged for two decades, congressional offices depend heavily on unpaid help, mainly college-age interns. On average, each House and Senate office uses about nine interns every year (see Appendix B for information on internships).

Congressional Allowances, 1999

	House	Senate
Compensation		
Salary[a]	$136,700	$136,700
Health, life insurance	Provided	Provided
Tax deduction for D.C. living expenses	$3,000 maximum	$3,000 maximum
Outside earned income	15% of salary (maximum)	15% of salary (maximum)
Honoraria	Prohibited	Prohibited
Official personnel and office allowance[b]	$952,777 (average)	$1.7–$3.0 million[b]
Administrative/clerical staff	Maximum 18: total $632,355	$1.2–$2.2 million[c]
Legislative staff	(included in above)	$396,477
Office expenses[d]	$194,888 (average)	$127,384–$470,272[c]
Office space	Provided	Provided
Travel (by formula)	Minimum $6,200; Maximum approx. $67,200	—[d]
Official mail allowance (average)	3 × 25¢ × number of district households	Included in above
Other office allowances		
Stationery	40,000 envelopes	1.8–30.4 million sheets; 180,000–1.9 million letterheads
Furnishings/equipment	Provided[d]	Provided[d]
District/state offices		
Rental	2,500 sq. ft.	4,800–8,000 sq.ft.[b]
Furnishings/equipment	Provided[d]	Provided[d]
Mobile office	—	one

Source: Paul E. Dwyer, *Salaries and Allowances: The Congress,* Congressional Research Service Report, No. RL30064, Feb. 16, 1999.

[a] Effective Jan. 1, 1998; leaders' salaries are higher.

[b] Funds for the operations of House members' offices are provided primarily from the *Members' Representational Allowances.* Funds for the operations of senators' offices are provided primarily from the *Official Personnel and Office Expense Allowances.* Generally, members may shift funds among categories. For senators, the amounts represent totals of three categories below: administrative clerical staff; legislative staff; and office expenses.

[c] A sliding scale linked to the state's population.

[d] Basic allowances are available in addition to those for office space and travel. House office expenses are no longer supplied; figure is authors' estimate.

Staff Organization. No two congressional offices are exactly alike. Each is shaped by the personality, interests, constituency, and politics of the individual legislator. State and district needs also influence staff composition. A senator from a farm state likely will employ at least one specialist in agricultural problems; an urban representative might hire a consumer affairs or housing expert.

Traditions are important. If a legislator's predecessor had an enviable reputation for a certain kind of service, the new incumbent will dare not let it lapse.

The member's institutional position also affects staff organization. Committee and subcommittee chairmen have committee staff at their disposal. Members without such aides rely heavily on personal staff for committee work.

Staff Functions. Most personal aides in the House and Senate are young, well educated, and transient. The average Senate aide in 1997 had been on the job just 3.6 years, although senior aides often have considerable longevity. Pay (Senate staffers average $39,500, House aides $39,100) is slightly above that for the average full-time worker in the United States, but well below that for comparably educated workers.[93]

The mix of personal staff functions is decided by each member. Most hire administrative assistants (AAs), legislative assistants (LAs), caseworkers, and press aides as well as a few people from the home state or district. The administrative assistant supervises the office and imparts political and legislative advice. Often he or she functions as the legislator's alter ego, negotiating with colleagues, constituents, and lobbyists. Legislative assistants work with members in committees, draft bills, write speeches, suggest policy initiatives, analyze legislation, and prepare position papers. They also monitor committee sessions that the member is unable to attend.

To emphasize the "personal touch," many members have moved casework staff to their home districts or states. Virtually all House and Senate members have home district offices in post offices or federal buildings; some members have as many as five or six. With the decline of party workers to assist local citizens, members' district staffs fill this need and, simultaneously, enhance members' reelection prospects. Senators have an average of four home state offices and deploy a third of their staff there. Representatives have an average of 2.3 offices and deploy no less than 43 percent of their aides in their districts.[94]

Many other reasons are cited for decentralizing constituent functions. Congressional office buildings on Capitol Hill are crowded. Field offices have lower staff salaries and lower overhead. They also are more convenient for constituents, local and state officials, and regional federal officers. Computers and fax machines make it easy for Washington offices and district offices to communicate. This decentralizing trend, which is likely to persist, implies a heightened division between legislative functions based on Capitol Hill and constituency functions based in field offices. In other words, "Office of the Member, Inc." is increasingly split into headquarters and branch divisions— with the Capitol Hill office dealing with legislative duties and the state or district office dealing with constituents.

Members and the Media

Office allowances in both chambers amply support lawmakers' unceasing struggle for media attention. A member's office bears some resemblance to the mail distribution division of a medium-size business. Nearly every day, stacks of printed matter and electronic messages are released for wide distribution. In addition to turning out press releases, newsletters, and individual and mass

mailings, members communicate through telephone calls, interviews, radio and TV programs, and videotapes. Most of the time, these publicity barrages are aimed not at the national media but at individual media outlets back in the home state or district.

"Think Direct Mail"

The traditional cornerstone of congressional publicity is the franking privilege—the right of members to send out mail at no cost to them with their signature (the frank) instead of a stamp. The practice, which in this country dates from the First Continental Congress in 1775, is intended to facilitate official communication between elected officials and the people they represent (a rationale accepted by federal courts in upholding the practice). In recent times members found that aggressive use of the frank could aid reelection. Former Republican representative Bill Frenzel of Minnesota noted that both parties teach newcomers three rules for getting reelected: "Use the frank. Use the frank. Use the frank."[95]

Reliable numbers on the extent of franking are hard to come by, but the Postal Service estimated that members sent out 363 million pieces of franked mail in fiscal 1994—nearly two items for every person in the country over the age of eighteen. And franking is not free: the price tag that year was $53 million.[96] (Congress reimburses the U.S. Postal Service for the mailings on a bulk basis.)

Critics point out that franked mail is largely unsolicited and politically motivated. First, outgoing mail volume is much higher in election years than in nonelection years (see Figure 5-2). Second, the bulk is in mass mailings rather than individual letters. When Charles McC. Mathias Jr. was Senate Rules and Administration chairman, he declared that mass mailings constituted 96 percent of the mail sent by senators; three-quarters of these mailings were constituent newsletters. Only 4 percent were individual letters responding to inquiries or requests.[97]

The majority of mass mailings are general-purpose newsletters blanketing home states or districts. These are upbeat accounts of the legislator's activities, replete with photos of the legislator greeting constituents or conferring with top decision makers. The member's committee posts are highlighted, as are efforts to boost the home area. Recipients are urged to share their views or contact local offices for help. Perhaps once a year the newsletter may feature an opinion poll asking for citizens' views on selected issues. Whatever the results, the underlying message is that the legislator really cares what folks back home think.

The current franking law confers wide mailing privileges but forbids use of the frank for mail "unrelated to the official business, activities, and duties of members." It also bars the frank for "mail matter which specifically solicits political support for the sender or any other person or any political party, or a vote or financial assistance for any candidate for any political office." In addition, chamber rules forbid mass mailings (500 or more pieces) sixty days (Senate) or ninety days (House) before a primary, runoff, or general election. In the

Figure 5-2   Volume of Outgoing Mail in House and Senate, Fiscal Years 1972–1996

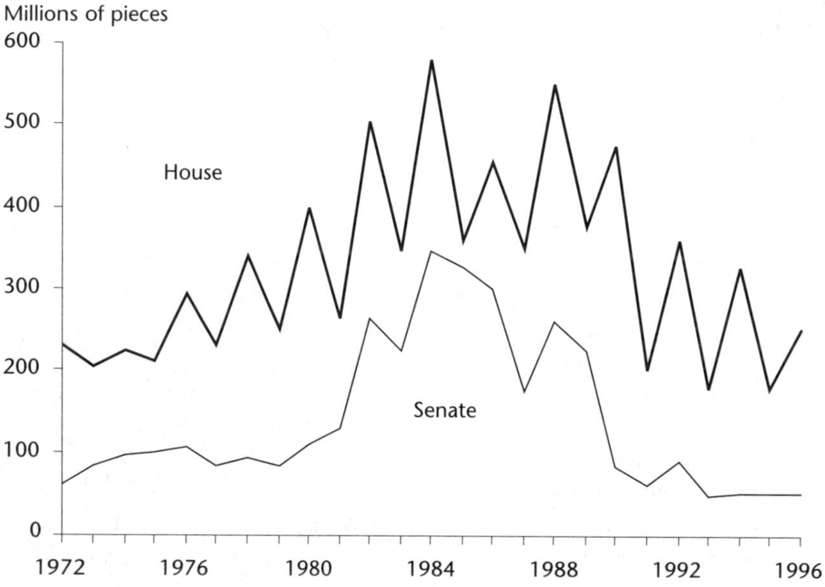

Millions of pieces

Source: John S. Pontius, Congressional Research Service.

two months just before the beginning of each cutoff period, streams of Postal Service trucks are seen pulling away from loading docks of the congressional office buildings. During the period, moreover, many members skirt the requirement by sending out similar letters in batches of 499 or fewer.

Criticisms of such abuses led both houses to impose new franking restrictions in the 1990s. Most important, mailing costs have been integrated into members' office allowances, which forces tradeoffs between mail and other expenditures, such as travel or staff. Caps have been placed on newsletters and on total outgoing mail—one piece for each address in the state for senators, three pieces for each address in the district for representatives. Rules governing newsletters curb their "advertising" features—for example, personal references or pictures of the member.

The recent reforms have reversed the upward spiral of congressional mail costs, saving an estimated $300 million or more in the 1990s.[98] Members have turned toward discounted bulk mailings and away from mass newsletters and first-class letters. Although it can still be abused, the franking privilege is essential to sustain communications between lawmakers and their constituents. A former chairman of a House oversight commission posed the issue: "How do you write rules and regulations that distinguish between a thoughtful discussion of some important public issue and a self-promoting thing with the photograph of a member on every other page?"[99]

Feeding the Local Press

News outlets in this country are highly decentralized and dispersed. About 10,000 newspapers are published in the United States; of these the 1,500 or so dailies are the most important in prestige and circulation. More than 12,000 periodicals are published. There are also more than 11,700 radio stations and 1,500 TV stations throughout the country.[100] These media outlets are locally based because of the vitality of local issues and local advertising.

Taken as a whole, local media outlets have inadequate resources for covering what their congressional delegations are doing in the nation's capital. Few of them have their own Washington reporters; most rely on syndicated or chain services that rarely follow individual members consistently. "If they report national news it is usually because it involves local personalities, affects local outcomes, or relates directly to local concerns," stated a Senate report.[101]

Relations with the press receive careful attention from members. Most legislators have at least one staffer who serves as a press aide; some have two or three. Their job is to generate coverage highlighting the member's work. Executive agencies often help by letting incumbents announce federal grants or contracts awarded in the state or district. Even if the member had nothing to do with procuring the funds, the press statement proclaims, "Senator So-and-So announced today that a federal contract has been awarded to XYZ Company in Jonesville." Many offices also prepare weekly or biweekly columns that small-town newspapers can reprint under the lawmaker's byline.

The House, the Senate, and the four Capitol Hill parties have fully equipped studios and satellite links where audio or video programs or excerpted statements (called "actualities") can be produced for a fraction of the commercial cost.[102] Some incumbents produce regular programs that are picked up by local radio or television outlets. More often, these outlets insert brief audio or TV clips on current issues into regular news broadcasts—to give the impression that their reporters have actually gone out and got the story. Members also create their own "news" reports and beam them directly to hometown stations, often without ever talking to a reporter. With direct satellite feeds to local stations, members regularly go "live at five" before local audiences.

Rep. Kenny Hulshof, R-Mo., typifies today's media-savvy lawmakers. Each week he holds a telephone conference with radio stations in his central Missouri district. Each month he hosts a half-hour television show in Columbia, his hometown and his district's largest city. Periodically he talks about the day's issues in links with local television outlets. A reporter described one such session:

> On the afternoon he appeared on satellite, from a GOP studio with red, white and blue drapes and a mural of the Capitol, Hulshof was questioned, in turn, by reporters from television stations in Quincy and Jefferson City about a bill to restructure the Internal Revenue Service (H.R.2676) that Republicans had just passed.[103]

Aggressive media outreach was a logical strategy for Hulshof. In 1996 he ousted, by a 2 percent margin, a twenty-year Democratic incumbent who was widely perceived as being out of touch with his constituency. Hulshof's strategy seemed to have worked: he won reelection handily two years later.

Some members invite controversy as a way of showing their accessibility. For example, Rep. Mark Souder, R-Ind., tapes five-minute reports every weekday for local airing and hosts an hour-long call-in show every Sunday—unofficially dubbed "Bark at Mark"—on a popular talk radio station in Fort Wayne.[104]

Like printed communications, radio and TV broadcasts pose ethical questions. House and Senate recording studios are supposed to be used only for communicating about legislation and other policy issues, but the distinction between legitimate constituent outreach and political advertising remains blurred. (Political party facilities, like the one used by Representative Hulshof, have no such limits.) Some radio and television news editors have qualms about using members' programs. "It's just this side of self-serving," said one television editor of the biweekly "Alaska Delegation Report."[105] Others claim to see little difference between these electronic communications and old-fashioned press releases: local editors and producers still have to decide whether to use the material, edit it, or toss it.

Local Press "Boosterism"?

In the eyes of home district media outlets, incumbents fare splendidly. Michael Robinson cites the case of "Congressman Press," a midlevel House member, untouched by scandal, who has an average press operation. One year Congressman Press issued 144 press releases, about three a week. That year the major paper in his district ran 120 stories featuring or mentioning him; more than half the stories drew heavily on the press releases. "On average, every other week, Congressman Press was featured in a story virtually written in his own office."[106]

Even when local stories are not drawn from press releases, they tend to be respectful if not downright laudatory. Hometown stories during one of the re-election campaigns of William Steiger, then a Republican representative from Wisconsin, were so fulsome in their praise, his press aide confessed, that no self-respecting press secretary would have dared put them out.[107] A detailed study of the local press corps in eighty-two contested races highlighted the journalists' tendency toward "safety and timidity." Incumbents were rendered respectful coverage based on their experience; in contested open seats, journalists tended to keep their distance.[108]

Electronic media are even more benign than print media. As one legislator said, "TV people need thirty seconds of sound and video at the airport when I arrive—that's all they want."[109] Most local reporters for radio and TV are on general assignment and do little preparation for interviews; their primary goal is to get the newsmaker on tape. This is especially true of outlets in smaller markets, few of which have access to a Washington bureau. As a Jef-

ferson City, Missouri, TV editor explained his station's handling of an appearance initiated by Representative Hulshof's office:

> He's trying to manage the information aspect of all of this [the IRS reform issue]. But we get the information we need, so we don't mind it too much. . . . We're in TV. We want to see him talk to us. We don't want phone calls.[110]

Local radio and television's weakness for congressionally initiated communications magnifies the advantages incumbents enjoy. ABC correspondent Cokie Roberts concludes, "The emergence of local TV has made some members media stars in the home towns and, I would argue, done more to protect incumbency than any franking privilege or newsletter ever could, simply because television is a more pervasive medium than print."[111] Representative Hulshof states blandly: "I've been treated very fairly back home by the media, who have been content to just report the facts."[112]

Reports on Congress from the national press corps are far more critical than those from local news organizations (see Chapter 15). Following the canons of investigative journalism, many national reporters are on the lookout for scandals or evidence of wrongdoing. The national press reports primarily on the institution of Congress, whereas the local press is interested mostly in local senators and representatives. Individual members tend to be reported far more favorably than the institution. The content and quality of press coverage underscore the two Congresses: Congress as collective policy maker, covered mainly by the national press, appears in a different light from the politicians who make up the Congress covered mainly by local news outlets.

Conclusion

In this chapter we have seen how members of Congress manage the two-Congresses dilemma in their daily tasks on Capitol Hill and in their home states or districts. Election is a prerequisite to congressional service. Incumbent legislators allocate much of their time and energy, and even more of their staff and office resources, to the care and cultivation of voters. Their Hill styles and home styles are adopted with this end in mind. Yet senators and representatives do not live by reelection alone. Not a few turn their backs on reelection to pursue other careers or interests. For those who remain in office, reelection usually is not viewed as an end in itself but as a lever for pursuing other goals—policy making or career advancement, for example. Fenno challenged one of the representatives whose constituency career he had followed, remarking that "sometimes it must be hard to connect what you do here with what you do in Washington." "Oh no," the lawmaker replied, "I do what I do here so I can do what I want to do there."[113]

Part 3

A Deliberative Assembly
of One Nation

A pride of Hill lions. House Republican leaders (above, left–right)—Conference Chair J. C. Watts Jr., Speaker Dennis Hastert, and Majority Leader Dick Armey—hold a news conference. Many think House chief GOP whip Tom DeLay (middle left) of Texas, nicknamed "The Hammer," is the Hill's best vote counter. Senate Republican leader Trent Lott (middle right) talks with reporters. Leaders of the minority Democrats, Sen. Tom Daschle and Rep. Richard A. Gephardt, work to thwart the GOP agenda and build their party's case for regaining control of their respective chambers.

6

Leaders and Parties
in Congress

Do leaders matter? Listen to what Rep. Sherwood Boehlert, R-N.Y., had to say about Newt Gingrich, R-Ga., who was then House Speaker and widely credited with ending forty years of Democratic control of the House in the November 1994 elections. "Gingrich is the one responsible for leading the Republican Party out of the wilderness of the minority . . . to the promised land of the majority," said Boehlert. "He is singularly responsible for us being where we are now."[1] Four years later Newt Gingrich was out as Speaker. Many of his former followers blamed him for the humiliating loss of GOP seats in the November 3, 1998, elections. (Defying electoral history, Democrats made a net gain of five House seats instead of suffering the usual midterm election losses for the party that holds the presidency.)

On November 6, 1998, only hours after Robert L. Livingston, R-La., the Appropriations Committee chairman, announced that he would contest for the speakership, Gingrich said he would step down as Speaker—and quit the House.[2] Six weeks later, on the same day the House impeached President Bill Clinton, Livingston stunned his colleagues by declaring he would no longer seek to become Speaker and that he too would resign from the House.

Two days before this statement on the House floor, Livingston had informed GOP colleagues that he had had several adulterous affairs during his marriage. Livingston's decision to reveal his extramarital liaisons was apparently prompted by an online news source that said a magazine was preparing a story on his affairs.[3] Although most Republicans defended Livingston after his confession, about a dozen conservatives were angry that he had not mentioned his marital indiscretions before being nominated for Speaker. Some even suggested that Livingston ought to give up the post or they might not vote for him as Speaker of the 106th House.[4]

House Republicans turned quickly to J. Dennis Hastert of Illinois, the GOP's chief deputy whip since 1995. A popular and well-liked lawmaker, Hastert moved so quickly to lock up the support of his partisan colleagues that he headed off any potential challengers.[5] On January 6, 1999, the opening day of the 106th Congress, Hastert was elected Speaker. "He's the right man at the right time," declared GOP Conference chairman J. C. Watts Jr., of Oklahoma. Or, as Rep. Ray LaHood, R-Ill., said, "He does not come into the job radioactive, controversial from the get go."[6]

These examples of the give and take between leaders and followers parallel the constant interaction between the two Congresses—between the law-

making institution and the representative assembly. In their "inside" role, party leaders guide institutional activities and influence policy. Leaders also must find ways of persuading members who represent different constituencies, regions, ideologies, values, and interests to support legislation that addresses national concerns. Good communications skills, a talent for coalition building, tactical and strategic competence, intelligence, parliamentary expertise, and sensitivity to the mood of the membership and of the electorate are important attributes of an effective leader. "The only thing that counts is 218 votes, and nothing else is real," once explained Minority Leader Richard A. Gephardt, D-Mo. "You have to be able [to attract a majority of the House] to pass a bill."[7]

In their "outside" role, party leaders formulate and publicize issue agendas designed to galvanize the support of partisans nationally. They help recruit candidates for Congress and assist in their campaigns. Leaders also must serve as the party's link to the president, the press, the public, and the partisan faithful. When Speaker Gingrich departed the House, GOP strategist Ralph Reed noted that Republicans "are losing someone who has probably raised, over the last four years, conservatively, a quarter of a billion dollars for the party, and those things are hard to replace."[8]

The leaders' inside and outside roles are in constant interaction and may complicate legislative strategy. For example, Senate Democratic leader Tom Daschle of South Dakota recognized that legislation establishing a permanent burial site for nuclear waste at Yucca Mountain in Nevada was supported by most senators. Daschle was also well aware that Democrats appeared to have a good chance to win back control of the Senate in the 2000 elections. Daschle's conundrum was that if the Senate approved the popular nuclear waste bill over the objections of Nevada Democrat Richard H. Bryan, Bryan's Senate seat could end up in Republican hands in 2000.[9] Bryan resolved Daschle's problem when he unexpectedly announced that he would not seek reelection. This decision, however, created an even bigger problem for Daschle: how to retain Democratic control of the Nevada seat.

Congress is a partisan body: the majority party in the House or the Senate controls not only the top leadership posts and each chamber's agenda of activities but also majorities on committees and subcommittees and all their chairmanships. In this chapter we identify party leaders, describe their jobs, and assess the sources of their influence; we also consider party structure— caucuses, committees, and informal groups. Finally, we look at continuity and change in the congressional party system.

Leaders of the House

Compared with the rules of the Senate, which emphasize minority rights, House rules permit a determined majority to achieve its policy objectives. During much of the nineteenth century, the struggle between majority rights and minority rights was paramount until the majoritarian principle became embedded in House procedures by the turn of the twentieth century. Stalling tactics by the minority during the pre- and post–Civil War House often prevented

action. Finally, in 1890 Republican Speaker Thomas "Czar" Reed of Maine broke the minority's nearly unstoppable capacity to frustrate House decision making. The House adopted new rules (the famous "Reed Rules") to facilitate majority rule and action. "No dilatory motion shall be entertained by the Speaker" is an 1890 House rule that remains in effect today.

The Speaker

No other member of Congress possesses the visibility and authority of the Speaker of the House. The Constitution states that the House "shall chuse their Speaker." Although the Constitution does not require the Speaker to be a House member, all of them have been. The Speaker is second in line behind the vice president to succeed to the presidency.

For a time former House Speaker Gingrich was a virtual rival to the White House in setting the nation's course. In an unprecedented event mirroring what presidents often do, Gingrich made a prime-time, nationally televised address on April 17, 1995, highlighting the accomplishments of Congress and outlining the country's future direction. Not since Speaker Henry Clay in the early 1800s put forward an agenda (titled "The American System") for strengthening the nation's infrastructure has a Speaker so exploited the position's "bully pulpit." No wonder scholars and commentators focused on the media leadership of the "public speakership."[10] Under Gingrich, the speakership became a platform for focusing public debate on crucial issues of national governance. Speaker Hastert, by contrast, maintained a lower public profile than Gingrich and shared with other Republicans the national spokesman's role. Hastert, noted one account, "is not known for the pithy sound bites that modern politics demands."[11]

The office of Speaker combines procedural and political prerogatives with policy and partisan leadership. Speakers preside over the House, rule on points of order, announce the results of votes, refer legislation to the committees, name lawmakers to serve on conference committees and select committees, and maintain order and decorum in the House chamber. In addition to these procedural prerogatives, they exercise important political powers. They set the House's agenda of activities, control the Rules Committee, chair their party's committee assignment panel (the Republican Steering Committee), bestow or withhold various tangible and intangible rewards, coordinate policy making with Senate counterparts, and, in this age of videopolitics, present party and House positions to the public at large.

Before 1899 it was not uncommon for Speakers to have only a few years of service as representatives. Whig Henry Clay of Kentucky was elected to the speakership on November 4, 1811—his first day in the House. Speakers elected since 1899 have served, on average, more than twenty years before their election to the post. Hastert, it is worth noting, served a dozen years before becoming Speaker on January 6, 1999.

Once in position, Speakers traditionally have been reelected as long as their party controlled the House. Not since 1923 has there been a floor battle

over the speakership because one party has always had a clear majority; typically, members vote for the speakership along straight party lines. As chief parliamentary officer and leader of the majority party (see Figure 6-1), the Speaker enjoys unique powers in scheduling floor business and in recognizing members during sessions. Occasionally, Speakers will relinquish the gavel to join in floor debate; usually they vote only in case of a tie.

The Speaker is also in charge of administrative matters. During the early 1990s, this responsibility embroiled Thomas Foley, D-Wash., then Speaker, in a bitter controversy involving management of the House restaurants, post office, and "bank." Some lawmakers ran up large unpaid bills at various House restaurants, and several employees at the post office pleaded guilty to embezzlement. Hundreds of lawmakers were charged with overdrawing their accounts at the now defunct House bank. The "perks and privileges" of lawmakers, epitomized by their ability to bounce checks, angered voters, prompted numerous retirements and defeats, and contributed to ending the forty years of Democratic control of the House in the November 1994 elections.

When Speaker Gingrich took office, he revamped the administrative structure and management of the House. Administrative units and positions were abolished, management was streamlined and modernized, an outside independent audit of the accounting systems was undertaken, and a new chief administrative officer—elected by the House at the start of each Congress—was assigned overall responsibility for running the House's administrative operations in a professional manner.[12]

Cannon and Rayburn. During the Republic's first 120 years, Speakers gradually accrued power. By 1910 Speaker Joseph G. Cannon, R-Ill., dominated the House. He assigned members to committees, appointed and removed committee chairmen, regulated the flow of bills to the House floor as chairman of the Rules Committee, referred bills to committee, and controlled floor debate. Taken individually, Cannon's powers were little different from those of his immediate predecessors, but taken together and exercised to their limits they bordered on the dictatorial. The result: a revolt against Cannon.

The House forced Cannon to step down from the Rules Committee in 1910. The next year, when Democrats took control of the House, the new Speaker ("Champ" Clark of Missouri) was stripped of his authority to make committee assignments, and his power of recognition was curtailed. The speakership then went into long-term eclipse. Power flowed to the majority leader, to the committee chairmen, and for a while to party caucuses.

Speakers after Cannon exhibited various leadership styles that reflected their personalities, the historical context in which they operated, and the partisan divisions and level of conflict within the chamber. Democrat Sam Rayburn of Texas (Speaker, 1940–1947, 1949–1953, 1955–1961) was a formidable leader because of his personal prestige as well as his long political experience and immense parliamentary skills. As he explained, "The old day of pounding on the desk and giving people hell is gone. . . . A man's got to lead by persuasion and kindness and the best reason—that's the only way he can

Figure 6-1 Organization of the House of Representatives, 106th Congress (1999–2001)

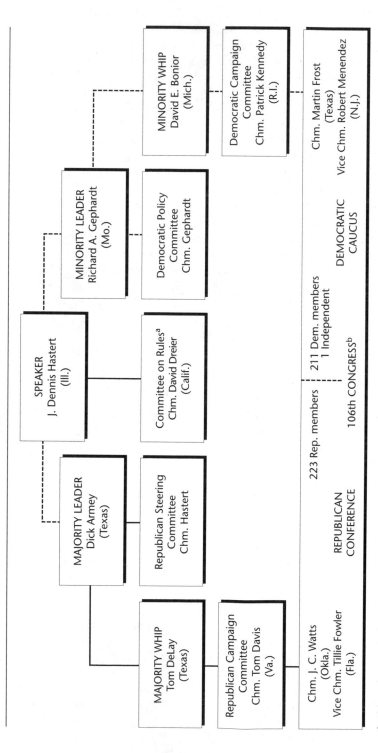

SPEAKER
J. Dennis Hastert
(Ill.)

MAJORITY LEADER
Dick Armey
(Texas)

MINORITY LEADER
Richard A. Gephardt
(Mo.)

MAJORITY WHIP
Tom DeLay
(Texas)

MINORITY WHIP
David E. Bonior
(Mich.)

Committee on Rules[a]
Chm. David Dreier
(Calif.)

Republican Steering
Committee
Chm. Hastert

Democratic Policy
Committee
Chm. Gephardt

Republican Campaign
Committee
Chm. Tom Davis
(Va.)

Democratic Campaign
Committee
Chm. Patrick Kennedy
(R.I.)

Chm. J. C. Watts
(Okla.)
Vice Chm. Tillie Fowler
(Fla.)

Chm. Martin Frost
(Texas)
Vice Chm. Robert Menendez
(N.J.)

223 Rep. members

211 Dem. members
1 Independent

REPUBLICAN
CONFERENCE

106th CONGRESS[b]

DEMOCRATIC
CAUCUS

[a] Although not strictly a party panel, the Rules Committee in modern times functions largely as an arm of the majority leadership.
[b] As of July 1999.

lead people."[13] Rayburn lent coherence to a House in which power was diffused among a relatively small number of powerful committee chairmen.

Revival of the Speakership. Although the legacy of the historic 1910 revolt was weak central party leadership, several Speakers gradually regained some of the former powers of the office. "In the few years [1947–1949, 1953–1955] that I served as Speaker," boasted Republican Joseph Martin of Massachusetts, "no Republican went on an important committee without my approval."[14] The key to effective leadership for Speakers during most of the post-Cannon period was to maximize their leverage over the standing committees and their influential chairmen. Even in the Rayburn House, "committees were certainly not autonomous in the sense of being unaccountable to their party."[15]

The distribution of internal power changed fundamentally after Rayburn. To curb the power of the committee "barons," lawmakers elected during the Vietnam War and the Watergate era combined forces with longtime members disgruntled with the status quo. The majority Democrats changed their party rules to require the election of committee chairmen by secret ballot of the Democratic Caucus. Chairmen were obligated to share power with subcommittee chairmen. At the same time the reformers in the late 1960s and 1970s strengthened the hand of the party leadership. The Speaker, for example, gained the right to name all the majority party members of the Rules Committee, including the chairman. House rules were further amended to permit the Speaker to refer measures to more than one committee.

The Modern Speakership: O'Neill (1977–1987).[16] Thomas P. "Tip" O'Neill Jr., D-Mass., held the speakership for ten consecutive years, the longest uninterrupted service of any Speaker. Using a "strategy of inclusion" to draw Democratic rank and file into the leadership orbit, he expanded the whip structure and encouraged junior Democrats to back partisan priorities by appointing them to leadership task forces.[17] During the first six years of the Reagan presidency, when the House was the only national governmental branch in Democratic hands, O'Neill became his party's national spokesman. In the process he transformed the speakership into an office of high national visibility. He even made a guest appearance on the hit TV show *Cheers.*

The Limits of Power: Wright (1987–1989). O'Neill's successor, Jim Wright, D-Texas, pushed the prerogatives of office even farther. In domestic and foreign policy, Wright took bold risks. Whereas O'Neill strived for consensus, Wright laid out an agenda and then worked diligently, by himself if necessary, to mobilize support. "The Congress," declared Wright, "should not simply react, passively, to recommendations from the president but should come forward with initiatives of its own."[18] His unyielding personal style and knack for making "minority status more painful," as one House GOP leader put it, embittered Republicans (and even some of his own party).[19]

"If Wright consolidates his power, he will be a very, very formidable man," said Representative Gingrich. "We have to take him on early to prevent that."[20] Gingrich brought ethics charges against the Speaker, and they were investigated by the Committee on Standards of Official Conduct. That panel eventu-

ally charged Wright with violating House rules by accepting gifts from a close business associate and circumventing limits on members' outside income through bulk sales of his 1984 book (*Reflections of a Public Man*) to lobbyists and interest groups. Wright did not survive these ethical and political challenges and left the House in June 1989. Eight years later—as political "payback"—many House Democrats tried to force Gingrich from the speakership for ethical violations (see discussion of Gingrich).

End of An Era: Foley (1989–1995). Next in line to succeed Wright as Speaker was Majority Leader Foley. Elected to the House in November 1964, Foley had risen through the ranks to become Speaker during an era of sharp partisan, political, and personal infighting. The new Speaker had a reputation for being a judicious, low-key, honest, and consensus-oriented leader. His initial objectives as Speaker were to restore civility, integrity, and bipartisan cooperation to the House and to provide policy direction. Although Republicans found Foley easier to deal with than Wright, they soon lamented the Speaker's willingness to use procedural rules to frustrate GOP objectives. When a Democrat was elected president in 1992, Foley's instincts for conciliation became an asset as he worked to foster harmony among House Democrats and good ties with the Clinton White House. In November 1994, after a thirty-year congressional career, Speaker Foley lost his reelection bid and Democrats lost the House.

Gingrich: A New Style of Speaker (1995–1999). There is little doubt that Newt Gingrich was a unique Speaker. His Democratic predecessors, he once said, were "essentially legislative leaders speaking to the press about legislative matters." He went on to say, "I on the other hand, was essentially a political leader of a grassroots movement seeking to do nothing less than reshape the federal government along with the political culture of the nation."[21] Gingrich, summarized a commentator, was "first a leader of a national movement, then a Republican spokesman and, only third, Speaker of the House."[22]

He was his party's unanimous choice for Speaker after its dramatic and surprising capture of Congress following the November 1994 elections. The large class of seventy-three freshmen GOP lawmakers, plus nearly all other Republicans, believed that they had won majority control of the House because of Gingrich. Indeed, since his 1978 election, Gingrich had worked to undermine Democratic control of the House. He even managed to become the minority whip in 1989, winning the post by one vote, despite being known as a "bomb thrower" and lacking a reputation for consensus building, committee work, or passing legislation.

As Speaker, Gingrich took the office to new heights. His Contract with America, which the House acted upon within the promised first 100 days of the 104th Congress, set the agenda for Congress and the nation. Three factors help explain his influence: recognition on the part of most GOP lawmakers that they owed their majority status to him; broad commitment on their part to the GOP's agenda, especially cutting spending and balancing the budget; and the new majority's need to succeed at governance after forty years in the minority.

A centralizing aspect of Gingrich's speakership was his influence over committees. Not only did Gingrich personally select certain Republicans to chair several standing committees, ignoring seniority in the process, but he required the GOP members of the Appropriations Committee to sign a written pledge that they would heed the Republican leadership's recommendations for spending reductions. Furthermore, he often bypassed committees entirely by establishing leadership task forces to process legislation.

Gingrich's speakership went through three phases. The first was characterized by the "triumphalism" of the first 100 days: everything in the ten-point contract passed the House (except term limits for lawmakers). It was a different story in the Senate, where lawmakers who had not signed the contract employed filibustering techniques to stall many of its items.

In the second phase, Gingrich's confrontational strategy with the White House produced political disaster for Republicans. In a face-off with President Clinton, Republicans were publicly blamed for twice shutting down the government in late 1995 and early 1996 (see Chapter 13). Further, their "revolutionary" plans for downsizing government by eliminating cabinet departments and reducing spending for education, environment, and health programs were successfully characterized by Democrats as "extreme." Gingrich's public popularity plummeted, and the Speaker became a campaign issue in many 1996 congressional races.

The lead-up to the November 1996 campaign ushered in the third phase of Gingrich's speakership. Worried that President Clinton would campaign against a "do-nothing" Congress, congressional Republicans and the White House cooperated and passed health, minimum wage, and welfare reform legislation. Each side wanted something positive to campaign on. The result was that Clinton won reelection to a second term, and the Republicans—although they lost nine House seats—held majority control of Congress.

A narrower majority was not Gingrich's only problem when the House convened in the 105th Congress (1997–1999). On December 21, 1996, he had admitted that he had provided inaccurate and incomplete information to the House ethics committee regarding his solicitation of tax-deductible contributions, which were used for partisan purposes contrary to federal law. Two weeks after Gingrich's reelection as Speaker, the House voted 395–28 to reprimand him for ethical misconduct and to fine him $300,000. He became the first Speaker formally disciplined by the House for ethical wrongdoing.

Weakened by the ethics charge, Gingrich no longer dominated the House as he once did. In the 105th Congress he decided on a modest agenda (keeping the House in session the fewest number of days in two decades) and focused on hot-button issues ("partial-birth" abortion, education vouchers, tax cuts) designed to energize the GOP electorate for the November 1998 midterm elections. Rank-and-file Republicans and his top leadership lieutenants became frustrated with Gingrich's impulsive leadership style. Rep. Peter T. King, R-N.Y., recommended that Gingrich step aside as Speaker because his low popular standing (below 30 percent job approval) made him unable to boost Republican priorities. "As roadkill on the highway of American politics," wrote

King, "Newt Gingrich cannot sell the Republican agenda."[23] *Time* magazine's 1995 "Man of the Year" had fallen far. Top GOP leaders and a small band of ideologically hard-line junior conservatives griped that Gingrich compromised too much with the Democrats. The result: a coup plot in the summer of 1997 was hatched by the hard-liners with the encouragement of some in the leadership. The plan to depose Gingrich was uncovered and averted, but it exposed the deep frustration with the Speaker among Republican ranks.[24]

On the eve of the November 3, 1998, elections, the Speaker took a high-risk political gamble. Despite polls showing the public was sick of hearing about President Clinton's sexual relationship with White House intern Monica Lewinsky, Gingrich gave the order to GOP campaign officials to blanket selected House districts with multimillion-dollar TV ads highlighting the scandal. When the House adjourned two weeks before the election, Clinton-preoccupied Republicans had no coherent agenda to promote. Furthermore, they allowed the president to win large spending increases in an omnibus appropriations bill nearly 4,000 pages in length, which no one had time to read and which was filled with "pork." Many Republicans and conservative voters were livid with the Speaker about this end-of-session budget deal.

When the midterm results came in, Republicans were shell-shocked at their poor showing. Scores of Republicans blamed Gingrich for another election in which they lost seats despite the early predictions, including those of the Speaker, that their party would gain seats and coast to victory. Gingrich became an early casualty of the election: he abruptly departed the race for the speakership and for the House. A skillful insurgent leader as a minority lawmaker, Gingrich had difficulty adjusting to the formidable job of governing the House.

The "Coach" as Speaker: Dennis Hastert (1999–). A former high school wrestling coach and Illinois state legislator, Hastert took office in the aftermath of the contentious House impeachment proceedings against President Clinton. The new Speaker promised to restore some semblance of bipartisanship between Democrats and Republicans and to unite his often fractious and divided party. Known as a patient, congenial, behind-the-scenes workhorse, Hastert excelled at counting votes as chief deputy whip to Majority Whip Tom DeLay, R-Texas, and at crafting compromises and winning coalitions. Employing the "coaching" metaphor, Hastert explained how he expected to fulfill his leadership role. "A good coach knows when to step back and let others shine in the spotlight," he said. "A coach worth his salt will instill in his team a sense of fair play, camaraderie, respect of the game and for the opposition. Without those, victory is hollow."[25]

A strong conservative, Hastert became Speaker without previously serving in an elective leadership post—something that had not occurred since the 1919–1925 period, when Frederick Gillett, R-Mass., was Speaker. Understandably, for much of the 106th Congress, Hastert's speakership was a work in progress as he developed new relationships with the other GOP leaders, the committee chairs, and the factional groups in the House. Among Hastert's new departures was "ceding substantial authority to committee chairmen, delegating his role as party spokesman to a variety of Members, hiring seasoned staff

who work well with the other leadership offices and playing a more active role in the day-to-day gruntwork of legislating."[26] In brief, Hastert's style of leadership was different from Gingrich's because each operated in a different legislative context and with different personal skills. Hastert, a low-key leader with a razor-thin majority, could not dominate the House as Gingrich initially did. (See box, p. 173, for a summary comparison of some of the differences between Gingrich and Hastert.)

Hastert's low-key style aroused some concern in late April 1999, when the House failed on a tie vote to support a Democratic proposal backing the NATO air war in the Serbian province of Kosovo. The Speaker stood in the back of the chamber and waited until the last minute to cast his vote in support of the air campaign, while DeLay urged Republicans to vote against the bombing. Some Republican lawmakers criticized Hastert for not providing an early signal on how they should vote. The Speaker later apologized to the GOP Conference and said he had learned an important leadership lesson: vote early and send a clear signal.[27]

The Speaker's Influence: Context and Style. Congressional analysts generally agree that the primary determinants of leadership are context and personal style or skills; however, they sometimes disagree over which is the more crucial. (See box, p. 174, for a brief review of the principal scholarly theories about congressional leadership.)

Context refers to the House's external and internal environment, which changes over time. External elements include the public's demand for legislation, the complexity of national problems, the popularity of the president, and the strength of partisan identification within the electorate. Internal elements that condition the Speaker's influence are the configuration of forces within the House, such as the size and cohesiveness of the majority party, the diffusion of power among members, and the autonomy of committees.

Personal style, on the other hand, refers to the skills, talents, and personality of the Speaker. Contrast the "iron fist" leadership of Wright with the "nice guy" approach of Hastert. Or compare the incremental reforms of some Speakers, such as O'Neill, with the dramatic and aggressive agenda changes pushed by Gingrich.

Advocates of the individualist rather than contextualist school of leadership stress that personally adroit and active Speakers can lead by molding circumstances and opportunities to their own objectives. Speakers' personal capacities, in short, allow them to exercise that elusive quality called leadership—persuading others to follow their lead. To be sure, the dynamic interaction between context and style is not easy to untangle; both context and personal talent are critical ingredients in shaping the limits and possibilities of leadership.[28]

Floor Leaders

The Speaker's principal deputy—the *majority leader*—is the party's floor leader, elected every two years by secret ballot of the party caucus. The floor

A Comparison of the Speakerships of Gingrich and Hastert

J. Dennis Hastert, R-Ill. (Speaker 1999–)	Newt Gingrich, R-Ga. (Speaker 1995–1999)
A pragmatic leader who returned to the "regular order" of lawmaking	A visionary leader who often set aside traditional legislative procedures
Restored committees' prerogatives	Decreased power of committees
Observed traditional seniority system in naming committee chairs	Set aside seniority in naming several committee chairs
Personally managed the floor schedule	Delegated floor management duties to the majority leader
Limited use of party task forces	Increased use of party task forces
Played relatively small role as public spokesman	Assumed large public spokesman role
Eased partisan tension in the House	Contributed to partisan rancor
Operated behind-the-scenes	Relished national spotlight
Exercised accommodating style of leadership	Exercised confrontational style of leadership
Relied on committee chairs	Bypassed committees on occasion to achieve his party's legislative ends

leader is not to be confused with a *floor manager.* The floor managers, usually two for each bill, are frequently the chairman and ranking minority member of the committee that reported the bill. They try to steer the bill to a final decision.

The House majority leader is usually an experienced legislator. Jim Wright and Thomas Foley, for example, each served twenty-two years before their election as majority leader. When Richard Gephardt took the office in June 1989, he had been in the House for more than a decade, had served as chairman of the Democratic Caucus for four years, and had been a 1988 presidential candidate. Dick Armey of Texas, the first Republican majority leader in forty years, was almost ejected from his post at the start of the 106th Congress because he was implicated in the 1997 aborted "coup" against Speaker Gingrich. Armey bested two challengers (Jennifer Dunn, Wash., and Steve Largent, Okla.) to remain majority leader.

By modern custom, neither the Speaker nor the Democratic or Republican floor leader chairs committees. The Speaker and minority floor leader are ex officio members of the Select Intelligence Committee. The majority and minority leaders, as well as the Speaker, may serve on informal task forces.

Theories of Congressional Leadership

Political scientists have developed different theories to explain why congressional leaders appear to be stronger during some eras than others. The most prominent is called "conditional party government."[a] A competing theory—the "pivotal voter" theory—suggests that the influence of party leaders is marginal with respect to their ability to shift policy outcomes away from what a majority of the chamber prefers toward the policy preferences of the majority party.[b]

Proponents of each theory view party leaders as "agents" of their "principals"— their rank-and-file partisans. Members want their party leaders to help them accomplish their fundamental goals: getting reelected, making good policy, and gaining—or maintaining—power in the House or Senate. A correspondence in leader-member views means that party leaders will work to advance the majority preferences of the rank and file. After all, party leaders hold their positions at the sufferance of their partisan colleagues and they usually want to be reelected to those leadership posts.

Conditional Party Government Theory. Under this model, the power of congressional leaders hinges on the degree of homogeneity within the majority party concerning policy and on the extent of interparty conflict between Democrats and Republicans. With both conditions in play, the theory goes, rank-and-file party members are supportive of changes that strengthen their party leaders, such as the Speaker. A cohesive majority party can pass legislation without any support from the minority party. Conversely, when parties' policy goals are fragmented, partisan lawmakers have little incentive to give their leaders more authority. They may use their power against the political and policy interests of many in the rank-and-file.

Pivotal Voter Theory. This theory challenges the conditional party government model by suggesting that policy outcomes on the floor rarely diverge from what is acceptable to the "pivotal voter"—the member who casts the 218th vote in the House. Rarely does everyone in the majority party support a particular policy. Why, then, should majority members change their policy views to back a party position with which they disagree? Instead, they will join with members of the other party to form the winning coalition. According to this theory, these "pivotal voters" determine chamber outcomes.

Moreover, if each party is internally united in its policy preferences, as the conditional party government theory states, there will be no difference between what the majority party wants and what the chamber membership will agree to. Simply observing party leaders engaged in frenetic activity—often seeking pivotal votes—does not mean they can skew legislative outcomes beyond what is acceptable to a majority of the entire membership.

a. See, for example, John H. Aldrich and David W. Rohde, "The Transition to Republican Rule in the House: Implications for Theories of Congressional Politics," *Political Science Quarterly* (winter 1997–1998): 541–567.
b. See Keith Krehbiel, *Pivotal Politics: A Theory of U.S. Lawmaking* (Chicago: University of Chicago Press, 1998).

House and party rules are largely silent about the majority leader's duties. By tradition, the primary duties are to be principal floor defender, negotiator, and spokesman for the party. The majority leader helps to plan the daily, weekly, and annual legislative agendas; consults with members to gauge sentiment on legislation; coordinates chamber action with the majority floor manager and other party leaders; confers with the president about administrative proposals, particularly when the president is of the same party; urges colleagues to support or defeat measures; and, in general, works hard to advance the purposes and programs of the majority party. To expand his awareness of the concerns and suggestions of his GOP colleagues, Armey created a new leadership post: "assistant majority leader." He appointed two trusted Republican colleagues—Rick Lazio, N.Y., and James Talent, Mo.—as assistant majority leaders to assist him on "floor scheduling, legislative and communications strategy, the policy agenda, and leadership decisions."[29]

The *minority leader* is the floor leader of the "loyal opposition." (Speakers assume that role for the majority.) Like the Speaker, these party leaders bring different styles to their roles. In general, minority leaders promote unity among party colleagues, monitor the progress of bills through committees and subcommittees, and forge coalitions with like-minded members of the opposition party. Bertrand Snell, R-N.Y., minority leader from 1931 to 1939, thus described the duties:

> He is spokesman for his party and enunciates its policies. He is required to be alert and vigilant in defense of the minority's rights. It is his function and duty to criticize constructively the policies and program of the majority, and to this end employ parliamentary tactics and give close attention to all proposed legislation.[30]

Perhaps the most important task of the minority leader is to work constantly to win back majority control of the House. This requires the confluence of a variety of forces, including maintaining partisan unity and mobilizing turnout among supporters in the electorate. At the start of the 106th Congress House Democrats found themselves lacking a woman as part of the elective party leadership. Yet forty-one of the House's fifty-eight females were Democrats. (Republicans recently had elected Rep. Tillie Fowler, Fla., as vice chair of the GOP Conference, the fifth-ranking post in the GOP's elective hierarchy.) So Minority Leader Gephardt established another leadership position—assistant to the Democratic leader—and worked successfully to ensure that the party caucus elected Rosa DeLauro of Connecticut to the post. DeLauro had lost her bid to chair the Democratic Caucus. DeLauro's job, said Gephardt, is to "oversee coordination of policy, communications and research for the party leadership" and to "serve as a liaison to freshmen members."[31] Additionally, Gephardt created a six-member Leadership Council, composed of members from the Black Caucus, the Hispanic Caucus, the Women's Caucus, the moderate New Democratic Coalition, the Progressive Caucus, and the conservative Blue Dogs" to be a support arm of the Democratic leadership.[32]

The Whips

Another elective party post is the *whip*. As the term implies, the jobs of a whip are to encourage party discipline, count votes, and, in general, mobilize winning coalitions on behalf of partisan priorities. These objectives are accomplished primarily through persuasion and hard work.

In recent years both parties have expanded their whip systems to include a variety of deputy, regional, or assistant whips who meet regularly to discuss issues and strategy. Naming more members as whips involves them in leadership decision making and gives them additional incentives to back their top leaders. Adding more whips also ensures leadership representation for important party groups.

Majority Whip DeLay and his chief deputy whip meet weekly with the other sixty-four deputy and assistant whips to count votes, share intelligence, and ensure that everything is being done to marshal support for GOP proposals. DeLay believes in the "rule of 200." During floor votes "the first side to get to 200 votes almost always wins."[33] He mobilized his formidable whip organization to line up party support first for Livingston's bid to be Speaker and then for Hastert.

Despite his acknowledged role in the aborted attempt to unseat Gingrich, DeLay has emerged largely unscathed because he admitted his complicity and continued to be the GOP's most accurate vote counter. For his combativeness in challenging Democrats (he was the most active GOP leader in urging President Clinton's impeachment and removal from office) and for his aggressiveness in campaign fund raising and lobbying, DeLay has earned the nickname "The Hammer."

In recognition of his skill and power, Speaker Hastert granted DeLay prime control over the party's operation on K Street (a street in the District of Columbia where numerous lobbying firms have their offices). DeLay "orchestrate[s] 'grow the vote' campaigns to bring together members, trade associations and activists to help push through legislation."[34] His whip office is also noted for lining up support for GOP lawmakers' pet projects and "providing food and drink during late nights on the floor."[35]

Minority Whip David E. Bonior of Michigan heads a large whip organization composed of about one-third of the Democratic membership, including four chief deputy whips who assist in vote counting and devising party strategy. They are named to reflect diversity within the Democratic Caucus and include a woman, an African American, a southerner, and a Hispanic. As the Democrats' top vote counter, Bonior has stayed "active in attacking Republican programs and policies and actions when [he thinks] they are hypocritical, excessive, and greedy."[36]

Each party's whip prepares weekly "whip notices" advising members of the upcoming floor agenda. Because scheduling changes can occur frequently, DeLay has introduced "The Whipping Post," a one-page daily bulletin. It identifies the time when the House is to convene and when the last vote is expected; it spells out what action is to occur that day on the floor, in the Sen-

ate, and in selective committees; and it forecasts the next day's schedule of floor business.

Leaders of the Senate

Today's Senate, far more than the House, is an institution that tolerates and even promotes individualism. Candidate-centered elections, the decline of partisan affiliation in the electorate, the proliferation of policy-oriented interest groups, the large role of money in campaigns, and the huge influence of the press and media in political life are among the factors that have led to today's individualistic Senate. Senators cherish their independence, which exacerbates the challenges faced by those elected to lead them. Unlike House leaders, Senate leaders lack the buttress of rules designed to expedite business and so must rely heavily on personal skills and negotiation with their colleagues.

Presiding Officers

The House majority's highest elected leader, the Speaker, presides over the House. By contrast, the Senate majority leader, the majority party's highest leader, almost never presides in the Senate chamber. In fact, the Senate has three categories of presiding officers.

First, the constitutional president of the Senate is the vice president of the United States (see Figure 6-2). Except for ceremonial occasions, the vice president seldom presides over Senate sessions, and he can vote only to break a tie. When votes on major issues are expected to be close, party leaders make sure that the vice president is presiding so that he can break tie votes. Vice presidents experienced in the ways of Congress, such as former senators Albert Gore, Dan Quayle, and Walter Mondale, can help bridge the gap between Capitol Hill and the White House.

Second, the Constitution provides for a *president pro tempore* to preside in the vice president's absence. In modern practice this constitutional officer is the majority party senator with the longest continuous service. By passing a simple resolution, the Senate sometimes appoints a deputy president pro tempore. This majority party official, who presides over the Senate in the absence of the vice president and president pro tempore, is part of the leadership group that meets periodically at the White House with the president.

Third, a dozen or so majority senators, typically junior members, serve approximately half-hour stints each day as the presiding officer. The opportunity to preside helps newcomers become familiar with Senate rules and procedures. None of these presiding officers has the influence or visibility of the House Speaker.

Floor Leaders

The majority leader is the head of the majority party in the Senate, its leader on the floor, and the leader of the Senate. Similarly, the minority leader heads the Senate's minority party. (Nowadays, minority leaders prefer to be called the "Republican leader" or the "Democratic leader," as the case may be.)

Figure 6-2 Organization of the Senate, 106th Congress (1999–2001)

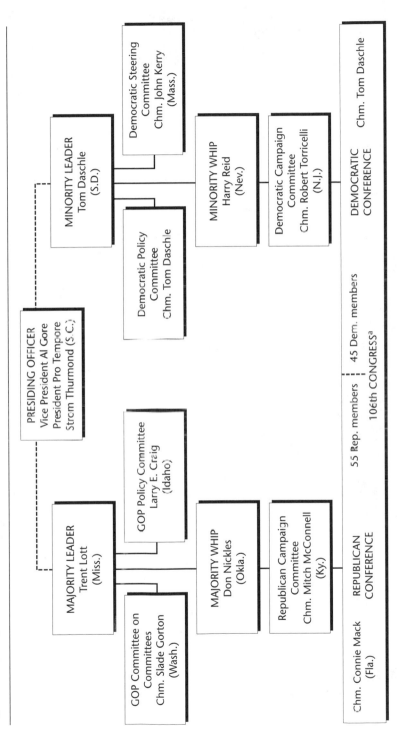

PRESIDING OFFICER
Vice President Al Gore
President Pro Tempore
Strom Thurmond (S.C.)

MINORITY LEADER
Tom Daschle
(S.D.)

Democratic Steering
Committee
Chm. John Kerry
(Mass.)

Democratic Policy
Committee
Chm. Tom Daschle

MINORITY WHIP
Harry Reid
(Nev.)

Democratic Campaign
Committee
Chm. Robert Torricelli
(N.J.)

DEMOCRATIC
CONFERENCE

Chm. Tom Daschle

MAJORITY LEADER
Trent Lott
(Miss.)

GOP Policy Committee
Larry E. Craig
(Idaho)

GOP Committee on
Committees
Chm. Slade Gorton
(Wash.)

MAJORITY WHIP
Don Nickles
(Okla.)

Republican Campaign
Committee
Chm. Mitch McConnell
(Ky.)

REPUBLICAN
CONFERENCE

Chm. Connie Mack
(Fla.)

55 Rep. members   45 Dem. members
106th CONGRESS[a]

a As of July 1999.

The majority and minority leaders are elected biennially by secret ballot of their party colleagues. Neither position is mentioned in the Constitution, and each is a relatively recent creation that came into being during the early 1900s.

Historically, the Senate has always had leaders, but no single senator exercised central management of the legislative process in the fashion of today's floor leader. During the Senate's first century or so—especially in the 1790s and early 1800s, when there was no system of permanent standing committees or organized senatorial parties—leadership flowed from the personal talents and abilities of individual legislators. The small size of the early Senate and its tradition of viewing members as "ambassadors" from sovereign states promoted an informal and personal style of leadership.

Throughout the nineteenth century scores of prominent senators were called "leaders" by scholars and other observers. Some were sectional or factional leaders; others headed important committees (by the mid- to late 1840s committees and their chairmen had become centers of power); and still others (the Clays, Calhouns, and Websters) exercised wide influence because of their special political, oratorical, or intellectual gifts. Even as late as 1885, however, Woodrow Wilson could write, "No one is *the Senator*. . . . No one exercises the special trust of acknowledged leadership."[37]

By the turn of the twentieth century the political landscape had changed. Party structures and leaders emerged as clearly identifiable forces in organizing and managing the Senate's proceedings. This important development occurred, according to a historian of the Senate, because of the influx of a "new breed" of senator who valued party unity and "the machinery of [party] organization," especially the party caucus.[38] Soon those senators who chaired their respective party caucuses acquired levers of authority over senatorial affairs. They chaired important party panels, shaped the Senate's agenda of business, and mobilized party majorities behind important issues. From the caucus chairmanship, scholars agree, the position of majority leader had informally emerged by 1913.[39]

Strong Leadership, 1953–1960. One turning point came in 1953, when Republican Robert A. Taft of Ohio became majority leader. Although Taft served less than a year before his death, he enhanced the stature of the office and underscored its potential as an independent source of authority. He "proved a master of parliamentary procedures" and contributed to his party's cohesiveness, which "showed more unity on key roll-call votes in 1953 than at any time in years."[40]

Unlike Taft, who served fourteen years before becoming party leader, Lyndon B. Johnson was elected minority leader in 1953 after only four years in the Senate. Johnson became majority leader in 1955, when the Democrats regained control of Congress. He possessed singular attributes that helped him gain the top party office. "He doesn't have the best mind on the Democratic side," declared Richard Russell of Georgia, the leader of southern Democrats. "He isn't the best orator; he isn't the best parliamentarian. But he's the best combination of all of these qualities."[41]

Known for his awesome persuasive abilities, Johnson transformed the Democratic leadership post into one of immense authority and prestige. His extensive network of trusted aides and colleagues made him better informed about more issues than any other senator. Opposition party control of the White House gave the aggressive Johnson the luxury of choosing which policies to support and which strategies to employ to get them enacted. And his pragmatic outlook, domineering style, and arm-twisting abilities made him the premier vote gatherer in the Senate. The majority leader's awesome display of face-to-face persuasion has been called the "Johnson Treatment" (see frontispiece).

> The Treatment could last ten minutes or four hours. It came, enveloping its target, at the LBJ Ranch swimming pool, in one of LBJ's offices, in the Senate cloakroom, on the floor of the Senate itself. . . . Its tone could be supplication, accusation, cajolery, exuberance, scorn, tears, complaint, the hint of threat. It was all of these together. It ran the gamut of human emotions. Its velocity was breathtaking, and it was all in one direction. Interjections from the target were rare. Johnson anticipated them before they could be spoken. He moved in close, his face a scant millimeter from his target, his eyes widening and narrowing, and his eyebrows rising and falling. From his pockets poured clippings, memos, statistics. Mimicry, humor, and the genius of analogy made The Treatment an almost hypnotic experience and rendered the target stunned and helpless.[42]

Buttressing Johnson was an "inner club," a bipartisan group of senior senators, mainly southern Democrats such as Russell. The club, observers said, wielded the real power in the Senate through its control of chairmanships and committee assignments.[43] There were even unwritten rules of behavior (for example, junior members should be seen and not heard) that encouraged new senators to defer to the "establishment."

Collegial Leadership, 1961–1991. Johnson's successor, Mike Mansfield, D-Mont. (1961–1977), sharply curtailed the role of majority leader. He viewed himself as one among equals. "I can see a Senate with real egalitarianism, the decline of seniority as a major factor, and new senators being seen and heard and not being wallflowers," Mansfield said.[44] He permitted floor managers and individual senators to take public credit when measures were enacted. Significant organizational and procedural developments, such as increases in the number of subcommittees and staff aides, occurred in the Senate during his leadership.

When Robert Byrd, D-W.Va., served as majority leader (1977–1981 and 1987–1989), the Senate remained egalitarian, individualistic, assertive, independent, and open to public view. Byrd's style fell somewhere between that of the flamboyant Johnson and the relaxed Mansfield. "Circumstances don't permit the Lyndon Johnson style," he observed. "What I am saying is that times and things have changed. Younger Senators come into the Senate. They are more independent. The 'establishment' is a bad word. Each wants to do his 'own thing.' "[45]

Byrd recognized that he had to cater to individual members. At the same time, the majority leader is charged with processing the Senate's workload. Caught between individual and institutional pressures, Byrd employed his formidable parliamentary skills and controls to accommodate colleagues and expedite the Senate's business.

During the Republicans' six years of controlling the Senate (1981–1987), majority leaders Howard Baker of Tennessee (1981–1985) and Bob Dole of Kansas (1985–1987) for the most part continued the Senate's tradition of collegial leadership. Like other majority leaders, Baker found it difficult to lead the Senate. He even formulated the theory that "being leader of the Senate was like herding cats. It is trying to make ninety-nine independent souls act in concert under rules that encourage polite anarchy and embolden people who find majority rule a dubious proposition at best."[46] Dole brought to the office experience, national visibility, quick wit, independence, and mastery of coalition building.

When George J. Mitchell, D-Maine, became majority leader in 1989, he involved other Democrats in leadership activities by dispersing to partisan colleagues power that previously had been consolidated in the majority leader's office. He consulted regularly with Minority Leader Dole about the Senate's agenda and worked to establish an atmosphere of civility and cooperation in the Senate. "The Senate is a unique institution," Mitchell said, "and with its rules, which permit unlimited debate and the unlimited right of amendments, it is very difficult to manage and organize in a constructive and productive way."[47] Mitchell voluntarily retired from the Senate at the end of the 103d Congress.

A More Partisan Senate: The 1990s. Sharp partisanship was plainly evident in the Senate during the 1980s, but it accelerated in the following decade. There were more party-line votes (a majority of Democrats facing off against a majority of Republicans) because of greater ideological cohesion within each party; there was more willingness to use the Senate's rules for partisan purposes; and there was a decline in the number of centrists, many of whom voluntarily leave the Senate because of its sharper partisan atmosphere. As former senator Dale Bumpers, D-Ark., wrote soon after he retired from the Senate, there is more mean-spiritedness and lack of collegiality in the Senate because of "the compulsion to put a partisan bent on every single issue."[48]

With Republicans in charge of the Senate during the mid-1990s, Senator Dole again became majority leader. This time around he was not only managing the dramatic agenda changes in the Senate but running for president as well. Dole, who served longer as Senate GOP leader than anyone else (eleven years), was the first Senate leader ever to win his party's presidential nomination. With his nomination a foregone conclusion by early 1996, Dole at first tried to campaign for the presidency while still at his post. In the end he could not manage the two tasks. As majority leader, he became embroiled in too many procedural, partisan, and ideological battles in the Senate. Moreover, the minority Democrats had little incentive to aid his legislative deal making. In a

surprise announcement on May 15, 1996, Dole stated his decision to resign from the Senate and campaign full time for the White House.[49]

Dole's successor, Trent Lott, R-Miss., brought a different style and emphasis to the majority leadership. Lott had an abundance of Capitol Hill experience as a former House staff aide, House GOP whip, and then Senate GOP whip. A gregarious, polished, and results-oriented lawmaker, he is skilled in consensus building, deal making, and negotiating. "I'd rather have 80 percent of something than 100 percent of nothing," he said.[50] With a penchant for order and organization, Lott is a strong partisan who favors "a team approach to leadership, with a changing set of Senate advisers dubbed the 'Council of Trent.' " Sen. Connie Mack, R-Fla., characterizes Lott's method of running the Senate as "participatory management."[51]

During the Senate's impeachment proceedings against President Clinton, Lott faced strong crosspressures. He had to weigh the pro-impeachment preferences of House and Senate conservatives and their outside supporters against the wishes of moderate lawmakers and the general public, who favored some form of rebuke to the president and a speedy end to the trial. "Welcome to the operations of the United States Senate," he said about managing the chamber. "It's never easy to get 100 senators to agree."[52]

Minority Leader. The Senate minority leader consults continually with the majority leader. If a member of the president's party, the minority leader has the traditional obligations of trying to carry out the administration's program and to rebut partisan criticisms of the president. The minority leader also exercises a "watchdog" role over the majority party, offering criticism, frustrating majority actions, formulating alternative proposals, and protecting the political interests of the minority party. "We [should] deal with the Republicans with some muscle and with some discipline that will cause them to sit up and listen," said Democratic leader Daschle.[53]

Daschle meets regularly with Senate Democrats and with his House counterpart to coordinate strategy, develop tactics to block or modify Republican initiatives, and devise an alternative Democratic agenda. In 1999 he appointed Richard J. Durbin of Illinois to be assistant party floor leader.[54] This relatively new post had been created two years earlier and filled first by Byron L. Dorgan of North Dakota.

The minority leader is always searching for ways to win back control of the Senate. Because Democrats believed the 2000 elections would be good for their party, Daschle announced that he would be more actively involved in the day-to-day operations of the Democratic Senatorial Campaign Committee.[55] His low-key, consensus-oriented leadership style involves many colleagues in decision making. In fact, Daschle was instrumental in developing a state-of-the-art TV studio for beaming party messages to the electorate and for expanding "the media visibility of Democrats in general and himself in particular."[56] The Daschle-led Democrats also have employed parliamentary procedures and communications strategies to stymie their opponents' objectives.

Party Whips. The Senate's whip system carries out functions that are similar to those of the House's system, such as "counting noses" before crucial votes. When Don Nickles, R-Okla., replaced Lott as majority whip near the end of the 104th Congress, he brought renewed energy, organization, and coordination to the GOP's whip system of deputy and regional whips. Not only were expenditures for the majority whip's office nearly doubled, but the majority leader assigned more coalition building and floor responsibilities to Nickles. "Trent has said that my title is 'assistant majority leader,' and that's what he is making the role," stated Nickles. Further, Nickles keeps in close touch with various outside groups that can help move the GOP's agenda.[57]

In a move designed to appeal to women and to reach out to nonsouthern GOP senators, Nickles named Olympia J. Snowe, R-Maine, to a new leadership post: "counsel" to the majority whip. "The gender gap continues to surface for Republicans as something that we have to address as we form our legislative strategy," remarked Senator Snowe about her new assignment.[58]

Minority Whip Harry Reid of Nevada is the Democrats' second in command. He heads a whip structure that includes a chief deputy whip and four regionally appointed deputy minority whips. Reid's primary objectives are to ensure party unity, devise party strategy, defend the floor against GOP criticisms of the Democratic Party, and assist the minority leader.

On occasion the Democratic and Republican whip organizations cooperate to expedite the Senate's floor business. One way they do this is by identifying which senators plan to offer floor amendments and encouraging them to come to the chamber in a timely manner to offer the proposals.

Selection of Leaders

Before the beginning of each new Congress, senators and representatives elect their top leaders by secret ballot in their party caucuses. Although the whole House votes for the Speaker, the election is a pro forma one. With straight party voting the unspoken rule on this and other organizational matters, the majority party has always elected the Speaker.

Since the 1980s candidates for party leadership positions have usually waged meticulous campaigns to win support from their partisan colleagues. Occasionally, to be sure, last-minute entrants successfully bid for leadership positions. A good example is Senator Lott. Just before the start of the 104th Congress, Lott decided to challenge the incumbent GOP whip, Alan K. Simpson of Wyoming. Lott ousted Simpson by one vote, which burnished Lott's credentials later to become majority leader. But whether short or long, campaigns for party leadership positions are intense. Members understand that a party leadership post can be a "career launching pad . . . either within the [Congress] or outside it."[59]

The two parties treat their hierarchies differently in the House: the Democrats as something like a ladder and the Republicans as a slippery slope. Democrats have a history of elevating their next-in-line officer—from whip to majority leader to Speaker—as vacancies occur. Republicans have had a his-

tory of pushing people off the ladder because of turmoil in their ranks. For example, in 1959 Charles Halleck ousted Joseph Martin as the GOP leader; in 1965 Gerald Ford turned the tables on Halleck; and in 1980 John Rhodes was persuaded by his colleagues to step down as party leader.

Length of service in Congress is not the only criterion that influences the election of party leaders. Other considerations are ideological or geographical balance within the leadership; reputation for hard work and competency in procedural and organizational matters; and personal attributes, such as intelligence, fairness, persuasiveness, political shrewdness, and media savvy.

For the most part, House and Senate leaders swim in the mainstream or center of their respective parties. When he was majority leader, Byrd explained why: "As a member of the leadership it is my duty to bring north and south, liberals and conservatives together; to work out compromises. . . . I think it takes a centrist to do that."[60] Leaders are not always centrists or moderates. At the beginning of the 104th, 105th, and 106th Congresses, for example, House GOP conservatives won all the top party leadership positions. Among the factors that accounted for the conservatives' victories were the large influx of ideologically committed Republicans and their desire for an aggressive leadership team to change the country's direction and confront the Democratic president.

Serving as a party leader in the House is a full-time position, although top party leaders sometimes serve ex officio on some committees. By contrast, every party leader in the Senate sits on several committees. The smaller size of the Senate allows leaders to participate in committee work while discharging their leadership duties. As majority leader, Johnson made a notable contribution on space policy, Mansfield and Baker on international affairs, Byrd on energy issues, Mitchell on environmental protection, Dole on tax questions, and Lott on transportation issues.

Leadership Activities

House and Senate leaders have basically the same job: to bring coherence, direction, and efficiency to a decentralized and individualistic legislative body. Leadership duties can be described in terms of "institutional maintenance" (ensuring that Congress and its members perform their lawmaking and oversight duties effectively) and "party maintenance" (crafting winning coalitions among partisan colleagues).[61] Both kinds of functions point toward the parties' objectives of influencing policy making in conformity with their political leanings.

Institutional Tasks

Organizing the Chamber. Party leaders influence congressional organization and procedure. They select the chief administrative officers of the House or Senate, oversee committee jurisdictional revisions, and revise congressional rules. Speaker Gingrich backed the abolition of three standing committees. Speaker Hastert supported a major recodification of House rules, the first since 1880; the recodification was authored by a bipartisan task force headed by Rules Committee chairman David Dreier, R-Calif. Senate majority leader Lott established a bipartisan task force on Senate reform at the start of the 105th

Congress to propose improvements in senatorial operations for consideration during the 106th Congress.[62]

Scheduling Floor Business. "The power of the Speaker of the House is the power of scheduling," Speaker O'Neill once declared.[63] Or, as Newt Gingrich put it, "When you are Speaker you get to set the agenda . . . you get to decide what legislation is up."[64] After consulting with committee leaders, interested members, the president, and others, party leaders decide what, when, and in which order measures should come up for debate. Only weeks after becoming Speaker, Hastert announced that the House would "vote on patient protection legislation in 1999."[65]

Once a bill is scheduled for action, the leaders' job is to see that members vote—a task more difficult than merely herding bodies into the chamber. Party leaders may seek out certain members to speak on an issue because their endorsement can persuade other legislators to support it. Or they may delay action until the bill's sponsors are present. "The leadership must have the right members at the right place at the right time," said Byrd when he was the Senate majority whip.[66] In short, the leaders' scheduling prerogatives mold policy; arranging the time that bills reach the floor can seal their fate. A week's delay in scheduling a controversial White House initiative, for instance, gives the president, lobbying groups, and others additional time to mobilize votes for the proposal.

Sometimes business is scheduled with elections in mind. Measures are postponed to avoid an electorally embarrassing defeat or, alternatively, they are brought to the floor to woo groups allied with each party. What better time to take up legislation revamping the Internal Revenue Service or a constitutional amendment affecting the internal revenue code than April 15, the filing deadline for paying federal income taxes? The period around July 4 is also popular for scheduling consideration of constitutional amendments banning the desecration of the American flag. In short, both parties commonly use the floor as an election platform to raise issues that appeal to their outside partisans. A party that fails to pass something can say to its bedrock supporters, "Look what we tried to do." Conversely, a party can say, "Look what we did for you," when it passes measures advocated by its electoral base.

Influencing Colleagues. Party leaders also have the task of persuading members to support their legislation. In the modern Congress "twisting arms" means pleading and cajoling to coax votes. "If you have no sense of what other people's judgments, values or goals are," stated former Speaker Foley about the negotiating process, "you're in a very poor position to evaluate how you might accommodate them."[67] Although leaders generally seek to influence members of their own party and chamber, they also try to win cooperation from the other chamber and from the opposition party. Majority Leader Lott and Speaker Hastert, and their top aides, meet regularly to coordinate agendas, priorities, and strategies.

Party leaders do not have to rely solely on their powers of persuasion, however. Informal political networks and access to strategic information give them an edge in influencing colleagues:

Because of an improved whip system and because members will respond more candidly to leadership polls than to lobbyist or White House polls, [leaders] have perhaps the most important information in a legislative struggle—information on where the votes are and (sometimes) what it will take to win certain people over.[68]

Top leaders can bestow or withhold a variety of tangible and intangible rewards. They can name legislators to special or select committees, influence assignments to standing committees, aid reelection campaigns, and smooth access to the White House or executive agencies.

Consulting the President. A traditional duty of party leaders is to meet with the president to discuss the administration's goals and to convey legislative sentiment about what the executive branch is doing or not doing. This consultative duty is performed mainly by leaders of the president's party. Presidents also consult with opposition leaders. At the invitation of GOP congressional leaders, President Clinton journeyed to Capitol Hill early in the 105th Congress to meet with Lott, Gingrich, and other Republican leaders. The purpose of the meeting was to find areas of agreement on several priority issues. Nothing much happened until a major breakthrough in May 1997, when both sides supported a plan to balance the budget (see Chapter 13).

Party Tasks

Organizing the Party. Top congressional leaders help to organize their party by selecting partisan colleagues for standing committees, revising party rules, choosing other party leaders, appointing party committees, and influencing policy formation.

Promoting Party Unity. Another leadership assignment is to encourage party unity in Congress on priority legislation. Everett Dirksen (minority leader, 1959–1969) used social gatherings to accomplish this goal:

Dirksen brought party members together in a series of social affairs. He held cocktail parties at a Washington country club, inviting all Republican senators and sometimes their wives too. These were calculated by Dirksen to improve party harmony and to build a friendly feeling for himself with the Republican senators.[69]

But party leaders' assistance to the rank and file goes far beyond extending them social invitations. Leaders schedule members' bills, provide them with timely political information, advise them on electoral issues, visit with their constituents, help them obtain good committee assignments, and work with them to forge policy agendas. Periodically, leaders organize partisan "retreats" where members discuss party and policy goals, consider specific legislative initiatives, air differences, and resolve disputes.

Publicizing Party Views. Leaders are expected to publicize their party's policies and achievements. They give speeches in various forums, appear on radio and television talk shows, write newspaper and journal articles, and hold press

conferences. The spokesperson's role has increased in importance in recent years in part because of the political effect of the mass media. "We've created a situation," noted a scholar, "where the real way you drive the legislative process is by influencing public opinion, rather than by trading for votes."[70]

The House Republican Conference, like the other party caucuses on Capitol Hill, provides its members with "talking points" for meetings with journalists or constituents. In 1995 the GOP Conference distributed informational packets explaining how Republicans can give their constituents confidence concerning the direction the GOP wants to take Medicare reform.[71] An eight-minute video was prepared, and Republicans were encouraged to show it at their town meetings. The video underscored that GOP lawmakers were working to save Medicare, the government's major health program for the elderly, from bankruptcy.[72] Democrats had their own information packets, which told them to emphasize that Republicans were slashing Medicare to pay for tax cuts. The Republicans lost this public relations battle—and nearly control of the 105th House. More successful in publicizing their views, the Democrats persuaded many that the GOP wanted to slash Medicare to provide tax cuts for the wealthy.

Providing Campaign Assistance. Leaders assist party members seeking reelection with campaign funds and endorsements. With Republicans in charge in 1995 for the first time in four decades, GOP lawmakers quickly turned their majority status into a fund-raising advantage. They were soon "eclipsing all records in raising campaign cash and proving the Washington adage that money follows power." Top GOP party leaders used their political clout both "to encourage interest groups to help [GOP] freshmen retire [campaign] debt" and to attract funds for their GOP colleagues' next campaign.[73] In fact, during the 1996 election cycle Republicans for the first time outraised the Democrats in political action committee (PAC) money.[74]

Members anticipating a run for a leadership post distribute campaign funds as standard operating practice. They create their own leadership PACs and donate money to various party candidates. As one account noted about a party leader's ability to raise money, "It seems that the job of fundraiser is becoming more important to senators' expectations of what a majority leader should do. The candidates thus are not trying to buy votes so much as to demonstrate how well they can fulfill that role."[75] The ability to raise funds for colleagues is an increasingly important criterion for judging prospective party leaders and another reminder that leaders stand at the conjunction of the two Congresses: the representative assembly, where money is needed to join, and the lawmaking body, where power calls the shots.

Party Caucuses, Committees, and Informal Groups

House and Senate leaders operate in different institutional contexts. In the larger, more impersonal House, majority party leaders sometimes ignore the wishes of the minority party. This seldom happens in the Senate, which emphasizes individualism, minority rights, reciprocity, and mutual accommoda-

tion. Partisan conflict, as a result, tends to be somewhat more muted than in the House, where bitter party battles are commonplace. Despite these differences between parties in the House and Senate, they are organized into the same three components: caucuses, committees, and informal party groups.

Party Caucuses

The organization of all partisans in a chamber is called the conference or (in the case of House Democrats) the caucus. Party conferences (caucuses) elect leaders, approve committee assignments, provide members with services, and debate party and legislative policies. In an explanation that applies equally well to both parties, a senior House Democrat explained how the caucus can serve to promote consensus on issues:

> The caucus is the place where a great deal of freewheeling debate over an issue takes place and where sometimes a consensus develops. . . . Most of the discussions, although they have taken place at leadership meetings and at chairmen's meetings and in whips' meetings, have ended up in the broader forum of the caucus where every member of the Democratic party partici pates. You don't take a vote, but you try to develop a consensus and make concessions where they're necessary and develop the strongest possible position that can be supported by the maximum number of Democrats.[76]

The House Republican Conference has also been active in working to attract national media attention to Republican priorities. For example, during a Republican Conference, party leaders urged the rank and file "to use TV news shows and 'news magazines' to spread the Republican message about the [federal] programs they feel waste taxpayer money."[77]

In brief, party caucuses are useful forums where party members and leaders can assess and sway sentiment on substantive or procedural issues. On rare occasions, party caucuses vote to strip members of their committee seniority or to oust committee leaders. Committee leaders are removed from their posts when legal action is taken against them (for example, if they are indicted). Sometimes presidents attend their party's House or Senate caucus to "rally the troops." Before the November 1998 elections President Clinton told the House Democratic Caucus, "We plan to raise issues, raise money and raise Cain!"[78]

Party Committees

Each of the four congressional parties establishes committees to serve partisan needs and objectives (see Table 6-1). All four parties on Capitol Hill have policy committees, for example. The committees do not actually make "policy," but they provide advice on scheduling, encourage party unity, research substantive and political issues, distribute policy papers, track party votes on issues, and discuss and implement party policy. Their influence has varied over the years, assuming greater importance when the party does not control the White House and thus needs policy guidance. The two Senate policy committees maintain Web sites that party members and staff can access at any time

Table 6–1 Party Committees in the Senate and House

Committee	Approximate number of members	Function
Senate Democratic		
Policy	24	Considers party positions on specific measures and assists the party leader in scheduling bills
Steering and Coordination	20	Assigns Democrats to committees and works to coordinate policy and legislative issues for the Democratic Conference
Campaign	15	Works to elect Democratic senatorial candidates to the Senate
Technology and Communications	13	Promotes internal and external communications among Democrats
Senate Republican		
Policy	26	Provides summaries of GOP positions on specific issues; researches procedural and substantive issues; drafts policy alternatives
Committee on Committees	9	Assigns Republicans to committees
Campaign	11	Works to elect Republican senatorial candidates to the Senate
House Democratic		
Policy	36	Assists the leadership and Democratic Caucus in establishing, implementing, re-searching, and communicating party priorities
Steering	44	Assigns Democrats to committees
Campaign	40	Aids in electing Democrats to the House
House Republican		
Policy	39	Considers policy alternatives to majority proposals and works for consensus among Republican members
Steering	27	Assigns Republicans to standing committees
Campaign	33	Seeks to elect Republicans to the House

Note: The official names of the parties' campaign committees are as follows: Democratic Senatorial Campaign Committee, National Republican Senatorial Committee, Democratic Congressional Campaign Committee, and National Republican Congressional Committee.

for pertinent information. Other important party panels are the campaign and committee assignment committees.

Informal Party Groups

In addition to party committees, a variety of informal groups operate on Capitol Hill. House and Senate leaders employ party task forces (see Chapter 7) to devise policy alternatives, formulate strategy, and coordinate floor action. In 1998 there were more than 175 informal groups on Capitol Hill (see Chapter 12). They are partisan or bipartisan, unicameral or bicameral in composition. The House Republicans' Conservative Action Team (the CATs) has a strong interest in "lower taxes, smaller government and a rollback of federal regulations."[79] A moderate group of Republicans called the Tuesday Lunch Bunch sometimes opposes the actions of its more conservative colleagues. GOP party leaders have the daunting task of trying to accommodate the concerns of each group, especially given the close partisan division of the 106th House. Banded together, even a half-dozen members can greatly influence the fate of legislation.

Party Continuity and Change

Several features of the contemporary party system on Capitol Hill stand out. Some reflect elements of continuity; others highlight change. Among these features are the vigor of the congressional parties, the persistence of the two-party system, and the advent of new coalition-building practices.

Vigorous Congressional Parties

By any test one can use, the four Capitol Hill parties—Senate and House Democrats, Senate and House Republicans—are flourishing. The organizational elements are healthy and active, leaders are increasingly prominent, and party voting is at relatively high levels. The congressional parties are assisted by well-staffed and professional congressional campaign committees whose ultimate task is either to win or to keep majority control of the House or Senate.[80] These campaign panels recruit and train candidates, raise money, engage in research on the opposition party, target competitive districts, furnish polling advice and services, develop election strategies, and, in general, do everything they can to support congressional campaigns by their party's candidates.[81]

Democrats and Republicans vote along party lines on more issues than ever before. There are several reasons for this trend. (Voting trends are discussed further in Chapter 9.) First, the Democratic Party has become more liberal and the Republican Party more conservative than in the past. As Sen. Orrin Hatch, R-Utah, put it, "Today, most Democrats are far left; most Republicans are to the right; and there are very few in between."[82] Demographic factors largely account for this development, which fosters voting cohesion within each party.

Constituency changes in the South have led to the election of Democrats who are more ideologically compatible with their party colleagues from the rest of the country. The once prominent conservative coalition of Republicans

and southern Democrats no longer is an important voting bloc in today's Congress. The South, as recent elections have shown, is now in the GOP camp. For the first time since Reconstruction, more lawmakers from the South are Republicans than Democrats. Meanwhile, the disappearance of liberal "Rockefeller Republicans" from GOP ranks has led to the dominance of conservative lawmakers in that party.

Second, as voting turnout has gone down, lawmakers from each party are more beholden to activists who vote in the primary and general elections. As a result, lawmakers may be reluctant to vote for bipartisan compromises that antagonize the vocal concerns of well-organized groups, such as the Christian Coalition, the National Rifle Association, or labor unions. As one analyst observed, moderate members of Congress in the Republican Party today,

> even popular incumbents who would win a general election by overwhelming margins, are hostage to the party's right wing. With few exceptions, they are vulnerable because of low turnouts in the primary elections, in which a relative handful of determined conservatives could oust the most popular incumbent while most voters are not paying attention.[83]

The heightened partisanship in Congress—fomented by the legislative and electoral prevalence of "attack politics"—motivates party leaders to demand, and often get, party loyalty on various votes. "Procedure is always a party vote," declared House GOP whip DeLay.[84]

Early in the 105th Congress the rancorous partisan atmosphere got so bad in the House (Speaker Gingrich and Minority Leader Gephardt refused to speak to each other for a year) that a bipartisan group of lawmakers organized a weekend retreat for all members and their families. The so-called civility retreat was designed to allow members with different partisan viewpoints to get to know each other better. This result might then encourage them to work together on a bipartisan basis to resolve the nation's problems. To further ease partisan hostilities, Hastert and Gephardt sponsored another civility retreat early in the 106th Congress. As Rep. Ray LaHood, R-Ill., one of the organizers, said, "Let's face it: The impeachment process [against President Clinton] has caused an awful lot of hard feelings."[85]

There have been episodes of sharp partisanship even in the usually sedate Senate. As Senator Snowe remarked, "The whole Congress has become far more polarized and partisan so it makes it difficult to reach bipartisan agreements. The more significant the issue, the more partisan it becomes."[86]

Under this kind of "policy partisanship," one of the two congressional parties advances substantive measures (abortion rights or affirmative action, for example) to foment political divisions within the other party and to unite their own partisans. "Process partisanship," on the other hand, involves efforts by party leaders to structure the procedural playing field to advance their party's agenda or, alternatively, to stymie the other party's goals.[87] Process partisanship is easier to invoke in the majority-run House (assuming unity within

the majority party) than in the Senate, where power is more evenly divided among all senators. Congress is, in short, a partisan body—perhaps more so than at any time in modern history.

The Two-Party System

The Democratic and Republican parties have dominated American politics and Congress since the mid-nineteenth century. Scholars have posited various theories for the dualistic national politics of a country as diverse as the United States. Some trace the origins of the national two-party system to early conflicts between Federalists (advocates of a strong national government) and Antifederalists (advocates of limited national government). This dualism continued in subsequent splits: North versus South, East versus West, agricultural versus financial interests, and rural versus urban areas.[88] Constitutional, political, and legal arrangements are other bases of the two-party system. Plurality elections in single-member congressional districts encouraged the creation and maintenance of two major parties. Under the winner-take-all principle, the person who wins the most votes in a state or district is elected to the Senate or House. This principle discourages the formation of third parties. In addition, many states have laws that make it difficult to create new parties.

Although partisanship is rampant on Capitol Hill, the trend is toward an increasingly independent-minded, ticket-splitting, nonpartisan electorate. The registration of more casual voters unaffiliated with any party, the political alienation of young voters, and candidate-centered elections are among the reasons for this development.[89] Neither party has solidified its control of the legislative branch. Therefore, congressional parties strive to appeal to the relatively small group in the electorate that can tip the balance of power their way. Both legislative parties jockey constantly to win public credit for their agenda and issue positions.

Whatever mix of causes produced the two-party system, one thing is clear: few third-party or independent legislators have been elected to Congress during the twentieth century. The 63d Congress (1913–1915) had the greatest minor-party membership during this century: one Progressive senator and nineteen representatives elected as Progressives, Progressive-Republicans, or independents. Since 1951 only three senators and four representatives have been elected from minor parties or as independents. Most legislators convert to one of the major parties or vote with them on organizational matters, which hinge on party control. Third-party members have no institutional status. Their participation in Democratic or Republican affairs is "by invitation only."

Rep. Bernard Sanders of Vermont, first elected in 1990, is the only independent to serve in Congress in four decades (and the first Socialist since 1923). Sanders contemplated joining the Democratic Caucus, but some party members objected that having a self-described Socialist in their midst might damage the party's image and cause reelection problems for Democrats in conservative districts. Although he did not become a member of the caucus, Sanders was assigned committees by the Democrats and usually votes with them.

Advances in Coalition Building

To get the legislative results they desire, party leaders increasingly use media strategies, omnibus bills, and strategic planning. Procedural innovations also are important elements in the arsenal of the party leaders. (Multiple referrals and ad hoc task forces will be discussed in Chapter 7. Creative "rules" from the House Rules Committee and innovative unanimous consent agreements in the Senate will be discussed in Chapter 8.)

Media Strategies. Party leaders understand that media strategies (the use of the press, television, radio, polls, speeches, and so on) are essential to move or block legislation. They form "issue teams," "message groups," or "theme teams" to orchestrate and organize political events and communications strategies that promote the party's message to the general public. No longer is the "inside" game—working behind the scenes to line up votes—sufficient to pass major, controversial measures. Also necessary is the "outside" game—influencing public opinion and creating grassroots support for policy initiatives.

In the 105th Congress Senate Democratic leader Tom Daschle orchestrated a successful media campaign for legislation aiding flood victims in the Midwest and the Dakotas. Congressional Republicans added two controversial "riders" (unrelated policy proposals) to the disaster relief bill. President Clinton carried out his promise to veto the bill if the riders (one dealing with the automatic funding of government programs and the other blocking use of statistical sampling for the 2000 census) were included in the legislation.

To dramatize the plight of the flood victims, many of whom were living in temporary shelters, the Daschle-led Democrats had planned to use the Senate floor, but Majority Leader Lott adjourned the Senate three times in one week to prevent that from happening. Therefore, "Daschle turned his office into a media center, calling on twenty-four Senate Democrats and sixteen House Democrats to stage an all-night vigil in which they took to the airwaves to plead for relief for Midwest flood victims."[90] With the polls and media blaming Republicans for delaying aid to the flood victims, the GOP Congress capitulated to the Democrats. The riders were dropped and a "clean" bill was sent to the White House where it was signed into law.

Omnibus Bills. A phenomenon of modern lawmaking is the rise of megabills—legislation that is hundreds or thousands of pages in length. Many of Congress's most significant policy enactments are sometimes folded into four or five omnibus bills. There are many reasons that account for the use of these "packages." For instance, some initiatives are incorporated into megabills to improve their chances of enactment. Bundling popular programs with painful spending cuts increases the chances of enacting megabills. This tactic limits the number of difficult votes lawmakers cast and provides them with political cover. Members can explain to angry constituents or groups that they had to support the "indivisible" whole because its discrete parts were not open to separate votes.

Joining several bills may increase the chances of garnering more support. (The reverse concern is that a megabill may attract a "coalition of minorities"

with the votes needed to reject the measure.) "Sweeteners" can be added to woo supporters, or provisions that are unable to win majority support in stand-alone bills can be buried in megabills. Megabills can also strengthen Congress's leverage with the executive branch. Recognizing that the Clinton administration wanted Congress to provide funds for the International Monetary Fund (IMF), House conservatives blocked the IMF bill until the White House accepted the abortion restrictions on international family planning that were contained in the measure. Secretary of State Madeleine K. Albright called this tactic "legislative blackmail."[91]

Party leaders command the resources and authority to exercise coordinative and substantive influence over the packaging process. "Omnibus bills place a huge amount of power in the hands of a few key leaders and their staffs," remarked one House member.[92] As a result, rank-and-file members look to party leaders for assistance in formulating a package acceptable to at least a majority of members. House and Senate leaders often appoint ad hoc party task forces to mobilize support behind these priority matters.

Strategic Planning and Coordination. On major policy issues, strategic planning and coordination are crucial to the leadership's ability to forge successful coalitions. The top House and Senate leaders meet regularly with their partisan allies to craft their plans, to anticipate the legislative moves of the opposition, and to develop their countermoves. At the beginning of the 106th Congress, Speaker Hastert unveiled a nine-point legislative agenda during a well-staged press conference. The agenda was deliberately structured to attract bipartisan support. It was "designed in part to finesse the opposition with their own issues, leaving Democrats limited opportunity to make their case for change [in the 2000] election."[93] Hastert holds "biweekly strategy sessions with committee chairmen" and, with an eye toward strengthening House-Senate coordination and communication, has invited a senior aide of Senate majority leader Lott to attend the House GOP leadership's weekly meetings.[94]

The minority Democrats also engage in strategic calculations, especially as they contemplate the elections of 2000. They need six more seats to win back the House. Should Democrats work to pin the "do nothing" label on the 106th House by using parliamentary "guerrilla warfare" tactics to slow down the GOP agenda or by making policy demands that Republicans are unlikely to accept? Or should they cooperate with Republicans so that the 106th House can produce significant legislative successes? As Rep. Barney Frank, D-Mass., once said:

> How do you govern in a relatively noncontroversial way . . . and simultaneously frame an appeal to the public so when the [legislative and political] breakout happens, it's your side that's in the majority?[95]

Conclusion

Congressional parties have elaborate organizations, and their leaders fulfill a multiplicity of roles and duties. The Senate majority leader, explained

Byrd when he held that post, "facilitates, he constructs, he programs, he schedules, he takes an active part in the development of legislation, he steps in at crucial moments on the floor, offers amendments, speaks on behalf of legislation and helps to shape the outcome of the legislation."[96] Party leaders can do many things, but they cannot command their colleagues. Their leadership rests chiefly on their skill in providing others with reasons to follow them.

As we have seen, the "party principle" organizes Congress. The "committee principle," however, shapes the measures Congress acts upon. These two principles are often in conflict. The first emphasizes aggregation, the second fragmentation. Party leaders struggle to manage an institution that disperses policy-making authority to numerous work groups. In short, leaders provide the centripetal force to offset committees' centrifugal influence.

Two faces of committee work. Above, House Commerce chair Thomas J. Bliley Jr. of Virginia confers with ranking Democrat (and former chair) John D. Dingell of Michigan. Below, the Senate Foreign Relations Committee holds a public hearing in the Hart Office Building. Behind the senators are staff aides, and between the senators and the witnesses are the press photographers—mediators between the "two Congresses."

7

Committees: Workshops of Congress

Committees serve two broad purposes: individual and institutional. Individually, lawmakers look for ways from their committee perches to benefit their constituents. "As far as I can see, there is really only one basic reason to be on a public works committee," admitted a House member. "Intellectual stimulation" is not it. "Most of all, I want to be able to bring home projects to my district."[1] With scores of representatives seeking assignment to this panel, it has grown to be the largest (seventy-five members) in congressional history. Members of Congress understand the reelection connection between their committee assignments and their electoral opportunities.

Committees also enable legislators to utilize or develop expertise in areas that interest them. A former teacher, for instance, may seek assignment to the education committee. And some panels, such as the tax and appropriations "power committees," enable members to wield personal influence among their colleagues. Members ask to be on the House Appropriations Committee, explained Rep. Dick Armey, R-Texas, because "instantaneously . . . they have a host of new friends, and we all know why": that panel controls the distribution of discretionary federal money.[2]

Institutionally, committees are the centers of policy making, oversight of federal agencies, and public education (largely through the hearings they hold). By dividing their membership into a number of "little legislatures," the House and Senate are able to consider dozens of proposed laws simultaneously.[3] Without committees a legislative body of 100 senators and 440 House members could not handle roughly 10,000 bills and nearly 100,000 nominations biennially, a national budget of around $1.8 trillion, and a limitless array of controversial issues. Although floor actions often refine legislation, committees are the means by which Congress sifts through an otherwise impossible jumble of bills, proposals, and issues.

Congressional committees serve another important institutional function in our political system: they act as "safety valves," or outlets for national debates and controversies. Military and economic responsibilities, demographic shifts, trade agreements, global environmental concerns, the drug war, the social dislocations caused by technological advances, and the rising cost of health care place enormous strains on the political system. As forums for public debates, congressional committees help to vent, absorb, and resolve these strains. Moreover, the safety-valve function gives the citizenry a greater sense of participation in national decision making and helps educate members about public problems.

The individual and institutional purposes of the committee system can conflict. Because members tend to gravitate to committees for constituency or career reasons, they are not the most impartial judges of the policies they authorize. "It's one of the weaknesses of the system that those attracted to a committee like Agriculture are those whose constituents benefit from farm programs," acknowledged Sen. Charles E. Schumer, a Democrat from New York. "And so they're going to support those programs and they're not going to want to cut them, even the ones that are wasteful."[4]

The Purposes of Committees

Senator Schumer's comment highlights an ongoing debate about the development and fundamental purposes of the committee system. To explain the organization of legislatures, scholars have advanced the distributional, informational, and party hypotheses.

The *distributional hypothesis* suggests that legislatures create committees to give lawmakers policy influence in areas critical to their reelection. Members seek committee assignments to "bring home the bacon" (public goods and services) to their constituents. Because lawmakers self-select these kinds of committees, the committees become filled with what scholars call "preference outliers" —members whose homogeneous preferences for benefits to their constituents put them out of step with the heterogeneous views of the membership as a whole. Chamber majorities, in brief, may need to rein in overreaching committees by rejecting or amending their recommended actions.[5]

The Agriculture Committees, among others, illustrate the distributional hypothesis. An important challenge for Republicans in the 104th Congress was whether they could cut subsidies for farm programs that benefit their rural supporters. But so many GOP farm-state lawmakers on the House Agriculture Committee opposed crop-subsidy cuts that Republican leaders had to step in to ensure that the reductions would be made. "If we can't cut federal spending on programs that benefit our own constituencies, I don't see how we get to a balanced budget," said Rep. Dan Miller, R-Fla.[6]

The *informational hypothesis* proposes that legislative bodies establish committees to provide lawmakers with the specialized expertise required to make informed judgments in a complex world. Furthermore, the division of labor under the committee system augments Congress's role in relation to the executive branch. Rather than being composed primarily of preference outliers, committees under this model will consist of a diverse membership with wide-ranging perspectives. The basic goal of committees, then, is to formulate policies that resolve national problems.[7]

The *party hypothesis* views committee members as agents of their party caucuses. According to this perspective, committee members are expected to support their party's programs.

Needless to say, the committee system encompasses aspects of all three models. Lawmakers are concerned with local issues, but every district and state is also affected by broad national concerns—the condition of the econ-

Three Views on the Role of Committees

Political scientist Forrest Maltzman has described three common views of committees: the committee autonomy perspective, the chamber dominated perspective, and the party dominated perspective.

The committee autonomy perspective portrays committees as "autonomous units that are able to control policy outcomes pertaining to their jurisdictions. Since members are allocated their committee seats in a fashion that is unresponsive to the chamber's policy preferences, and, after being assigned, . . . accept committee norms and receive biased information, [they may] . . . advance policies that are contrary to the preferences of the chamber as a whole." According to this view, the committee system is "a locus of institutionalized parochialism and logrolling."

The chamber dominated perspective is based on the premise that members of the House want to belong to an effective institution and create good public policy. "In order to accomplish these goals, the institution needs information and expertise. Through the division of labor, the committee system provides such expertise," explains Maltzman. As a check on the committees' use of their position to benefit their own members, "the chamber retains the right to amend or reject committee recommendations and, if necessary, abolish or restructure its committees."

The party dominated perspective is based upon two premises: all members of Congress seek electoral success for their party, and this success depends upon a party's capacity to form and enact a platform. According to this view, "the party caucuses organize the chamber so as to promote the party agenda. In order to prevent contingents from shirking their collective party responsibilities, the party appoints loyal members to committees and punishes those that ignore the needs of the party."

Source: Based on Forrest Maltzman, "Committee-Chamber-Party Relations in the Post-Reform House" (Paper presented at the annual meeting of the Midwest Political Science Association, Chicago, April 9–11, 1992), 2–3. See also Forrest Maltzman, *Competing Principals: Committees, Parties and the Organization of Congress* (Ann Arbor: University of Michigan Press, 1997), chap. 2.

---

omy and the environment, for example. Issues may lend themselves on occasion more to the distributional than to the informational or party theory of policy making. (For a review of comparable hypotheses, see box, this page.)

Because good public policy may be impeded by the parochial orientations of individual members, Congress has a small number of "control," or centralizing, committees that promote institutional and policy integration over committee and programmatic particularism. For example, each house has a Budget Committee, which proposes limits on how much Congress can spend for designated functional areas.[8]

However committees are characterized, they focus and concentrate the policy and oversight activities of individual lawmakers. In this chapter we will show how committees fit into the theme of the "two Congresses"—the lawmaking institution and the representative assembly. We also will address the following questions: How have committees changed since the First Congress? What are the different types of committees, and how are members assigned to

them? What reforms have transformed the workings of the committee system? How do committees make policy, and what duties do the staffs perform? In short, we will describe what happens in these busy workshops of Congress.

Evolution of the Committee System

Committees in the early Congresses generally were temporary panels created for specific tasks. Proposals were considered on the House or Senate floor and then were referred to specially created panels that worked out the details—the reverse order of today's system. The Senate, for example, would "debate a subject at length on the floor and, after the majority's desires had been crystallized, might appoint a committee to put those desires into bill form."[9] About 350 ad hoc committees were formed during the Third Congress (1793–1795) alone.[10] The parent chamber closely controlled these temporary committees: it assigned them clear-cut tasks, required them to report back favorably or unfavorably, and dissolved them when they had completed their work.

The Senate by about 1816—and the House a bit later—had developed a system of permanent, or standing, committees, some of which are still in existence. Standing committees, as historian DeAlva Alexander explained, were better suited than ad hoc groups to cope with the larger membership and wider scope of congressional business. Another scholar, George Haynes, pointed out that the "needless inconvenience of the frequent choice of select committees" taxed congressional patience. Lawmakers recognized that debating bills one at a time before the whole chamber simply was an inefficient way of processing Congress's legislative business. Perhaps, too, legislators came to value standing committees as counterweights to presidential influence in setting the legislative agenda.[11]

Permanent committees changed the way Congress made policy and allocated authority: the House and Senate now reviewed and voted upon recommendations made by specialized, experienced committees. Standing committees also encouraged oversight of the executive branch. Members have called them "the eye, the ear, the hand, and very often the brain" of Congress.[12]

As committees acquired expertise and authority, they became increasingly self-reliant and resistant to chamber and party control. After the House revolted against Republican Speaker Joseph G. Cannon in 1910, power flowed to the committee chairmen, who took on substantial powers. Along with a few strong party leaders, they held sway over House and Senate policy making during much of the twentieth century. In rare instances committee members rebelled and diminished the chairman's authority. But most members heeded the advice that Speaker John McCormack (1962–1971) gave to freshmen: "Whenever you pass a committee chairman in the House, you bow from the waist. I do."[13]

The chairmen's authority was buttressed by the custom of seniority that flourished with the rise of congressional careerism. The majority party member with the most years of continuous service on a committee automatically be-

came its chairman. There were no other qualifications, such as ability or party loyalty. As a result, committee chairmen owed little or nothing to party leaders, much less to presidents. This automatic selection process produced experienced, independent chairmen but concentrated authority in a few hands. The "have nots" wanted a piece of the action and objected that seniority promoted the competent and incompetent alike. They objected, too, that the system promoted members from "safe" one-party areas—especially conservative southern Democrats and midwestern Republicans—who could ignore party policies or national sentiments.

The late 1960s and 1970s saw a rapid influx of new members, many from the cities and suburbs, who opposed the conservative status quo. Allying themselves with more senior members seeking a stronger voice in Congress, they pushed through changes that diffused power and shattered seniority as an absolute criterion for leadership posts. Today House and Senate committee chairmen (and ranking minority members) must be elected by their party colleagues. No longer free to wield arbitrary authority, they must abide by committee and party rules and be sensitive to majority sentiment within their party's caucus or conference. For example, the House Republican Conference adopted party rules for the 106th Congress that state, "The Chairman on each committee has an obligation to ensure that each measure on which the Republican Conference has taken a position is managed in accordance with such position on the Floor of the House of Representatives."

Types of Committees

Congress today has a shopper's bazaar of committees—standing, select, joint, and conference—and within each of these general types there are variations. Standing committees, for example, can be characterized as *authorizing* or *appropriating* panels. Authorizing committees (Agriculture, Banking, Commerce, and so on) are the policy-making centers on Capitol Hill. As substantive committees, they propose solutions to public problems and advocate what they believe to be the necessary levels of spending for the programs under their jurisdictions. The House and Senate Appropriations Committees recommend how much money agencies and programs will receive. Unsurprisingly, there is continuing conflict between the two types of panels. Typically, authorizers press for full funding for their recommendations, while appropriators are in the habit of recommending lower spending levels (see Chapter 13).

Standing Committees

A *standing committee* is a permanent entity created by public law or House or Senate rules. Standing committees continue from Congress to Congress, except in those infrequent instances when they are eliminated or new ones are created. Table 7-1 compares the standing committees in the 106th Congress in terms of their sizes, party ratios, and number of subcommittees.

Standing committees process the bulk of Congress's daily and annual agenda of business. Seldom are measures considered on the House or Senate

Table 7-1 Standing Committees of the House and Senate, 106th
Congress (1999–2001)

Committee	Size and party ratio	Number of subcommittees
	House	
Agriculture	51 (R 27/D 24)	4
Appropriations	61 (R 34/D 27)	13
Armed Services	60 (R 32/D 28)	5
Banking and Financial Services	59 (R 32/D 27)	5
Budget	43 (R 24/D 19)	—
Commerce	53 (R 29/D 24)	5
Education and the Workforce	49 (R 27/D 22)	5
Government Reform	43 (R 24/D 19)	7
House Administration	9 (R 6/D 3)	—
International Relations	49 (R 26/D 23)	5
Judiciary	37 (R 21/D 16)	5
Resources	52 (R 28/D 24)	5
Rules	13 (R 9/D 4)	2
Science	47 (R 25/D 22)	4
Small Business	36 (R 19/D 17)	5
Standards of Official Conduct	10 (R 5/D 5)	—
Transportation and Infrastructure	75 (R 41/D 34)	6
Veterans' Affairs	31 (R 17/D 14)	3
Ways and Means	39 (R 23/D 16)	5
	Senate	
Agriculture, Nutrition, and Forestry	18 (R 10/D 8)	4
Appropriations	28 (R 15/D 13)	13
Armed Services	20 (R 11/D 9)	6
Banking, Housing, and Urban Affairs	20 (R 11/D 9)	5
Budget	22 (R 12/D 10)	—
Commerce, Science, and Transportation	20 (R 11/D 9)	7
Energy and Natural Resources	20 (R 11/D 9)	4
Environment and Public Works	18 (R 10/D 8)	4
Finance	20 (R 11/D 9)	5
Foreign Relations	18 (R 10/D 8)	7
Governmental Affairs	16 (R 9/D 7)	3
Health, Education, Labor and Pensions	18 (R 10/D 8)	4
Judiciary	18 (R 10/D 8)	7
Rules and Administration	16 (R 9/D 7)	—
Small Business	18 (R 10/D 8)	—
Veterans' Affairs	12 (R 7/D 5)	—

Source: CQ Weekly, March 13, 1999.

floor without first being referred to, and approved by, the appropriate committees. Put negatively, committees are the burial ground for most legislation. Stated positively, committees select from the thousands of measures introduced in each Congress those that merit floor debate. Of the hundreds of bills that clear committees, fewer still are enacted into law.

Sizes and Ratios. At the beginning of each new Congress, each chamber adopts two separate resolutions, one offered by the Democrats and the other by the Republicans, that elect members to the committees and thus set their sizes and ratios (the number of majority and minority members on a panel). In practice, committee sizes and ratios are set in the House by the majority leadership and are negotiated in the Senate by the majority and minority leaders. In the 1996 elections Democrats lost a net of two seats in the Senate, changing the party ratio from 53–47 in the 104th Congress to 55–45 in the 105th. Because of their party's weaker position, Senate Democratic leaders "agreed to let the majority have a two-seat advantage on all major committees to reflect the GOP's 55–45 advantage. Republicans had held a one-seat advantage on key panels."[14] Because there was no change in the partisan makeup of the Senate following the 1998 elections, the ratios on committees stayed virtually the same for the 106th Senate.

The House was a different story. Democrats picked up five seats after the 1998 elections, and their leaders negotiated for weeks with their GOP counterparts to increase Democratic representation on the standing committees. The ranking Democrat on the Rules Committee, for example, complained that Republicans controlled 54.9 percent of all committee seats with only 51 percent of the House's membership. "The Republican leadership has taken 30 committee seats away from Democratic Members," complained Rep. Joe Moakley, D-Mass.[15] GOP leaders provided a few additional committee seats, far short of what the Democrats wanted. There was little GOP support for changing the ratios because some Republicans might have been "bumped" from their committee places to make room for the Democrats added. As one Republican said, "We have to let them make their noise and voice their outrage and eventually that goes away."[16]

In the Senate, noted for more reciprocity and comity among members, panels may be enlarged to accommodate senators seeking membership on the same committees. Or senators may be granted waivers from Senate rules limiting them to service on no more than two major standing committees. Waivers are sometimes granted to permit senators to sit on an extra major committee that they deem important to their reelection prospects. This is another example of the "two Congresses," the institution bending to suit individual preferences.

House committee enlargements are engineered, scholars suggest, by majority party leaders who want to accommodate their colleagues' preferences. They recognize that party harmony can be maintained by boosting the number of committee seats. When he was Speaker (1995–1999), Newt Gingrich, R-Ga., expanded the number of slots to entice conservative Democrats to

switch parties. At the beginning of the 104th Congress, he allowed five representatives who switched to the GOP in 1995—all southerners—to keep the seniority they had accumulated as Democrats rather than to be assigned, as custom usually dictates, to the last slot on the panel's GOP membership roster. In the Senate Ben Nighthorse Campbell of Colorado and Richard Shelby of Alabama switched to the Republican Party after the 1994 elections.

Party ratios influence committee work as much as panel size does. Biennial election results frame the bargaining between majority and minority leaders. On most committees, ratios normally reflect party strength in the full House or Senate. Because the majority party has the votes, it can be the final arbiter if the minority protests its allotment of committee seats. If the full committee is "stacked" against the minority, that situation will repeat itself in subcommittee assignments. Other practices can affect ratios. Some House committees, such as Appropriations, Budget, Rules, and Ways and Means, traditionally have disproportionate ratios to ensure majority party control.

Subcommittees. Subcommittees perform much of the day-to-day lawmaking and oversight work of Congress. Like standing committees, these subunits of committees vary widely in rules and procedures, staff arrangements, modes of operations, and relationships with other subcommittees and the full committee. Subcommittees are created for various reasons, such as lawmakers' need to subdivide a committee's wide ranging policy domain into manageable pieces, their desire to chair these panels and to have a platform to shape the legislative agenda, and their wish to respond to the policy claims of specialized constituencies. During the 106th Congress the nineteen House standing committees together created eighty-four subcommittees; the sixteen Senate standing committees collectively established sixty-nine subcommittees (see Table 7-1).

Under House rules adopted in 1999, Republicans limited all standing committees (except Appropriations, Government Reform, and Transportation and Infrastructure) to no more than five subcommittees. However, committees may create a sixth subcommittee provided that it is devoted to oversight. This move, championed by Speaker Dennis Hastert, R-Ill., was intended to encourage his GOP-run committees to shift from political oversight (the search for scandal in the Democratic administration) to programmatic oversight (evaluating agency and program performance). Another House rule limits members to no more than four subcommittees. These limits on the number of subcommittees for each standing committee and subcommittee assignment restrictions for each member are designed to make Congress "more deliberative, participatory, and manageable by reducing scheduling conflicts and jurisdictional overlap."[17]

In stark contrast to the practice when Democrats ran the House, GOP committee chairmen manage their committees without having to contend with independent subcommittee chairmen. The chairmen run their panels as they see fit. As House Commerce chairman Thomas J. Bliley Jr., R-Va., stated, the "chairman controls the staff, the chairman has the right to name subcommittee chairmen and has much more power than the . . . Democratic chairmen [had] when they were in the majority."[18]

Although silent on the number of subcommittees that standing committees may establish, Senate rules set subcommittee assignment limits for senators and prohibit them from chairing more than one subcommittee on any one committee. Unsurprisingly, the number of subcommittees often equals the number of majority party members on a committee. On occasion, the Senate grants waivers so that senators may chair an extra subcommittee if, for example, there are more subcommittees than majority party senators. Under a GOP Conference rule most standing committee chairmen are prohibited from chairing any subcommittee.

Select, or Special, Committees

Select, or special, committees (the terms are interchangeable) are usually temporary panels that go out of business after the two-year life of the Congress in which they were created. But some select committees take on the attributes of permanent committees. The House, for example, has a Permanent Select Intelligence Committee. Select committees usually do not have legislative authority (the right to receive and report out measures); they can only study, investigate, and make recommendations. In 1998 the House created a select committee to investigate China's attempts to acquire U.S. military technology, and the Senate established a special committee to address the year 2000 technology problem. (Computers programmed to recognize only the last two digits of a year might assume that January 1, 2000, was January 1, 1900.)

Select panels are created for several reasons. First, they accommodate the concerns of individual members. The chairmen of these panels may attract publicity that enhances their political careers. For example, Harry S. Truman of Missouri came to the public's (and President Franklin Roosevelt's) attention as head of a special Senate committee investigating World War II military procurement practices. Second, special panels can be a point of access for interest groups, such as the elderly and owners of small businesses. Third, select committees supplement the standing committee system by overseeing and investigating issues that the permanent panels lack time for or prefer to ignore. Finally, select committees can be set up to coordinate consideration of issues that overlap the jurisdictions of several standing committees. This approach is intended to reduce jurisdictional bickering.

Joint Committees

Joint committees, which include members from both chambers, have been used since the First Congress for study, investigation, oversight, and routine activities. Unless their composition is prescribed in statute, House members of joint committees are appointed by the Speaker, and senators are appointed by that chamber's presiding officer. (See Chapter 6 for a discussion of the persons who can serve as the Senate's presiding officer.) The chairmanship of joint committees rotates each Congress between House and Senate members. In 2000 there were four joint committees: Economic, Library, Printing, and Taxation. The Joint Library Committee and the Joint Printing Committee

oversee, respectively, the Library of Congress and the Government Printing Office. The Joint Taxation Committee is essentially a "holding company" for staff who work closely with the tax-writing committees of each house. The Joint Economic Committee conducts studies and hearings on a wide range of domestic and international economic issues.

Conference Committees

Before legislation can be sent to the president to be signed, it must pass both the House and the Senate in identical form. Conference committees, sometimes called the "third house of Congress," reconcile differences between similar measures passed by both chambers. They are composed of members from each house. A representative highlighted their importance:

> When I came to Congress I had no comprehension of the importance of the conference committees which actually write legislation. We all knew that important laws are drafted there, but I don't think one person in a million has any appreciation of their importance and the process by which they work. Part of the explanation, of course, is that there never is a printed record of what goes on in conference.[19]

Conference bargaining roughly can be classified in four ways: *traditional, offer-counteroffer, subconference,* and *pro forma.* Traditional conferences are those in which the participants meet face to face, haggle among themselves about the items in bicameral disagreement, and then reach an accord. The bulk of conferences are of this type. In offer-counteroffer conferences, often used by the tax-writing committees, one side suggests a compromise proposal; the other side recesses to discuss it in private and then returns to present a counteroffer. Conferences with numerous participants (on omnibus bills, for example) usually break into small units, or subconferences, to reconcile particular matters or to address special topics. Pro forma conferences are those in which issues are resolved informally—by preconference negotiations between conferee leaders or their staffs. The conference itself then ratifies the earlier decisions.[20]

Some scholars argue that congressional committees are influential because they possess unilateral authority at the conference stage to veto or negotiate alterations in legislation. Others dispute this contention and claim that the so-called "ex post veto is not a significant institutional foundation of congressional committee power."[21] Another model suggests that conferees serve as agents of their respective chamber majorities and advocate their policy positions rather than committee viewpoints.[22] Increasingly, the top party leaders in each chamber are taking a more direct and active role in determining who should (or should not) be a conferee. (Selection of conferees, rules changes affecting conference committees, and conference reports are discussed in Chapter 8.)

The Assignment Process

Every congressional election sets off a scramble for committee seats. As noted earlier, legislators understand the linkage between winning desirable as-

signments and winning elections. Newly elected representatives and senators quickly make their preferences known to party leaders, to members of the panels that make committee assignments, and to others. At the same time, incumbents may be trying to move to more prestigious panels.

The Pecking Order

The most powerful, and so most desirable, standing committees are House Ways and Means and Senate Finance, which pass on tax measures, and the House and Senate Appropriations Committees, which hold the federal purse strings. The Budget Committees, established in 1974, also have become sought-after assignments because of their important role in economic and fiscal matters and their guardianship of the congressional budgeting process.

Among those that seldom have waiting lists are the Senate Ethics and House Standards of Official Conduct Committees. The House and Senate ethics panels are required to have an equal number of Democrats and Republicans. These committees in both chambers are unpopular because legislators are reluctant to sit in judgment of their colleagues. "Members have never competed for the privilege of serving on the ethics committee, and I am no exception," remarked Rep. Howard L. Berman, D-Calif., after Democratic leader Richard A. Gephardt of Missouri prevailed on him to join the ethics panel. Or as Rep. James V. Hansen, R-Utah, said after serving as ethics chairman during the 105th Congress, "I've paid my debt to society. It's time for me to be paroled."[23]

The attractiveness of committees can change. The House Science Committee, not considered a popular assignment in past years, attracted keen interest in the 1990s in part because of President Clinton's emphasis on high-tech investment and lawmakers' desire to woo scientific projects and jobs to their districts.[24]

Preferences and Politicking

In an analysis of six House committees, Richard F. Fenno Jr. found that three basic goals of lawmakers—reelection, influence within the House, and good public policy—affect the committee assignments that members seek. Reelection-oriented members were attracted to committees such as Resources (then called the Interior Committee). Appropriations and Ways and Means attracted influence-oriented members. Policy-oriented members sought membership on what are now called the Education and the Workforce Committee and the International Relations Committee. Members with similar goals find themselves on the same committees, Fenno concluded. This homogeneity of perspectives may result in harmonious but biased committees.[25]

Since Fenno's study, scholars have elaborated on the relationship between members' goals and committee assignments. They have divided House committees into reelection (or constituency), policy, and power panels and concur that some mix of the three goals motivates most activity on the committees. They agree too that members' goals "are less easily characterized in the Senate than in the House."[26] Almost every senator has the opportunity to serve on one

Table 7-2 House and Senate Committee Comparison

Category	House	Senate
Number of standing committees	19	16
Committee assignments per member	About 5	About 7
Power or prestige committees	Appropriations, Budget, Commerce, Rules, Ways and Means	Appropriations, Armed Services, Commerce, Finance [a]
Treaties and nominations submitted by the president	No authority	Committees review
Floor debate	Representatives' activity is somewhat confined to the bills reported from the panels on which they serve	Senators can choose to influence any policy area regardless of their committee assignments
Committee consideration of legislation	More difficult to bypass	Easier to bypass [b]
Committee chairmen	Subject to party and speakership influence that limits their discretionary authority over committee operations	Somewhat freer rein to manage committees
Committee staff	Less assertive in advocating ideas and proposals	More aggressive in shaping the legislative agenda
Subcommittee chairmanships	Representatives of the majority party usually must wait at least one term	Majority senators, regardless of their seniority, usually chair subcommittees

[a] Almost every senator is assigned to one of these committees.
[b] For example, by allowing "riders"—unrelated policy proposals—to measures pending on the floor.

of these top committees: Appropriations, Armed Services, Commerce, and Finance. Hence the power associated with a particular committee assignment is less important for senators than for representatives (see Table 7-2).

In the weeks after an election, members campaign vigorously for the committees they prefer. Freshman representative Robert B. Aderholt, R-Ala., elected in 1996, set out to win a coveted spot on the Appropriations Committee. He solicited the help of Majority Leader Dick Armey, R-Texas, and lobbied

each member who sat on the GOP's committee assignment panel. "It was almost like this was another congressional campaign," Aderholt explained. "While a lot of [new] members were driving around house hunting and interviewing staff members, I was working" to win appointment to Appropriations.[27] Rep. Jennifer Dunn, R-Wash., provided all incoming GOP freshmen with a "how to" booklet on securing committee assignments. She suggested a three-part strategy emphasizing personal, political, and geographical factors. For example, Dunn suggested face-to-face meetings with members of the Steering Committee, letters and phone calls to committee chairmen, and personal contact with party leaders. "Do not be afraid to go to each Member of the Leadership to let them know of your political needs. Leadership has proven . . . open to placing freshmen Members on key committees," she advised the newcomers. Dunn also suggested that the freshmen seek help from key GOP members in their state or region.[28]

Although both parties try to accommodate assignment preferences, some members inevitably receive unwelcome assignments. A classic case involved Democratic representative Shirley Chisholm of Brooklyn (1969–1983), the first African American woman elected to Congress. She was assigned to the House Agriculture Committee her first year in the House. "I think it would be hard to imagine an assignment that is less relevant to my background or to the needs of the predominantly black and Puerto Rican people who elected me," she said. Chisholm's protests won her a seat on the Veterans' Affairs Committee. "There are a lot more veterans in my district than there are trees," she later observed.[29] Yet some urban lawmakers welcome service on the Agriculture Committee, where they can fuse metropolitan issues with rural issues through food stamp, consumer, and other legislation.

How Assignments Are Made

Each party in each house has its own panel to review members' committee requests and hand out assignments: the Steering Committee for House Republicans, the Steering Committee for House Democrats, the Republican Committee on Committees for Senate Republicans, and the Steering and Coordination Committee for Senate Democrats (see boxes, pp. 210 and 211). The decisions of these panels are the first and most important acts in a three-step procedure. The second step involves approval of the assignment lists by each party's caucus. Finally, there is pro forma election by the full House or Senate.

Formal Criteria. Both formal and informal criteria guide the assignment panels in choosing committee members. Formal criteria are designed to ensure that each member is treated equitably in committee assignments. For example, the House Republican Conference divides committees into three classes: exclusive, nonexclusive, and exempt. A member assigned to an exclusive panel (Appropriations, Budget, Commerce, Rules, and Ways and Means) may not serve on any other standing committee unless the GOP Conference waives this party rule for certain members. Republicans may serve on only two nonexclu-

The Senate GOP Assignment Process

Briefly, the [Senate committee assignment] procedure generally works like this: after the election the total number of Republicans and Democrats are compared to determine a ratio. That ratio is then applied to each of the various committees, and adjustments in the size of the committee and the Republican/Democrat ratio are made.

The vacancies caused by the election results, plus any changes in the number of seats each party controls, provide the actual number of vacancies for the next Congress. A list of all committees and vacancies is compiled. Each Republican Senator and Senator-elect is asked to notify the Committee on Committees as to their preferences for committee assignment. Incumbent Senators may indicate that they wish to retain their current committee assignments, or they may want to move from one committee to another. If they want to change, they indicate in writing the committee(s) they wish to relinquish and their preferences, in order of priority, for new assignment. Newly elected Senators indicate, in order of priority, their desired assignments.

These letters are all compiled, through the use of a computer, into a list indicating each Senator, beginning with the most senior member, and on down the line, with his or her committee preferences.

When the Committee on Committees meets, after the reorganization of the Republican leadership, the two lists are compared. The Committee looks at the letter from the most senior Senator. If he requests any changes they look to the list of committees and, if the assignments he requests are available, they are made. The positions he is giving up are then reflected as vacancies on whatever committees he has relinquished, and the Committee turns to the next Senator, and so on through all incumbent Senators.

After each incumbent Senator is given his committee assignments, the Committee turns to the most senior freshman Senator. Each freshman Senator is allowed to make one committee selection before the most senior freshman Senator is permitted to make two committee selections.

Source: Letter to then senator (now secretary of defense) William S. Cohen, R-Maine, from Howard Baker, then GOP Senate leader. See William S. Cohen, *Roll Call, One Year in the United States Senate* (New York: Simon and Schuster, 1981), 30–31. This outline of the process is still valid.

---

sive panels: Agriculture, Banking and Financial Services, Budget, Education and the Workforce, Government Reform, International Relations, Judiciary, Armed Services, Resources, Science, Small Business, Transportation and Infrastructure, and Veterans' Affairs. The exempt committees are House Administration, Select Intelligence, and Standards of Official Conduct. The intent of the Conference provision is to prevent members who receive the "plum" assignments from crowding members out of other spots.

Since 1953, when Senate Democratic leader Lyndon B. Johnson announced his "Johnson rule," all Senate Democrats are assigned one major committee before any party member receives a second major assignment. In 1965 Senate Republicans followed suit.

Informal Criteria. Many informal criteria affect committee assignments, including the members' own wishes. Sen. Max Cleland, D-Ga., sought assign-

Party Assignment Committees

House Republicans. Before the 104th Congress began, incoming Speaker Newt Gingrich revamped his party's committee on committees, which he chaired. Gingrich renamed it the Steering Committee; transformed it into a twenty-six-member, leadership-dominated panel; eliminated a weighted voting system wherein a GOP member of the assignment panel cast as many votes as there were Republicans in his or her state delegation; and granted the Speaker control over about one-fourth of the total votes on the panel with the Speaker personally casting the most votes (five). These reforms continued in the 105th and 106th Congresses. The Speaker also appoints all GOP members of the Rules and House Administration Committees.

House Democrats. Democrats on the House Ways and Means Committee functioned as their party's committee on committees from 1911 until 1974, when the Democratic Caucus voted to transfer this duty to the Steering and Policy Committee. Renamed the Steering Committee at the beginning of the 104th Congress, the thirty-nine-member assignment panel is chaired by Minority Leader Richard A. Gephardt of Missouri.

Senate Republicans. The chairman of the Republican Conference appoints the assignment panel of about eight members. In addition, the floor leader is an ex officio member. Washington senator Slade Gorton chaired the panel during the 106th Congress.

Senate Democrats. The Steering and Coordination Committee makes assignments for Democrats. Its size (about twenty-five members) is set by the party conference and may fluctuate from Congress to Congress. The party's floor leader appoints the members of this panel and its chairman (Sen. John Kerry of Massachusetts, for the 106th Congress).

---

ment to the Armed Services Committee, in part because Georgia has a large military population. He was also following the tradition of distinguished Georgians who made their reputations in Congress on military matters. Equally significant, Cleland is a Vietnam War veteran who has overcome grievous injuries—he lost both legs and an arm in a grenade explosion. Gender may affect assignments as well. With Clinton impeachment hearings on the horizon in the fall of 1998, party leaders recruited Rep. Mary Bono, R-Calif., the widow of Rep. Sony Bono, to serve on the Judiciary Committee as the panel's only female Republican. They hoped she might "soften the harsh image projected by some committee conservatives" and demonstrate the party's gender sensitivity at hearings where allegations of sexual exploitation could play a role.[30]

Worth underscoring is the reality of the "two Congresses" in assignment decisions. Each party seeks through the appointments process to give electoral advantage to lawmakers of their party. For example, two Senate incumbents targeted for defeat by the opposition in 1998, Lauch Faircloth, R-N.C., and Barbara Boxer, D-Calif., were given coveted seats on the Appropriations Committee, "which would allow them to pursue funds for their home states."[31] Boxer won her contest, but Faircloth lost his. Members also seek assignment

to certain committees because they can raise "campaign cash that can help their reelection prospects." Members of the top House and Senate committees took in more political action committee (PAC) money from 1993 to 1998 than did their colleagues on less high-profile panels."[32]

Seniority. Normally, the assignment panels observe seniority when preparing committee membership lists. The member of the majority party with the longest continuous committee service is always listed first. Senate Republicans, unlike House Republicans and House and Senate Democrats, apply seniority rigidly when two or more GOP senators compete for a committee position. Republicans in both chambers have diminished the role of seniority in chairmanship selection. When he was Speaker, Gingrich on several occasions bypassed the seniority custom to give chairmanships to ideological loyalists.

In 1995 the House imposed a six-year term limit on committee and subcommittee chairmen. Three years later Resources Committee chairman Don Young, R-Alaska, called term limits "a dumb idea to begin with." Republicans now face the prospect of "musical chairs"—chairmen trading their committee leadership roles to become the chairs on other panels, assuming the GOP retains majority control of the House.[33] Another problem is that term-limited chairmen—like Bill Archer, R-Texas, of Ways and Means—could opt to retire, perhaps jeopardizing safe GOP seats in a hard-fought election year like 2000.

Senate Republicans followed the House's term limit decision by adopting a party rule, effective in 1997, limiting committee chairmen to six years of service. "The whole thrust behind this," said Sen. Connie Mack, R-Fla., the author of the term limit change, "is to try to get greater participation, so new members of the Senate don't have to wait until they've been here 18 years to play a role."[34]

Biases. The decisions made by the assignment panels inevitably determine the geographical and ideological composition of the standing committees. Committees can easily become biased toward one position or another. Farm areas are overrepresented on the Agriculture Committees and small business interests on the Small Business Committees. No wonder committees are policy advocates: they propose laws that reflect the interests of their members and the outside groups and agencies that gravitate toward them.

Who gets on a panel or who is left off affects committee policy making. Committees that are carefully balanced between liberal and conservative interests can be tilted one way or the other by new members. A committee's political philosophy influences its success on the House or Senate floor. Committees ideologically out of step with the House or Senate as a whole are more likely than others to have legislation defeated or significantly revised by floor amendments.

Approval by Party Caucuses and the Chamber

For most of the twentieth century each chamber's party caucuses either ratified the assignment decisions of their committees on committees or took no action on them at all. Beginning in the 1970s, however, party caucuses be-

came major participants in the assignment process. Chairmen and ranking minority members were subjected to election by secret ballot of their partisan colleagues. Clearly, committee leadership is no longer an automatic right.

Although seniority still encourages continuity on committees, the seniority system has now become more flexible and is under caucus control. House GOP rules for the 106th Congress stated that the "Conference shall vote by secret ballot on each recommendation of the . . . Steering Committee for the position of Chairman. If the Republican Conference fails to approve a recommendation . . . the matter shall be automatically recommitted without instruction to [the Steering] Committee." In the Senate the parties can exercise control over committees but nearly always defer to the seniority rankings of lawmakers in determining who heads a committee or subcommittee.

Each chamber's rules require that all members of standing committees, including chairmen, be elected by the entire House or Senate. The practice, however, is for each party's leaders to offer the caucus-approved assignment lists to the full chamber. Normally, these are approved quickly by voice vote.

Committee Leadership

Committee leaders are usually the chairmen and the ranking minority members. Committee chairmen call meetings and establish agendas, hire and fire committee staff, arrange hearings, recommend conferees, act as floor managers, allocate committee funds and rooms, develop legislative strategies, chair hearings and markups, and regulate the internal affairs and organization of the committee.

The procedural advantages of a chairman are hard for even the most forceful minority members to overcome. The chairman may be able to kill a bill simply by refusing to schedule it for a hearing. Or a chairman may convene meetings when proponents or opponents of the legislation are unavoidably absent. The chairman's authority derives from the support of a committee majority and a variety of formal and informal resources, such as substantive and parliamentary experience and control over the agenda, communications, and financial resources of the committee. When told by a committee colleague that he lacked the votes on an issue, former House Commerce chairman John D. Dingell, D-Mich., once replied, "Yeah, but I've got the gavel."[35] Dingell banged his gavel, adjourned the meeting, and the majority had no chance to work its will before the legislative session ended.

More than a decade later a Republican was at the helm of the Commerce Committee, and he too exercised his leadership prerogatives. At the request of the Speaker, Chairman Bliley acted with dispatch to report legislation overhauling the Medicare and Medicaid programs. Sweeping aside pleas for more hearings from Democrats, including ranking minority member Dingell, Bliley had his panel mark up the legislation and report it to the floor.[36]

The top minority party member on a committee is also an influential figure. Among his or her powers are nominating minority conferees, hiring and firing minority staff, sitting ex officio on all subcommittees, appointing mi-

nority members to subcommittees, assisting in setting the committee's agenda, and managing legislation on the floor.

Policy Making in Committee

Committees foster deliberate, collegial, fragmented decisions. They encourage bargaining and accommodation among members. To move bills through Congress's numerous decision points from subcommittee to committee, authors of bills and resolutions typically make compromises in response to important committee members. These "gatekeepers" may exact alterations in a bill's substance. The proliferation of committees also multiplies the points of access for outside interests.

Overlapping Jurisdictions

The formal responsibilities of a standing committee are defined by the rules of each house, various public laws, and precedents. Committees with overlapping jurisdictions sometimes formulate a written "memorandum of understanding" that informally outlines how policy topics are to be referred among them.[37] Committees do not have watertight jurisdictional compartments. Any broad subject overlaps numerous committees. The Senate has an Environment and Public Works Committee, but other panels also consider environmental legislation; the same is true in the House. These House bodies, along with a brief sketch of some of their environmental responsibilities, are outlined in the following list:

Agriculture: pesticides; soil conservation; some water programs

Appropriations: funding for environmental programs and agencies

Banking and Financial Services: open space acquisition in urban areas

Commerce: health effects of the environment; environmental regulations; solid waste disposal; clean air; safe drinking water

Government Reform: federal executive branch agencies for the environment

International Relations: international environmental cooperation

Resources: water resources; power resources; land management; wildlife conservation; national parks; nuclear waste; fisheries; endangered species

Science: environmental research and development

Small Business: effects of environmental regulations on business

Transportation and Infrastructure: water pollution; sludge management

Ways and Means: environmental tax expenditures

Jurisdictional overlaps can have positive results. They can enable members to develop expertise in several policy fields, prevent any one group from dominating a topic, and promote healthy competition among committees. On

the other hand, "healthy competition" can quickly turn to intercommittee warfare.

In recent Congresses the House Commerce, Resources, and Science Committees have clashed over issues that do not fit neatly into any single panel's area of responsibility (energy and environmental issues, for instance). Committees' formal jurisdictional mandates have not kept pace with change—nor can they. Another trigger of turf battles is "forum shopping" by outside interests who want their carefully drafted bills referred to sympathetic committees.

The expansionist tendency of some committees also can create intercommittee tussles. In the mid-1990s the House Banking panel indicated it planned to review the statutes governing the Securities and Exchange Commission (Commerce shares jurisdiction with Banking) and the Commodity Futures Trading Commission (under the Agriculture Committee's aegis) because it was considering merging the two commissions. In a letter to the Banking chairman, the Agriculture and Commerce chairmen wrote, "We strongly urge you to reconsider [your plans] because it is our position that such actions would clearly constitute a violation of [House rules] and would compromise the good working relationship our committees have developed thus far."[38]

Multiple Referrals

When a bill is introduced in the House, it usually is referred to a single committee. Until 1975 House rules made no provision for multiple referrals, although informally there were occasions when more than one panel reviewed the same bill. In that year, however, the rules were changed to permit several types of multiple referrals. This change augmented the Speaker's authority and granted him additional flexibility in referring measures to various committees.

When Republicans assumed control of the 104th Congress, they streamlined multiple referrals and placed them firmly under the Speaker's control. The Speaker must "designate a committee of primary jurisdiction upon the initial referral of a measure to a committee." The "primary committee" concept is designed to increase accountability for legislation while retaining for the Speaker flexibility in determining whether, when, and for how long other panels can receive the measure.

At the time of initial referral, the Speaker identifies the primary committee; it has predominant responsibility for shepherding the legislation to final passage. The Speaker may also send the measure to secondary panels. The House parliamentarian calls this practice an "additional initial referral." In the following example of referral language, the Judiciary Committee is the primary committee and Resources is the additional initial panel:

> H.R. 2555. A bill to preserve the authority of the States over waters within their boundaries . . . to the Committee on the Judiciary, and in addition to the Committee on Resources, for a period to be subsequently determined by the Speaker, in each case for consideration of such provisions as fall within the jurisdiction of the committee concerned.

Multiple referrals may promote integrated policy making, broader public discussion of issues, access to the legislative process, and consideration of alternative approaches. They also enhance the Speaker's scheduling prerogatives. The Speaker can use the referral power to intervene more directly in committee activities and even to set deadlines for committees to report multiply referred legislation. The reverse is also possible: the Speaker can delay action on measures by referring them to other committees. Thus, multiple referrals can be employed to slow down legislative decision making.

The Senate usually sends measures to a single committee—the committee with jurisdiction over the subject matter that predominates in the legislation. Although multiple referrals have long been permitted by unanimous consent, they are infrequently used, mainly because senators have many opportunities to influence policy making on the floor.

Where Bills Go

Many bills referred to committee are sent by the chairman to a subcommittee. Others are retained for review by the full committee. In the end committees and subcommittees select the measures they want to consider and ignore the rest. Committee consideration usually consists of three standard steps: public hearings, markups, and reports.

Hearings. When committees or subcommittees conduct hearings on a bill, they listen to a wide variety of witnesses. These include the bill's sponsors, federal officials, pressure group representatives, public officials, and private citizens—sometimes even celebrities. Movie-star witnesses can help give a bill national visibility. When Elizabeth Taylor appeared before a Senate panel to testify on AIDS, the chairman said of the press coverage, "I haven't seen anything like this in the 30 days we have had hearings."[39] Or as Sen. Arlen Specter, R-Pa., put it, "Quite candidly, when Hollywood speaks, the world listens. Sometimes when Washington speaks, the world snoozes."[40]

Equally important are witnesses who can add drama to hearings because of their first-hand experience with an issue or problem. The Senate Finance Committee, for example, attracted national headlines with its hearings on wrongdoings by the Internal Revenue Service. Innocent taxpayers recounted their horrendous experiences, and IRS agents donned black hoods to tell about the organization's mistreatment of taxpayers.[41]

Hearings provide opportunities for committee members to be heard on the issues. Frequently, lawmakers present their views on legislation in the guise of asking questions of witnesses. Most hearings follow a traditional format. Each witness reads a prepared statement. Then each committee member has a limited time (often five minutes) to ask questions before the next witness is called. To save time and promote give-and-take, committees occasionally use a panel format in which witnesses sit together and briefly summarize their statements.

After 1997 new House rules were adopted to promote opportunities for longer exchanges between lawmakers and witnesses; the majority and minor-

ity on a committee now can designate one of their panel members or committee staff aides to question a witness for a total of one hour.

Gradually, committees are beginning to harness contemporary technology to conduct Capitol Hill hearings. Several House and Senate panels have used interactive video, teleconferencing, and other technology to collect testimony from witnesses who may be located in other parts of the nation or world. The Internet has been used to transmit testimony, and cable television viewers have e-mailed or faxed questions to witnesses.[42] The House Agriculture Committee in September 1998 became "the first congressional panel to broadcast its proceedings in live audio format over the internet."[43]

The overlapping purposes served by hearings are many:

- to explore the need for legislation;
- to build a public record in support of legislation;
- to publicize the role of committee chairmen;
- to review executive implementation of public laws; and
- to provide a forum for citizens' grievances and frustrations.

Sometimes committees hold joint hearings with other House or Senate panels or conduct field hearings around the country to generate and assess public support for measures. In 1995 House Democrats conducted their own ad hoc "field" hearing on the Capitol lawn to protest GOP plans for revamping Medicare and Medicaid and to demonstrate that their requests for committee hearings on specific bills dealing with those issues had been denied by the Republican leadership.[44]

Hearings are shaped mainly by the chairman and staff, with varying degrees of input from party leaders, the ranking minority member, and others. By revealing patterns of support or opposition and by airing substantive problems, hearings indicate to members whether a bill is worth taking to the full chamber. Chairmen who favor bills can expedite the hearings process; conversely, they can "kill with kindness" legislation they oppose by holding endless hearings. When a bill is not sent to the full chamber, the printed hearings are the end product of the committee's work.

Committee chairmen can also use hearings to try and win reelection. Facing a tough (and ultimately unsuccessful) battle in 1998 against Democratic challenger Charles E. Schumer, then a U.S. representative, Sen. Alfonse M. D'Amato, R-N.Y., turned his chairmanship of the Banking Committee into "the ideal election-year platform for a number of populist issues." For example, to attract the support of Jewish groups in New York, he staged highly publicized hearings that criticized the Swiss government "for protecting Nazi gold stored in its banks during World War II."[45] The gold had been taken from Holocaust victims.

Markups. After hearings have been held, committee members decide the bill's actual language; the bill is "marked up." Proponents try to craft a bill that will muster the backing of their colleagues, the other chamber, lobbyists, and

the White House. This process can be arduous because members often face the "two Congresses" dilemma: whether to support a bill that might be good for the nation or oppose it because of the opposition of their constituents. Not surprisingly, the bill that emerges from markup is usually the one that can attract the support of the most members. As former representative Dan Rostenkowski, D-Ill., said when he chaired the House Ways and Means Committee, "We have not written perfect law; perhaps a faculty of scholars could do a better job. A group of ideologues could have produced greater consistency. But politics is an imperfect process."[46]

Outside pressures are often intense during markup deliberations. Under House and Senate "sunshine" rules, markups must be conducted in public, except on national security or related issues. (House Republicans in the mid-1990s strengthened the sunshine rules by permitting television and radio coverage of open committee sessions, as a matter of right and not committee approval.) Compromises can be difficult to achieve in markup rooms filled with lobbyists watching how each member will vote. Hence, committees sometimes conduct "pre-markups" in private to work out their positions on various issues.

After conducting hearings and markups, a subcommittee sends its recommendations to the full committee. The full committee may conduct hearings and markups on its own, ratify the subcommittee's decision, take no action, or return the matter to the subcommittee for further study.

Reports. If the full committee votes to send the bill to the House or Senate, the staff prepares a report, subject to committee approval, describing the purposes and provisions of the legislation. Reports emphasize arguments favorable to the bill, summarizing selectively the results of staff research and hearings. Reports are noteworthy documents. The bill itself may be long, highly technical, and confusing to most readers. "A good report, therefore, does more than explain—it also persuades," commented a congressional staff aide.[47] Furthermore, reports may guide executive agencies and federal courts in interpreting ambiguous or complex legislative language.

The Policy Environment

Executive agencies, pressure groups, party leaders and caucuses, and the entire House or Senate form the backdrop against which a committee makes policy. These environments may be consensual or conflictual: some policy questions are settled fairly easily, while others are bitterly controversial. Environments also may be monolithic or pluralistic: some committees have a single dominant source of outside influence, while others face numerous competing groups or agencies.

Environmental factors influence committees in at least four ways. First, they shape the content of public policies and thus the likelihood that these policies will be accepted by the full House or Senate. The Judiciary Committees are buffeted by diverse and competing pressure groups that feel passionately on volatile issues such as abortion, school prayer, and gun control. The

committees' chances for achieving agreement among their members or on the floor depend to a large extent on their ability to deflect such issues altogether or to accommodate diverse groups through artful legislative drafting.

Second, policy environments foster mutual alliances among committees, federal departments, and pressure groups—the "iron triangles" (see Chapter 12). The House and Senate Veterans' Affairs Committees, for example, regularly advocate legislation to benefit veterans' groups. This effort is backed by the Department of Veterans Affairs. At the very least, "issue networks" emerge. These are rather fluid and amorphous groups of policy experts who try to influence any committee that deals with their subject area.[48]

Third, policy environments establish decision-making objectives and guidelines for committees. Clientele-oriented committees, such as the House and Senate Small Business Committees, try to promote the policy views of their satellite groups, such as small-business enterprises. Alliances between committees and federal departments also shape decisions.

Finally, environmental factors influence the level of partisanship on committees. Some committees are relatively free of party infighting. But other committees—such as the Health, Education, Labor and Pensions Committee in the Senate and the Education and the Workforce Committee in the House—consider contentious social issues like poverty and welfare that often divide the two parties. The aforementioned Judiciary Committee is a polarized panel filled with conservative Republican and liberal Democratic firebrands. Their sharp ideological clashes got wide publicity during the panel's nationally televised impeachment proceedings against President Clinton.[49]

In recent Congresses party infighting has engulfed committee deliberations. The widening ideological differences between the parties and the assertiveness of new lawmakers have exacerbated partisan tensions.

Committee Staff

Throughout the three principal stages of committee policy making—hearings, markup, and report—staff aides play an active part. Representatives and senators (to a greater degree because there are fewer of them) cannot handle the large workload on their own and so must rely heavily on the "unelected lawmakers."

As part of their Contract with America, House Republicans in 1995 cut committee staff by one-third, a reduction of 621 congressional jobs.[50] In addition, they reduced committee spending and provided the committee minority with more staff and resources (often one-third of the total) than they had received in previous years. The GOP-controlled Senate cut committee staff by 20 percent.[51] The committee funding process in both the Senate and House has been changed from an annual to a biennial cycle.

Staff reductions may have been too severe. The Republicans "went too far in downsizing committee staffs, hurting their ability to advance their own agenda," wrote a former GOP staff aide.[52] In the opinion of Sen. Robert C. Byrd,

D-W.Va., staff reductions are "affecting the ability of Members to adequately address issues of national importance which arise in Congress every day."[53]

The discretionary agenda of Congress and its committees is powerfully shaped by the congressional staff. Their influence can be direct or indirect, substantive or procedural, visible or invisible. In the judgment of one former senator, "most of the work and most of the ideas come from the staffers. They are predominantly young men and women, fresh out of college and professional schools. They are ambitious, idealistic, and abounding with ideas."[54] Staff turnover on Capitol Hill is fairly high; House personal staff members, for example, "have an average of only 2.7 years of experience in their current jobs."[55] Many committee and leadership aides use their experience as a stepping-stone to other jobs, such as lobbying.

Policy proposals emanate from many sources—the White House, administrative agencies, interest groups, state and local officials, scholars, and citizens—but staff aides are strategically positioned to advance or hinder these proposals. As one Senate committee staff director recounted, "Usually, you draw up proposals for the year's agenda, lay out the alternatives. You can put in some stuff you like and leave out some you don't. I recommend ideas that the [chairman's] interested in and also that I'm interested in."[56] Many committee staff are active in outside communications and issue networks (health or environment, for example) that enhance lawmakers' ability to make informed decisions.[57]

Staff aides negotiate with legislators, lobbyists, and executive officials on issues, legislative language, and political strategy. Sometimes they travel to foreign countries to conduct investigations. Congress's investigative power undergirds its ability to make informed judgments on policy matters. And staff members are the ones who do the essential spadework that can lead to changes in policy or new laws. Staff aides sometimes make policy decisions. Consider their crucial role on a defense appropriations bill.

> The dollar figures in the huge piece of legislation [were] so immense that House-Senate conferees, negotiating their differences . . . , relegated almost every item less than $100 million to staff aides on grounds that the members themselves did not have time to deal with such items, which Sen. Ted Stevens (R-Alaska) called "small potatoes."[58]

During hearings, aides recruit witnesses, on their own or at the specific direction of the chairman, and plan when and in what order they appear. In addition, staff aides commonly accompany committee members to the floor to give advice, draft amendments, and negotiate compromises. The number of aides who can be present on the floor is limited, however, by House and Senate regulations.

For information, analyses, policy options, and research projects, committee staff can turn to the three legislative support agencies: the Congressional Research Service, established in 1914; the General Accounting Office, estab-

lished in 1921; and the Congressional Budget Office, established in 1974. The Office of Technology Assessment, a support agency created in 1972 to assist lawmakers in making scientific and technological policy, was abolished by the Republican-controlled Congress in 1995. One factor in the office's demise was the perception that its research duplicated that performed by other public and private organizations.[59] Unlike committee or personal aides, the Congressional Research Service, the General Accounting Office, and the Congressional Budget Office operate under strict rules of nonpartisanship and objectivity. Staffed with experts, they provide Congress with analytical talent matching that in executive agencies, universities, or specialized groups.

Some members and scholars contend that unelected staffs are overactive in shaping policy and thus undercut the lawmaking role of elected members. We are "elected Senators and we should try to do our business, occasionally, with ourselves and among ourselves and between ourselves," remarked Alan K. Simpson of Wyoming when he was a senator.[60] On the other hand, lawmakers recognize and appreciate the value of experienced and knowledgeable staff aides.

Staffing reflects members' dual roles in the "two Congresses": individual policy maker and constituency representative. It can be a controversial process. Sen. Robert G. Torricelli, D-N.J., was criticized by black clergy in New Jersey for "failing to appoint blacks to important positions on his personal staff" as he had promised during his 1996 senatorial campaign. Torricelli responded that he had hired professional black staffers and "defended his efforts to hire members of racial minorities."[61]

Committee Reform and Change

Since passage of the Legislative Reorganization Act of 1946, Congress has made numerous attempts to reform the committee system but has only rarely succeeded. In 1973 and 1974 the Select Committee on Committees, headed by Richard Bolling (House, 1949–1983), tried to eliminate several standing committees and make extensive changes in the jurisdiction of other committees. Instead, because of strong opposition from members who stood to surrender subcommittee chairmanships or favored jurisdictions, the House adopted only a watered-down version of the committee proposal. In 1977 a Senate select committee, chaired by Adlai E. Stevenson (Senate, 1970–1981), tried committee reform with somewhat greater success.

Since then, given the decidedly mixed results of these earlier efforts, Congress has moved gingerly to restructure committees. A House select committee proposal in 1979 to create a standing committee on energy failed, and a Senate select panel, created in 1984 to address committee reform and assignment limitations, had few of its recommendations acted upon by the full Senate.

Many witnesses who appeared before the 1993 Joint Committee on the Organization of Congress urged a major overhaul of the House and Senate committee systems. Others argued for modest changes: reducing committee sizes, eliminating subcommittees, or restricting the use of multiple referrals.

Neither the House nor the Senate acted during the 103d Congress on the reform recommendations of the joint committee.[62] Then came the electoral earthquake of November 1994. Republicans revamped the committee system, especially in the House. Some of the changes were formal (amendments to House rules) and others occurred informally. The informal developments reflect a trend that has been under way for years—namely, a weakening in the autonomy of the standing committees.

Committee Structure

Rep. David Dreier, R-Calif., had just gone to bed after the exhilarating 1994 election day victory for Republicans, when Speaker-to-be Gingrich telephoned: "David, this is Newt. I want you to reform the committees."[63] (Dreier had been vice chairman of the 1993 Joint Committee on the Organization of Congress.) The jurisdictional changes adopted on the first day of the 104th Congress were the most significant committee changes since enactment of the Legislative Reorganization Act of 1946. Three standing committees in the House with Democratic constituencies— District of Columbia, Merchant Marine and Fisheries, and Post Office and Civil Service—were abolished and their functions assigned to other standing committees.

Returning Power to Committee Chairmen

"In 1995 House Republican leaders marched into control of Congress intent on slashing the power and number of committees that had flourished under the Democrat's reign. Two years later Speaker [Gingrich] and his leadership team wanted to return authority to the chairmen, allowing them greater leeway to set the agenda and to take the GOP's case to the voters," noted one congressional observer.[64] Under Speaker Hastert the internal distribution of power has continued to shift away from the speakership to committee chairs and other GOP leaders and activists. Indeed, the chairs have regained much of the power they had lost to Gingrich. Hastert also holds "biweekly strategy sessions with committee chairmen" as a way to more directly involve them in advancing the GOP's agenda.[65]

Committee Chairmanship Prerogatives

Although committee chairmen's terms are now limited to six years, their powers have been strengthened in various ways. Democrats, when they were in the majority, had deliberately encouraged the rise of strong subcommittee chairmen, but Republicans granted their full committee chairmen significant leverage over their subcommittees.

Standing committee chairmen name their subcommittee leaders, assign members to subcommittees, hire all majority staff (ending the Democrats' practice of allowing subcommittee chairs to hire their own staffers), and control the committee budget. Gone are the subcommittee fiefdoms and staff baronies prevalent on certain committees when Democrats were in control. The

enhancement of chairmen's authority comports with Speaker Hastert's general leadership style of involving and delegating responsibility to chairmen and others for implementing the GOP agenda hammered out in discussions among the members and in leadership circles.

The Senate GOP Conference took a different tack with respect to the authority of committee chairmen. Junior Republicans wanted more of a say in how committees are run, and they had the votes to pass a party rule, effective October 1, 1999. The rule permits subcommittee chairmen on the standing committees to hire their own staff, with the concurrence of the committee chairmen. Not surprisingly, committee chairmen opposed this dilution of their authority, but a majority backed the initiative sponsored by Sen. Rod Grams of Minnesota. "The new GOP rule is a radical change from the practice of most committees, where the chairmen do the hiring and firing and decide which staffers are assigned to each Senator."[66]

Committee Procedures

When the Republicans assumed control of the 104th Congress, they passed a House rule banning proxy (absentee) voting in committee and subcommittee. They prohibited proxy voting to promote greater participation in committees so that the product would reflect the work of all members, rather than a few. This ban, however, is not popular with everyone. Given the frenetic pace and heavy workload, and the narrow GOP majority on most committees, the ban on proxy voting has made life difficult for committees and their members. Many lawmakers must sprint to cast votes in committees that are conducting business simultaneously. Or they must run back and forth from committee to the House floor to cast their votes. Even some GOP chairmen have expressed dismay with the ban on proxy voting. As Judiciary chairman Henry J. Hyde, R-Ill., stated, "If they are going to let people serve on more than one committee and if they are going to simultaneously debate and vote on amendments on the floor [and in committee], then they should allow proxies."[67]

Task Forces

Although Speaker Hastert has used task forces less than did his predecessor, they remain a useful way to facilitate the leadership's control over the party's policy priorities. Task forces can forge consensus, draft legislation, coordinate strategy, promote intraparty communication, and involve noncommittee members and junior members in issue areas.

Gingrich's use of task forces provides a practical look at the three theories of legislative organization mentioned earlier in this chapter: the distributional hypothesis, the informational hypothesis, and the party hypothesis. The Speaker's Task Force on California was established in large measure to ensure that the politically important state of California received its fair share of federal funds from the GOP-controlled House. This panel's formation buttressed the committee autonomy or distributive politics view of congressional organization: committees

are designed to accommodate important constituencies. The Task Force on Immigration highlights the chamber-dominated, or informational, perspective. Its work enhanced the expertise of all members by providing them with specialized information on the complexities of immigration policy. Finally, the Task Force on the Environment was formed in part to promote the GOP's deregulatory agenda. A partisan perspective shaped much of its work.

Senate majority leader Trent Lott, R-Miss., formed GOP task forces on education, campaign finance, Senate reform, and even plutonium disposition. "Disposition of the current 50 tons of Russian excess weapons-grade plutonium," he said, "is an important national goal."[68] This bipartisan task force was created to guard against the danger of plutonium falling into the hands of terrorists or rogue states. Task forces are "more directed over here," explained Sen. Pat Roberts, R-Kan., a former House member elected to the Senate in November 1996. "I don't expect task forces on task forces, like we had in the House."[69]

Conclusion

Several generalizations can be made about committees today. First, they shape the House and Senate agendas. Not only do they have negative power—pigeonholing legislation referred to them—but positive power as well. The bills they report largely determine what each chamber will debate and in what form. As one House chairman stated in his testimony before the Joint Committee on the Organization of Congress:

> [Committees] provide Congress with the expertise, skill, and organizational structure necessary to cope with the increasingly complex and technical questions in both the domestic and international arenas. They also ensure a forum for the broadest possible participation of diverse interests and constituencies in the formative stages of the legislative process. They are, in short, the window through which much of the democratic participation in lawmaking is made possible.[70]

Second, committees differ in their policy-making environments, mix of members, decision-making objectives, and ability to fulfill individual members' goals. Recruitment methods reinforce the committees' autonomy. Committees frequently are imbalanced ideologically or geographically. They are likely to advocate policies espoused by agencies and outside groups interested in their work.

Third, committees often develop an esprit de corps that flows across party lines. Committee members usually will defend their panels against criticisms, jurisdictional trespassing, or any attempt to bypass them.

Fourth, committees typically operate independently of one another. This longtime custom fosters an attitude of "mutual noninterference" in the work of other committees. Needless to say, multiple referrals of bills spawn broader interrelationships among committees.

Finally, the committee system contributes fundamentally to policy fragmentation, although a few committees—Rules and Budget, for example—act as policy coordinators for Congress (see Chapters 8 and 13). "This is one of the anomalies here," remarked Rep. George E. Brown Jr., D-Calif. "In order to attain legislative efficiency, we say that we have to break down into committees with specialized jurisdictions. When you do that, you lose your ability to grapple with the big problems."[71] Party leaders, as a result, are more involved than ever in coordinating policy making and forging winning coalitions in committees and on the floor.

The Speaker's rostrum with mace in the House chamber. In early sessions of Congress the sergeant-at-arms would lift the staff from its pedestal and "present" it before an unruly member to restore order.

8

Congressional Rules
and Procedures

"We're determined to get a date for the Chemical Weapons Convention, and unless we get some sort of date, we're not going to be inclined to move any additional legislation," declared Tom Daschle, D-S.D., the Senate minority leader.[1] Sure enough, Senate majority leader Trent Lott, R-Miss., set a date for Senate action on the chemical arms treaty, which attracted the necessary two-thirds vote for passage. Lott took Daschle's threat seriously because senators can bring the Senate and even its committees to a virtual standstill by employing an awesome array of parliamentary procedures—debating bills at length, offering scores of amendments, requesting time-consuming roll-call votes, and so on. This episode underscores the weight of parliamentary procedures in making policy. Daschle threatened to use parliamentary rules to stall the Senate until treaty supporters won their policy objective.

Congress needs written rules to do its work. Compiling the Senate's first parliamentary manual, Thomas Jefferson stressed the importance of a known system of rules:

> It is much more material that there should be a rule to go by, than what the rule is; that there may be uniformity of proceeding in business not subject to the caprice of the Speaker or captiousness of the members. It is very material that order, decency, and regularity be preserved in a dignified public body.[2]

Jefferson understood that how Congress operates affects what it does. Thus Congress's rules protect majority and minority rights, divide the workload, help contain conflict, ensure fair play, and distribute power among members. Because formal rules cannot cover every contingency, *precedents*—accumulated decisions of House Speakers and Senate presiding officers—fill in the gaps. These precedents are codified by House and Senate parliamentarians, printed, and distributed. There are also informal, unwritten codes of conduct such as courtesy to other members. These *folkways* are transmitted from incumbent members to newcomers.[3] (See Chapter 5 for a discussion of folkways.)

Before bills become laws, they must pass successfully through several veto points in each house (see Figure 8-1). Bills that fail to attract majority support at any critical juncture may never be passed. Congress, in short, is a procedural obstacle course that favors opponents of legislation and hinders proponents. This "defensive advantage" promotes bargaining and compromise at each decision point.

Figure 8-1 How a Bill Becomes Law

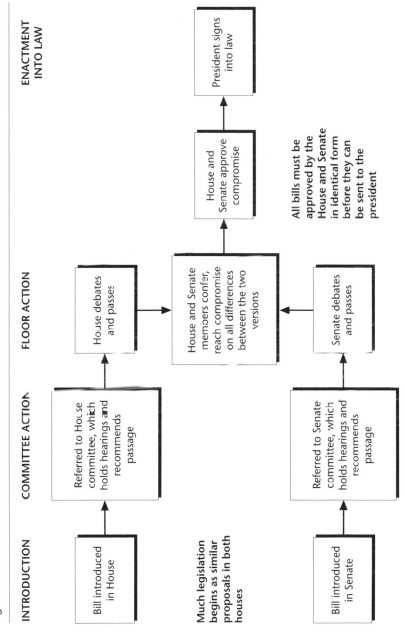

INTRODUCTION

COMMITTEE ACTION

FLOOR ACTION

ENACTMENT INTO LAW

Bill introduced in House

Referred to House committee, which holds hearings and recommends passage

House debates and passes

House and Senate members confer, reach compromise on all differences between the two versions

House and Senate approve compromise

President signs into law

Bill introduced in Senate

Referred to Senate committee, which holds hearings and recommends passage

Senate debates and passes

Much legislation begins as similar proposals in both houses

All bills must be approved by the House and Senate in identical form before they can be sent to the president

Rules are not neutral. They can be employed to advance or block actions in either chamber. They are also used to advance policy agendas and accomplish other goals. For example, when Republicans won control of the House in the mid-1990s, they amended House rules to eliminate three standing committees, reduce the number of committee staff by one-third, and restrict the number of subcommittees. A major purpose of these changes was to enhance the majority party's influence over committee policy making. Republicans also required committees, to the maximum extent practicable, to make their publications available over the Internet. This change was designed to provide constituents with more information about congressional policies and the work of their elected representatives.

Congressional rules are not independent of the policy and power struggles that lie behind them. There is very little that the House and Senate cannot do under the rules so long as the action is backed by votes and inclination. Yet votes and inclination are not easily obtained, and the rules persistently challenge the proponents of legislation to demonstrate that they have both resources at their command. There is little to prevent obstruction at every turn except the tacit understanding that the business of the House and Senate must go on. Members recognize that the rules can be redefined and prerogatives taken away or modified. Rules can also be employed against those who use them abusively.

Introduction of Bills

Only members of Congress can introduce legislation. The reasons that they introduce the bills they do are fascinating and numerous:

> Lawmakers are led to their choice of legislation by many factors: parochial interest, party preference and, often, crass calculation connected to campaign fund raising. But there is a motivator that is rarely discussed that can be just as potent: a personal brush with adversity. Congress is an intensely human place where personal experience sometimes has powerful repercussions.[4]

For example, Sen. Strom Thurmond, R-S.C., a frequent foe of government regulation, became the chief sponsor of legislation "that would require warning labels on all print and broadcast advertising for alcoholic beverages."[5] Thurmond's eldest daughter was killed by a drunken driver as she crossed a street in Columbia, South Carolina. No doubt this searing experience also contributed to Thurmond's subsequent introduction of legislation that would reverse a federal agency's approval of bottling labels touting the health benefits of moderate wine drinking.[6] Personal experience, however, is not the only source of legislative proposals. Often members get ideas for bills from the executive branch, interest groups, scholars, state and local officials, and their own staff.

A member who introduces a bill becomes its *sponsor.* This member may seek cosponsors to demonstrate wide support for the legislation. Outside

groups also may urge members to cosponsor measures. "We were not assured of a hearing," said a lobbyist of a bill that his group was pushing. "There was more hostility to the idea, so it was very important to line up a lot of cosponsors to show the over-all concern."[7] As important as the number of cosponsors is their leadership status and ideological stance. Cosponsors are not always like-minded politically. Massachusetts senator Edward M. Kennedy, a liberal Democrat, once said of conservative senator Thurmond, "Whenever Strom and I introduce a bill together, it is either an idea whose time has come, or one of us has not read the bill."[8]

Although it is easy to identify a bill's sponsors, it may be difficult to pinpoint its real initiators. Legislation is "an aggregate, not a simple production," wrote Woodrow Wilson. "It is impossible to tell how many persons, opinions, and influences have entered into its composition."[9] President John F. Kennedy, for example, usually is given credit for initiating the Peace Corps. But Theodore Sorensen, Kennedy's special counsel, recalled that the Peace Corps was

> based on the Mormon and other voluntary religious service efforts, on an editorial Kennedy had read years earlier, on a speech by General Gavin, on a luncheon I had with Philadelphia businessmen, on the suggestions of [Kennedy's] academic advisers, on legislation previously introduced and on the written response to a spontaneous late-night challenge he issued to Michigan students. [10]

In short, the ideas behind many bills have tangled histories.

Required legislation, particularly funding measures, makes up much of Congress's annual agenda. Bills that authorize programs and specify how much money can be spent on them (*authorization bills*) and bills that actually provide the money (*appropriation bills*) appear on Congress's schedule at about the same time each year. Other matters recur at less frequent intervals, every five years perhaps. Emergency issues require Congress's immediate attention. Activist legislators also push proposals onto Congress's program. Bills not acted upon die automatically at the end of each two-year Congress. "Anybody can drop a bill into the hopper [a mahogany box near the Speaker's podium where members place their proposed bills]," Rep. Dick Armey, R-Texas, said. "The question is, Can you make something happen with it?"[11]

Drafting

"As a sculptor works in stone or clay, the legislator works in words," declared one member.[12] Words are the building blocks of policy, and legislators frequently battle over adding, deleting, or modifying terms and phrases. Members sometimes give their bills eye-catching titles. The Republicans' celebrated Contract with America bristled with items such as the American Dream Restoration Act (tax code reform), the Common Sense Legal Reforms Act (tort and product liability changes), and the Taking Back Our Streets Act (crime control). Lawmakers sometimes use the names of famous sports figures to gain

publicity and support for their ideas, such as the "Mark McGwire Interstate Route 70" act and the "Muhammad Ali Boxing Reform Act." Instead of proposals to reduce "estate taxes," they are called bills to end "death taxes." "Whoever controls the language controls the debate," asserted one commentator.[13]

Although bills are introduced only by members, anyone may draft them.[14] Expert drafters in the House and Senate offices of legislative counsel assist members and committees in writing legislation. Executive agencies and lobby groups often prepare measures for introduction by friendly legislators. Many home state industries, for instance, draft narrowly tailored tariff or regulatory measures that enhance their business prospects. These proposals are then introduced by the local lawmakers—another instance of the two-Congresses linkage. As a senatorial aide said, the senator "just introduces it as a courtesy to his constituents."[15] The box, p. 232, outlines the four basic types of legislation: bills, joint resolutions, concurrent resolutions, and simple resolutions.

Nowadays Congress frequently acts on comprehensive bills or resolutions (called "packages" or megabills by the press). Packages contain an array of issues that once were handled as separate pieces of legislation. Their increasing use stems in part from members' reluctance to make hard political decisions without a package arrangement. A House Budget Committee chairman once explained their attractiveness:

> You can use large bills as a way to hide legislation that otherwise might be more controversial, as a way to be able to slam-dunk issues that otherwise might be torn apart, as a way to avoid hard votes that Members would have to account for at election time, as a way to avoid angering special-interest groups that use votes [to decide] contributions to campaigns and as a way to guarantee that the President will have to accept it.[16]

Recent Congresses have enacted fewer but lengthier laws than in the past. For example, from the 1950s through the mid-1960s, "the average number of pages was approximately 2.5. The average jumped to approximately 5 pages in the mid-1970s, reached 7 pages [in 1975], and jumped to between 8 and 9 pages in [the late 1970s and 1980s]. That more than doubled to 19.1 pages in the [mid-1990s]."[17]

Timing

"Everything in politics is timing," the late Speaker Thomas P. O'Neill Jr. used to say. A bill's success or failure often hinges on when it is introduced or brought to the floor. A bill that might succeed early in a session could fail as adjournment nears. On the other hand, it is sometimes possible to rush through controversial legislation during the last hectic days of a Congress.

Elections greatly influence the timing of legislation. Policy issues can be taken off or kept on Congress's agenda because of electoral circumstances—a good illustration of how the "two Congresses" are inextricably connected. For example, most House Republicans endorsed the Contract with America dur-

Types of Legislation

Bill. Most legislative proposals before Congress are in a bill form. Bills are designated H.R. (House of Representatives) or S. (Senate) according to where they originate, followed by a number assigned in the order in which they were introduced, from the beginning of each two-year congressional term. *Public bills* deal with general questions and become public laws if approved by Congress and signed by the president. *Private bills* deal with individual matters, such as claims against the government, immigration and naturalization cases, and land titles. They become private laws if approved and signed.

Joint Resolution. A joint resolution, designated H. J. Res. or S. J. Res., requires the approval of both houses and the president's signature, just as a bill does, and has the force of law. There is no significant difference between a bill and a joint resolution. The latter generally deals with limited matters, such as a single appropriation for a specific purpose. Joint resolutions also are used to propose constitutional amendments, which do not require presidential signatures but become a part of the Constitution when three-fourths of the states have ratified them.

Concurrent Resolution. A concurrent resolution, designated H. Con. Res. or S. Con. Res., must be passed by both houses but does not require the president's signature and does not have the force of law. Concurrent resolutions generally are used to make or amend rules applicable to both houses or to express their joint sentiment. A concurrent resolution, for example, is used to fix the time for adjournment of a Congress and to express Congress's annual budgeting plan. It might also be used to convey the congratulations of Congress to another country on the anniversary of its independence.

Resolution. A simple resolution, designated H. Res. or S. Res., deals with matters entirely within the prerogatives of one house. It requires neither passage by the other chamber nor approval by the president and does not have the force of law. Most resolutions deal with the rules of one house. They also are used to express the sentiments of a single house, to extend condolences to the family of a deceased member, or to give "advice" on foreign policy or other executive business.

---

ing the 1994 election and promised voters that they would place its agenda items (line-item veto, balanced-budget constitutional amendment, term limits for lawmakers, welfare reform, and more) "at the top of their legislative calendars" if they succeeded in winning the House.[18] Their victory was interpreted by many as a mandate for action; the contract dominated the House's agenda for the first hundred days and colored deliberations throughout the 104th Congress and succeeding Congresses.

By 1999, however, adverse election results signaled to GOP leaders that the hard edges of the contract needed to be softened to what some called "compassionate conservatism." In an effort to ease the partisan passions triggered by the impeachment of President Clinton, House Speaker J. Dennis Hastert began the 106th Congress with floor action on a number of measures that many Democrats could support and that demonstrated the House's ability to set aside party differences and pass legislation. Hastert added that, on the

deadline-driven, must-pass money measures, "My mantra is that we get our work done on time."[19]

Referral of Bills

After bills are introduced, they are referred to appropriate standing committees (see Chapter 7) by the Senate presiding officer or the House Speaker. A bill's phraseology can affect its referral and hence its chances of passage. This political fact of life means that members use words artfully when drafting legislation. The objective is to encourage the referral of their measures to sympathetic rather than hostile committees. If a bill mentions taxes, for example, it invariably is referred to the tax panels. To sidestep these committees, Sen. Pete V. Domenici, R-N.M., avoided the word *tax* in a bill proposing a charge on waterborne freight:

> If the waterway fee were considered a tax—which it was, basically, because it would raise revenues for the federal treasury—the rules would place it under the dominion of the Senate's tax-writing arm, the Finance Committee. But Finance was chaired by Russell B. Long, of Louisiana, whose state included two of the world's biggest barge ports and who was, accordingly, an implacable foe of waterway charges in any form. Domenici knew that Long could find several years' worth of bills to consider before he would voluntarily schedule a hearing on S. 790 [the Domenici bill]. For this reason, [Domenici staff aides] had been careful to avoid the word *tax* in writing the bill, employing such terms as *charge* and *fee* instead.[20]

Domenici's drafting strategy worked; his bill was jointly referred to the Commerce and Environment Committees on which he served.

Of the thousands of bills introduced annually, Congress takes up relatively few. During the 105th Congress, 7,732 public bills and joint resolutions were introduced; of these only 394 became public laws (see Table 8-1). Many reasons can be cited for the enactment of fewer laws: the public's disenchantment with federal initiatives, legislative interest in reducing the role of the national government, an emphasis on community action and volunteerism for resolving problems, the complexity of issues, the intensity of partisanship, divided government, the narrow party divisions in Congress, and significant sentiment in both chambers that more laws are not the answer to the nation's problems.

The recent decline also reflects the House prohibition against commemorative legislation (bills designating special days, weeks, or months—National Dairy Goat Awareness Week or National Tap Dance Week, for example). The majority Republicans amended House rules to say, "No bill or resolution, and no amendment to any bill or resolution, establishing or expressing any commemoration may be introduced or considered in the House."

Lawmaking, too, is hard work. As Majority Leader Lott noted, "That's the way Congress works. You work for two years and finally you get to the end and either it all collapses in a puddle or you get a breakthrough."[21]

Table 8-1   **Bills introduced and Legislation Enacted, 80th–105th Congresses (1947–1999)**

Congress and years		Bills and joint resolutions introduced			Laws enacted	
		Total	House	Senate	Public	Private
80th	(1947–1949)	10,797	7,611	3,186	906	458
81st	(1949–1951)	14,988	10,502	4,486	921	1,103
82d	(1951–1953)	12,730	9,065	3,665	594	1,023
83d	(1953–1955)	14,952	10,875	4,077	781	1,002
84th	(1955–1957)	17,687	13,169	4,518	1,028	893
85th	(1957–1959)	19,112	14,580	4,532	936	784
86th	(1959–1961)	18,261	14,112	4,149	800	492
87th	(1961–1963)	18,376	14,328	4,048	885	685
88th	(1963–1965)	17,479	14,022	3,457	666	360
89th	(1965–1967)	24,003	19,874	4,129	810	173
90th	(1967–1969)	26,460	22,060	4,400	640	362
91st	(1969–1971)	26,303	21,436	4,867	695	246
92d	(1971–1973)	22,969	18,561	4,408	607	161
93d	(1973–1975)	23,396	18,872	4,524	649	123
94th	(1975–1977)	21,096	16,982	4,114	588	141
95th	(1977–1979)	19,387	15,587	3,800	634	170
96th	(1979–1981)	12,583	9,103	3,480	613	123
97th	(1981–1983)	11,490	8,094	3,396	473	56
98th	(1983–1985)	10,559	7,105	3,454	623	52
99th	(1985–1987)	9,885	6,499	3,386	664	24
100th	(1987–1989)	9,588	6,263	3,325	713	48
101st	(1989–1991)	10,352	6,683	3,669	650	16
102d	(1991–1993)	10,513	6,775	3,738	590	20
103d	(1993–1995)	8,544	5,739	2,805	465	8
104th	(1995–1997)	6,808	4,542	2,266	333	4
105th	(1997–1999)	7,732	5,014	2,718	394	10

Source: Rozanne M. Barry, *Bills Introduced and Laws Enacted: Selected Legislative Statistics, 1947–1992,* Congressional Research Service Report, Jan. 15, 1993, 2. See also U.S. Congress, *Congressional Record,* daily ed., 106th Cong., 1st sess., Jan. 19, 1997, D29.

Under House and Senate rules a majority of the full committee must be physically present to report out any measure. If this rule is violated, a point of order can be made against the proposal on the floor. (A point of order is a parliamentary objection that halts the proceedings until the chamber's presiding officer decides whether the contention is valid.)

Bills reported from committee have passed a critical stage in the lawmaking process. The next major step is to reach the House or Senate floor for debate and amendment. We begin with the House because tax and appropriation bills originate there—the first under the Constitution, the second by custom.

Scheduling in the House

All bills reported from committee are listed in chronological order on one of several *calendars*—lists that enable the House to put measures into convenient categories. Bills that raise or spend money are assigned to the Union Calendar. The House Calendar contains all other major public measures. Private bills, such as immigration requests or claims against the government, are assigned to the Private Calendar, and generally noncontroversial bills are placed on the Corrections Calendar. There is no guarantee that the House will debate legislation placed on any of these calendars. The Speaker, in consultation with other party leaders, largely determines if, when, and in what order bills come up (see Chapter 6).

Shortcuts for Minor Bills

Whether a bill is major or minor, controversial or noncontroversial, influences the procedure employed to bring it before the House. Most bills are relatively minor and are taken up and passed through various shortcut procedures.

One shortcut is the designation of special days for considering minor bills. Measures on the *Corrections Calendar,* for example, are in order for floor consideration on the second and fourth Tuesdays of the month. The Corrections Calendar is an innovation of Speaker Newt Gingrich (1995–1999). He wanted an expeditious way to repeal the silliest rules, regulations, and laws currently on the books. The House adopted the calendar on June 20, 1995, by amending its rules. The Speaker has sole authority to determine whether a bill, which must have been favorably reported from a committee, is to be on the Corrections Calendar. A three-fifths vote (261 votes) is required to pass corrections legislation.

Another shortcut is the *suspension-of-the-rules* procedure (informally referred to as the "suspension calendar"), which is controlled by the Speaker through his power of recognizing who may speak. Today roughly 50 percent of the measures passed by the House are considered under suspension, compared with about 8 percent a quarter-century ago. Members may use this time-saving device every Monday and Tuesday to pass relatively noncontroversial measures. The procedure permits only forty minutes of debate, allows no amendments, and requires a two-thirds vote for passage. The procedure is favored by bill managers who want to avoid unfriendly amendments and points of order against their legislation.

House members sometimes complain that weighty bills are rushed through under suspension of the rules, often late in the session. As journalist Elizabeth Drew observed:

> The theory is that [the suspension procedure] is an efficient way of clearing noncontroversial proposals, but [it] is used also for other purposes: to slip bills through or to deny members an opportunity to amend them, under the pretense that if a bill is on the suspension calendar it is by definition noncontroversial.[22]

There are occasions, too, when the Speaker can use the procedure to frustrate action on unwanted measures. Under pressure from his own rank-and-file and Democratic lawmakers, Speaker Gingrich felt compelled to schedule floor action in March 1998 on a controversial campaign finance reform measure (banning "soft money") that he and other GOP leaders opposed. (Recall that in June 1995 Gingrich and President Clinton shook hands in New Hampshire and promised to establish a blue ribbon commission on campaign reform.) To make good on his promise without fear that the legislation would attract the two-thirds vote for passage, Gingrich brought the bill to the floor under the suspension procedure. Democrats and some Republicans denounced the successful use of this parliamentary tactic as a "sham" and "fraud."[23]

The current rules of the House Republican Conference establish some guidelines for the Speaker in using the suspension procedure. For example, the Speaker cannot schedule any bill or resolution under suspension of the rules that "fails to include a cost estimate, has not been cleared by the minority, was opposed by more than one-third of the committee members [who] reported the bill, and exceeds $100,000,000 in authorized appropriated, or direct or indirect loan commitments or guarantees."

Major measures reach the floor by different procedures. Budget, appropriation, and certain other measures are considered privileged and may be called up from the appropriate calendar for debate at almost any time. Most major bills, however, do not have an automatic "green light" to the floor. Before they reach the floor they are assigned a "rule" by the Rules Committee.

The Strategic Role of the Rules Committee

Since the very first Congress there has been a House Rules Committee. During its early years the committee prepared or ratified a biennial set of House rules and then dissolved. As House procedures became more complex, the committee became more important. In 1858 the Speaker became a member of the committee and the next year its chairman. In 1880 Rules became a permanent standing committee. Three years later the committee launched a procedural revolution: it began to issue rules (sometimes called *special rules*), which are privileged resolutions that grant priority for floor consideration to virtually all major bills.

Arm of the Majority Leadership. In 1910 the House rebelled against the arbitrary decisions of Speaker Joseph Cannon, R-Ill., and removed him from the Rules Committee. During the subsequent decades, as the committee became an independent power, it extracted substantive concessions in bills in exchange for rules, blocked measures it opposed, and advanced those it favored, often reflecting the wishes of the House's conservative coalition of Republicans and southern Democrats.

The chairman of the Rules Committee from 1955 to 1967, Howard W. "Judge" Smith, D-Va., was a master at devising delaying tactics. He might abruptly adjourn meetings for lack of a quorum, allow requests for rules to languish, or refuse to schedule meetings. House consideration of the 1957 civil

rights bill was temporarily delayed because Smith absented himself from the Capitol. His committee could not meet without him. Smith claimed he was seeing about a barn that had burned on his Virginia farm. Retorted Speaker Sam Rayburn, "I knew Howard Smith would do most anything to block a civil rights bill, but I never knew he would resort to arson."[24]

Liberals' frustration with the coalition of conservatives who dominated the committee boiled over. After President Kennedy was elected in 1960, Speaker Rayburn realized he needed greater control over the Rules Committee if the House was to advance the president's activist New Frontier program. Rayburn proposed enlarging the committee from twelve members to fifteen. This proposal led to a titanic struggle between Rayburn and the archconservative Rules chairman:

> Superficially, the Representatives seemed to be quarreling about next to nothing: the membership of the committee. In reality, however, the question raised had grave import for the House and for the United States. The House's answer to it affected the tenuous balance of power between the great conservative and liberal blocs within the House. And, doing so, the House's answer seriously affected the response of Congress to the sweeping legislative proposals of the newly elected President, John Kennedy.[25]

In a dramatic vote the House agreed to expand the Rules Committee. Two new Democrats and one Republican were added, which loosened the conservative coalition's grip on the panel.

During the 1970s the Rules Committee came under even greater majority party control. In 1975 the Democratic Caucus authorized the Speaker to appoint, subject to party ratification, all Democratic members of the committee. (Thirteen years later Republicans authorized their leader to name the GOP members of the Rules Committee.) The majority party maintains a disproportionate ratio on the panel (nine Republicans and four Democrats in the 106th Congress). The Rules Committee, in short, has become the Speaker's committee. As GOP Rules vice chairman Porter J. Goss of Florida said about the panel's relationship with Speaker, "How much is the Rules Committee the handmaiden of the Speaker? The answer is, totally."[26] Rep. David Dreier, R-Calif., chairs the panel in the 106th Congress.

The Speaker's influence over the Rules Committee ensures that he can both bring measures to the floor and shape their procedural consideration. Because House rules require bills to be taken up in the chronological order listed on the calendars, many substantial bills would never reach the floor before Congress adjourned. The Rules Committee can put major bills first in line. Equally important, a rule from the committee sets the conditions for debate and amendment.

A request for a rule usually is made by the chairman of the committee reporting the bill. The Rules Committee conducts hearings on the request in the same way that other committees consider legislation, except that only mem-

Example of a Rule from the Rules Committee

The following "open" rule (H. Res. 44) set the terms for debating and amending the Presidential and Executive Financial Accountability Act of 1999.

Resolved. That at any time after the adoption of this resolution the Speaker may, pursuant to clause 2(b) of rule XVIII, declare the House resolved into the Committee of the Whole House on the state of the Union for consideration of the bill (H.R. 437) to provide for a Chief Financial Officer in the Executive Office of the President. The first reading of the bill shall be dispensed with. General debate shall be confined to the bill and shall not exceed one hour equally divided and controlled by the chairman and ranking minority member of the Committee on Government Reform. After general debate the bill shall be considered for amendment under the five-minute rule. The bill shall be considered as read. During consideration of the bill for amendment, the chairman of the Committee of the Whole may accord priority in recognition on the basis of whether the Member offering an amendment has caused it to be printed in the portion of the Congressional Record designated for that purpose in clause 8 of rule XVIII. Amendments so printed shall be considered as read. The chairman of the Committee of the Whole may: (1) postpone until a time during further consideration in the Committee of the Whole a request for a recorded vote on any amendment; and (2) reduce to five minutes the minimum time for electronic voting on any postponed question that follows another electronic vote without intervening business, provided that the minimum time for electronic voting on the first in any series of questions shall be 15 minutes. At the conclusion of consideration of the bill for amendment the Committee shall rise and report the bill to the House with such amendments as may have been adopted. The previous question shall be considered as ordered on the bill and amendments thereto to final passage without intervening motion except one motion to recommit with or without instructions.

Source: U.S. Congress, *Congressional Record*, daily ed., 106th Cong., 1st sess., Feb. 11, 1999, H613.

---

bers testify. The House parliamentarian usually drafts the rule after consulting with committee leaders and staff. The rule is considered on the House floor and is voted on in the same manner as regular bills (see box, this page).

Types of Rules. Traditionally, the Rules Committee has granted open, closed, or modified rules as well as waivers. An *open rule* means that any germane amendments can be proposed. A *closed rule* prohibits the offering of amendments. A *modified rule* permits amendments to some parts of the bill but not to others. *Waivers of points of order* set aside technical violations of House rules to allow bills to reach the floor.

During the 1980s and early 1990s the Democratic majority on the Rules Committee displayed great procedural creativity and imagination:

Instead of choosing from among a few patterns the Rules Committee has demonstrated a willingness to create unique designs by recombining an in-

creasingly wide array of elements, or by creating new ones as the need arises, to help leaders, committees, and members manage the heightened uncertainties of decision making on the House floor.[27]

The trend toward creative use of complex rules reflected several developments: the desire of majority party leaders to exert greater control over floor procedures, members' restlessness with dilatory floor challenges to committee-reported bills, the rise of megabills hundreds of pages in length, and efforts by committee leaders either to limit the number of amendments or to keep unfriendly amendments off the floor.

The sharp rise in partisanship, especially since the early 1980s, also triggered an increase in restrictive rules. GOP lawmakers, when they were in the minority, sometimes sponsored floor amendments designed to embarrass Democrats and to supply GOP House challengers with campaign ammunition. In response, the Rules Committee restricted GOP opportunities to offer floor amendments, a move that led to angry outcries from Republican members.

When Republicans took control of the House, they remembered their bitter experience with rules that restricted their right to offer amendments. The Rules Committee under GOP control has generally tried to provide all lawmakers with more opportunities for amendment. Of 142 rules granted during the 105th Congress for the initial consideration of legislation, 72 were open (see Table 8-2). Nevertheless, the Democrats contend that the Republicans have fallen far short of meeting their claims of more open rules.

Open rules, however, sometimes clash with a fundamental objective of any majority party: passage of priority legislation even at the cost of restricting members' amending opportunities. The minority Democrats, trying to hold the GOP firmly to the new openness they promised, regularly lambaste Republicans for providing anything less than a completely open and unrestricted amendment process. Under an open rule, Democrats could offer scores of dilatory amendments to stall action on the GOP's agenda. Such actions prompted a Rules chairman to say, "It looks like we're going to have to increasingly restrict rules if the Democrats won't cooperate."[28]

Indeed, the Republicans not only have used most of the creative rules noted in the box on p. 241 but also have devised new rules of their own. When they were in the minority, Republicans opposed the so-called king-of-the-hill rules crafted by the Democrats. These rules made in order a limited number of major amendments but stipulated that only the last alternative voted on is the one that counts for purposes of accepting or rejecting national policy. The yeas and nays on the other amendments were "free votes"; they provided "political cover" to lawmakers who could explain them however they wished. Republicans argued that these rules "violated the democratic principle that the position with the strongest support should prevail."[29] The GOP-controlled Rules Committee now issues "queen of the hill" rules, by which the major amendment that wins the most votes in the Committee of the Whole (discussed later in this chapter) is forwarded to the full House for a vote on final passage.

Table 8-2   Open and Restrictive Rules, 95th–105th Congresses
(1977–1999)

Congress and years	Total rules granted	Open rules		Restrictive rules	
		Number	Percent	Number	Percent
95th (1977–1979)	211	179	85	32	15
96th (1979–1981)	214	161	75	53	25
97th (1981–1983)	120	90	75	30	25
98th (1983–1985)	155	105	68	50	32
99th (1985–1987)	115	65	57	50	43
100th (1987–1989)	123	66	54	57	46
101st (1989–1991)	104	47	45	57	55
102d (1991–1993)	109	37	34	72	66
103d (1993–1995)	104	31	30	73	70
104th (1995–1997)	151	86	57	65	43
105th (1997–1999)	142	72	51	70	49

Sources: U.S. Congress, *Congressional Record,* daily ed., 103d Cong., 2d sess., Oct. 7, 1994, H11278. For the 104th see Dec. 10, 1996, press release, House Rules Committee. For the 105th Congress, the Rules Committee issued a total of 207 rules, but many did not directly involve bills and resolutions. As a result, the authors selected 142 as the number of rules granted for bills and resolutions. Minority Democrats have made their own calculation of the kinds of rules granted by the committee. They identify a total of 163 rules of which 38 are open (23 percent) and 115 (77 percent) are restrictive. See *Survey of Activities of the House Committee on Rules,* 105th Cong., 2d sess. (Washington, D.C.: U.S. Government Printing Office, 1999).

The Republican leadership devised a queen-of-the-hill rule to frustrate House approval of campaign reform legislation that would prohibit the national parties from receiving or spending "soft money." To kill this proposal, the Rules Committee made in order eleven substitute amendments, forcing the soft money ban to compete against all the other reform recommendations. For example, one of the substitutes proposed the creation of a bipartisan commission on campaign finance reform. GOP leaders expected this generally noncontroversial idea to receive an overwhelming number of "yes" votes and easily trump the soft money proposal. However, many who supported the commission idea voted either "no" or "present" because they preferred the soft money amendment and realized that under the queen-of-the-hill procedure the amendment that gets the most votes becomes the House bill. "The reason [members] will vote 'present' or 'no' [on the commission recommendation] is because they know that this is simply an attempt to undercut" the soft money ban, said Rep. Sam Gejdenson, D-Conn.[30]

Another GOP innovation, the time-structured rule, allows lawmakers to offer their amendments but only within specified time limits set by the Rules Committee. A ten-hour cap for debating and voting on amendments is an ex-

Examples of Creative Rules

Queen-of-the-Hill Rule. Under this special rule, a number or major alternative amendments—each the functional equivalent of a bill—are made in order to the underlying legislation, with the proviso that the substitute that receives the most votes is the winner. If two or more alternatives receive an identical number of votes, the last one voted upon is considered as finally adopted by the membership.[a]

Self-Executing Rule. This special rule provides that when the House adopts a rule it has also agreed simultaneously to pass another measure or matter. Adoption of a self-executing rule means that the House has passed one or more other proposals at the same time it agrees to the rule. Whether this rule is controversial or not usually depends on the nature of the policy being agreed to in the "two for one" vote.

Restrictive Rule. The essential feature of the restrictive rule is that it limits the "freedom of Members to offer germane amendments to the bills made in order by those rules."[b] During the 1980s and 1990s there has been an increase in the number of restrictive rules. Rank-and-file members often rail against these rules because they restrict their opportunities to amend committee-reported measures or majority party initiatives.

Multiple-Step Rule. This type of rule facilitates an orderly amendment process. One variation is for the Rules Committee to report a rule that regulates the debating and amending process for specific portions of a bill and then report another follow-on rule to govern the remainder of the measure and amendments to it.[c] Another variation is for the Rules Committee to state publicly that if a measure encounters difficulties on the floor, the panel "reserves its right to report a subsequent rule . . . which might limit time for further debate or further amendments."[d]

Anticipatory Rule. To expedite decision making on the floor, the Rules Committee may grant a rule even before the measure or matter to which it would apply has been reported by a House committee or conference committee. "In past years we used to call this buying a pig in a poke," said one Rules opponent of an anticipatory rule, "but now the language has been updated."[e]

[a] U.S. Congress, *Congressional Record,* 105th Cong., 2d sess., May 21, 1998, H3722-3.
[b] U.S. Congress, *Congressional Record,* 100th Cong., 2d sess., July 7, 1988, H5352.
[c] For an example, see U.S. Congress, *Congressional Record,* 100th Cong., 2d sess., April 26, 1988, H2496.
[d] U.S. Congress, *Congressional Record,* 98th Cong., 1st sess., October 20, 1983, H8473.
[e] U.S. Congress, *Congressional Record,* 100th Cong., 2d sess., May 26, 1988, H3689.

ample of such a rule. Democrats criticize this type of rule as not being genuinely open. They argue, for instance, that a ten-hour cap may actually leave only seven hours for amendments because the time for voting is counted against the overall time restriction.

In summary, rules establish the conditions under which most major bills are debated and amended. They determine the length of general debate, permit or prohibit amendments, and may waive points of order. They are sometimes as important to a bill's fate as a favorable vote out of committee.

Dislodging a Bill from Committee

Committees do not necessarily reflect the point of view of the full chamber. What happens when a standing committee refuses to report a bill or when the Rules Committee does not grant a rule? To circumvent committees, members have three options, but they are extraordinary actions and are seldom successful: the discharge petition, the Calendar Wednesday rule, and a device that enables the Rules Committee to extract a bill from committee.

The *discharge petition* permits the House to relieve a committee from jurisdiction over a stalled measure. This procedure also provides a way for the rank-and-file to force a bill to the floor even if the majority leadership opposes it. If a committee does not report a bill within thirty days after the bill was referred to it, any member may file a discharge motion (petition) requiring the signature of 218 members, a majority of the House. Once the signatures are obtained, the discharge motion is placed on the Discharge Calendar for seven days; it can then be called up on the second and fourth Mondays of the month by any member who signed the petition. If the discharge motion is passed, the bill is taken up right away. Since 1910, when the discharge rule was adopted, only two discharged measures ever have become law. Its threatened use, however, may stimulate a committee to act on a bill and the majority leadership to schedule it for floor action.

A combination of Democratic and Republican lawmakers used the discharge petition strategy to force House action on the campaign finance reform bill we have been discussing. When the GOP leadership used the suspension route to block the bill, advocates of reform turned to the discharge petition. As the number of signatures on the discharge petition reached 204, the GOP leadership, confronting a rebellion in their own party ranks, successfully urged twelve Republicans who had signed the petition to remove their names from it. In exchange, the Speaker promised to bring the bill to the floor under an "open" rule. The bill was then taken up by the House.[31]

The minority also uses discharge petitions to spotlight the "two Congresses." Democrats during the late 1990s identified their high-priority issues and circulated discharge petitions "in an attempt to force House votes—and provide a contrast with Republicans in an election year."[32] At the same time, outside groups, such as the National Right to Life Committee, ran ads in selected lawmakers' districts to discourage them from signing discharge petitions on campaign reform legislation. The measure would have restricted a group's ability "to spend unlimited sums airing 'issue-advocacy' ads just before an election."[33]

The discharge rule also applies to the Rules Committee. A motion to discharge a "rule" is in order after seven legislative days, rather than thirty days, as long as the bill made in order by the rule has been in committee for thirty days. Any member may enter a discharge motion. When Rep. Chris Shays, R-Conn., signed a discharge petition in 1999 to force faster action on a campaign finance reform bill than Speaker Hastert wanted, there were charges of

"treason" against Shays and rumblings that he might face a primary challenge in 2000.[34]

Adopted in 1909, the *Calendar Wednesday rule* provides that on Wednesdays committees may bring up from the House or Union calendar their measures that have not received a rule from the Rules Committee. Calendar Wednesday is cumbersome to employ, seldom used, and generally dispensed with by unanimous consent. Since 1943 fewer than fifteen measures have been enacted into law under this procedure.[35]

Finally, the Rules Committee has the power of *extraction*. The committee can propose rules that make bills in order for House debate even if the bills have neither been introduced nor reported by standing committees. Based on an 1895 precedent, this procedure is akin to discharging committees without the 218 signatures requirement. It stirs bitter controversy among members who think it usurps the rights of the other committees and is seldom used.

House Floor Procedures

The House meets Monday through Friday, usually convening at noon. In practice, it conducts the bulk of its committee and floor business during the middle of the week—the so-called Tuesday to Thursday Club. This scheduling pattern helps representatives juggle legislative business with weekend trips to their districts—weekly testimony to the "two Congresses."

At the beginning of each day's session, bells ring throughout the Capitol and the House office buildings, summoning representatives to the floor. The bells also notify members of votes, quorum calls, recesses, and adjournments. Typically, the opening activities include a daily prayer; recitation of the Pledge of Allegiance; approval of the *Journal* (a constitutionally required record of the previous day's proceedings); receipt of messages from the president (such as a veto message) or the Senate; announcements, if any, by the Speaker; and one-minute speeches by members on any topic. There is also a period of "morning hour" debate, on Mondays and Tuesdays, which occurs after the opening preliminaries but before the start of formal legislative business.

The practice of reciting the Pledge of Allegiance, which began in the fall of 1988, grew out of partisan politics. House Republicans, wanting to embarrass Democrats and aid their presidential nominee, George Bush, introduced a surprise resolution on the floor to require daily recitation of the pledge. (On the campaign trail Bush repeatedly had criticized Michael Dukakis, the Democratic nominee, for vetoing a state law requiring teachers to lead their pupils in the pledge when he was governor of Massachusetts.) The Democrats voted to quash the resolution but quickly recognized their electoral predicament. They did not want to appear unpatriotic (especially those facing tough reelection contests) or to seem to oppose Dukakis's position. Ultimately, the Democratic majority leadership instituted the practice of having a Democrat and a Republican alternate in leading the House in the pledge.[36] When Republicans won majority control, House rules were amended to require it.

After these preliminaries, the House generally begins considering legislation. For a major bill, a set pattern is observed: adopting the rule, convening in Committee of the Whole, allotting time for general debate, amending, voting, and moving the bill to final passage.

Adoption of the Rule

The Speaker, after consulting the majority leader and affected committee chairmen, generally decides when the House will debate a bill and under what kind of rule. When the scheduled day arrives, the Speaker recognizes a majority member of the Rules Committee for one hour to explain the rule's contents. By custom, the majority member yields half the time for debate to a minority member of the Rules Committee. At the end of the debate, which usually takes less than the allotted hour, the House votes on the rule.

Opponents of a bill can try to defeat the rule and avert House action on the bill itself. But rules seldom are defeated because the Rules Committee is sensitive to the wishes of the House. Once the rule is adopted, the House is governed by its provisions. Most rules state that "at any time after the adoption of [the rule] the Speaker may declare the House resolved into the Committee of the Whole."

Committee of the Whole

The Committee of the Whole House on the State of the Union is a parliamentary artifice designed to expedite consideration of legislation. It is simply the House in another form with different rules. For example, a quorum in the Committee of the Whole is only 100 members, compared with 218 for the House. The Speaker appoints a majority party colleague to preside over the committee, which then begins general debate of a bill.

General Debate

A rule from the Rules Committee specifies the amount of time, usually one to two hours, for a general discussion of the bill under consideration. Controversial bills will require more time, perhaps four to ten hours. Control of the time is divided equally between the majority and minority floor managers—usually the chairman and ranking minority member of the committee that reported the legislation. (When bills are referred to more than one committee, a more complex division of debate time is allotted among the committees that had charge of the legislation.) The majority floor manager's job is to guide the bill to final passage; the minority floor manager may seek to amend or kill the bill.

After the floor managers have made their opening statements, they parcel out several minutes to colleagues on their side of the aisle who wish to speak. General debate rarely lives up to its name. Most legislators read prepared speeches; give-and-take exchange occurs infrequently at this stage of the proceedings.

The Amending Phase

The amending process is the heart of decision making on the floor of the House. Amendments determine the final shape of bills and often dominate public discussion. Illinois Republican Henry J. Hyde, for example, repeatedly and successfully has proposed amendments barring the use of federal funds for abortions.

An amendment in the Committee of the Whole is considered under the *five-minute rule,* which gives the sponsor five minutes to defend it and an opponent five minutes to speak against it. The amendment then may be brought to a vote. Amendments are routinely debated for more than ten minutes, however. Legislators gain the floor by saying, "I move to strike the last word" or "I move to strike the requisite number of words." These pro forma amendments, which make no alteration in the pending matter, simply serve to give members five minutes of debate time.

If there is an open rule, opponents may try to load a bill with so many objectionable amendments that it will sink of its own weight. The reverse strategy is to propose "sweetener" amendments that attract support from other members. Offering many amendments is an effective dilatory tactic because each amendment must be read in full, debated for at least five to ten minutes, and then voted on.

In this amending phase the interconnection of the "two Congresses" is evident: amendments can have electoral as well as legislative consequences. Floor amendments enable lawmakers to take positions that enhance their reputations with the folks back home, put opponents on record, and shape national policy. For example, "put them on the spot amendments," as Rep. (now Sen.) Charles Schumer, D-N.Y., dubbed them, can be artfully fashioned by minority lawmakers to force the majority Republicans to vote on issues (such as Social Security or veterans' benefits) that can be used against them in the next campaign.[37]

The minority party's policy preferences often are expressed through amendments. "Since the . . . leadership more often than not refuses to schedule hearings on our bills," wrote a House member, "we counter by offering our legislation in the form of amendments to other bills scheduled for consideration by the House."[38]

The minority also guards the floor to demand explanations or votes on amendments brought up by the majority. When Republicans were in the minority, one of their floor guardians wrote, "So long as a floor watchdog exists all members of the House are afforded some additional protection from precipitous actions."[39] With Democrats in the minority since the mid-1990s, Rep. Barney Frank, D-Mass., and others assumed this role for their party.

Voting

Before the 1970 Legislative Reorganization Act was passed, the Committee of the Whole adopted or rejected amendments by voice votes or other votes with no public record of who voted and how. Today any legislator sup-

ported by twenty-five colleagues can obtain a *recorded* vote. (The member who requested a recorded vote is counted as one of the twenty-five who rise to be counted by the chair.) How members decide which way to vote is discussed in detail in Chapter 9; here we focus on the mechanics of voting.

Since the installation of an electronic voting system in 1973, members can insert their personalized cards (about the size of a credit card) into one of more than forty voting stations on the floor and press the Yea, Nay, or Present button (see photo, p. 256). A large electronic display board behind the press gallery provides a running tally of the total votes for or against a motion. The voting tally, said a representative, is watched carefully by many members:

> I find that a lot of times, people walk in, and the first thing they do is look at the board, and they have key people they check out, and if those people have voted "aye," they go to the machine and vote "aye" and walk off the floor.
>
> But I will look at the board and see how [members of the state delegation] vote, because they are in districts right next to me, and they have constituencies just like mine. I will vote the way I am going to vote except that if they are both different, I will go up and say "Why did you vote that way? Let me know if there is something I am missing."[40]

After all pending amendments have been voted on, the Committee of the Whole "rises." The chairman hands the gavel back to the Speaker, and a quorum once again becomes 218 members.

Final Passage

As specified in the rule, the full House must review the actions of its agent, the Committee of the Whole. The Speaker announces that under the rule the *previous question* has been ordered; this parliamentary term means that no further debate is permitted on the bill or its amendments. The Speaker then asks whether any representative wants a separate vote on any amendment. If not, all the amendments agreed to in the committee will be approved.

The next important step is the *recommittal motion,* which provides a way for the House to return, or recommit, the bill to the committee that reported it. By precedent, the request is always made by a minority party member who opposes the legislation. Recommittal motions rarely succeed, but they do serve to protect the rights of the minority. In fact, when Republicans won majority control, they amended House rules to guarantee the minority leader or his designee the right to offer a recommittal motion with instructions (the instructions embody the minority's policy alternative).

The recommittal motion, as noted, is usually defeated. The Speaker then declares, "The question is on passage of the bill." Final passage is usually by recorded vote. Passage by the House marks about the halfway point in the lawmaking process. The Senate must also approve the bill, and its procedures are strikingly different from those of the House.

Scheduling in the Senate

Compared with the larger and more clamorous House, which needs and follows well-defined rules and precedents, the Senate operates more informally. And, unlike the House, where the rules permit a determined majority to make decisions, the Senate's rules emphasize individual prerogatives and minority rights—those of the minority party, a faction, or even a single senator. "The Senate," said one member, "is run for the convenience of one Senator to the inconvenience of 99."[41] By informal but studiously observed convention, senators can halt consideration of a measure or nomination by placing a "hold" on it. A hold is a request by a senator to his or her party leader to delay floor action on the matter in question. Moreover, a motion that requires a simple majority to pass the House may require a supermajority in the Senate. Proponents of legislation may need to attract sixty votes to break a filibuster before they can get a final vote on the measure. No wonder some commentators say the Senate has only two rules—unanimous consent and exhaustion—and three speeds—slow, slower, and slowest.

The scheduling system for the Senate is relatively simple: the Calendar of Business is used for all public and private bills and the Executive Calendar for treaties and nominations. The Senate has nothing comparable to the scheduling duties of the House Rules Committee, and the majority and minority leadership actively cooperate in scheduling. The Senate majority leader is responsible for setting the agenda and is aided in controlling the scheduling by the priority given him when he seeks recognition on the floor. Despite the Senate's smaller size, it is actually harder to establish a firm agenda of business in the Senate than in the House. As a former majority leader once said:

> The ability of any Senator to speak without limitations makes it impossible to establish total certainty with respect to scheduling. When there is added to that the difficulty and very demanding schedules of 100 Senators, it is very difficult to organize business in a way that meets the convenience of everybody.[42]

Senators, like House members, lament the absence of predictability in their schedules. Facing scores of meetings every day, lawmakers have little time to study the issues and converse with their colleagues. They race from one appointment to another and from committees to the floor to cast votes. "Life is miserable," said Sen. Bob Kerrey, D-Neb., about a legislative schedule filled with conflicts.[43] Senators' daily schedules are jam-packed. Many legislators have urged party leaders to support changes that cut down meeting conflicts, promote "family friendly" scheduling, and strengthen their quality of work.

Legislation typically reaches the Senate floor in two ways: by unanimous consent or by motion. Unanimous consent is of utmost importance, and its use is regulated by the majority leader in consultation with the minority leader.

Example of a Unanimous Consent Agreement

2.—*Ordered,* That at 11:00 a.m. on Wednesday, May 5, 1999, the Senate resume consideration of S. 900, to enhance competition in the financial services industry by providing a prudential framework for the affiliation of banks, securities firms, insurance companies, and other financial service providers; that the time until 12:00 noon be equally divided between the Senator from Texas (Mr. Gramm) and the Senator from Maryland (Mr. Sarbanes); and that at 12:00 noon the Senator from Texas (Mr. Gramm) be recognized to make a motion to table the pending Sarbanes amendment to S. 900.

Ordered further, That no amendments or motions to commit or recommit be in order during the pendency of the Sarbanes substitute, amendment No. 302; and that if the amendment is agreed to, it be considered as original text for the purpose of further amendment.

Ordered further, That following the disposition of the Sarbanes substitute, the next two amendments in order be the first degree amendments to be offered by the Chairman or his designee.

Ordered further, That following the disposition of the two Republican amendments, the Senator from Maryland (Mr. Sarbanes) or his designee be recognized to offer an amendment, the text of which is the CRA provisions of S. 753, substituting for the CRA provisions of S. 900; and that no amendments or motions to commit or recommit be in order during the pendency of the Sarbanes/CRA amendment.

Ordered further, That all amendments in order to S. 900 be relevant to the Financial Services Legislation.

Source: U.S. Senate, Calendar of Business, 106th Cong., 1st sess., May 5, 1999, 2.

Unanimous Consent Agreements

The Senate frequently dispenses with its formal rules and instead follows privately negotiated agreements submitted to the Senate for its unanimous approval (see box, this page). The objective is to expedite work in an institution known for extended debate, to impose some measure of predictability on floor action, and to minimize dilatory activities. As Democratic leader Tom Daschle of South Dakota observed:

> We aren't bringing [measures] to the floor unless we have [a unanimous consent] agreement. We could bring child-care legislation to the floor right now, but that would mean two months of fighting. We want to maximize productive time by trying to work out as much as we can in advance [of floor action].[44]

It is not uncommon for party leaders to negotiate piecemeal unanimous consent agreements—limiting debate on a specific amendment, for example—and to hammer them out in public on the Senate floor.

Unanimous consent agreements (also called time-limitation agreements) limit debate on the bill, any amendments, and various motions. Occasionally, they specify the time for the vote on final passage and impose constraints on the amendment process. For example, to facilitate enactment of an omnibus crime package that contained provisions with widespread Senate support, sen-

ators agreed to a unanimous consent request barring floor amendments on controversial issues such as gun control or the death penalty.[45]

The Senate's unanimous consent agreements are functional equivalents of special rules from the House Rules Committee. They waive the rules of their respective chambers, and each must be approved by the members—in one case by majority vote and in the other by unanimous consent. Senators and aides often negotiate and draft unanimous consent agreements privately, whereas the Rules Committee hears requests for special orders in public session.

Ways to Extract Bills from Committee

If a bill is blocked in committee, the Senate can do one of several things to obtain floor action: it can add the bill as a nongermane floor amendment to another bill, bypass the committee stage by placing the bill directly on the calendar, suspend the rules, or discharge the bill from committee. Only the first procedure is effective; the other three are somewhat difficult to employ and seldom succeed.[46]

Because the Senate has no general germaneness (or relevancy) rule, senators can take an agriculture bill that is stuck in committee and add it as a nongermane floor amendment to a pending health bill. "Amendments may be made," Thomas Jefferson noted long ago, "so as to totally alter the nature of the proposition." Most unanimous consent agreements, however, prohibit nongermane amendments.[47]

Senate Floor Procedures

The Senate, like the House, regularly convenes at noon, sometimes earlier, to keep pace with the Senate's workload. Typically, it opens with a prayer. This is followed by "leader's time" (usually ten minutes each to the majority leader and the minority leader to discuss various issues). If neither leader wants any time, the Senate typically either permits members who have requested time to make five-minute statements or it resumes consideration of old or new business under terms of a unanimous consent agreement. The Senate, too, must keep and approve the Journal of the previous day's activities. Commonly, the Journal is "deemed approved to date" by unanimous consent when the Senate adjourns or recesses at the end of each day.

Normal Routine

For most bills the Senate follows four steps:

- The majority leader secures the unanimous consent of the Senate to an arrangement that specifies when a bill will be brought to the floor and the conditions for debating it.
- The presiding officer recognizes the majority and minority floor managers for opening statements.
- Amendments are then in order, with debate regulated by the terms of the unanimous consent agreement.
- A roll call vote takes place on final passage.

As in the House, amendments in the Senate serve various purposes. For example, floor managers might accept "as many amendments as they can without undermining the purposes of the bill, in order to build the broadest possible consensus behind it."[48] Some amendments bestow benefits to the electorate and can embarrass members who must vote against them. "My amendment can be characterized as a 'November amendment,' " remarked Sen. Jesse Helms, R-N.C., "because the vote . . . will provide an opportunity for Senators to go home and say, 'I voted to reduce Federal taxes' and 'I voted to cut Federal spending.' "[49] Unless constrained by some previous unanimous consent agreement, senators generally have the right to offer an unlimited number of floor amendments.

A bill is brought to a final vote whenever senators stop talking. This can be a long process, particularly in the absence of a unanimous consent agreement. On some bills unanimous consent agreements are foreclosed because of deliberate obstructive tactics, particularly the filibuster. In these instances bills cannot be voted upon until the filibuster has ended.

Holds, Filibusters, and Cloture

The old-style filibuster has long been associated with the 1939 movie *Mr. Smith Goes to Washington,* which featured Jimmy Stewart conducting a dramatic solo talkathon to inform the public about political wrongdoing. In its new incarnation the filibuster is usually threatened more than invoked to gain bargaining power and negotiating leverage.

Filibusters involve many blocking tactics besides extended debate in which senators hold the floor for hours of endless speeches. Many contemporary filibusters are waged by those who skillfully use Senate rules. For example, senators might offer scores of amendments, raise points of order, or demand numerous and consecutive roll call votes. Holds also function as a form of silent filibuster.

Holds. A hold permits one or more senators to block floor action on measures or matters by asking their party leaders not to schedule them. Neither Senate rules nor precedents make provision for holds; they are an informal custom honored by party leaders at their discretion. The power of holds, however, is grounded in the implicit threat of senators to conduct filibusters or to object to unanimous consent agreements.

Holds have come under criticism because they often lead to delays or even the death ("choke holds") of measures or nominations. Originally intended as a way for senators to get information about when the majority leader planned action on a measure, holds have become devices to kill measures by delaying them indefinitely or to gain political leverage by, for instance, holding up action on presidential nominations. On one occasion, there were so many holds on nominations pending before the Senate that Minority Leader Tom Daschle, D-S.D., felt left out. As he explained: "I'm going to have to pick out a nominee to get to know him or her a lot better because it works that way. I mean, it's 'Hello, I'm your holder . . . come dance with me.' "[50]

Soon after the 106th Congress began, Majority Leader Lott and Minority Leader Daschle ended the much criticized use of secret holds. Previously, senators could impose confidential holds against a bill, and the sponsor might not know which of his or her colleagues was blocking floor consideration of the legislation. The two leaders jointly informed all senators of the new policy in a "Dear Colleague" letter that was printed in the *Congressional Record:*

> At the beginning of the first session of the 106th Congress all members wishing to place a hold on any legislation or executive calendar business shall notify the sponsor of the legislation and the committee of jurisdiction of their concerns. Further, written notification should be provided to the respective Leader stating their intentions regarding the bill or nomination.[51]

Worth emphasis is that it is up to the majority leader to decide whether, or for how long, he will honor a colleague's hold.

Filibusters and Cloture. The right of extended debate is unique to the Senate. Any senator or group of senators can talk continuously in the hope of delaying, modifying, or defeating legislation. In 1957 Sen. Strom Thurmond, then a Democrat, set the record for the Senate's longest solo performance— twenty-four hours and eighteen minutes—trying to kill a civil rights bill.

The success of a filibuster depends not only on how long it takes but also on when it is waged. A filibuster can be most effective late in a session because there is insufficient time to break it.[52] Even the threat of a filibuster can encourage accommodations or compromises between proponents and opponents of legislation.

Defenders of the filibuster say it protects minority rights, permits thorough consideration of bills, and dramatizes issues. Critics contend that talkathons enable minorities to extort unwanted concessions. During most of its history, the Senate had no way to terminate debate except by unanimous consent, exhaustion, or compromise. In 1917 the Senate adopted Rule XXII, its first *cloture* (debate ending) rule. After several revisions, Rule XXII now permits three-fifths of the Senate (sixty members) to shut off debate on substantive issues or procedural motions. (A two-thirds vote is required to invoke cloture on a proposal to change the rules of the Senate.) Once cloture is invoked, thirty hours of debate time remain before the final vote.

Senators complain about the frequent use of filibusters and cloture attempts. In the past, filibusters generally occurred on issues of great national importance; today they occur on a wide range of less momentous topics. As one majority leader pointed out:

> Not long ago the filibuster or threat of a filibuster was rarely undertaken in the Senate, being reserved for matters of grave national importance. That is no longer the case. . . . The threat of a filibuster is now a regular event in the Senate, weekly at least, sometimes daily. It is invoked by minorities of as few as one or two Senators and for reasons as trivial as a Senator's travel schedule.[53]

Attempts to invoke cloture also have increased. Moreover, the norm of one cloture vote per measure has changed. The modern Senate reached a record of eight cloture votes (all unsuccessful) on a controversial campaign financing measure during the 100th Congress (1987–1989).

This upward trend reflects the willingness of senators today to employ their procedural prerogatives to gain concessions, delay the consideration of legislation, or accomplish other objectives through greater use of filibusters and threatened filibusters (as well as holds and nongermane amendments). Two examples illustrate the point. First, the majority leader usually requests and overwhelmingly receives unanimous consent to bring legislation to the Senate floor. If senators object to that request, perhaps signaling that blocking actions will be taken on the measure, the majority leader may then offer a debatable motion to take up the legislation. Recent Congresses have witnessed an increase in the number of cloture petitions filed on the leader's motion to take up measures. From only two cloture motions filed during the 96th Congress (1979–1981), the 1990s have regularly seen cloture motions in the double digits on the leader's motion to bring legislation to the floor. The high-water mark was thirty-five cloture petitions filed during the 102d Congress (1991–1993) on the leader's motion to take up legislation.

Second, the majority leader regularly asks and receives unanimous consent to adjourn or to recess the Senate. Today, however, senators do not hesitate to threaten to force roll call votes on this procedural motion. For instance, Sen. Paul Wellstone, D-Minn., made it plain to Majority Leader Lott that unless a clear timetable was established for bringing campaign finance reform legislation to the floor, he would "start to take amendments, campaign finance reform amendments, and attach those [nongermane] amendments to other bills." Senator Wellstone added, "I want colleagues to know that this time I am not objecting to the UC [unanimous consent] for recess. But— and this is plenty of warning—that may very well happen." Lott made it equally clear to Wellstone that picking a date certain for campaign finance reform simply was not possible. Lott warned that he did not "want to start the cloture wars this year" by filing cloture petitions on measures as soon as they are called up to thwart senators' efforts to offer nongermane amendments to legislation. One effect of invoking cloture is to impose a germaneness, or relevancy, requirement on all amendments.[54]

These actions reflect the Senate's shift away from its norm of collegiality and accommodation. There are various explanations for this development; among them are the heightened demands placed on senators by constituents and lobbyists and the escalating costs of campaigns. "Daily priorities [are] shaped more by personal agendas—campaign needs, interest-group demands, personal staff, obligations to meet constituents, and off-the-Hill speeches— and less by the expectations of colleagues and the needs of Senate colleagues," wrote a congressional scholar. "Pressed by constituencies and lobbyists and more strongly motivated to grab a headline, senators now more routinely and more fully exploit their procedural prerogatives than at any other time in the Senate's history."[55]

Resolving House-Senate Differences

Before bills can be sent to the president, they must be passed by the House and the Senate in identical form. If neither chamber will accept the other's changes, a House-Senate conference committee is appointed to reconcile the differences. Conference committees meet to resolve the matters in dispute; they cannot reconsider provisions already agreed to. Nor can they insert new matter. However, parliamentary rules are not self-enforcing, and either chamber can waive or ignore them. It is not unusual for conference reports to contain new matter that neither chamber had ever debated or amended in committee or on the floor. "In other words," said Sen. Robert C. Byrd, D-W.Va., on one of these occasions, the first time emergency funding for Kosovo "has been before the Senate is today in the form of this conference agreement."[56]

Most public laws are approved without conferences; either they pass each chamber without any changes, or the House and Senate amends a bill in turn until both chambers agree on the wording. Only about 10 to 15 percent of the measures passed by Congress—usually the most important and controversial—are subject to bicameral reconciliation by conference committees.

Selection of Conferees

Conferees usually are named from the committee or committees that reported the legislation. Congressional rules state that the Speaker and the Senate presiding officer select conferees; in fact, that decision typically is made by the relevant committee chairmen and the ranking minority members. When Gingrich was Speaker, he took a strong role in the selection of House conferees. In precedent-setting events for the modern House, Gingrich several times even named conservative minority Democrats (in part to woo them to convert to the Republican Party) to serve as conferees on the House Republican conference delegation.

Each chamber may name as many conferees as it wants, and in recent years some conference delegations have grown quite large. The 1981 omnibus reconciliation conference set the record, with more than 250 House and Senate conferees working in fifty-eight subconferences to resolve more than 300 matters in bicameral disagreement.

Today's conference committees represent a sharp departure in size and composition from the pre-1980 era, when conference delegations generally ranged from five to twelve conferees from each house. And before the mid-1970s conferees nearly always were the most senior lawmakers from the committees that reported the legislation. Today, conferees commonly are chosen from many standing committees and sometimes reflect intricate selection arrangements. For example, conferees may be named to negotiate only certain items in disagreement rather than the entire bill. Multiple referrals and megabills are the driving forces behind these two developments.

In conference each chamber has a single vote determined by a majority of its conferees, who are expected generally to support the legislation as it passed their house. But, a senator confessed, as conference committees drag on, the "individual attitudes of the various members begin to show."[57] House confer-

ees on some occasions have a "knowledge advantage" over Senate conferees. Because representatives serve on fewer committees than do senators, they have greater opportunities to specialize in various policy areas. This means that representatives on conference committees often find that they are "arguing with Senate staff. For a House member, that's a frustrating experience."[58]

The ratio of Republicans to Democrats on a conference committee generally reflects the proportion of the two parties in the House or Senate. Seniority frequently determines who the conferees will be, but it is not unusual for junior and even first-term members to be conferees.

Openness

Secret conference meetings were the norm for most of Congress's history. In 1975 both houses adopted rules requiring open meetings unless the conferees from each chamber voted in public to close the sessions. Two years later the House went further, requiring open conference meetings unless the full House agreed to secret sessions. Sometimes C-SPAN will televise conference proceedings (see box, p. 255).

The open conference is yet another instance of individual-institutional cleavage. Under the watchful eye of lobbyists, conferees fight harder for provisions they might have dropped quietly in the interest of bicameral agreement. Needless to say, private bargaining sessions still permeate conference negotiations. As one senator noted:

> When we started the openness thing we found it more and more difficult to get something agreed to in the conferences; it seemed to take forever. So what did we do? We would break up into smaller groups and then we would ask our [conference] chairman . . to see if he could find his opposite number on the House side and discuss this matter and come back and tell us what the chances would be of working out various and sundry possibilities.[59]

Senators and representatives expect certain bills to go to conference and plan their strategy accordingly. For example, whether to have a recorded vote on amendments can influence conference bargaining. In the absence of a recorded vote, amendments may be easier to drop in conference.

The Conference Report

A conference ends when its report (the compromise bill) is signed by a majority of the conferees from each chamber. The House and Senate then vote on this report without further amendment. If either chamber rejects the conference report—an infrequent occurrence—a new conference may be called or another bill introduced. Once passed, the compromise bill is sent to the president for approval or disapproval.

Conclusion

The philosophical bias of House and Senate rules reflects the character of each institution. Individual rights are stressed in the Senate, majority rule in

Appropriations, Live

For true legislative junkies, there was nothing quite like C-SPAN's coverage of the exhaustive House-Senate negotiations May 11–13 over the midyear supplemental spending package. It televised a rare glimpse of the good, the bad, and the ugly in the normally closed world of congressional appropriations.

The show got better ratings than "E.R." in the Capitol, alerting Speaker J. Dennis Hastert to a surprise development and inspiring other members to rush to the floor and demand special votes to affect the talks.

Reviews from those in the camera's gaze were decidedly mixed, raising the question of whether the appropriators will invite C-SPAN back. "The answer is, I don't know," said Senate Appropriations chairman Ted Stevens, who was visibly angry at several points.

What galled Stevens was that, while one lawmaker would be speaking, C-SPAN cameras panned the room showing others chatting, reading, or just relaxing. Sometimes microphones picked up the sounds of lawmakers laughing and joking. All that is normal in any lengthy meeting, but, Stevens said in an interview, "When you're having a private conversation or chewing out a staffer, we don't want that picked up."

Stevens, whose language is not always G-rated, added: "My wife told me I had to stop swearing."

C-SPAN officials said they have covered high-profile appropriations conferences in the past. What was different in this case was that the appropriators did not boot out the press and public, as they are wont to do.

Source: Carroll J. Doherty, *CQ Weekly*, May 22, 1999, 1185.

---

the House. In both chambers, however, members who know the rules and precedents have an advantage over procedural novices in affecting policy outcomes. Senator Byrd is an acknowledged procedural expert in the Senate. Byrd understands that passing measures often involves unorthodox processes and procedures (for example, foregoing committee hearings or markups or even floor debate).[60]

In addition to congressional rules, persistence, strategy, timing, compromise, and pure chance are also important elements in the lawmaking process. To make public policy requires building majority coalitions at successive stages where pressure groups and other parties can advance their claims. Political, procedural, personal, and policy considerations shape the final outcome. Passing laws, as one former representative said, is like the "weaving of a web, bringing a lot of strands together in a pattern of support which won't have the kind of weak spots which could cause the whole fabric to fall apart."[61] In the next chapter we explore further the weaving of laws by analyzing factors that influence how Congress and its individual members make decisions.

The House employs an electronic system to record votes. Members insert plastic cards in voting boxes at stations throughout the chamber and vote "yea," "no," or "present." Their votes are displayed on the wall above the House gallery.

9

Decision Making in Congress

The House of Representatives took formal action in October 1998 to deal with the scandal involving President Bill Clinton and White House intern Monica Lewinsky. Since it had been revealed nine months earlier, the scandal had fascinated the public and commandeered nonstop media coverage. Independent counsel Kenneth Starr's controversial report, with supporting documents, was sent in August to the House, which referred it to the Judiciary Committee. On October 11 the committee released Starr's report to the public and the Internet. By the end of the following day, 25 million people had viewed the report online; the conventional media brought it to millions more.

On October 18 the issue reached the House floor in the form of H. Res. 581, a Republican-sponsored resolution directing the Judiciary Committee to conduct an open-ended impeachment investigation of the president. Now individual lawmakers had to take stands on the matter. One of them was Gerald D. Kleczka, a seven-term Democrat from Milwaukee's south side:

> Kleczka stood transfixed in the center of the House, voting card in hand and eyes on the tote board above him. Should he support the third presidential impeachment inquiry in the nation's history?
>
> Kleczka . . . hesitated for several minutes and talked to a couple of Judiciary Committee members. Finally, he punched in his card.[1]

The vote that Kleczka cast was "no." All but thirty-one Democrats voted against impeachment, as Kleczka did. But the Republican resolution was approved, 258–176. Earlier a Democratic alternative that would have limited the scope of the investigation and finished it by the end of the year, was voted down, 198–236.

The vote on H. Res. 581 was the most fateful and symbolic action taken by the ideologically divided 105th Congress. It set Congress and the nation on a five-month course that led to impeachment by the House and acquittal by the Senate. It ensured that the whole process would be marked by boisterous partisanship: the vote itself was accompanied by catcalls and angry exchanges. Even without the Democratic defectors, the unanimous Republican majority commanded the votes to conduct the impeachment process on their own terms. But with only thirty-one Democrats supporting them at the outset, it was going to be a bitter, partisan affair to the very end.

The agonizing votes on the impeachment inquiry were a reminder that members of Congress are free agents obliged, according to the Constitution, to make public commitments that they alone can answer for, regardless of the ap-

peals of party leaders, lobbyists, or even the president of the United States. These votes also show that, at this point in history, lawmakers tend to follow their party's direction. "Can I trust the Republicans to conduct this in a fair and expeditious manner?" Kleczka asked himself. His answer: "They are content to draw this out as far into next year as possible."[2]

The Power to Choose

Although not all votes command as much attention as the impeachment of a president, every decision has the capacity to shape government. In both chambers every legislator has the right, indeed the obligation, to vote. Legislators cast their own votes; no colleague or staff aide may do it for them. To exchange their votes for money or for any other thing of value would be to accept a bribe, a federal crime.

Recorded votes on the House or Senate floor or in committee, though the most visible decisions made by legislators, are imperfect clues to their beliefs. From his study of members' committee activity, Richard L. Hall distinguishes between formal and informal modes of participation.[3] Much of Congress's decision making is a matter of public record: voting, of course, but also participation in formal meetings, markups, debates, and amending activities. But equally important are the complex informal negotiations that surround nearly every enactment—away from the prying eyes of reporters and lobbyists and often conducted by staff aides. For a fuller measure of members' performance, one must also consider not only how members participate in floor or committee deliberations but also how much effort they expend. How much attention do they pay to issues, how do they gain expertise on them, and how do they attend to party or caucus affairs? How do they allocate time between legislative and constituent duties and hire and supervise staff? Countless such decisions— some reached with the solemnity of a vote to commit troops abroad (see Chapter 14), others made hastily or inadvertently—define what it means to be a member of Congress.

Capitol Hill norms strongly underscore lawmakers' independence. Although party leaders may plead, coax, or warn, using "roughhouse" tactics against members can backfire. When House GOP leaders took freshman representative Mark W. Neumann, R-Wis., to the woodshed in the fall of 1995, he ended up with a plum assignment. Neumann, a member of the Appropriations Subcommittee on National Security, had fought for an amendment requiring congressional approval before President Clinton could deploy U.S. troops in Bosnia. Because the House-Senate conference had dropped the provision, Neumann voted against the conference report, which failed on the House floor. The irate Appropriations chairman, Robert L. Livingston, R-La., fired off a letter reassigning Neumann to the less important Military Construction Subcommittee. But the seventy-three GOP freshmen rallied to Neumann's cause, citing an early leadership promise that no members would ever have to vote against their conscience. Livingston would not rescind his decision, but the leadership compensated Neumann with a coveted place on the House Budget Committee—two seats for the price of one.[4]

Nor are there any legal grounds for attacking legislators for performing their duties, at least in legislative deliberations and votes. Anxious to prevent reprisals against legislators in the conduct of office, the Constitution's authors specified in Article I, Section 6, that "for any speech or debate in either House, they shall not be questioned in any other place."

Types of Decisions

One of the most basic decisions made by legislators is how much time to spend in the nation's capital. Members within air-commuting range often remain at their home base, commuting to Washington for midweek sessions. Many of these "Tuesday to Thursday Club" members rarely if ever spend a weekend in Washington. For them, life in the Washington community is as alien as in a foreign country. Others, with varying degrees of enthusiasm, plunge into the capital's social and political activities. Such individuals rarely "go back to Pocatello," as the saying goes. Between these two extremes are many variations.

A more subtle question for lawmakers is how to spend their time and energies while in the nation's capital. Some members work hard to digest the mountains of studies and reports that cross their desks; in the parlance of Capitol Hill, they "do their homework." By comparison, others seem to know or care little about legislative matters. They prefer other aspects of the job (correspondence, outreach, and visits with constituents or lobby groups, for example). Such members rarely contribute to committee or floor deliberations; their votes are usually prompted by cues from colleagues, staff members, the White House, or interested groups. They are found in the ranks of the "Obscure Caucus," a list of unnoticed members compiled periodically by *Roll Call,* a Capitol Hill newspaper. "These members kept their noses down for the most part, made the welfare of their district their number one priority, and largely avoided joining any contentious national debates."[5]

Although either of these strategies can be successfully pursued, and distressingly few voters can tell the difference, most legislators claim to prefer legislative tasks, as we saw in Chapter 5. Whatever the distractions, they strive to make time for their legislative duties.

Specializing

Within the legislative realm, members may dig deeply in a particular area or range widely across issues and policies. Senators are more apt to be generalists, while representatives are inclined to cultivate a few specialties.

In both houses key policy-making roles are played by those whom Rep. David E. Price, D-N.C., a political scientist, calls policy entrepreneurs: those recognized for "stimulating more than . . . responding" to outside political forces in a given field.[6] Often nearly invisible to the mass of citizens, these legislators are known to specialized publics for their contributions to specific policies—for example, Sen. John D. Rockefeller IV, D-W.Va., on health care; Sen. Mitch McConnell, R-Ky., on campaign finance; Rep. Henry A. Waxman, D-Calif., on health and the environment; and Rep. Tom DeLay, R-Texas, on regulatory reform.

Legislative specialties are often dictated by constituency concerns. Alaska lawmakers focus on the policies toward government-controlled Alaska lands, while the delegation from Washington state (the home of Boeing and Microsoft) must be attuned to needs of the aerospace and software industries.

Committee assignments themselves may shape members' interests. Sens. Richard G. Lugar, R-Ind., and Chuck Hagel, R-Neb., use their seats on the Foreign Relations Committee to express thoughtful, independent views on foreign affairs. Such specialties are hardly calculated to appeal to home state voters, but their assignments challenge them to undertake serious legislative work.

Specializations may also reflect personal interests nurtured by background or experience. As former senator Warren Rudman explained:

> Who are we when we're elected to the Senate? . . . We are men and women. We are not bland, neutral, blank-slate people who never suffered, and never were happy. You tend to be influenced by the sum total of life's experiences.[7]

Past experiences impel members to specialize in particular issues. Rep. Floyd D. Spence, R-S.C., one of the first people in the country to undergo a double-lung transplant, became a champion of fetal tissue research—something opposed by many of his anti-abortion GOP colleagues. Sens. Pete V. Domenici, R-N.M., and Paul Wellstone, D-Minn., both of whom have family members suffering from mental illness, led a 1996 fight to require health plans to offer the same coverage for severe mental disorders as for physical disorders. They agree on so little else that they were dubbed the "odd couple of health care." Wellstone and House Speaker J. Dennis Hastert, both former school wrestlers, formed another unexpected team. They come together to support provisions of higher education bills that bolster the place of "nonrevenue-producing sports" such as wrestling, gymnastics, tennis, or track "Wrestling really saved me," Wellstone confesses. "It gave me self-confidence and self-respect." Hastert, a high school wrestling coach for sixteen years, deplores cutting back small sports programs as "an unintended consequence" of collegiate efforts to comply with Title IX's efforts to promote athletic opportunities for women.[8]

Before the reforms of the 1960s and 1970s, lawmakers faced formidable obstacles if they wanted to affect policies not handled by their committees. Today, however, members have avenues of influence besides committee assignments—speeches, floor amendments, caucuses, and task forces, to name a few. When only in his second term, and not a member of the Armed Services Committee, Rep. Dick Armey, R-Texas, devised an ingenious scheme (involving an outside commission) for closing unneeded military bases; his proposal smoothed political sensitivities and won bipartisan support for passage in 1988. Such spectacular feats are not everyday occurrences, but the fluidity of today's procedures makes even the most junior member a potential policy entrepreneur. (A few years later Armey became House majority leader.)

Whatever a member's specialty, the ability to influence the decision-making process is what really counts, as the late senator Edmund S. Muskie, D-Maine, explained:

People have all sorts of conspiratorial theories on what constitutes power in the Senate. It has little to do with the size of the state you come from. Or the source of your money. Or committee chairmanships, although that certainly gives you a kind of power. But real power up there comes from doing your work and knowing what you're talking about. Power is the ability to change someone's mind. . . . The most important thing in the Senate is credibility. Credibility! That is power.[9]

Staking Out Positions

Lawmakers, of course, do more than specialize in a particular policy field. Sooner or later they must adopt positions or take stands—what Richard F. Fenno Jr. has called the "politics of timing."[10]

From his examination of a 1981 vote on selling AWACS (airborne warning and control system) reconnaissance planes to Saudi Arabia, Fenno identified three types of decision makers: early deciders, active players, and late deciders. Early deciders are fervent supporters who want to get out front in the debate. "I'd rather come out early and be part of the fight," said Rep. Peter King, R-N.Y., of his ready support of "fast track" trade authority in 1997.[11] These members are bypassed by most lobbyists, because their fixed positions are known at the outset from declarations, bill sponsorship, or prior voting records. Active players, in contrast, delay their commitment, inviting bids from various sides of the issue at hand and often giving them leverage over the final language of legislation. Late deciders delay their decision (or reconsider an earlier commitment) until the very last moment. Although they have little influence over the basic framework of the measure, they are eagerly courted by all sides and may gain other concessions. Late deciders are concerned not only about political payoffs and their need for political cover but also about their reputation for independence.

Introduction and sponsorship of bills vary widely among individual senators and representatives. Some lawmakers are inveterate initiators of bills and resolutions; others shy away from sponsoring measures. A Senate study by Wendy Schiller found that bills were most likely to be introduced by senior senators, those who are chairs or ranking members of high-volume committees (like Commerce), and those who represent large, diverse states.[12]

According to Senate and House rules, bills and resolutions may have an unlimited number of cosponsors. And cosponsorship has become quite common. A majority of bills introduced in both chambers were cosponsored, according to a study of the 99th Congress; the average such bill had 7.2 cosponsors in the Senate, and 22.2 cosponsors in the House.[13] Authors of measures will often circulate a "Dear Colleague" letter detailing the virtues of the bill and soliciting cosponsors to demonstrate broad support and force committee action. According to one study, House members circulated no fewer than 5,400 "Dear Colleagues" during 1993—an average of just over twelve letters per member.[14]

Cosponsorship, no less than sponsorship, is politically motivated, as freshman Dan Quayle (R-Ind., Senate 1981–1989) well understood when he asked liberal Edward M. Kennedy, D-Mass., to cosponsor his first major bill,

the 1982 Job Training Partnership Act. Soliciting Kennedy's cooperation was a daring move for a young conservative embarking on his first subcommittee chairmanship. "The decision to travel the bipartisan route . . . was his earliest strategic decision," wrote Fenno of Quayle's eventual legislative success. "It caused him a lot of trouble, but he never looked back."[15] Despite right-wing opposition and stonewalling from President Ronald Reagan's administration, Quayle's decision won him passage of the job training act—his greatest Senate achievement.

Occasionally, however, cosponsors are shunned. Introducing his waterway users' fee bill, Senator Domenici decided against seeking cosponsors for several reasons.[16] First, as ranking Republican on the subcommittee, he could arrange for hearings without the support of cosponsors. Second, single sponsorship would be easier. ("If you've got cosponsors you have to clear every little change with them.") Third, if by chance he found no cosponsors, his effort might suffer a devastating initial setback. And, finally, if the bill became law, he would get full, undiluted credit. Thus, for a time, Domenici fought alone for his bill. In the end it was signed into law by President Jimmy Carter at a Democratic rally crowded with politicians who initially had opposed it. Domenici's role was barely mentioned. Such are the ironies of politics.

Do legislators actually favor the bills and resolutions they introduce? Normally they do, but as Sportin' Life, the *Porgy and Bess* character, said, "It ain't necessarily so." Members may introduce a measure to stake out jurisdiction for their committee or to pave the way for hearings and deliberations that will air a public problem. Or they may introduce measures they do not personally favor in order to oblige an executive agency or to placate a given interest.

Taking Part

As in any organization, some members of Congress take a passionate interest in what goes on, others pay selective attention to issues; a few seem just to be going through the motions. In his detailed study of three House committees, Richard Hall uncovered varying levels of participation among members, among the committees and subcommittees, and among types of involvement.

Although members' attendance at committee and subcommittee sessions was quite respectable (about three-quarters of the members showed up for at least part of each session), active participation—taking part in markup debate, offering amendments, and the like—was far less common. Perhaps half a subcommittee's members could be considered "players," by a generous counting. The rest are "nonplayers." As a subcommittee staffer remarked, "On a good day half of [the members] know what's going on. Most of the time it's only five or six who actually mark a bill up."[17]

Constituency interests, as might be predicted, strongly propel members' participation in committee business. This is true even when the negotiations are informal, out of the public's sight. In formal subcommittee markup sessions, "the public forum has the benefit of allowing members to at once promote—through their votes, arguments, amendments, obstructionism—con-

stituency interests and be seen doing so."[18] Constituency-driven activity was most pronounced in the Agriculture Committee, a panel historically driven by regional and commodity pressures. That committee also witnessed the most "biased" participation in that participants were unrepresentative of the full committee (much less the full House). Decisions on programs for dairy farmers and peanut growers, for example, were strongly tilted toward producers in those agricultural areas. Not even full committee or floor deliberations muted the enthusiastic advocacy of the dozen or so lawmakers from districts where those commodities were concentrated. In debates over job training legislation participating members tended to represent areas with higher unemployment rates than those of nonparticipants. In the three other cases, where concentrated district benefits were not at stake, Hall did not discern participatory biases.

Casting Votes

Lawmakers' most visible choices are embodied in the votes they cast. Voting is a central ritual in any legislative body. Members place great stock in their voting records, under the assumption (sometimes borne out) that constituents will judge them at reelection time. Outside groups are keen-eyed followers of the votes on specific measures. Scholars, too, have a longstanding love affair with legislative voting, no doubt because votes provide concrete, quantifiable indicators that lend themselves to statistical analysis.

Senators and representatives strive to be recorded on as many floor and committee votes as they can. The average member participates in nineteen of every twenty recorded votes on the floor. Members seek to cultivate a record of diligence to buttress their home styles and to forestall charges of absenteeism by opponents. House and Senate leaders have in recent years made it easier for members to compile such records by avoiding votes on Mondays and Fridays, "stacking" votes back to back in midweek, and promising no votes several evenings each week.[19] (The details of how members vote are found in Chapter 8.)

If members cannot vote in person, they can still be recorded on an issue. They may announce their views in floor statements or in press releases. Or they may pair themselves with someone on the opposite side of an issue. *Pairing* is a voluntary arrangement that allows members to go on record without actually voting or affecting the final tabulation.

The practice of allowing absent members to vote by proxy—entrusting their votes to an ally who is present at the session—has never been permissible in floor deliberations, and in 1995 it was suspended in House committees. During their forty years in the minority, House Republicans resented the fact that their members in attendance invariably were outvoted by chairmen voting the proxies they had collected beforehand from busy Democrats (though the tactic was used by both parties). By abolishing proxies, the new majority hoped to encourage members to attend their committee meetings, even though it made life more hectic for everyone.

Offering Amendments

A chief strategy for shaping legislation during committee or floor deliberations is to offer amendments. Sometimes amendments are intended to provide a test of strength. In 1993, during debate on reauthorizing the National Aeronautics and Space Administration, a junior committee member, Rep. Tim Roemer, D-Ind., introduced an amendment to cancel the costly space station program. Instead of losing by a comfortable margin—as had happened in previous years—the amendment failed by a single vote, signaling plunging support for the space station and other "big science" projects such as the superconducting super collider.[20]

Some amendments are designed to force members to declare themselves on symbolic issues that command public attention. Amendments on abortion funding or balanced budgets are prime examples. Others are "killer amendments," intended to make a bill so unpalatable that it will fail. During House debates on term limits in 1995 and 1997, minority Democrats, most of whom opposed the idea, floated amendments to apply a twelve-year term limit retroactively. If passed, the amendments would have booted many sitting members out of office. These amendments failed by wide margins.[21] Killer amendments upset the sponsors and managers of bills, but in fact such roadblocks rarely alter a measure's ultimate fate. During 1996 debate on a controversial shipbuilding trade agreement, a bipartisan amendment was proposed to provide U.S. shipbuilders with thirty months of transition assistance once the agreement took effect. Supporters of the trade agreement warned that the amendment would force a new round of international negotiations. Ron Dellums, then a Democratic representative from California, disputed the threat:

> "Killer amendment." I have not seen anything die in the twenty-five years I have been around here, and I have gone after some things to try to kill them, so that is a bunch of hyperbole, Mr. Chairman.[22]

The House passed both the amendment and the shipbuilding agreement, but the Senate took no action.

In the House, majority party leaders can shape outcomes by determining which, if any, members' floor amendments will be in order. The outcome of the 1997 debate over funding for the National Endowment for the Arts (NEA) hinged on the single floor amendment permitted by the leadership. Conservatives urged GOP leaders to honor their commitment to ax the NEA and uphold the Appropriations Committee's bill, which in essence ended the agency's funding. But fearing defeat by a bipartisan, pro-arts coalition, Republican leaders seized upon an amendment proposed by Rep. Vernon J. Ehlers, R-Mich., and incorporated it into the Rules Committee's "rule" for the debate. This amendment would have eliminated the agency, but it would have sent $80 million directly to the states for arts and education grants. The amendment satisfied neither of the warring camps, who pleaded for an up-or-down vote on NEA. By twisting arms, the leaders eked out a victory for the rule by one

vote, 217–216. But the next day the Ehlers amendment itself went down to defeat, 155–271. And the bill went to the Senate with no NEA funding at all.[23]

In the Senate, which cherishes individual senators' prerogatives, amendments are more freely offered and form a central part of floor debate. With elections looming in 1996, Sen. Edward Kennedy won passage of two popular measures by vowing to introduce them as amendments for a variety of floor bills. These were a hike in the minimum wage and a provision that insurance companies could not drop coverage when people switch jobs or deny coverage for preexisting medical conditions (the latter cosponsored with Sen. Nancy Landon Kassebaum, R-Kan.). GOP leaders strongly opposed both measures but allowed them to be voted on rather than face repeated embarrassments in an election year.

Amendments can also derail legislation. President Clinton's 1993 economic stimulus package came unglued in the Senate under a barrage of hostile amendments. While the bill's Democratic managers labored to keep the measure intact, Republicans put forward amendments to drop what they claimed were "pork" projects. When Democrats shut off amendments by a parliamentary maneuver, the Republicans' opposition hardened, and cloture could not be invoked.

What Do Votes Mean?

Like other elements in the legislative process, voting is open to manifold interpretations. A vote may or may not be what it seems to be. Therefore, one must be very cautious in analyzing legislative votes.

House and Senate floor votes are crude channels for registering members' views. Votes are frequently taken on procedural matters that evoke responses independent of the issue at hand. Or members may favor a measure but feel constrained to vote against the version presented on the floor. Conversely, as with the 1997 balanced-budget resolution, members may go along because "on the whole" they deem it a step forward, even though they dislike specific portions. Or they may vote for a questionable proposal to prevent enactment of something worse. Or they may support a harmful amendment expecting that the other chamber or the conference committee will kill it. Finally, they may accede to party leaders' wishes on measures so long as their actions do not adversely affect their constituencies.

The dilemmas of voting were brought home to Rep. Steny H. Hoyer, D-Md., when he struggled late in the 1983 session to push a civil service health care bill desired by federal workers (65,000 of whom resided in his district). To facilitate action, Hoyer offered an amendment limiting abortions under federal health plans. His tactic was aimed at forestalling even stronger anti-abortion provisions, and in any event he expected the amendment to be scuttled in a House-Senate conference. But the Senate fooled him, voting 44–43 to accept his amendment and adopting the House bill without a conference. So the "Hoyer amendment" became law, to the chagrin of its author and the anger of his pro-choice allies.[24]

In some cases recorded votes are wholly misleading. A favorable vote may really be negative, or vice versa. A Senate vote to attach a school prayer amendment sponsored by Jesse Helms, R-N.C., to a 1979 measure dealing with Supreme Court jurisdiction was really a vote to kill the amendment: it was expected that the House would scuttle the bill. Later that year a vote against automobile air bags was only a token vote: it was tied to an authorizing bill that would have expired before the National Highway Traffic Safety Administration's air-bag regulations were to take effect. In such cases legislators' votes must be decoded to reveal their real meaning.

Sometimes voting conceals a legislator's true position. Given the multiplicity of votes—procedural as well as substantive—on many measures, it is entirely possible for lawmakers to come out on more than one side of an issue, or at least appear to do so. For instance, members may vote for authorizing a program but against funding it. Or they may vote against final passage of a bill but for a substitute version. This tactic assures the bill's backers that a lawmaker favors the concept, while pleasing voters who oppose the bill. Such voting patterns may reflect either a deliberate attempt to obscure one's position or a thoughtful response to complex questions. As in so many aspects of human behavior, lawmakers' motivations can be judged fully only in light of specific cases.

Lawmakers' voting rationales are sometimes hard to explain to outsiders. In some cases members face a dilemma: either vote their convictions and face the consequences or swallow their reservations and vote for appearance' sake. Rep. Mark Sanford, R-S.C., chose the former course in 1998, when he joined fourteen other Republicans in voting against a popular bill authorizing U.S. sanctions against nations that persecute religious minorities—an appealing idea but fraught with problems, "This was an awfully awkward vote, and I know I'll hear from the folks back home," he explained. "But the devil was in the details."[25] More often lawmakers decide to go with the crowd. Regarding a highly appealing constitutional amendment requiring a balanced budget, Sen. Ernest F. Hollings, D-S.C., admitted that he planned to vote for it because he got "tired of explaining" its deficiencies. It was easier "just to say put it in."[26]

This point is important for students to understand because scholars often treat votes as if they were unambiguous indicators of legislators' views. It is important for citizens because lobbyists and reporters frequently assess incumbents on the basis of floor votes. As we will detail in Chapter 12, many groups construct voting indexes to label "friendly" or "unfriendly" legislators. Citizens are well advised to examine such indexes closely. How many votes does the index comprise, and are they a fair sample of the group's concerns? Does the index embody a partisan or ideological agenda, hidden or otherwise? The bottom line: beware of an interest group's voting scorecards, even if you agree with its policy leanings.

Determinants of Voting

Votes, particularly on single issues, should be examined, interpreted, and labeled with caution. With these caveats in mind, we turn to several factors

Figure 9-1 Party Unity Votes in Congress, 1970–1998

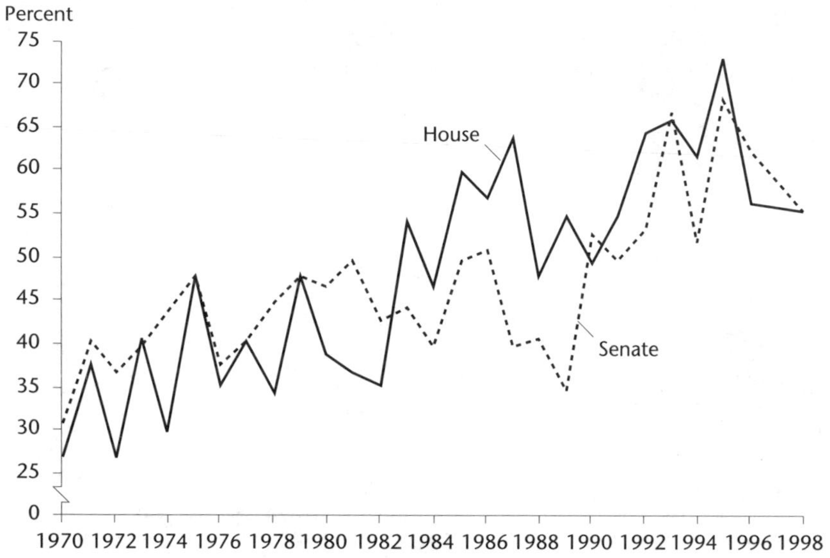

Percent

Source: *CQ Weekly,* Jan. 9, 1999, 79.

Note: Party unity votes are defined as the percentage of all House and Senate votes in which a majority of Democrats opposed a majority of Republicans.

that shape congressional voting: party affiliation, ideological leanings, constituents' views, and presidential leadership.

Party and Voting

One way for members to reach voting decisions is to consult the views of their political party colleagues. Party affiliation is the strongest single correlate of members' voting decisions, and in recent years it has reached surprisingly high levels. Of the nearly 2,000 floor votes cast by House and Senate members on articles of impeachment against President Clinton, for example, 92 percent followed partisan battlelines—Republicans favoring impeachment, Democrats resisting it.

In a typical year nearly two-thirds of all floor votes could be called *party unity votes,* defined by Congressional Quarterly as votes in which a majority of voting Republicans oppose a majority of voting Democrats. Figure 9-1 depicts such House and Senate party votes from 1970 through 1998. Today's revival of party voting recalls the militant parties era of a century ago. At that time at least two-thirds of all roll calls were party unity votes. In several sessions a majority of the votes found 90 percent of one party arrayed against 90 percent of the other; today such sharp partisan divisions appear in about one roll call vote in ten.[27]

Figure 9-2   Levels of Party Voting in Congress, 1970–1998

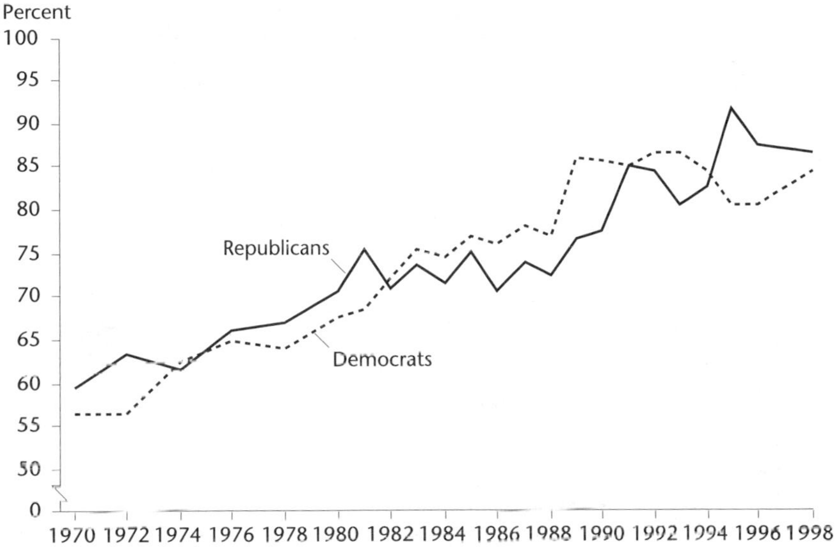

Percent

Sources: Derived from voting studies in *Congressional Quarterly Weekly Report,* Dec. 22, 1990, 4212; Dec. 19, 1992, 3849, 3905; Dec. 18, 1993, 3432; Jan. 27, 1996, 245; Dec. 21, 1996, 3432; Jan. 9, 1999, 80.

Note: The graph shows the percentage of times the average Democrat or Republican in Congress voted with his or her party majority in partisan votes for the years listed. These *composite party unity scores* are based on votes that split the parties in the House and Senate— a majority of voting Democrats opposing a majority of voting Republicans. We have recomputed the scores to correct for absences.

Unlike parliamentary systems, however, the U.S. Congress rarely votes along absolutely strict party lines and never brings down the government in power (unless one counts impeachment of the president). In a typical year the minority party wins perhaps a third of all party unity votes, thus indicating the looseness of party ranks.

It is possible to calculate party unity scores for individual members—the percentage of party unity votes in which each member voted in agreement with the majority of his or her party colleagues. According to these scores the average legislator now sticks with the party line on at least four of every five votes. Aggregate party unity scores for Democrats and Republicans from 1970 through 1998 are displayed in Figure 9-2. Partisan voting blocs are evident also in many committees. From their painstaking study of voting in eight House committees during the mid-1970s, Glenn and Suzanne Parker concluded that partisanship was a major explanatory variable in all of the panels except for Foreign Affairs, which has a bipartisan tradition.[28]

Party voting levels in both houses, which were relatively high in the 1950s, fell in the 1960s and rose again perceptibly in the 1970s. Sharpened partisanship has marked congressional politics since then, to the point that "partisan gridlock" has become a buzzword in campaigns of the 1990s.[29]

Partisan strength in voting is rooted in several factors. Some students argue that party loyalty is mainly a shorthand term for constituency differences; that is, partisans vote together because they reflect the same kinds of political and demographic areas. According to this reasoning, legislators stray from party ranks when they feel their constituents will not benefit from the party's policies. Today's Democratic mavericks tend to be from nonminority southern districts, whose voters typically are to the right of the party's mainstream. Six of them—five representatives and one senator—decamped to the GOP after the 1994 elections. Republican mavericks are mostly from New England and the Northeast corridor, where voters fall to the left of the party's center. Of the ten freshmen Republicans who gave less than 90 percent support to the Republican program during the first hundred days of 1995, eight were northeasterners.[30] To win in these areas, elected officials must lean away from their parties' main thrust.

Sorting out the two parties' constituency differences also helps explain the recent upsurge in lawmakers' party loyalty. Among Democratic representatives, increasing numbers of their southern flank are African Americans. The dwindling number of Democrats representing conservative districts (including the self-named Blue Dog Democrats) try to put distance between themselves and their leaders. By the same token, the Republican congressional party is more uniformly conservative than it used to be. In the South the most conservative areas now tend to elect Republicans, not Democrats. Elsewhere many areas once represented by GOP liberals have been captured by Democrats. The decline of archconservative Democrats and liberal Republicans, especially in the House, underlies much of the ideological cohesion within, and chasm between, today's Capitol Hill parties.[31]

Party cohesion also flows from shared policy goals shaped early in a politician's career. Those who entered politics through the civil rights, environmental, or antiwar movements gravitated toward the Democratic Party and displayed their shared values in voting. By contrast, individuals who became active to slash taxes, downsize the government, or safeguard traditional values tended to gather under the GOP banner, underscoring that party's historic approach to such issues.

Constituency and recruitment are not, however, the sole sources of Capitol Hill partisanship. Another source is institutional: the congressional parties and their activities to promote partisanship. New-member socialization is dominated by party organizations. Incoming members attend party-sponsored orientations, rely on party bodies for their committee assignments, and often organize into partisan "class clubs." When seeking out cues for voting, moreover, legislators tend to choose party colleagues as guides for their own behavior.[32]

Party leaders, as we saw in Chapter 6, repeatedly contact members to solicit views and urge them to support the party. The more visible an issue, the harder leaders must compete against other pressures for members' votes. Rep. Mark Souder, R-Ind., described the exhortations of Newt Gingrich, then House Speaker, and his lieutenants during the GOP's first year in power:

> They pull us into a room before almost every vote and yell at us. . . . They say, "This is a test of our ability to govern," or "This is a gut check," or "I got you here and you hired me as your coach to get you through, but if you want to change coaches, go ahead."[33]

Leaders are more likely to muster votes if the issue is defined in procedural terms than if the issue is presented substantively. Whatever the legislator's personal leanings, the institutional push toward partisan voting cannot be ignored.

Finally, party leaders exploit each chamber's rules and procedures to encourage favorable outcomes. David W. Rohde calls this *process partisanship*, which means "the degree to which each institution is structured or operates in a partisan fashion."[34] House procedures sharpen partisanship, inasmuch as a cohesive majority party can usually work its will. Through their control of key committees, their scheduling powers, and the use of special rules to structure floor debate and voting, majority party leaders can arrange votes they are likely to win and avoid those they are apt to lose. Senate leaders have fewer opportunities to engineer victories because that chamber's rules and procedures distribute power more evenly between the parties and among individual senators than does the House. Yet Senate floor leaders can regulate the timing of debates to their advantage and (through their right to be recognized first to speak or offer amendments on the floor) influence the order and content of floor deliberations.

Ideology and Voting

Just as lawmakers are committed partisans, they also tend to harbor ideological views. From roll call votes and interviews, Jerrold Schneider concluded that much congressional voting is ideological, that voting coalitions form because members carry with them well-developed ideological positions. Since then Keith T. Poole and Howard Rosenthal have derived from roll call votes ideological scores for all members of Congress from 1789 to the present.[35] They find stable cleavages along two dimensions: race and government intervention in the economy.

When political scientists began to do serious voting analysis in the 1950s, it was obvious that party and ideology were quite distinct ingredients, despite measurable differences between the parties. The reason was deep ideological splits within the two parties. In the late 1930s a conservative coalition of Republicans and southern Democrats emerged in a reaction against the New Deal.[36] Historically, this coalition was stronger in the Senate than in the House, but its success rate in both chambers was formidable during the 1938–1964

period—no matter which party controlled the White House or Capitol Hill. In 1981 the coalition reappeared as President Ronald Reagan captured votes of conservative Democrats on budget, tax, and social issues, while pulling mainstream Democrats toward conservative positions on the other issues.[37]

Today the conservative coalition appears in less than one vote of every ten. But in those rare instances when conservatives of both parties stand together, they almost always win.[38]

The underlying reason for the decline of bipartisan conservatism, of course, is the hardening ideological consistency of both political parties. The Republicans are more uniformly conservative, and the Democrats more liberal, than they were in the period between the late 1930s and the mid-1980s. "Democrats are perched on the left, Republicans on the right, in both the House and the Senate as the ideological centers of the two parties have moved markedly apart," writes Sarah A. Binder.[39] In other words, the two parties are more cohesive internally and farther apart externally than they were in the recent past.

Partisan repositioning has shrunk the ideological center in the two chambers. The proportion of centrists—conservative Democrats and moderate Republicans—hovered at about 30 percent in the 1960s and 1970s. (Binder's definition of centrists is those members who are closer to the ideological midpoint between the two parties than to the ideological center of their own party.) Only about one in ten of today's lawmakers fall into this centrist category.[40] Conservative Democrats, the larger of the two centrist groupings, once represented a third of their party's members; a mere handful remain today. Also few in number, moderate to liberal Republicans account for no more than 6 percent of all House GOP members and 15 percent of senators.

Faced with increasing resistance within their respective parties, many of these centrists have left Capitol Hill. Many of them speak bitterly of their frustration with the wrangling and partisanship that have characterized recent Congresses. "I thought the essence of good government was reconciling divergent views with compromises that served the country's interests," wrote Senator Rudman, who retired in 1992. "But that's not how 'movement conservatives' or far-left liberals operate. The spirit of civility and compromise was drying up."[41] Retiring moderates are no longer assured of being replaced by new faces like them; increasingly their successors are more ideologically rigid than they—oftentimes representing the opposition party.

Constituency and Voting

To consider the potency of constituency, we need only consider how House members voted on an uncommonly partisan agenda: the fourteen-point Contract with America in 1995. Fealty to the contract hinged mainly on partisanship and ideology, according to James G. Gimpel's multivariate analysis of the voting. Southern Democrats, for example, were more supportive than were nonsoutherners. Also significant were district characteristics: racial composition, median income, percentage of rural inhabitants, and percentage who

voted for independent presidential candidate Ross Perot in 1992. Gimpel summarizes his findings:

> The plurality of legislators who found themselves on the losing side of these votes [on the contract] were from northern and western urban districts with significant minority and low-income populations. In this sense, the Contract with America was a legislative program supported most consistently by members from predominantly white, middle- and upper-income suburban and rural districts.[42]

Constituencies control lawmakers' choices in two ways. First, people can elect representatives whose views so mirror their own that floor votes automatically reflect the will of the constituents. In other words, representatives vote their constituency because they are simply transplanted locals. Certain constituency issues invariably override party or ideology—for example, farm subsidies, public lands management, and immigration.

A second form of constituency control is the ever present threat of electoral defeat. Only rarely do politicians' careers hang on a single vote, but it happens. Pennsylvania Democrat Marjorie Margolies-Mezvinsky lost her swing district in 1994 because of her deciding vote that passed President Clinton's budget. Her constituents regarded her vote as a broken promise to oppose tax and spending increases. Naturally skittish in calculating voters' reactions, politicians usually play it safe. The choices they make, taken cumulatively, offer opportunities to expand or contract their electoral base of support. To explain how politicians calculate the electoral effect of their decisions, R. Douglas Arnold draws upon the distinction between attentive and inattentive publics first described by V. O. Key Jr.[43]

Attentive publics are those citizens who are aware of issues facing Congress and harbor decided opinions about what Congress should do. Such people usually, though not always, belong to interest groups that reinforce, mobilize, and voice their preferences. Politicians have little trouble discerning who is paying attention to a given issue and even grasping what the electoral consequences may be. Yielding to a group's strongly voiced preferences is a politician's natural instinct—unless the issue in question has mobilized two equally vociferous but opposing interests. Especially feared are single-interest groups that threaten to withhold electoral support if their preferences are not followed. Abortion and gun control are recent issues that have evoked such threats. Happily for lawmakers, most citizens, even highly motivated ones, are interested in a range of issues. Thus politicians can cultivate support over the long haul and encourage voters to gloss over "wrong" votes on particular issues.

Inattentive publics are people who lack extensive knowledge and firm preferences about a specific issue. This describes most of us most of the time. We pay attention to only a small fraction of the issues being decided by Congress. Yet a reelection-minded legislator cannot afford to ignore people who seemingly are indifferent to an issue. "Latent or unfocused opinions," Arnold cau-

tions, "can quickly be transformed into intense and very real opinions with enormous political repercussions. Inattentiveness and lack of information today should not be confused with indifference tomorrow."[44]

Previously "invisible" issues—the savings and loan scandal in the 1980s, the House "bank overdrafts," and personal ethical lapses, for example—may leap to the public spotlight, especially when prompted by aggressive media coverage or interest group activity. Thus legislators are well advised to approach even the most minor choices with this question in mind: Will my decision be defensible if somehow it appears on the front pages of major newspapers in my state or district?

Calculating the electoral consequences of a lawmaker's multitude of daily decisions is no easy task. Arnold summarizes the components of such calculations:

> To reach a decision, then, a legislator needs to (1) identify all the attentive and inattentive publics who might care about a policy issue, (2) estimate the direction and intensity of their preferences and potential preferences, (3) estimate the probability that the potential preferences will be transformed into real preferences, (4) weight all these preferences according to the size of the various attentive and inattentive publics, and (5) give special weight to the preferences of the legislator's consistent supporters.[45]

Fortunately, lawmakers do not have to repeat these calculations every time they face a choice. Most issues have been around for some time: the preferences of attentive and even inattentive publics are fairly well known. Moreover, Congress is well structured to amass and assess information about individual and group preferences. And prominent officials—party leaders and acknowledged policy experts, for example—can often legitimize members' choices and give them "cover" in explaining those choices to voters.

The Presidency and Voting

Although Congress often pursues an independent course and few members feel a deep loyalty to the occupant of the White House, presidents do influence voting. Not only do presidents shape the legislative agenda, but they can persuade members to lend support. Figure 9-3 depicts the percentage of times presidents from Dwight D. Eisenhower to Bill Clinton have prevailed in congressional roll call votes on which the president announced a position. (Presidents take an unambiguous stance on only a fraction of the issues that reach the House or Senate floor.) Although this index includes many routine and noncontroversial matters, it still roughly gauges the presidents' standing on Capitol Hill and suggests several patterns.

First, modern presidents see their position prevail in two-thirds to three-fourths of House and Senate votes, though support levels can vary wildly from year to year. Their successes probably spring not so much from popularity or skill as from the routine nature of many of their initiatives. Yet some presi-

Figure 9-3   **Presidential Success History, 1953–1998**

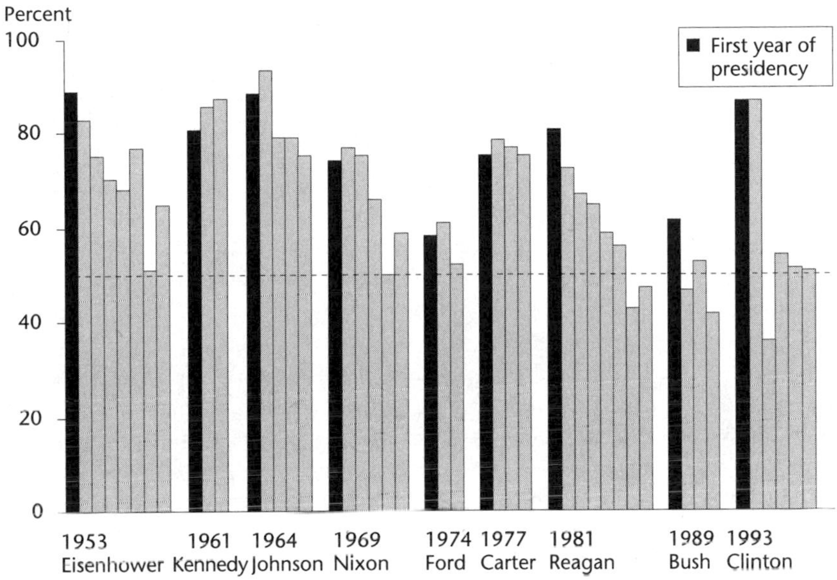

Percent

100 ▪ First year of presidency

80

60

40

20

0

1953   1961   1964   1969   1974 1977 1981   1989 1993
Eisenhower Kennedy Johnson Nixon   Ford Carter Reagan   Bush Clinton

Source: CQ Weekly, Jan. 9, 1999, 76.

Note: Presidential success is defined as the percentage of times the president won his way on roll-call votes on which he had taken a clear position.

dents—such as Eisenhower, Johnson, and Clinton during their first two years, Kennedy during his three years in office, and Reagan in 1981—enjoy extraordinary success in steering their proposals through Congress.

Second, presidents do better with their own partisans than with those of the opposition party. In 1998 the average House Democrat supported President Clinton 74 percent of the time, the average Democratic senator 82 percent of the time. For Republicans, the figures were 26 percent for House members and 41 percent for GOP senators.[46]

Third, partisan swings affect presidential success rates. As long as their party controls Congress, presidents win at least three of every four votes on which they have taken positions; when the government is divided, presidents fall well below that level. In his first two years in office, with Democrats controlling both chambers, President Clinton prevailed on 86.4 percent of all roll calls—the best record since Lyndon Johnson's Great Society juggernaut of 1965. Success smiled even upon Jimmy Carter, whose reputation on Capitol Hill was clouded by his stance as an outsider and the initial ineptness of his legislative liaison staff. With heavy partisan majorities in both chambers, Carter had a legislative record that actually was quite strong.[47]

When partisan control of the White House and Congress is divided, presidents' success levels are far less reliable. President Clinton's success rates on

Capitol Hill plummeted to a modern-day low in 1995. His overall success rate was 36 percent; the previous low was President George Bush's 43 percent in 1993, his last year in office.[48] President Eisenhower's success rate fell 24 percent after the Democrats' victories in the 1958 congressional elections. Building on the 1964 Democratic landslide, President Johnson achieved a modern high of 93 percent success. (Johnson's success rate was boosted by his habit of sending up messages supporting measures he already knew would pass.)

Fourth, presidents tend to lose congressional support as their administrations age. Reagan's experience dramatically confirmed this finding: his support score fell thirteen points after his first year and dropped still further after the 1982 midterm elections boosted the Democrats' majority in the House. After the Democrats recaptured the Senate in 1986 and his administration was damaged by the Iran-contra revelations, Reagan's success rate sagged to 43.5 percent.

Finally, although presidents have taken clear-cut stands on an increasing number of issues over time, these represent a declining percentage of congressional votes because the workload of members is much heavier than it used to be.[49] In 1998 President Clinton took a position on about 18 percent of all House and Senate votes; at a comparable stage in his administration Eisenhower was taking positions on about three of five congressional votes.

Giving and Taking Cues

Scholars have devised various legislative voting models to explain how members of Congress make up their minds. As the following models show, party, constituency, ideology, and presidential support are not the only cues that influence members' voting decisions.

Cleo Cherryholmes and Michael Shapiro divided legislative decision making into two phases: *predisposition* and *conversation*. In the initial phase, party, region, committee, and other variables predispose each legislator for or against each measure. If the predisposition is indecisive, the lawmaker seeks cues from colleagues—the conversation stage. Cherryholmes and Shapiro assigned weights to various predispositions as well as to the probability that members would accept cues from colleagues. When applied to votes on federal activism and foreign aid in the 1960s, this model predicted 84 percent of the results in both areas.[50]

In their study of selected votes from 1958 to 1969, Donald Matthews and James Stimson estimated the significance of nine sources of voting cues: state party delegations, party leaders, party majority, president, House majority, committee chairmen, ranking minority members, the conservative coalition, and the liberal Democratic Study Group. In both parties, state party delegations proved to have the highest correlations with voting. Party and committee leaders were also effective cue givers, as were party and House majorities. Democratic presidents were potent cue givers for the Democrats, and Republican presidents were moderately powerful in influencing their Hill partisans. In short, partisan cues were most potent when the White House and Congress were controlled by the same party. Taken as a whole, the Matthews-Stimson model was able to predict 88 percent of the votes actually cast.[51]

Policy dimensions form the basis of Aage Clausen's model, which he drew from analyzing roll call votes in the 1950s and 1960s. Clausen examined voting on government management, social welfare, international involvement, civil liberties, and agricultural aid. Scoring legislators on each policy dimension, he discovered great stability in members' positions over time and in the impact of various cue sources. Political party was an effective predictor for some issues (especially government management). Constituency controlled others (civil liberties, in particular). In still other cases a combination of factors was at work: party and constituency dominated social welfare and agricultural aid votes, while constituency and presidential influenced international decisions. Clausen's work demonstrated that stable forces such as party, constituency, and presidential support induce members to assume long-term positions on legislative policy.[52]

These three models are based on, or tested with, aggregate voting statistics. To compile these figures, researchers compare individual members' votes with factors such as the party majority or the president's position; high correlations are described as influence. Thus the models are based on inferences gleaned from the conjunction of members' votes and other factors. A few researchers have tackled the arduous job of trying to tap the actual processes by which voting cues are given or received.

David Kovenock's communications audit supported the notion of cue giving and cue taking within Congress. "Most of the messages congressmen received, and most of those which influence them," he found, "originate at least in the first instance from sources within the Congress."[53] Nearly two-thirds of all incoming communications originated on Capitol Hill—from fellow representatives, staff aides, or senators. Of those communications dealing with subcommittee business and regarded as influential, 99 percent came from members and staff, governmental agencies, or organized interest groups. The kinds of communications lawmakers received depended on their positions. For example, the more vulnerable their electoral position, the less they focused on lawmaking messages and the more they communicated with folks back home.

John Kingdon's model of representatives' decisions is based on interviews with members immediately after their votes on specific issues.[54] Legislators have little difficulty making up their minds when they have strong personal convictions or when party leaders and interest groups agree and point them in the same direction. If all the actors in their field of vision concur, members operate in a "consensus mode" of decision making. Fellow members emerge as the most influential cue givers, with constituencies ranking second. As one lawmaker observed:

> I think that the other members are very influential, and we recognize it. And why are they influential? I think because they have exercised good judgment, have expertise in the area, and know what they are talking about.[55]

When members deviate from the consensus stance indicated by their cue givers, it is usually to follow their own consciences. Adding up these short-

term forces, Kingdon in his model successfully predicted about 90 percent of the decisions.

Legislative voting models, no matter how elegant, cannot capture the full range of factors shaping decisions. "The two biggest political lies," former senator Thomas Eagleton, D-Mo., once declared, are "one, to say a senator never takes into account the political ramifications of a vote and secondly, almost an equal lie, is to say the only thing a senator considers is politics."[56] To unravel the chain of causality involved in congressional decision making would require a comprehensive model embracing demographic, sociological, psychological, and political motivations. Simplified models, without a doubt, pinpoint important components of legislators' decisions. As with all complex human behavior, however, such decisions elude wholly satisfactory description.

Legislative Bargaining

Legislators decide on a staggering variety of matters, in relatively short periods of time, often with inadequate information. First, each legislator has separate and sometimes conflicting goals and information. Second, whatever their goals or information levels, every legislator wields a single vote with which to affect the outcome.[57]

Such a state of affairs—disparate goals and widely scattered influence—is hazardous. Conflict may flare out of control if the contending policy objectives are not adequately met. On the other hand, stalemate is a constant threat, as when irresistible forces clash with immovable objects. To overcome such a predicament, members have to resort to politicking: that is, they must trade off goals and resources to get results. No wonder, then, that Congress is "an influence system in which bargain and exchange predominate."[58]

Implicit and Explicit Bargaining

Bargaining is a generic term that refers to several related types of behavior. In each case an exchange takes place: goals or resources pass from a bargainer's hands in return for other goals or resources that he or she values. Bargains may be implicit or explicit.

Implicit bargaining occurs when legislators take actions designed to elicit certain reactions from others, even though no negotiation may have taken place. For example, legislators may introduce a bill or sponsor hearings not because they think the bill will pass but because they hope the action will prod someone else—an executive branch official, perhaps, or a committee chairman with broader jurisdiction on the question—into taking action on the problem. Or a bill's managers may accept a controversial amendment knowing full well that the objectionable provision will be dropped in the other chamber or in conference. These are examples of the so-called law of anticipated reactions.[59]

Another type of implicit bargaining occurs when legislators seek out or accept the judgments of colleagues with expertise on a given matter, expecting that the situation will be reversed in the future. What is being traded is information. As Sen. Carl Levin, D-Mich., said of former senator Sam Nunn of Geor-

gia, then chairman of the Armed Services Committee, "He knows more about the subject he talks about than anybody else by the time he starts talking about it."[60] The exchange not only saves the recipient the time and trouble of mastering the subject matter; it may also provide a credible "cover" in defending the vote. During the 1986 tax reform debates, Bill Bradley, then a Democratic senator from New Jersey, was a trailblazer who gave members across the ideological spectrum guidance on tax issues. When conservative Republican Charles E. Grassley of Iowa made decisions on tax policy, he said there was always "another factor to consider: How does Bradley look at this?"[61] As we have seen already, exchanges of voting cues are endemic in both chambers.

Explicit bargains also take several forms. In making compromises legislators agree to split their differences. Compromises are straightforward in measures containing quantitative elements that can easily be adjusted upward or downward—for example, funding levels or eligibility criteria. Compromise on substance is also possible. For example, members who favor a major new program and members who oppose any program at all may agree to a two-year pilot project to test the idea.

"You cannot legislate without the ability to compromise," declared Sen. Alan Simpson, R-Wyo., who retired in 1996 with harsh words for some of the militant junior members of his party. He illustrated his point with the following tale from the 104th Congress:

> On a recent bill, I went to [conservative House members] and said: "Here's what I'm doing. I've got six senators who will vote this far, and then the next time if you go any further, they will not be there." So [Sen.] Larry Craig [R-Idaho] and I delivered on this singular bill, and they said, "We want you to get more." And we said, "There is no more to get." Next vote on this bill, we lost six votes. Then they came in and said, "We are going to probably kill the whole thing." . . . [A]nd they got nothing.[62]

The lesson is that compromise is inevitable in crafting laws; those who are unwilling to give ground are bound to be disappointed.

Logrolling

Logrolling is bargaining in which the parties trade off support so that each may gain its goal. The term originated in the nineteenth century when neighbors helped each other roll logs into a pile for burning. In its most visible form, trading is embodied in a something-for-everyone enactment—known as "pork barrel"—on subjects such as public works, omnibus taxation, or tariffs and trade. Describing the classic logroll, former representative Edward J. Derwinski, R-Ill., explained how the country's two million farmers put together a majority coalition every five years to pass the omnibus farm bill's basket of price supports, acreage allowances, and marketing agreements:

> What [the farmers] do is very interesting. The agriculture people from North Carolina, where agriculture means tobacco, discuss their problems with the

man representing the rice growers in Arkansas or California. The sugar beet growers in Minnesota and sugar cane interests in Louisiana and Hawaii and the wheat and corn and soybean and other producers just gather together in one great big happy family to be sure there is a subsidy for every commodity. They put those numbers together again so that they have at least 218 supporters in the House and 51 in the Senate. A supporter of the tobacco subsidy automatically becomes a supporter of the wheat subsidy, or the sugar quota, or the soybean subsidy, or whatever else follows.[63]

One of the most successful logrolling achievements in the farm bill was the food stamp program. It brought together farm lobbies that wanted to boost the agricultural market and urban welfare interests that wanted to feed low-income people. Environmentally minded lawmakers were lured to the farm bill because subsidies are linked to prudent land use. This logroll has proved inclusive and durable. In 1998 a House-Senate agriculture conference report included a crop insurance provision for farmers and a provision restoring food stamps to a quarter-million immigrants who had lost them in the 1996 welfare overhaul. House Republican leaders decided to strip the food stamp provision from the agreement—a move calculated to please conservatives. The rule for debate was soundly defeated by an urban-rural coalition of 98 Republicans and 190 Democrats. "It was wrong to try to use procedure to amend a conference report that had such overwhelming bipartisan support," said Rep. Lincoln Diaz-Balart, R-Fla. "After today's vote, there is no doubt about food stamps."[64]

At the personal level, logrolling draws individual lawmakers into the finished legislative product by embracing (or anticipating) their special interests, proposals, or amendments. The late senator Henry "Scoop" Jackson, D-Wash., when asked how he had assembled a majority for a new proposal, responded something like this: "Maggie said he talked to Russell, and Tom promised this if I would back him on Ed's amendment, and Mike owes me one for last year's help on Pete's bill."[65] Such reciprocity especially pervades the Senate, dominated as it is by individuals. Sponsors of a Senate bill often must placate most or all of the interested legislators in order to gain clearance to bring a bill to the floor.

Lawmakers who enter into, and stand to profit from, a logroll are expected to support the final package, regardless of what that package looks like. A broad-based logroll is hard to stop. "It's not a system of punishment. It's a system of rewards," explained former representative Bill Frenzel, R-Minn., about the House tax-writing process.[66] The 1998 transportation bill, crafted mainly by House Transportation Chair Bud Shuster, R-Pa., embraced so many highway and mass transit projects in so many congressional districts that it was impossible to stop—despite the fact that it bent earlier budget figures out of shape.

Fiscal constraints since the 1980s, however, have shifted the goal of logrolling. In a hostile fiscal environment, logrolling is often aimed at equalizing sacrifices rather than distributing rewards. Broad-spectrum bills—authorizations, omnibus tax measures, continuing resolutions, and budget resolutions—may include numerous less than optimal provisions, many of which

would fail if voted on separately. Such a negative logroll enables lawmakers to support the measure as "the best deal we can get." In other words, members find it easier to accept damage to their favorite programs as long as they are sure that everyone else is "taking their lumps" through cutbacks or across-the-board formulas that limit other programs or benefits. Former Senate Appropriations Committee chairman Mark O. Hatfield, R-Ore., explained that he would "hold my nose and do certain things here for the purpose of getting the job done, but certainly not with enthusiasm or anything other than recognizing that we are doing things under emergency."[67]

In a time of fiscal stringency, legislators have fewer opportunities to claim credit for sponsoring new programs or obtaining added funding. Avoiding blame can displace claiming credit as a legislative objective, and these omnibus reverse logrolls are a result.[68] Aside from its political value, logrolling can have policy virtues. As Douglas Arnold notes,

> It can draw under a single umbrella coalition a whole series of programs, each of which targets funds according to need. Districts then receive substantial benefits where their needs are greatest and nothing where they are marginal.[69]

Logrolling, however, can turn narrowly targeted programs into broad-scale ones. In negotiating for passage of two high-priority measures—crime reduction and a national service corps—the Clinton administration had to scatter benefits so broadly that their effectiveness was severely impaired. The 1994 crime bill provided for 100,000 more police officers on the nation's streets, but it was rendered less effective by spreading the funds throughout the entire country, not just in high-crime, inner-urban areas. Similarly, funds in the Americorps program were spread too thinly among too many sites to be successful.[70]

In a time logroll, members agree to support one measure in exchange for later support for another measure. Sometimes the logroll specifies an exchange; at other times it is open ended until the donor decides to call in the chips. That is why President Clinton failed to gain passage of "fast track" trade negotiation authority late in 1997. Four years earlier, Clinton had won a narrow victory for the North American Free Trade Agreement (NAFTA) by promising wavering Democrats programs that would help workers and industries hurt by freer trade; now members complained that the bargains had not been carried out. Explained Rep. Xavier Becerra, D-Calif., "I was one of those opposed to NAFTA, and I gave the president the benefit of the doubt." Clinton had pledged to negotiate side agreements protecting labor and the environment. "There was an utter failure to implement those proposals."[71]

In a logroll with side payments, support is exchanged for benefits on an unrelated issue—for example, a federal project for the state or district, a better committee assignment, inclusion in an important conference, or access to the White House. White House officials are adept at such maneuvering. In the aforementioned 1997 debate on fast-track authority, the following exchange

took place on the House floor between Robert L. Livingston, then Appropriations chair, and his ranking minority member, Rep. David R. Obey, D-Wis.:

> Mr. OBEY: Does the gentleman know how many bridges the president has promised today for fast-track votes?
>
> Mr. LIVINGSTON: The gentleman does not have enough fingers for that.[72]

Although the side benefits of bargains often seem trivial or parochial, in many cases such payoffs help the member to achieve other valued goals.

Bargaining Strategy

Are there limits to negotiation? According to bargaining theory, a measure's sponsors will yield only what they absolutely must to gain a majority of supporters. Under this "size principle," a minimum winning coalition occurs in ideal legislative bargaining situations—that is, when the bargainers act rationally and with perfect information.[73] Recounting Senate majority leader Lyndon Johnson's meticulous vote counting before a floor fight, political scientist John G. Stewart concluded, "And once a sufficient majority had been counted, Johnson would seldom attempt to enlarge it: Why expend limited bargaining resources which might be needed to win future battles?"[74]

Most legislative strategists, however, lack Johnson's extraordinary skills. Uncertainty about outcomes leads them to line up more than a simple majority of supporters. Moreover, at many points in the legislative process supermajorities are required—for example, in voting on constitutional amendments, in overriding vetoes, or in ending Senate filibusters. Not surprisingly, therefore, minimum winning coalitions are not typical of Congress, even in the majoritarian House of Representatives.[75] Yet coalition size is the crux of legislative strategy. Bargainers repeatedly face the dilemma of how broadly or how narrowly to frame their issues and how many concessions to yield in an effort to secure passage.

Conclusion

For bargaining to take place, participants must be reasonably certain of each other's intentions and likely future actions. Listen to Senator Simpson, a conservative Republican, describing his liberal Democratic colleague Senator Kennedy:

> If I tell people in Wyoming that I trust Ted Kennedy, they'll say, "What kind of an idiot are you?" But it just means you work with him for seventeen years. And when you say, "Ted, what are we going to do with legal immigration and the family preference system and chain migration?" he answers, "You're right, and here's the farthest I can go." . . . He's never once blindsided me, but his philosophy is different than mine.[76]

For bargaining to succeed, the participants must agree on the desirability of a legislative product. That is, the benefits of reaching a decision must exceed

the costs of failing to do so. In the vast majority of cases—where there is sharp disagreement, or concerted opposition—a negative political cost-benefit ratio results in no action at all: think of the thousands of proposed laws that fall short of enactment. In other cases politicians may prefer a course of strategic disagreement, which John B. Gilmour describes as "efforts of politicians to avoid reaching an agreement when compromise might alienate supporters, damage their prospects in an upcoming election, or preclude getting a better deal in the future."[77] Needless to say, such strategies are shaped by our fragmented political structures. The result often lends an appearance of stalemate or gridlock.

The enterprise of lawmaking rests, however, on the premise that at least where urgent matters are concerned, bargainers will normally prefer some sort of new outcome to none at all. Especially is this the case with actions facing deadlines or imperiling government functions if not approved—reauthorizations, appropriations, debt ceiling adjustments, and the like.

The ultimate consequence of nonaction is government shutdown. Since 1981 budget confrontations between executive and legislative branches controlled by different political parties have left the government temporarily without funds to operate on sixteen separate occasions. Such "funding gaps" typically have lasted only a few hours or days, but in the winter of 1995–1996 the stalemate between the Clinton White House and GOP congressional majorities caused major disruptions. When the parties realized the escalating costs of inaction, the bargaining resumed; but breakdowns in bargaining reflected deep political divisions.

Bargaining is reflected not only in the substance of legislation but also in many attributes of the legislative process—delay, obfuscation, compromise, and norms such as specialization and reciprocity. It is no exaggeration to say that bargaining is endemic to the legislative way of life. Legislative bargaining shapes the character of bills, resolutions, and other forms of congressional policy making. It is yet another point of contact and conflict between the two Congresses—the Congress of individual wills and the Congress of collective decisions.

Part 4

Policy Making and Change
in the Two Congresses

The president and Congress. In the midst of scandal and impeachment, President Bill Clinton (inset) delivers his State of the Union message in January 1999. Earlier that month, Rep. Henry J. Hyde, R-Ill. (above, right), accompanied by House Judiciary Committee chief of staff Thomas E. Mooney and other House managers, arrives at the Senate chamber to present two articles of impeachment against the president. Both articles later were rejected. As party lines hardened, House Democratic leader Richard A. Gephardt (Mo.), below, leads his party colleagues out of the Capitol to protest the GOP-sponsored impeachment.

10

Congress and
the President

"$\mathbf{W}$e are intent on making [a national missile defense system] the official
policy of the United States with or without the support of the Clinton
Administration," declared Curt Weldon, R-Pa., chairman of the House Armed
Services Subcommittee on Military Research and Development.[1] Congressional Republicans have advocated such a system ever since President Ronald
Reagan first proposed a "Star Wars" missile defense shield. The White House
initially threatened to veto a missile defense bill. President Clinton said he
would not decide on deployment of a missile defense system until June 2000.
By then the administration would have assessed its cost, technological feasibility, effect on arms control agreements, and the seriousness of a missile threat
from rogue nations such as North Korea or an accidental missile launch from
Russia. The president dropped his veto threat after the Senate adopted compromises that made deployment contingent on technological feasibility while
negotiations continued with Russia on nuclear arms reductions.[2]

Tensions between the executive and legislative branches are inevitable.
These two branches are organized differently; they have divergent responsibilities; they have different constituencies and terms of office; and they are jeal-
ous of their prerogatives. Executive officials see Congress as inefficient and
meddlesome. Legislators perceive the executive branch as arrogant and arbitrary. At times these differences lead to conflicts that the media dramatize as
"battles on the Potomac."

Yet day in and day out Congress and the president work together. Even
when their relationship is guarded or hostile, bills get passed and signed into
law. Presidential appointments are approved by the Senate. Budgets are eventually enacted and the government is kept afloat. This necessary cooperation
goes on even when control of the White House and the Capitol is divided
between the two major parties. Conversely, as President Jimmy Carter sadly
learned—and President Clinton learned during his first two years in office—
unified partisan control of both branches is no guarantee of harmony. Indeed,
David Mayhew has asserted that it "does not seem to make all that much difference whether party control of the American government happens to be unified or divided" in influencing the productivity of laws and investigations.[3]

Conflict between Congress and the president is embedded in our system
of separation of powers and checks and balances. But the Founders also expected their governmental arrangement to promote accommodation between
the branches. Historical patterns have veered between these two extremes. The

two branches worked together in the early days of Woodrow Wilson's progressive New Freedom (1913–1916), during the New Deal (1933–1937) and World War II (1941–1945), in the brief Great Society years (1964–1966) following John Kennedy's assassination (1963), and for the even briefer Reaganomics juggernaut during Ronald Reagan's first year in office (1981). At other times they fought fiercely: during Woodrow Wilson's second term (1919–1921); after 1937 for Franklin Roosevelt; after 1966 for Lyndon B. Johnson; and for most of Richard Nixon's, Reagan's, and George Bush's tenures.[4]

The President as Legislator

Presidents are sometimes called the "chief legislators" because they are closely involved in the decisions Congress makes. Article II, Section 3, of the Constitution directs the president from time to time to "give to the Congress Information of the State of the Union and recommend to their Consideration such Measures as he shall judge necessary and expedient." (Today this means annually and during prime-time television.) Soon after delivering the annual State of the Union address, the president sends to Congress draft "administration bills" for introduction on his behalf. By enlarging the list of messages required from the president—the annual budget and economic reports, for example—Congress has further involved the chief executive in designing legislation. Crises, partisan considerations, and public expectations all make the president an important participant in congressional decision making. And the president's constitutional veto power ensures that White House views will be listened to, if not always heeded, on Capitol Hill.

The concept of the legislative presidency did not become widespread until after World War II. Only then could it be said that the role was institutionalized, performed not because of some unique combination of personality and circumstance but because everyone—including Congress, the press, and the public—expected it.[5] This expectation could change, and governance at the national level might revert to a pattern common to much of the nineteenth century: a strong Congress and a weak president.

Setting the Agenda

From the beginning, presidents have shaped Congress's agenda in varying degrees. The first Congress of "its own volition immediately turned to the executive branch for guidance and discovered in [Treasury Secretary Alexander] Hamilton a personality to whom such leadership was congenial."[6] Two decades later (from 1811 to 1825) the "initiative in public affairs remained with [Speaker Henry] Clay and his associates in the House of Representatives" and not with the president.[7]

Dominance in national policy making may pass from one branch to the other. Strong presidents sometimes provoke efforts by Congress to reassert its own authority and to restrict that of the executive. Periods of presidential ascendancy often are followed by eras of congressional assertiveness.

Presidents Carter and Reagan. Recent presidents have followed very different patterns in setting agendas. Agenda control was the hallmark of Reagan's leadership during his first year in office. The president shrewdly limited the number of his legislative priorities. Most were encapsulated as "Reaganomics"—tax and spending cuts—introduced soon after the 1980 election. This period was both a political honeymoon for the president and a time of widespread anticipation of a new era of GOP national political dominance. Reagan dealt skillfully with Congress to mobilize support and public backing through dramatic television appeals. Later, when his control over the agenda slackened, Congress was still confined to a playing field largely demarcated by the president. It was forced to respond to, although not always accept, the positions the president had staked out on taxes, spending, defense, and social issues.

By contrast, Reagan's predecessor in the White House, Jimmy Carter, quickly overloaded Congress's agenda and never made clear what his priorities were. Three major consequences resulted:

> First . . . there was little clarity in the communication of priorities to the American public. Instead of galvanizing support for two or three major national needs, the Carter administration proceeded on a number of fronts. . . . Second, and perhaps more important, the lack of priorities meant unnecessary waste of the President's own time and energy. . . . Third, the lack of priorities needlessly compounded Carter's congressional problems. . . . Carter's limited political capital was squandered on a variety of agenda requests when it might have been concentrated on the top of the list.[8]

President Bush. After eight years of often sharp confrontation between President Reagan and Congress, President George Bush skillfully courted Democrats and Republicans in Congress to establish a more congenial tone for legislative-executive relations. But unlike Reagan, who made the most of his honeymoon with Congress by winning enactment of his economic agenda, Bush did not push quickly for major policy changes or even articulate two or three major goals that he wanted to accomplish. If Carter overloaded the congressional agenda, Bush underutilized it.

Needless to say, the policy-making context in which Bush operated differed from that of Reagan. Reagan entered the White House in 1981 with Republicans in charge of the Senate, while Bush faced Democratic control of both houses. Furthermore, Reagan began his presidency with deficits in the tens of billions of dollars, while Bush had to contend with deficits in the hundreds of billions. Both factors influenced the policy-making abilities of each administration.

By the end of Bush's four-year term (1989–1993), the president and Congress were deadlocked on numerous issues. Bush's success rate with Congress was the lowest of any president in forty years. Although Bush achieved successes such as the Clean Air Act of 1990 and congressional authorization of the Persian Gulf war, the improved tenor of the legislative-executive relation-

ship at the beginning of his presidency did not last. Finger pointing, bickering, and confrontation increased. Not surprisingly, the theme of "government gridlock" pervaded the November 1992 election and contributed to Bill Clinton's election as the nation's "agent of change."

President Clinton. After twelve years of GOP control of the White House, and elected with a Congress controlled by his own party, Clinton laid out an ambitious agenda. The president planned to "end welfare as we know it," to revamp the nation's health care system, to foster economic growth and productivity, and to end business as usual in Washington. Clinton soon learned, however, how hard it is to concentrate on a few goals. Instead of a focused agenda, the president found himself, like Carter, with an overloaded agenda. As two journalists wrote, "President Clinton promised to focus like a 'laser' on the economy, but the first 100 days of his administration . . . looked more like a light show, flickering from Russian aid to national service, the reinvention of government to gays in the military to Bosnia."[9]

Despite the rocky start of his first term, Clinton enjoyed a high success rate in getting legislation through the Democratic-controlled Congress. In 1993 he won enactment of a major deficit-reduction package and the North American Free Trade Agreement (NAFTA); he succeeded in passing the Family and Medical Leave Act, which had been vetoed by Republican presidents.

The next year was different, however. Clinton trumpeted health care reform as his top priority. He and his wife, Hillary Rodham Clinton, devoted enormous time and energy to it. They devised a complex, expensive, and—during a time when the public's confidence in government was low—highly bureaucratic plan to provide universal health care coverage for all Americans. In the end their health care effort collapsed.[10] According to Stanley Greenberg, then the president's pollster, Clinton's health care plan "helped stamp him and the Democrats as the party of big government, and those perceptions contributed significantly to the [dramatic] Republican victory" in November 1994.[11]

The clashing views of the 104th Republican Congress (1995–1997) and the Democratic president twice forced the federal government into temporary shutdowns in late 1995 and early 1996. Republicans wanted to balance the budget in seven years (proposing $1 trillion in deficit reduction over that period), but Clinton disagreed with essential points of their plan. Although both sides agreed on the need to restrain spending and balance the budget, they differed sharply about how to achieve those objectives.

As the November 1996 elections loomed closer, and with the public generally blaming Republicans and not Clinton for gridlock in Washington, GOP congressional leaders agreed to cooperate with the president to pass important legislation (welfare and health reform and a hike in the minimum wage, for instance). Republicans wanted to ensure that the 104th could not be tagged in the campaign as a "do nothing Congress" by Democrats. Clinton wanted to demonstrate his capacity to govern "from the center" and to work with an opposition-controlled Congress. He succeeded, winning reelection by 49.2 percent of the popular vote, an increase from his 43 percent showing in 1992.

Clinton became the first Democrat since Franklin D. Roosevelt to win re-election. He also became the first Democrat ever to face a GOP-controlled Congress for more than two years. For their part, Republicans retained consecutive control of Congress for the first time since the 1927–1931 period (see Appendix A).

During the 105th Congress, neither elective branch had the political clout or the votes to force into law policies unwanted by the other. Mindful that they tried to do too much too quickly during the 104th Congress, congressional Republicans in the 105th deliberately slowed their legislative pace and waited for Clinton to take the lead on many issues. One was the budget. "We made a decision in November [1996] to wait for Bill Clinton to send his budget" to Capitol Hill, said House GOP Conference chairman John A. Boehner of Ohio.[12] With Clinton and congressional Republicans in general agreement on balancing the budget and shrinking governmental activism, they often ended up skirmishing over smaller issues to highlight their ideological identities.[13] As for Clinton, his legislative program, in one scholar's words, was "the policy equivalent of miniature golf. Long drives had been supplanted by short strokes, such as promoting 'V-chips' to block violent programming on television and endorsing the use of school uniforms. The president invested most of his efforts blocking Republican initiatives, not pursuing his own."[14]

Stymied by Congress on issues such as antismoking legislation, a patients' bill of rights, and subsidies for school construction, Clinton expanded the use of executive authority. Issuing executive orders—a form of administrative lawmaking to carry out authority delegated by the legislative branch, including the issuance of rules for the executive branch—was a favorite technique of the president to bypass the GOP-controlled Congress. Presidents have long employed executive orders. President Harry S. Truman, for example, issued an executive order to integrate the armed forces. But Clinton rewrote the manual on how to use executive authority. "His formula includes pressing the limits of his regulatory authority, signing executive orders and using other unilateral means to obtain his policy priorities when Congress fails to embrace them."[15] To dramatize the importance of trigger locks on guns, a proposal that stalled in Congress, Clinton issued an executive order requiring trigger safety locks on new guns purchased for federal law enforcement officers.[16] Congressional Republicans railed against Clinton's "go it alone" governing.

After the impeachment turmoil of 1998 and early 1999—Clinton became the first elected president to be impeached by the House, although he was acquitted by the Senate—the question was whether the White House could or would work with the GOP-controlled Congress. To be sure, there were incentives for both branches to cooperate. After the November 1998 elections, House Republicans had a slimmer and internally divided majority with which to forge winning coalitions, plus a new Speaker—Dennis Hastert—who said he would reach out to Democrats to pass legislation. Electorally, Republicans also worried that public opinion polls identified them as the anti-Clinton party with no coherent agenda; they feared that the November 2000 elections could

cost them majority control unless they delivered legislative successes. For his part, President Clinton, concerned about his legacy in the aftermath of the Monica Lewinsky scandal, had reason to work with congressional Republicans on issues such as education, Social Security, and Medicare, especially when projected budget surpluses could make it easier to reconcile partisan differences. "If the Republican-controlled Congress works with the president to produce meaningful legislation, that's a win for everybody," said a House GOP aide, "but that's a win for Republicans as well."[17]

Both legislative chambers moved quickly to pass popular bipartisan legislation, such as pay hikes for military personnel, greater flexibility for states to spend federal education money, and disaster assistance for communities. However, given the high political stakes of the November 2000 election, there were also countervailing pressures that worked against cooperative lawmaking. Although a "lame duck" president interested in creating a legacy other than his impeachment, Clinton wanted Vice President Albert Gore to succeed him in the White House and the Democrats to recapture majority control of Congress. Thus, in the lead-up to the 2000 elections, each side calculated how to balance two competing imperatives: the need for bipartisan policy successes as well as partisan political victories.

Presidential Priorities

The divergent agendas of Carter, Reagan, Bush, and Clinton remind us that presidential leadership is an amalgam of personal and political ingredients. An engineer by profession, Carter preferred to work with a large number of technically detailed issues. Reagan, who had no patience for details, believed he had an electoral mandate to achieve a small number of fundamental changes. Bush had few firm policy commitments and ran a campaign in 1988 that targeted his opponent more than it highlighted his own objectives. Early in his administration, Clinton's restless intellect and personal style immersed him in many issues. Known as a "policy wonk," Clinton found it hard to keep to a few specific themes.

Hoping to change the public's perception that the White House was disorganized and that he was lurching from one issue to the next, Clinton replaced his chief of staff, Thomas F. "Mack" McLarty with Leon Panetta, a former House member and director of the Office of Management and Budget. With the White House running smoothly, Panetta resigned at the beginning of Clinton's second term. Erskine Bowles, a businessman friend of Clinton's, succeeded Panetta. Bowles continued to impose discipline on Clinton's schedule, ensuring that meetings began and concluded on time and that the president stayed "on message" in his public pronouncements. When Bowles departed, John Podesta, the deputy chief of staff, took over as the fourth of Clinton's chiefs of staff.[18]

Proposal and Disposal. A wide gap separates what presidents want from what they can get. Congress can influence what, when, how, or even whether executive recommendations are sent to Capitol Hill. White House agendas frequently are shaped by expectations of what will pass Congress. This indirect

priority-setting power of the House and Senate can affect whether the president even transmits certain proposals to Congress. It also works in the other direction: recommendations may be forwarded or endorsed because the White House knows they have broad legislative support. "The president proposes, Congress disposes" is an oversimplified adage.

Central Clearance. In fashioning a legislative program, presidents do not lack advice. Externally, ideas come from Congress, the executive branch, and the pressures of current events and crises. In addition, cues are taken from public opinion, the president's party, interest groups, and the media. Internally, the campaign platform and the president's staff are sources of ideas.[19] Coordinating and sifting through these recommendations ("central clearance") is a responsibility primarily of the Office of Management and Budget. Central clearance enables the president "to monitor department requests to ensure that they are not in conflict with his own."[20]

Outside Events. National and international developments influence a president's agenda. In the 1930s the Great Depression promoted President Franklin Roosevelt's agenda-setting role. When Roosevelt took office in 1933, Congress wanted him to tell it what to do. And he did. During his first hundred days, Roosevelt sent Congress fifteen messages and signed fifteen bills into law—an astonishing number for those days. (Later New Deal initiatives had more congressional input.)

The Constitution gives the president the authority to convene one or both houses of Congress "on extraordinary occasions." A few days after taking office, FDR called a special session of Congress to consider his emergency banking legislation. "The House had no copies of the bill; the Speaker recited the text from the one available draft, which bore last minute corrections scribbled in pencil." After thirty-eight minutes of debate, "with a unanimous shout, the House passed the bill, sight unseen."[21] Passing President Reagan's revised budget package in 1981 took Congress a little longer, but that legislation featured the same kind of swift support from the House and Senate.

Contrast these bold strides with the small steps taken by Clinton during his second term. Once again, the tenor of the times shaped the agenda. Clinton faced a GOP-controlled Congress hostile to government activism. Recall from Chapter 9 that Clinton had the lowest success rate with Congress of any recent president in his sixth year in office—51 percent in 1998 compared with Eisenhower's 76 percent in 1958. The country was at peace and in a period of economic growth. The public seemed satisfied with the status quo and ambivalent toward, if not skeptical of, government. A leading national newspaper characterized Clinton's 1999 State of the Union message: "With a blizzard of small initiatives and one big proposal on Social Security" [reserving most of a projected surplus for Social Security], Clinton's goals in the post-impeachment environment were to frame the political debate, "seize the initiative from the Republicans and keep his own party united."[22] Little surprise that in the twilight of his presidency Clinton generally advocated modest forms of government activism, such as reducing class sizes in the early grades of school.

Legislative Delegations. Congress often delegates legislative responsibility to the president. A few examples illustrate the point. In the Budget and Accounting Act of 1921, Congress directed the president to prepare an annual national budget. In 1946 Congress asked the president to report annually on ways to keep the nation's economy healthy.[23] Since 1932 Congress has periodically granted the president authority to reorganize the executive branch subject to congressional approval.

The decision to delegate authority to the president typically occurs because Congress cannot overcome its own shortcomings—its decentralized committee structure, which inhibits swift and comprehensive policy formulation; its lack of technical expertise; and its members' vulnerability to reelection pressures. Congress also appreciates the strengths of the White House, including its capacity for negotiation and coordination.

The Veto Power

Article I, Section 7, of the Constitution requires the president to approve or disapprove of bills passed by Congress. In the case of disapproval, the measure dies unless it "shall be repassed by two thirds of the Senate and House of Representatives." Because vetoes are so difficult to override, the veto power makes the president, in Woodrow Wilson's words, a "third branch of the legislature."[24] Presidents usually can attract one-third plus one of their supporters in Congress to sustain a veto, and so presidential vetoes are not very often overridden (see Table 10-1).

The decision to veto is a collective administration judgment. Presidents seek advice from numerous sources, such as agency officials, the Office of Management and Budget, and White House aides. Five reasons commonly are given for vetoing a bill: (1) the bill is unconstitutional; (2) it encroaches on the president's independence; (3) it is unwise public policy; (4) it cannot be administered; and (5) it costs too much. Political considerations may permeate any or all of these reasons. The cost rationale is a favorite of recent presidents.

The veto is more than a negative power, however. Presidents also use it to advance their policy objectives. Veto threats, for example, often encourage committees and legislators to accommodate executive preferences and objections. Presidents also practice the "politics of differentiation" in using their vetoes. A veto fight with Congress may be just fine with presidents who want to underscore for voters how their views differ from the other party's.

For its part, Congress can discourage vetoes by adding its desired items to "must pass" legislation or to measures strongly favored by the president. Opposed to a defense appropriations bill that would spend $7 billion more than he had requested, President Clinton in 1995 reluctantly accepted its terms because the measure contained funding for an administration priority: deploying American troops to Bosnia to keep the peace.[25]

Veto Options. Once the president receives a bill from Congress, he has ten days (excluding Sundays) in which to exercise four options.

Table 10-1 Number of Presidential Vetoes, 1789–1998

Years	President	Regular vetoes	Pocket vetoes	Total vetoes	Vetoes overridden
1789–1797	George Washington	2	0	2	0
1797–1801	John Adams	0	0	0	0
1801–1809	Thomas Jefferson	0	0	0	0
1809–1817	James Madison	5	2	7	0
1817–1825	James Monroe	1	0	1	0
1825–1829	John Q. Adams	0	0	0	0
1829–1837	Andrew Jackson	5	7	2	0
1837–1841	Martin Van Buren	0	1	1	0
1841	W. H. Harrison[a]	0	0	0	0
1841–1845	John Tyler	6	4	0	1
1845–1849	James K. Polk	2	1	3	0
1849–1850	Zachary Taylor	0	0	0	0
1850–1853	Millard Fillmore	0	0	0	0
1853–1857	Franklin Pierce	9	0	9	5
1857–1861	James Buchanan	4	3	7	0
1861–1865	Abraham Lincoln	2	5	7	0
1865–1869	Andrew Johnson	21	8	29	15
1869–1877	Ulysses S. Grant	45	48	93	4
1877–1881	Rutherford B. Hayes	12	1	3	1
1881	James A. Garfield[b]	0	0	0	0
1881–1885	Chester A. Arthur	4	8	2	1
1885–1889	Grover Cleveland	304	0	414	2
1889–1893	Benjamin Harrison	19	25	44	1
1893–1897	Grover Cleveland	42	128	70	5
1897–1901	William McKinley	6	36	42	0
1901–1909	Theodore Roosevelt	42	40	82	1
1909–1913	William H. Taft	30	9	39	1
1913–1921	Woodrow Wilson	33	1	44	6
1921–1923	Warren G. Harding	5	1	6	0
1923–1929	Calvin Coolidge	20	30	50	4
1929–1933	Herbert Hoover	21	6	37	3
1933–1945	Franklin D. Roosevelt	372	263	635	9
1945–1953	Harry S. Truman	180	70	250	12
1953–1961	Dwight D. Eisenhower	73	108	81	2
1961–1963	John F. Kennedy	12	9	21	0
1963–1969	Lyndon B. Johnson	16	4	30	0
1969–1974	Richard M. Nixon	26	7	43	7
1974–1977	Gerald R. Ford	48	8	66	12
1977–1981	Jimmy Carter	13	8	31	2

(Table continues on next page)

Table 10-1   (continued)

Years	President	Regular vetoes	Pocket vetoes	Total vetoes	Vetoes overridden
1981–1989	Ronald Reagan	39	39	78	9
1989–1993	George Bush[c]	29	17	46	1
1993–1998	Bill Clinton	25	0	25	1
Total		1,473	1,067	2,540	105

Sources: Presidential Vetoes, 1789–1976, compiled by the Senate Library (Washington, D.C.: U.S. Government Printing Office, 1978), ix; and Gary L. Galemore, Congressional Research Service.

[a] Harrison served from March 4 to April 4, 1841.

[b] Garfield served from March 4 to September 19, 1881.

[c] Bush claimed that he pocket vetoed two bills (H.R. 2712 in 1989 and H.R. 1699 in 1991); in fact, he returned them to Congress, which attempted to override the veto on the first bill. Because these vetoes were returned to Congress, they are counted here as regular vetoes. Congress argued that Bush's other two pocket vetoes (of H.J. Res. 390 in 1989 and S. 1176 in 1991) were invalid and that the bills became law. Because the National Archives does not recognize these bills as enacted into law, they are counted here as pocket vetoes. Courtesy of Louis Fisher, Congressional Research Service.

- He can sign the bill. Most public and private bills presented to the president are signed into law. Presidents sometimes issue "signing statements" that express their interpretation of a new law's provisions.[26]
- He can return the bill with his veto message to the originating house of Congress.
- He can take no action, and the bill will become law without his signature. This option, seldom employed, is reserved for bills the president dislikes but not enough to veto (see box, p. 295).
- He can "pocket veto" the bill. Under the Constitution, if a congressional adjournment prevents the return of a bill, the bill cannot become law without the president's signature.

During the 1970s and 1980s Congress and the president sharply disagreed over the meaning of prevents in the fourth option. A federal appeals court ruled that President Reagan acted unconstitutionally when he pocket vetoed a measure during the holiday season between the first and second sessions of the 98th Congress. Congressional attorneys argued that during legislative recesses both chambers designate officials to receive executive communications, including veto messages. Pending action by the Supreme Court, the appeals court ruling makes clear that pocket vetoes are constitutional only when Congress adjourns sine die (that is, adjourns finally) at the end of its second session. President Bush tried to expand the pocket veto to include midsession recesses and adjournments between the first and second sessions of a Congress, but congressional leaders disputed such actions.

An Unsigned Bill Becomes Law

In November 1995 President Clinton opposed legislation (S.1322) that would re-locate the U.S. embassy in Israel from Tel Aviv to Jerusalem. Clinton did not object in principle to moving the embassy to Jerusalem, which Israel has regarded as its capital since 1950. But he warned that ordering the shift would risk derailing the Middle East peace process because Arab nations strongly objected to the idea.

Both chambers of Congress approved S.1322 by wide margins. Clinton decided not to veto the measure and face an almost certain override. Instead, he announced that he would allow the bill to become law without his signature and would make use of a provision added in the Senate after closed-door negotiations that would enable him to delay the move indefinitely for national security reasons.

Clinton's decision to distance himself from the embassy bill without actually veto-ing it was by no means unprecedented, although it is an option rarely used by chief ex-ecutives. S.1322 is only the sixth bill to become law in this way since 1973.

Source: Adapted from Amy D. Burke, "An Unsigned Bill to Become Law Today," *CQ's Congressional Monitor,* Nov. 7, 1995, 3.

Veto Strategies. President Bush was among the most successful chief exec-utives in employing the veto against an opposition Congress. He used it to block unwanted legislation and as a potent bargaining weapon to get conces-sions from the Democratic-controlled Congress. Not until his term was nearly over (on October 5, 1992), and after thirty-five consecutive veto victories, did Congress manage to override Bush's veto of a popular bill to reregulate the cable television industry. Part of the explanation for Bush's veto successes was that he announced his intentions early and stuck by them unless the compro-mises he wanted were agreed to. Furthermore, he convinced congressional Re-publicans that their strength depended on sustaining the president's vetoes. Frustrated by their inability to override presidential vetoes, congressional Demo-crats devised their own strategy: win by losing. To sharpen the policy differ-ences between the two parties before the November 1992 election, they sent the president bills that he was certain to veto.

By contrast, President Clinton did not veto a single measure during his first two years in office—something that had not happened since the days of Millard Fillmore in the 1850s. Part of the explanation is that Congress was then controlled by Democrats. (Clinton had threatened to veto his health re-form plan unless it was passed as he wanted, but the 103d Congress never acted upon it.)

Clinton used his veto pen for the first time on June 7, 1995, rejecting an appropriations bill. Subsequently, the president either exercised or threatened to use the veto against numerous Republican-sponsored bills.

Clinton even vetoed a bill he did not oppose: funding for the legislative branch. His reason was that "it would be inappropriate to provide full-year

regular funding for Congress . . . while funding for most other activities of Government remains incomplete, unresolved, and uncertain."[27] Congress had deliberately acted first on its own funding to set a governmentwide example by cutting its own expenditures before cutting spending for other federal entities and programs. The president turned that argument against the GOP leadership and, for the first time in congressional history, vetoed a free-standing appropriations bill for the legislative branch.

Postveto Action. Just as there may be strong pressure on the White House to veto or sign a bill, there can be intense political heat on Congress after it receives a veto message. A week after President Richard Nixon's 1970 televised veto of a bill funding welfare programs, House members received more than 55,000 telegrams, most of them urging support for the veto. Congress upheld the veto, in part because of Nixon's televised appeal. On the other hand, despite a massive telephone campaign to congressional offices (as many as 80,000 calls an hour) urging support for President Reagan's veto of a 1988 civil rights bill, the House and Senate easily overrode the veto.[28]

Congress need not act at all upon a vetoed bill. If party leaders believe they lack the votes to override, the chamber that receives a bill may refer it to committee or table it. Even if one house musters the votes to override, the other body may do nothing. No amendments can be made to a vetoed bill— it is all or nothing at this stage—and the Constitution requires votes on vetoed bills to be recorded.

The Line-Item Veto. Congress's habit of combining numerous items into a single measure puts the president in the position of having to accept or reject the entire package. Presidents and supporters of executive power have long touted the advantages of allowing the president to veto items selectively. The legislative line-item veto was a mid-1990s priority in the GOP's Contract with America. Proponents argued that it would give the president an effective way to eliminate wasteful spending and reduce the federal deficit. Opponents countered that the item veto is really about interbranch power and not fiscal restraint. Granting the item veto to the president, they said, would undermine Congress's "power of the purse" and give chief executives added bargaining leverage over lawmakers. "The president could say, 'I'm going to zap your dam, but I've got another piece of legislation coming around, and I won't be so inclined to do that [if you support me],' " said Rep. Jack Kingston, R-Ga.[29] After much debate, the 104th Congress expanded the president's rescission (cancellation of spending) authority. It eventually passed the line-item veto despite some concern among congressional Republicans that President Clinton might use it against GOP-passed "riders" (extraneous policy provisos) in appropriations bills.

The Line-Item Veto Act gave the president another option besides the four described earlier. After a president signed a bill into law, he could exercise the line-item veto prerogative to (1) cancel dollar amounts specified in any appropriations law or even in the accompanying House or Senate committee reports; (2) strike new entitlement programs or expansions of existing programs;

and (3) delete tax breaks limited to 100 or fewer beneficiaries. After taking these actions, the president was required to send a special message to Congress identifying what he had rescinded. To overturn these decisions, Congress would have to pass another bill that the president could then veto, requiring Congress to override it by a two-thirds vote of each chamber. Under the law the president could block something if he had the support of only one-third plus one of the members of each chamber. The act became effective January 1, 1997, and was to expire at the end of 2004.

Right after the bill took effect, however, a bipartisan group of lawmakers filed a lawsuit challenging the law's constitutionality. The group argued that the law allowed the president to repeal statutory provisions unilaterally and that it eroded Congress's constitutional power of the purse.[30] Without addressing the law's constitutionality, the Supreme Court ruled that year that members of Congress lacked legal standing to bring the suit. They had suffered no specific personal injury—a requirement if the Court is to decide cases or controversies—because Clinton had never exercised the line-item's cancellation authority. The Court's decision cleared the way for the president to exercise the line-item veto option, and he did so for the first time in August 1997.[31]

Contrary to expectations, President Clinton exercised caution in his use of the line-item veto. Apparently, the president chose not to anger lawmakers whose support he might need later to enact administration priorities. As one account noted, the president "has deferred to Congress on the overwhelming majority of projects that members added to budget bills, even when the Administration could find no compelling public interest to justify them."[32]

Moreover, as everyone expected, several lawmakers brought another suit challenging his use of the line-item veto. On June 25, 1998, in the case of *Clinton v. New York City,* the Supreme Court by a 6–3 vote declared the Line-Item Veto Act unconstitutional because it gave the president "unilateral authority to change the text of duly enacted statutes," wrote Justice John Paul Stevens for the majority.[33] The administration soon announced that it would release funding for projects that had been subject to the line-item veto. Subsequently, several lawmakers introduced line-item veto alternatives, including a constitutional amendment. As the chairman of the House Ways and Means Committee said, "I am deeply concerned that our commitment to fiscal discipline will be eaten away" unless we enact a constitutional line-item veto amendment.[34] Now that the federal government appears to be entering the era of budget surpluses (see Chapter 11), however, momentum for further legislative action on the line-item veto is likely to decline.

Lobbying Congress

Many factors influence how members vote on issues important to the White House. Although the personal legislative skills of presidents are significant, other considerations—members' constituency interests, policy preferences, and ideological dispositions, as well as public opinion and the number of partisan seats in each house—usually are more important in shaping con-

gressional outcomes. As a result, the White House legislative liaison operation is concerned less with specific "arm twisting" and more with the "longer-term strategic task of creating an atmosphere of cooperation between the White House and Congress."[35]

No president has an easy task persuading Congress to act in a certain way. "Merely placing a program before Congress is not enough," President Lyndon Johnson once declared. "Without constant attention from the administration, most legislation moves through the congressional process at the speed of a glacier."[36] Johnson regularly (and sometimes crudely) admonished his aides and departmental officers to work closely with Congress. "[Get off] your ass and see how fast you can respond to a congressional request," he told his staff. "Challenge yourself to see how quickly you can get back to him or her with an answer, any kind of an answer, but goddamn it, an answer."[37]

White House liaison activities with Congress, patronage services, and public appeals for support are some of the ways presidents enhance their bargaining power with the legislative branch. These activities help presidents exercise their constitutional and persuasive powers, and they also may minimize the delay and deadlock built into executive-legislative relationships.

White House Liaison

Presidents have always maintained informal contacts with Congress. George Washington dispatched Alexander Hamilton, his secretary of the Treasury, to consult with members; Thomas Jefferson socialized with his congressional allies. But not until the Truman administration, in 1949, did any president create an office to maintain ties with Congress. Truman's liaison unit consisted of two persons inexperienced in legislative politics.

In 1961 President John F. Kennedy upgraded the congressional relations unit. He realized that without aggressive liaison his New Frontier program faced tough sledding in a Congress dominated by conservatives. Every president since Kennedy has had his own system for lobbying Congress. Carter's liaison unit used computers to analyze congressional votes and target members who could be coaxed for votes on certain issues. In the Reagan White House overall legislative strategy on major issues was formulated by his Legislative Strategy Group. The group's objectives were to promote enactment of the president's agenda by building winning coalitions on Capitol Hill. Reagan, like Carter before him and Bush and Clinton after, appointed White House aides to contact groups and constituencies needed to win legislative battles. Their job, in effect, was to "lobby the lobbyists."

Patronage Services

To win congressional support for their programs, presidents commonly grant or withhold their patronage resources. Broadly conceived, patronage involves not only federal and judicial positions but also federal construction projects, location of government installations, campaign support, availability of strategic information, plane rides on *Air Force One,* White House access for im-

portant constituents, and countless other favors, large and small. The actual or potential award of favors enables presidents to amass political IOUs they can cash in later for needed support in Congress. Some presidents even keep records of the political favors they grant to members. A story illustrates the dynamics of trading:

> John Kennedy was trying to make a case to Senator Robert Kerr [D-Okla.] for an investment credit tax bill that was bottled up in the Senate Finance Committee, of which Kerr was an influential member. Kerr responded by asking why the administration opposed his Arkansas River project and by demanding a trade. Kennedy smiled and replied, "You know, Bob, I never really understood that Arkansas River bill before today." Kerr got his project as well as several other benefits. In return, he provided Kennedy with important support and managed the president's high-priority Trade Expansion Act in the Senate.[38]

Sen. Everett M. Dirksen, R-Ill., an influential minority leader from 1959 to 1969, insisted that patronage was a "tremendous weapon" of the president. "It develops a certain fidelity on the part of the recipient," he said.[39] Yet there are limitations. Presidents try to avoid the irritation of members whose requests are turned down, sometimes assigning to other officials the job of saying "no." As President Clinton's one-time head of congressional liaison said, "The problem with Congressional relations is that with every good intention, at the end of the day you can't accommodate all the requests that you get."[40]

Presidents who try to punish lawmakers may see their attempts backfire. Witness President Clinton's "lesson" to Alabama senator Richard C. Shelby, then a Democrat, who lost some federal funding for programs in his state because he opposed the president's economic program. Shelby began to vote regularly with the opposition; finally, he formally switched parties and became a Republican. And when Shelby became chairman of the Senate Select Intelligence Committee in 1997, he vehemently opposed Clinton's choice of Anthony Lake (the president's national security adviser during his first term) to be head of the Central Intelligence Agency. The upshot: Lake withdrew his nomination. "Kicking Bill Clinton in the shins," one analyst said, reinforced Shelby's strong electoral standing in Alabama.[41]

Public Appeals for Support

"With public sentiment, nothing can fail; without it nothing can succeed," Abraham Lincoln once observed.[42] "Going public" on an issue, however, is not without its risks. The president can raise expectations that cannot be met, make inept presentations, lose control over issues, infuriate legislators whose support he needs, or further stiffen the opposition. Furthermore, many legislators are more popular than the president in their districts or states. The president goes public to gather support, because "if he had the votes he would pass the measure first and go to the public only for the bill-signing ceremonies."[43]

President Reagan was an acknowledged master at using the electronic media to orchestrate public support. The Hollywood actor turned president was at home in front of cameras and microphones, and he had a keen sense of public ritual and symbolism as means of rallying support. Reagan's adroitness with the media, primarily during his first year in office, is where his legacy will loom large for future presidents and Congresses. He showed that "one man using the White House's immense powers of communication can lift the mood of the nation and alter the way it does business."[44]

President Bush's public relations techniques "abandoned the elaborate, tightly controlled machinery developed in recent years to project, manipulate and polish a presidential image" in the television age.[45] Instead, Bush used traditional methods—meeting with small groups of reporters, inviting journalists to lunch, or traveling outside Washington—to build public support through communications.

President Clinton, by contrast, was innovative in using media technologies to reach voters and in employing campaign-style practices to generate public support for his programs. The April 1995 Oklahoma City bombing—and Clinton's empathetic response—reminded the public of the human face of the federal government, the very entity Republican "revolutionaries" were warring against. When Republicans added provisions to a flood relief bill that Clinton opposed, the president used the bully pulpit to paint the GOP position as "extreme" and generated a flurry of favorable publicity for his position. As one account noted:

> News accounts portrayed Republicans as, well, crazy extremists bent on playing games with flood victims. Rank-and-file Republicans writhed in political agony. Michigan Republican Fred Upton's mother watched the news accounts with alarm and warned her son, "You're getting killed." "When your mom tells you that, you know you're in trouble," said Upton [46]

The White House uses "nightly tracking polls and weekly focus groups to help determine its daily message and the approach President Clinton should take to important national issues."[47] One controversial issue was the chemical weapons treaty. The contending sides took to the airwaves to mobilize public support for their positions. Senate Foreign Relations chairman Jesse Helms, R-N.C., successfully prevented action on the treaty during the 104th Congress. His committee staff fought an effective grassroots campaign, "sending by fax nearly 1,000 press releases . . . to local newspapers, radio and television stations in key states across the country." The treaty, he argued, would have "devastating" effects, especially on small chemical businesses. When the 105th Congress began, President Clinton made ratification of the treaty a top priority. His administration conducted its own grassroots campaign and won passage of the treaty, which banned the use, storage, or production of chemical weapons.[48]

The Clinton administration and the GOP Congress continued to wage the battle for public opinion. Both sides struggled to frame the national debate in

ways that mobilize public support behind their policy and political objectives. Throughout the impeachment events of 1998, the White House waged an aggressive campaign to portray the president as taking care of the public's business and to stigmatize his accusers. It was a battle the White House won, as the president's job approval ratings remained high, Congress's ratings sagged, and a majority of citizens opposed impeachment. Mindful that Clinton still held the megaphone and excelled at taking his message to the public, House and Senate Republicans scheduled more than 500 town meetings over the 1999 Easter recess to tout their proposals on Social Security and other issues. "There is a great deal of effort and involvement going into [having all GOP lawmakers] talk about the same message," said a Senate Republican official.[49] In short, the line between campaigning and governing has virtually disappeared at both ends of Pennsylvania Avenue.

Sources of Legislative-Executive Cooperation

Unlike national assemblies where executive authority is lodged in the leader of parliament—called the prime minister or premier—Congress truly is separate from the executive branch. Yet the executive and legislative branches are mutually dependent in policy making. The 110 volumes of the *United States Statutes at Large* underscore the cooperative impulses of the two branches. Each volume contains the joint product of Congresses and presidents over the years, from the 108 public laws enacted by the First Congress (1789–1791) to the 394 enacted by the 105th Congress (1997–1999). These accomplishments are the result of party loyalties and public expectations, bargaining and compromise, and informal links between the president and lawmakers.

Party Loyalties and Public Expectations

Presidents and congressional leaders have met informally to discuss issues ever since the First Congress, when George Washington frequently sought the advice of Rep. James Madison. But meetings between the chief executive and House and Senate leaders did not become common until Theodore Roosevelt's administration. Today congressional party leaders are two-way conduits who communicate legislative views to the president and inform members of executive preferences and intentions.

Presidents and members of their party are linked psychologically and ideologically. This means that "bargaining 'within the family' has a rather different quality than bargaining with members of the rival clan."[50] During Reagan's first term, for instance, the president and his chief aides relied heavily on Howard H. Baker Jr., the Senate majority leader, to marshal support. "Before we move on anything up there, we pick up the phone and get Howard Baker's judgment on what will or won't fly," said White House chief of staff James Baker (no relation to the senator).[51]

Presidents and their partisan colleagues on Capitol Hill sometimes have divergent goals, however, especially when the president's party is in the minority. The need for legislative results impels presidents to deal with whichever is the

majority party. As one Clinton adviser explained, the "president must present himself as a national leader, as opposed to a Democratic leader, to an electorate increasingly dominated by voters who feel no allegiance to either party."[52]

Presidents' relations with Congress are also made difficult by pervasive anxiety and alienation among many citizens (most of whom stay away from the polls), combative interest groups, and an aggressive and often critical press. Presidents sometimes can overcome these forces and successfully reach out to lawmakers in both parties. Clinton, for instance, relied heavily on Republican lawmakers and conservative Democrats to pass legislation in the summer of 1997 implementing the balanced-budget plan agreed to that spring.

Bargaining and Compromise

The interdependence of the two branches provides each with the incentive to bargain. Legislators and presidents have in common at least three interests: shaping public policy, winning elections, and attaining influence within the legislature. In achieving these goals, members may be helped or hindered by executive officials. Agency personnel, for example, can heed legislators' advice in formulating policies, help them gain favorable publicity back home, and give them advance notice of executive actions. Executive officials, on the other hand, rely on legislators for help in pushing administrative proposals through the legislative process.

An illustration of effective presidential bargaining with Congress occurred on May 7, 1981, when the Democratic-controlled House adopted President Reagan's controversial budget package, intended to cut federal spending for social programs and to raise military spending. The plan easily passed the House because of Reagan's popularity and skill in dealing with representatives. The "greatest selling job I've ever seen," said Speaker Thomas P. "Tip" O'Neill Jr. On the key House vote all 191 GOP members and 63 Democrats backed the president's budget scheme.

The president's victory was made possible by a multipronged strategy. Reagan bolstered the support of wavering Republicans. He persuaded several governors to meet with representatives from their states who were opposing the program. He met or phoned conservative Democrats whose support was needed. Top executive officials were sent into targeted Democratic districts to drum up public support. Finally, a few days before the House vote, and in his first public appearance since he had been shot in an assassination attempt, Reagan made a nationally televised address before a joint session of Congress and appealed for support of his economic program.

During intense legislative-executive negotiations in late 1995, President Clinton and the GOP Congress played a game of "fiscal chicken." Each side sought public support and twice refused to yield on their budget blueprints. The immediate result was the shutdown of major parts of the federal government. Bargaining between the branches continued as Congress passed temporary funding measures that provided full-year funding for several departments. Neither side, however, budged very much from their positions. Finally, as the

public began to blame Republicans more than the president for the deadlock, the stand-off ended and the government was funded and reopened.

Informal Links

Some presidents are able to deal with Congress more adeptly than others. Lyndon Johnson assiduously courted members. He summoned legislators to the White House for private meetings, danced with their wives at parties, telephoned greetings on their birthdays, and hosted them at his Texas ranch. He also knew how to "twist arms" to win support for his programs. Johnson's understanding of what moved members and energized Congress was awesome. "There is only one way for a President to deal with the Congress," he said, "and that is continuously, incessantly, and without interruption."[53]

In contrast, President Carter, who was elected as a Washington "outsider," never developed an affinity for Congress. Although by one measurement Congress sided with Carter on 75 percent of the votes on which he took a position during 1977, the margin was low for a first-year president whose party also controlled the Congress (see Figure 9-3, p. 274). A House Democrat recalled:

> When I came here President Kennedy would have six or seven of us down to the White House every evening for drinks and conversation. Johnson did the same thing, and they created highly personal, highly involved relationships. With Carter, he has 140 people in for breakfast and a lecture.[54]

In this respect Carter was like Nixon who, despite his service in Congress, dealt clumsily with lawmakers. Nixon shunned informal contacts with members, rarely telephoned them, and "could not bring himself to ask for votes."[55]

Other chief executives were more at ease with members. President Reagan enjoyed swapping stories with Democrats and Republicans alike. As former Senate majority leader Baker described him:

> In dealing with Congress, he's closer to Lyndon Johnson than anyone else. . . . Carter never understood the legislative process. Ford understood but he couldn't do anything about it. Nixon never paid enough attention to it to be successful. For give-and-take with Congress, Reagan is the best I've ever served with.[56]

Bush's personal style with Congress fell somewhere between President Carter's (impersonal and detail oriented) and President Reagan's (friendly and focused on the big picture). Bush was more involved in day-to-day policy making and personally consulted with many members of Congress and friends around the country. "He makes and takes scores of phone calls each day," one report noted, "talking to an army of people in and out of government, from Congressmen to civil rights leaders to cronies from the Texas oil fields."[57]

Clinton had an activist style of courting Congress but claimed few close allies in the House or Senate. The president periodically journeyed to Capitol Hill to talk with lawmakers about the budget, the crisis in Bosnia, and other

issues. Early in the 105th Congress the president went to Capitol Hill to meet with the bipartisan congressional leadership to discuss developing an agenda of commonly shared goals. As the crisis in the Balkans grew intense in spring 1999, Clinton invited the bipartisan congressional leadership to the White House twice in four days to explain why it might be necessary for the United States to become more involved in the war in Kosovo.[58]

Ultimately, however, presidential style and skills affect legislative success only "at the margins."[59] Far more important, as we have seen in Chapter 9, are contextual factors, the most important of which is the president's partisan strength in Congress.

Sources of Legislative-Executive Conflict

Legislative-executive conflicts were evident in 1789; they are present today; and they can be expected in the future for at least three reasons. First, the Constitution specifies neither the precise policy-making roles of Congress and the president nor the manner in which they are to deal with one another. Second, presidents and Congresses serve different constituencies. Third, there are important variations in the timetables under which the two branches operate.

Constitutional Ambiguities

Article I invests Congress with "all legislative Powers," but it also authorizes the president to recommend and to veto legislation. In several specific areas the Constitution splits authority between the president and Congress. The Senate, for example, is the president's partner in treaty making and nominations under "advice and consent" clauses. And, before treaties can take effect, they require the concurrence of two-thirds of the Senate. The Constitution is silent, however, on how or when the Senate is to render its advice to the president.[60]

In 1919 and 1920 a historic confrontation occurred when the Senate vehemently opposed the Treaty of Versailles negotiated by President Wilson. The treaty contained an agreement binding the United States to the proposed League of Nations. Many senators had warned the president against including the league provision in the treaty, and during floor deliberations the Senate added several "reservations" that were strongly opposed by the president. Spurning compromise, Wilson launched a nationwide speaking tour to mobilize popular support for the treaty. Not to be outdone, senators opposed to the pact organized a "truth squad" that trailed the president and rebutted his arguments. During his tour Wilson suffered a stroke from which he never fully recovered. In the end the treaty was rejected. The Constitution, in short, intermingles presidential and congressional authority but also assigns each branch special duties.

Different Constituencies

Presidents and their vice presidents are the only public officials elected nationally. To win, they must create vastly broader electoral coalitions than is

necessary for legislators, who represent either states or districts. Only presidents, then, can claim to speak for the nation at large. It is important to note, however, that

> there is no structural or institutional or theoretical reason why the representation of a "single" broader constituency by the President is necessarily better or worse than the representation of many "separate" constituencies by several hundred legislators. Some distortion is inevitable in either arrangement, and the question of the good or evil of either form of distortion simply leads one back to varying value judgments.[61]

Presidents and legislators tend to view policies and problems from different perspectives. Members often subscribe to the view that "what's good for Portland is good for the nation." Presidents are apt to say that "what's good for the nation is good for Portland." In other words, public officials may view common issues differently when they represent diverging interests.

For example, a president might wish to reduce international trade barriers. A representative from a district where a manufacturer is threatened by imported Japanese products is likely to oppose the president's policy, while importers and retailers of Italian shoes are likely to support the president. The challenge to national policy making is to forge consensus within an electorate that simultaneously holds membership in two or more competing constituencies.

Disparities in constituencies are underscored by differences in the ways voters judge presidents and members of Congress. Studies of presidential popularity ratings suggest that presidents are judged on the basis of general factors—economic boom or bust, the presence or absence of wars or other crises, the impact of policies on given groups.[62] Legislators, by contrast, tend to be assessed on the basis of their personalities, their communication with constituents, and their service in material ways to the state or district. Not only do presidents and legislators serve different constituencies; they labor under divergent incentives.

Different Time Perspectives

Finally, Congress and the president operate on different timetables. Presidents have four years, at most eight, to win adoption of their programs. They are usually in a hurry to achieve all they can before they leave office. In practice, they have even less time—in view of the typical fall-off of presidential support after the initial honeymoon. In reality, presidents and their advisers have a year, perhaps less, to sell their basic program to Congress and the public.

Congress, on the other hand, typically moves slowly. Seldom does it pass presidential initiatives quickly. Moreover, many legislators are careerists. Once elected, House members are likely to be reelected, and senators serve six-year terms. Most members hold office a good deal longer than the presidents they deal with. Skeptical legislators, reluctant to follow the president, realize that if they resist long enough someone else will occupy the White House. In addi-

tion, the lawmakers' attitude toward the president depends on whether the chief executive is up for reelection. Comparing Reagan's first and second terms, one congressional Republican said:

> The main political undercurrent is that Ronald Reagan will not run for re-election. His agenda is now a little bit different from Republicans in Congress. In the first term Ronald Reagan's agenda was the same as the Republicans—to get re-elected. Now it's a little different. While there's certainly times when both want the same thing, members of Congress ask, "Is this really in my best interest if I want to get re-elected?" Reagan doesn't have to ask that question any more.[63]

Or as Rep. Barney Frank, D-Mass., said following Clinton's election to a second term: "I don't have to worry anymore about the consequences of my actions on Bill Clinton's reelection."[64] Whereas "governing" will be a major focus of Clinton's second term, a "campaigning" perspective will suffuse many actions of congressional Democrats. They must calculate whether their strategic choices advance or hinder the likelihood of reclaiming the House in 2000 or thereafter.

The Balance of Power

"The relationship between the Congress and the presidency," wrote Arthur M. Schlesinger Jr., "has been one of the abiding mysteries of the American system of government."[65] Part of the mystery inheres in the Constitution, which enumerates many powers for Congress as well as those "necessary and proper" to carry them out, while leaving the president's powers largely ambiguous. Where does the balance of power lie? There is no easy answer, but at certain times the scale has tipped toward Congress and at other times toward the president. Scholars have even identified periods of "congressional government" or "presidential government."[66]

Several points need to be remembered about the ups and downs of Congress and the presidency. First, the power balance is in constant flux. The stature of either branch can be influenced by issues, events, or personalities. Partisan circumstances also come into play. In the recent past, congressional Republicans generally supported executive authority because their party had won the White House so often (five of the seven elections from 1968 to 1992). During that period Republicans acted as the "executive party" and Democrats as the "congressional party." After 1992 these roles have been reversed.

Even during periods when one branch appears to dominate, actual relationships in specific policy areas may be far more complex. The mid-1960s and early 1970s, for example, are cited as a time of "imperial presidents" and compliant Congresses.[67] But Congress was by no means passive during this period. While it enacted much of President Johnson's Great Society program, it also initiated scores of laws, including consumer, environmental, health, and civil rights legislation. Nor did executive actions go unchallenged. Nationally

televised hearings conducted in 1966 by the Senate Foreign Relations Committee helped to mobilize congressional and public opposition to Johnson's Vietnam War policies.

Split control of the legislative and executive branches did not hamper legislative productivity during the period of mutual hostility between President Nixon and the Democratic Congress. Among the major laws passed during this period were the National Environmental Policy Act of 1969, the Occupational Safety and Health Act of 1970, the War Powers Resolution of 1973, and the Congressional Budget and Impoundment Control Act of 1974—not to mention the Twenty-sixth Amendment to the Constitution, which grants eighteen-year-olds the right to vote. Although Nixon is viewed as a conservative president, his record with Congress was expansive and liberal.

Second, legislative-executive relationships are not zero-sum games. If one branch gains power, the other does not necessarily lose it. If one branch is up, the other need not be down. The expansion of the federal government since World War II has augmented the authority of both branches. Their growth rates were different, but each expanded its ability to address complex issues, initiate legislation, and frustrate proposals of the other.

Third, events contribute significantly to policy-making power. Conventional wisdom states that wars, crises, nuclear weapons, military expansion, and public demands fostered the imperial presidency. Such factors certainly enlarge the likelihood of executive dominance, but we should note that in the wars of 1812 and 1898, military action was encouraged in part by aggressive Congresses. Economic panics and depressions under Presidents James Monroe, James Buchanan, and Ulysses S. Grant did not lead to losses of congressional power.

Fourth, shifts of power occur within each branch. In Congress aggressive leaders may be followed by less assertive leaders. In the executive branch the forces for White House leadership regularly battle the forces for agency decentralization. These internal power fluctuations clearly affect policy making. As recently as the Eisenhower presidency in the 1950s, powerful committee and party leaders could normally deliver blocs of votes to pass legislation. Today, the president can never be quite sure which of the 535 members will form a winning coalition.

Fifth, pendulum swings associated with shifting public opinion shape issue areas and how they are addressed by the two branches. In foreign relations, cycles of isolationism and internationalism, noninterventionism and interventionism, have succeeded each other at fairly regular intervals. Debates on health policy may shift from emphasizing government-run programs to approaches stressing private-sector competition. Or Congress may grab the policy-making initiative away from the president.

Congress and the president are institutions shaped by diverging imperatives. Executive officials want flexibility, discretion, and long-range commitments from Congress. They prefer few controls and consultations with a limited number of legislators. The executive tends to be hierarchical in decision

making, whereas Congress is collegial. One of the legislative branch's strengths, however, is to give voice and visibility to diverse viewpoints that the executive branch may have overlooked or ignored. The dispersion of power can slow down decision making, but it can also promote public acceptance of the nation's policies. Hence what are often viewed as Congress's vices have genuine virtue.

Conclusion

Legislative-executive relations are characterized by accommodation, conflict, and flux. Of these, accommodation is the most important. Neither branch is monolithic. Presidents find supporters in Congress even when they are opposed by a majority of either house. Both branches seek support for their policy preferences from each other and from outside allies.

It is also true that confrontation is a recurring element in dealings between Capitol Hill and the White House. The framers of the Constitution consciously distributed and mixed power among the three branches. They left it unclear how Congress or the president was to assert control over the bureaucracy and over policy making. No wonder these two branches tend to be adversaries even when they are controlled by the same party.

Finally, legislative-executive relations are constantly in flux. Either branch may be active on an issue at one time and passive on the same or different issues at another time. So many circumstances affect how, when, what, or why changes are brought about in their relationship that it is impossible to predict the outlook.

It is clear, however, that over the past generation Congress has equipped itself with a formidable arsenal of resources. As a result, it can play a more active role and even initiate policies of its own. This development need not be a formula for stalemate. "Our proper objective," counseled the late senator J. William Fulbright, D-Ark., "is neither a dominant presidency nor an aggressive Congress but, within the strict limits of what the Constitution mandates, a shifting of the emphasis according to the needs of the time and the requirements of public policy."[68]

The Executive and Congress: Advocacy and Defense. Donna Shalala, secretary of health and human services, tries to sell the Clinton administration's health care plan to the House Energy and Commerce Committee's Health Subcommittee. Critics of the Internal Revenue Service, below, are sworn in before the Senate Finance Committee, where they testified on alleged abusive practices.

11

Congress, the Bureaucracy, and the Courts

A fter the Republicans captured control of Congress in the 1994 elections, they immediately began to carry out their core objective: shrinking the size, reach, and cost of the federal government. Their "revolution" in trimming the government, however, soon went off track. The public blamed them for forcing two shutdowns of the federal government in 1995 and early 1996. President Bill Clinton effectively portrayed the proposed GOP reductions as "extreme" and highlighted the benefits to the populace of many federal services and programs.[1] He was quick to recognize, however, the popularity of the GOP's smaller government message. Instead of advocating broad federal initiatives, the president favored "incremental" ideas for providing individuals and communities with assistance (for instance, tax incentives to corporations that train workers poorly prepared for the information age).

In his State of the Union message in 1996, Clinton declared that "the era of big government is over," successfully co-opting the GOP's message. He then used his veto pen to foil Republican plans for any dramatic retrenchment of governmental agencies or programs. In this way the Democratic White House and the GOP-controlled Congress feuded over how best to reduce the government's roles and responsibilities. Whereas many Republicans favored a meat axe, Clinton proposed a scalpel for making bureaucratic cuts.

Why is it so difficult for presidents or Congress to shrink the government? One reason is the ambivalence of the citizenry. Although professing to want to get government off their backs, Americans of virtually all ideological persuasions turn to government to fulfill their goals and to provide assistance during times of need. After a tragic crash of a passenger airline, former senator William Cohen, secretary of defense in Clinton's second term, put it this way: "the government is the enemy until one needs a friend."[2] Needless to say, lawmakers defend governmental programs supported by their constituents. The paradox, then, is that citizens understandably oppose the idea of "big government" (after all, most people do not like to pay taxes), but they support the government's role—and may even welcome its selective expansion—in ensuring clean air and water, a strong national defense, quality health care, the safety of prescription drugs, or crime prevention.

Even the GOP-controlled Congress, which vowed to devolve power to the states and localities, has consolidated authority in Washington "when it proved the best way to implement [the Republican] agenda."[3] In state capitols across the nation, many people have noted "how limited the transfer of power to the

states has been so far, at least compared with the scale of the promises once held out for the idea."[4] As Sen. Fred Thompson, R-Tenn., has noted, "It's much easier to devolve when someone else is in power. When you've got the ball, the temptation is to replace those bad, old regulations with your good, new regulations, instead of sending it back to the states."[5] Except in the areas of welfare and unfunded federal mandates for the states, devolution has even given way to counterdevolution as the national government preempts state authority to tax Internet businesses, regulate electricity, or define what constitutes drunk driving. Moreover, nationwide corporations often lobby for federal regulation because then they do not have to contend with the different rules of the fifty states.

Congress Organizes the Executive Branch

Both the president and Congress are responsible for the "fourth branch of government"—the bureaucracy. The Constitution requires presidents to implement the laws, and by implication it empowers them to give managerial direction to the executive branch. But just as the president is a key player in the lawmaking process, so Congress "has at least as much to do with executive administration as does an incumbent of the White House."[6] Congress is constitutionally authorized to organize the executive branch. But the Framers could not have foreseen that their sparse references to "executive departments" would nurture the huge modern bureaucracy. George Washington supervised only three departments (State, War, and Treasury); President Clinton heads fourteen. Congress establishes the departments and creates the independent agencies, government corporations, and intergovernmental commissions (see Figure 11-1).

The complex federal structure periodically undergoes four basic forms of reorganization. First, executive agencies are created or abolished by law. Second, the president can recommend administrative changes, such as new strategies for management improvements. President Clinton, for instance, appointed Vice President Al Gore to undertake a "national performance review" of the government with an eye toward "reinventing," restructuring, and downsizing the federal bureaucracy. Third, Congress can authorize departments and agencies to reorganize themselves. Finally, Congress can authorize the president to propose reorganization plans subject to some form of congressional review.[7]

Reorganizations have political as well as administrative results. Congress is unlikely to approve such plans if they disrupt committee relations with favored agencies and programs. "If by this [executive] reorganization you affect in a major way the powers of the various committees in the Congress, you may as well forget it," a House committee chairman once told President Richard Nixon.[8] The difficulty of abolishing departments and agencies has prompted some lawmakers, such as Senate Finance chairman William V. Roth Jr., R-Del., to propose that an outside commission be established to recommend how Congress can do it.[9]

Figure 11-1   The Government of the United States

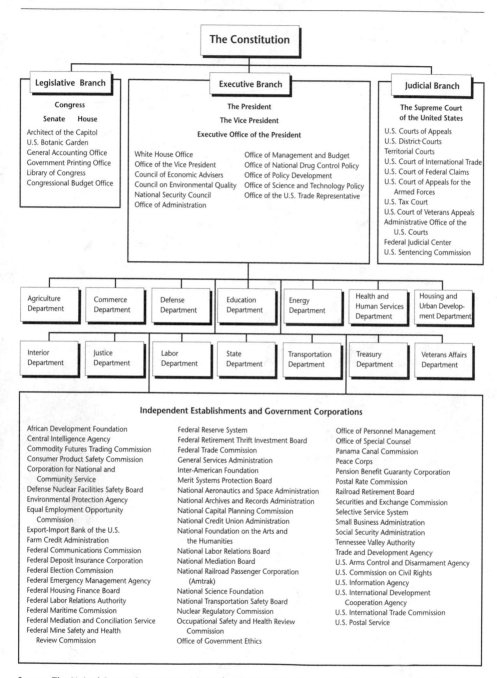

Source: *The United States Government Manual, 1998/1999* (Washington, D.C.: U.S. Government Printing Office, 1998), 22.

Figure 11-2   The Appointments Process

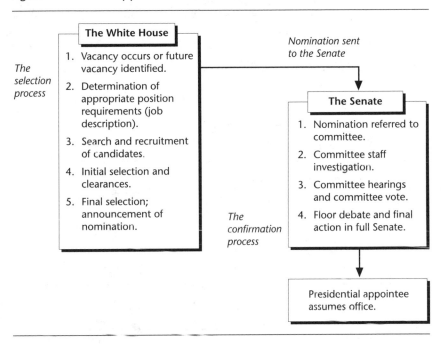

Source: G. Calvin Mackenzie, *The Politics of Presidential Appointments* (New York: Free Press, 1981), xv. Reprinted with permission of Macmillan Publishing Company. Copyright © 1981.

Senate Confirmation of Presidential Appointees

High-level federal appointments are subject to the Senate's "advice and consent" under Article II, Section 2, of the Constitution. After the president has decided whom to nominate, the Senate decides whether to confirm (see Figure 11-2). Senate committees usually elicit the following promise from nominees they have confirmed: "The nomination was approved subject to the nominee's commitment to respond to any requests to appear and testify before any duly constituted committee of the Senate."[10] The confirmation process also reflects the "two Congresses" principle. As a top Senate official once remarked, "It looks very, very good in California or some place to put out a press release that says, 'Today, I questioned the new Secretary of Transportation about the problems of our area.' "[11]

Presidents sometimes circumvent the Senate's role by making "recess appointments" during breaks in the Senate's session. (Recess appointees serve until the end of the next Senate session; for example, a person named in 2000 might serve until late 2001.) The Senate resents presidential use of this constitutional option (see Article II, Section, 2), and its opposition to some recess appointees has caused them to give up their posts. Another way for the administration to circumvent the confirmation process is to appoint officials on an "acting" basis. In 1998, 20 percent of the Cabinet-level jobs requiring Senate confirmation (64

of 320 slots) were held by "acting" officials.[12] Anger at this practice, including the president's designation in December 1997 of Bill Lann Lee as "acting" assistant attorney general for civil rights after the Senate did not act on his nomination, precipitated enactment of the Vacancies Act of 1998. This law identifies individuals subject to the "advice and consent" of the Senate who can be named on an "acting" basis and sets limits on the length of their tenure.

Nominations to high executive posts today are subject to standards of judgment and evaluation that go beyond questions of competence or conflict of interest. Nominees' personal lives and morality are scrutinized as well. As one commentator explained:

> These days, if you want to run for office or accept a position of public trust, everything is relevant. Your moral, medical, legal and financial background, even your college records, become the subject of public scrutiny. In the old days, the scrutiny was done in private, and certain transgressions could be considered irrelevant.[13]

This shift in standards stems in part from a shift in attitudes by the press and public. The press now reports more aggressively than in years past the private activities of public officials.[14]

President Clinton's nominee to be director of the Central Intelligence Agency, Anthony Lake, withdrew in March 1997 from consideration for the position, calling the confirmation process "nasty and brutish without being short."[15] Although the vast majority of presidential appointments are confirmed with little difficulty, critics of the process decry the rough treatment of many nominees. They lament the intrusion in the confirmation process of ideological interest groups that organize "attack campaigns" to defeat nominees who appear unsupportive of their agenda.

Another factor contributes to confirmation struggles: the legislative-executive tug of war. Some say the purpose of confirmation hearings in Congress "seems less to ensure that nominees are fit than to cripple the chief executive's political leadership. A defeated nomination can embarrass a president, demoralize his supporters, and reduce public confidence in his judgment."[16] To be sure, others argue that the confirmation process may be tough, but so are the positions for which nominees seek assignment. "If you can't fight your way through the process," stated former CIA director Robert Gates, "you might not just do a hot job as director."[17]

Judicial appointments are subject to even closer Senate scrutiny than are high-level executive appointments. President Ronald Reagan's 1987 nomination of Robert Bork to the Supreme Court underscored the Senate's intensive role in the advice-and-consent process. During nationally televised hearings, members of the Senate Judiciary Committee probed Bork's constitutional and philosophical views in minute detail. Because Bork's nomination to a lifetime position came at a time of great public concern about the Supreme Court's ideological balance, and because Bork's views were perceived as too conservative and controversial by many senators and interest groups, the Senate rejected the nomination.[18]

Even more controversial was President George Bush's 1991 nomination to the Supreme Court of Clarence Thomas, narrowly approved by the Senate, 52–48. Law professor Anita Hill, who previously had worked for Thomas, charged that he had sexually harassed her at work. The charges and counter-charges, played out on national television during the Senate confirmation hearings, riveted the nation's attention.[19] Since then the process has been re-formed. Future nominees to the Supreme Court are asked to respond to allegations against them in closed session and under oath rather than in the circus atmosphere of televised public hearings.

When Clinton began his second term in 1997, Senate Republicans de-layed scheduling hearings on the president's judicial appointments. One of their reasons was that they did not want the president to be able to appoint a majority of the judges on the federal bench by the end of his second term. Additionally, Senate Republicans vowed to block appointment of "activist" judges who give less deference to decisions made by legislatures and executives. Senate Judiciary chairman Orrin G. Hatch, R-Utah, even scheduled unusual "re-hearings" on judicial nominations his committee had already approved.[20]

Sen. Patrick J. Leahy of Vermont, ranking Democrat on the Judiciary panel, repeatedly lamented this slow pace. One judicial confirmation "took 41 months to complete—the longest-pending judicial nomination" in the Senate's history.[21] "In fairness to [Senator Hatch], if it was just left to the two of us, we would be moving them a lot faster," Leahy said. "Their [GOP] Caucus keeps much tighter control on what the chairman is allowed to do or not allowed to do."[22]

In 1998 the Senate confirmed sixty-five judges and significantly reduced the federal judicial vacancy rate. In 1999, however, controversy again sur-rounded Senate action on Clinton's judicial nominees. Chairman Hatch de-manded that Clinton nominate a conservative aide to Utah's GOP governor as a federal judge. Clinton balked, and Hatch "declined to hold confirmation hearings" on any of the thirty-six federal judgeship nominations still pend-ing.[23] President Clinton did succeed in placing more women and minorities on the federal bench "than any other president in American history."[24]

As in the past, political, patronage, and policy considerations permeate the confirmation process. Plum ambassadorial positions, for instance, are often given to campaign donors. According to one account, "About 30 percent of the more than 160 ambassadorial posts filled by Mr. Clinton have gone to politi-cal appointees, about the average over the last three decades." President Nixon once put the price of an ambassadorship at $250,000.[25]

The Senate may refuse to consider a nominee if members invoke "senato-rial courtesy." This tradition, dating from President Washington's administra-tion, generally means that the Senate will delay or not act upon nominations if a senator of the president's party opposes them.[26] Senators also may place "holds" on nominees (see Chapter 8). Holds are an unwritten, informal cus-tom, that senators use to block or delay nominations, sometimes to gain lever-age in negotiations with the administration.

Table 11-1   Political Appointments by Type and Work Schedule, September 1998

Type	Work Schedule		
	Full Time	Part Time	Total
Presidential appointments:			
Requiring Senate approval	536	110	646
Not requiring Senate approval	71	125	196
Other executive-level appointments	38	5	43
Other ambassadors	156	0	156
Total presidential appointments	801	240	1,041
Other political appointments:			
Noncareer senior executives	661	0	661
Schedule C[a]	1,335	11	1,346
Total political appointments[b]	2,797	251	3,048

Source: Central Personnel Data File (CPDF), Office of Workforce Information, U.S. Office of Personnel Management, December 18, 1998. Prepared by Roger Garcia of the Congressional Research Service.

[a] Employees in policy-determining positions and/or those who are required to have a close, confidential working relationship with the head of an agency or other key appointed officials.

[b] Less than 0.2 percent of civilian, nonpostal, executive branch employees.

The Senate never took action on President Clinton's openly gay nominee for ambassador to Luxembourg; several senators placed holds on the nominee. Alfonse D'Amato, R-N.Y., pleaded with GOP leaders to schedule a vote. In response, Sen. Jesse Helms, R-N.C., chided: "Senator D'Amato has a very large homosexual population in his state and he's trying to get their vote."[27] D'Amato did not win reelection in 1998, but his plea illustrates the two Congresses theme by linking senatorial action and vote getting. (In 1999 the nominee became ambassador by a recess appointment.)

The Personnel System

Congress wields wide authority—constitutionally, legally, informally—over the federal personnel system. The assassination of President James Garfield in 1881 by a disgruntled job seeker prompted Congress to curb the abuses of the "spoils system," the practice of handing out federal jobs to supporters of the party that had won the presidency. In 1883 Congress passed the first civil service law that substituted merit for patronage. The modern equivalent of the early patronage practices is the political-appointee system. Currently, there are more than 3,000 political appointments (see Table 11-1).

Political Appointees. In the 1970s, writes Paul C. Light, "Congress discovered executive structure . . . and began to mine it."[28] Since then Congress, and the president, have made numerous changes in the top four layers of officials

in Cabinet departments (secretary, deputy secretary, under secretary, and assistant secretary). In fact, 1998

> was a record-setter in more than just home runs and independent counsel reports. It also marked a new record in the number of job titles at the top of the federal government. Never have so many senior executives, political and career, occupied so many layers between the president and the front lines of government.[29]

Among the numerous new titles are deputy to the deputy secretary, principal assistant deputy under secretary, and associate principal deputy assistant secretary.[30] As a result of "title creep," it is becoming "impossible for the bottom to hear the top when messages go through dozens of interpretations on their journey down."[31]

With more top managers it takes longer for presidents to get their bureaucratic team confirmed and on the job. Top appointees in the Bush and Clinton administrations were confirmed, on average, more than eight months after the presidential inauguration; by contrast, confirmation of President John F. Kennedy's appointees averaged two and a half months.[32]

The number of political appointees is small compared with the total number of federal employees (about 2.8 million nondefense federal workers). Yet there is concern about the "politicization" of high-level jobs in the civil service. "We entrust the administration of the largest 'company' in the country . . . to a cast of well-meaning political loyalists with little or no management experience," wrote a career civil servant with thirty-four years of federal service. "We accept the rather mindless notion that any bright and public-spirited dilettante can run a government agency, bureau, or office."[33]

Sens. Russell D. Feingold, D-Wis., and John McCain, R-Ariz., proposed that the number of political appointees be capped at 2,000.[34] In their judgment there are too many for the president to manage effectively. Far from enhancing responsiveness, said Sen. Trent Lott, R-Miss., the large number of political appointees undermines "presidential control of the executive branch."[35] Not everyone agrees. Some contend that more political appointees are needed "to monitor the permanent government" and "to develop aggressively new policies."[36]

Pay and Other Legal Standards. By law, Congress has wide control over federal employees. It can establish special requirements for holding office; employee performance standards; wages, benefits, and cost-of-living adjustments; personnel ceilings; and protections from reprisals for "whistleblowers" (employees who expose waste and corruption). The 1939 Hatch Act, named for Carl Hatch, a Democratic senator from New Mexico, restricts federal employees' partisan activity. The act was passed during the New Deal after reports that civil servants were being coerced to back President Franklin Roosevelt in his reelection efforts. Congress tried unsuccessfully several times to revamp the law and give federal employees wider opportunities to participate in the political process. Finally, in 1993, President Clinton signed into law the Hatch Act reform amendments. They encourage civil servants to participate in political activity in accordance with regulations prescribed by the Office of Personnel Management.

Under the Constitution, Congress determines its own pay. It legislates pay raises or accepts pay hikes recommended by the statutorily created Citizens' Commission on Public Service and Compensation. Members of Congress may also receive automatic cost-of-living adjustments by statute. COLAs were intended to remove politics from the pay hike issue. However, there are still periodic battles waged in Congress—often in election years—over the cost-of-living adjustments, and lawmakers have several times been successful in passing legislation to deny the increase. Public criticism of pay hikes is a real concern, as is the threat that potential opponents will seize upon the issue in the next election.[37]

Under the 1989 Ethics Reform Act, "lawmakers are entitled to an annual raise equivalent to half a percentage point below the employment cost index, a gauge used to measure inflation."[38] Subsequent legislation prohibited senators as well as representatives from accepting speaking fees, or honorariums, from special interests and other groups.

In 1992 the Twenty-seventh Amendment to the Constitution (first proposed by James Madison in 1789) was ratified: "No law varying the compensation for the services of the Senators and Representatives shall take effect, until an election of Representatives shall have intervened." This amendment permits voters an opportunity to render their verdict on the pay hike before lawmakers receive it.[39]

After leaving public office, members, legislative staffers, and executive officers often pass through the "revolving door" to jobs with private firms that deal with the government. Responding to procurement abuses at the Pentagon, Congress restricted federal officials who leave public service from immediately joining a private company to work on projects or contracts they managed while in government service. Former federal employees who were "personally and substantially" involved in trade or treaty negotiations with a foreign government cannot lobby on behalf of foreign governments for a year after they leave office. When Congress passed the Lobby Disclosure Act of 1995, it prohibited the U.S. trade representative and his or her deputies from ever lobbying on behalf of foreign interests. The 1995 act also repealed the Ramspeck Act (named after a former House member), which allowed congressional employees who lost their jobs on Capitol Hill to enter the civil service without meeting the competitive requirements for government positions.

Size of Government. Americans have debated the size and scope of the federal government since the nation's founding. There are the perennial debates over what functions (defense, welfare, education, and so on) each level of government (local, state, or national) should be responsible for; in addition, people disagree about whether the federal government is bigger or smaller today than it was a few decades ago. Much of the disagreement centers on how governmental size is measured, such as federal expenditures as a share of the gross domestic product, the magnitude of the federal budget, or the number of federal employees. As to the first standard, "federal spending has shrunk relative to the size of the American economy," from 22 percent of gross domestic product in 1990 to 20 percent in 2000 and a projected 18.8 percent in 2002.[40] The federal budget keeps growing ($1.8 trillion in 2000), but so too have other things, including the population and the economy.

Contrary to many people's ideas, the federal work force has remained relatively constant in size. Since 1993 employment trends have headed downward, with much of the downsizing in the Pentagon and in low-grade positions.[41] (There are about 1.9 million full-time permanent civil servants, 1.5 million uniformed personnel, and 850,000 postal service workers.) In comparison, state and local jobs have mushroomed—from 13.3 million in 1980 to 16.6 million in 1999—and they may soar higher still if federal functions are returned to the states and localities.

How can the government continue to perform services while keeping its size down? One answer is that much of what the federal government does is to transfer money to eligible recipients, such as the elderly who receive Social Security. This function does not require large numbers of federal workers. Another answer is that many subnational governments and private organizations perform federal functions indirectly. Weapons systems, for example, are built by private companies under contract to the government. The job of Defense Department personnel, like that of many federal workers, consists of "planning, coordinating, preparing and issuing regulations and contracts for, negotiating, paying for, overseeing, inspecting, auditing, and evaluating the work of others."[42] The "others" include state and local governments, universities, businesses, hospitals, and private firms. Federal work, in brief, is being "outsourced" to contract employees.

When everyone who works directly or indirectly for the federal government is counted, it is much bigger than twenty years or thirty years ago, according to Light. He puts its "true size" at 17 million employees: the 4.25 civilian, military, and postal workers plus the 12.7 "shadow" workers who are "off the books" because they "work under federal contracts and grants or mandates imposed on state and local governments."[43] An academic dean at Harvard University, however, disagrees. He argues that whom and how many people the federal government employs are "poor surrogates" for the size and scope of government. The conclusion he reaches is that the "federal government—measured by direct and indirect employment, by the dollars it spends and how it spends them—is doing less today than a generation ago."[44]

However this debate about governmental size is reconciled, it is plain that privatizing the work of the federal government has advantages and disadvantages. Because companies under contract to the government are not directly responsible to Congress, so-called third-party or shadow government presents serious problems of accountability.[45] Some believe certain functions are inherently governmental and ought not to be turned over to outside organizations. Yet third parties are sometimes faster, more flexible, and cheaper than the governmental machine.

The Rulemaking Process

Although Congress creates executive agencies and lays down their mandates by law, it rarely can specify the details needed to implement policies. The landmark Telecommunications Act of 1996, for example, made it illegal to

make "indecent" material available to minors. What material is indecent? That question rests with government regulators (the Federal Communications Commission already bars "seven dirty words" from broadcasts) and ultimately the federal courts. In such cases, specifications must be written, details filled in, and procedures set forth. Thus agencies are empowered to make rules for carrying out the mandates contained in laws.[46]

In the Administrative Procedures Act of 1946 and later changes to it, Congress established standards for rulemaking by government agencies. Interested parties can take part in the process by testifying in public about the merits or demerits of proposed regulations. Regulations have all the force and effect of law. All regulations, explained Sen. Charles E. Grassley, R-Iowa,

> are based ultimately on authority granted by this Congress. When an agency promulgates a rule, it is engaging in a legislative task—in effect, filling in the gaps on the implementation of policies that we in Congress have established through statute. Accordingly, all regulations must be accountable to this Congress.[47]

In other words, rulemaking is a legislative process authorized by Congress but located in the executive branch or in independent regulatory bodies.

Since the mid-1990s, several laws give members more ability to call regulation writers to account. For example, the Congressional Review Act of 1996 requires regulators to submit all proposed new rules to the House and Senate. Lawmakers then have sixty legislative days to take steps to disapprove the regulations; otherwise, they go into effect.[48] Under the Small Business Regulatory Enforcement Fairness Act of 1996, agencies must take specific steps "to ensure that small business has a voice in the drafting of rules—and is aware of and understands the final version."[49] To be sure, federal regulations may be overturned or even declared unconstitutional, as occurred with air quality standards promulgated by the Environmental Protection Agency (EPA). A federal appeals court in May 1999 ruled that Congress had delegated "too much legislative-like authority" to the EPA.[50]

Congress and the White House frequently skirmish over rulemaking. During the Clinton administration, Republicans put the rollback of federal regulations high on their agenda. "Regulatory agencies have run amok and need to be reformed," House majority whip Tom DeLay, R-Texas, declared.[51] This sentiment was triggered in large measure by business's animus toward regulatory growth (see Table 11-2).

Business groups successfully delayed the Occupational Safety and Health Administration (OSHA) from implementing ergonomic standards. (Ergonomics is the science of designing job practices that suit each worker and thus minimize repetitive motion and other injuries.) In 1999, one account noted, "OSHA will unveil proposed 'ergonomics' standards after eight years of study and false starts. It has faced relentless opposition from business and from Republicans in Congress, who have three times written into appropriations laws language that barred the agency from preparing rules on the subject."[52]

Table 11-2 Code of Federal Regulations Page Count by Selected Presidencies

President	Average annual number of pages in the *Code of Federal Regulations*
Ford	71,982
Carter	94,777
Reagan	109,599
Bush	125,664
Clinton	134,173

Source: Office of Federal Register. [From] Cornelius M. Kerwin, *Rulemaking: How Government Agencies Write Law and Make Policy,* 2d ed. (Washington, D.C.: CQ Press, 1999), 21.

The Office of Management and Budget (OMB) is obligated by a 1998 law (P.L. 105-277) to issue an analysis of the costs and benefits of all federal regulations. Noting the limitations and difficulties of fulfilling this mandate, OMB "estimated the net benefits from health, safety and environmental regulation at between $30 billion and $3.3 trillion annually. Costs fall somewhere between $170 billion and $230 billion."[53]

Today the impetus for regulation often comes from the judiciary. Given inequities in the marketplace, individuals look to the courts rather than to traditional bureaucratic rulemaking to redress their grievances, such as discriminatory harassment in the workplace, unfairness in hiring practices, or unresponsive health maintenance organizations. "The main regulators are . . . claimants and lawyers and judges and juries, all working independently to spin, in the fashion of a mass of caterpillars, a cocoon of intricate social regulation that enfolds even the most minute details of everyday life."[54] Restaurants nationwide, for instance, are likely to regulate the hotness of their coffee given a 1992 court decision that awarded punitive damages to a woman scalded by McDonald's brew.

How valuable are regulations? Lawmakers, like their constituents, are of two minds. Some, like Sen. Barbara Boxer, D-Calif., emphasize their positive achievements:

> The purpose of the Federal regulatory process is to improve and protect the high quality of life that we enjoy in our country. Every day, the people of our Nation enjoy the benefits of almost a century of progress in Federal laws and regulations that reduce the threat of illness, injury, and death from consumer products, workplace hazards, and environmental toxins.[55]

Others, like Senator Roth, call for "more rational regulations," with "better analysis of costs, benefits, and risks, so that regulators will issue smarter, more cost-effective regulations."[56] A difficult challenge is to distinguish between inflexible,

pointless, or overly burdensome and costly regulations and beneficial regulations that are necessary to promote and protect the public's health and safety.

Regulatory agencies, like the Federal Trade Commission and the Consumer Product Safety Commission, are insulated from direct White House control. Commission members, including the chairs, are appointed by the president, subject to the advice and consent of the Senate. Because regulatory commissions are located outside executive departments, they are immune from the president's general authority to remove federal officials.

In addition, Congress has established a variety of quasi-governmental corporations. (One example is Sallie Mae, the Student Loan Marketing Association.) These entities are normally exempt from requirements imposed on other federal agencies, such as civil service rules, salary limits, presidential orders, and OMB clearance of their legislative or regulatory proposals. "Profound constitutional questions are raised by the vesting of governmental duties and authorities in quasi-governmental institutions," warned one administrative expert.[57] These institutions have the luxury of behaving like private companies when it suits them and claiming the privileges of quasi-governmental status when they are challenged. Such exemptions erode accountability to elected officials.

The Electoral Connection

Some observers suggest that Congress enlarged the executive establishment by passing vague laws that bureaucrats had to embellish with rules and regulations. Many regulatory laws, for example, call for a "reasonable rate," without defining "reasonable." Frustrated by government rules, people turn to their senators and representatives for help. Lawmakers thus "take credit coming and going"—they claim credit for getting programs enacted and then for untangling the bureaucratic snarls they create.[58]

This electoral explanation of overall bureaucratic growth is unproved. There is little support for the argument that "congressmen's incessant quest for local benefits has somehow contributed to growth in government spending." In fact, the most costly federal programs, such as Medicare and Medicaid, "deliver benefits as a matter of right, not privilege, and congressmen have fewer opportunities to claim responsibility for them."[59]

Many considerations affect how federal benefits are distributed. An agency may process the requests of the president's congressional backers quickly, while other members' proposals are encased in red tape. Or influential members of the committees with jurisdiction over certain agencies may receive the lion's share of federal benefits. Lawmakers eagerly "earmark" money in appropriations bills for projects in their states or districts. Presidential pork is also commonplace as chief executives promise jobs and projects in states crucial to their reelection.

GOP members of California's congressional delegation were angry with the Federal Emergency and Management Administration because an internal memorandum suggested that Democratic senator Boxer be given "prior notice of $65 million in grants so that she could announce them."[60] At the time, Boxer was locked in a tight 1998 reelection battle, which she won.

Not all federal projects are worth attracting. Members compute the political risks of backing a missile base, hazardous waste dump, nuclear power plant, or other controversial project strongly resisted by their constituents. Some lawmakers oppose spending for projects even if they are in their own district. They have formed a "Porkbusters Coalition" to oppose what they view as wasteful federal expenditures on unjustified constituency projects. Senator McCain is especially vigilant in targeting what he considers to be wasteful spending. "McCain's Internet web site posts his floor statements decrying the pork that his staff aides find when scouring" legislation. Still other members want to challenge unnecessary tax and spending subsidies for businesses and industries ("corporate welfare").[61]

Whatever their view of federal projects, legislators must act as intermediaries between constituents and federal agencies. Constituents' problems are handled by personal staff aides called caseworkers (see Chapter 5). In addition to courting the electoral payoff of effective casework, the "two Congresses" once again, some members appreciate its value in oversight. "The very knowledge by executive officials that some Congressman is sure to look into a matter affecting his constituents acts as a healthy check against bureaucratic indifference or arrogance," wrote a former senator.[62]

Congressional Control of the Bureaucracy

"Congressional power, like chastity," explained a scholar, "is never lost, rarely taken by force, and almost always given away."[63] Congress gives away to executive officials considerable discretion in interpreting and implementing the laws it passes. This entrustment of authority is because legislators lack the knowledge and expertise to address the complexities of contemporary society (licensing interstate communications, for example), and no law can be sufficiently detailed to cover every conceivable circumstance.

In fact, Congress is sometimes criticized for drafting vague or sloppy legislation that gives executive officials and judges too much leeway in interpretation and administration. "Administration of a statute is, properly speaking, an extension of the legislative process," and therefore Congress must watch over its programs lest they undergo unintended change.[64] Given the size and reach of the executive establishment, Congress's oversight role is more important today than when Woodrow Wilson wrote, "Quite as important as lawmaking is vigilant oversight of administration."[65]

The Constitution does not refer explicitly to the oversight role; it is implicit in Congress's right to, among other things, make laws, raise and appropriate money, give "advice and consent" to executive nominations, and impeach federal officials. Congress, however, has formalized its oversight duties. The Legislative Reorganization Act of 1946 directed all House and Senate committees to exercise "continuous watchfulness" over the programs and agencies under their jurisdiction. Subsequent statutes and House and Senate rules extended Congress's authority and resources for oversight.

Members understand their review responsibilities. "Congress' duty didn't end in passing this law," remarked Sen. Phil Gramm, R-Texas. "We have to

make sure the law works." Or as Senate majority leader Lott said: "I have always felt that one-third of the role of Congress should be in oversight."[66] Speaker Dennis Hastert, R-Ill., has made it clear that he wants committees to focus more of their attention on oversight. Hastert's "not so much interested in scandal as he is in how departments are being run, what programs work and which don't," said the Speaker's spokesperson.[67]

To ensure that laws are working, Congress utilizes an impressive array of formal and informal processes and techniques. Much of its oversight activities are indirect, ad hoc, and not subject to easy quantification or even recognition. "Oversight isn't necessarily a hearing," said John D. Dingell, D-Mich., a noted House overseer. "Sometimes it's a letter. We find our letters have a special effect on a lot of people."[68]

Hearings and Investigations

Many of Congress's most dramatic moments have occurred in legislative probes into administrative misconduct. Examples include the Teapot Dome inquiry (1923), the Senate Watergate hearings (1973–1974), the Iran-contra investigation (1987), and the investigations undertaken in 1997–1998 into illegal and improper campaign fund-raising practices during the 1996 election cycle. But Congress's investigative authority is not without limits. Earl Warren, when he was chief justice, wrote in *Watkins v. United States* (1957):

> There is no general authority to expose private affairs of individuals without justification in terms of the functions of Congress. . . . Nor is the Congress a law enforcement or trial agency. These are functions of the executive and judicial departments of government. No inquiry is an end in itself; it must be related to, and in furtherance of, a legitimate task of the Congress.[69]

By collecting and analyzing information, House and Senate inquiries can clarify whether specific legislation is needed to address public problems. They also sharpen Congress's ability to scrutinize executive branch activities, such as the expenditure of funds, the implementation of laws, and the discharge of duties by administrative officials. And they inform the public by disseminating and revealing information. "Congress provides a forum for disclosing the hidden aspects of governmental conduct," wrote two Senate members of the Iran-contra investigating committee. It allows a "free people to drag realities out into the sunlight and demand a full accounting from those who are permitted to hold and exercise power."[70] Hearings and investigations, in short, are valuable devices for making government accountable to the people. They can spawn new laws or their functional equivalent: unwritten laws that change bureaucratic operations.

Congressional Vetoes

With unelected executive officials necessarily involved in the complexities of modern decision making, Congress has little choice but to delegate sweeping authority to administrative agencies. There are strings attached, however.

One of the most popular strings is the *legislative veto* (or *congressional veto*), a statutory enactment that permits presidents or agencies to take certain actions subject to later approval or disapproval by one or both houses of Congress (or in some cases by committees of one or both houses). Legislative vetoes are arrangements of convenience for both branches: executives gain decision-making authority they might not have otherwise, and Congress retains a second chance to examine the decisions.

In 1983, in *Immigration and Naturalization Service v. Chadha,* the Supreme Court declared many forms of the legislative veto unconstitutional. The Court majority held that the device violated the separation of powers, the principle of bicameralism, and the "presentation" clause of the Constitution (legislation passed by both chambers must be presented to the president for his signature or veto). The decision, wrote Justice Byron White in a vigorous dissent, "strikes down in one fell swoop provisions in more laws enacted by Congress than the court has cumulatively invalidated in its entire history."[71]

Congress repealed some legislative vetoes, amended others, and employed its wide range of oversight techniques to monitor executive actions. Yet despite the *Chadha* decision, legislative vetoes continue to be enacted into law. Public law scholar Louis Fisher sums up the status of legislative vetoes:

> Are they constitutional? Not by the Court's definition. Will that fact change the behavior between committees and agencies? Probably not. An agency might advise the committee: "As you know, the requirement in this statute for committee prior-approval is unconstitutional under the Court's test." Perhaps agency and committee staff will nod their heads in agreement. After which the agency will seek prior approval of the committee.[72]

In short, self-interest requires that agencies pay close attention to the wishes of members of Congress, especially those who sit on their authorizing or appropriating panels.

Mandatory Reports

Congress requires the president, federal agencies, and departments to assess programs and report their findings.[73] Reports can act "as a mechanism to check that laws are having the intended effect." They can "drive a reluctant bureaucracy to comply with laws it would otherwise ignore."[74] Periodically, Congress passes legislation to eliminate obsolete or unnecessary reports. But, as Senator McCain noted, "Congress assigns about 300 new reports to the agencies each year."[75] By one estimate, executive agencies prepare more than 5,000 reports for submission to Congress annually.

Nonstatutory Controls

Congressional committees also use informal means to review and influence administrative decisions. These range from telephone calls, letters, personal contacts, and informal understandings to statements in committee and conference reports, hearings, and floor debates.[76] Committee reports frequently con-

tain phrases such as "the committee clearly intends that the matter be reconsidered," or "the committee clearly intends for the Secretary to promote," or "the committee clearly expects."

On occasion, OMB directors tell federal agencies to ignore appropriations report language because it is not legally binding. Lawmakers of both parties and chambers (and even executive officials) mobilize to thwart such directives, however. Sometimes they threaten to make all report language legally binding on agencies, thus limiting the agencies' flexibility and discretion in resolving issues.[77] Although there is no measure of their usage, nonstatutory controls may be the most common form of congressional oversight.

Inspectors General

In 1978 Congress created a dozen independent offices for inspectors general (IGs). Since then Congress has established inspector general offices in nearly every federal department and agency. Inspectors general submit directly to Congress reports on their efforts to root out waste, fraud, and abuse. "It is the IG's job," said a high executive official, "to offer independent analysis to Congress and the public on how the agency and the agency head are doing." Some IGs meet regularly with legislative officials. The State Department's IG, for instance, "meets with congressional staffers at least every other week to discuss his work and, as a result, is often asked by congressional committees to conduct specific audits and investigations."[78]

The Appropriations Process

Congress probably exercises its most effective oversight of agencies and programs through the appropriations process. By cutting off or reducing funds (or threatening to do so), Congress can abolish agencies, curtail programs, or obtain requested information. By the same token, Congress can build up program areas by increasing their appropriations—sometimes beyond what the administration has requested.

The appropriations power is exercised mainly through the Appropriations Committees in the House and Senate (and especially through each panel's thirteen standing subcommittees). These panels annually recommend funding levels for federal agencies and departments, so they have the money to carry out their program responsibilities. The budgetary recommendations of the Appropriations Subcommittees are generally accepted by their parent committee and by the House or Senate.

The Appropriations Committees and Subcommittees, or members from the House or Senate floor, may offer amendments that limit the purposes for which money may be spent or that impose other expenditure restrictions on federal agencies. The spending bills also may contain various policy directives to federal agencies—for example, imposing airline smoking bans. Such policy directives are often in the form of floor amendments called *riders*. "These amendments," wrote Sens. Larry E. Craig, R-Idaho, and Slade Gorton, R-Wash., "are an important way for Congress to save taxpayers from wasteful agency spending, and they enjoy a long-standing precedent because of their use by Re-

publican and Democratic Congresses alike to rein in the excesses of Republican and Democratic administrations."[79] (For further discussion of the appropriations and authorization process, see Chapter 13.)

Impeachment

Article II, Section 4, of the Constitution states:

> The President, Vice President, and all Civil Officers of the United States, shall be removed from office on Impeachment for, and Conviction of, Treason, Bribery, or other high Crimes and misdemeanors.

The ultimate governmental "check" is this removal power, and it is vested exclusively in Congress.[80] The House has the authority to impeach an official by majority vote. It then tries the case before the Senate, where a two-thirds vote is required for conviction.

Only in seventeen cases has the House voted to impeach; the Senate convicted seven persons, all of them federal judges.[81] The House impeached President Andrew Johnson in 1868, after Radical Republicans in the House charged that he had violated the Tenure of Office Act by dismissing the secretary of war. The Senate acquitted Johnson by a single vote. President Richard Nixon resigned in 1974, after the House Judiciary Committee voted articles of impeachment; he faced probable impeachment and conviction. In December 1998 President Clinton became the first elected president to be impeached by the House. (Johnson was not elected; he became president when Abraham Lincoln was assassinated.) The charges against President Clinton were perjury and obstruction of justice. Two months later the Senate voted acquittal on both these articles of impeachment.

Oversight: An Evaluation

Congress's greater willingness in recent years to conduct oversight stems from several factors: the public's dissatisfaction with government, revelations of executive agency abuses, the influx of new legislators skeptical of government's ability to perform effectively, the availability of congressional staff, and recognition by Congress that it must make every dollar count.[82]

Electoral and political incentives also encourage members to oversee the bureaucracy. One of these is the opportunity to receive favorable publicity back home (the "two Congresses" connection). Another is prodding by interest groups and the media. Committee and subcommittee chairmen "seek a high pay off—in attention from both the press and other agencies—when selecting federal programs to be their oversight targets."[83]

Divided government—the president of one party, the Congress of another—fosters vigorous congressional oversight. Opposition lawmakers, for example, may monitor and supervise agency activities and at the same time be on the lookout for ways to bash the administration's politics. President Clinton's press secretary complained that House Republicans requested information "not so they can evaluate the effectiveness of the government's perfor-

mance but so that they can. . . [gum] up the works in order to intimidate and thwart those who might be carrying out the laws as they've been properly passed by Congress." In response, the press secretary to House Republican leader Dick Armey of Texas said, "They've gotten nothing from Democratic oversight chairmen [when that party was in charge] but postcards from Hawaii saying, 'Wish you were here.' Now they have to deal with the same type of oversight the Democrats had during the Reagan-Bush years."[84]

Congressional Republicans highlighted the oversight potential inherent in a little-known law passed by the Democratic-controlled 103d Congress: the Government Performance and Results Act of 1993 (GPRA). Under the law, federal agencies are required to submit strategic plans to Congress specifying how they intend to measure the achievement of their goals. Republicans recognize that GPRA gives them "a powerful framework for establishing agency priorities and analyzing how [the agencies] perform."[85] House GOP leaders, especially Majority Leader Armey, have urged their committee chairmen to eliminate wasteful and duplicative programs. To make this point Armey held up a pizza box: "If this were a cheese pizza, it would be inspected by the [Food and Drug Administration]. If it were a pepperoni pizza, it would be inspected by the [U.S. Department of Agriculture]. . . . We definitely have a great deal of duplication here."[86]

On occasion, congressional oversight may not be as tough as some members would wish. "Sweetheart" alliances can develop between the committees that authorize programs, the agencies that administer them, and the interest groups that benefit from the services. Many committees are biased toward the programs or agencies they oversee: they want to protect and nurture their progeny and make program administration "look good." Without concrete allegations of fraud or mismanagement, committees may lack the incentive to scrutinize and reevaluate their programs. This kind of "cooperative" oversight can dissuade committees from conducting hard-hitting inquiries.

A standard rationale for oversight is that it ensures that laws are carried out according to congressional intent. Because many laws are vague and imprecise, however, they are difficult to assess. Moreover, evidence that programs are working as intended can take years to emerge. Congressional patience may wane as critics charge that there are no demonstrable payoffs for the taxpayer. Alternatively, oversight may identify program flaws but may not reveal what will work or even whether there is any ready solution.

Each oversight technique has limitations. Hearings, for example, tend to be episodic with minimal follow-up. The appropriations process is usually hemmed in by programmatic needs for financial stability. And statutes are often blunt instruments of control. Other obstacles to effective oversight include inadequate coordination among committees that share jurisdiction over a program; unsystematic review by committees of departmental activities; and frequent turnover among committee staff aides, a situation that limits their understanding of programs passed by Congress.

Critics who fault Congress's oversight may be erecting unattainable standards. Many analysts are looking for what scholars have come to call "police

patrol" oversight—active, direct, systematic, regular, and planned surveillance of executive activities. Instead, Congress often waits until "fire alarms" go off from interest groups, the press, staff aides, and others about administrative violations before it begins to review in detail agencies' activities.[87]

Micromanagement

Because oversight tends to be specific rather than general, committees are open to complaints about "micromanagement"—legislative intrusion into administrative details. Perhaps to the chagrin of executive officials, Congress's focus on administrative details is as old as the institution itself. The structural fragmentation of the House and Senate encourages examination of manageable chunks of executive actions. Members understand that power inheres in details, such as prescribing personnel ceilings for agencies. Presidents who oppose certain programs can "starve" them to death by shifting employees to favored activities. Thus Congress may specify personnel ceilings for some agencies. "It is one of the anomalies of constitutional law and separated powers," writes Louis Fisher, "that executive involvement in legislative affairs is considered acceptable (indeed highly desirable) while legislative involvement in executive affairs screams of encroachment and usurpation."[88]

Congress and the Courts

Given our constitutional system of separate institutions sharing power combined with each branch's ability to impose limits on the other, it is no surprise that Congress and the federal courts interact with each other in numerous direct and indirect ways. (Recall our earlier discussion on the Senate confirmation of judicial appointments, probably the most visible form of interaction between the legislative and judicial branches.)

In 1999 Chief Justice William Rehnquist made headlines as the constitutional presiding officer of the Senate during its impeachment trial of President Clinton. Rehnquist also attracted national visibility in the late 1990s for other things he had to say to Congress. For one thing, he asked Congress "not to make the federal judiciary's budget a hostage in the fight between Congress and the White House over how to conduct the 2000 census."[89] For another, he criticized the Senate for moving too slowly on filling federal judicial vacancies. Then the chief justice urged Congress to curb the politically popular practice of federalizing crimes (drug possession, murder, rape, and so on) that states can handle. As Rehnquist said in an address to the American Law Institute:

> In my annual report for [1997], I criticized the Senate for moving too slowly in filling vacancies on the federal bench. This criticism received considerable public attention. I also criticized Congress and the president for their propensity to enact more and more legislation which brings more and more cases into the federal court system. . . . And yet the two are closely related: We need vacancies filled to deal with the cases arising under existing laws, but if Congress enacts, and the president signs, new laws allowing more cases to be brought into the federal courts, just filling the vacancies will not be enough. We will need additional judgeships.[90]

Friction between the legislative and judicial branches has been a common feature of American politics from our very beginning. The Supreme Court, after all, serves as both the "referee" between the two nationally elective branches and as the "umpire" in federal-state relations. Ever since the Court claimed the power of judicial review and struck down an act of Congress in *Marbury v. Madison* (1803), it has considered a large number of separation of powers issues, most notably during the New Deal period and in the past few decades. "Super legislature" is the oft repeated criticism against the Court when it makes decisions that others believe should be settled by the elective branches of government.[91]

As the federalism "umpire," the Supreme Court has lately taken a more limited view of federal authority in relation to state prerogatives. The Tenth Amendment to the Constitution (powers not delegated to the national government, nor prohibited to the states, are reserved to the states or to the people) has been somewhat revived by the Court. For example, in *United States v. Lopez* (1995), the Supreme Court overturned a federal law banning guns near school grounds; it was the "first time since the New Deal that the Court found Congress to have exceeded the bounds of its constitutional authority to regulate interstate commerce"—in this case the movement of guns across state lines that could end up on school playgrounds.[92] Quickly, Congress moved to pass legislation that made clear its authority under the Commerce Clause to restrict guns from school zones. In 1996 it enacted a measure, which the president signed, that said, "It shall be unlawful for any individual knowingly to possess a firearm that has moved in or that otherwise affects interstate or foreign commerce at a place that the individual knows, or has reasonable cause to believe, is a school zone."[93]

Statutory interpretation and legislative checks on the judiciary are two traditional features of the Court-Congress connection.

Statutory Interpretation. Communications between Congress and the federal courts are less than perfect. Neither branch understands the workings of the other very well.[94] Judges often are unaware that ambiguity, imprecision, or inconsistency may be the price for winning enactment of legislative measures. The more members try to define a bill, the more they may divide or dissipate congressional support for it. Abner Mikva, a three-term House Democrat from Chicago who went on to become a federal judge and later counsel to President Clinton, recounted an example from his Capitol Hill days; the issue involved a controversial strip-mining bill being managed by Arizona Democrat Morris K. Udall, then chairman of the House Interior Committee (now called the Resources Committee):

> They'd put together a very delicate coalition of support. One problem was whether the states or the feds would run the program. One member got up and asked, "Isn't it a fact that under this bill the states will continue to exercise sovereignty over strip mining?" And Mo replied, "You're absolutely right." A little later someone else got up and asked, "Now is it clear that the Federal Government will have the final say on strip mining?" And Mo replied, "You're absolutely right." Later, in the cloakroom, I said, "Mo, they can't both be right." And Mo said, "You're absolutely right."[95]

Called upon to interpret statutes, judges may not appreciate the efforts required to get legislation passed on Capitol Hill or understand how to divine *legislative history,* as manifested in hearings, floor debate, and reports.

A group of federal judges, led by Supreme Court justice Antonin Scalia, argues that legislative history is open to "manipulation" by individual members of Congress, executive officials, congressional staff members, and lobbyists and therefore is unreliable as an indicator of congressional intent.[96] Scalia contends that judges should follow a "textualist" approach and look at the words of laws or constitutional clauses and interpret them according to what they meant at the time of their enactment.[97] Other federal judges, including Supreme Court justice Stephen G. Breyer, defend the value of legislative history, finding it useful in statutory interpretation.

A good example of the dispute over legislative history involves Congress's response to a Supreme Court decision. The Civil Rights Act of 1991 overturned, in whole or in part, seven civil rights cases decided by a conservative-leaning Supreme Court.[98] Yet the 1991 legislation was filled with ambiguities, and so lawmakers created their own legislative history during floor debate. A memorandum was even put in the *Congressional Record* stating that the written statement was the exclusive legislative history for certain contested provisions. During debate on the legislation, John Danforth, then a Republican senator from Missouri, pointed out the pitfalls of relying on legislative history. His position essentially endorsed Justice Scalia's view that Congress should state clearly what it means or wants in the law itself rather than in floor debate or explanatory statements.[99]

Justice John Paul Stevens expressed a contrary opinion, saying that a "stubborn insistence on 'clear statements' [in the law] burdens the Congress with unnecessary reenactment of provisions that were already plain enough." Rep. Barney Frank, D-Mass.—who once stopped committee members from putting explanatory language in a committee report by saying "Justice Scalia"—added that if Scalia's view on legislative history became dominant, Congress would be required to develop a new category of legislation: "the 'No, we really meant it' statute."[100]

Legislative Checks on the Judiciary. Decisions of the Supreme Court can have profound effects on Congress and its members. Cases involving the redistricting of House seats, the line-item veto, and term limits for lawmakers are recent examples. Sometimes court actions trigger hostile reactions on the part of Congress, as in recent years. We have already mentioned the partisan fights that may embroil judicial nominations, the redraft of laws overturned by the Court, and the threat of impeachment lodged against some judges.[101] In addition, Congress may threaten to withdraw the Supreme Court's authority to hear certain cases. Under Article III, Section 2, of the Constitution, "the supreme Court shall have appellate Jurisdiction, both as to Law and Fact, with such Exceptions, and under such Regulations, as the Congress shall make." While the authority to withdraw is seldom used, some lawmakers today are

not reluctant to propose legislation that limits what they consider overreaching on the part of judges who substitute their judgment for that of Congress or the public. Senate Judiciary chairman Hatch, for instance, recommended that a single judge no longer should have the authority to issue "an order halting the implementation of a state referendum."[102]

On four occasions, Congress successfully used the arduous process of amending the Constitution to overturn decisions of the Supreme Court. In *Chisholm v. Georgia* (1803), the Court held that citizens of one state could sue another state in federal court. To prevent a rash of citizen suits against the states, the Eleventh Amendment reversed this decision. It guarantees the states immunity from these kinds of citizen suits. The *Dred Scott v. Sandford* (1857) decision that denied African Americans citizenship under the Constitution was nullified by the Thirteenth (abolishing slavery) and Fourteenth (granting African Americans citizenship) Amendments. The Sixteenth Amendment overturned *Pollock v. Farmer's Loan and Trust Co.* (1895), which struck down a federal income tax. Lastly, the Twenty-sixth Amendment invalidated *Oregon v. Mitchell* (1970), which said that Congress had exceeded its authority by lowering the minimum voting age to eighteen for state elections.[103]

The size and structure of the federal court system is also within the purview of Congress as is the salary of federal judges. As Article III, Section 1, of the Constitution states: "The judicial Power of the United States, shall be vested in one supreme Court, and in such inferior Courts as the Congress may from time to time ordain and establish." Article III also stipulates that the compensation of judges "shall not be diminished during their Continuance in Office." However, Congress can deny federal judges cost-of-living adjustments. Today Congress actively scrutinizes the fiscal administration of the judicial branch. Sen. Charles E. Grassley, R-Iowa, is particularly keen on promoting cost efficiencies within the federal judicial system. As chairman of the Judiciary Subcommittee on Administrative Oversight of the Courts, Senator Grassley has highlighted his responsibility "to review federal court processes and procedures."[104]

Conclusion

Because of continual shifts in the balance of legislative, executive, and judicial prerogatives, the age-old issue of executive and judicial independence versus congressional scrutiny cannot be settled conclusively. The Republicans' control of the House and Senate, according to Senator McCain, "changed the climate around here and made Congress more aggressive in its oversight of all taxpayer money."[105] Yet the recent interest in oversight has had little discernible effect on the size and scale of the executive branch or on the main roles and responsibilities of the judicial and legislative branches. After all, committees are not disinterested overseers but guardians of the agencies and programs under their jurisdictions. Together with their satellite interest groups, committees and agencies form "subgovernments" or "issue networks" that dominate many policy-making areas. In the next chapter we focus on these complex relationships.

Capitol Hill clashes of interest (clockwise from upper left): Microsoft chairman Bill Gates and Scott McNealy of Sun Microsystems air their differences over Internet monopoly before the Senate Judiciary Committee; former White House press secretary James Brady (foreground) with President Clinton before signing the handgun control bill, known as the Brady bill; demonstrators support NATO military action against Serb atrocities in Yugoslavia; and lobbyists line up to snare seats for a committee session.

12

Congress and
Organized Interests

A subcommittee markup of the House Banking Committee attracted scores of lobbyists representing Wall Street and other interests. Early each morning before a scheduled markup session, people formed long lines outside the meeting room for the limited number of seats. "Places on the line [were] being held for [the $300-an-hour] lobbyists by some people being paid almost $20 an hour."[1] As one line-stander said, "The lobbyists pay us, and then the interest groups and corporations seeking tax breaks pay the lobbyists."[2]

Capitol Hill lobbyists regularly fill committee hearings and markups, jam into conference committee rooms, and pack House and Senate galleries. These emissaries of organized interests do more than observe congressional events. They wield their vast resources—money, personnel, information, and organization—to win passage of legislation they favor and to reward the politicians who help them. Practically every major corporation, trade association, and professional group has Washington lobbyists. They even have their own associations: the American Society of Association Executives and the American League of Lobbyists. Like many other groups, both are based in Washington, D.C., home to more national associations than any other city.

Looking in the Washington telephone directory under "associations" reveals as much about what moves Congress as the Constitution does. More than 80,000 employees work for various associations. Numerous law firms have moved to the District of Columbia, and growing cadres of consultants and lawyers represent diverse clients, including foreign governments. The lobbying community probably constitutes the third largest "industry" employer in the nation's capital behind government and tourism. In 1997 lobbies in Washington spent an estimated $1.2 billion pressing their clients' cases.[3]

A Nation of Joiners

Americans' zest for joining groups was observed long ago by the French chronicler Alexis de Tocqueville. Americans of all "conditions, minds, and ages daily acquire a general taste for association and grow accustomed to the use of it," he wrote in 1825.[4] During the 1990s about 65 percent of the population belonged to at least one organization.[5] All told, the United States is home to more than 138,000 national, regional, and local organizations.[6]

The First Amendment protects the people's right to "petition the Government for a redress of grievances." Throughout American history, groups speaking for different subsets of "the people" have swayed public policies and poli-

tics. The nineteenth-century abolitionists fought to end slavery. The Anti-Saloon league crusaded for Prohibition in the 1900s. Movements of the 1960s and 1970s protested the Vietnam War, racial discrimination, and abuse of the environment. Interest groups galvanized support for women's rights and anti-abortion efforts in the 1980s and for term limits for lawmakers and balanced-budget amendments in the 1990s.

A free society nurtures politically active groups. "Liberty is to faction what air is to fire," wrote James Madison in *The Federalist,* Number 10. In recent years interest groups have grown in number and diversity. In particular, there are more narrow-based groups that focus on single issues such as abortion, gun control, or animal rights. Many factors account for proliferation of interest groups of all kinds: social and economic complexity, the surge in scientific and technological developments, the government's regulatory role, the competition for scarce federal dollars, and the diffusion of power in Congress and throughout the government, which enhances access for outside interests.

For decades the American Medical Association dominated health lobbying. Today hundreds of health advocacy groups woo lawmakers and orchestrate grassroots efforts. In 1975 there were about 90 health groups; today there are nearly 750. "You name a disease, there's probably a Washington lobby for it," said an official of the American Heart Association.[7] Lobbyists for specific diseases use an innovative technique: "placement spots" on television shows watched nationwide. For example, they might lobby Hollywood producers to use a story line on *ER* that dramatizes certain afflictions, such as AIDS or Hodgkin's disease. A mention on a hit show encourages viewers to donate money to the relevant health advocacy group.[8]

Some scholars contend, however, that people's civic engagement has declined. Harvard University's Robert Putnam argues that citizen participation in associations is on the wane, and he employs a good example to highlight his contention: more people are bowling but they are bowling alone, resulting in a drop in the number of bowling leagues.[9] "People would rather be alone in front of a television set than out with a group," added Putnam.[10]

Putnam's views about the lack of civic engagement and community involvement have been challenged by other scholars. "Civic America is in fact being renewed and extended, not diminished," states Professor Everett Ladd. Putnam rightly notes, says Ladd, that membership in longtime organizations, such as the Lions Club, Elks, or Masons, is down. By contrast, membership is on the rise in newer organizations, such as environmental or youth soccer groups. Furthermore, other important indicators of civic engagement—especially volunteering and charitable giving—register increases in participation.[11]

There is, however, a clear difference in the activity levels of the advantaged and the disadvantaged. A bias in political participation advantages the well off and the well educated in our society compared with those who are not so fortunate. Lawmakers hear disproportionately from the former rather than the latter. Each group is interested in different things. The advantaged talk about taxes, government spending, or social issues, while the disadvantaged are pri-

marily concerned about "basic human needs . . . poverty, jobs, housing, and health."[12] Elected officials are inundated with messages from groups that represent the politically active (the elderly, veterans, small-business owners, for example). Lawmakers receive comparatively little information about the policy preferences of the needy, who often are only marginally engaged in civic life.

Pressure Group Methods

Groups have influenced congressional decisions from the beginning. During the nation's early technological and industrial expansion, railroad interests lobbied for federal funds and land grants to build their routes. Some of the lobbyists' methods—offering bribes, for example—helped foster the traditional public suspicion of pressure tactics. In 1874 Sen. Simon Cameron, R-Pa., described an honest politician as one who "when he is bought, stays bought" (or stays "rented" with a long lease).[13] Samuel Ward, the "king of the lobby" for fifteen years after the Civil War, once wrote to his friend Henry Wadsworth Longfellow:

> When I see you again I will tell you how a client, eager to prevent the arrival at a committee of a certain member before it should adjourn, offered me $5,000 to accomplish this purpose, which I did, by having [the congressman's] boots mislaid while I smoked a cigar and condoled with him until they could be found at 11:45. I had the satisfaction of a good laugh [and] a good fee in my pocket.[14]

Lobbying methods during the twentieth century became more varied, urbane, and subtle. But the move from limited government to big government deepened the mutual dependence of legislators and lobbyists:

> Groups turn to Congress as an institution where they can be heard, establish their positions, and achieve their policy goals. Members of Congress in turn rely on groups to provide valuable constituency, technical, or political information, to give reelection support, and to assist strategically in passing or blocking legislation that the members support or oppose. Groups need Congress, and Congress needs groups.[15]

Modern-day methods vary according to the nature and visibility of the issue and the groups' resources. Among the most important practices are direct and social lobbying, group alliances, grassroots support, and electronic advocacy.

These diverse techniques typically overlap. For example, a small group of business lobbyists regularly meet privately with House majority whip Tom DeLay, R-Texas, to formulate GOP strategy on the party's issues and goals. The lobbyists then mobilize grassroots support for these GOP initiatives through petition drives, rallies, radio and television advertising blitzes, national door-to-door campaigns, and other techniques.[16] DeLay has asked his closest lobbying allies to bankroll his "Retain Our Majority Program" (ROMP), which will help reelect vulnerable Republicans in the 2000 elections.[17]

Direct Lobbying

In the traditional method of direct lobbying, lobbyists present their clients' cases directly to members and congressional staff. If a group hired a prominent lawyer or lobbyist, such as Ken Duberstein, Anne Wexler, or Tom Korologos, the direct approach would involve personal discussions with senators or representatives. An aide to former Speaker Thomas P. "Tip" O'Neill Jr. explained the importance of the personal touch:

> [Lobbyists] know members of Congress are here three nights a week, alone, without their families. So they . . . [s]chmooze with them. Make friends. And they don't lean on it all the time. Every once in a while, they call up—maybe once or twice a year—ask a few questions. . . . Anne Wexler [a former official in the Carter White House, now a lobbyist] will call up and spend half an hour talking about . . . politics, and suddenly she'll pop a question, pick up something. They want that little bit of access. That's what does it. You can hear it. It clicks home. They'll call their chief executive officer, and they've delivered. That's how it works. It's not illegal. They work on a personal basis.[18]

Particularly effective at direct lobbying are Hollywood movie stars (Charlton Heston heads the National Rifle Association), the children of powerful members, former staff aides and government luminaries, famous sports figures (boxer Evander Holyfield, car racer Bobby Unser, or football star Jerome Bettis), prominent business executives (such as Microsoft's Bill Gates), and some former members of Congress.[19] "Since I will continue to be active in the Congressional Prayer Breakfast Group, in the House gym, the members' Dining Room and on the House Floor, I will maintain contact with my good friends who affect legislation," a just-retired representative of twenty years wrote to prospective clients. He promised to "unravel red tape, open doors, make appointments, work with the Administration or government agencies, influence legislation, and assist in any other service required."[20]

Member-to-member lobbying can be uniquely effective: no outsider has the same access to lawmakers (or to certain areas of Congress) that former colleagues have. But some members are offended by the entrée that former legislators who are lobbyists have to the floor and to other Capitol Hill locations not generally open to the public.[21] Since 1991 former lawmakers have been prohibited for one year from lobbying members of Congress directly, although they may plan strategy and advise others who do so.

Direct lobbying takes many forms. Lobbyists monitor committees and testify at hearings; interpret Hill decisions to clients and clients' interests to legislators; perform services, such as writing speeches for members; and give campaign assistance. The House offers more occasions for contacting members directly than does the Senate, where lobbyists are more likely to target the staff who surround each member. "Essentially, we operate as an extension of congressmen's staff," explained one lobbyist. "Occasionally we come up with the legislation, or speeches—and questions [for lawmakers to ask at hearings] all

the time. We look at it as providing staff work for allies."[22] Or, as one of Washington's premier lobbyists, Thomas Hale Boggs Jr. (son of former House majority leader Hale Boggs, D-La., and former representative Lindy Boggs, D-La.) explained, "Congressional staffs are overworked and underpaid. Lobbyists help fill the information vacuum."[23]

The direct approach is limited, however, by rapid turnover in Congress. Nonetheless, lobbyists are major players in congressional policy making. "Lobbyists contribute a lot to democracy," stated Rep. James P. Moran, D-Va. "They provide continuity and institutional memory. Most of them have been around longer than members."[24]

Social Lobbying

Although the Washington social circuit is vastly overrated, some lobbyists gain access to members at dinner parties or receptions. "When you want to make an end run, meet someone at a party," explained an experienced power dealer.[25] Because of the public's clamor and members' concern about free gifts, meals, and trips from lobbyists, the House and Senate in 1995 imposed tighter restrictions on gift giving. "By themselves, gifts and meals are not sufficient to corrupt the whole system," remarked Sen. Russell D. Feingold, D-Wis. "But they create a psychological feeling that you are obliged. Somebody might not be aware of it, but I think it does have that effect."[26]

Under the amended 1995 House rules, virtually all gifts—free meals, free trips, and free presents—were banned. Representatives then complained about the complexities associated with the strict ban on free meals and gifts. (For example, is a gift of a pie or a can of popcorn unacceptable?) This confusion led the House four years later to again amend its gift rules to bring them into alignment with those of the Senate. The Senate's rules include a number of exceptions for meals and gifts. For example, senators may accept gifts, including meals, if the gift has a value of less than $50. Senators may not accept a gift, however, from any one source that exceeds $100 annually. Items of little monetary value, such as baseball caps or T-shirts, are exempt from the gift limitation. Neither chamber bans gifts to political organizations or to members' campaigns. Gifts of liquor flow freely to lawmakers' fund-raising events.[27]

A variation on social lobbying is offering legislators speaking fees (honorariums). Although members now are banned by law from pocketing honorariums, they still may accept speaking fees if they donate them to charities or other tax-exempt groups. Some critics suggest that this arrangement enables members to "obtain political benefits by directing contributions to favored organizations, and some tax-exempt groups are affiliated with politicians."[28]

House and Senate gift rules permit lawmakers and staff aides to travel on fact-finding missions or to make speeches if they are connected with their official duties and the trips are disclosed within thirty days of their completion. Special interests and foundations sponsor many trips to locations throughout the United States and abroad. For lawmakers and staff aides, special interests pay the way "for 4,000 trips per year to destinations that vary from the Florida cane fields to Paris and Beijing."[29] Corporations frequently provide lawmakers

with subsidized travel aboard company jets; the members or their campaign committees pay the equivalent of the first-class rate or the charter rate in "case of a destination not served by commercial airlines."[30] Congressional leadership aides "routinely maintain lists of a dozen or more friendly companies that put their multimillion-dollar jets at their bosses' disposal."[31]

Members are becoming wary of overseas travel, however. "If you travel a lot, your opponent will put a map of the world on the screen and have you, like a pingpong ball, zigging and zagging all over the world," remarked Rep. Ileana Ros-Lehtinen, R-Fla. No matter who pays for it—special interests or taxpayers—travel can be a political liability, she noted.[32]

Campaign fund-raising events are another important aspect of social lobbying. "With politicians wanting money and lobbyists wanting access, lobbyists are paying big sums to spend time in fancy places with lawmakers." These getaways are legal "because the money comes as a campaign contribution and not as a gift."[33] One lawmaker invited lobbyists to attend a four-day "winter conference" in Vail, Colorado. Here is a chance, the lawmaker said in his invitation, for "members of the PAC [political action committee] community to make a $3,000 . . . contribution to my . . . Leadership PAC."[34] To raise money for their reelection, lawmakers sometimes invite lobbyists to hang out with them informally—on a Super Bowl weekend, a summer trip to Nantucket, or a spring baseball training excursion in Florida, for example.

Coalition Lobbying

"We have no permanent friends or permanent enemies—only permanent interests." This oft repeated truism helps to explain why "coalitions, like politics, make strange bed fellows."[35] Rival lobbying interests sometimes forge temporary coalitions to promote or defend shared goals. House Budget Committee chairman John R. Kasich, R-Ohio, forged an unusual coalition of about a dozen organizations spanning the ideological spectrum, "from the libertarian Cato Institute and the antigovernment Americans for Tax Reform on the right to Friends of the Earth and various Ralph Nader groups on the left." Kasich's bipartisan coalition, dubbed "Stop Corporate Welfare," is intent on cutting back government subsidies that inappropriately benefit large corporations. It believes spending on corporate welfare, like spending on public welfare, should be reduced.[36]

Coalitions bring advantages—more resources, contacts, and money—to lobbying efforts, but one advantage is especially significant. With the diffusion of power on Capitol Hill, coalitions are better able than a single group to "touch all the legislative bases." A drawback is that coalitions are marriages of convenience: it is difficult to keep them working in harness for very long. To coordinate their activities and keep all participants informed, some coalitions post Web sites on the Internet.[37]

Grassroots Lobbying

Instead of contacting members directly, many organizations mobilize citizens to pressure their senators and representatives—perhaps the most effective

lobbying technique. Masters of grassroots lobbying know how to be very specific. Here is what one lobbyist said when he called a sportsman about a proposal to make hunting a nondeductible business expense: "Hello, Johnny Bob? This is J. D. in Washington. Got a pencil handy? Now, this is who your congressman is. This is how you write him."[38]

Interest groups often send mass mailings to targeted congressional districts with enclosed letters or postcards for constituents to sign and mail to their legislators. Legislators understand that lobby groups orchestrate this "spontaneous" outpouring of mail, but they do not wholly disregard it:

> Members have to care about this mail, even if it's mail that is almost identically worded. Labor unions do this sort of thing a lot. The congressman has to care that somebody out there in his district has enough power to get hundreds of people to sit down and write a postcard or a letter—because if the guy can get them to do that, he might be able to influence them in other ways. So, a member has no choice but to pay attention. It's suicide if he doesn't.[39]

Lawmakers sometimes have to distinguish between genuine grass roots and astroturf. Many so-called grassroots groups function as front organizations for their financial backers. For example, a group called the Citizens for Sensible Control of Acid Rain was funded by the coal and electric industry to lobby against the Clean Air Act.[40] When the House debated a major telecommunications bill in the mid-1990s, lawmakers were flooded with bogus "constituent" mail from children, dead people, and constituents who said they had not sent the mailgrams. The uproar from members led to an investigation of the incident by the Capitol police.[41]

Mass mobilizations have become so common that some firms specialize in "grass tops" lobbying. Whereas the goal of grassroots lobbying is to mobilize the masses, the goal of grass tops lobbying "is to figure out to whom a member of Congress cannot say no: his chief donor, his campaign manager, a political mentor. The lobbyist then tries to persuade that person to take his client's side" during talks with the lawmaker.[42] Big corporations may also hire "stealth lobbyists"—public relations specialists who work quietly to "influence the news media, sponsor grassroots activities and generate favorable scientific reports."[43]

Electronic Lobbying

"Through their computers [lobbying] groups get to more of my voters, more often, and with more information than any elected official can do," complained one House member. "I'm competing to represent my district against the lobbyists and the special interests."[44] Indeed, many lobbyists today orchestrate support at the local level by means of sophisticated electronic technology. As one account noted:

> The mobile telephone allows a lobbyist sitting in a congressional hearing to alert a lobbying group's head office; the fax machine can be used to send out a "broadcast fax" to hundreds of sympathizers with one push of a button. . . . A laptop and printer can be set up at a protest meeting, so that people can type

their name, address and a personal message into a standard letter which can then be printed and signed on the spot.[45]

Talk-radio hosts, such as Rush Limbaugh (who is heard weekly on 660 stations by about 20 million listeners), can trigger an outpouring of letters, telegrams, e-mails, and faxes to lawmakers. The potent combination of technology and politics makes "it easier to organize and send a political message across the country at warp speed."[46]

Many groups use computers to identify supporters, target specific constituencies, or generate "personalized" mass mailings. Cyber-lobbying through the Internet is fast becoming an important form of grassroots activism. For example, opponents of a ban on "indecent" material on-line rallied Internet users and "orchestrated 20,000 phone, fax or e-mail messages to House and Senate offices in a single day."[47] With the emergence of interactive Web sites, lobbyists can communicate directly with prospective supporters, recruit volunteers, assign tasks, and get immediate feedback on any issue.[48]

With software programs, such as "In-House Lobbyist," computer users—students and homemakers as well as business professionals and interest groups—can send targeted letters to scores of lawmakers or organize a "billion byte march" on Capitol Hill.[49] Washington law firms and lobbying shops increasingly are using the Internet to reach clients and to distribute their research. Sen. Max Cleland, D-Ga., informed his colleagues about a Web site on the Internet called INCONGRESS, which "enables interest groups that lobby Congress to put their policy statements and press releases—on issues and legislation before the Congress—on one single Web site in an organized and targeted manner."[50]

Rep. Jesse L. Jackson Jr., D-Ill., may be the only member to use his Web site (www.jessejacksonjr.org) to create an electronic network of outside political activists and organizations to lobby Congress on behalf of his policies they support. His e-mail network of external allies can quickly be mobilized to launch lobbying blitzes. Members will be "getting ready to do something against my bill, and I'll go straight to the computer and I'll say, 'All right, folks, we're having a problem over here,' " explained Representative Jackson. "And then, whoomp!"[51] A flood of e-mails, faxes, letters, personal visits, or telephone calls will inundate lawmakers' offices.

Groups and the Electoral Connection

In the fall of 1995 an unusual event occurred: a group of congressional candidates descended on Capitol Hill to learn how to win elections. What made the group unusual was its members. They were not Democratic or Republican recruits but members of the National Federation of Independent Business, an organization that had handpicked them to run for Congress. "It's the final stage of sophistication when [interest groups] train their members to actually run for office," declared a business PAC official.[52] Labor unions, as well as business groups, are making the electoral connection (see box, p. 343).

Union Workers Trained As Lobbyists

The AFL-CIO brings a group of legislative interns to the capital four times a year. It pays them what they make in their normal jobs plus expense allowances, lodges them in hotels, and gives them desks in the Steel Workers' Offices near DuPont Circle. The visitors are technically on sabbaticals authorized by the union's collective bargaining agreements.

The program combines schooling and work. Interns often are sent to Capitol Hill to track down lawmakers or congressional aides to make the union's case on legislative issues. During a typical week, they also study congressional procedures and history, attend hearings, and observe union policy meetings. The purpose is to give rank-and-file workers a deeper knowledge of Congress and to inspire activism at the local level. The union hopes its interns will go home more politically savvy and better prepared to rally co-workers on union issues and at election time.

The steel union's program is unusual in intensity, length, and agenda. The union wants to bolster its grassroots efforts and deepen its pool of potential candidates for elected offices. Gary Hubbard, spokesman for the Steel Workers, said the union hopes the two-year-old program will "get more plumbers and steamfitters and electricians into public office."

Source: Matthew Tully, "Union Program Fields Blue-Collar Washington Lobbyists," *CQ Daily Monitor,* March 29, 1999, 7.

Interest groups help reelect members to Congress in three main ways. They raise funds and make financial contributions through political action committees, they conduct their own independent campaigns for or against issues and candidates, and they rate the voting record of legislators.

Groups and Campaign Fund Raising

Legislators who dislike raising money—seemingly a majority of them—turn to lobbyists or professional fund-raisers to sponsor parties, luncheons, dinners, or other social events where admission is charged. Lobbyists buy tickets or supply lists of people who should be invited.

Fund-raising events have consumed more and more of legislators' limited time and created new scheduling conflicts—further evidence of the imperatives of the "two Congresses," the representative assembly and the lawmaking institution. Members cannot "chase money" and vote on bills at the same time. To minimize these conflicts between members' electoral and lawmaking responsibilities, "windows" are opened in the Senate schedule:

> A window is a period of time in which it is understood that there will be no roll-call votes. Senators are assured that they won't be embarrassed by being absent for a recorded vote. Windows usually occur between six and eight in the evening, which is the normal time for holding fundraising cocktail parties.[53]

Veteran senator Robert C. Byrd, D-W.Va., complained that members must spend more time raising money than legislating.[54] A former senator said that he "had to become an expert [at fund raising] to survive in California politics." He described three principles of raising money based on his experiences. First, "people who give once are likely to give again." If you stop asking, they will stop giving or give to someone else. Second, "it's a compliment . . . to ask someone for a large sum." But many people "can never bring themselves to ask for really large amounts." Third, "people who have given to other causes may give to yours." For this reason, "keep track of all who give what to whom."[55]

Congressional critics, and even legislators and lobbyists, question the propriety of fund-raising practices. Members are concerned about implied obligations when they accept help or money from groups. For their part, lobbyists resent pressure from members to give repeatedly, and in ever higher amounts, to congressional campaigns. To date, there is no congressional consensus on how to reform campaign financing in a way that all parties and interests view as fair.

Groups and Their Own Campaigns

Before the 2000 elections interest groups began to mount especially aggressive campaigns to elect lawmakers sympathetic to their point of view and to influence the legislative agenda. The AFL-CIO, for instance, said it planned to spend up to $46 million to elect pro-labor Democrats in 2000 and to return the House and Senate to Democratic control. Labor's announcement prompted business groups to try to safeguard the GOP-controlled Congress by electing pro-business lawmakers and educating workers on "how a pro-business agenda benefits workers. In this way, business will try to cut in on the influence labor has on employees."[56]

To win, congressional candidates must broaden their sights beyond their partisan opponents to well-funded "issue advocacy" media campaigns. "We don't just run against our opponent anymore," explained the political adviser to Sen. Tom Daschle, D-S.D. "We run against anybody who wants to come in and run ads."[57] Today lobbyists use congressional staff "focus groups" to determine what arguments will most appeal to lawmakers.[58] Jim Smith, president of a telephone trade association, described the importance of keeping congressional staffers informed. He even organized a retreat for congressional aides in part to glean political intelligence about how best to frame his association's issues on Capitol Hill.[59]

Something like "reverse lobbying" also occurs. Lawmakers try to pass legislation designed to appeal to the outside groups aligned with their partisan and policy objectives. To ensure that a minimum wage bill (backed by organized labor) would be made palatable to corporate and small-business interests (traditional GOP supporters), Newt Gingrich, R-Ga., then House Speaker, met with officials of the National Federation of Independent Business: "So you guys need to tell us items on your agenda" that will make this bill acceptable to you. "Just give us the list."[60] In short, lawmakers aggressively solicit from their interest group allies legislative input as well as campaign funds.

Groups and the Policy Payoff

Today there are about 4,000 political action committees, and they play a significant role in financing the election of lawmakers, especially incumbents (see Chapter 3). Journalists and campaign reform groups often posit a "direct linear correlation" between a member's vote and the amount he or she has received from a PAC. The Center for Responsive Politics, a nonprofit research group, analyzed fourteen heavily lobbied votes and found that "corporations that poured money into Congress typically got the votes they wanted."[61] The nonpartisan and nonprofit Center for Public Integrity also reported that "lawmakers devote themselves to protecting the industries that do them favors and pay for their campaigns."[62]

Other researchers have had a hard time proving such a cause-and-effect relationship. For one thing, groups tend to give money to members who are already favorably disposed to their objectives; contributions cement a relationship more often than they create one. Moreover, the influence of money must be weighed against other considerations that influence how members vote. These include constituency pressures, party ties, friendship with fellow legislators or lobbyists, conscience, and personal idiosyncrasies and prejudices.[63] As Rep. Barney Frank, D-Mass., put it:

> Votes will beat money any day. Any politician forced to choose between his campaign contributions and strong public sentiment is going to vote public sentiment. Campaign contributions are fungible, you can get new ones. You can't get new voters.[64]

Access is another matter. "There is no question—if you give a lot of money, you will get a lot of access. All you have to do is send in the check," explained one corporate executive.[65] Or as one senator explained:

> If someone came in and said, "I contributed $1,000, or am about to contribute $1,000, to your campaign and I expect you to vote No," I think most Members would, if not kick 'em out of the office, at least make an outraged statement. But, a contributor calls you on a busy day when your inclination is not to take any calls, and if that person says, "I must speak to you urgently," the chances are you will take that call when you wouldn't have taken any other calls. So to that extent I think money does have impact.[66]

Rating Legislators

About a hundred groups keep pressure on legislators by issuing "report cards" on their voting records. Groups select major issues and then publicize the members' scores (0–100) based on their "right" or "wrong" votes on those issues. Members are often warned by colleagues that certain votes will be scored. "You'll hear this as you walk into the chamber: 'This is going to be a scored vote. The environmentalists are going to score this vote, or the AFL-CIO is going to score this vote,'" stated Rep. Joel Hefley, R-Colo.[67] Congressional aides also telephone lobbying groups to determine if certain votes will be scored.

Scorecards not only attract the attention of lawmakers; they are used by interest groups to influence members' decisions on selected issues. The liberal Americans for Democratic Action (ADA) and the conservative American Conservative Union (ACU) issue score-based ratings that are well known and widely used. One must beware of the "ratings game," however (see Chapter 9). It is always simplistic. The selected issues often are biased, self-serving, and in any case inadequate to judge a member's record. Group strategists, however, defend ratings as "a shorthand way for voters to tell something about their congressman."[68] Many groups that target members for electoral assistance or defeat assign them attention-catching names based on their scorecards: "heroes and zeroes" (from consumer advocates) or the "dirty dozen" (environmental polluters).

Groups use legislative scorecards to determine which candidates will win endorsements and which will receive campaign contributions. Incumbents who hold closely contested seats are usually careful when casting their votes. As a lawmaker who represents a marginal district once said, "If I cast a vote, I might have to answer for it. It may be an issue in the next campaign. Over and over I have to have a response to the question: Why did you do that?"[69] Some of the groups that rate lawmakers maintain Web sites where visitors can register "how they would have voted on the scorecard issues and then compare their own voting record to that of their senators or representatives."[70]

Groups and Legislative Politics

The lobbyist's job is time consuming because power in Congress is diffused. "Instead of selling his idea to a few senior members," observed one lobbyist, "he must work all members of a committee, on both sides of the aisle, and repeat that work when legislation reaches the floor."[71] Reflecting on the changing styles of modern lobbying, a former lawyer lobbyist said.

> Because of the increasing sophistication of staff, you have to be armed with facts, precedents and legal points. Sure it's a political environment, but it's much more substantive. The old-style, pat-'em-on-the-back lobbyist is gone, or at least going.[72]

An annual survey conducted by the American League of Lobbyists underscored this observation. Lobbyists rated "good information/analysis" given directly to the member as the most effective way to influence a lawmaker.[73]

An open, decentralized institution, Congress affords lobbyists multiple opportunities to shape the fate of legislation. Groups affect, directly or indirectly, virtually every feature of the congressional environment, such as committee activities, legislative agendas, and floor decision making.

Lobbyists and Committees

Many congressional committees reflect the concerns of specific groups, such as farmers, teachers, or veterans. As long as an outside group wields political clout, Congress is unlikely to eliminate the committee it supports.

Members, too, seek assignments to prestigious panels, because they provide a good perch from which to raise money from political action committees. "Members of top Senate and House committees took in more political action (PAC) money from 1993 to 1998 than did their colleagues on less high-profile panels," according to an analysis by the Center for Responsive Politics.[74] In campaigning for choice committee assignments, legislators sometimes enlist the support of outside organizations. Lobbyists also encourage friendly legislators to bid for committees and subcommittees that handle issues important to their group's interests.

At committee hearings lobbyists employ the usual techniques to win support for their issues. They enlist the assistance of their "champions" on committees and encourage favorite witnesses to testify. Finding a celebrity witness ensures members' attendance and media attention. An official of a health advocacy group made this observation:

> Let me tell you, at hearings where Elizabeth Taylor has testified about AIDS, there wasn't a seat in the house. There were members there not even on the committee. The minute she left, they left.[75]

Or as Sen. Arlen Specter, R-Pa., put it: "Quite candidly, when Hollywood speaks, the world listens. Sometimes when Washington speaks, the world snoozes."[76]

Committees often form alliances with the bureaucrats and lobbyists who regularly testify before them and with whom members and staff aides periodically meet. Scholars and journalists use the term *subgovernment* for the three-way, policy-making alliances of committees, executive agencies, and interest groups.

These triangular relationships dominate policy arenas less today than in the past. Other contending forces (citizens' groups, aggressive journalists, assertive presidents) have ended their policy monopoly. Fluid "issue networks," in which diverse participants and groups influence decision making, better characterize the relationships within and among policy domains. When Democrats ruled Capitol Hill, favored clusters of interest groups embraced such issues as welfare programs, environmental protection, and civil rights. With the GOP in charge, the insiders tend to represent such interests as small business, the "family" lobby, and the military. But many lobbying clusters—for example, big business and veterans—seem equally at home with both political parties.

Lobbyists and Legislation

Lobbyists are active during all phases of the legislative process. During the committee phase, they draft bills and amendments for members and testify at hearings. They often "help the policy-making process by pointing out how different industries and regions might be affected by various provisions, perhaps in ways unintended by those who drafted them."[77] Sometimes groups blanket Capitol Hill with materials or devices to make a point. The Sierra Club, for instance, sent Hill offices a letter with a condom attached. "I'm sending you this

condom," wrote the Club's president, "to reinforce our message that international family planning programs, free speech, and environmental protection deserve extra protection."[78]

When measures reach the House and Senate floor, groups focus on influencing votes. They plan strategy with friendly lawmakers, prepare arguments for and against expected floor amendments, work to round up their supporters for key votes, and draft floor statements and amendments. The wording of legislation can be all important. The deletion of one word—*nonprofit*—from an obscure passage of a 400-page welfare bill produced an immediate scramble for federal dollars. For-profit orphanages competed with nonprofit foster homes "for the billions of dollars that the Government spends each year to support poor children who are taken away from homes judged unfit."[79]

Groups help to frame Congress's policy and oversight agenda by pushing the House and Senate to address their concerns. Many legislative preoccupations of the past several decades—civil rights, abortion, environmental and consumer protection, deregulation, and child care among them—reflect vigorous lobbying. On the other hand, a lobbyist's job is often to stop things from happening. "Most of the stuff that we do in this business is protection—negative stuff," stated Tom Korologos, one of Washington's premier lobbyists. "For the most part, it's stop this regulation, stop that tax, stop this crazy scheme."[80]

For their part, members sponsor bills and amendments that win them group support—again the "two Congresses." Sen. Jesse Helms, R-N.C., has been successful in using these techniques. Helms offers amendments on controversial social issues such as abortion and school prayer and forces votes on them. "His amendments," wrote Elizabeth Drew, "gave him a kind of publicity that was useful, firmed up his relationships with a cluster of 'New Right' groups, helped him raise money, and provided material with which he and his allies could try to defeat opponents."[81]

Informal Groups of Members

Congress always has had informal groups, caucuses, coalitions, clubs, alliances, blocs, and cliques. What makes today's informal congressional groups different from earlier ones is their greater number (about 180 in the late 1990s), diversity, and capacity to monitor developments that affect their interests.[82]

Some state delegations, often including House and Senate members, meet frequently on either a partisan or bipartisan basis. At a weekly breakfast or lunch they discuss state and national issues and internal congressional politics, plan strategies to capture their share of federal funds and projects, champion colleagues for coveted committee assignments, or back candidates for party leadership positions.

Types of Groups

Many informal congressional groups have ties with outside interests. Not surprisingly, the Steel Caucus maintains links with the steel industry and the Textile Caucus with textile manufacturers. Interest groups can be instrumen-

tal in forming these informal legislative entities. The idea for the Mushroom Caucus (to protect mushroom producers from foreign imports) originated at a May 1977 luncheon sponsored for House members by the American Mushroom Institute.[83] The Black, Hispanic, and Women's Caucuses were established to give their national constituencies—and the members themselves—more recognition and clout in Congress.

Other groups have a regional purpose. Members of the Northeast-Midwest Congressional Coalition want to retain their share of energy supplies, encourage federal aid to cities, and promote manufacturing in the Frost Belt states. The Sunbelt Caucus, a southern representative explained, was established in 1979 "in large part to counter lobbying and information-disseminating activities of the Northeast-Midwest Coalition."[84] Each move to protect a region's interests is likely to prompt a countermove from another region.

Similarly, moves and countermoves are evident on substantive matters. When a group of moderate House Republicans established the Tuesday Lunch Bunch to function as a swing bloc to temper the more conservative policy stances of their party, conservative GOP lawmakers responded in kind. They formed the Conservative Action Team (CATs) to press their views with party leaders. Caucuses also are formed to focus on issues that overlap several committees' jurisdictions or that fail to receive sufficient committee attention. Sometimes caucuses can buttress their members' strength back home. The House Coal Caucus offered its initiator, Rep. Nick J. Rahall II, D-W.Va., significant political benefits in his coal-producing district.

Legislative Effect of Caucuses

The effect of informal groups on policy making is not clear. Some legislators believe they undermine party unity and lead to the "balkanization" of the institution. Nonetheless, informal groups can shape Congress's policy agenda and influence policy making. For example, members of Congress who are on the Internet Caucus—many from rural areas—have been instrumental in shaping telecommunications legislation. The rural members of this caucus want to ensure that their constituencies are not left behind technologically. "There is a common theme with the belief that telecommunications can be a bridge for rural areas into the American economic mainstream," remarked Rep. Rick Boucher, D-Va., co-chairman of the Internet Caucus.[85] To be sure, caucus members want to attract high-tech industries to their states or districts.

Informal groups serve as contact points for liaison officers in the executive branch. They provide executive and White House officials with information and can play an essential role in coordinating a legislative strategy and building coalitions. Caucuses permit members to discuss common strategies and join with other groups to pass or defeat legislation. Finally, caucuses enable lawmakers to align themselves publicly with a cause or interest; for many, these memberships are simply another way of taking a position. Paradoxically, informal groups foster both decentralizing and integrative tendencies in Congress.

Regulation of Lobbying

For more than a hundred years Congress intermittently considered ways to regulate lobbying—a right, as noted earlier, protected by the First Amendment: "the right of the people . . . to petition the Government for a redress of grievances." Not until 1946, however, did Congress enact its first comprehensive lobbying law, the Federal Regulation of Lobbying Act (Title III of the Legislative Reorganization Act of that year). This law's ineffectiveness finally led to passage of the Lobby Disclosure Act of 1995.

The 1946 Lobbying Law

The main objective of the 1946 act was to disclose lobbying activities to the public. Persons trying to influence Congress were required to register with the clerk of the House or the secretary of the Senate and to report quarterly on the amount of money received and spent for lobbying. The law's authors, although loath to propose direct control of lobbying, believed that "professionally inspired efforts to put pressure upon Congress cannot be conducive to well-considered legislation." Hence the law stressed registration and reporting:

> The availability of information regarding organized groups and full knowledge of their expenditures for influencing legislation, their membership and the source of contributions to them of large amounts of money, would prove helpful to Congress in evaluating their representations without impairing the rights of any individual or group freely to express its opinion to the Congress.[86]

The lobby law soon proved ineffective. In 1954 the Supreme Court upheld its constitutionality, but the decision (*United States v. Harriss*) significantly weakened the law. First, the Court said that only lobbyists paid to represent someone else must register, exempting lobbyists who spent their own money. Second, the Court held that registration applied only to persons whose "principal purpose" was to influence legislation. As a result, many trade associations, labor unions, professional organizations, consumer groups, and Washington lawyers avoided registering because lobbying was not their principal purpose. Some lobbyists claimed immunity from the law on the pretext that their job was to inform, not influence, legislators. Finally, the Court held that the act applied only to lobbyists who contacted members directly. This interpretation excluded lobbying activities that generated grassroots pressure on Congress.

Lawmakers tried repeatedly to plug the loopholes of the 1946 law. These attempts foundered largely because it was difficult to regulate lobbying without trespassing on citizens' rights to contact their elected representatives. Finally, after repeated efforts to "change the way Washington does business"—a campaign theme advocated by many members—the two parties came together to enact the first major overhaul of the 1946 act. Then-Speaker Gingrich and President Clinton, at a June 11, 1995, rally in New Hampshire, shook hands and promised to propose campaign finance and lobby reforms. The latter, but not the former, was enacted into law.

Lobbying Reforms

The Lobby Disclosure Act of 1995 tightened the rules for lobbyists. An outline of the major changes follows:

- A "lobbyist" is defined as anyone who spends 20 percent or more of his or her time in paid lobbying.
- Lobbying activities include preparation and research intended to influence policy as well as direct contacts with policy makers and their staff.
- Lobbyists are required to register with Congress. They must disclose the names of their clients and the issues they are lobbying on and state approximately how much clients are paying for their services.[a]
- Lobbyists must file disclosure reports every six months. Those who fail to comply are subject to civil fines up to $50,000.
- Nonprofit groups under IRS Section 501(C)4 that lobby cannot receive direct federal grants.
- Former U.S. trade representatives and deputies are banned for life from lobbying for foreign interests.

Source: Washington Times, Nov. 30, 1995, A14.

[a] There are some exemptions; for example, lobbyists paid $5,000 or less in six months are not required to register.

The Lobby Disclosure Act of 1995

Under the Lobby Disclosure Act of 1995, which became effective on January 1, 1996, new rules apply to individuals and firms who lobby the Congress and senior executive branch officials (see box, this page). Significantly, the law broadened the definition of people who must register as lobbyists (all those who spend one-fifth of their time trying to influence lawmakers, congressional aides, or high executive officials). Registrations of lobbyists quickly soared. A study by the General Accounting Office determined that when the law took effect "only 6,078 individuals and organizations had registered" under the outdated 1946 act. "After the new law took effect, a total of 14,912 lobbyists registered" with 10,612 being first-time registrants.[87] The law is administered by the public records offices of the House and Senate.

Lobbyists are required to "provide semiannual disclosures showing who their clients are, what policies they are trying to influence and roughly how much money they are spending for lobbying."[88] Civil fines of up to $50,000 can be imposed on those who fail to comply. Grassroots lobbying is exempt from the law, as are lobbyists paid $5,000 or less semiannually and organizations that use their own employees to lobby. The 1995 lobby disclosure law was amended three years later to make several technical corrections, such as clarifying the definition of "lobbying contact."

Although the 1995 lobby law is better than the old one, it is minimally enforced, according to some analysts. Not a single firm or lobbyist has yet to receive an official notice for failure to file the required reports. Some firms and

organizations even underreport their lobbying expenditures. "Companies, trade associations, and lobby firms often misreport—intentionally or inadvertently—how much money they shell out or take in." Administrators of the law contend, however, that there have been no serious cases of noncompliance or evasion.[89]

Foreign Lobbying

The 1995 law also amended the Foreign Agents Registration Act of 1938, which required those who lobby on behalf of foreign governments or political parties to register with the Justice Department. The 1995 law broadened the definition of foreign lobbyists to include individuals who lobby on behalf of foreign-owned commercial enterprises. It required them to register with the clerk of the House and the secretary of the Senate. About 600 lobbyists have registered with the Justice Department as "agents" representing foreign governments or parties.

Understandably, given the role of the United States in the global economy and in military security, many foreign nationals and Americans who work for foreign clients spend a lot of time and money lobbying Capitol Hill and promoting their interests nationwide. In 1996 foreign governments, corporations, and individuals reported that they spent $678 million in the United States on various endeavors, such as trade promotion, public relations, and the distribution of materials. Of that amount $64 million was spent specifically on lobbying governmental entities.[90] These figures probably understate the full range of foreign lobbying activities and expenditures. Covert campaign contributions by foreign governments and foreign nationals to American elections is a problem that congressional committees have investigated.

The American Israel Public Affairs Committee (AIPAC) is not a registered foreign lobby because it is independent of foreign sponsorship and composed of American citizens who have a keen interest in the "mother country." Yet AIPAC is one of the most influential lobbying groups in the United States. To preserve a positive relationship between the United States and Israel, it has a staff of more than 100, an annual budget of about $14.2 million, and a membership of 55,000 people. AIPAC "sponsors tours of Israel for legislators and keeps in touch with all departments of the United States Government with the slightest involvement in Israel. It has student affiliates at more than 200 campuses."[91] To be sure, many other nations and international interests have covered the costs of lawmakers and congressional aides who visit their countries on fact-finding missions.

The "globalization" of American lobbying efforts is also occurring. Worried that international restrictions and regulations might adversely affect the gun trade and the ability of Americans to acquire firearms, the National Rifle Association formed a transnational organization of gun groups and firearms manufacturers from eleven other countries (the World Forum).[92] The organization's objectives are to fend off international pressure for tighter gun controls in the United States and to defend the right to bear arms worldwide. Many U.S.-based corporations also hire lobbyists who can operate globally to protect their interests in Europe or other parts of the world when disputes arise about trade, agriculture, antitrust laws, the environment, and other issues.[93]

Globalization of the world's economy also influences congressional lobbying. In the late 1990s U.S. antitrust officials approved the Boeing aircraft company's merger with rival McDonnell Douglas in part because the global marketplace seems to require firms to be larger and more efficient to survive. This global imperative enhanced Boeing's political clout on Capitol Hill by broadening its ties beyond lawmakers in its home base in the state of Washington to include "congressional delegations from California, Missouri, Texas, Alabama, and Pennsylvania. . . . Through subcontractors and their employees, they can bring direct influence to bear on virtually every other delegation in Congress."[94] For example, Boeing executives enlisted machine and tool subcontractors in El Monte, California, to lobby their representatives to support the renewal of China's favorable trade status with the United States. Boeing executives said the suppliers readily agreed to lobby Congress because "their firms depend as much as Boeing does on business generated by aircraft sales to China."[95]

Conclusion

From the nation's beginning, lobbying and lawmaking have been twin phenomena. Lobbying "has been so deeply woven into the American political fabric that one could, with considerable justice, assert that the history of lobbying comes close to being the history of American legislation."[96]

Recent years have witnessed an explosion in the number and types of groups organized to pursue their ends on Capitol Hill. Compared with a decade ago, more industry associations, public affairs lobbies (such as Common Cause), single-issue groups, political action committees, and foreign agents are engaged in lobbying. Some of these groups employ new grassroots and technological lobbying techniques. Many victories today are won in Washington because of sophisticated lobbying campaigns back in home states or districts.

No one questions that groups and lobbyists have a rightful public role, but some aspects of lobbying warrant concern. Groups push Congress to pass laws that benefit the few and not the many. They exaggerate their members' views and hinder compromise. They frequently misrepresent the voting records of legislators in their rating schemes and pour money into campaigns of their allies (mainly incumbents). Lawmakers who defy single-issue groups find at election time that these organizations pull out all the stops to defeat them.

Built-in checks constrain group pressures, however. Legislators can play one competing group off against another, and knowledgeable staff aides can forearm members to counter the lobbyists' arguments. Lawmakers' own expertise is another informal check on lobbyists. Finally, there are self-imposed constraints. Lobbyists who misrepresent issues or mislead members soon find their access permanently closed off.

Many interest groups are especially active when government funding for their programs is under review. During the recent struggles between Congress and the White House to reach a balanced budget accord, lawmakers and the president mobilized supporters to convince the public that their fiscal approach represented the best choice for the nation. The next chapter examines the dynamics of domestic policy making and congressional budgeting.

Budget politics. President Bill Clinton (above) holds a White House news conference to announce his plan for using budget surpluses to finance Social Security and Medicare. Congressional appropriators Sonny Callahan (R-Ala.), chair of the Foreign Operations Subcommittee, and David R. Obey, ranking Democrat on the full Appropriations Committee, review strategy while drafting a funding bill for the contentious House floor.

13

Congress, Budgets, and Domestic Policy Making

The cold war defined defense and foreign policy from the end of World War II in 1949 until the fall of the Berlin Wall in 1989. Similarly, the huge fiscal deficits of the past twenty-five years defined domestic policy. Today the federal budget is in surplus, and this apparent reality has the capacity to reshape the political and economic landscape dramatically. "It's a world I never thought I'd live to see," admitted Sen. Charles E. Grassley, R-Iowa, who has served in Congress since 1974. "The deficit put us in an era of limits. That has been replaced by a debate over what to do in a time of plenty."[1] Whether the surplus will materialize to any significant degree and how long it may last are unclear, but the political squabbles over what do to with the money have already begun. "We haven't quite figured out the politics of surplus," says Sen. Joseph I. Lieberman, D-Conn.[2]

Before discussing the fiscal surplus and congressional budgeting, we will first look at the issues behind the budget. What are public policies and how does Congress make them? What are the principal stages and characteristics of policy making? We then examine how the annual budget establishes the nation's policy priorities.

Definitions of Policy

Because policies ultimately are what government is about, it is not surprising that definitions of policy and policy making are diverse and influenced by the beholder's eye. David Easton's celebrated definition of public policy as society's "authoritative allocations" of values or resources is one approach to the question. To put it another way, policies can be regarded as reflecting "who gets what, when, and how" in a society. A more serviceable definition of policy is offered by Randall Ripley and Grace Franklin: policy is what the government says and does about perceived problems.[3]

How do we recognize policies? The answer is not as simple as it may seem. Many policies are explicitly labeled and recognized as authoritative statements of what the government is doing, or intends to do, about a particular matter. The measures may be far reaching (financing the Social Security system, for example); they may be trivial (naming federal buildings after deceased public officials). Nonetheless, they are obvious statements of policy. They are usually written down, often in painfully precise legal language. They boast documented legislative histories in committee hearings, reports, or floor deliberations that indicate what lawmakers had in mind as they hammered out the policy's final provisions.

Not all policies, however, are formal enough to be considered "the law of the land." Some are articulated by officials but, for one reason or another, are never set down in laws or rules. The Monroe Doctrine, which declared U.S. resistance to European intervention in the Western Hemisphere, was inserted into the president's 1823 State of the Union report (written, in those days) by Secretary of State John Quincy Adams; it has been adhered to ever since by successive generations of policy makers. Other policies, especially of a symbolic or exhortatory nature, gain currency in the eyes of elites or the public without formal or legal elaboration.

Some policies stress substance—programs designed to build the nation's defense, for example. Others stress procedure, such as those imposing personnel ceilings on federal agencies, mandating program management standards, or requiring contractors' insurance for military weapons. Still others are amalgams of substance and procedure, such as "fast track" provisions written into trade laws and other laws that expedite committee and floor action in each house. Ways of putting legislation on a fast track include time limits on committee consideration of a bill and on floor debate of the measure, prohibitions on the offering of floor amendments, and requirements obligating each chamber to pass identical legislation, thus obviating the need for a conference committee to iron out bicameral differences.

Finally, some policies are made by negation. Doing nothing about a problem often has results that are as profound as passing a law about it. The United States had no general immigration law before 1924 and no overall medical care program before 1965, but its policies on those matters—mainly favoring unregulated private activity—were unmistakable.

The process of arriving at these policies is *policy making*. The process may be simple or complex, highly publicized or nearly invisible, concentrated or diffuse. It may happen suddenly, as when President Bill Clinton decided in March 1999 to have the United States and its NATO allies launch an air war against Serbian military forces engaged in "ethnic cleansing" in Kosovo. Or it may require years or even decades to formulate, as in the case of civil rights or Medicare for the elderly.[4]

Stages of Policy Making

Whatever the time frame, policy making normally has four distinct stages: setting the agenda, formulating policy, adopting policy, and implementing policy.

Setting the Agenda

At the initial stage, public problems are spotted and moved onto the national agenda, which can be defined as "the list of subjects to which government officials and those around them are paying serious attention."[5] In a large, pluralistic country like the United States, the national agenda at any given moment is extensive and vigorously debated.

How do problems get placed on the agenda? Some are heralded by a crisis or some other prominent event—the bombing of a building by terrorists, a schoolyard shooting, a national disaster, or a campaign-funding scandal. Others are occasioned by the gradual accumulation of knowledge—for example, increasing awareness of an environmental hazard like acid rain or ozone depletion. Still other agenda items represent the accumulation of past problems that no longer can be avoided or ignored. Finally, agendas may be set in motion by political processes—election results, turnover in Congress, or shifts in public opinion.[6] The 1994 election results gave the GOP control of Congress and a chance to pursue its "revolution" in downsizing government. The next two elections conveyed quite a different message—generally caution and compromise—to both the Democratic president and the GOP Congress.

Agenda items are pushed by *policy entrepreneurs,* people willing to invest time and energy to promote a particular issue. Numerous Washington "think tanks" and interest groups, especially at the beginning of a new president's term, issue reports that seek to influence the economic, social, or foreign policy agenda of the nation. Usually, however, elected officials and their staffs or appointees are more likely to shape agendas than are career bureaucrats or nongovernmental actors.[7] Notable policy entrepreneurs on Capitol Hill are party and committee leaders who push their party's policy initiatives.

Lawmakers frequently are policy entrepreneurs because they are expected to voice the concerns of constituents and organized groups and to seek legislative solutions. Politicians generally gravitate toward issues that are visible, salient, and solvable. Tough, arcane, or conflictual problems may be shunned because they offer few payoffs and little hope of success.

Sometimes only a crisis, such as the oil price increases in the 1970s, can force lawmakers to address difficult questions. Yet, despite enactment of legislation designed to ameliorate future energy problems, Americans today are as dependent on imported oil as they were three decades ago. Forecasters predict another energy crisis unless steps are taken to develop alternative fuels, change habits of consumption, and reduce the spiraling demand for oil, especially from the volatile Middle East. This kind of "creeping crisis" is often difficult for members of Congress to grapple with, in part because of the "two Congresses" dilemma. As conscientious lawmakers, members might want to forge long-term solutions. But as representatives of their constituents, they are deterred from acting when most citizens see no problems with the immediate situation.

Formulating Policy

In the second stage of policy making, items on the political agenda are discussed and potential solutions are explored. Members of Congress and their staffs play crucial roles by conducting hearings and writing committee reports. They are aided by policy experts in executive agencies, interest groups, and the private sector.

Another term for this stage is *policy incubation,* which entails "keeping a proposal alive while it picks up support, or waits for a better climate, or while

a consensus begins to form that the problem to which it is addressed exists."[8] Sometimes this process takes only a few months; more often it requires years. During Dwight D. Eisenhower's administration, for example, congressional Democrats explored and refined domestic policy options that, while not immediately accepted, were ripe for adoption by the time their party's nominee, John F. Kennedy, was elected president in 1960.[9]

The incubation process not only brings policies to maturity but also refines solutions to the problems. The process may break down if workable solutions are not available. The seeming intractability of many modern issues complicates problem solving. Thomas S. Foley, D-Wash. (Speaker, 1989–1995), held that issues had become far more perplexing since he came to Congress in 1965. At that time "the civil rights issue facing the legislators was whether the right to vote should be federally guaranteed for blacks and Hispanics. Now members are called on to deal with more ambiguous policies like affirmative action and racial quotas."[10] Added to those are such complex contemporary topics as physician-assisted suicide, human cloning, and genetic discrimination.

Solutions to problems normally involve "some fairly simple routines emphasizing the tried and true (or at least not discredited)."[11] A repertoire of proposals exists—for example, blue-ribbon commissions, trust funds, or pilot projects—that can be applied to a variety of unsolved problems. Problem solvers also must guard against recommending solutions that will be viewed as worse than the problem.

Adopting Policy

Laws are ideas whose time has come. The right time for a policy is what scholar John Kingdon calls the *policy window*: the opportunity presented by circumstances and attitudes to enact a policy into law. Policy entrepreneurs must seize the opportunity before the policy window closes and the idea's time has passed.

Once policies are ripe for adoption, they must gain popular acceptance. This is the function of *legitimation*, the process through which policies come to be viewed by the public as right or proper. Inasmuch as citizens are expected to comply with laws or regulations—pay taxes, observe rules, or make sacrifices of one sort or another—the policies themselves must appear to have been properly considered and enacted. A nation whose policies lack legitimacy is in deep trouble.

Symbolic acts, such as members voting on the House or Senate floor or the president signing a bill, signal to everyone that policies have been duly adopted according to traditional forms. Hearings and debates, moreover, serve not only to fine-tune policies but also to cultivate support from affected interests. Responding to critics of Congress's slowness in adopting energy legislation, Sen. Ted Stevens, R-Alaska, asked these questions:

> Would you want an energy bill to flow through the Senate and not have anyone consider the impacts on housing or on the automotive industry or on the energy industries that provide our light and power? Should we ignore the

problems of the miner or the producer or the distributor? Our legislative process must reflect all of the problems if the public is to have confidence in the government.[12]

Legitimating, in other words, usually demands a measured pace and attention to procedural details. Another strategy is to move quickly in response to a public outcry—before opposition forces can mobilize—to enact bold changes, knowing that the details will have to be refined and adjusted later.

Implementing Policy

In the final stage, policies shaped by the legislature and the highest executive levels are put into effect, usually by a federal agency. Policies are not self-executing: they must be promulgated and enforced. A law or executive order rarely spells out exactly how a particular policy will be implemented. Congress and the president usually delegate most decisions about implementation to the responsible agencies under broad but stated guidelines. Implementation determines the ultimate effect of policies. Officials of the executive branch can thwart a policy by foot dragging or sheer inefficiency. By the same token, overzealous administrators can push a policy far beyond its creators' intent.

Congress therefore must exercise its oversight role (see Chapter 11). It may require executive agencies to report or consult with congressional committees or to follow certain formal procedures. Members of Congress get feedback on the operation of federal programs through a variety of channels: media coverage, interest group protests, and even casework for constituents. With such information Congress can and often does pass judgment by adjusting funding, introducing amendments, or recasting the basic legislation governing a particular policy.

Types of Domestic Policies

One way to understand public policies is to analyze the nature of the policies themselves. Scholars have classified policies in many different ways.[13] Our typology identifies three types of domestic policies: distributive, regulatory, and redistributive.

Distributive Policies

Distributive policies or programs are government actions that convey tangible benefits to private individuals, groups, or firms. Invariably, they bestow subsidies, tax breaks, or advantageous regulatory provisions upon favored individuals or groups. The benefits are often called "pork" (usually special-interest spending for projects in members' states or districts), although that appellation is sometimes difficult to define. After all, "one person's pork is another person's steak." The projects come in several varieties:

> Dams, roads and bridges, known as "green pork," are old hat. These days, there is also "academic pork" in the form of research grants to colleges, "defense pork" in the form of geographically specific military expenditures and

lately "high-tech pork," for example the intense fight to authorize research into super computers and high-definition television (HDTV).[14]

The presence of distributive politics—which makes many interests better off and few, if any, visibly worse off—is natural in Congress, which as a non-hierarchical institution must build coalitions in order to function. A textbook example was the $1-billion-plus National Parks and Recreation Act of 1978. Dubbed the "Park Barrel" bill, it created so many parks, historical sites, seashores, wilderness areas, wild and scenic rivers, and national trails that it sailed through the Interior (now Resources) Committee and passed the House by a 341–61 vote. "Notice how quiet we are. We all got something in there," said one House member, after the Rules Committee cleared the bill in five minutes flat. Another member quipped, "If it had a blade of grass and a squirrel, it got in the bill."[15] Distributive politics of this kind throws into sharp relief the "two Congresses" notion: national policy as a mosaic of local interests.

The politics of distribution works best when tax revenues are expanding, fueled by high productivity and economic growth. When productivity declines or tax cuts squeeze revenues, it becomes difficult to add new benefits or expand old ones. Such was the plight of lawmakers in the 1980s and much of the 1990s. Yet distributive impulses remained strong, adding pressure to wring distributive elements out of "red ink" federal budgets. Even in the tight-fisted Republican Congresses, lawmakers in both parties managed to ensure that money would be spent for particular purposes in their districts or states. For example, during the late 1990s, scores of House members asked the Transportation and Infrastructure Committee to funnel money for highway and transit projects to their districts. According to one account, "Republicans and Democrats alike are now lining up at the trough. After putting out a call for proposals, the Transportation and Infrastructure Committee says it has received nearly 1,500 project requests from about 90 percent of House members."[16]

Senate majority leader Trent Lott, R-Miss., highlighted the "two Congresses" theme and the prevailing appeal of distributive policy making to members of Congress when he remarked: "Mississippi is getting tired of dirt roads; we want some asphalt. I also want some more asphalt for my buddies in Florida, Texas, and Alabama."[17] Or, as Lott's colleague Rick Santorum, R-Pa., said: "Republicans feel very strongly about infrastructure. It's an area where we feel real comfortable spending money."[18]

Regulatory Policies

Regulatory policies are designed to protect the public against harm or abuse that might result from unbridled private activity. For example, the Food and Drug Administration (FDA) monitors standards for foodstuffs and tests drugs for purity, safety, and effectiveness, and the Federal Trade Commission (FTC) guards against illegal business practices, such as deceptive advertising.

Federal regulation against certain abuses dates from the late nineteenth century, when the Interstate Commerce Act and the Sherman Antitrust Act

were enacted to protect against transport and monopoly abuses. As the twentieth century dawned, scandalous practices in slaughterhouses and food processing plants led to meatpacking, food, and drug regulations. The stock market collapse in 1929 and the Great Depression paved the way for the New Deal legislation that would regulate the banking and securities industries and labor-management relations. Consumer rights and environmental protection came of age in the 1960s and 1970s. Dramatic attacks on unsafe automobiles by Ralph Nader and others led to new laws mandating tougher safety standards. Concern about smog produced by auto exhausts led to the Clean Air Act of 1970. And concern about airline delays, congestion, and safety prompted Congress to consider new regulatory controls for the nation's air traffic system.

Recently, growing public frustration with lost luggage, canceled flights, and other inconveniences associated with airline travel prompted President Clinton and congressional lawmakers to propose a passenger "bill of rights." This would, among other things, require airlines to give passengers accurate information about flight delays or to compensate passengers who are kept locked for hours in planes sitting on the tarmac. The airlines "need to start treating their passengers like human beings," declared Rep. Bud Shuster, R-Pa., chairman of the Transportation panel.[19]

Regulation is not popular with the recent GOP-controlled Congresses. Republicans wanted to cut back the government's role by repealing or modifying many federal regulations that they viewed as overly costly and burdensome, especially to businesses. Much of the clean-air debate, for instance, involves the basic issue of costs versus benefits: do the public health benefits of cleaner air outweigh the financial costs?[20] The Clinton administration argued that tougher standards for regulating air pollution will prevent suffering and save the lives of thousands who are afflicted with asthma and other lung diseases. Industries and conservative groups attack these claims and contend that the "regulations are unnecessary, would be too costly and would yield only marginal health benefits."[21]

The Republicans' efforts in the mid-1990s to cut back environmental rules produced a political backlash in the electorate, which supports environmental protection even more than regulatory reform. The issue sharply divided GOP ranks. "I'll be real straight with you—we have lost the debate on the environment," conceded House majority whip Tom DeLay, R-Texas. "There was a regulatory reform strategy that deteriorated into an environmental issue and it cost us."[22]

Redistributive Policies

Redistribution, which visibly shifts resources from one group to another, is the most difficult of all political feats. Because they are controversial, redistributive policies engage a broad spectrum of political actors—not only in the House and Senate chambers but also in the executive branch and among interest groups and the public at large. Redistributive issues tend to be ideological: they often separate liberals and conservatives because they upset relation-

ships between social and economic classes. Theodore R. Marmor described the fight over medical care for the aged as "cast in terms of class conflict":

> The leading adversaries . . . brought into the opposing camps a large number of groups whose interests were not directly affected by the Medicare outcome. . . . [I]deological charges and countercharges dominated public discussion, and each side seemed to regard compromise as unacceptable.[23]

Most of the divisive socioeconomic issues of the past generation—civil rights, affirmative action, school busing, welfare, homelessness, abortion, tax reform—were redistributive problems. A looming redistributive issue for the twenty-first century concerns the increasing share of the federal budget that goes to the elderly compared with everyone else in society. Tax dollars spent on entitlement programs such as Social Security and Medicare absorb an ever increasing proportion of federal dollars, which then are unavailable for other important social and defense needs.

Federal budgeting is marked not only by conflict but also by techniques to disguise the redistributions or make them more palatable. Omnibus budget packages permit legislators to approve cuts en bloc rather than one by one, and across the board formulas (like "freezes") give the appearance of spreading the misery equally to affected groups. In all such vehicles, distributive elements are added to placate the more vocal opponents of change.

Characteristics of Congressional Policy Making

As a policy-making body, Congress displays the traits and biases of its membership and structure and of the larger political system. Congress is bicameral with divergent electoral and procedural traditions. It is representative, especially where geographic interests are concerned. It is decentralized, having few mechanisms for integrating or coordinating its policy decisions. It sometimes is inclined toward enacting symbolic measures rather than substantive ones. And it is generally reactive, mirroring conventional perceptions of problems.

Bicameralism

Several differences between the House and Senate—their terms of office, the character of their constituencies, and the size of their legislative bodies— powerfully influence the policies they make. Six-year terms, it is argued, allow senators to play the statesman for at least part of each term before they are forced by oncoming elections to concentrate on fence mending. This distinction may be more apparent than real, but empirical studies of senators' voting habits lend some support to it.

The various constituencies unquestionably pull in divergent directions. The more homogeneous House districts often promote clear and unambiguous positions on a narrower range of questions than those considered by senators, who must weigh the claims of many competing interests on a broad range of matters. The sizes of the two chambers, moreover, dictate procedural

characteristics. House rules are designed to allow majorities to have their way. In contrast, Senate rules give individual senators great latitude to influence action. Minority Democratic senators, for example, can employ their formidable filibustering weapons to block Senate action on many bills passed by the GOP-controlled House.

Are the biases of the two chambers consistent? Probably not. For years the Senate appeared more "liberal" than the House because of the presence of urban configurations in most of the states and the lingering effects of malapportionment favoring rural areas in drawing House districts.[24] Today that generalization would be hard to defend.

The two chambers, in short, differ in outlook, constituency, and strategy. Bicameralism is less important in promoting or discouraging particular kinds of policies, writes Benjamin Page, than in "the furtherance of deliberation, the production of evidence, and the revealing of error."[25]

Localism

Congressional policies respond to constituents' needs, particularly those that can be mapped geographically. Sometimes these needs are pinpointed with startling directness. For example, an aviation noise control bill required construction of a control tower "at latitude 40 degrees, 43 minutes, 45 seconds north and at longitude 73 degrees, 24 minutes, 50 seconds west"—the exact location of a Farmingdale, New York, airport in the district of the Democratic representative who requested the provision.[26]

Usually, however, programs are directed toward states, municipalities, counties, or geographic regions. Funds are often transferred directly to local government agencies, which in turn deliver the aid or services to citizens. Lawmakers for a time required states and localities to fund some national programs. These "unfunded mandates" strained state budgets and aroused the ire of state and local officials, who generated significant public opposition to them. In 1995 President Clinton signed into law the Unfunded Mandates Reform Act, which governs any proposed mandate that the Congressional Budget Office estimates will cost state and local governments $50 million or more. Congress must either "make provision to pay for the mandate . . . or take a separate recorded vote to waive the requirement, thus holding members of Congress accountable for their decision."[27] A few years later Congress was considering extending limits on unfunded mandates to the private sector.

In short, lawmakers must now consider the costs of any federal requirements they impose on state and local governments. Not surprisingly, members of Congress often share local policymakers' views on such matters as having communities rather than the federal government take a larger role in education, crime, or job training. But both liberals and conservatives have had reason to push for national policies. To deal with crime, liberals support gun control; conservatives have greatly expanded the federal criminal code and prison regulation.

National and local policies are necessarily intertwined. National policies can be advanced by state and local governments, or states and localities can

develop innovations that can spur national action. For example, Maine, California, Colorado, and other states have taken the lead over Congress in enacting campaign finance reform. "The states are the laboratories that will lead us to reform on Capitol Hill," argued the president of the League of Women Voters.[28] On other issues as well, the states are the testing ground for social, economic, and political experiments.

Many policy debates revolve around not only which governmental level can most effectively carry out a responsibility but which level best promotes particular values. Liberals, for example, seek a significant role for the national government in the enforcement of civil rights and environmental protection. Conservatives support an activist national government on defense and intelligence matters. Although "empowerment" and "decentralization" are popular concepts among today's conservatives, in previous decades they were powerful slogans for liberals who supported equal rights for women and local Head Start programs for children. When it suits their purposes, both liberals and conservatives are capable of advocating either national actions or local preferences, depending on which level of government would best serve their objective.

Piecemeal Policy Making

Policies all too often mirror Congress's scattered and decentralized structure. Typically, they are considered piecemeal, reflecting the patchwork of committee and subcommittee jurisdictions. Congress's segmented decision making is typified by authorizing and appropriating processes in which separate committees consider the same programs often without consulting each other.

The structure of a policy frequently depends on which committees have reported it. Working from varying jurisdictions, committees can take different approaches to the same problem. A program from the taxing committees will feature tax provisions, from the Appropriations Committees a fiscal approach, from the commerce panels a regulatory approach, and so forth. The approach may be well or ill suited to the policy objective. It all depends on which committee was best positioned to promote the bill.

Symbolic Policy Making

At heart, congressional policy making often concerns appearances more than substance. Symbolic actions are important to all politicians. Often bills are passed to give the impression that action is being taken when the impact or efficacy of the measure is wholly unknown. Groups outside Congress continually demand, "Don't just stand there, do something." Doing "something" is often the only politically feasible choice, even when no one really knows what to do or whether inaction might be just as effective.[29]

Reactive Policy Making

Elected officials are seldom far ahead of or far behind the collective views of the citizenry. Hence it would be misguided to expect the national legislature routinely to express "radical" solutions to problems. Members know that rad-

ical views are unlikely to attract widespread public support. Congress, in short, is essentially a reactive institution. As one House member explained:

> When decision rests on the consent of the governed, it comes slowly, only after consensus has built or crisis has focused public opinion in some unusual way, the representatives in the meantime hanging back until the signs are unmistakable. Government decision, then, is not generally the cutting edge of change but a belated reaction to change.[30]

The reactive character of Congress's policy making is evident in its budget process. Under pressures to reform, Congress reacted in 1974, 1985, and again in the 1990s with changes in the way it makes budget decisions. The current budget process, dating from the mid-1970s, was intended to bring coherence to the way standing committees handle the president's budget. It has decisively shaped both Congress's internal decision making and its relations with the executive.

Congressional Budgeting

Congressional budgeting is a complex process that involves virtually all House and Senate members and committees, the president and executive branch officials, and scores of other participants. That congressional budgeting is usually contentious and conflict-laden should come as no surprise considering the high political and policy stakes associated with fiscal decision making. In this section we will outline the major procedural features of the legislative budget process and discuss how that process has changed in recent times. The box on p. 366 outlines some of the terminology used in budgeting.

Authorizations and Appropriations

Congress has a two-step financial procedure: *authorizations* and *appropriations*. Generally, Congress first passes authorization laws that establish federal agencies and programs and recommends funding them at certain levels. It then enacts appropriation laws that allow agencies to spend money. An authorization is like an IOU that must be validated by an appropriation.

The authorization-appropriation sequence is an invention of Congress. It is required not by the Constitution, but by House and Senate rules. The dual procedure dates from the nineteenth century and stems from inordinate delays caused by adding *riders*—extraneous policy amendments—to appropriation bills. "By 1835," wrote a legislator, "delays caused by injecting legislation [policy] into these [appropriation] bills had become serious and John Quincy Adams suggested that they be stripped of everything save appropriations."[31] Two years later the House required authorizations to precede appropriations. The Senate followed suit.

Authorizations and appropriations can be annual, multiyear, or permanent. Through the end of World War II most federal agencies and programs were permanently authorized; they were reviewed annually by the House and

A Budget Glossary

Appropriations. The process by which Congress provides budget authority, usually through the enactment of thirteen separate appropriations bills.

Budget authority. The authority for federal agencies to spend or otherwise obligate money, accomplished through enactment into law of appropriations bills.

Budget outlays. Money that is actually spent in a given fiscal year, as opposed to money that is appropriated for that year. One year's budget authority can result in outlays over several years, and the outlays in any given year result from a mix of budget authority from that year and prior years. Budget authority is similar to putting money into a checking account; outlays occur when checks are written and cashed.

Discretionary spending. Programs that Congress can finance as it chooses through appropriations. With the exception of paying entitlement benefits to individuals (see mandatory spending below), almost everything the government does is financed by discretionary spending. Examples include all federal agencies, Congress, the White House, the courts, the military, and programs supporting space exploration and child nutrition. About a third of all federal spending falls into this category.

Fiscal year. The federal government's budget year. For example, FY 2000 runs from October 1, 1999, through September 30, 2000.

Mandatory spending. Made up mostly of entitlements, which are programs whose eligibility requirements are written into law. Anyone who meets those requirements is entitled to the money until Congress changes the law.

Examples are Social Security, Medicare, Medicaid, unemployment benefits, food stamps, and federal pensions. Another major category of mandatory spending is the interest paid to holders of federal government bonds. Social Security and interest payments are permanently appropriated. And although budget authority for some entitlements is provided through the appropriations process, appropriators have little or no control over the money. Mandatory spending accounts for about two-thirds of all federal spending.

Pay-as-you-go rule (PAYGO). This rule requires that all tax cuts, new entitlement programs or expansions of existing entitlement programs be budget-neutral—offset either by additional taxes or by cuts in existing entitlement programs.

Reconciliation. The process by which tax laws and spending programs are changed, or reconciled, to reach outlay and revenue targets set in the congressional budget resolution. Established by the 1974 Congressional Budget Act (P.L. 93-344), it was first used in 1980.

Rescission. The cancellation of previously appropriated budget authority. This is a common way to save money that already has been appropriated. A rescissions bill must be passed by Congress and signed by the president (or enacted over his veto), just as an appropriations bill is.

Revenues. Taxes, customs duties, some user fees and most other receipts paid to the federal government.

Sequester. The cancellation of spending authority as a disciplinary measure to cut off spending above preset limits. Appropriations that exceed annual spending caps can trigger a sequester that will cut all appropriations by the amount of the excess. Similarly, tax cuts or new or expanded entitlement spending programs that are not offset under pay-as-you-go rules will trigger a sequester of nonexempt entitlement programs.

Source: Adapted from *CQ Weekly*, Feb. 6, 1999.

Senate Appropriations Committees but not by the authorizing panels (such as Agriculture, Banking, or Commerce). Since the 1970s the trend has been toward short-term authorizations, giving the authorizing committees more chances to control agency operations.[32]

The Two Stages. Here is what happens after an authorizing committee approves a new program or policy. Suppose, for example, that the authorizing committee recommends $20 million for an Energy Department solar research and development program. Under the authorization-appropriation procedure the bill must pass both houses and be signed by the president before the Energy Department has the "authorization" to establish the program.

Then the House Appropriations Committee (usually one of its thirteen subcommittees) must propose how much money the solar program should receive. The proposed amount is the *budget authority* (BA). It is equivalent to depositing money in a checking account. The *budget outlay* (BO) is the actual check written by the Treasury to meet a financial commitment. The Appropriations Committee can provide the whole $20 million (but not more), or propose cuts, or refuse to fund the program at all. Let's assume that the House goes along with the Appropriations Committee and votes to approve $15 million. The Senate Appropriations Committee, acting somewhat like a court of appeals, then hears agency officials asking the Senate to approve the full $20 million. If the Senate accedes, a House-Senate compromise is worked out under the procedure described in Chapter 8.

In practice, it is hard to keep the two stages distinct. Authorization bills sometimes carry appropriations, and appropriation bills sometimes contain legislation (or policy provisions). In the House *limitation riders* make policy under the guise of restricting agency use of funds. Phrased negatively ("None of the funds . . ."), limitations bolster congressional control of bureaucracy. The Senate, too, is not reluctant to add extraneous policy proposals to appropriations bills. Often controversial, policy riders trigger disputes with the other body and veto threats from the president.

Committee Roles and Continuing Resolutions. Among the authorizing committees, House Ways and Means and Senate Finance have especially powerful roles in the budget process. Both House and Senate tax panels have access to the staff experts of the Joint Taxation Committee. Because the House initiates revenue measures, it usually determines whether Congress will act on measures to raise, lower, or redistribute taxes. Occasionally, however, the Senate takes the lead. The Senate technically can comply with the Constitution by taking a minor House-passed revenue bill and adding to it a major tax measure. In 1981 the Republican-controlled Senate employed this tactic to act on President Ronald Reagan's sweeping tax-cut plan; it used the same ploy the next year on the president's tax-increase package. But the House jealously guards its constitutional authority to originate tax measures and may return to the Senate any bills that violate the origination clause.

Whenever Congress cannot complete action on one or more of the thirteen regular appropriations bills (one for each subcommittee) by the beginning

of the fiscal year, it provides temporary, stopgap funding for the affected federal agencies through a joint resolution known as a *continuing resolution*. In the past, continuing resolutions were usually employed to keep a few government agencies in operation for short periods (usually one to three months). Some years Congress has packaged all thirteen regular appropriations bills into one massive continuing resolution.

After their political black eye for twice shutting down the federal government in late 1995 and early 1996, Republicans tried unsuccessfully to enact an automatic continuing resolution. "A repeat of [government shutdowns] is not acceptable to anybody," declared Senate majority whip Don Nickles, R-Okla.[33] Democrats and the Clinton administration opposed the antishutdown proposal. They argued that Republicans, who favor domestic spending cuts, would have little incentive to pass regular appropriations bills if this backup spending provision were in place.[34] An automatic stopgap spending provision would undercut the Democrats' bargaining leverage with Republicans by removing the threat of a government shutdown if Congress could not enact all thirteen regular spending bills by the beginning of the fiscal year.

Backdoor Spending Techniques

To sidestep the appropriations ax, authorizing committees have evolved "backdoor" funding provisions that are outside the appropriations process. There are three types of back doors. *Contract authority* permits agencies to enter into contracts that subsequently must be covered by appropriations. *Borrowing authority* allows agencies to spend money they have borrowed from the public or the Treasury. And *mandatory entitlements* grant eligible individuals and governments the right to receive payments from the national government.

The fastest growing of these three techniques is entitlements, which establish legally enforceable rights without reference to dollar amounts. In other words, spending for entitlement programs (Medicare, Medicaid, and Social Security, for example) is determined by the number of citizens who qualify and the benefit levels established by law; no fixed dollar amount is established.

Entitlements are the real force behind the escalation of federal spending (see Figure 13-1). More than half of all federal spending consists of entitlements that bypass the annual appropriations process review. Interest on the federal debt is another uncontrollable expenditure. Unlike defense or domestic discretionary programs—for which the Appropriations Committees recommend annual amounts and on which all lawmakers may vote—entitlement spending occurs automatically under the terms outlined in the statute. Moreover, four-fifths of these programs "are not 'means tested,' or linked to the incomes of recipients."[35]

Congress has done a good job of containing discretionary spending. It is trying to rein in expenditures for costly entitlements, a much more difficult task. In 1996 Congress passed legislation ending a decades-old national welfare entitlement program—Aid to Families with Dependent Children.[36] Benefits to the elderly make up the largest share of entitlement spending. Given an

Figure 13-1 Federal Spending by Major Category, Fiscal Years 1965 and 2000 (in billions)

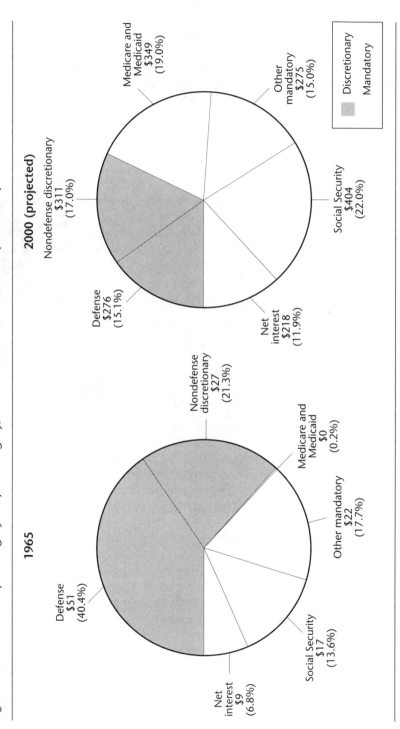

Source: For 1965 data, Robert Keith, Government Division, Congressional Research Service, Library of Congress, May 1997. For 2000 data, Congressional Budget Office, *The Economic and Budget Outlook: Fiscal Years 2000–2009*, January 1999.

aging society and longer lived population (thanks to advances in often expensive medical technology), spending for Social Security and Medicare is sure to escalate until steps are taken to revise these entitlement programs.

Mindful of this fiscal predicament, the Senate made a politically bold decision in 1997 by passing major initiatives to restrain entitlement spending for the elderly. Senators voted to raise the eligibility age for Medicare from sixty-five to sixty-seven and to "means test" the program by requiring affluent retirees to pay more for their doctors' insurance. The counterpart bill in the House did not contain these provisions. Both proposals were dropped in conference; later the Clinton administration dropped "means testing" as too controversial.

The Bipartisan Commission on the Future of Medicare, chaired by Sen. John B. Breaux, D-La., and co-chaired by Rep. Bill Thomas, R-Calif., spent a year exploring how to pay for the program's spiraling costs. It disbanded in March 1999 in deadlock. A majority of its members could not agree on a recommendation to shore up the long-term solvency of Medicare.[37] The result: the challenge of reforming the politically sensitive Medicare program shifted back to the president and Capitol Hill.

The 1974 Budget Act

Loose control of Congress's purse strings in the 1960s gave rise to charges of financial irresponsibility. President Richard Nixon blamed Congress for annual deficits, consumer price hikes, high joblessness, and inflation. He also refused to spend—*impounded*—monies duly appropriated by Congress. Although his administration lost every court challenge to the impoundments, Nixon won the political high ground. These diverse pressures prompted Congress to restructure its budget procedures.

The Budget and Impoundment Control Act of 1974 created the House Budget Committee, the Senate Budget Committee, and the Congressional Budget Office. (The CBO prepares economic forecasts for Congress, scores the costs of proposed legislation, and issues fiscal, monetary, and policy reports.) The 1974 act also established a timetable for action on authorization, appropriation, and tax measures.

Under the budget act, Congress was required to adopt at least two concurrent budget resolutions each year, but the resolutions had no legal effect and required no action by the president. The first budget resolution was supposed to be adopted by May 15. Its purpose was to recommend fixed targets or aggregates for overall federal spending and revenue during the government's fiscal year and divide the spending among various functional categories (defense, energy, and international affairs, for example). By September 15 the Budget Committees were to report a second resolution that was shaped by Congress's previous spending decisions and the needs of the economy. This resolution would establish binding budgetary totals for Congress.

If the spring and summer spending decisions exceed these binding totals, budgetary discipline can be imposed through a *reconciliation process* that forces

appropriate committees to report bills that raised revenue or reduced spending. Reconciliation "forces committees that might not want to reduce spending for the entitlements under their jurisdiction to act and report legislation."[38] Stated differently, reconciliation requires committees to report legislation that changes, or "reconciles," tax, entitlement, or other programs in order to meet the fiscal targets established in the congressional budget resolution.

During the first stage of this reconciliation process, Congress adopts a concurrent budget resolution, giving each designated committee a dollar figure for mandated savings and a deadline for reporting legislation to achieve the savings. During the second stage the budget panels compiles the legislative recommendations of the instructed committees into an omnibus reconciliation bill.

Reconciliation bills are treated in the Senate differently from other bills or amendments. Reconciliation bills cannot be filibustered (there is a statutory time limit of twenty hours for debate); passage requires a simple majority rather than the supermajority (sixty votes) needed to stop a talkathon. Amendments to the reconciliation bill must be germane (the Senate has no general germaneness rule). Furthermore, the so-called Byrd rule (named for its author, Sen. Robert C. Byrd, D-W.Va.) "makes it possible to strike extraneous provisions [those not related to deficit reduction] added by committees; the rule can only be waived with 60 votes."[39]

The 1974 act also limited presidential use of impoundments. Impoundments are divided into two categories: *rescissions* and *deferrals*. A rescission is an executive branch recommendation to cancel congressionally approved spending for a program. Presidents propose deferrals if they want to delay temporarily the spending of certain funds.

Changes in the Budget Process

In 1982 Congress dropped the fall budget resolution, leaving the spring resolution as the major vehicle for budgeting. There simply was not enough time for legislators to consider two major budget resolutions. For the first time ever, Congress in 1998 failed to adopt a budget resolution. Each chamber passed a dramatically different budget resolution that House and Senate Republicans could not reconcile because they disagreed over what to do with the surplus. As one analyst explained: "For years everyone agreed the budget resolution would be used to control spending to help fight the deficit. The surplus was like the Berlin Wall coming down. Nobody could decide what to accomplish next—and there weren't the votes to accomplish any one thing."[40]

During President Jimmy Carter's last year in office, Congress moved the reconciliation process to the beginning of the budget timetable (in tandem with the first budget resolution) rather than to the end. The result of these changes is a budget resolution that generally consists of three main parts: fiscal aggregates (broad totals for spending and revenue), functional categories (spending divided among about twenty allocations), and, on an optional basis, reconciliation instructions.

Reagan and the 1981 Reconciliation

President Reagan's economic plan dominated the 1981 reconciliation process. GOP leaders drafted a reconciliation package that dictated deep, multiyear reductions in domestic spending. Not long afterward, Congress also agreed to the Economic Recovery Tax Act of 1981, which sharply cut tax rates for individuals and businesses. The revenue losses caused by the tax cuts, increased defense spending, and insufficient funding reductions in other areas soon pushed annual budget deficits into the $200 billion range. Never before had the nation seen such huge deficits during an economic expansion (following the 1982 recession). The catch phrases of this period—*borrow* and *spend* and *debt* and *consumption*—affected more than just the national government. As economist Lester Thurow commented:

> The federal government is not strange. The federal government is going into debt. Consumers are going into debt. Firms are going into debt. It isn't as though the federal government is being profligate and the rest of us are not. It's a consistent national pattern of behavior.[41]

As budgetary deficits mounted, so did disagreement on how to address the problem. It was this political and economic stalemate that prompted passage in late 1985 of a deficit-reduction plan sponsored by Sens. Phil Gramm, R-Texas, Ernest Hollings, D-S.C., and Warren Rudman, R-N.H., who retired in 1992.

The Gramm-Rudman-Hollings Plan

The objective of the Gramm-Rudman-Hollings bill was to change the political dynamics between the legislative and executive branches. The core concept of the plan was *sequestration*: if neither branch could support a spending blueprint that would meet the annual deficit-reduction target, the president would have to sequester funds—that is, to impose across-the-board spending cuts evenly divided between domestic and defense programs. But nearly 70 percent of the budget was exempt from sequestration.

In the end GRH was incapable of eliminating the deficit. Congress and the president remained at loggerheads. President Reagan vowed to veto any tax increases. Congress objected to further cuts in domestic discretionary programs. The deficit continued to escalate and triggered enactment of another major budgetary reform: the Budget Enforcement Act of 1990, which later was extended through 2002.

The Budget Enforcement Act of 1990

The Budget Enforcement Act (BEA) once again changed the fiscal procedures of Congress. It shifted Congress's attention from deficit reduction to spending control by setting strict spending caps for three discretionary categories—domestic, defense, and international—and by forbidding any shifting of funds between the categories. This "firewalls" prohibition was designed

to prevent Congress from raiding the defense category to fund domestic programs. However, the three categories were soon merged into one pot of discretionary spending, and all programs had to compete for scarce federal dollars. The BEA retained overall deficit targets and a general sequestration procedure, but it removed the threat of an automatic fiscal guillotine if conditions beyond Congress's control (inflation, a worsening economy, or emergency funding for disasters or crises) pushed the deficit upward.

In addition, the BEA subjected taxes and entitlement programs to a new "pay as you go" (PAYGO) procedure. Spending increases for existing entitlements or funding for new entitlements must be offset either by cuts in other mandatory spending programs or by tax hikes. Tax increases or cuts must also be accomplished in a deficit-neutral manner. The Budget Enforcement Act has worked well in controlling the discretionary side of federal spending and slowing the growth of entitlements.

Clinton and Congress: Act One

A new fiscal and political dynamic occurred with the Republican takeover of the 104th Congress. The November 1994 elections filled the House and Senate with "deficit hawks" intent upon slashing spending and balancing the budget within seven years. As one account noted:

> Ending three decades of deficit spending became the overarching goal of the Republicans, because in doing so they would realize the rest of their aspirations: to dismantle dozens of domestic programs; reverse the capital's regulatory tide; dole out an array of tax cuts; and staunch the growth of welfare and health care entitlements to the poor, the young and the elderly.[42]

On December 6, 1995, President Clinton vetoed the ambitious GOP-crafted budget reconciliation bill passed by Congress—the first reconciliation bill ever vetoed by a president. As part of their political game plan to compel Clinton to agree to their plan to balance the budget in seven years, Republicans employed two "hardball" strategies. The first was shutting down the federal government twice: for six days in November 1995 and for nearly a month from mid-December to early January 1996. The cost of the two shutdowns was estimated at more than $1.25 billion, mostly for back pay for furloughed federal workers.[43] Congress eventually had to pass several short-term continuing resolutions to keep the government running. The second strategy was imposing restrictions on raising the statutory debt ceiling. Each strategy was designed to force the president to support major cutbacks in government spending and to control entitlement spending. Neither one worked.

Congressional Republicans believed that Clinton would be blamed for any hardships caused by a government shutdown, which would occur if he vetoed the appropriations bills and continuing resolutions. They were wrong. After surveys showed the public blaming Republicans for the closures, and with cracks emerging in their ranks, GOP congressional leaders changed their combative approach and reopened the government.

Congressional Republicans also threatened to foreclose the government's ability to borrow more money. The total amount of permissible outstanding debt (currently at $5.6 trillion) is established by statute; the debt ceiling must be raised when the legal limit is reached. (The national debt reflects the cumulative annual deficits—the shortfall between revenues and expenditures—from 1789 until today.) Failure to raise the ceiling would force an unprecedented default on the federal government's financial obligations (for example, interest on U.S. savings bonds or Treasury notes).

In November 1995 Congress sent the president a bill to raise the debt ceiling, but the legislation limited the Treasury secretary's ability to use federal trust funds to avoid a default. Clinton vetoed the bill. In response, Robert Rubin, then the Treasury secretary, applied creative accounting practices—borrowing money from the federal employee retirement fund—to avoid default by the national government. Like the GOP's shutdown plan, the debt ceiling strategy failed to achieve agreement with the president on a long-term plan to balance the budget. On April 26, 1996, the standoff finally ended when the president signed into law the last continuing resolution (there were fourteen earlier versions) providing full-year funding for the departments and agencies then operating on a short-term, stopgap basis.

The fierce budget battles of the 104th Congress reflected profound policy differences between the two parties and between the Democratic president and GOP-controlled Congress. In seeking their budgetary goals, Republicans confronted other hurdles: a conflicted electorate and a divided government. The failure to agree to a deficit-eliminating plan by the designated (and arbitrary) year of 2002 set the stage in the next Congress for another round of revenue and expenditure discussions. Would the White House and lawmakers be able to achieve what had not been achieved since 1969: a national budget in balance?

Clinton and Congress: Act Two

In 1997 the 105th Congress got off to a slow legislative start. After nearly losing control of Congress, Republicans lacked a focused agenda and Clinton appeared uncertain how to deal with the majority party while accommodating his Democratic allies in Congress. Yet despite the fitful start, the two sides made a fiscal and policy breakthrough that might prove to be the fundamental legacy of the 105th Congress and President Clinton's second term. On May 2, 1997, they announced their broad agreement to a joint plan to balance the budget by 2002.[44]

Pundits talked a lot about the pain and sacrifice that balancing the budget would entail, but this budget agreement required little of either. What brought the two sides together was an eleventh-hour, rosy economic forecast by the Congressional Budget Office. The booming economy had generated an extra $225 billion in revenues. This unexpected windfall enabled both sides to achieve their fiscal objectives with minimal difficulty. For Clinton, more money was available to spend on domestic programs. For Republicans, the extra revenue eased the cost of their planned tax cuts. In effect, economic

growth rather than spending reductions, tax hikes, or some combination thereof largely accounted for the relative ease of reaching the balanced-budget accord. "The fact is that a lot of the deficit solved itself," remarked former Labor secretary Robert Reich.[45]

Clinton and Congress: The Unexpected Act

The possibility of a balanced budget became reality sooner than anyone expected. By the end of September 1998 the national budget was $70 billion in the black. "And with the expiration of the [1998] fiscal year came some of the most welcome and almost unbelievable news that, for the first time since 1969, the . . . Federal budget was in surplus," exclaimed Senator Byrd.[46] David Stockman, President Reagan's director of the Office of Management and Budget, once predicted deficits as far as the eye could see. Now economic forecasters were predicting surpluses as far as the eye could see, with estimates of about $4.5 trillion accumulating over fifteen years.[47] In a celebration at the White House, President Clinton exclaimed: America has put "an end to three decades of deficits and launches a new era of balanced budgets and surpluses. America can now turn off the deficit clock and turn on the surplus clock."[48]

Why the surge of black ink and the apparent dawn of the surplus era? Several important factors contributed to the fiscal turnaround. First, the end of the cold war led to reductions in defense expenditures and thus to a cumulative "peace dividend" of $1 trillion.[49] Second, despite some soft spots, the American economy was strong and healthy and entering its ninth year of expansion. This factor, combined with a booming stock market, flooded the federal Treasury with tax and capital gains dollars provided mainly by the richest 1 percent of the population. Third, the Federal Reserve kept inflation and interest rates under control through an effective monetary policy that promoted economic expansion. Fourth, presidential and congressional budgetary decisions, such as passage of the BEA of 1990 during George Bush's administration and Clinton's 1993 deficit-reduction plan, encouraged fiscal restraint and led to budgetary savings. Finally, luck and timing contributed to the fiscal mix. "Just about everything broke right that could have broken right" is how Robert Reischauer, a former director of the Congressional Budget Office, explained the deficit-free picture.[50]

Of course, not everyone believed that the politics of plenty had arrived or, if so, that it would last indefinitely. Another economic recession could be just around the corner. Economic forecasters always like to dance with "rosy scenarios," and their projections are often unreliable or just plain wrong. An international economic crisis could undermine the optimistic fiscal projections. A prolonged war in the Balkans or elsewhere could send military expenditures skyrocketing and erode any budgetary surplus. In fact, some analysts and lawmakers flatly deny a surplus exists. "The truth is there is no surplus," contends Senator Hollings, D-S.C. "We continue to borrow money from federal trust funds—mainly Social Security—to mask the budget deficits. Meanwhile, the national debt skyrockets."[51]

Most of the surplus is generated from the payroll taxes of workers and their employers earmarked for deposit in the Social Security trust fund. More payroll taxes are going into the trust fund than are needed to pay benefits for elderly retirees. The "extra" Social Security money is then used to cover, or "mask," part of the deficit in the government's operating budget. This favorable condition is projected to last for another decade or so until 76 million "baby boom" retirees (those born between 1946 and 1964) begin to draw down Social Security's excess revenues. Not until the early 2000s will the government's general revenues (individual and corporate taxes, for example) be sufficient to cover its spending obligations and produce a surplus without relying on Social Security's excess revenues. In other words, the surplus has two parts:

> One is generated by surplus Social Security revenues; the other, known as the "on-budget" surplus, will begin to accumulate in 2001, when the amount of all other revenues (excluding Social Security) will begin to exceed what is spent to finance the rest of the government's programs."[52]

Both parties are busy making plans based on the risky assumption that the extra revenues will emerge in the projected amounts. Two important dimensions—policy-political and procedural—overlay the new "surplus era" in Washington.

The Policy-Political Dimension. For twenty-five years almost every policy debate in Washington was influenced by deficit considerations. "All of our policy for years was driven by nickel-and-diming the deficit rather than asking what's the right policy," said the former chief economist of the House Budget Committee."[53] On the other hand, the consensus strategy for dealing with the deficit was straightforward: reduce it. Today no broad consensus exists about what to do with the projected surplus. Some want to spend it. Some want to return it to taxpayers in the form of tax cuts. Some want to save it and pay down the $5.6 trillion national debt. Still others want a mix of the three choices. Post-deficit politics and policy making will be as difficult and contentious as during the deficit years. "No matter what the surplus is," remarked Rep. Gary A. Condit, D-Calif., "it won't be enough to do what everyone wants to do."[54]

President Clinton advocated allocating most of the administration's projected $4.4 trillion surplus to bolster the nation's largest and most popular social programs—Social Security (62 percent) and Medicare (15 percent). His plan assigned 11 percent to additional domestic spending on defense, education, and research and the remainder to create a voluntary and supplemental government-assisted retirement savings account for taxpayers. The president's plan ensures that under the government's accounting rules the money would be used to reduce the national debt. Politically, this demonstration of frugality prepared the groundwork for Clinton's familiar opposition to Republican tax-cut proposals.[55]

For their part congressional Republicans have their own ideas on how to spend the surplus—ideas that reflect the party's desire to accomplish its pol-

icy goals and inoculate itself electorally against Democrats' allegations that it is "raiding" Social Security and Medicare to pay for tax cuts. The GOP said it wanted to boost defense spending (especially in light of the war in Kosovo in 1999), strengthen education (by reducing the federal role and enhancing state and local control), preserve Social Security, and cut taxes. On Social Security, Republicans agreed to use most of the surplus to shore up the program, but they proposed to "trump" Clinton's plan by creating a "lock box"—locking away 100 percent of the Social Security surplus, thus prohibiting its use to fund the general operations of the government. "We will lock up every penny of the Social Security surplus for retirement security programs," declared House Budget chairman John R. Kasich, R-Ohio.[56] Republicans also have suggested ways to "privatize" Social Security, such as allowing workers to create an individual account for investment in the financial markets.

On the revenue side, the GOP's plan to shrink government by cutting taxes significantly (a 10 percent reduction in federal income tax rates) did not generate partisan consensus or much public support. Some Republicans worried that their plan for cutting taxes by $800 billion over ten years might pass the House but not the Senate with the result that Republicans would be blasted yet again by Democrats for handing out tax breaks to the wealthy. Moreover, polls indicated that the public, when asked what the government should do with the surplus, said "tax relief is a less attractive option than shoring up the Social Security system, improving education, or reducing the $5.6 trillion national debt."[57]

Finally, concern about a prolonged intervention in Kosovo slowed legislative action on the GOP's tax reduction plan. The possibility of a lengthy military conflict even fostered debate about whether defense should replace tax reduction as the GOP's "signature issue for the next few years."[58] In discussing additional spending for Kosovo, House majority leader Dick Armey, R-Texas, said "tax reduction might have to be less than it otherwise might be."[59]

Lawmakers in both parties understand the electoral stakes in the surplus debate. With the 2000 elections as the backdrop, they often play a "political chess match with each party trying to counter the other" by preempting or neutralizing their opponents' most popular positions.[60] This is the essence of the policy-political dimension.

The Procedural Dimension. Lawmakers face the prospect of large surpluses, but their budget rules are designed for deficit reduction. Unless the budget rules are changed, and there is sentiment on Capitol Hill to do that, the tax and spending plans of many lawmakers collide with budgetary rules that lock them in a fiscal straitjacket. In particular, two features of the Budget Enforcement Act of 1997—spending caps and PAYGO rules—are frustrating lawmakers' fiscal goals.

Take the issue of spending caps. Congress and the president agreed to impose strict caps on discretionary spending as a way to hold down expenditures and bring the budget into balance by 2002. House and Senate appropriators, who are in charge of the discretionary budget, are statutorily assigned a $536

billion cap for fiscal year 2000. (For fiscal year 1999, discretionary spending was $573 billion.) What this means is that the $536 billion cap is "so tough that it will force Congress to cut at least $9 billion below current spending levels, and more than $20 billion from what it would take to keep all programs even with inflation."[61] Yet scores of lawmakers, expecting large surpluses, want to boost discretionary spending for defense and many domestic programs, such as education.

Unless the spending caps or more revenues are raised (or are predicted), members must make deep cuts in agencies and projects both to stay within the caps and to find the money to fund the large increases in other program areas that many lawmakers strongly support. In short, lawmakers confront a zero-sum budgetary dilemma. "There's no will for nondefense spending to go down, [but] there's an absolute will for defense spending to go up," remarked Senate Appropriations chairman Ted Stevens, R-Alaska. Rep. C. W. Bill Young, R-Fla., chairman of the House Appropriations Committee, put it this way: "I can live with the caps. Can 218 members of the House live with the caps?"[62] Unless extended, the caps are slated to expire in 2002.

Another option to permit spending above the caps is for Congress and the president to declare the extra expenditures "emergency"—an often debatable label. "It used to be called smoke and mirrors. Now it's called emergency spending," said Rep. E. Clay Shaw Jr., R-Fla.[63] This budgetary designation (or "loophole," in the judgment of some lawmakers) permits additional spending without the need to find offsets, or funding reductions or freezes, in other discretionary programs.[64] Money for the air and missile assault in Yugoslavia was designated emergency spending. "If the president of the United States says it's an emergency," said Senator Stevens, "he's going to get the [money] as far as I'm concerned."[65] An emergency appropriation will either reduce any surplus or add to the deficit.

Like the spending caps, deficit reduction is also the focus of the "pay as you go" requirement, which deals with taxes and entitlements. Recall that any bill that adds to the deficit by cutting taxes or increasing entitlement spending has to be offset by an equivalent tax hike or entitlement reduction. "We have surpluses and the [PAYGO] rules ought to be updated to meet the current situation," stated Senate Finance chairman William V. Roth Jr., R-Del.[66] Especially annoying to Republicans are PAYGO rules that state that reductions in discretionary spending cannot be used to offset tax cuts. There is a bias, they say, toward spending rather than saving money. The budget rules need to be changed, argues Sen. Sam Brownback, R-Kan., to eliminate the provision that makes it "illegal to use cuts in inefficient government spending to pay for tax cuts. . . . [We need] to allow for tax cuts to be implemented in the amount of program eliminations."[67] However, non–Social Security surpluses can be used for tax cuts or entitlement increases.

In both parties and in both chambers of Congress there is opposition to changing the caps and pay-as-you-go rules. The argument boils down to the importance of maintaining fiscal discipline. Many believe that any surplus is

short term and will quickly evaporate when the baby boom generation begins to retire, Medicare costs escalate, and demands grow for spending on other programs. People need to realize, said Sen. Bob Kerrey, D-Neb., "that the more we spend on entitlements, the fewer tax dollars will be available for education and training of our children, or the research and development of new medicinal drugs or space exploration."[68]

Conclusion

Budget surpluses provide lawmakers with the breathing room to rethink their procedures for ensuring fiscal prudence. The continual "graying" of the national budget—the escalating health and retirement expenditures for elderly retirees—is a serious concern. These expenditures need to be reassessed in light of the investment needs and tax preferences of future generations.

Congress's revamped budget process has promoted budgetary coherence within the House and Senate and strengthened the legislature's financial capabilities in dealing with presidential budgets. (In recent years presidential budgets have tended to be negotiating instruments rather than firm statements of national priorities.)

The annual national budget is not one document but many—appropriations bills, tax bills, and reconciliation measures—that in the aggregate produce the nation's fiscal blueprint. As Rep. David E. Price, D-N.C., a political scientist, once said: "The budget situation centralizes power. It affects everything we do: it affects what initiatives are viable, it affects who has power, it determines the preoccupation of the party leaders."[69]

Today lawmakers are preoccupied with the projected surpluses. Will they endure and, if so, what should be done with them? Governing means making choices. Thus future decisions about budgeting and national priorities will surely reflect the values, goals, and priorities that result from the confrontations and accommodations inherent in our pluralist policy-making system.

Two sides of national security. Defense Secretary William S. Cohen and Secretary of State Madeleine K. Albright (above) testify on NATO expansion. U.S. Marines enter Macedonia on a NATO peacekeeping mission in the Kosovo region of Yugoslavia, even as Congress was debating whether to fund the effort.

14

Congress and National Security Policies

Voting to send your nation into war is the most solemn decision a lawmaker can make, and the 1991 Persian Gulf War was no exception. On the eve of congressional voting on the question, senators and representatives struggled to make up their minds and justify their decisions for colleagues and constituents. As the nation watched the riveting and emotional debates, hawks and doves explained why they supported, or opposed, President George Bush's request for authority to use military force against Iraqi president Saddam Hussein.

Less visible were lawmakers who were undecided—"agonizers," one observer called them. Theirs was the task of balancing conflicting pressures, which ranged from personal ambition and party loyalty to long-held convictions about Middle East affairs or the effectiveness of force versus economic sanctions.

One of the agonizers was Vermont's senator James M. Jeffords, a Republican maverick who wanted to support his president, but who had learned that 500 people were gathered outside his Montpelier office to protest the war. Shunning reporters, Al Gore—then a Democratic senator from Tennessee—pondered whether his hawkishness, a major theme of his failed presidential bid in 1988, would harm his future White House aspirations.[1]

Both chambers approved the military action, Operation Desert Storm, in historic votes on January 12, 1991. The House vote was 250–183, the Senate's a narrow 52–47. Jeffords and Gore both voted "aye." Gore's vote reinforced his promilitary credentials and aided him eighteen months later when Democratic presidential nominee (and Vietnam War no-show) Bill Clinton was searching for a running mate. Ironically, the members may have agonized unduly. Six months after Congress voted on the gulf war, only a fifth of the public could recall whether their senators or representatives had favored or opposed the use of force.[2]

These events, admittedly more dramatic than most, contain important lessons about the making of U.S. foreign and national security policies. Congress and the president share in these duties just as they do in domestic and budgetary matters. Congress has sweeping constitutional authority to participate in making foreign and defense decisions. Even the most decisive chief executives can find themselves constrained by active, informed, and determined policy makers on Capitol Hill.

Constitutional Powers

The Constitution is "an invitation to struggle for the privilege of directing American foreign policy."[3] In other words, foreign and military powers are divided: "while the president is usually in a position to *propose,* the Senate and Congress are often in a technical position at least to *dispose.*"[4] The struggle over the proper role of each branch in shaping foreign policy typically focuses on two broad issues: conflict over policy and conflict over process.

Presidents command formidable constitutional powers. They manage day-to-day relations with foreign governments, nominate ambassadors and other emissaries, receive other nations' representatives, and negotiate treaties and other agreements. When duly concluded and ratified, treaties are the law of the land, but not all treaties signed by the president are accepted by the Senate. Because treaties are so difficult to ratify—requiring as they do a two-thirds vote of the Senate—presidents tend to use *executive agreements* to reach accords with other nations. Although not mentioned in the Constitution, such agreements are binding and are used six times as often as treaties.

Presidential leadership in conducting diplomacy leads some observers to presume that foreign affairs are the president's exclusive domain. Two historical sources are cited by advocates of presidential supremacy in foreign affairs. One is a statement by John Marshall in 1800, before he became chief justice: "The president is the sole organ of the nation in its external relations, and its sole representative with foreign nations."[5] But note that Marshall did not claim that the president *makes* foreign policy single-handedly, he merely observed that the president *executes* foreign policy. It is formulated jointly.

The second source is a misleading statement by Justice George Sutherland in *United States v. Curtiss-Wright Export Corp.* (1936): legislation dealing with foreign affairs "must often accord to the president a degree of discretion and freedom from statutory restriction which would not be admissible were domestic affairs alone involved."[6] Because this decision dealt with a president's implementation of a congressional enactment, Justice Sutherland's expansive language was beside the point, and it certainly does not support a claim of exclusive presidential domain in foreign affairs. The most that can be said, as Justice Robert Jackson later noted in *Youngstown Sheet and Tube Co. v. Sawyer* (1952), is that "the president might act in external affairs without congressional authority, but not that he might act contrary to an act of Congress."[7]

Congress has an awesome arsenal of explicit constitutional duties, such as the power to declare war, to regulate foreign commerce, and to raise and support military forces. The president's explicit international powers are to serve as commander in chief, to negotiate treaties and appoint ambassadors (a power shared with the Senate), and to receive ambassadors. Throughout our history, presidents have claimed not only these powers but others not spelled out in the Constitution. Whether they are called *implied, inherent,* or *emergency powers,* they have been invoked by presidents to conduct foreign policy in part because of the innate advantages of the executive office. As John Jay wrote in

The Federalist, No. 64, the office's unity, its superior information sources, and its capacity for secrecy and dispatch give the president daily charge of foreign intercourse.[8] In Jay's time, of course, Congress was not in session the whole year, whereas the president was always on hand to make decisions.

The president's advantages are especially marked in times of warfare or crisis. The legislature's clumsy management of affairs during the Revolutionary War led the Founders to champion an independent, energetic executive and to designate the president as commander in chief. Because wars and conflicts tend to centralize authority, presidential powers have been at their zenith during armed conflict. This held true during the so-called cold war—hostilities between the United States and the Soviet Union—and the "hot wars" that ignited in Korea (1950–1953) and Vietnam (1965–1974). Throughout this period, from the late 1940s through the 1980s, presidents vigorously exploited their powers as commander in chief—buttressed by the nation's place as a world leader and by a military and intelligence establishment that was, by historical standards, enormous for a period in which there were no declared wars.

After hostilities cease, presidential powers have tended to dissipate. As bipolar tensions lessened after the collapse of the Soviet Union in 1991, for example, U.S. presidents' ability to rally the nation behind foreign commitments was curtailed.

Types of Foreign and National Security Policies

Foreign policy is the sum total of decisions and actions governing a nation's relations with other nations. The major foreign policy ingredients are *national goals* to be achieved and *resources* for achieving them. *Statecraft* is the art of formulating realistic goals and marshaling appropriate resources to attain them.

Ascertaining a nation's goals is no simple matter. Many of the great congressional debates have been over divergent and even incompatible foreign policy goals—over ties to old-world powers such as England and France during our nation's first decades, over high tariffs versus low ones, over American expansionism and industrialization abroad, and over involvement in foreign wars. Among a nation's resources for achieving its goals are its military strength and preparedness (national security policies), but other assets (for example, economic wealth and productivity) may be even more potent

In balancing national goals and national resources, policy makers must manipulate several different types of foreign and national security policies. *Structural policies* involve deploying resources or personnel; *strategic policies* advance the nation's interests militarily or diplomatically; and *crisis policies* protect the nation's vital interests against specific foreign threats.

Structural Policies

Foreign and military programs employ millions of people and billions of dollars annually. Decisions about deploying such vast resources are called *structural policy decisions.* Examples include decisions on specific weapons systems, contracts with private suppliers, location of military installations, sales

of weapons and surplus goods to foreign countries, and trade policies that affect domestic industries and workers. Structural policy making on foreign and defense issues is virtually the same as distributive policy making in the domestic realm (see Chapter 13).

Structural decisions engage varied political interests. Defense projects and installations, for example, are pursued by business firms, labor unions, local communities, and their representatives on Capitol Hill. The Defense Department's muscle is toned by the immense volume of structural decisions it controls: it is the nation's largest employer and its most generous purchaser of goods and services. By contrast, the State Department makes few distributive decisions.

The "Congressional-Industrial Complex"

Lobbying for military projects comes naturally to members of Congress who, as we have seen, are expected to champion local interests. The impulse is bipartisan. Historically, southern Democrats relied upon defense dollars to lift their economically depressed communities. Republicans, many of whom now represent these areas, tend to favor military expansion even as they want other federal programs scaled back. For example, GOP leaders seized on the 1999 Kosovo conflict as an opening for boosting military budgets. "Clinton bled defense," House majority leader Dick Armey, R-Texas, told his colleagues. "As we consider funding for the Kosovar War, we cannot make the mistake of merely replacing bomb for bomb and missile for missile. We must take urgent steps to improve our military capabilities across the board."[9]

Needless to say, Pentagon procurement officers have learned to anticipate congressional needs in planning and designing projects. The perfect weapons system, it is said, is one with a component manufactured in every congressional district in the nation. Indeed, many weapons are made of components produced by widely scattered subcontractors. The F-22 Raptor is assembled at a Georgia factory from parts made in forty-three states. "What it means to the company is the technology and the jobs," explained the factory's manager.[10]

Even when military planners decide to phase out a weapon, they may be pressured by lawmakers into keeping the item in production. The result can be both wasteful and expensive. Consider the V-22 Osprey, a tilt-rotor aircraft that flies like a conventional plane but takes off and lands like a helicopter. After spending $1.3 billion to develop the plane, the Pentagon decided that it (along with the F-14 Tomcat) was too costly to be continued in a time of drastic cutbacks. But the Osprey and the Tomcat live on. A coalition of representatives from regions in which both planes were manufactured—especially from Pennsylvania, Texas, and New York—worked with contractors to keep the projects alive, even against the dogged opposition of Pentagon managers.[11] The "military pork barrel," contends Lawrence J. Korb, former assistant secretary of defense for manpower, "costs the taxpayer at least $10 billion a year, things we don't want, things we don't need, but are in there to protect vested interests."[12]

The proliferation and geographic dispersion of military installations are another example of distributive military policy making. L. Mendel Rivers, one-

time chairman of the House Armed Services Committee, kept defense money flowing to bases in Charleston, South Carolina, and campaigned on the slogan "Rivers Delivers!" More recently, Senate majority leader Trent Lott described a Pascagoula, Mississippi, firm that keeps busy building ships for the navy: "It's one of the most important shipyards in the country, and if I were not supportive of my hometown, that shipyard and the workers in that shipyard, I wouldn't deserve to be in Congress, now would I?" [13]

In the post–cold war era, Congress cut back military spending and struggled with the politically unpalatable problem of reducing rather than expanding military installations. In 1988 Congress passed a law intended to insulate decisions on base closures from congressional pressure by delegating them to a bipartisan Base Realignment and Closing Commission (BRAC). This agency drew up a list of installations targeted for closure; to make the decisions hard to overturn, the list had to be accepted or rejected as a whole by the president and Congress.

Four rounds of BRACs (between 1989 and 1995) reduced or eliminated some 250 defense installations. Each round was more contentious than the last. The third one "cast its net so broadly that it snared bases in areas represented by some of the most ardent budget-cutters in Congress as well as by critics of meddling in military affairs." [14] Political pressures were intense: the last commission chair, former senator Alan J. Dixon, D-Ill., was greeted at base entrances by parents holding children who, they said, would starve if the base closed. [15] Senators and representatives from affected areas fought the closure lists and nearly succeeded in overturning them; everyone seemed relieved when the agency closed its doors at the end of 1995, having succeeded in closing some 100 major facilities at home and more than 600 abroad.

Yet the base-closing issue resurfaced when William Cohen, secretary of defense, called for two additional BRAC rounds in 1999 and 2001. "Over my dead body!" exclaimed Joel Hefley, a Republican member of the House Armed Services Committee and normally a vocal foe of pork barrel spending. His Colorado Springs district bristles with military installations (some of them obsolete). [16] Subsequently, a Senate proposal for a BRAC in 2001 was defeated in a rare floor vote on the issue.

Structural decisions, like distributive ones in the domestic realm, are typically reached in congressional subcommittees. Legislators from areas containing major military installations or defense contractors lobby with executive agencies for continued support, and subcommittee decisions are reached with local needs in mind. Referring to military bases, Rep. Tom Allen, D-Maine, explained how constituency interests attracted him to the Armed Services Committee as a freshman: "There are enough jobs dependent [on defense] that I believed it was important to be present when those issues are discussed." [17] Rarely do these issues spill out on the House or Senate floor; interested members can usually craft agreements at the subcommittee or committee stage on how to allocate defense resources.

Trade Politics

In foreign policy the most conspicuous arena for distributive politics is foreign trade. Since the very first Congress, the power "to regulate commerce with foreign nations" has been used to protect and enhance the competitive position of domestic goods and industries—whether cotton or wheat or textiles or automobiles. From 1789 through the early 1930s, tariff legislation was fiercely contested on Capitol Hill by the political parties and economic regions. Increasingly, however, Congress delegated the details of tariff negotiations to the executive branch, especially following the Reciprocal Trade Agreements Act of 1934. After World War II tariffs were reduced dramatically as U.S. industries sought to extend their dominance by exporting throughout the world.

Yet the politics of protectionism revived in the 1970s: many U.S. industries lost (or squandered) their competitive advantages, trade imbalances soared, and pressures mounted for protecting domestic firms—and the jobs they provided. Congress began pressing the executive branch to "get tough" with foreign competitors and ensure open markets for U.S. goods.[18]

Congress found itself impaled on a dilemma. Having delegated most trade decisions to the executive for four decades, lawmakers wanted to get back into the act by acting upon specific trade provisions. At the same time, members understood that trading partners needed assurances that their agreements could be ratified quickly and as a package. The Trade Act of 1974 addressed this dilemma. Presidents, it said, must actively consult, notify, and involve Congress as they negotiate trade agreements. These agreements take effect only after an implementing bill is enacted. Such legislation would be handled under an expedited "fast track" procedure, including required steps and deadlines, limits on debate, and prohibition of amendments. Congress's involvement in trade decisions continued with passage of the Omnibus Trade and Competitiveness Act of 1988, which strengthened its oversight of trade agreements.[19]

All manner of trade interests are represented on Capitol Hill. As representatives of the business community, Republicans tend to favor lowering trade barriers at home and combating them abroad. Democrats from areas of union strength worry about exporting jobs abroad. But other foreign policy concerns can fragment these lines. In the late 1990s debates over U.S.–China trade status found representatives divided across the political spectrum. Those responsive to big business favored normal trade relations because of China's vast potential market for U.S. goods. Liberals incensed at China's poor human rights record found themselves aligned with conservatives who despised the nation's communist regime and accused it of stealing U.S. technological secrets.

When the bill implementing the controversial North American Free Trade Agreement (NAFTA) reached Capitol Hill in late 1993, a bipartisan effort was needed to approve it. Many Democrats opposed the treaty, including the House majority leader and chief whip. President Clinton launched a high-profile public relations campaign, trumpeted the bill's job-creation benefits, welcomed support from Republican leaders, and cut deals to meet individual legislators'

objections. In the end, only 40 percent of House Democrats supported the president, but their 102 votes along with those of 132 Republicans were enough to gain House passage. NAFTA then easily passed the Senate.

Five years later, the president's drive to reinstate fast-track authority (which had lapsed) fell short. Democratic suspicions of free trade had hardened, with many lawmakers complaining that the administration had failed to carry out programs to soften NAFTA's effect on U.S. producers and workers. Republican leaders finally decided it was futile to continue the president's fight. "It's enormously frustrating," said Samuel R. Berger, President Clinton's national security adviser. "Nobody gets told when they are hired: 'You owe your job to the fact that we're doing more business in China.' " [20]

Whenever American firms and producers—from wheat growers to airplane manufacturers—encounter problems abroad, lawmakers are hard pressed to resist lobbying for trade concessions with the International Trade Commission or the Office of the U.S. Trade Representative. In the thirteen months preceding completion of the NAFTA negotiations, U.S. trade representative Carla A. Hills logged forty consultations with individual lawmakers and no fewer than 199 meetings with congressional groups, from the House Ways and Means and Senate Finance Committees to the Northeast-Midwest Coalition and the Senate Textile Group. [21] The legislation that Congress approved to implement NAFTA was a huge patchwork of provisions aimed at placating disparate interests. It included a $140 million job retraining program to help U.S. workers who lose their jobs because of competition with Mexico. [22]

Distributive politics infuse many other foreign and defense programs. For example, P.L. 480 dispenses agricultural surpluses to needy nations. This law not only serves humanitarian purposes but also provides outlets for subsidized farm production at home. Selling arms to other countries profits the U.S. government and private firms and also affects civil and military affairs in every corner of the globe.

Strategic Policies

To protect the nation's interests, decision makers design strategies toward other nations. Strategic policies are concerned with spending levels for international and defense programs; total military force levels; the basic mix of military forces and weapons systems; arms sales to foreign powers; foreign trade inducements or restrictions; allocation of economic, military, and technical aid to developing nations; treaty obligations to other nations; U.S. responses to human rights abuses abroad; and America's basic stance toward international bodies such as the United Nations (UN), the North Atlantic Treaty Organization (NATO), and world financial agencies.

Strategic policies embrace most major foreign policy questions; they engage not only top-level executive decision makers but also congressional committees and midlevel executive officers. The State Department is a key agency for strategic decision making, as is the Office of the Secretary of Defense and the National Security Council. Strategic issues generally are accorded less at-

tention from the public and the media than are crisis situations; however, they can capture citizens' ideological, ethnic, racial, or economic interests.[23] Although they may have distributive elements, strategic issues typically involve broad themes and invoke policy makers' long-term attitudes and beliefs.

The Power of the Purse

The spending power gives Congress the leverage to establish overall spending levels for foreign and defense purposes. Within these ceilings, priorities must be assigned—among military services, among weapons systems, between uniformed personnel and military hardware, and on economic, cultural, or military aid, to name just a few of the choices. The president exerts leadership by presenting an annual budget, lobbying for the administration's priorities, and threatening to veto options deemed unacceptable. Yet Congress is now equipped to write its own budgets down to the smallest detail. And the omnibus character of appropriations measures places pressure on presidents to accede to the outcome of legislative bargaining on expenditures. To get the 95 percent of the budget they need, presidents may have to swallow the 5 percent they oppose. For example, to support his peacekeeping deployments of U.S. forces in Bosnia (1995) and Kosovo (1999), President Clinton was obliged to sign military spending bills that included projects he and his defense secretary had resisted.

National defense consumes a sizable portion of federal outlays; funding for international affairs represents a relatively small expenditure (see Figure 14 1). The notable exception occurred in the immediate post–World War II years, 1947–1951, when programs to rebuild devastated Europe and Japan consumed as much as 16 percent of our annual spending. In recent years, such spending—for Department of State operations, the diplomatic service, and foreign aid—has accounted for less than 1 percent of all expenditures. (Opinion surveys show that citizens grossly overestimate foreign aid spending, which is one-third of 1 percent of the federal budget.)

Congress responds both to perceived levels of international tension and to public moods that swing from wanting "preparedness" to demanding cutbacks. Congress in the 1990s was whipsawed by conflicting goals. On the one hand, the cold war's end raised hopes that a sizable "peace dividend" could be shifted from defense to budget-starved domestic needs. On the other, downsizing the military establishment is politically and economically disruptive. Besides, the military can be deployed in a wide variety of politically useful tasks, from security duty at Atlanta's 1996 Olympic games to rescue and peacekeeping missions and highly visible military operations in places like Bosnia and Kosovo. Thus post–cold war defense budgets will decline less sharply than the swift conversion of the post–World War II years.

Another gauge of defense priorities is the size of the military forces authorized by Congress. During the first decade of the new nation, about 4,000 men were in arms. For most of the nation's history (that is, until World War II), Congress allowed the peacetime active military to grow only as fast as, or a lit-

Figure 14-1 Defense and Foreign Policy Spending as Percentage of Total Budget Outlays, 1940–2000

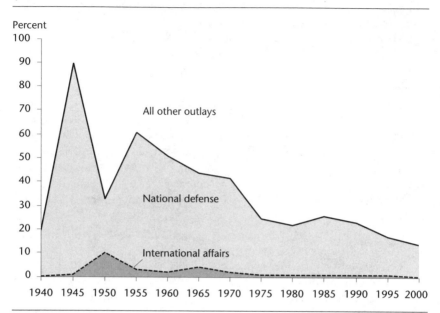

Source: Office of Management and Budget, *Budget of the United States Government, Fiscal Year 1998, Historical Tables,* 19–20.

Note: Figures are fiscal year outlays, according to current statistical conventions for treating off-budget items. The total budget in billions of dollars was $9.5 in 1940, $42.6 in 1950, $92.2 in 1960, $195.6 in 1970, $590.9 in 1980, $1,253.2 in 1990, and $1,814.4 in 2000.

tle faster than, the general population. The pattern was a series of wartime mobilizations followed by ever higher plateaus after the wars ended. As Christopher J. Deering notes, "Demobilization inevitably occurred at the close of each conflict, but rarely to prewar levels."[24] The nation's global burdens after World War II shattered this pattern, resulting in a peacetime military far larger than ever before. Today's military force stands at about 1.3 million men and women, down from 2 million during the Reagan years and destined for even lower levels after 2000. Force levels pose underlying strategic issues concerning, for example, how many and what kinds of conflicts military planners envision.[25]

International operations, too, grew in magnitude and importance as America's international leadership solidified after World War II. Until then the nation's foreign operations had required relatively little money. The situation changed radically after 1945, when the United States became a major provider of economic, military, and technical aid throughout the world.

In the final analysis, no major foreign or military enterprise can be sustained unless Congress provides money and support. Presidents can conduct an operation for a time using existing funds and supplies, as Lyndon Johnson

did at first in Vietnam, but sooner or later they must ask Congress for funding. The United States' role in South Vietnam ended, belatedly, when Congress refused to provide emergency aid funds. Many of the Reagan administration's clashes with Congress took the form of fights over funding—for example, for aid to anticommunist "freedom fighters" in Nicaragua and Angola and for arms to Saudi Arabia and Jordan. Clinton's requests for special funds for operations in Bosnia and Kosovo were granted, but only after Congress added its own spending priorities.

The dependence of foreign and defense policies on economic resources heightens Congress's leverage. It also has equalized the role of the House in comparison with that of the Senate. Because the House traditionally originates taxing and funding legislation, its key panels—especially Ways and Means and the Appropriations subcommittees on national security and foreign operations—usually set forth the detailed specifications and dollar amounts. The Senate serves as the court of appeals, ratifying or modifying the House committees' products.

The Treaty Power

The Constitution makes Congress a full-fledged partner with the president in one form of strategic policy: treaties with foreign powers. Although initiated by the president, treaties are made "by and with the advice and consent of the Senate." The Senate's consent is signified by the concurrence of two-thirds of the senators present and voting.

Congress may or may not be taken into the president's confidence when treaties and executive agreements are negotiated. To avoid President Woodrow Wilson's humiliation when the Senate rejected the Versailles treaty after World War I, modern chief executives usually inform key senators during the negotiation process.

The Chemical Weapons Agreement, negotiated and signed during President George Bush's administration and signed by 161 nations, illustrates the Senate's active role in ratification. Although the treaty had broad bipartisan support, a group of hawkish advocates argued that the agreement was filled with loopholes and would not prevent such "rogue states" as Iraq or Libya from making and using chemical weapons. Simply to get the measure to the Senate floor required arcane negotiations with its archenemy, Foreign Relations chairman Jesse Helms, R-N.C. Negotiations were spearheaded by Secretary of State Madeleine K. Albright and mediated by Majority Leader Trent Lott. The administration not only agreed to twenty-eight clarifications demanded by the conservatives, but it made other major concessions—including a State Department reorganization, UN reform, and submission of other arms control treaties to the Senate—that would strengthen Lott's and Helms's hands in future bargaining. During the floor debate, President Clinton and his aides worked the phones, trumpeted support from such Republican luminaries as retired general Colin Powell and former senator Bob Dole, and sent a last-minute letter to Lott promising to withdraw from the treaty if it subverted

U.S. interests in any way. The multiple offensive paid off when Lott brought in enough skeptical Republicans to ratify the treaty in April 1997. Five days later it went into effect.[26]

Although the Senate may reject a treaty outright, it rarely does so. The Senate has turned down only nineteen treaties since 1789. One study found that the Senate had approved without change 944 treaties, or 69 percent of those submitted to it.[27] As for the rest, the Senate attaches reservations to the treaty, amends it, or simply postpones action. After the chemical weapons pact was ratified, nearly fifty other treaties negotiated and signed by various presidents were languishing without Senate approval—including pacts dealing with the oceans, women's and children's rights, global warming, and biological diversity.[28]

The hurdle of obtaining a two-thirds Senate vote has led presidents to rely increasingly on *executive agreements*—international accords that are not submitted to the Senate for its advice and consent. Of the approximately 13,000 U.S. international accords signed between 1946 and 1992, more than 12,000 were executive agreements.[29] (Executive agreements are enforceable under international law, which regards a "treaty" as any binding agreement among nations.) Most executive agreements might better be termed congressional-executive agreements: they are made pursuant to legislative authority of some type, and many subsequently are approved by Congress. According to the Case-Zablocki Act of 1972, copies of all executive agreements must be transmitted to Congress within sixty days of their going into effect. From time to time a constitutional amendment requiring Senate ratification of executive agreements has been proposed.

Other Policy-Making Powers of Congress

In addition to controlling the purse strings, Congress employs an array of techniques to shape or influence strategic policies. Sometimes the techniques are used to support presidential initiatives; often, however, Congress ventures on its own and challenges the president to respond. The most common tools of congressional policy leadership are (1) informal advice, (2) legislative prodding through nonbinding resolutions or policy statements, (3) policy oversight, (4) legislative directives or restrictions, (5) structural or procedural changes, and (6) "hostage taking."[30]

Congressional leaders and key members routinely provide the president and other executive officials with *informal advice*. Sometimes this advice proves decisive. In 1954 President Dwight D. Eisenhower decided not to intervene militarily in Indochina (Vietnam) after a meeting between Secretary of State John Foster Dulles and a small bipartisan group of congressional leaders. The leaders unanimously declined to sponsor a resolution favoring involvement until other nations indicated their support of military action. Lacking assurances from either Congress or foreign allies, Eisenhower decided against intervening.[31]

Congress engages in *legislative prodding* by passing nonbinding resolutions that state positions or give advice about foreign policy. Recent Congresses have

approved, on average, more than fifty simple or concurrent resolutions that were not legally binding or enforceable. Such pronouncements may lend support to the executive branch, advance certain policies, or signal assurances or warnings to other nations. Occasionally, nonbinding resolutions put forward fresh policy ideas; at other times they are little more than posturing. Some of both were embedded in the House resolution backing troops for the Kosovo crisis in 1999. The resolution—supported by 174 Democrats, 44 Republicans, and 1 independent—authorized the president to deploy troops with the NATO peacekeeping force, but it also instructed the president to explain to Congress an "exit strategy" from the area and to ensure that U.S. troops would answer only to American commanders.[32]

Congress shapes foreign policy through *oversight* of the executive branch's performance. Hearings and investigations often focus on foreign policy issues. The Senate Foreign Relations Committee's hearings beginning in 1966 raised doubts in the public's mind about the Vietnam War. Recurrent hearings on authorizing and funding State Department and Defense Department programs offer many opportunities for lawmakers to voice their concerns, both large and small. Another oversight technique is requiring that certain decisions or international agreements be submitted to Congress before they go into effect. Or Congress and its committees can require reports from the executive that "provide not only information for oversight but also a handle for action."[33] Some 600 foreign policy reporting requirements are embedded in current legislation.

Congress sometimes makes foreign policy by *legislative directives*—to launch new programs, to authorize certain actions, or to set guidelines. A cornerstone enactment of the cold war era was the Jackson-Vanik amendment to the Trade Act of 1974 (named for Sen. Henry M. "Scoop" Jackson, D-Wash., and Rep. Charles Vanik, D-Ohio). Prompted by concern over the Soviet Union's treatment of its Jewish minority, the amendment denied government credits and most-favored-nation trade status to any communist country that restricted free emigration of its citizens.

Foreign policy statutes may include explicit *legislative restrictions*—perhaps Congress's most effective weapon. Often they are embedded in authorization or appropriation bills that the president is unlikely to veto. Throughout the Reagan years, for example, Congress passed many limits on military aid to Central American countries. Most notable were the "Boland amendments" (named for House Intelligence Committee chairman Edward Boland, D-Mass.) that were attached to various bills after 1982 to forbid nonhumanitarian aid to the contra rebels in Nicaragua. In the 1987 Iran-contra scandal, President Reagan and his National Security Council staff were accused of violating this prohibition.

Even the threat of passing legislation may bring about the desired result. Dissatisfied with the Reagan administration's "constructive engagement" policy toward South African apartheid (a brutal form of racial separation), a pro–civil rights coalition on Capitol Hill threatened to pass legislation imposing economic and other sanctions. In 1985, just before a sanctions bill was to be ap-

proved, President Reagan issued an executive order imposing limited sanctions. (The next year, over Reagan's veto, Congress enacted tougher restrictions.)

Legislation also shapes the *structures and procedures* through which policies are carried out. "Congress changes the structure and procedures of decision making in the executive branch in order to influence the content of policy," writes James M. Lindsay.[34] When lawmakers wanted to reform military procurement, they restructured the Defense Department to clarify and streamline the process; when they wanted more say in trade negotiations, they wrote themselves into the process with the 1974 and 1988 trade laws.

Finally, in the extreme tactic of *hostage taking,* Congress may place international initiatives on hold until the executive compromises or capitulates to lawmakers' demands. In the mid-1990s Senate Foreign Relations chairman Helms pushed for consolidation into the State Department of three foreign policy agencies—the Agency for International Development, the Arms Control and Disarmament Agency, and the U.S. Information Agency—to downsize their missions. Ambassadorial nominations and treaty actions were halted for the better part of a year by a stalemate over Senator Helms's reorganization scheme. Stonewalled at first by the Clinton administration, Helms simply placed "holds" on nominations and other actions to prevent them from being considered on the Senate floor. At one point 15 percent of U.S. embassies worldwide were left without new ambassadors. The standoff ended in 1997, when the administration announced its own reorganization plan for the three agencies.[35] Helms's tactics enraged Democrats and discomforted some of his GOP colleagues, but they forced the administration to pay attention to his proposal.

Crisis Policies: The War Powers

Self-preservation is not the only goal of foreign or military policy, but when the nation is directly threatened, other goals are shunted aside. One definition of an international crisis is a sudden challenge to the nation's safety and security. Examples range from Japan's attack on the U.S. naval fleet in Pearl Harbor in 1941 to Iran's seizure of American citizens at the U.S. embassy in Tehran in 1979.

Crisis policies engage decision makers at the very highest levels: the president, the secretaries of state and defense, the National Security Council, and the Joint Chiefs of Staff. Occasionally, congressional leaders are brought into the picture; sometimes, as in the failed 1980 attempt to rescue the American hostages in Iran, no consultation is undertaken. Even more rarely, congressional advice is sought and heeded—as in President Eisenhower's 1954 decision against military intervention in Indochina. Often when executive decision makers fear congressional opposition, they simply neglect to inform Capitol Hill until the planned action is under way.

As long as a crisis lingers, policy makers keep a tight rein on information flowing upward from line officers. The attention of the media and the public is riveted upon crisis events. Patriotism runs high; citizens hasten to "rally round the flag" and support whatever course their leaders choose.[36]

The so-called war powers are shared by the president and Congress. The president is the commander in chief (Article II, Section 2), but Congress has the power to declare war (Article I, Section 8). Congress has declared war in only five conflicts: the War of 1812 (1812–1814), the Mexican War (1846–1848), the Spanish-American War (1898), World War I (1917–1918), and World War II (1941–1945). In all but one case (the Mexican War), Congress assented eagerly to the president's call for war, acknowledging in the declaration that a state of war already existed. Only once did Congress actually delve into the merits of waging war, and that was in 1812, when the vote was rather close. In two cases—the Mexican and Spanish-American conflicts—lawmakers later had reason to regret their haste.

More problematic than formal declarations of war are the more than 270 instances when U.S. military forces have been deployed abroad. The examples range chronologically from an undeclared naval war with France (1798–1800) to NATO air strikes over Yugoslavia in March 1999.[37] (The number is uncertain because of quasi engagements involving military or intelligence "advisers.") Since the end of our last declared war—World War II—in 1945, there have been numerous military interventions abroad (see box, p. 395). Some of them were massive prolonged wars (Korea, 1950–1953; Vietnam, 1964–1975). Others were brief actions (for example, military coordination of medical and disaster relief after U.S. embassies in Kenya and Tanzania were bombed in 1998). Still others were rescue or "peacekeeping" missions, some of which involved casualties (Lebanon, 1983; Somalia, 1992–1993).

Most of these interventions were authorized by the president as commander in chief on the pretext of protecting American lives, property, or interests abroad. Some were justified on the grounds of treaty obligations or "inherent powers" derived from a broad reading of executive prerogatives; others were peacekeeping efforts under UN or NATO sponsorship. In virtually every armed intervention in our history, constitutional questions have generated "lively disagreement among the president, Congress, and the Supreme Court, and between the central government and the states."[38]

Members of Congress, though wary of armed interventions, are reluctant to halt them: "No one actually wants to cut off funds when American troops are in harm's way," in the words of a House leadership aide. "The preferred stand is to let the president make the decisions and, if it goes well, praise him, and if it doesn't criticize him," observed former House International Relations chairman Lee H. Hamilton, D-Ind.[39] Interventions "go well" if they come to a swift, successful conclusion with few American lives lost. Actions that drag on without a satisfactory resolution or that cost many lives will eventually tax lawmakers' patience. As the sense of urgency subsides, competing information appears that may challenge the president's version of the event; congressional critics are emboldened to voice their reservations. This reaction occurred as the undeclared wars in Korea and Vietnam dragged on, and after U.S. troops suffered casualties in Lebanon and Somalia.

The War Powers Resolution in Action

Each time a president has used military forces abroad in near-combat situations or on rescue missions that might have led to combat, members of Congress have cited the resolution, if only to elicit from the executive a complete explanation of the operation. Below are some examples.

Indochina. In the spring of 1975 President Ford conducted a series of rescue missions from Danang, Saigon, and Phnom Penh as U.S. involvement ceased and hostilities increased. Ford maintained he had authority as commander in chief to use troops to rescue citizens and others, but he "took note" of the resolution by giving Congress advance notice and later submitting reports.

Iran. When President Carter, in April 1980, ordered a rescue of the forty-nine hostages held in the American Embassy in Tehran, he did not consult with members of Congress beforehand or inform them of the mission until after it had been aborted. Leaders of both parties said Carter had not complied with the resolution, although his aides said they would have consulted eventually.

Grenada. The U.S.-led invasion of Grenada in October 1983 occurred without advance consultation with Congress: briefings for key congressional leaders took place only when the operation was imminent. But the exercise appeared to fit the resolution's definition of an emergency, in which the president was authorized to use troops. The hostilities ceased within several days.

Lebanon. In 1983 Congress established a timetable for the withdrawal of a U.S. Marine peacekeeping force in Lebanon. The troops, however, were unilaterally pulled out by President Reagan in early 1984 after more than 200 servicemen lost their lives in a terrorist attack.

Somalia. President Bush in late 1992 reported, "consistent with the War Powers Resolution," that U.S. forces had entered Somalia in response to a humanitarian crisis. Six months later President Clinton reported that troops had participated in military action after UN forces there were attacked by a factional leader.

Bosnia. Fulfilling a U.S.-brokered peace agreement, President Clinton in 1995 committed up to 20,000 troops as part of a NATO force to keep peace among warring Yugoslav factions. After several congressional efforts to forestall the mission, the House voted a resolution opposing the mission but expressing support for the troops. The Senate adopted a resolution saying the president could fulfill his commitment to send the troops. Neither chamber was willing to cut off funds once the troops were deployed.

Yugoslavia. On March 26, 1999, President Clinton notified Congress that he had ordered U.S. military forces, in coalition with NATO allies, to begin air strikes against Yugoslavia in response to that government's campaign of violence and repression against the ethnic Albanian people of Kosovo.

Source: Richard F. Grimmett, *War Powers Resolution: Presidential Compliance,* Congressional Research Service Issue Brief, No. 81050, April 19, 1999, 10–14.

Backlash against the Vietnam War made lawmakers skeptical of presidential initiatives abroad. In 1973 Congress passed the War Powers Resolution (P.L. 93-148) over President Nixon's veto. Under this law the president must (1) consult with Congress before introducing U.S. troops into hostilities; (2) report any commitment of forces to Congress within forty-eight hours; and

(3) terminate the use of forces within sixty days if Congress does not declare war, does not extend the period by law, or is unable to meet. (The president may extend the period to ninety days, if necessary.)

By 1999 U.S. presidents had submitted sixty-seven reports to Congress that troops had been deployed abroad.[40] In several other cases the military action was brief, and no report was filed. In still other cases the executive branch claimed that reports were not required because U.S. personnel were not confronting hostilities or imminent hostilities. Thus the Reagan administration declined to comply with congressional reporting requirements when it sent military advisers to El Salvador in 1981 and when it provided protection for oil tankers in the Persian Gulf in 1987 and 1988.

The resolution is an awkward compromise of executive and legislative authority, and presidents still intervene as they see fit. In some cases, members of Congress sit on the sidelines, only later questioning presidential initiatives. One action, the 1983 invasion of Grenada—a Caribbean island whose repressive regime was menacing U.S. citizens there—proved so popular and successful that widespread misgivings were effectively silenced. Other actions are debated heatedly. President Reagan dispatched 2,000 Marines to Lebanon in 1982, but it was not until the troops came under hostile fire in 1983 that Congress seriously debated invoking the War Powers Resolution. Finally, a compromise was reached: the president signed congressional legislation invoking the War Powers Resolution, and Congress authorized U.S. troops to remain in Lebanon for eighteen months (P.L. 98-119). Shortly afterward, 241 Marines were killed by a suicide truck bombing, raising new complaints from Congress and the public. The president withdrew the troops early in 1984.

The War Powers Resolution figured prominently in the Persian Gulf War of 1991—a real war involving forces from the United States and the United Nations. A week after Iraqi troops invaded Kuwait in August 1990, President Bush notified Congress that he had deployed troops to the region. Although the president did not consult with congressional leaders before acting, both chambers later adopted measures supporting the deployment and urging Iraqi withdrawal from Kuwait. The United Nations, prodded by the Bush administration and strengthened by U.S.-Russian cooperation, passed resolutions setting a deadline of January 15, 1991, for Iraqi withdrawal and authorizing member states to use "all necessary means" to restore peace and security to the area. A week before the deadline President Bush, urged by congressional leaders, asked for a resolution supporting the use of all necessary means to implement the UN decrees. As enacted, P.L. 102-1 was a statutory authorization of military action under the War Powers Resolution.

Why did Congress not simply declare war on Iraq? Lawmakers understood they were authorizing a war. Indeed, four days after the congressional vote President Bush launched the military campaign that eventually forced Iraqi troops to abandon Kuwait. Conceding that the resolution was militarily the same as declaring war, Thomas S. Foley, D-Wash., who was then House Speaker, later explained that "there is some question about whether we wish

to excite or enact some of the domestic consequences of a formal declaration of war—seizure of property, censorship, and so forth, which the president neither sought nor desired."[41]

Similar issues arose when the United States joined a NATO assault against Yugoslavia in an attempt to halt the "ethnic cleansing" of ethnic Albanians in Kosovo. As with the Persian Gulf War, the events showed the interplay of presidential initiatives and congressional responses. For months President Clinton, beleaguered by impeachment at home, relied upon threats to goad Yugoslav president Slobodan Milosevic into ending the persecution. Only in March 1999 was the White House ready to face the problem. On March 11 the House adopted, by a 219–191 vote, a resolution authorizing the president to deploy U.S. troops to Kosovo as part of a NATO peacekeeping operation. Twelve days later the Senate, in a 58–41 vote, authorized him to conduct "military air operations and missile strikes" in a NATO operation. Believing (like Bush, his predecessor) he possessed the authority to act, Clinton had not encouraged these votes, but the "sense of the Congress" resolutions conveyed a cautious complicity on the part of the two chambers.

The day after the Senate resolution, the president authorized U.S. forces to begin air strikes against Yugoslavia. In reporting his actions, Clinton noted that he had taken into account the "views and support expressed by the Congress" in the two resolutions.

As in other post-Vietnam interventions, executive branch decision makers fretted about U.S. (and other) casualties—and the possible fallout in congressional and public support.[42] Thus the White House and NATO shied away from committing ground troops in Kosovo. Reports of atrocities against ethnic Albanians in Kosovo, however, fueled surprisingly favorable public reaction to the NATO assaults. Many prominent figures, notably Sen. John McCain, R-Ariz., faulted the administration's strategy as slow and timid. Yet Congress remained fragmented and indecisive: some called for more vigorous action, others were content to "support the troops," and still others regarded it as "Clinton's war" to win or lose. When the House got around to a full debate on the matter, members voted to bar the president from sending ground troops to Yugoslavia and then on a tie vote declined to support NATO air strikes against Serbia—a month after such strikes had begun. "The House today voted no on going forward, no on going back and they tied on standing still," remarked a White House aide.[43]

With each new crisis the War Powers Resolution is attacked or defended, depending on the view held of the proposed intervention. Presidents continue to insist on flexibility and to resist congressional "meddling." Lawmakers strive vainly to be consulted; they support the action as long as it is politically feasible. If the crisis persists and the president's actions backfire, however, Congress moves in and sometimes curtails the action by refusing funds.

Although the resolution has few outright defenders, members of Congress hesitate to repeal or replace it. Democratic leaders vowed to rewrite the statute in the 103d Congress but fell short. In the 104th Congress Republican leaders

in both chambers introduced repeal bills; the House measure, authored by Judiciary chairman Henry J. Hyde, R-Ill., was brought to the floor. Closing the debate, then-Speaker Newt Gingrich argued for passage. But in a rare rebuff to the leadership, the measure was rejected, 217–201. Forty-four Republicans joined 172 Democrats to retain the War Powers Resolution. "The power of the purse is not equivalent to Congress sharing the critical decision, up front, to send troops or not," argued Representative Hamilton, then ranking Democrat on the International Relations Committee. "Congress should hold tenaciously to the power of sharing the decision." Rep. Fred Upton of Michigan, one of three Republicans who spoke against repeal, contended that the resolution, even when not invoked, forces presidents to work with Congress. "The biggest vote that I ever cast was to give President Bush the authority to go into the Gulf War," he said. "I'm not so certain he would have done that [consulted Congress] if there had not been a war powers act."[44] For the time being, then, the War Powers Resolution stands as a reminder of the ultimate need to gain congressional acquiescence, if not approval, for military commitments.

Who Speaks for Congress?

In the spring of 1999, after a House select committee found that China had used U.S. technology to build powerful long-range weapons, a number of House and Senate panels scrambled to claim jurisdiction over various aspects of the scandal—from intelligence and law enforcement to currency transfers and weapons research. In fact, the wide-ranging subjects of foreign policy and military affairs fall within the purview of sixteen committees (see Table 14-1). In addition, at least nine other House panels and six Senate panels consider matters related to foreign and military policy.

The foreign affairs and national security panels are among the most visible on Capitol Hill. The Senate Foreign Relations and House International Relations committees get more time on the nightly television newscasts than do other committees.[45] The Senate and House Armed Services Committees rank fourth, still relatively high TV exposure.

The Senate Foreign Relations Committee considers treaties and nominations of many foreign policy officials. It has normally seen itself as a working partner and adviser to the president, but during the height of dispute over the Vietnam War in the late 1960s and early 1970s, the committee became a forum for antiwar debate under the leadership of Chairman J. William Fulbright, D-Ark. Senator Helms, who became chair in 1995, repeatedly locked horns with the Clinton administration. Despite the committee's prestige, its subject matter is sometimes hazardous for its members. Not a few of them, Fulbright included, were defeated for reelection in part because their work was portrayed as irrelevant to constituents' concerns. As Sen. Richard G. Lugar, R-Ind., observed of a more recent issue, "There's almost no political sex appeal to issues like Bosnia. For those who get involved it's strictly a pro bono service."[46] Indeed, the panel's stock fell so low in the late 1990s that the Republican Conference talked about downgrading its status.

Table 14-1   Major Congressional Committees Dealing with
International Affairs

House	Senate	Jurisdiction
Agriculture	Agriculture, Nutrition, and Forestry	Agricultural marketing and food in foreign countries
Appropriations	Appropriations	Funding of foreign policy agencies and programs
Armed Services	Armed Services	National defense and security
Banking and Financial Services	Banking, Housing, and Urban Affairs	International finance
International Relations	Foreign Relations	State Department and other foreign affairs agencies; foreign aid program; foreign relations
Judiciary	Judiciary	Immigration
Select Committee on Intelligence	Select Committee on Intelligence	Intelligence community
Ways and Means	Finance	Tariffs and trade agreements

For most of its history the House Foreign Affairs (now International Relations) Committee worked in the shadow of its Senate counterpart. This situation changed after World War II, when foreign aid programs thrust the House—with its special powers of the purse—into virtual parity with the Senate.[47] Today the House committee addresses nearly as wide a range of issues as does the Senate committee. It tends, however, to attract members who are more liberal and internationalist in outlook than the House as a whole. Consequently, its reports sometimes generate fierce debate on the House floor.

The Senate and House Armed Services Committees oversee the nation's military establishment. Annually, they authorize Pentagon spending for research, development, and procurement of weapons systems; construction of military facilities; and civilian and uniformed personnel. This last-mentioned jurisdiction includes the Uniform Code of Military Conduct, which governs

the lives of uniformed personnel—and which has attracted congressional scrutiny of such diverse matters as sexual harassment and the right of Jewish officers to wear yarmulkes with military headgear. Although global strategy may interest some members of the Armed Services and National Security Committees, what really rivets their attention is structural policy making—force levels, military installations, and defense contracts—issues closer to home. Thus constituency politics often drives military policy.

Because defense spending is the single largest controllable segment of the yearly federal budget, Appropriations subcommittees exert detailed control over foreign and defense policies. Senate and House oversight committees review intelligence activities. Tariffs and other trade regulations are the province of the taxing committees (House Ways and Means, Senate Finance). Banking committees handle international financial and monetary policies; the commerce committees have jurisdiction over "foreign commerce generally."

The profusion of congressional power centers leads chief executives to contend that they don't know whom to consult when crises arise and that leaks of sensitive information are inevitable with so many players. This viewpoint was expressed in retiring secretary of state George P. Shultz's farewell address:

> What we have to fear today is not the imperial Congress but the chaotic Congress. Dialogue between the branches cannot yield productive results when, no matter what the apparent agreement, any faction, any staffer, any subcommittee, any member of Congress, can delay, and impede even the will of the majority.[48]

Congress's organization for policy making is, of course, far from tidy. But the notion that the president, executive strategists, or even a few congressional experts "know best" is no longer an acceptable notion on Capitol Hill. As the late secretary of state Dean Rusk once noted, participatory decision making "has made communication between the executive and legislative branches all the more important."[49] In fact, chief executives are free to consult with as few or as many lawmakers as they like—in some cases with only the joint party leaders, in others with chairmen of the relevant committees (Armed Services, Foreign Relations/International Relations, Select Intelligence).

The Ebb and Flow of Power

From the nation's earliest days, foreign policy initiative and influence have ebbed and flowed between the two branches. Relations have been especially volatile since World War II. Given the United States' world leadership role, not to mention the vast resources needed to fulfill this responsibility, the stakes are as high as they have ever been.

The Cold War Era

The closing years of World War II and the immediate postwar years (1943–1950) were a time of *accommodation*: "close cooperation was initiated

between high-level executive officials and the committee and party leaders of Congress."[50] This cooperation fostered consistent postwar policy. It permitted speedy approval of unprecedented numbers of American pledges of economic and military aid; for a time it kept foreign policy insulated from partisan politics. In this era statesmen such as Arthur H. Vandenberg, R-Mich., and Tom Connally, D-Texas, chaired the Senate Foreign Relations Committee and set an example of bipartisanship.

The next period (1950–1953) was characterized by *antagonism*. Partisan squabbling broke out over the "loss" of China to the communists, the Korean War, and President Harry S. Truman's dismissal of a World War II hero, Gen. Douglas MacArthur. This period saw the meteoric rise and subsequent fall of one of the Senate's most vicious demagogues, Republican senator Joseph R. McCarthy of Wisconsin, whose speeches were peppered with unsupported charges of communist influence in the State Department, universities, churches, and finally even the U.S. Army.

Following Eisenhower's election as president, a period of *acquiescence* began in 1953. A national consensus favored the policy of containment— keeping communism within its existing borders. Congress got into the habit of ratifying the president's plans; it cut marginal amounts from program budgets but generally supported presidential initiatives. Aaron Wildavsky's "two presidencies" hypothesis captured the temper of the times: "Since World War II, presidents have had much greater success in controlling the nation's defense and foreign policies than in dominating its domestic policies."[51] This period of acquiescence lasted into the 1960s. The high-water mark occurred in 1964, when President Johnson persuaded Congress to support the Gulf of Tonkin Resolution, a vague grant of authority to act militarily in Southeast Asia. The next year, without further consulting Congress, Johnson began escalating the number of U.S. troops sent to Vietnam.

Controversy over Vietnam brought a period of *ambiguity* (1969–1970). At first Americans supported the war as a method of containing communism. But the conflict dragged on, claiming more lives and money for purposes that seemed increasingly elusive. By the end, 58,000 U.S. service men and women had died in the conflict, their names now inscribed on the stark Vietnam Memorial in Washington, D.C. Shifting public sentiment helped to drive Johnson from office in 1968. Members of Congress lagged behind the shift in public sentiment, but at last a majority of lawmakers turned against the war. The period of ambiguity ended decisively when President Nixon ordered the invasion of Cambodia in 1970 without consulting Congress. The following period of *acrimony* (1970–1976) was marked by disputes over Vietnam and almost every other phase of foreign policy. Congressional reassertions of authority in trade pacts and war powers, among other subjects, date from this period.

The Post-Vietnam Era

By refusing to approve more funds, Congress in 1975 finally halted American participation in the Vietnam War. Since then Congress has shown little

desire to follow blindly wherever the president leads. I. M. Destler described the new relationship between Congress and the president:

> The congressional revolution against presidential foreign policy dominance began as a revolt against the people, ideas, and institutions held responsible for the Vietnam War debacle. In terms of its objectives, this revolution was highly successful. Congress reined in the president and constrained the use of military and paramilitary power. It also elevated policy goals the executive had neglected, such as human rights and nuclear nonproliferation.[52]

This congressional activism and assertiveness survived the Reagan administration, which witnessed a renewed level of foreign intervention not seen since before the Vietnam War. Reagan ordered the invasion of Grenada in 1983 and attacked Libya in 1986—acts taken with neither prior consultation nor authorization after the fact. But Congress struggled over MX missile funding, research on the Strategic Defense Initiative (known as "Star Wars"), aid to anticommunist "freedom fighters" in Nicaragua and elsewhere, and arms sales in the Middle East. And Congress pushed the president toward arms control talks, human rights activism (especially in South Africa), and trade protection for certain domestic industries.

The Iran-Contra Affair

In 1985 and 1986 White House staffers launched and carried out a highly secret foreign policy, apparently with President Reagan's blessing: Arms were shipped to Iran in exchange for the release by terrorists of American hostages in the Middle East; the payment of money was channeled through third parties. Some of this money eventually reached the contra forces fighting the leftist Nicaraguan government in Central America. The vehicle for this policy was "the Enterprise," a shadowy network of private arms dealers and soldiers of fortune working under the aegis of White House operatives. Here is how Congress's investigating committee described this singular operation:

> The Enterprise, functioning largely at [Lt. Col. Oliver] North's direction, had its own airplanes, pilots, airfield, operatives, ship, secure communications devices, and secret Swiss bank accounts. For sixteen months, it served as the secret arm of the [National Security Council] staff, carrying out with private and non-appropriated money, and without the accountability or restrictions imposed by law on the CIA, a covert contra aid program that Congress thought it had prohibited.[53]

After a small Lebanese newspaper blew the cover off this operation in late 1986, "Iran-contra" became the biggest scandal of the Reagan administration. Because it violated explicit statutes, it raised grave issues of constitutional comity. It was, arguably, as subversive of the policy-making process as the Watergate fiasco had been to the political process some twenty years earlier. Articles of impeachment were not seriously considered, however, because there

was no "smoking gun" (however implausibly, Reagan denied knowledge of the plot), and because congressional leaders dared not bring down such a popular figure. Nonetheless, the scandal undermined the president's image of firmness in dealing with terrorists and in managing his own administration. It also eroded the trust and deference that members of Congress tend to show the president, even of the opposite party. Congress was outraged that the president had deceived it; the public was puzzled because the president had betrayed his own pledge—no concessions to terrorists.

After the Cold War

The collapse of the Soviet Union and its communist alliance in 1991 ended the cold war and profoundly altered foreign policy. On the one hand, it removed what President Reagan once had called the "evil empire" as an archfoe of U.S. interests. On the other hand, it unleashed racial and ethnic factions in Eastern Europe that had been repressed by Soviet domination—for example, in the former Yugoslavia and the former Soviet Union. It means a less predictable world and, in that sense, one no less hazardous than that of the cold war era.

With the threat of conflict between the superpowers removed, many lawmakers have concluded that their constituents are preoccupied with domestic good times and uninterested in world affairs. This seems to be a misreading of public sentiment. A strong majority of citizens support an active role for the United States in world affairs. Although people are reluctant to use U.S. troops overseas, they support fights against international terrorism, nuclear proliferation, and drug trafficking.[54] Scant evidence of isolationism among the American public was found by Steven Kull and I. M. Destler in an ingenious study comparing national surveys with opinions in four House districts whose members had anti-internationalist public records. In every district the citizens supported the United Nations, foreign aid, and a generally active role in world trouble spots. Their findings undermined such assumptions that "members necessarily mirror their districts" or that "the aggregate behavior of Congress, in particular its move away from international engagement, is a good indicator of American public opinion as a whole."[55]

Unfolding developments promise to enhance Congress's role in foreign policy. First, the United States, as the world's remaining superpower, continues to exert influence in every corner of the world through its actions—and its inactions as well. Second, the end of the cold war means that the public will be more inclined toward legislative dissent in foreign affairs than it was in the past. Legislators more likely will oppose the president if they believe the voters will not punish them for doing so. Third, global interdependence blurs the line that once demarked domestic policy from foreign policy. Insofar as the resulting issues trespass upon traditional domestic matters, such questions are bound to encourage congressional intervention and influence. Finally, the gap between the nation's international commitments and its ability (or willingness) to pursue them will lead Congress to insist upon limits to foreign policy spending and other commitments.[56]

Conclusion

Members of Congress dare not abandon their interest in foreign and national security policies. As the world grows interdependent, these policies are increasingly important to every citizen and to every local community. An internationally minded electorate—sensitive to famines in Africa, massacres in the Balkans, deforestation in the Amazon, and foreign competition for jobs and trade—will draw fewer distinctions between domestic and global matters than in the past. Far more than their predecessors, today's senators and representatives do care about world issues: they realize that global developments touch their local constituencies, and they believe (rightly or wrongly) that they will be judged to some degree on their mastery of those subjects. "In Lyndon Johnson's age, you just had to be able to say [Soviet Premier Nikita] Khrushchev," remarked Sen. Bob Kerrey, D-Neb. Now, "you need to know the leaders in sixteen former Soviet Union States." Most of Nebraska's exports, mostly farm related, go to foreign customers. As the state's junior senator, Chuck Hagel, a Republican, told college students in Kearney: "We are living in a global village, undergirded by a global economy." [57]

Conclusion

Congress, often belittled by media elites and ignored by preoccupied citizens, remains the world's strongest legislative body. Here news media representatives await House votes on the Clinton impeachment.

15

The Two Congresses and the American People

At 12:39 p.m. on Friday, February 12, 1999, the impeachment of President Bill Clinton came to an end. In two roll calls the Senate voted, 55–45 and 50–50, to acquit the president on the two articles of impeachment approved and presented by the House of Representatives. Unlike the impeachment of Andrew Johnson 131 years before, virtually the entire impeachment drama played out before the American public.

The failed impeachment effort will be judged by future historians. Political scientists see it as a paramount example of what Benjamin Ginsberg and Martin Shefter call "politics by other means": political conflict waged not by electoral battles decided by voters but by attacks in court cases, investigations (congressional and others), and media disclosures.[1] But the process also reminds us of Congress's centrality as an engine of public policy. The United States is not, as some have claimed, a "presidential nation"; rather, it is a "separated system" that is marked by the ebb and flow of power among the policy-making branches of government.[2] As former Speaker Newt Gingrich said about the nation's complex and frustrating governing arrangements:

> We have to get the country to understand that at the heart of the process of freedom is not the presidential press conference. It is the legislative process; it is the give and take of independently elected, free people coming together to try to create a better product by the friction of their passions and the friction of their ideas.[3]

Citizens' ambivalent feelings toward the popular branch of government bring us back to the dual character of Congress—the theme that has pervaded our explanations of how Congress and its members work. This notion of the two Congresses manifests itself in public perceptions and assessments: citizens look at the Congress in Washington through different lenses from those with which they view their individual senators and representatives.[4] This same dualism appears in media coverage. In fact, the two Congresses are covered by different kinds of reporters working for different kinds of media organizations.

Individual senators and representatives present themselves to their constituents largely on their own terms—through advertising, self-promotion, and uncritical coverage by local or regional news media. Citizens tend to regard their own legislators as agents of personal or localized interests. Legislators are judged on their service to the state or district, their communication with constituents, and their home style—that is, the way they deal with the home folks.

The institutional Congress, by contrast, is covered mainly by the national press—the wire services, radio and television networks, and a few prestigious newspapers. It is viewed by the public as a lawmaking instrument and judged primarily on the basis of citizens' overall attitudes about policies and the state of the nation. Such national concerns typically lead people to conclusions at variance with their evaluations of their own senators and representatives.

Congress-as-Politicians

We opened this book with the story of Rep. Carolyn McCarthy. She was the suburban nurse and housewife who gained national fame when she won a House seat in the aftermath of the tragic shooting death of her husband and the wounding of her son by a gunman on a Long Island commuter train. A registered Republican who ran on the Democratic ticket, McCarthy was soon targeted by GOP officials hoping to oust her in subsequent elections. "She is somebody who is quite knowledgeable on the gun issue," remarked the county GOP chairman. "But I've got to tell you: there's more than one issue in Congress."[5]

Members of Congress these days are a beleaguered band. Citizens' ambivalence toward politics and politicians is nothing new, but the level of indifference and distrust today is alarming, at least by modern standards (that is, since the advent of mass opinion surveys in the late 1930s). The phenomenon is not confined to Capitol Hill or even to the United States. Mounting unrest among voters is reported in nearly every Western democracy.

Despite the pressures, elected representatives are not yet an endangered species. The hours are killing, the pay relatively modest, and the psychic rewards fleeting, but diligence and attentive home styles yield dividends at the polls. As we have said, if voters regard elected officials as a class as rascals, they tend to be more charitable toward their own elected officials. Nor do they seem eager to "throw the rascals out." Since World War II, 92 percent of all incumbent representatives and 78 percent of incumbent senators running for reelection have been returned to office (see Table 3-1 in Chapter 3). Even in the anti-incumbent 1990–1994 period, fewer members went down to defeat than retired. (Some, to be sure, beat a strategic retreat.) More than nine of ten senators and representatives who took the oath of office on January 6, 1999, were returnees from the previous Congress.

This return rate does not mean, as some have suggested, that the membership of the two chambers is stagnant or unresponsive. For one thing, members of Congress scan reelection rates less calmly than do scholars and reporters sitting on the sidelines. They never feel secure. Bent on maintaining their vote margins, members see themselves as "unsafe at any margin."[6] Moreover, high reelection rates do not always reflect low turnover in membership. Voluntary retirements, including those in which members seek other offices, keep turnover brisk.

In addition to the frantic pace and damage to family life, many retirees fault the decline in comity and erosion of the arts of bargaining and compromise. "We used to have friends on both sides of the aisle," observed Rep. John T.

Myers, R-Ind., a fifteen-term member who exited at the close of the 104th Congress. "Today's attitude is that you can't be friends with someone whose opinion is different. And you can't compromise."[7] From retiring senator (now secretary of defense) William S. Cohen, R-Maine, came this assessment:

> We are witnessing a gravitational pull away from center-based politics to the extremes on both the right and left. Those who seek compromise and consensus are depicted with scorn as a "mushy middle" that is weak and unprincipled. By contrast, those who plant their feet in the concrete of ideological absolutism are heralded as heroic defenders of truth, justice, and the American way.[8]

Incivility had become so rife in the House that a bipartisan group of lawmakers sponsored a retreat in Hershey, Pennsylvania, in 1997 and again in 1999, for some 200 representatives and their families. The objective was to build bipartisan friendships and relationships. The retreats, however, did little to smooth the sharp-edged partisanship that characterizes today's Congress. As one commentator wrote:

> Pressure has been strong within parties to continue grenades-as-usual operations in the House. . . . The one-minute "attack ads" continue on the House floor at the start of each day's session; House leaders have [few] bipartisan dealings, formal or otherwise; and there's been no apparent rebound in the public's esteem for lawmakers or interest in their work.[9]

Whether the shift toward the extremes and the coarsening of legislative life is a transitory phenomenon or a long-term one is not clear. What does seem apparent is that constituents, who see themselves as less partisan than in the past, expect Congress to avoid internal partisan gridlock and to pass legislation. "Compromise may be a dirty word in Washington," remarked pollster Peter D. Hart. "But out among the public it is a very positive term."[10]

Members' Bonds with Constituents

The visibility that members of Congress enjoy in their states or districts helps explain the support they command from potential voters. A majority of citizens report contacts with their House members by receiving mail from them, reading about them in a newspaper or magazine, or seeing them on television. Incumbents, moreover, lose no opportunities to do favors for constituents—gestures that are remembered or at least appreciated by most recipients.

Another bond between members and voters is forged out of perceived mutual agreement on important issues facing the constituency and the nation. The recruitment process we described in Chapters 3 and 4 yields lawmakers who reflect local views and prejudices. Contacts with voters throughout the campaign and while in office reinforce this convergence of views, as do representational norms adopted by most members. Whatever the source, the result is that voters believe their views are shared by their representatives.

Members and their staffs, as we observed in Chapter 5, devote constant attention to generating publicity and local press. Most members employ one or more press aides and regularly use Capitol Hill studios, where audio or video programs or excerpts can be produced for a fraction of their commercial cost. With the advent of low-cost technology to transmit messages by tape or satellite, local media outlets no longer have to rely on network or news service coverage of major events, especially ones with a local angle. What easier way of covering the local story than airing a statement from a senator or representative? "I am never too busy to talk to local TV," said a prominent House member. "Period. Exclamation point."[11] A survey of House press secretaries showed virtually unanimous agreement: "We'd rather get in [the hometown paper] than on the front page of the *New York Times* any day."[12]

Elected officials are at an advantage in impromptu interviews. Local reporters, especially for the electronic media, usually are on general assignment and are ill prepared to question the lawmaker in detail about issues or events. (Sometimes they begin an interview by asking what the lawmaker wants to discuss.) Moreover, local reporters tend to treat national figures with deference and respect. Often their overriding goal is simply to get the legislator on tape or film. For politicians this is an ideal situation: they can express their views in their own words with a minimum of editing and few challenges from reporters.

As a result, individual members of Congress are normally portrayed in a favorable light by the local media, often getting a free ride from reporters eager for a good quote or "news bite." Or they are presented to their constituents through their own press releases, newsletters, targeted mailings, Web pages, or recorded radio or television appearances. Individual members thus receive a large measure of low-cost, uncritical publicity. Is it little wonder, then, that in their home districts lawmakers have a positive public image?

Questions of Ethics

Another question mark in our assessment of individual lawmakers is the recurrence of doubts about members' personal ethics (see box, p.411). The vast majority of lawmakers are dedicated and ethical in their behavior, and there is no reason to think that overall ethical standards are not as high as, or higher than, at any time in history. As Norman J. Ornstein points out, "most observers would suggest that real corruption on the Hill has in fact *declined* significantly over the past 20 or 30 years, whether the misbehavior is licentiousness or bribery or financial chicanery."[13] Among the reasons he cites are the rising quality of members, broader scrutiny by the public, and reforms in campaign finance, disclosure, and ethics procedures. Why, then, do ethical questions continue to loom so large in public and media commentary about members of Congress?

First, organized interests and lobbies of all kinds are no less eager than in past eras to manipulate lawmakers and bend public policy to their wishes. Indeed, the public policy stakes are higher as government advances into more and more sectors of our economic and social life. Huge sums of money find their

Congressional Ethics

Members of Congress are bound by the Constitution, federal laws, party provisions, and House and Senate rules and conduct codes. Although many observers criticize loopholes, the panoply of regulations is extensive.

Constitution. Each chamber has the power to punish its members for "disorderly behavior" and, by a two-thirds vote, to expel a member. Members are immune from arrest during attendance at congressional sessions (except for treason, felony, or breach of peace); and "for any speech or debate in either house, they shall not be questioned in any other place" (Article I, Section 6). This latter provision protects lawmakers from any reprisals for expressing their legislative views.

Criminal Laws. Federal laws make it a crime to solicit or accept a bribe; to solicit or receive "anything of value" for performing any official act, service, or for using influence in any proceeding involving the federal government; to enter into or benefit from any contracts with the government; or to commit any fraud against the United States. Defendants in the so-called Abscam affair were convicted in 1981 for violating these laws.

Ethics Codes. Adopted in 1968 and substantially tightened in 1977, 1989, and 1995, the House and Senate ethics codes apply to members and key staff aides. The codes require extensive financial disclosure; restrict members' outside earned income (15 percent of salaries); prohibit unofficial office accounts that many members used to supplement official allowances; impose stricter standards for using the frank; and ban lawmakers from accepting virtually all meals and gifts from lobbyists. The House Committee on Standards of Official Conduct and the Senate Select Ethics Committee implement the codes, hear charges against members, issue advisory opinions, and recommend disciplinary actions.

Party Rules. Congressional parties can discipline members who run afoul of ethics requirements. House Democratic and Republican rules require a committee leader who is indicted to step aside temporarily; a leader who is censured or convicted is automatically replaced.

Federal Election Campaign Act Amendments of 1974. As amended again in 1976 and 1979, FECA imposes extensive requirements on congressional incumbents as well as challengers.

---

way to Capitol Hill in the form of political contributions and other perquisites. Fearful of raising their own salaries because of expected backlash from voters, some members can fall prey to the blandishments of money and favors.

Many of the most blatant financial abuses, however, have been curtailed or subjected to disclosure requirements. Direct gifts and honoraria have been virtually eliminated, and lobbying by former members or staff has been restricted. Formerly, money flowed under the table. "Back in the old days, it was a common occurrence that you walked around with envelopes of cash in your pocket" to hand out to powerful lawmakers, recalled a Washington lobbyist.[14] Today most of it—campaign contributions and direct lobbying expenses, for example—is reported and subject to scrutiny by reporters and civic groups.

Although loopholes remain, contemporary financial practices unquestionably are tame by the standards common before, let us say, the 1970s.

Second, changing standards of behavior have cast new light upon issues of personal habits and conduct. Sexual misconduct and substance abuse, for example, are less tolerated today than they were a generation ago; certainly, colleagues and journalists are less inclined to look the other way. An adulterous affair led would-be House Speaker Bob Livingston to resign from the House. At the same time President Bill Clinton was impeached and nearly removed from office on charges relating to sexual misconduct. Allegations of adultery against earlier public figures—for example, Presidents John F. Kennedy and Lyndon B. Johnson—were kept largely out of public view.

Third, ethical lapses and scandals are the glaring exceptions to our conclusion that the media exert little enterprise or energy in covering individual senators and representatives. The rise of investigative journalism over the past generation has increased the odds that ethics violations—or even allegations—will be headline news. When Sen. Daniel Brewster, D-Md., was indicted in 1969 and convicted on corruption charges, Ornstein relates, "it was a middle-of-the-book story, meriting a few column inches at best and a grand total over two years of 170 seconds on network evening news shows."[15] Not until 1991 did the House "bank" (actually, a disbursing office that offered check-writing and check-cashing services) become a front-page story. The bank, which dated back to 1830, had been honoring overdrafts on members' checks as a draw against the following month's net salary deposits for at least forty years.[16] After the bank scandal, other perquisites were targeted as well: members' and staff's restaurants, barber and beauty shops, gymnasiums, and free parking spaces. Though modest in comparison with private-sector standards, such benefits titillate the public's interest and sell newspapers and air time.

Finally, intensified regulation of public life has itself opened windows for press coverage and citizens' reaction. So many laws, rules, and regulations govern the public activities of lawmakers that they can unintentionally run afoul of them. As law professor Cass Sunstein puts it:

> If the law books were taken entirely seriously and every American were fully investigated with an unlimited budget for crimes committed within the past two decades, we could probably manage to put a high percentage of Americans behind bars and bring the economy to a grinding halt. High-level public officials are particularly good targets for investigation, if only because of the complex network of statutes that regulate their behavior.[17]

Elected officials are scrutinized by the Federal Election Commission, the House and Senate ethics committees, and occasionally by the Justice Department and federal prosecutors. Reports, investigations, hearings, and even court proceedings are not uncommon. All can bring unwanted publicity to officials. Some of these inquiries uncover genuine wrongdoing that warrants legal punishment or defeat at the polls. Other cases are politically motivated—by electoral foes,

Table 15-1   High Approval for Members, Low Approval for
Congress

Individual members	Congress as institution
Serve constituents	Resolves national issues only with difficulty or not at all
Run against Congress	Has few defenders
Emphasize personal style and outreach to constituents	Operates as collegial body that is difficult for citizens to understand
Covered by local media in generally positive terms	Covered by national media, often negatively (with focus on scandals and conflicts)
Respond quickly to most constituent needs and inquiries	Moves slowly with cumbersome processes that inhibit rapid responses
Are able to highlight personal goals and accomplishments	Has many voices but none can speak clearly for Congress as a whole

Sources: Timothy E. Cook, "Legislature vs. Legislator: A Note on the Paradox of Congressional Support," *Legislative Studies Quarterly* (February 1979): 43–52; Glenn R. Parker and Roger H. Davidson, "Why Do Americans Love Their Congressmen So Much More Than Their Congress?" *Legislative Studies Quarterly* (February 1979): 53–61; and Richard Born, "The Shared Fortunes of Congress and Congressmen: Members May Run from Congress but They Can't Hide," *Journal of Politics* (November 1990): 1223–1241.

by regulators seeking partisan advantage, or by ambitious prosecutors hoping to bag a high-profile trophy. In other words, ethics charges and countercharges are another means of waging political warfare.

Congress-as-Institution

If individual members get respectable marks, people now seem ready to flunk Congress as a whole (see Table 15-1). The institutional Congress usually ranks well below the respondents' own representatives in public esteem. Citizens' approval of Congress rises or falls with economic conditions, scandals, wars and crises, and waves of satisfaction or cynicism (see Figure 15-1). Support for Congress surged briefly after it handled the Watergate affair in 1974 and again after the Republican takeover twenty years later. But these surges soon subsided.

The public's approval of Congress often follows approval of presidents. Perhaps people use the more visible presidency as a handle for assessing Con-

Figure 15-1   Public Assessments of the "Two Congresses," 1974–1999

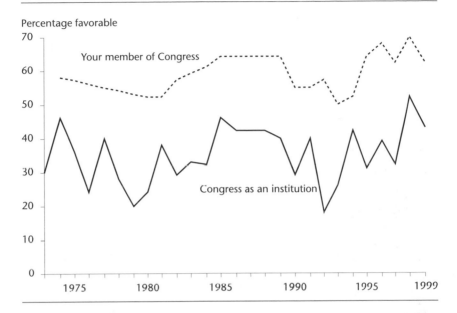

Percentage favorable

Sources: Authors' interpolations of surveys of the Gallup Organization and the Harris Survey for the years 1974–1992 as summarized in "Public Opinion and Demographic Report," *American Enterprise,* November-December 1992, 86–87. Recent figures are from *National Journal,* May 13, 1995, 1180; April 26, 1997, 842; March 21, 1998, 642; Oct. 31, 1998, 2559.

Note: The Gallup Organization's questions are "Do you approve of the way the U.S. Congress is handling its job? Do you approve or disapprove of the way the representative from your own congressional district is handling his/her job?" The Harris Survey's questions are "How would you rate the job done this past year by [Congress] [your member of Congress]—excellent, pretty good, only fair, or poor?" Responses are dichotomized as favorable ("excellent," "pretty good") or unfavorable ("only fair," "poor"). The plotted points in the figures indicate respondents who approve of or are favorable toward congressional performance.

gress and the rest of the government. More likely, they form overall impressions of how the government is doing and rate both institutions accordingly.[18] Thus economic prosperity in the mid-1980s buoyed citizen approval of Congress as well as of President Reagan. Similarly, euphoria over the Persian Gulf War in 1991 briefly lifted public assessments of Congress as well as of President George Bush. Congress's relative popularity in the late 1990s reflected a populace happy with sustained economic growth and satisfied with President Clinton's leadership—which carried over into optimism and confidence in other parts of the federal government. These positive assessments sustained Clinton throughout the Lewinsky scandal and tended to depress support for his enemies—including Republican congressional leaders who were seen as waging partisan warfare against him.

Although the American public's views of Congress change over time, its expectations of Congress remain relatively demanding. People expect Congress to exert a strong, independent policy-making role. This has been a consistent finding of surveys over a number of years. People want Congress to check the president's initiatives and to examine the president's proposals carefully.[19] They often have expressed support for the notion of divided government: the White House controlled by one party but checked by another party controlling Capitol Hill.

Media Coverage

The most open and accessible of the branches of government, Congress is covered by a large press corps containing many of the nation's most skillful journalists. (Capitol Hill is, after all, the best news beat in Washington.) But neither reporters nor their editors can convey in the mass media the internal subtleties or the external pressures that shape lawmaking.

The problem is compounded because the major mass media outlets have curtailed their coverage of Congress and indeed of national politics in general. These outlets include the major news services, the large radio and television networks, the national news magazines, and a few of the daily newspapers of national repute (including the *New York Times, Washington Post, Los Angeles Times,* and *Wall Street Journal*). The decline has been especially dramatic in television, where most Americans receive their news about government and politics. In the early 1970s the three major networks ran about 124 stories a month on Congress; twenty years later, only 42 stories appeared each month.[20] Some of the slack may have been taken up by round-the-clock news channels, but they, too, tend to prefer nonpolitical stories.

The focus of the shrinking coverage has shifted: there are fewer stories on policy issues, and more on scandal, wrongdoing, or corruption. Following the canons of investigative journalism, reporters play the role of suspicious adversaries on the lookout for good guys and bad guys, winners and losers. Ethical problems, congressional pay and perquisites, campaign war chests, and foreign junkets are frequent targets of their investigations. Their stories reinforce popular negative stereotypes about Congress as an institution.

A recent survey of 331 experienced members of the national news media bears out this picture, though with some instructive exceptions. The journalists were asked to rate the performance of the current Congress, and from their comments a twelve-point "hostility index" toward the institution was constructed. The vast majority of the journalists fell in the middle—with television reporters slightly more critical of Congress than were print, radio, or wire service people. The small number of reporters who covered Capitol Hill full time were significantly more favorable toward the institution. At the other end were hosts of radio talk shows, who were far more hostile toward Congress than were those in any other group. Most radio talk show hosts are not active journalists, although they tend to see themselves as purveyors of information

rather than as entertainers.[21] Needless to add, their listeners regard Congress as negatively as do the talk show hosts.

Former Speaker Thomas S. Foley tells a story about how his remarks to a new-member orientation session were covered by the press. Foley advised the freshmen to avoid the mistake of some former members who had promised perfect attendance for floor votes. You're going to miss a procedural vote someday, he said; get it over with and don't drive yourself crazy trying to make every vote. The Speaker also counseled that foreign travel, though a cheap political target, was a good way to learn about world conditions and, incidentally, to get acquainted with colleagues from the opposing party. The next day's headline in his district proclaimed: "Foley tells freshmen: Take a junket, miss a vote."[22]

Divergent press coverage thus widens the gap between the two Congresses' distinct images: less negative for individual members than for the institution. It is still true that "American's love their congressmen much more than they love their Congress."[23] Individual lawmakers tend to be well known, sympathetically judged, respectfully covered by the local media, and—most important—reelected. Congress the institution, in contrast, is covered by the national press with considerable skepticism and cynicism. In short, the two Congresses are viewed through different lenses, reported by different channels of communication, and judged by different criteria.

Citizens' Attitudes toward Congress

Although extensively reported in the media, Congress is not well understood by the average American. Partly to blame are the size and complexity of the institution, not to mention the arcane twists and turns of the legislative process. Indeed, what many citizens find distasteful are the core attributes of lawmaking: controversy, messiness, and compromise (so much deal making to achieve anything).

The public's distrust of the institution goes far deeper than unhappiness with specific policies or disgust with scandals, if we are to believe the sobering findings of John R. Hibbing and Elizabeth Theiss-Morse:

> People do not wish to see uncertainty, conflicting opinions, long debate, competing interests, confusion, bargaining, and compromised, imperfect solutions. They want government to do its job quietly and efficiently, sans conflict and sans fuss. In short . . . they often seek a patently unrealistic form of democracy.[24]

In other words, people abhor the very attributes that are the hallmarks of robust representative assemblies such as Congress. As Hibbing and Theiss-Morse observe, Congress "is structured to embody what we dislike about modern democratic government, which is almost everything."[25]

This unfavorable judgment reflects more than outrage at scandals and distrust of politicians. Surveys have uncovered critical views of virtually all pub-

lic institutions and doubts about the effectiveness of government. "Americans increasingly suspect the worst about their government," according to one nationwide survey.[26] Another survey portrayed voters as feeling remote from Washington politics despite (or perhaps because of) their sense of personal satisfaction and economic confidence. "Politics in Washington doesn't seem to affect me directly," commented an electrician who was interviewed. "It's all too remote. My job and the traffic and the kids swamp out national politics."[27]

Into the Third Century

The U.S. Congress is now in its third century. Survival for more than two centuries is no mean feat. Perhaps like Dr. Johnson's dog (noted not for its skill at standing on hind legs but for doing so at all), Congress's longevity is proof enough of its worth. Congress has withstood repeated stress and turbulence including a civil war, political assassinations, domestic scandals, and tenuous foreign involvement. It is sobering to realize that our government charter is far older than most of the world's governments. "Our present Congress was invented before canned food, the first Wright brothers flight, refrigeration, photography, the Bessemer furnace, the typewriter and telephone; before the automobile, radio and TV; before Hiroshima and Auschwitz and computers."[28]

Mere survival, though, is not enough. Congress must help America thrive in a world where all countries increasingly face similar or interrelated problems. National borders and the authority of national governments are becoming less potent than in the past. In a global economy, "firms have more freedom over where to locate. Activities that require only a screen, a telephone and a modem can be located anywhere. This will make it harder for a country to tax businesses much more heavily than its competitors."[29]

The U.S. Congress struggles to maintain its autonomy by crafting its own legislation and monitoring the governmental apparatus. Yet many people question whether, realistically, Congress can retain meaningful control given the complex, interdependent character of current problems. "The real problem [members of Congress] face," wrote a political observer, "is that local and national politics have now become irretrievably global because their economies are locked into the global system."[30]

Also debatable is whether representative assemblies are relevant to twenty-first century challenges. Representative assemblies rest on the principle of geographic representation; this idea made sense when land was the basic productive resource. Indeed, for much of our history local and regional fissures were translated into political divisions. Today America's divisions tend to be more economic, social, intellectual, or ideological than geographic. As we saw in Chapter 5, states and even districts now tend to be microcosms of the nation as a whole in terms of the diversity of interests they embrace.

Some contend that too much is expected of members of Congress. How can elected generalists render intelligent judgments on the dizzyingly complex problems of governance? "People shouldn't expect those in office to be at the forefront of new developments," observed Rep. Barney Frank, D-Mass.

"The best we can do is to be adapters. No one has the intellectual energy to be an elected official and simultaneously break new intellectual ground."[31]

When the first Congress convened, the United States had a tiny population, mostly rural and uneducated; its social and industrial structure was simple. Changes occurred slowly, and the government's tasks were few. Nothing could be farther from the contemporary situation. "Today," reflected Nancy Landon Kassebaum, discussing her retirement as a Republican senator from Kansas, "there's an almost information overload, a bombardment by news, by faxes. Everything is instantaneous with too little time for thoughtful reflection."[32]

This observation about Congress applies with equal force to many other public and private institutions. Congress has responded to its overload of work by making organizational changes, primarily more division of labor, more staff assistance, and more technology. It may be, however, that the challenges are so fundamental that they cannot be met with organizational tinkering.

Finally, is it possible that the very concept of national policy is unrealistic and outmoded? The foes of technology originally feared that mass production, mass communication, and other advances would create a single homogeneous society in which individuals, brought together and exposed to the same stimuli, would march in lockstep and forfeit their individuality. If anything, the opposite has occurred: technology has "demassified" society and fostered diversity. While erasing geographical isolation, technology has made possible the pursuit of all manner of other human diversities. Far from being a single mass society, America is increasingly "sliced into dozens of different geographic, economic, social, and cultural markets."[33] According to one source, roughly 55,000 different mailing lists of citizens are available for rental by marketers, politicians, or interest groups. There are lists for gun owners, classical music lovers, biblical archeologists, physicists, and signers of petitions for a balanced-budget amendment. And with a simple mouse click, Internet users can access a vast number of Web sites covering virtually all subjects.

Our society is being reshaped structurally by this splitting-apart process. Diversification in the media is well under way: a few national magazines and journals have been supplanted by thousands of special-interest publications, and the national TV networks are waging a rearguard action against cable- and satellite-based systems. The growth of voluntary associations and interest groups—always a hallmark of our nation—has been so startling in recent years that commentators speak of a "participation revolution."[34]

In light of all this buzzing profusion, a single national assembly of generalists elected by majority votes from geographical areas may seem anomalous indeed. Perhaps Congress inadequately mirrors the real-world "democracy of . . . complex, multiple and transient minorities."[35] Perhaps we are witnessing not a retreat from participation or from civic involvement but a movement away from older forms—mass political parties and elections—toward more varied, personal, and adaptable modes of participation than we have seen before. And perhaps the movement is away from government itself and toward

more fluid, decentralized nongovernmental entities. One thoughtful observer has even suggested that "Congress is so unpleasantly noisy these days not because it has too much to do, but because it has too little."[36]

Some have urged the United States to reduce its reliance upon historic representational forms—legislatures, adversarial courts, secret ballots—and move toward these more varied methods of citizen participation in decision making. Such modes, many of them already heavily used by citizens, would be given more formal recognition in political theory and practice. Benjamin R. Barber's program for "strong democracy" stresses participatory models such as neighborhood assemblies, electronic civic-communications networks, national initiative and referendum processes, and selective experiments with voucher systems for schools, public housing projects, and transportation systems.[37] Not all of these proposals will be workable or desirable; some could result in even greater problems than the current system engenders. More important than the content of the proposed remedies, however, is the challenge that they pose to traditional forms of representative government.

We have no solutions to these dilemmas, and so we end our discourse with questions for the twenty-first century. Are the two Congresses ultimately compatible? Or are they diverging, each detrimental to the other? Even if the federal government is downsized (an uncertain prospect), the burden placed on both Congresses will remain heavy by historical standards. Congress-as-Institution is expected to resolve all manner of problems, not only by processing legislation but also by monitoring programs and serving as an all-purpose watchdog. By all outward signs of activity—such as numbers of committees and subcommittees, hearings, reports, votes, and hours in session—legislators are struggling valiantly to keep abreast of these demands.

At the same moment, Congress-as-Politicians is busier than ever. In part because of the sheer scope of modern government, in part because of constituents' uncertainties about the future, citizens are insisting that senators and representatives communicate with them more often, serve their states or districts materially, play the role of ombudsmen, and adhere to strict standards of personal conduct. Legislators have accepted and profited electorally from these functions, but not without misgivings and not without detriment to their legislative tasks. As former senator and vice president Walter Mondale observed:

> Constituent service can . . . be a bottomless pit. The danger is that a member of Congress will end up as little more than an ombudsman between citizens and government agencies. As important as this work is, it takes precious time away from Congress's central responsibilities as both a deliberative and a lawmaking body.[38]

The intensified demands on the two Congresses could well lie beyond the reach of average men and women. Reflecting on the multiplicity of presidential duties, Woodrow Wilson once remarked that we might be forced to pick

our leaders from among "wise and prudent athletes"—a small class of people.[39] The same can now be said of senators and representatives. And if the job specifications exceed reasonable dimensions, can we expect even our most talented citizens to perform these tasks successfully?

In the longer view the question is whether an institution embracing so many disparate motives and careers can continue to function as a coherent whole. Can policies patched together from many discrete interests really guide the nation on its course? Since 1787 people have wondered about these questions. History is only mildly reassuring, and the future poses new and delicate challenges for which the margin of error may be narrower than ever before. And yet representative democracy itself is a gamble; the proposition that representation can yield wise policy making remains a daring one. As always, it is an article of faith whose proof lies inevitably in the future.

Reference Materials

Appendix A   Party Control: Presidency, Senate, House, 1901-2001

Congress	Years	President	Senate			House		
			D	R	Other	D	R	Other
57th	1901-1903	McKinley/T. Roosevelt	31	55	4	151	197	9
58th	1903-1905	T. Roosevelt	33	57	—	178	208	—
59th	1905-1907	T. Roosevelt	33	57	—	136	250	—
60th	1907-1909	T. Roosevelt	31	61	—	164	222	—
61st	1909-1911	Taft	32	61	—	172	219	—
62d	1911-1913	Taft	41	51	—	228	161	1
63d	1913-1915	Wilson	51	44	1	291	127	17
64th	1915-1917	Wilson	56	40	—	230	196	9
65th	1917-1919	Wilson	53	42	—	216	210	6
66th	1919-1921	Wilson	47	49	—	190	240	3
67th	1921-1923	Harding	37	59	—	131	301	1
68th	1923-1925	Coolidge	43	51	2	205	225	5
69th	1925-1927	Coolidge	39	56	1	183	247	4
70th	1927-1929	Coolidge	46	49	1	195	237	3
71st	1929-1931	Hoover	39	56	1	167	267	1
72d	1931-1933	Hoover	47	48	1	220	214	1
73d	1933-1935	F. Roosevelt	60	35	1	313	117	5
74th	1935-1937	F. Roosevelt	69	25	2	319	103	10
75th	1937-1939	F. Roosevelt	76	16	4	331	89	13
76th	1939-1941	F. Roosevelt	69	23	4	261	164	4
77th	1941-1943	F. Roosevelt	66	28	2	268	162	5
78th	1943-1945	F. Roosevelt	58	37	1	218	208	4
79th	1945-1947	Truman	56	38	1	242	190	2
80th	1947-1949	Truman	45	51	—	188	245	1
81st	1949-1951	Truman	54	42	—	263	171	1
82d	1951-1953	Truman	49	47	—	234	199	1
83d	1953-1955	Eisenhower	47	48	1	211	221	1
84th	1955-1957	Eisenhower	48	47	1	232	203	—

Appendix A   *(continued)*

Congress	Years	President	Senate D	R	Other[a]	House D	R	Other
85th	1957-1959	Eisenhower	49	47	—	233	200	—
86th[a]	1959-1961	Eisenhower	65	35	—	284	153	—
87th[a]	1961-1963	Kennedy	65	35	—	263	174	—
88th	1961-1963	Kennedy/Johnson	67	33	—	258	177	—
89th	1965-1967	Johnson	68	32	—	295	140	—
90th	1967-1969	Johnson	64	36	—	247	187	—
91st	1969-1971	Nixon	57	43	—	243	192	—
92d	1971-1973	Nixon	54	44	2	254	180	—
93d	1973-1975	Nixon/Ford	56	42	2	239	192	1
94th	1975-1977	Ford	60	37	2	291	144	—
95th	1977-1979	Carter	61	38	1	292	143	—
96th	1979-1981	Carter	58	41	1	276	157	—
97th	1981-1983	Reagan	46	53	1	243	192	—
98th	1983-1985	Reagan	45	55	—	267	168	—
99th	1985-1987	Reagan	47	53	—	252	183	—
100th	1987-1989	Reagan	55	45	—	258	177	—
101st	1989-1991	Bush	55	45	—	260	175	—
102d	1991-1993	Bush	57	43	—	268	166	1
103d	1993-1995	Clinton	56	44	—	258	176	1
104th	1995-1997	Clinton	47	53	—	204	230	1
105th	1997-1999	Clinton	45	55	—	207	227	1
106th	1999-2001	Clinton	45	55	—	211	223	1

☐ Republican control   ▨ Democratic control

Source: Encyclopedia of the United States Congress, ed. Donald C. Bacon, Roger H. Davidson, and Morton Keller (New York: Simon and Schuster, 1995), 1556–1558.

Note: Figures are for the beginning of the first session of each Congress and do not include vacancies, subsequent shifts, or changes in party affiliation.

[a] The House in the 86th and 87th Congress had 437 members because of an at-large representative given to both Alaska (January 3, 1959) and Hawaii (August 21, 1959) prior to redistricting in 1962.

Appendix B

Internships: Getting Experience on Capitol Hill

Capitol Hill is an excellent place to obtain first-hand experience with the U.S. government. With 540 lawmakers (representatives, senators, delegates, and resident commissioners); hundreds of committees and subcommittees; scores of informal caucuses; and three congressional support agencies (the Congressional Research Service, General Accounting Office, and Congressional Budget Office), intern opportunities abound for students interested in experiencing Congress and its members "up close and personal."

Undergraduates will find useful information about landing an internship on Capitol Hill in several sources. One of the best is published under the auspices of the American Political Science Association and is titled *Storming Washington: An Intern's Guide to National Government*. Political scientist Stephen E. Frantzich discusses how to get a good internship, make the most of the experience, and find a place to live in Washington, D.C.

From our own years of "soaking and poking" on Capitol Hill, we offer five observations about getting congressional experience. First, there is no central clearinghouse for internships. Every congressional office, committee, caucus, and support agency manages its own internship program. You must be persistent, patient, and determined to find a position that will be a rewarding learning experience. Not only should you determine what duties and functions will be assigned to you as a volunteer intern (it is sometimes possible to find paid internships), but you need to remember that you have something useful to offer. Most congressional offices and committees are understaffed and subject to high staff turnover. Although the market for interns is competitive, congressional lawmakers, committees, and staffers want and need your talent.

Second, develop some notion as to where you would like to intern. Do research on the committee, lawmaker, support agency, or caucus that you would like to intern with. Remember that every office has its own personality. Senate offices, for instance, are often large enterprises with many staff aides, while House offices generally are smaller. Interns thus will have more opportunities for personal, day-to-day contact with House members than with senators. The best way to determine the office environment is by interviewing people who have worked in a particular office, talking with intern coordinators at your college or university, or visiting the office yourself.

Third, target your own representative and senators. Many congressional members prefer interns from their own state or district who are likely to be familiar with the geography and concerns of that area. In addition, potential in-

terns probably will have family and friends who are constituents of the law-maker. Don't hesitate to use your contacts. You might also volunteer to work in a state or district office of the lawmaker. Before accepting an internship, consider your own views and ideals. If your views are conservative, working for a lawmaker who espouses liberal causes may be difficult. On the other hand, if you are tactful and open-minded, working for someone whose views differ from yours may be instructive. Because you are a student, an internship with someone who holds divergent ideological views probably will not be held against you later in landing a position.

Fourth, intern placement opportunities are plentiful. Many colleges and universities sponsor semester programs in Washington. Several schools, in-cluding the American University, Boston University, Hamilton College, the State University of New York, the University of Southern California, and sev-eral University of California campuses run programs in Washington; some ac-cept students from other accredited colleges and universities. The Washington Center for Internships and Academic Seminars, in existence since 1975, has placed thousands of students from hundreds of colleges.

Finally, Congress needs and welcomes the influx of new ideas and experi-ences that interns bring with them. The work at times may be drudgery—answering mail and telephones, entering information into computers, and run-ning errands—but the opportunity to learn about Congress and to pick up "po-litical smarts" not easily available from textbooks is nearly without equal. You may even want to keep a private journal of your experiences: what you have done and what you have learned. In sum, a volunteer job on Capitol Hill is likely to be rewarding intellectually and in other ways that are impossible to predict.

Resources

Frantzich, Stephen E. *Storming Washington: An Intern's Guide to National Government.* 4th ed. Washington, D.C.: American Political Science Association, 1994.

Internships in Congress. Annual survey of internships in lawmakers' offices. Available from the Graduate Group, P.O. Box 370351, West Hartford, CT 06137-0351. Tele-phone: (860) 233–2330.

Jimenez, Rita. *Internships and Fellowships: Congressional, Federal, and Other Work Experience Opportunities.* Congressional Research Service, Library of Congress. Report No. 98-654C. August 5, 1998. Provides extensive listings and bibliographies of internships.

Maxwell, Bruce. *Insider's Guide to Finding a Job in Washington: Contacts and Strategies to Build Your Career in Public Policy.* Washington, D.C.: CQ Press, 1999.

Oldman, Mark. *Student Advantage Guide to America's Top Internships, 1998.* New York: Random House, 1997.

Peterson's Internships. Princeton, N.J.: Peterson's Guides. Annual.

The Washington Center for Internships and Academic Seminars, 2000 M Street, N.W., Suite 750, Washington, D.C. 20036. Telephone: (202) 336-7600 or (800) 486-8921; Fax: (202) 336-7609; e-mail: info@twc.edu and Internet: http://www.twc.edu

Washington Information Directory. Washington, D.C.: Congressional Quarterly. Annual publication that provides information about governmental and nongovernmental groups as well as addresses and phone numbers for congressional offices and committees.

Notes

Chapter 1 (pages 3–10)

1. Dan Barry, "L.I. Widow's Story: Next Stop Washington," *New York Times*, Nov. 7, 1996, B1.
2. Robin Toner, "A Most Curious Kind of Democrat," *New York Times*, Oct. 12, 1996, 25.
3. Steven Greenhouse, "Labor Musters Infantry for Long Island Race," *New York Times*, Nov. 2, 1996, 30.
4. David M. Halbfinger, "McCarthy Is Re-elected by a Slim Margin," *New York Times*, Nov. 5, 1998, B14.
5. James Madison, *The Federalist*, No. 51, ed. Edward Mead Earle (New York: Modern Library, n.d.), 338.
6. Ibid., 343.
7. Sam Rayburn, *Speak, Mr. Speaker*, ed. H. G. Dulaney and Edward Hake Phillips (Bonham, Texas: Sam Rayburn Foundation, 1978), 263–264. Rayburn was Speaker from 1940 to 1947, 1949 to 1953, and 1955 to 1961.
8. Glenn R. Parker, *Homeward Bound: Explaining Campaign Changes in Congressional Behavior* (Pittsburgh: University of Pittsburgh Press, 1986), 18.
9. U.S. Congress, House Committee on Administrative Review, *Administrative Management and Legislative Management*, 2 vols., H. Doc. 95-232, 95th Cong., 1st sess. Sept. 28, 1977, 2:18–19.
10. Alan Abramowitz, "A Comparison of Voting for U.S. Senator and Representative in 1978," *American Political Science Review* 74 (September 1980): 633–640; Richard F. Fenno, Jr., *The United States Senate: A Bicameral Perspective* (Washington, D.C.: American Enterprise Institute, 1982), 29ff.
11. U.S. Congress, Joint Committee on the Organization of Congress, *Organization of the Congress, Final Report*, 2 vols., H. Rept. No. 103-14, 103d Cong., 1st sess., December 1993, 2:275–287. See Table 5-2 in this book.
12. Glenn R. Parker and Roger H. Davidson, "Why Do Americans Love Their Congressmen So Much More Than Their Congress?" *Legislative Studies Quarterly* 4 (February 1979): 53–61; Kelly D. Patterson and David B. Magleby, "Public Support for Congress," *Public Opinion Quarterly* 56 (winter 1992): 539–540; Randall B. Ripley et al., "Constituents' Evaluations of U.S. House Members," *American Politics Quarterly* 20 (October 1992): 442–456.
13. Edmund Burke, "Speech to Electors at Bristol," in *Burke's Politics*, ed. Ross J. S. Hoffman and Paul Levack (New York: Knopf, 1949), 116.
14. Ibid.
15. Quoted in *Roll Call*, Sept. 9, 1993, 16.
16. *U.S. Term Limits v. Thornton*, 115 S. Ct. 1842 (1995).
17. Quoted by Mark Carl Rom in "Why Not Assume that Public Officials Seek to Promote the Public Interest?" *Public Affairs Report* 37 (July 1996): 12.
18. Woodrow Wilson, *Congressional Government* (1885; reprint, Baltimore: Johns Hopkins University Press, 1981), 210.

19. Richard F. Fenno, Jr., *Home Style: House Members in Their Districts* (Boston: Little, Brown, 1978), 168.

Chapter 2 *(pages 13–39)*

1. Alvin M. Josephy, Jr., *On the Hill: A History of the American Congress* (New York: Simon and Schuster, 1908), 41–48.
2. Charles A. Beard and John P. Lewis, "Representative Government in Evolution," *American Political Science Review* (April 1932): 223–240.
3. Ibid.
4. Jock P. Green, ed., *Great Britain and the American Colonies, 1606–1763* (New York: Harper TorchBooks, 1970), xxxix.
5. Edmund C. Burnett, *Continental Congress* (New York: Norton, 1964).
6. *Congressional Quarterly's Guide to Congress*, 4th ed. (Washington, D.C.: Congressional Quarterly, 1991), 8.
7. Burnett, *Continental Congress*, 171.
8. Jack N. Rakove, *The Beginnings of National Politics: An Interpretive History of the Continental Congress* (New York: Knopf, 1979), 43.
9. Charles C. Thach, Jr., *The Creation of the Presidency, 1775–1789: A Study in Constitutional History* (Baltimore: Johns Hopkins University Press, 1969), 34.
10. James Sterling Young, "America's First Hundred Days," *Miller Center Journal* 1 (winter 1994): 57.
11. John Locke, *Two Tracts on Government*, ed. Philip Abrams (New York: Cambridge University Press, 1967), 374.
12. James Madison, *The Federalist*, No. 48, ed. Edward Mead Earle (New York: Modern Library, n.d.), 321.
13. Joseph Story, *Commentaries on the Constitution of the United States*, 5th ed. (Boston: Little, Brown, 1905), 1:396. For Jackson's comments, see *Youngstown Sheet and Tube Co. v. Sawyer*, 343 U.S. 579, 635 (1952).
14. *Nixon v. United States*, 506 U.S. 224 (1993).
15. See Sidney M. Milkis and Michael Nelson, *The American Presidency: Origins and Development, 1776–1998*, 3d ed. (Washington, D.C.: CQ Press, 1999), 34–36.
16. Alexander Hamilton, *The Federalist*, No. 65, 423–424.
17. Van Tassel, Emily Field, and Paul Finkelman, *Impeachable Offenses: A Documentary History from 1787 to the Present* (Washington, D.C.: Congressional Quarterly, 1999).
18. *Marbury v. Madison*, 1 Cranch 137 (1803).
19. *The Constitution of the United States of America: Analysis and Interpretation*, S. Doc. 92-80, 92d Cong., 2d sess., 1973, 1597–1619. Recent figures are courtesy of George Costello, Congressional Research Service.
20. William N. Eskridge, Jr., "Overriding Supreme Court Statutory Interpretation Decisions," *Yale Law Journal* 101 (November 1991): 331–455. See also R. Shep Melnick, *Between the Lines: Interpreting Welfare Rights* (Washington, D.C.: Brookings Institution, 1994).
21. Louis Fisher, *Constitutional Dialogues: Interpretation as Political Process* (Princeton: Princeton University Press, 1988), 275.
22. Quoted in Charles Warren, *The Making of the Constitution* (Boston: Little, Brown, 1928), 162.
23. Quoted in Charles Warren, *The Supreme Court in United States History* (Boston: Little, Brown, 1919), 195.
24. Lindsay Rogers, *The American Senate* (New York: Knopf, 1926).

25. Charles A. Kromkowski and John A. Kromkowski, "Why 435? A Question of Political Arithmetic," *Polity* 24 (fall 1991): 129–145; David C. Huckabee, *House of Representatives: Setting the Size at 435*, Congressional Research Service Report, No. 95-791GOV, July 11, 1995.

26. Alexander Hamilton, *The Federalist*, No. 27, 168.

27. Joe Martin, *My First Fifty Years in Politics*, as told to Robert J. Donovan (New York: McGraw-Hill, 1960), 49–50.

28. Sam Rayburn, *Speak, Mister Speaker*, ed. H. G. Dulaney and Edward Hake Phillips (Bonham, Texas: Sam Rayburn Foundation, 1978), 466.

29. Norman J. Ornstein, Thomas E. Mann, and Michael J. Malbin, *Vital Statistics on Congress, 1997–1998* (Washington, D.C.: CQ Press, 1998), 167.

30. Ibid., 160–163.

31. U.S. Congress, House Commission on Administrative Review, *Administrative Reorganization and Legislative Management*, 2 vols., H. Doc. 95-232, 95th Cong., 1st sess., Sept. 28, 1977, 2:17; Senate Commission on the Operation of the Senate, *Senators: Offices, Ethics, and Pressures*, 94th Cong., 2d sess., 1977, Committee Print, xi.

32. See Jefferson's Manual, Section XI; House, *Rules of the House of Representatives*, H. Doc. 103-342, 103d Cong., 2d sess., 1995, 143–146.

33. George B. Galloway, *History of the House of Representatives* (New York: Crowell, 1961), 67.

34. Barbara Sinclair, *Legislators, Leaders, and Lawmaking* (Baltimore: Johns Hopkins University Press, 1995), 75.

35. Neil MacNeil, *Forge of Democracy: The House of Representatives* (New York: McKay, 1963), 306.

36. Elaine K. Swift, *The Making of an American Senate* (Ann Arbor: University of Michigan Press, 1996), 5.

37. David C. King, *Turf Wars: How Congressional Committees Claim Jurisdiction* (Chicago: University of Chicago Press, 1997).

38. Noble Cunningham, Jr., ed., *Circular Letters of Congressmen, 1789–1839*, 3 vols. (Chapel Hill: University of North Carolina Press, 1978).

39. Quoted in Galloway, *History of the House*, 122.

40. Quoted in Anthony Champagne, "John Nance Garner," in *Masters of the House: Congressional Leaders over Two Centuries*, ed. Roger H. Davidson, Susan Webb Hammond, and Raymond W. Smock (Boulder: Westview Press, 1998), 148.

41. Martin, *My First Fifty Years*, 101.

42. James Sterling Young, *The Washington Community, 1800–1828* (New York: Harcourt Brace Jovanovich, 1966), 89.

43. Cunningham, *Circular Letters*, 57.

44. Roy Swanstrom, *The United States Senate, 1787–1801*, S. Doc. 99-19, 99th Cong., 1st sess., 1985, 80.

45. Nelson W. Polsby, "The Institutionalization of the House of Representatives," *American Political Science Review* 62 (March 1968): 146–147; Randall B. Ripley, *Power in the Senate* (New York: St. Martin's, 1969), 42–43.

46. Peter Swenson, "The Influence of Recruitment on the Structure of Power in the U.S. House, 1870–1940," *Legislative Studies Quarterly* 7 (February 1982): 7–36.

47. Woodrow Wilson, *Congressional Government* (1885; reprint, Baltimore: Johns Hopkins University Press, 1981).

48. Martin, *My First Fifty Years*, 49.

49. Ripley, *Power in the Senate*, 43–44.
50. David W. Brady, "After the Big Bang House Battles Focused on Committee Issues," *Public Affairs Report* 32 (March 1991): 8. See also Samuel Kernell, "Toward Understanding the Nineteenth Century Congressional Career Patterns: Ambition, Competition, and Rotation," *American Journal of Political Science* 21 (November 1977): 669–693; and Nelson W. Polsby, Miriam Gallagher, and Barry S. Rundquist, "The Growth of the Seniority System in the U.S. House of Representatives," *American Political Science Review* 63 (September 1969): 794.
51. Swanstrom, *United States Senate*, 283.
52. Young, *Washington Community*, 126–127.
53. Ornstein, Mann, and Malbin, *Vital Statistics on Congress*, 133.
54. On the development of congressional "platforms," see John B. Bader, *Taking the Initiative: Leadership Agendas in Congress and the "Contract with America"* (Washington, D.C.: Georgetown University Press, 1996).

Chapter 3 (pages 43–86)

1. *U.S. Term Limits v. Thornton*, 115 S. Ct. 1842 (1995). When a constitutional amendment limiting terms subsequently failed in the House, the U.S. Term Limits group spearheaded a series of state laws aimed at pressuring officeholders into supporting a cap of three terms (six years) for representatives, two terms (twelve years) for senators. As a result, Arkansas and eight other states passed referenda—dubbed scarlet letter provisions—requiring members of Congress who failed to support that version to be labeled on future ballots as having "disregarded voter instruction on term limits." The Arkansas Supreme Court struck down the referendum as an unauthorized means of amending the Constitution. In February 1997 the U.S. Supreme Court refused to hear an appeal, seemingly nullifying that stratagem. The case was *Arkansas Term Limits v. Donovan* (96-903), 1997. Again thwarted, USTL turned to the tactic of exacting term-limit pledges from candidates and shaming incumbents (some of whom were having second thoughts) into honoring their earlier pledges. See Francis X. Clines, "Keeping Politicians True to Their Inner Selves," *New York Times*, March 15, 1999, A12.
2. Quoted in David S. Broder, "Escape from the Term-Limits Trap," *Washington Post*, Feb. 19, 1997, A21. The authors of the *Federalist* discuss election qualifications and arrangements in detail. See Nos. 53, 56, 57, 58, 59, 60, and 61 of *The Federalist*, ed. Edward Mead Earle (New York: Modern Library, n.d.).
3. Amy Keller, "In Sign on Times, Negative Ads Score Big Success at 'Pollie' Awards," *Roll Call*, Jan. 23, 1997, 11.
4. Quoted in Judith Havemann, "Moynihan Poses Questions of Balance," *Washington Post*, Aug. 14, 1995, A15.
5. This method is only one of several mathematical formulas that could be employed. Another, the major fractions method, was used from 1911 until 1940. The methods yield slightly different results. For example, in 1992 Montana faced the prospect of losing its second House seat. The state challenged the apportionment formula in the courts but was rejected by the Supreme Court, which found no conclusive answer to the question of "what is the better measure of inequality." *Department of Commerce v. Montana*, 503 U.S. 442 (1992). See also Linda Greenhouse, "Supreme Court Upholds Method Used in Apportionment of House," *New York Times*, April 1, 1992, B8. The methods are examined in David C. Huckabee, *House Apportionment Following the 1990 Census: Using the Official Counts*, Congressional Research Service Report, No. 91-130, Feb. 4, 1991.

6. *Wisconsin v. City of New York,* 116 S. Ct. 1091 (1996).

7. *Growe v. Emison,* 507 U.S. 25 (1993). See Susan B. Glasser, "Supreme Court Voids Minnesota Redistricting," *Roll Call,* Feb. 25, 1993, 1.

8. Alan Ehrenhalt, "Redistricting and the Erosion of Community," *Governing,* June 1992, 10.

9. Dennis Farney, "Phil Burton Has Cut Many Political Deals: Is It One Too Many?" *Wall Street Journal,* Sept. 28, 1982, 1.

10. John W. Swain, Stephen A. Borelli, and Brian C. Reed, "Partisan Consequences of the Post-1990 Redistricting for the U.S. House," *Political Research Quarterly* 51 (December 1998): 945–967.

11. Bruce E. Cain and David Butler, "Redistricting Myths Are at Odds with Evidence," *Public Affairs Report* 32 (September 1991): 6. See also Cain, "Assessing the Partisan Effects of Redistricting," *American Political Science Review* 79 (June 1985): 320–333.

12. This discussion is drawn from Michael Lyons and Peter F. Galderisi, "Incumbency, Reapportionment, and U.S. House Districting," *Political Research Quarterly* 48 (December 1995): 857–871.

13. *Davis v. Bandemer,* 478 U.S. 109 (1986).

14. *Hunt v. Cromartie,* 526 U.S. ___ (May 17, 1999).

15. *Miller v. Ohio,* 117 S. Ct. 504 (1996).

16. Cain and Butler, "Redistricting Myths," 7.

17. *Thornburg v. Gingles,* 478 U.S. 30 (1986).

18. Paul Taylor, "GOP Will Aid Civil Rights Groups in Redistricting," *Washington Post,* April 1, 1990, A6; and Richard L. Berke, "Strategy Divides Top Republicans," *New York Times,* May 9, 1991, A17.

19. Quoted in Randall Smothers, "Two Strangely Shaped Hybrid Creatures Highlight North Carolina's Primary," *New York Times,* May 3, 1992, 28.

20. Lani Guinier, "What Color Is Your Gerrymander?" *Washington Post,* March 27, 1994, C3.

21. Abigail M. Thernstrom, "A Republican–Civil Rights Conspiracy," *Washington Post,* Sept. 23, 1991, A11. See also Thernstrom, *Whose Votes Count? Affirmative Action and Minority Voting Rights* (Cambridge: Harvard University Press, 1987).

22. *Shaw v. Reno,* 509 U.S. 630 (1993).

23. Ehrenhalt, "Redistricting," 10.

24. Carol M. Swain, "The Voting Rights Act: Some Unintended Consequences," *Brookings Review* 10 (winter 1992): 51. See also David Lublin, *The Paradox of Representation: Racial Gerrymandering and Minority Interests in Congress* (Princeton: Princeton University Press, 1997).

25. Charles S. Bullock, "Affirmative Action Districts: In Whose Faces Will They Blow Up?" *Campaigns and Elections* (April 1995): 22.

26. Ibid., 23.

27. Lublin, *Paradox of Representation.*

28. *Gomillion v. Lightfoot,* 364 U.S. 339 (1960).

29. *Shaw v. Reno.*

30. *Miller v. Johnson,* 115 S. Ct. 2475 (1995).

31. Quotations from Kevin Sack, "Victory of Five Redistricted Blacks Recasts Gerrymandering Dispute," *New York Times,* Nov. 23, 1996, 1.

32. Charles S. Bullock and Richard E. Dunn, "The Demise of Racial Redistricting and the Future of Black Representation" (paper presented at the annual meeting of the American Political Science Association, Washington, D.C., 1997), 28.

33. Sack, "Gerrymandering Dispute," 10. The figures were compiled by David A. Bositis of the Joint Center for Political and Economic Studies, Washington, D.C.

34. See David T. Canon, Matthew M. Schousen, and Patrick J. Sellers, "The Supply Side of Congressional Redistricting: Race and Strategic Politicians, 1972–1992," *Journal of Politics* 58 (August 1996): 846–861.

35. *DeWitt v. Wilson*, 515 U.S. (1995).

36. The decision was described by Linda Greenhouse in "Court Gives Wiggle Room to Racially Drawn Districts," *New York Times*, May 18, 1999, A12.

37. Quoted in Holly Idelson, "It's Back to Drawing Board on Minority Districts," *Congressional Quarterly Weekly Report*, Oct. 7, 1995, 3065–3067.

38. Everett C. Ladd, ed., *America at the Polls, 1998* (Storrs, Conn.: Roper Center, University of Connecticut, 1999), 12. Longitudinal figures are from David C. Huckabee, *Elections for House, Senate, and President, 1990–1994: Nationwide Vote Totals and Seats Won,* Congressional Research Service Report, No. 95-978GOV, Sept. 15, 1995, 4–7, 11–12.

39. Louis Sandy Maisel, *From Obscurity to Oblivion: Running in the Congressional Primary* (Knoxville: University of Tennessee Press, 1982), 34.

40. Alan Ehrenhalt, *The United States of Ambition* (New York: Random House, 1991), 17.

41. The four Capitol Hill campaign committees are the National Republican Senatorial Committee (NRSC), the Democratic Senatorial Campaign Committee (DSCC), the National Republican Congressional Committee (NRCC), and the Democratic Congressional Campaign Committee (DCCC). See Paul S. Herrnson, *Congressional Elections: Campaigning at Home and in Washington*, 2d ed. (Washington, D.C.: CQ Press, 1998), especially chaps. 4–5.

42. Edward Walsh, "To Every Campaign, There Is a Recruiting Season," *Washington Post*, Nov. 12, 1985, A1.

43. Quoted in Richard L. Berke, "Run for Congress? Parties Find Rising Stars Are Just Saying No," *New York Times*, March 15, 1998, 27.

44. Connie Bruck, "The Politics of Perception," *New Yorker,* Oct. 9, 1995, 61.

45. Quoted in ibid., 63.

46. Alice A. Love, "Small Business Group Helps Grow Its Own Grassroots Candidates at Meeting Next Week," *Roll Call*, Oct. 16, 1995, 22.

47. David T. Canon, *Actors, Athletes, and Astronauts: Political Amateurs in the United States Congress* (Chicago: University of Chicago Press, 1990), 2–3, 25–31.

48. Maisel, *From Obscurity to Oblivion,* 23.

49. Michael Janofsky, "Two Congressional Candidates Know They'll Lose, but It's Still Fun," *New York Times*, Oct. 31, 1992, 27.

50. The seminal work on strategic politician theory is Gary C. Jacobson and Samuel Kernell, *Strategy and Choice in Congressional Elections*, 2d ed. (New Haven: Yale University Press), 1983.

51. Gary C. Jacobson, *The Politics of Congressional Elections,* 4th ed. (New York: Longman, 1997), 20.

52. Gary C. Jacobson, "The Marginals Never Vanished: Incumbency and Competition in Elections to the U.S. House of Representatives, 1952–1982," *American Journal of Political Science* 31 (February 1987): 126–141.

53. Norman J. Ornstein, Thomas E. Mann, and Michael J. Malbin, *Vital Statistics on Congress, 1997–1998* (Washington, D.C.: Congressional Quarterly, 1998), 61–63.

54. Donald Gross and David Breaux, "Historical Trends in U.S. Senate Elections: 1912–1988," *American Politics Quarterly* 19 (July 1991): 284–309.

55. On the first view mentioned in this paragraph, see Morris P. Fiorina, *Congress: Keystone of the Washington Establishment,* 2d ed. (New Haven: Yale University Press, 1989); and Bruce Cain, John Ferejohn, and Morris Fiorina, *The Personal Vote: Constituency Service and Electoral Independence* (Cambridge: Harvard University Press, 1987), esp. chaps. 6–7. For more on the second view, see Glenn R. Parker and Roger H. Davidson, "Why Do Americans Love Their Congressmen So Much More Than Their Congress?" *Legislative Studies Quarterly* 4 (February 1979): 53–61. On the question of whether incumbents' resources are directly tied to votes, see John R. Johannes, *To Serve the People: Congress and Constituency Service* (Lincoln: University of Nebraska Press, 1984), esp. chap. 8.

56. Jacobson, *Politics of Congressional Elections,* 43. Italics in original.

57. Jacobson and Kernell, *Strategy and Choice,* chap. 3.

58. Gary C. Jacobson, "The 105th Congress: Unprecedented and Unsurprising," in *The Elections of 1996,* ed. Michael Nelson (Washington, D.C.: CQ Press, 1997), 154.

59. Rachel Van Dongen, "Ripken Helped Dems Break Streak," *Roll Call,* Nov. 19, 1998, 13.

60. Peverill Squire, "Challengers in U.S. Senate Elections," *Legislative Studies Quarterly* 14 (November 1989): 531–547.

61. Kenneth J. Cooper, "Riding High Name Recognition to Hill," *Washington Post,* Dec. 24, 1992, A4.

62. Linda L. Fowler and Robert D. McClure, *Political Ambition: Who Decides to Run for Congress* (New Haven: Yale University Press, 1989).

63. Quoted in Burt Solomon, "A Daunting Task: Running for House," *National Journal,* March 21, 1992, 712.

64. Maisel, *From Obscurity to Oblivion,* 23.

65. L. Sandy Maisel, Cary T. Gibson, and Elizabeth J. Ivry, "The Continuing Importance of the Rules of the Game: Subpresidential Nominations in 1994 and 1996," in *The Parties Respond,* 3d ed., ed. L. Sandy Maisel (Boulder: Westview Press, 1998), 148–151.

66. Tim Curran, "Hastert: An Effective Legislator Who Lacks Enemies," *Roll Call,* Dec. 21, 1998, 21.

67. Maisel, Gibson, and Ivry, "Subpresidential Nominations," 162–164.

68. Harvey L. Schantz, "Contested and Uncontested Primaries for the U.S. House," *Legislative Studies Quarterly* 5 (November 1980): 559. The linkage between interparty and intraparty competition is sometimes referred to as "Key's Law." See V. O. Key Jr., *Parties, Politics and Pressure Groups,* 5th ed. (New York: Crowell, 1964), 438, 447.

69. Austin Ranney, "Parties in State Politics," in *Politics in the American States,* ed. Herbert Jacob and Kenneth Vines (Boston: Little, Brown, 1976), 61–99.

70. Quoted in Guy Gugliotta, "In Some Early Contests, Party Elders Get No Respect from Voters," *Washington Post,* April 11, 1996, A12.

71. Herrnson, *Congressional Elections,* 128.

72. Unless otherwise indicated, 1997–1998 figures are from Federal Election Commission, "1998 Congressional Financial Activity Declines," press release, Dec. 29, 1998, and supporting tables. See also Ornstein, Mann, and Malbin, *Vital Statistics on Congress, 1997–1998,* 81–93.

73. Gary C. Jacobson, "Money in the 1980 and 1982 Congressional Elections," in *Money and Politics in the United States,* ed. Michael J. Malbin (Chatham, N.J.: Chatham House, 1984), 58.

74. Christopher Buchanan, "Candidates' Campaign Costs for Congressional Contests Have Gone Up at a Fast Pace," *Congressional Quarterly Weekly Report,* Sept. 29, 1979, 2154–2155.
75. Jacobson, "Money in the 1980 and 1982 Congressional Elections," 57.
76. Quoted in Andy Plattner, "The High Cost of Holding—and Keeping—Public Office," *U.S. News and World Report,* June 22, 1997, 30.
77. Federal Election Commission, "Political Party Fundraising Continues to Climb," press release, Jan. 26, 1999, 2. The U.S. Supreme Court has devalued the force of these restrictions by permitting unlimited independent expenditures by party organizations. See *Colorado Republican Federal Campaign Committee v. Federal Election Commission,* 116 S. Ct. 2039 (1996).
78. Federal Election Commission, "Political Party Fundraising."
79. A. B. Stoddard, "Linder to Ask Colleagues for $2M by Friday," *The Hill,* Aug. 5, 1998, 3.
80. Jacobson, "Money in the 1980 and 1982 Congressional Elections," 58–59.
81. Federal Election Commission, "1998 Congressional Financial Activity Declines."
82. Case studies of political action committees are found in Robert Biersack, Paul Herrnson, and Clyde Wilcox, *Risky Business? PAC Decisionmaking and Congressional Elections* (Armonk, N.Y.: M. E. Sharpe, 1994).
83. Quoted in Jonathan D. Salant and David S. Cloud, "To the '94 Election Victors Go the Fundraising Spoils," *Congressional Quarterly Weekly Report,* April 15, 1995, 1055.
84. Quoted in Jonathan D. Salant, "Business PACs Pick Their Cause," *Congressional Quarterly Weekly Report,* May 6, 1995, 1234.
85. Jim Vande Hei, "Home Builders, Pressured by GOP, Stay Out of N.Y.," *Roll Call,* Oct. 23, 1997, 1; and "Pressure Pays Off: Corporations Hear GOP Plea to Give Less to Democrats," *Roll Call,* Oct. 30, 1997, 11.
86. Quoted in Leslie Wayne, "Business Is Biggest Campaign Spender, Study Says," *New York Times,* Oct. 18, 1996, A1, A26.
87. Scott Turow, "The High Court's 20-Year-Old Mistake," *New York Times,* Oct. 12, 1997, E15.
88. E. J. Dionne, "Politics as Public Auction," *Washington Post,* June 19, 1998, A25.
89. Gary C. Jacobson, *Money in Congressional Elections* (New Haven: Yale University Press, 1980).
90. Quoted in Brooks Jackson, "Loopholes Allow Flood of Campaign Giving by Business, Fat Cats," *Wall Street Journal,* July 5, 1984, 1.
91. Eric Schmitt, "Diverse Groups Fight to Shape Financing Issue," *New York Times,* Oct. 19, 1997, 1.
92. Chuck Alston, "A Field Guide to Election Spending Limits," *Congressional Quarterly Weekly Report,* May 22, 1990, 1621–1626.

Chapter 4 (pages 89–125)

1. Stuart Rothenberg, "The Fabulous Five TV Spots of 1994: No Gimmicks Here," *Roll Call,* Dec. 1, 1994, 13.
2. Elizabeth Kolbert, "Campaign in California: Little but Commercials," *New York Times,* May 22, 1992, A1.
3. See Richard G. Niemi, Lynda W. Powell, and Patricia L. Bickell, "The Effects of Congruity between Community and District on Salience of U.S. House Candidates," *Legislative Studies Quarterly* 11 (May 1986): 187–201; and James E. Camp-

bell, John R. Alford, and Keith Henry, "Television Markets and Congressional Elections," *Legislative Studies Quarterly* 9 (November 1984): 665–678.

4. Robin Toner, "In a Cynical Election Season, the Ads Tell an Angry Tale," *New York Times,* Oct. 24, 1994, A1.

5. These examples are drawn from Stuart Rothenberg, "This Year's Early Ads: They're Not as Fluffy as They May Look," *Roll Call,* Jan. 30, 1997, 13; Richard L. Berke, "Candidates Find that Experience Isn't a Liability," *New York Times,* July 13, 1998, A12.

6. Michael Barone and Grant Ujifusa, *The Almanac of American Politics, 1996* (Washington, D.C.: National Journal, 1995), 517.

7. Quoted in *Campaigns and Elections,* December–January, 1999, 17.

8. R. W. Apple Jr., "Battle for Mitchell's Maine Seat Reveals Democrats' Senate Woes," *New York Times,* Sept. 5, 1994, 7.

9. Howard Kurtz, "On the Defensive, Republicans Go Their Own Way in Ads," *Washington Post,* Oct. 3, 1996, A10.

10. Numbers from EMILY's List Web site: www.emilyslist.org.

11. Thomas B. Edsall, "In Tight Races, Early Cash Means Staying Competitive," *Washington Post,* July 14, 1998, A6.

12. Robin Toner, "In Final Rounds, Both Sides Whip Out Bare-Knuckle Ads," *New York Times,* Oct. 21, 1996, B7.

13. Sara Fritz and Dwight Morris, *Gold-Plated Politics: Running for Congress in the 1990s* (Washington, D.C.: Congressional Quarterly, 1992), 28.

14. Figures on incumbents' and challengers' disbursements calculated from Federal Election Commission, "1998 Congressional Financial Activity Declines," news release, Dec. 29, 1998.

15. Gary C. Jacobson, *The Politics of Congressional Elections,* 4th ed. (New York: Longman, 1997), 77.

16. Gary C. Jacobson, "The Effects of Campaign Spending on Congressional Elections," *American Political Science Review* 72 (June 1978): 469–491.

17. Quoted in Herbert E. Alexander and Brian A. Haggarty, "Misinformation on Media Money," *Public Opinion* 11 (May–June 1988): 7.

18. Paul Houston, "TV and High Tech Send Campaign Costs Soaring," *Los Angeles Times,* Oct. 2, 1986, 121.

19. Jamie Stiehm, "Ben and Jerry's State Offers a Choice of Three Flavors," *The Hill,* Nov. 22, 1995, 26.

20. Glenn R. Simpson, "In Rhode Island, Everyone Goes to Bristol Parade," *Roll Call,* July 9, 1990, 1; Simpson, "Judging from July 4th Bristol Parade in R.I., Chafee Looks Well-Positioned for November," *Roll Call,* July 11, 1994, 21.

21. Richard E. Cohen, "Costly Campaigns: Candidates Learn that Reaching Voters Is Expensive," *National Journal,* April 16, 1983, 782–788.

22. Edie N. Goldberg and Michael W. Traugott, *Campaigning for Congress* (Washington, D.C.: CQ Press, 1984), 93.

23. Craig Karmin, "Campaign Funds Used for Private Expenses," *The Hill,* Sept. 6, 1995, 1.

24. See E. J. Dionne Jr., "Radical," *Washington Post Magazine,* Jan. 19, 1997, 8ff.

25. David T. Canon, "The Wisconsin Second Congressional District: History in the Making," in *The Battle for Congress,* ed. James A. Thurber (Washington, D.C.: Brookings Institution, 1999).

26. Goldenberg and Traugott, *Campaigning for Congress,* 23.

27. Richard F. Fenno Jr., *Home Style: House Members in Their Districts* (Boston: Little, Brown, 1978), 46.

28. Larry J. Sabato and Glenn R. Simpson, *Dirty Little Secrets: The Persistence of Corruption in American Politics* (New York: Times Books, 1996), 156.

29. Merle Miller, *Lyndon: An Oral Biography* (New York: Putnam, 1980), 120.

30. John Mercurio, "Kentucky Senate Race No Picnic," *Roll Call*, Aug. 6, 1998, 14.

31. Ron Faucheux, "Candidate Canvassing," *Campaigns and Elections*, May 1997, 43.

32. Neil MacFarquhar, "In New Jersey, Meeting the Voters Is a Luxury," *New York Times*, Nov. 1, 1996, A1.

33. These figures came from Competitive Media Reporting's "Ad Detector," which monitors all TV advertising in the top seventy-five markets. Cited in Amy Keller, "Shop Talk," *Roll Call*, Nov. 16, 1996, 15.

34. Peter Clarke and Susan H. Evans, *Covering Campaigns: Journalism in Congressional Elections* (Stanford: Stanford University Press, 1983).

35. "Media Mix," *Campaigns and Elections*, May 1998, 44.

36. Burdett A. Loomis, "The Kansas Third District: Pros from Dover Set Up Shop," in Thurber, *The Battle for Congress*.

37. Barone and Ujifusa, *Almanac*, 1445–1446.

38. Canon, "The Wisconsin Second."

39. Lynda L. Kaid and Dorothy K. Davidson, "Elements of Videostyle: Candidate Presentation through Television Advertising," in *New Perspectives on Political Advertising*, ed. L. L. Kaid, D. Nimmo, and K. R. Sanders (Carbondale: Southern Illinois University Press, 1986), 184–209. See also Dorothy Davidson Nesbit, *Videostyle in Senate Campaigns* (Knoxville: University of Tennessee Press, 1988).

40. Loomis, "The Kansas Third District."

41. Howard Kurtz, "Attack Ads Carpet TV; High Road Swept Away," *Washington Post*, Oct. 20, 1998, A1.

42. Kolbert, "Campaign in California," A1.

43. Stephen Ansolabehere and Shanto Iyengar, *Going Negative: How Attack Ads Shrink and Polarize the Electorate* (New York: Free Press, 1996), 128.

44. Charles E. Cook, "Christensen's Low Blow Holds a Lesson for Other Campaigns," *Roll Call*, May 18, 1998, 8.

45. Benjamin Sheffner, "Minn. Candidate Can't Be Charged for Misleading Ad," *Roll Call*, March 7, 1996, 13; John E. Yang, "Oregon Rep. Cooley Indicted for Lying about Military Service," *Washington Post*, Dec. 12, 1996, A3.

46. Norman J. Ornstein, "Should Liars Be Seated? It's Not Up to Congress," *Roll Call*, May 17, 1993, 12.

47. Richard W. Stevenson, "A Campaign to Build Influence," *New York Times*, Oct. 29, 1996, D1.

48. Thomas B. Edsall, "Issues Coalitions Take On Political Party Functions," *Washington Post*, Aug. 9, 1996, A1.

49. Michael Weisskopf, "Small Business Lobby Becomes a Big Player in Campaigns," *Washington Post*, Aug. 9, 1996, A1.

50. Ruth Marcus, "Political Ads Test the Limits," *Washington Post*, April 8, 1996, A4.

51. David S. Broder and Thomas E. Edsall, "Amid Election Apathy, Parties Bet on Core Voters," *Washington Post*, Sept. 7, 1998, A12.

52. Edsall, "Issues Coalitions," A1.

53. Leslie Wayne, "A Back Door for the Conservative Donor," *New York Times*, May 22, 1997, A24.

54. Raymond E. Wolfinger and Steven J. Rosenstone, *Who Votes?* (New Haven: Yale University Press, 1980), 18ff.

55. B. Drummond Ayres Jr., "Easier Voter Registration Doesn't Raise Participation," *New York Times,* Dec. 3, 1995, 22. Registration data from Committee for the Study of the American Electorate, news release, Nov. 6, 1998.

56. Lynn Ragsdale and Jerrold G. Rusk, "Who Are Nonvoters? Profiles from the 1990 Senate Elections," *American Journal of Political Science* 37 (August 1993): 721–746; Associated Press, "Many More Non-Voters in '96 Were 'Too Busy,'" *Washington Post,* Aug. 17, 1998, A4.

57. Wolfinger and Rosenstone, *Who Votes?* See also Steven J. Rosenstone and John Mark Hansen, *Mobilization, Participation, and Democracy* (New York: Macmillan, 1993); Ruy Teixeira, *The Disappearing Voter* (Washington, D.C.: Brookings Institution, 1992).

58. Sidney Verba, Kay Lehman Schlozman, and Henry E. Brady, *Voice and Equality. Civic Voluntarism in American Politics* (Cambridge: Harvard University Press, 1995).

59. M. Margaret Conway, "Political Participation in Mid-Term Congressional Elections," *American Politics Quarterly* 9 (April 1981): 221–244.

60. Milton C. Cummings Jr., *Congressmen and the Electorate* (New York: Free Press, 1966).

61. Charles O. Jones, "The Role of the Campaign in Congressional Politics," in *The Electoral Process,* ed. M. Kent Jennings and L. Harmon Zeigler (Englewood Cliffs, N.J.: Prentice-Hall, 1966), 21–41.

62. Everett Carll Ladd et al., *America at the Polls 1998* (Storrs, Conn.: Roper Center, 1999), 61.

63. Ibid., 69–73.

64. Warren E. Miller, Donald R. Kinder, Steven J. Rosenstone, and the National Election Studies, *American National Election Study, 1990. Post-Election Survey,* 2d ed (Ann Arbor, Mich.: Inter-University Consortium for Political and Social Research, January 1992), 193–194.

65. Gary C. Jacobson, *The Electoral Origins of Divided Government: Competition in U.S. House Elections, 1946–1988* (Boulder: Westview Press, 1990), 20.

66. Ibid., 10.

67. Martin P. Wattenberg, *The Rise of Candidate-Centered Politics* (Cambridge: Harvard University Press, 1991), 36–39.

68. Norman J. Ornstein, Thomas E. Mann, and Michael J. Malbin, *Vital Statistics on Congress, 1997–1998* (Washington, D.C.: Congressional Quarterly, 1998), 71; Rhodes Cook, "Actual District Votes Belie Ideal of Bipartisanship," *Congressional Quarterly Weekly Report,* April 12, 1997, 859–862.

69. Cook, "Ideal of Bipartisanship," 860.

70. Jacobson, *Politics of Congressional Elections,* 132–133.

71. Angus Campbell, "Surge and Decline: A Study of Electoral Change," in *Elections and the Political Order,* ed. Angus Campbell et al. (New York: Wiley, 1966), 40–62; and Raymond E. Wolfinger, Steven J. Rosenstone, and Richard A. McIntosh, "Presidential and Congressional Voters Compared," *American Politics Quarterly* 9 (April 1981): 245–255.

72. Eric M. Uslaner and Margaret Conway, "The Responsible Electorate: Watergate, the Economy, and Vote Choice in 1974," *American Political Science Review* 79 (September 1985): 788–803; and Samuel Kernell, "Presidential Popularity and Negative Voting: An Alternative Explanation of the Midterm Congressional De-

cline of the President's Party," *American Political Science Review* 71 (March 1977): 44–46.

73. Alan I. Abramowitz, "A Comparison of Voting for U.S. Senator and Representative in 1978," *American Political Science Review* 74 (September 1980): 633–650.

74. David S. Broder and Claudia Deane, "Poll: Clinton Critics More Likely to Vote," *Washington Post*, Sept. 30, 1998, A6.

75. Ceci Connolly and Howard Kurtz, "Gingrich Orchestrated Lewinsky Ads," *Washington Post*, Oct. 30, 1998, A18.

76. Thomas B. Edsall and Claudia Deane, "Poll Shows Democratic Gains with Key Voters," *Washington Post*, Nov. 4, 1998, A27.

77. Committee for the Study of the American Electorate, news release, Nov. 6, 1998, 2.

78. Edsall and Deane, "Poll Shows Democratic Gains."

79. David Brady, Brian Gaines, and Douglas Rivers, "The Incumbency Advantage in the House and Senate: A Comparative Institutional Analysis," Stanford University, August 1994, unpublished paper; Robert S. Erikson, "The Advantage of Incumbency in Congressional Elections," *Polity* 3 (spring 1971): 395–405; Robert S. Erikson, "Malapportionment, Gerrymandering, and Party Fortunes in Congressional Elections," *American Political Science Review* 66 (December 1972): 1234–1245.

80. Jacobson, *Electoral Origins of Divided Government,* 28–29.

81. Jacobson, *Politics of Congressional Elections,* 33.

82. Warren Lee Kostroski, "Party and Incumbency in Postwar Senate Elections: Trends, Patterns, and Models," *American Political Science Review* 67 (December 1974): 1233.

83. Mark C. Westlye, "Competitiveness of Senate Seats and Voting Behavior in Senate Elections," *American Journal of Political Science* 27 (May 1983): 253–283.

84. Thomas E. Mann and Raymond E. Wolfinger, "Candidates and Parties in Congressional Elections," *American Political Science Review* 74 (September 1980): 623; Alan I. Abramowitz, "Name Familiarity, Reputation, and the Incumbency Effect in a Congressional Election," *Western Political Quarterly* 28 (December 1975): 668–684; Abramowitz, "Comparison of Voting," 633–650; and Thomas E. Mann, *Unsafe at Any Margin: Interpreting Congressional Elections* (Washington, D.C.: American Enterprise Institute, 1978).

85. David R. Mayhew, *Congress: The Electoral Connection* (New Haven: Yale University Press, 1974).

86. Michael J. Robinson, "Three Faces of Congressional Media," in *The New Congress,* ed. Thomas E. Mann and Norman J. Ornstein (Washington, D.C.: American Enterprise Institute, 1981), 91.

87. Gary C. Jacobson, "Incumbents' Advantages in the 1978 U.S. Congressional Elections," *Legislative Studies Quarterly* 6 (May 1981): 198.

88. Mann, *Unsafe at Any Margin.*

89. Donald E. Stokes and Warren E. Miller, "Party Government and the Saliency of Congress," *Public Opinion Quarterly* 26 (winter 1962): 531–546.

90. Patricia A. Hurley and Kim Quaile Hill, "The Prospects for Issue Voting in Contemporary Congressional Elections," *American Politics Quarterly* 8 (October 1980): 425–448; Lynda W. Powell, "Analyzing Misinformation: Perceptions of Congressional Candidates' Ideologies," *American Journal of Political Science* 33 (May 1989): 272–293.

91. Miller et al., *American National Election Study, 1990,* 126–129, 171.

92. Abramowitz, "Comparison of Voting," 635.

93. Gerald C. Wright Jr. and Michael B. Berkman, "Candidates and Policy in United States Senate Elections," *American Political Science Review* 80 (June 1986): 567–588.

94. John B. Bader, *Taking the Initiative: Leadership Agendas in Congress and the "Contract with America"* (Washington, D.C.: Georgetown University Press, 1996).

95. These quotes are from James G. Gimpel, *Fulfilling the Contract: The First 100 Days* (Boston: Allyn and Bacon, 1996), 28. Gimpel presents a balanced insider's view of the origin, development, and effects of the Contract with America.

96. Quoted in Judy Newman, "Do Women Vote for Women?" *Public Perspective* 7 (February–March 1996): 10.

97. See Felicia Pratto, Stanford University, and Jim Sidanius, UCLA, e-mail news release, Dec. 2, 1996.

98. Barbara Vobejda, "Fragmentation of Society Formidable Challenge to Candidates, Report Says," *Washington Post,* March 7, 1996, A15.

99. Fenno, *Home Style.*

100. Mann and Wolfinger, "Candidates and Parties," 630.

101. Figures are from Everett Ladd et al., *America at the Polls, 1998,* 14–18.

102. David W. Brady, "Electoral Realignments in the U.S. House of Representatives," in *Congress and Policy Change,* ed. Gerald C. Wright Jr., Leroy N. Reiselbach, and Lawrence C. Dodd (New York: Agathon Press, 1986), 46–69.

103. Stephen Earl Bennet and Linda L. M. Bennet, "Out of Sight, Out of Mind: Americans' Knowledge of Party Control of the House of Representatives, 1960–1984," *Political Research Quarterly* 46 (March 1993): 67ff.

104. Citizen's responses to interviewers' questions about divided government depend on the wording of the questions and on current election results—a fact that underscores the impression that such views lack salience and stability. Survey results are summarized in "Two Cheers: United Government," *American Enterprise,* January–February 1993, 107–108. The 1996 results are reported in Helen Dewar, "Balance of Power Appeals to Many Voters," *Washington Post,* Oct. 27, 1996, A1.

105. Gary C. Jacobson, "Meager Patrimony: The Reagan Era and Republican Representation in Congress," in *Looking Back on the Reagan Presidency,* ed. Larry Berman (Baltimore: Johns Hopkins University Press, 1990), 288–316; and Jacobson, *Electoral Origins of Divided Government,* 105ff.

106. Warren E. Miller and Donald E. Stokes, "Constituency Influence in Congress," *American Political Science Review* 57 (March 1963): 45–57.

107. John L. Sullivan and Robert E. O'Connor, "Electoral Choice and Popular Control of Public Policy: The Case of the 1966 House Elections," *American Political Science Review* 66 (December 1972): 1256–1268.

108. Mann and Wolfinger, "Candidates and Parties," 629.

Chapter 5 (pages 127–160)

1. Catherine Eisele, "Rep. Strickland Consoles Flood-Ravaged Victims," *The Hill,* April 2, 1997, 1.

2. Richard F. Fenno Jr., *The Making of a Senator: Dan Quayle* (Washington, D.C.: CQ Press, 1989), 119.

3. Michael M. Lazerow, "Millionaires Now 14 Percent of House," *Roll Call,* July 10, 1995, 3; Rachel Van Dongen and John Mercurio, "40% of the Senate Looks Like a Million Bucks," *Roll Call,* June 16, 1997, 3.

4. Commission on Executive, Legislative and Judicial Salaries, *Fairness for Our Public Servants* (Washington, D.C.: U.S. Government Printing Office, 1988), 23.

5. Data on characteristics of the 106th Congress are found in Mildred L. Amer, *Membership of the 106th Congress: A Profile,* Congressional Research Service Report, No. RS20013, Jan. 7, 1999.

6. Joseph Schlesinger, "Lawyers and American Politics: A Clarified View," *Midwest Journal of Political Science* 1 (May 1957): 26–39; and Allen G. Bogue et al., "Members of the House of Representatives and the Processes of Modernization, 1789–1960," *Journal of American History* 63 (September 1976): 284.

7. George Gallup, Jr., "Religion in America," *Public Perspective,* October–November 1995, 4–5.

8. The pioneering study of this subject is Irwin N. Gertzog, *Congressional Women: Their Recruitment, Treatment, and Behavior* (New York: Praeger, 1984). Two more recent studies are Barbara C. Burrell, *A Women's Place Is in the House* (Ann Arbor: University of Michigan Press, 1994); and Richard Logan Fox, *Gender Dynamics in Congressional Elections* (Thousand Oaks, Calif.: Sage Publications, 1997).

9. Betsy Rothstein, "Congresswomen Press Women's Health Issues," *The Hill,* Feb. 24, 1999, 19; Maureen Dowd, "Growing Sorority in Congress Edges into the Ol' Boys' Club," *New York Times,* March 5, 1993, A1, A18.

10. Jamie Stiehm, "In Senate, Sisterhood Can Override Party," *The Hill,* Nov. 22, 1995, 16.

11. Quoted in Erika Niedowski, "Four Walk Out of the Closet and Toward the House," *Congressional Quarterly Weekly Report,* April 25, 1998, 1051.

12. Amer, *Membership of the 106th Congress,* 1.

13. Charles S. Bullock and Burdett A. Loomis, "The Changing Congressional Career," in *Congress Reconsidered,* 3d ed., ed. Lawrence C. Dodd and Bruce I. Oppenheimer (Washington, D.C.: CQ Press, 1985), 66–69, 80–82.

14. Quoted in: Adam Clymer, "G.O.P. Revolution Hits Speed Bumps on Capitol Hill," *New York Times,* Jan. 21, 1996, 14.

15. Quoted in Lizette Alvarez, "Lawmaker Hedging on Term Limit Vow," *New York Times,* Feb. 22, 1998, 16.

16. Hannah Finichel Pitkin, *The Concept of Representation* (Berkeley: University of California Press, 1967), 166.

17. Susan Welch and John R. Hibbing, "Hispanic Representation in the U.S. Congress," *Social Science Quarterly* 64 (June 1984): 328–335; Charles Tien and Deny Levy, "Asian-American and Hispanic Representation in the U.S. House of Representatives" (paper presented at the Midwest Political Science Association, 1998).

18. L. Marvin Overby and Kenneth Cosgrove, cited in Carol Swain, "The Future of Black Representation," *American Prospect* 23 (fall 1995): 81.

19. Roger H. Davidson, *The Role of the Congressman* (Indianapolis: Bobbs-Merrill, 1969), 199.

20. Arturo Vega and Juanita Firestone, "The Effects of Gender on Congressional Behavior and the Substantive Representation of Women," *Legislative Studies Quarterly* 20 (May 1995): 213–222.

21. Quoted in: Adam Nagourney, "Upbeat Schumer Battles Polls, Turnouts and His Image," *New York Times,* May 16, 1998, A14.

22. Frank E. Smith, *Congressman from Mississippi* (New York: Pantheon, 1964), 129–130.

23. Donald R. Matthews, *U.S. Senators and Their World* (Chapel Hill: University of North Carolina Press, 1960), chap. 5; and Ross K. Baker, *House and Senate,* 2d ed. (New York: Norton, 1995), chap. 2.

24. Herbert B. Asher, "The Learning of Legislative Norms," *American Political Science Review* 67 (June 1973): 499–513.

25. Eric M. Uslaner, *The Decline of Comity in Congress* (Ann Arbor: University of Michigan Press, 1993), 5.

26. Thomas E. Cavanagh, "The Two Arenas of Congress," in *The House at Work*, ed. Joseph Cooper and G. Calvin Mackenzie (Austin: University of Texas Press, 1981), 65.

27. Quoted in *New York Times*, Aug. 14, 1980, B9.

28. Damon Chappie, "The New Look of Pork in the 104th," *Roll Call*, Jan. 22, 1996, B19.

29. Quoted in Louis Jacobson, "For Arkansas, No Abundance of Clout," *National Journal*, Feb. 20, 1999, 475.

30. James S. Fleming, "The House Member as Teacher: An Analysis of the Newsletters of Barber B. Conable, Jr.," *Congress and the Presidency* 20 (spring 1993): 53–74.

31. Smith, *Congressman from Mississippi*, 127. See also David Mayhew, *Congress: The Electoral Connection* (New Haven: Yale University Press, 1974).

32. Davidson, *Role of the Congressman*, 98; Senate Commission on the Operation of the Senate, *Toward a Modern Senate*, S. Doc. 94-278, 94th Cong., 2d sess., 1977 committee print, 27; and House Commission on Administrative Review, *Final Report*, 2 vols., H. Doc. 95-272, 95th Cong., 1st sess., Dec. 31, 1977, 2:874–875.

33. Joint Committee on the Organization of Congress, *Organization of Congress, Final Report*, H. Rept. 103-413, 103d Congress, 1st sess., December 1993, 2:231–232.

34. Ross A. Webber, "U.S. Senators: See How They Run," *Wharton Magazine* (winter 1980–1981): 38.

35. Senate Commission on the Operation of the Senate, *Toward a Modern Senate*.

36. Quoted in Lindsay Sobel, "Former Lawmakers Find Trade Association Gold," *The Hill*, Nov. 26, 1997, 14.

37. Webber, "U.S. Senators," 37.

38. Center for Responsive Politics, *Congressional Operations: Congress Speaks—A Survey of the 100th Congress* (Washington, D.C.: Center for Responsive Politics, 1988), 47–49.

39. Quoted in *Washington Post*, Oct. 18, 1994, B3.

40. Center for Responsive Politics, *Congressional Operations*, 62–64.

41. Joint Committee, *Organization of Congress*, 2: 281–287.

42. Quoted in Vernon Louviere, "For Retiring Congressmen, Enough Is Enough," *Nation's Business*, May 1980, 32.

43. John R. Hibbing, *Congressional Careers: Contours of Life in the U.S. House of Representatives* (Chapel Hill: University of North Carolina Press, 1991), 117 (italics in original).

44. Ibid., 126, 128.

45. William H. Riker, *The Theory of Political Coalitions* (New Haven: Yale University Press, 1962), 24–38.

46. Pitkin, *The Concept of Representation*, 166.

47. Davidson, *Role of the Congressman*, 80.

48. Ross J. S. Hoffman and Paul Levack, eds., *Burke's Politics* (New York: Knopf, 1949), 114–116.

49. Henry J. Hyde, "Advice to Freshmen: 'There Are Things Worth Losing For,'" *Roll Call*, Dec. 3, 1990, 5.

50. Quoted in Jamie Stiehm, "Ex-Rep Mike Synar, Who Fought Lobbyists, Succumbs to Brain Tumor," *The Hill,* Jan. 10, 1996, 5.
51. Cited in Richard Morin, "Unconventional Wisdom," *Washington Post,* Feb. 29, 1999, B5.
52. Jim McGee, "D'Amato's Pothole Politics and Paper Trails," *Washington Post,* April 22, 1990, A1, A16.
53. Clifford D. May, "Image of a Senator: D'Amato Ties to Local Interests," *New York Times,* May 11, 1988, B5.
54. Thomas E. Cavanagh, "The Calculus of Representation: A Congressional Perspective," *Western Political Quarterly* 35 (March 1982): 120–129.
55. John W. Kingdon, *Congressmen's Voting Decisions,* 3d ed. (Ann Arbor: University of Michigan Press, 1989), 47–54.
56. Lawrence N. Hansen, *Our Turn: Politicians Talk about Themselves, Politics, the Public, the Press, and Reform,* pt. 2 (Washington, D.C.: Centel Public Accountability Project, 1992), 9.
57. Richard F. Fenno Jr., *Home Style: House Members in Their Districts* (Boston: Little, Brown, 1978), 1.
58. David C. Huckabee, *Districts of the 103d Congress: Income Data and Rankings,* Congressional Research Service Report, No. 93-285GOV, March 1, 1993.
59. Authors' calculations from Huckabee, *Districts of the 103d Congress,* 14–32.
60. Rebecca Carr, "GOP's Election Year Worries Cooled Partisan Rancor," *Congressional Quarterly Weekly Report,* Dec. 21, 1995, 3432–3435.
61. Fenno, *Home Style,* 4–8.
62. John F. Bibby and Thomas M. Holbrook, "Parties and Elections," in *Politics in the American States,* ed. Virginia Gray and Herbert Jacob (Washington, D.C.: CQ Press, 1996), 109.
63. Albert D. Cover and David R. Mayhew, "Congressional Dynamics and the Decline of Competitive Congressional Elections," in *Congress Reconsidered,* 3d ed., 62–82.
64. James L. Payne, "The Personal Electoral Advantage of House Incumbents, 1936–1976," *American Politics Quarterly* 8 (October 1980): 465–482; Robert S. Erikson, "Is There Such a Thing as a Safe Seat?" *Polity* 8 (summer 1976): 623–632.
65. Thomas E. Mann, *Unsafe at Any Margin: Interpreting Congressional Elections* (Washington, D.C.: American Enterprise Institute, 1978).
66. Fenno, *Home Style,* 8–27.
67. Thomas P. O'Neill Jr., with William Novak, *Man of the House* (New York: St. Martin's, 1987), 25.
68. Robert Schlesinger, "Free Pass to Reelection Presents Incumbents with Dilemma: How to Energize their Troops," *The Hill,* March 18, 1998, 27.
69. Richard F. Fenno Jr., *Senators on the Campaign Trail* (Norman: University of Oklahoma Press, 1996), 131–132.
70. Fenno, *Home Style,* 24–25.
71. Fenno, *Senators on the Campaign Trail,* 189.
72. Fenno, *Home Style,* 153.
73. Ibid., 56.
74. Anthony Champagne, *Congressman Sam Rayburn* (New Brunswick, N.J.: Rutgers University Press, 1984), 28.
75. Kingdon, *Congressmen's Voting Decisions.*
76. Fenno, *Home Style,* 153.

77. Rhodes Cook, "The Safe and the Vulnerable: A Look Behind the Numbers," *Congressional Quarterly Weekly Report,* Jan. 9, 1982, 35–38.
78. Quoted in Lloyd Grove, "For Bill Cohen, a Midlife Correction," *Washington Post,* Jan. 26, 1996, F2.
79. Susan B. Glasser, "Introducing the Class of 1994," *Roll Call,* Nov. 14, 1995, B1.
80. E. Michael Myers, "Millions of Miles from Home," *The Hill,* June 14, 1995, 8.
81. Fenno, *Home Style,* 36, 209; and ibid.
82. Hibbing, *Congressional Careers,* 139.
83. Quoted in Jim Wright, *You and Your Congressman* (New York: Coward-McCann, 1965), 35.
84. John R. Johannes, *To Serve the People: Congress and Constituency Service* (Lincoln: University of Nebraska Press, 1984), chap. 5.
85. Richard E. Cohen, "Assertive Freshmen," *National Journal,* May 2, 1987, 1061.
86. Graeme Browning, "Return to Sender," *National Journal,* April 1, 1995, 794.
87. Johannes, *To Serve the People,* 34–36.
88. House Commission on Administrative Review, *Final Report,* 1:655; and Janet Breslin, "Constituent Service," in *Senators: Offices, Ethics, and Pressures,* in Senate Commission on the Operation of the Senate, 94th Cong., 2d sess., 1977 committee print, 21.
89. Warren E. Miller, Donald R. Kinder, Steven J. Rosenstone, and the National Election Studies, *American National Election Study, 1990: Post-Election Survey,* 2d ed. (Ann Arbor, Mich.: Inter University Consortium for Political and Social Research, January 1992), 166–170.
90. Morris P. Fiorina, *Congress: Keystone of the Washington Establishment,* 2d ed. (New Haven: Yale University Press, 1989), 45; and Miller et al., *Post-Election Survey,* 171.
91. George Serra and David Moon, "Casework, Issue Positions, and Voting in Congressional Elections: A District Analysis," *Journal of Politics* 56 (February 1994). 211.
92. Paul E. Dwyer, *Salaries and Allowances: The Congress,* Congressional Research Service Report, No. RL30014, Feb. 16, 1999. See also Congressional Management Foundation, *1997 Senate Staff Employment* (Washington, D.C.: CFM, 1997), 70–71; and Congressional Management Foundation, *1998 House Staff Employment Study* (Washington, D.C.: CFM, 1998), 48–49.
93. Congressional Management Foundation, *Senate Staff Employment,* 88–89; CFM, *House Staff Employment,* 64–65.
94. Congressional Management Foundation, *Setting Course: A Congressional Management Guide* (Washington: CFM, 1996), 336; Congressional Management Foundation, *Senate Staff Employment,* 38–39; and Congressional Management Foundation, *House Employment,* 34–35.
95. Charles R. Babcock, "Frankly, an Election-Year Avalanche," *Washington Post,* Sept. 19, 1988, A19.
96. John S. Pontius, *Congressional Mail: History of the Franking Privilege and Options for Change,* Congressional Research Service Report, No. 96-101, March 11, 1997, 2.
97. U.S. Congress, *Congressional Record,* daily ed., 97th Cong., 2d sess., Dec. 20, 1982, S15806–8.
98. John S. Pontius, *Official Congressional Mail Costs,* Congressional Research Service Report, No. 97-36GOV, Dec. 26, 1996, 2. See remarks of Rep. Vic Fazio, D-Calif., in U.S. Congress, *Congressional Record,* daily ed., 103d Cong., 2d sess., May 26, 1994, H4112.
99. Quoted in Burnham, "Congress's Computer Subsidy," 98.

100. Editor and Publisher, *International Yearbook 1995*; *Broadcasting and Cable Yearbook 1995* (New Providence, N.J.: R. R. Bowker, 1995), xxi.

101. Charles Bosley, "Senate Communications with the Public," in U.S. Senate, Commission on the Operation of the Senate, *Senate Communications with the Public*, 94th Cong., 2d sess., 1977, 17.

102. For descriptions of the studios, see Michael J. Robinson, "Three Faces of Congressional Media," in *The New Congress*, ed. Thomas E. Mann and Norman J. Ornstein (Washington, D.C.: American Enterprise Institute, 1981), 62–63; and Martin Tolchin, "TV Studio Serves Congress," *New York Times*, March 7, 1984, C22.

103. Jeffrey L. Katz, "Studios Beam Members from Hill to Hometown," *Congressional Quarterly Weekly Report*, Nov. 29, 1997, 2946.

104. Marcia Gelbert, "Call-in Show: Hoosiers 'Bark at Mark,'" *The Hill*, Feb. 1, 1995, 41.

105. Tolchin, "TV Studio Serves Congress."

106. Robinson, "Three Faces of Congressional Media," 80–81.

107. John F. Bibby and Roger H. Davidson, *On Capitol Hill: Studies in the Legislative Process*, 2d ed. (Hinsdale, Ill.: Dryden Press, 1972), 72.

108. Peter Clarke and Susan H. Evans, *Covering Campaigns: Journalism in Congressional Elections* (Stanford, Calif.: Stanford University Press, 1983). See also Charles M. Tidmarch and Brad S. Karp, "The Missing Beat: Press Coverage of Congressional Elections in Eight Metropolitan Areas," in *Congress and the Presidency* 10 (spring 1983): 47–61.

109. Robinson, "Three Faces of Congressional Media," 84.

110. Katz, "Studios Beam Members."

111. Cokie Roberts, "Leadership and the Media in the 101st Congress," in *Leading Congress: New Styles, New Strategies*, ed. John J. Kornacki (Washington, D.C.: CQ Press, 1990), 94.

112. Katz, "Studios Beam Members."

113. Fenno, *Home Style*, 99.

Chapter 6 (pages 163–195)

1. A. B. Stoddard, "Rejuvenated Gingrich Mounts Media Offensive," *The Hill*, July 10, 1996, 24.

2. Guy Gugliotta and Juliet Eilperin, "Gingrich Steps Down as Speaker in Face of House GOP Rebellion," *Washington Post*, Nov. 7, 1998, A1.

3. Larry Flynt, the publisher of *Hustler* magazine, placed an ad in the *Washington Post* in October 1998 offering $1 million to anyone who could document an affair with a member of Congress. See Steve Proffitt, "Interview: Larry Flynt," *Los Angeles Times*, Dec. 27, 1998, M3.

4. See, for example, Dan Carney, Karen Foerstel, and Andrew Taylor, "A New Start for the House," *CQ Weekly*, Dec. 22, 1998, 3333–3335; Edward Walsh and Eric Pianin, "Shadows from Livingston's Past Fall across Impeachment Debate," *Washington Post*, Dec. 18, 1998, A1; and Nancy Roman, "House Shellshocked as Livingston Resigns," *Washington Times*, Dec. 20, 1998, A1.

5. See, for example, Bob Gravely and Lori Nitschke, "Shell-Shocked GOP Settles on Hastert as a Source of Calm," *CQ Monitor*, Dec. 21, 1998, 3; Ceci Connolly, "Plain-Talking Hastert Poised to Be Speaker," *Washington Post*, Dec. 21, 1998, A1; and Art Pine, "It's Official: GOP Picks Hastert as New Speaker," *Los Angeles Times*, Jan. 6, 1999, A10.

6. Juliet Eilperin, "Speaker-to-Be Hastert Vows Civility and Unity for House," *Washington Post*, Jan. 6, 1999, A8.

7. *Wall Street Journal*, Jan. 30, 1985, 56.

8. Leslie Wayne, "The Speaker: Gingrich's Midas Touch to Be Missed," *New York Times*, Nov. 19, 1998, A26.

9. National Journal's *Congress Daily/PM*, Jan. 13, 1999, 2.

10. Douglass B. Harris, "The Rise of the Public Speakership," *Political Science Quarterly* (summer 1998): 193–212.

11. Ceci Connolly and Juliet Eilperin, "Hastert Steps Up to Leading Role," *Washington Post*, Jan. 5, 1999, A4.

12. See Graeme Browning, "The Steward," *National Journal*, Aug. 5, 1995, 2004–2007.

13. *U.S. News and World Report*, Oct. 13, 1950, 30.

14. Joe Martin, *My First Fifty Years in Politics* (New York: McGraw-Hill, 1960), 181.

15. Gary Cox and Mathew McCubbins, *Legislative Leviathan: Party Government in the House* (Berkeley: University of California Press, 1993), 58.

16. The descriptive subheadings on O'Neill, Wright, Foley, and Gingrich are from Matt Pinkus, *How Congress Works*, 3d ed. (Washington, D.C.: Congressional Quarterly, 1998).

17. See, for example, Barbara Sinclair, *Majority Leadership in the U.S. House* (Baltimore: Johns Hopkins University Press, 1983).

18. John M. Barry, *The Ambition and the Power: The Fall of Jim Wright* (New York: Viking Penguin, 1989), 4.

19. Tom Kenworthy, "House GOP Signals It's in a Fighting Mood," *Washington Post*, Dec. 26, 1988, A8.

20. Barry, *The Ambition and the Power*, 6.

21. Newt Gingrich, *Lessons Learned the Hard Way* (New York: HarperCollins, 1998), 37.

22. David Rogers, "Gingrich's New Style as Speaker Has a Few Hitches," *Wall Street Journal*, June 2, 1997, A24.

23. Peter King, "Why I Oppose Newt," *Weekly Standard*, March 31, 1997, 23.

24. See, for example, Ceci Connolly, David Broder, and Dan Balz, "GOP's House Divided," *Washington Post*, July 28, 1997, A1; Sandy Hume, "Gingrich Foils Coup by Deputies," *The Hill*, July 16, 1997, 1; and Jackie Koszczuk, "Party Stalwarts Will Determine Gingrich's Long-Term Survival," *Congressional Quarterly Weekly Report*, July 26, 1997, 1751–1755.

25. See Robert Pear, Pam Belluck, and Lizette Alvarez, "Humble Man at the Helm: John Dennis Hastert," *New York Times*, Jan. 7, 1999, A20.

26. Jim VandeHei, "Hastert Takes Gavel, Promises Cooperation," *Roll Call*, Jan. 7, 1999, 22.

27. *CQ Daily Monitor* May 6, 1999, 1.

28. Joseph Cooper and David W. Brady, "Institutional Context and Leadership Style: The House from Cannon to Rayburn," in *Understanding Congressional Leadership*, ed. Frank H. Mackaman (Washington, D.C.: CQ Press, 1981).

29. *CQ Monitor*, Jan. 21, 1999, 8.

30. Floyd M. Riddick, *Congressional Procedure* (Boston: Chapman and Grimes, 1941), 345–346.

31. *CQ Monitor*, Jan. 8, 1999, 4.

32. *Roll Call*, Jan. 7, 1999, 3.

33. National Journal's *CongressDaily/PM*, May 15, 1998, 4.

34. Jim VandeHei, "King of the Hill?" *Roll Call*, Nov. 23, 1998, 18.

35. Eric Planin, "GOP Whip's Skill Counted for Survival," *Washington Post,* Nov. 10, 1998, A1.
36. Kevin Merida, "Bonior Barks at the Capitol's New Masters," *Washington Post,* Jan. 9, 1995, A4; Lloyd Grove, "The Whip Lashes Out," *Washington Post,* Dec. 26, 1995, C1.
37. Woodrow Wilson, *Congressional Government* (Boston: Houghton Mifflin, 1885), 223.
38. David J. Rothman, *Politics and Power: The United States Senate, 1869–1901* (Cambridge: Harvard University Press, 1966), 5–7.
39. Margaret Munk, "Origin and Development of the Party Floor Leadership in the United States Senate," *Capital Studies* 2 (winter 1974): 23–41; and Richard A. Baker and Roger H. Davidson, eds., *First among Equals: Outstanding Senate Leaders of the Twentieth Century* (Washington, D.C.: Congressional Quarterly, 1991).
40. James T. Patterson, *Mr. Republican: A Biography of Robert A. Taft* (Boston: Houghton Mifflin, 1972), 593.
41. Robert L. Peabody, *Leadership in Congress* (Boston: Little, Brown, 1976), 323.
42. Rowland Evans and Robert Novak, *Lyndon B. Johnson: The Exercise of Power* (New York: New American Library, 1966), 104.
43. See John G. Stewart, "Two Strategies of Leadership: Johnson and Mansfield," in *Congressional Behavior,* ed. Nelson W. Polsby (New York: Random House, 1971), 61–92; William S. White, *Citadel: The Story of the United States Senate* (New York: Harper and Bros., 1956); Joseph S. Clark, *The Senate Establishment* (New York: Hill and Wang, 1963); and Randall B. Ripley, *Power in the Senate* (New York: St. Martin's, 1969).
44. Richard E. Cohen, "Marking an End to the Senate's Mansfield Era," *National Journal,* Dec. 25, 1976, 1803. See also U.S. Congress, *Congressional Record,* daily ed., 88th Cong., 1st sess., Nov. 27, 1963, 21754–21764.
45. U.S. Congress, *Congressional Record,* daily ed., 96th Cong., 2d sess., April 18, 1980, S3294.
46. U.S. Congress, *Congressional Record,* daily ed., 105th Cong., 2d sess., July 16, 1998, S8375. Baker made these remarks when he addressed senators at the leadership lecture series sponsored by Senate majority leader Trent Lott.
47. Claudia MacLachlan, "The Senate's Majority Head a Believer in Consensus," *National Law Journal,* June 3, 1991, 8. See also Richard E. Cohen, "The Judge's Trials," *National Journal,* July 13, 1991, 1726–1730.
48. Dale Bumpers, "How the Sunshine Harmed Congress," *New York Times,* Jan. 3, 1999, E9. Also see, for example, Sarah Binder, "The Disappearing Political Center," *Brookings Review* (fall 1996): 36–39; Binder, *Minority Rights, Majority Rule: Partisanship and Development of Congress* (New York: Cambridge University Press, 1997); and Barbara Sinclair, *The Transformation of the U.S. Senate* (Baltimore: Johns Hopkins University Press, 1989).
49. See, for example, *Washington Post,* May 16, 1996, A1.
50. Matthew Cooper, "The Making of Senator Smoothe," *Newsweek,* Jan. 27, 1997, 42.
51. David Rogers, "Sen. Lott Becomes GOP's New Standard-Bearer, but His Style Will Be Tested in the Next Congress," *Wall Street Journal,* Nov. 15, 1996, A16. Senator Mack is quoted in James Barnes, "The Senate Broker," *National Journal,* Dec. 21, 1996, 2733.
52. David Von Drehle, "For Senators, Exits Aren't Clearly Marked," *Washington Post,* Jan. 26, 1999, A8.
53. Jamie Stiehm, "Daschle Leadership Tested," *The Hill,* April 12, 1995, 4. See also Stiehm, "Senate Democrats Stall the Contract," *The Hill,* Aug. 16, 1995, 1; and

Sarah Pekkanen, "Consensus-Minded Leader Diffuses Power," *The Hill,* March 8, 1995, 15.

54. "The 106th Senate," *Roll Call,* Dec. 3, 1998, 16.

55. John Bresnahan and Rachel Van Dongen, "Daschle Expands DSCC Role," *Roll Call,* Dec. 7, 1998, 1.

56. Ed Henry, "Daschle's Media Empire Grows," *Roll Call,* July 18, 1996, 21.

57. Peter H. Stone, "Playing Second Fiddle," *National Journal,* July 11, 1998, 1612–1616.

58. Jennifer Senior, "Whip Job Gets Nickles Extra Dollars," *The Hill,* July 24, 1996, 3; and Ed Henry, "Snowe Gets a New GOP Leadership Post," *Roll Call,* Dec. 16, 1996, 15.

59. *New York Times,* Dec. 6, 1988, B13.

60. U.S. Congress, *Congressional Record,* daily ed., 94th Cong., 2d sess., Feb. 16, 1976, S3137.

61. Barbara Sinclair, *Majority Leadership in the U.S. House* (Baltimore: Johns Hopkins University Press, 1983).

62. Helen Dewar, "Will Brass Spittoons Survive Move to Modernize Senate?" *Washington Post,* Jan. 15, 1997, A17.

63. U.S. Congress, *Congressional Record,* daily ed., 98th Cong., 1st sess., Nov. 15, 1983, H9856.

64. Thomas B. Rosenstiel and Edith Stanley, "For Gingrich, It's 'Mr. Speaker!'" *Los Angeles Times,* Nov. 9, 1994, A2.

65. *National Journal's Congress Daily/AM,* Jan. 21, 1999, 1.

66. U.S. Congress, *Congressional Record,* daily ed., 94th Cong., 1st sess., Jan. 26, 1973, S2301.

67. Christopher Madison, "The Heir Presumptive," *National Journal,* April 29, 1989, 1036.

68. Sidney Waldman, "Majority Leadership in the House of Representatives," *Political Science Quarterly* 95 (fall 1980): 377.

69. Neil MacNeil, *Dirksen: Portrait of a Public Man* (New York: World, 1970), 168–169.

70. *New York Times,* June 7, 1984, B16.

71. *National Journal's Congress Daily/A.M.,* July 31, 1995, 5.

72. Nancy E. Roman, "Congressmen's Recess Is Medicare Mission," *Washington Times,* Aug. 22, 1995, A4.

73. Jim Drinkard, "Republican-led House Members PAC-ing It In," *USA Today,* Aug. 30, 1995, 8A. See also Glenn R. Simpson, "'Leadership PACs' for Republicans in the House Are Popular, but Critics Warn of Backlash," *Wall Street Journal,* Aug. 29. 1995, A16.

74. Connie Cass, "GOP Leads in Cash from PACs on Hill," *Washington Post,* May 14, 1997, A19.

75. Stephen Gettinger, "Potential Senate Leaders Flex Money Muscles," *Congressional Quarterly Weekly Report,* Oct. 8, 1988, 2776.

76. Sinclair, *Majority Leadership in the U.S. House,* 96–97.

77. *CQ Monitor,* April 18, 1996, 5.

78. Guy Gugliotta, "They Didn't Ask, He Didn't Tell," *Washington Post,* Aug.448 6, 1998, A13.

79. Christopher Georges, "'CATs' in Congress Push for Right-Wing Agenda despite Tricky Rapport with GOP Leadership," *Wall Street Journal,* Aug. 28, 1995, A14.

80. Robin Kolodny, *Pursuing Majorities: Congressional Campaign Committees in American Politics* (Norman: University of Oklahoma Press, 1998).

81. See Paul S. Herrnson, "National Party Organizations and the Postreform Congress," in *The Postreform Congress*, ed. Roger H. Davidson (New York: St. Martin's, 1992), 48–70.

82. Kathy Kiely and Wendy Koch, "Committee Shaped by Party Ties," *USA Today*, Oct. 5, 1998, 2A.

83. Lars-Erik Nelson, "The Republicans' War," *New York Review of Books*, Feb. 4, 1999, 7.

84. David Rogers and Jeannie Cummings, "Democrats Aim to Stir Public as Impeachment Nears," *Wall Street Journal*, Dec. 14, 1998, A20.

85. Jeffrey Katz, "Partisan Tensions, Already High, Are Unlikely to End When Trial Does," *CQ Weekly*, Jan. 30, 1999, 239.

86. Elizabeth Shogren, "Will Welfare Go Way of Health Reform?" *Los Angeles Times*, Aug. 10, 1995, A18.

87. See David W. Rohde, "Electoral Forces, Political Agendas, and Partisanship in the House and Senate," in *Parties and Leaders in the Postreform Congress* (Chicago: University of Chicago Press, 1991), 27–47.

88. See V. O. Key Jr., *Politics, Parties, and Pressure Groups*, 5th ed. (New York: Crowell, 1964); and Austin Ranney and Willmoore Kendall, *Democracy and the American Party System* (New York: Harcourt Brace, 1956).

89. Michael Grunwald, "Voters Shunning Party Identification, Loyalty," *Washington Post*, Jan. 3, 1999, p. A1.

90. Ed Henry, "On Graveyard Shift with Daschle: Senate Democrats Pull All-Nighter," *Roll Call*, June 12, 1997, 1.

91. Donna Cassata, "Key Measures Still Hostage to Abortion Dispute," *Congressional Quarterly Weekly Report*, Feb. 14, 1998, 401.

92. *U.S. Congress*, Congressional Record, daily ed., 104th Cong., 1st sess., Oct. 11, 1995, E1926. Rep. Lee Hamilton, D-Ind., who made the comment, strongly opposed the overuse of omnibus bills.

93. Jim VandeHei, "Hastert Plans Bipartisan Bills at Start," *Roll Call*, Feb. 1, 1999, 1.

94. *Roll Call*, Jan. 21, 1999, 3.

95. E. J. Dionne Jr., " 'Leverage' on the Hill," *Washington Post*, Nov. 29, 1996, A27.

96. Richard E. Cohen, "Byrd of West Virginia: A New Job, a New Image," *National Journal*, Aug. 20, 1977, 1294.

Chapter 7 *(pages 197–225)*

1. *Washington Post*, May 14, 1987, A23.

2. U.S. Congress, *Congressional Record*, daily ed., 100th Cong., 1st sess., June 25, 1987, H5564.

3. *Little legislatures* was a term coined by Woodrow Wilson in Congressional Government (Boston: Houghton Mifflin, 1885), 79.

4. *New York Times*, July 11, 1988, A14.

5. See, for example, Kenneth A. Shepsle and Barry R. Weingast, "The Institutional Foundations of Committee Power," *American Political Science Review* (1978): 85–104.

6. David R. Sands, "Reform of Farm Legislation Is Crucial Test for Congress," *Washington Times*, Sept. 4, 1995, A7. See also David Sands, "Axing Farm Subsidies Triggers GOP Rebellion," *Washington Times*, Oct. 25, 1995, A8.

7. See Keith Krehbiel, *Information and Legislative Organization* (Ann Arbor: University of Michigan Press, 1991); and Bruce Bimber, "Information as a Factor in Congressional Politics," *Legislative Studies Quarterly* (1991): 585–606.

8. John W. Ellwood, "The Great Exception: The Congressional Budget Process in an Age of Decentralization," in *Congress Reconsidered*, 3d ed., ed. Lawrence C. Dodd and Bruce I. Oppenheimer (Washington, D.C.: CQ Press, 1985), 329. For the classic discussion of committee and member roles, see Richard F. Fenno Jr., *Congressmen in Committees* (Boston: Little, Brown, 1973).

9. Roy Swanstrom, *The United States Senate, 1787–1801*, S. Doc. 64, 87th Cong., 1st sess., 1962, 224.

10. Lauros G. McConachie, *Congressional Committees* (New York: Crowell, 1898), 124.

11. DeAlva Stanwood Alexander, *History and Procedure of the House of Representatives* (Boston: Houghton Mifflin, 1916), 228; George H. Haynes, *The Senate of the United States: Its History and Practice*, vol. 1 (Boston: Houghton Mifflin, 1938), 272; and Ralph V. Harlow, *The History of Legislative Methods in the Period before 1825* (New Haven: Yale University Press, 1917), 157–158.

12. *Cannon's Procedures in the House of Representatives*, H. Doc. 122, 80th Cong., 1st sess., 1959, 83.

13. *Wall Street Journal*, May 3, 1979, 1.

14. Jackie Koszczuk, "Democrats' Fortunes Tied to Clinton," *Congressional Quarterly Weekly Report*, Dec. 7, 1996, 3332.

15. U.S. Congress, *Congressional Record*, daily ed., 106th Cong., 1st sess., Jan. 6, 1999, H196.

16. *Inside the New Congress*, Dec. 4, 1998, 5. This Washington, D.C.–based newsletter is issued every Friday.

17. U.S. Congress, *Congressional Record*, daily ed., 104th Cong., 1st sess., Jan. 4, 1995, H33.

18. Kirk Victor, "Mr. Smooth," *National Journal*, July 8, 1995, 1759.

19. Charles L. Clapp, *The Congressman: His Job as He Sees It* (Washington, D.C.: Brookings Institution, 1963), 245.

20. Lawrence D. Longley and Walter J. Oleszek, *Bicameral Politics: Conference Committees in Congress* (New Haven: Yale University Press, 1989), 196.

21. Keith Krehbiel, Kenneth A. Shepsle, and Barry R. Weingast, "Why Are Congressional Committees Powerful?" *American Political Science Review* 81 (September 1987): 935.

22. Roderick Kiewiet and Mathew McCubbins, *The Logic of Delegation: Congressional Parties and the Appropriations Process* (Chicago: University of Chicago Press, 1991).

23. James Bornemeier, "Berman Accepts Seat on House Ethics Panel," *Los Angeles Times*, Feb. 5, 1997, B1; *CQ Daily Monitor*, Dec. 11, 1999, 1.

24. Kenneth J. Cooper, "Future Is Now for House Science Committee," *New York Times*, Jan. 26, 1993, A15.

25. Fenno, *Congressmen in Committees*. See also Heinz Eulau, "Legislative Committee Assignments," *Legislative Studies Quarterly* (November 1984): 587–633.

26. Christopher J. Deering and Steven S. Smith, *Committees in Congress*, 3d ed. (Washington, D.C.: CQ Press, 1997), 61–62, 78.

27. Nancy Roman, "Freshman Nets Prized Panel by Seeking Leader's Support," *Washington Times*, Dec. 3, 1996, A4. See also Greg Hitt, "Ways and Means: An Illinois Republican Staged Hard Campaign for Key House Panel," *Wall Street Journal*, Jan. 3, 1997, A1.

28. Office of Rep. Jennifer Dunn, Washington, D.C.

29. Shirley Chisholm, *Unbought and Unbossed* (Boston: Houghton Mifflin, 1970), 84, 86.

30. See Kirk Victor and Eliza Carney, "Lights, Camera, History!" *National Journal*, Oct. 10, 1998, 2375; and T. R. Goldman, "Anatomy of a Committee," *Legal Times*, Sept. 14, 1998, 19.

31. Donna Cassata, "GOP Positions Itself to Expand Margin of Control in Two Years," *Congressional Quarterly Weekly Report*, Dec. 7, 1996, 3333.

32. Mary Lynn F. Jones, "Panel Assignments Bring Respect, Dollars," *The Hill*, Feb. 10, 1999, 10.

33. Lindsay Sobel, "GOP Chairs: 'Term Limits a Mistake,'" *The Hill*, May 20, 1998, 1. Also see Lindsay Sobel, "House Chairmen May Play Musical Chairs after 2000," *The Hill*, May 27, 1998, 1.

34. Paul Gigot, "Mack Uses Knife on Old Senate Order," *Wall Street Journal*, July 14, 1995, A12.

35. *Washington Post*, Nov. 20, 1983, A9.

36. See, for example, Spencer Rich and Eric Pianin, "Democrats Stage Walkout over Medicare," *Washington Post*, Oct. 3, 1995, A4.

37. See David King, *Turf Wars* (Chicago: University of Chicago Press, 1997).

38. National Journal's *Congress Daily/A.M.,* Nov. 1, 1995, 1.

39. Elizabeth Kastor, "The Capital Star System," *Washington Post*, May 9, 1986, D8.

40. Bob Pool, "Survivors Take Stock of Gains against Cancer," *Los Angeles Times*, May 30, 1997, B1.

41. Ralph Vartabedian, "Senate Panel Is Ready to Take IRS to Task," *Los Angeles Times*, Sept. 22, 1997, A1.

42. Sean Piccoli, "Hill Samples 'Third Wave,'" *Washington Times*, June 13, 1995, A8.

43. *Washington Post*, Sept. 23, 1998, A23.

44. Katharine Seelye, "Capitol Lawn Is the Stage as Democrats Play Outsiders' Role," *New York Times*, Sept. 23, 1995, 1.

45. Karen Foerstel, "D'Amato: A Street Fighter Prepares for Battle," *CQ Weekly*, June 6, 1998, 1510. D'Amato lost his senatorial seat to Schumer.

46. *Washington Post*, Nov. 25, 1985, A4. See also Richard L. Hall, *Participation in Congress* (New Haven: Yale University Press, 1997).

47. Eric Redman, *The Dance of Legislation* (New York: Simon and Schuster, 1973), 140.

48. Hugh Heclo, "Issue Networks in the Executive Establishment," in *The New American Political System*, ed. Anthony King (Washington, D.C.: American Enterprise Institute, 1978), 87–124. See also David E. Price, "Policy Making in Congressional Committees: The Impact of 'Environmental Factors,'" *American Political Science Review* (fall 1978): 548–574.

49. David Hosansky and Andrew Taylor, "Judiciary's 'Fateful Leap,'" *CQ Weekly*, Dec. 12, 1998, 3290–3294.

50. Bill Thomas, "Putting Our Own House in Order," *Washington Times*, March 31, 1995, A23.

51. U.S. Congress, *Congressional Record*, daily ed., 104th Cong., 1st sess., Feb. 10, 1995, S2455.

52. Bruce Bartlett, "Downsizing Staff with Painful Results," *Washington Times*, Nov. 22, 1996, A18.

53. U.S. Congress, *Congressional Record*, daily ed., 105th Cong., 1st sess., July 30, 1996, S9117.

54. Norris Cotton, *In the Senate* (New York: Dodd, Mead, 1978), 65.

55. Guy Gugliotta, "House Aides' Experience Drops, 'Pay Gap' Grows," *Washington Post*, Nov. 12, 1998, A19.

56. *Washington Post*, March 20, 1977, E9.
57. David Whiteman, *Communication in Congress: Members, Staff, and the Search for Information* (Lawrence: University Press of Kansas, 1995).
58. *Washington Post*, Nov. 20, 1983, A13.
59. See Eliza Newlin Carney, "Losing Support," *National Journal*, Sept. 23, 1995, 2353–2357.
60. U.S. Congress, *Congressional Record*, daily ed., 100th Cong., 2d sess., July 8, 1988, S9134.
61. Brett Pulley, "Black Clerics Criticize Torricelli on Minority Hiring for His Staff," *New York Times*, March 21, 1997, A25.
62. See C. Lawrence Evans and Walter J. Oleszek, *Congress under Fire: Reform Politics and the Republican Majority* (Boston: Houghton Mifflin, 1997).
63. Weston Kosova, "On the Hill: Slash and Burn," *New Republic*, Jan. 2, 1995, 12.
64. Allan Freedman, "Returning Power to Chairmen," *Congressional Quarterly Weekly Report*, Nov. 23, 1996, 3300.
65. *Roll Call*, Jan. 21, 1999, 3.
66. John Bresnahan, "GOP Senators Pass New Conference Rule," *Roll Call*, April 15, 1999, 21.
67. Gabriel Kahn, "GOP to Rethink Proxy Voting Ban," *Roll Call*, June 26, 1995, 30.
68. U.S. Congress, *Congressional Record*, daily ed., 105th Cong., 2d sess., Sept. 29, 1998, S11120.
69. Jennifer Senior, "For Leader Lott, It's Rule by Task Force," *The Hill*, Jan. 29, 1997, 5.
70. *Committee Structure*, Hearings before the Joint Committee on the Organization of Congress (Washington, D.C.: U.S. Government Printing Office, 1993), 779.
71. Curt Suplee, "The Science Chairman's Unpredictable Approach," *Washington Post*, Oct. 15, 1991, A21.

Chapter 8 (pages 227–255)

1. Nancy Roman, "Daschle Warns against Treaty Delay," *Washington Times*, March 20, 1997, A4.
2. *Constitution, Jefferson's Manual, and Rules of the House of Representatives*, House Doc. 103–342, 103d Cong., 2d sess., 1995, 119–120. The rules of the Senate are contained in *Standing Rules of the Senate*, Senate Doc. 104-8, 104th Cong., 1st sess., 1995.
3. Donald R. Matthews, *U.S. Senators and Their World* (Chapel Hill: University of North Carolina Press, 1960), chap. 5.
4. *Wall Street Journal*, Oct. 2, 1987, 1.
5. Martha Angle, "The Human Truth about Politics," *Congressional Quarterly Weekly Report*, May 22, 1993, 1326.
6. David Stout, "Senator Seeks to Block Labels Hinting about Wine's Benefits," *New York Times*, Feb. 23, 1999, A12.
7. *National Journal*, April 10, 1982, 632.
8. Julie Rovner, "Senate Committee Approves Health Warnings on Alcohol," *Congressional Quarterly Weekly Report*, May 24, 1986, 1175.
9. Woodrow Wilson, *Congressional Government* (Boston: Houghton Mifflin, 1885), 320.
10. Theodore Sorensen, *Kennedy* (New York: Harper and Row, 1965), 184.
11. *Wall Street Journal*, June 2, 1988, 56.

12. U.S. Congress, *Congressional Record,* daily ed., 95th Cong., 1st sess., May 17, 1977, E3076.

13. Peter Baker, "White House Finds 'Fast Track' Too Slippery," *Washington Post,* Sept. 14, 1997, A4. See also U.S. Congress, *Congressional Record,* daily ed., 105th Cong., 2d sess., Sept. 29, 1998, S11133 (the McGwire bill) and 106th Cong., 1st sess., Jan. 25, 1999, S979 (the Ali measure); and Ceci Connolly, "Consultant Offers GOP a Language for the Future," *Washington Post,* Sept. 4, 1997, A1.

14. For information on the drafting process, see Lawrence E. Filson, *The Legislative Drafter's Desk Reference* (Washington, D.C.: Congressional Quarterly, 1992).

15. *CQ Monitor,* July 24, 1998, 5.

16. Lawrence J. Haas, "Unauthorized Action," *National Journal,* Jan. 2, 1988, 20.

17. Norman J. Ornstein, Thomas E. Mann, and Michael J. Malbin, eds., *Vital Statistics on Congress, 1997–1998* (Washington, D.C.: Congressional Quarterly, 1998), 157.

18. James G. Gimpel, *Fulfilling the Contract: The First 100 Days* (Boston: Allyn and Bacon, 1996), 5.

19. *Washington Post,* Feb. 22, 1999, A3.

20. T. R. Reid, *Congressional Odyssey: The Saga of a Senate Bill* (San Francisco: W. H. Freeman, 1980), 17.

21. Carroll J. Doherty, "Lots of Inertia, Little Lawmaking as Election '98 Approaches," *CQ Weekly,* July 18, 1998, 1925.

22. Elizabeth Drew, "A Tendency to 'Legislate,' " *New Yorker,* June 26, 1978, 80.

23. Jeffrey Katz, "Campaign Finance," *Congressional Quarterly Weekly Report,* April 4, 1998, 863.

24. Jonathan Salant, "Under Open Rules, Discord Rules," *Congressional Quarterly Weekly Report,* Jan. 28, 1995, 277.

25. *National Journal,* Jan. 21, 1995, 183.

26. Lizette Alvarez, "Campaign Finance Measure Soundly Rejected by House," *New York Times,* June 18, 1998, A26.

27. Stanley Bach and Steven Smith, *Managing Uncertainty in the House of Representatives: Adaptation and Innovation in Special Rules* (Washington, D.C.: Brookings Institution, 1988), 87.

28. Alfred Steinberg, *Sam Rayburn* (New York: Hawthorn, 1975), 313.

29. Neil MacNeil, *The Forge of Democracy* (New York: McKay, 1963), 411.

30. David Rosenbaum, "Tax Bill Faces Fight, but First the Rules," *New York Times,* April 2, 1995, 20.

31. Jeffrey Katz, "Petition Pushes House GOP Leadership to Schedule Campaign Finance Debate," *CQ Weekly,* April 25, 1998, 1057–1058.

32. Lindsay Sobel, "Democrats Weight Discharge Petition Barrage," *The Hill,* July 1, 1998, 2.

33. Joan Lowy, "Abortion Foes Anger Hill Allies with Ads on Campaign Reform," *Washington Times,* Dec. 21, 1997, A4.

34. Alison Mitchell, "6 Republicans Break Ranks on Campaign Finance Issue," *New York Times,* May 27, 1999, A1.

35. Information courtesy of Richard Beth, Congressional Research Service.

36. Susan F. Rasky, "For House Democrats, a Pledge Lesson," *New York Times,* Sept. 10, 1988, 1; Tom Kenworthy, "Pledge Makes House Debut; A Long Run Appears Likely," *Washington Post,* Sept. 14, 1988, A10; and Matt Pinkus, "Gonzalez Was Right," *Roll Call,* July 15, 1993, 5.

37. National Journal's *Congress Daily/P.M.,* Jan. 13, 1995, 4.

38. *Mt. Vernon* [Ohio] *News,* Sept. 20, 1980, 2.

39. Robert S. Walker, "Why House Republicans Need a Watchdog," *Roll Call,* Jan. 19, 1987, 10.

40. John F. Bibby, ed., *Congress off the Record* (Washington, D.C.: American Enterprise Institute, 1983), 23.

41. J. Bennett Johnston, D-La., Senate (1972–1995), quoted in *New York Times,* Nov. 22, 1985, B8.

42. U.S. Congress, *Congressional Record,* daily ed., 101st Cong., 2d sess., July 20, 1990, S10183.

43. Kevin Merida, "Calling Time Out on Capitol Hill," *Washington Post,* May 16, 1993, A1.

44. Susan F. Rasky, "With Few Bills Passed or Ready for Action, Congress Seems Sluggish," *New York Times,* May 14, 1989, 24.

45. U.S. Congress, *Congressional Record,* daily ed., 98th Cong., 2d sess., Jan. 27, 1984, S328–S329.

46. Walter J. Oleszek, *Congressional Procedures and the Policy Process,* 4th ed. (Washington, D.C.: CQ Press, 1996), 263–266. See also Lewis A. Froman Jr., *The Congressional Process* (Boston: Little, Brown, 1967); and Terry Sullivan, *Procedural Structure: Success and Influence in Congress* (New York: Praeger, 1984).

47. *Constitution, Jefferson's Manual, and Rules of the House of Representatives,* 231.

48. Elizabeth Drew, *Senator* (New York: Simon and Schuster, 1979), 158.

49. U.S. Congress, *Congressional Record,* daily ed., 97th Cong., 2d sess., May 20, 1982, S5648.

50. Helen Dewar, " 'Hold' Likely for IRS Pick, Daschle Says," *Washington Post,* Oct. 30, 1997, A11.

51. U.S. Congress, *Congressional Record,* daily ed., 106th Cong., 1st. sess., March 3, 1999.

52. See comments by Alan Cranston, then Senate Democratic whip, in *New York Times,* July 17, 1986, A3.

53. U.S. Congress, *Operations of the Congress: Testimony of House and Senate Leaders,* Hearing before the Joint Committee on the Organization of Congress, 103d Cong., 1st sess., Jan. 26, 1993 (Washington, D.C.: U.S. Government Printing Office, 1993), 50.

54. U.S. Congress, *Congressional Record,* daily ed., 105th Cong., 1st sess., Feb. 13, 1997, S1417–S1418.

55. Testimony of Steven S. Smith, University of Minnesota, before the Joint Committee on the Organization of Congress, 103d Cong., 1st sess., May 20, 1993, 14.

56. U.S. Congress, *Congressional Record,* 106th Cong., 1st. sess., May 20, 1999, S5646.

57. Randall B. Ripley, *Power in the Senate* (New York: St. Martin's, 1969), 128.

58. Janet Hook, "In Conference: New Hurdles, Hard Bargaining," *Congressional Quarterly Weekly Report,* Sept. 6, 1986, 2081.

59. U.S. Congress, *Congressional Record,* daily ed., 99th Cong., 2d sess., Feb. 20, 1986, S1463.

60. Barbara Sinclair, *Unorthodox Lawmaking: New Legislative Processes in the U.S. Congress* (Washington, D.C.: CQ Press, 1997).

61. Barber B. Conable, "Weaving Webs: Lobbying by Charities," *Tax Notes,* Nov. 10, 1975, 27–28.

Chapter 9 (pages 257–282)

1. Jeffrey L. Katz, "Politically Charged Vote Sets Tone for Impeachment Inquiry," *CQ Weekly,* Oct. 10, 1998, 2712.
2. Ibid.
3. Richard L. Hall, *Participation in Congress* (New Haven: Yale University Press, 1996), 27–30.
4. Dan Morgan, "House Leadership Bends to Backbenchers' Muscle," *Washington Post,* Oct. 13, 1995, A14.
5. Craig Winneker and Glenn R. Simpson, "Obscure Caucus, Year Five," *Roll Call,* Sept. 12, 1994, A25–26. The listing omits senators: "senators are by definition not obscure, although there are several who seem to strive for it." To be listed in the "Obscure Caucus," House members must have served at least three terms.
6. David Price, *Who Makes the Laws?* (Cambridge, Mass.: Schenkman Publishing, 1972), 297.
7. Quoted in Laura Blumenfeld, "When Politics Becomes Personal," *Washington Post,* June 19, 1996, C1, 2. See also Sarah Pekkanen, "From Drunk Driving to Health Care, Lawmakers' Bills Have Personal Roots," *The Hill,* April 17, 1996, 10.
8. Guy Gugliotta, "On the Hill, Ex-Wrestlers Go to the Mat for the Sport," *Washington Post,* April 30, 1998, A19.
9. Bernard Asbell, *The Senate Nobody Knows* (Garden City, N.Y.: Doubleday, 1978), 210.
10. Richard F. Fenno Jr., "Observation, Context, and Sequence in the Study of Politics," *American Political Science Review* 80 (March 1976): 3–15.
11. Lindsay Sobel, "Early Fast-Track Support Cost Members Leverage," *The Hill,* Nov. 12, 1997, 33.
12. Cited in Philippe Shepnick, "Moynihan Is Champion Bill Writer," *The Hill,* March 10, 1999, 6.
13. Rick K. Wilson and Cheryl D. Young, "Cosponsorship in the U.S. Congress," *Legislative Studies Quarterly* 22 (February 1997): 25–43.
14. The study was released by Congressional Connection, an online database. Reported in *Roll Call,* June 16, 1994, 4.
15. Richard F. Fenno Jr., *The Making of a Senator: Dan Quayle* (Washington, D.C.: CQ Press, 1989), 43–45.
16. T. R. Reid, *Congressional Odyssey: The Saga of a Senate Bill* (San Francisco: W. H. Freeman, 1980), 15.
17. Quoted in Hall, *Participation in Congress,* 139; see also 119.
18. Ibid., 126–127.
19. See Elana Mintz, "Members' Roll Call Attendance Sets Election-Year Record," *Congressional Quarterly Weekly Report,* Dec. 21, 1996, 3489.
20. U.S. Congress, *Congressional Record,* daily ed., 103d Cong., 1st sess., June 23, 1993, H3941–3973.
21. John E. Yang, "Term Limits Fail Again in the House," *Washington Post,* Feb. 2, 1997, A1.
22. Quoted in John D. Wilkerson, " 'Killer' Amendments in Congress" (Paper presented at the annual meeting of the Midwest Political Science Association, Chicago, March 1998), 31.
23. Allan Freedman, "Elimination of NEA Squeaks By as House Passes Interior Rule," *Congressional Quarterly Weekly Report,* July 12, 1997, 1615–1618.

24. Margaret Shapiro, "Hoyer Unwittingly Led Antiabortion Cause in Bill Snafu," *Washington Post,* Nov. 15, 1983, E1.

25. Quoted in Eric Schmitt, "House Votes to Bar Religious Abuse Abroad," *New York Times,* May 15, 1998, A1.

26. Albert R. Hunt, "Balanced-Budget Measure Is Likely to Pass Senate Next Week, Faces Battle in House," *Wall Street Journal,* July 30, 1982, 2.

27. Norman J. Ornstein, Thomas E. Mann, and Michael J. Malbin, *Vital Statistics on Congress, 1997–1998* (Washington, D.C.: Congressional Quarterly, 1998), 210–213.

28. Glenn R. Parker and Suzanne L. Parker, "Factions in Committees: The U.S. House of Representatives," *American Political Science Review* 73 (March 1979): 85–102.

29. For an authoritative analysis of the decline and resurgence of congressional partisanship, see David W. Rohde, *Parties and Leaders in the Postreform House* (Chicago: University of Chicago Press, 1991), esp. 3–11.

30. *Roll Call,* Aug. 17, 1995, 7.

31. David W. Rohde, "Electoral Forces, Political Agendas, and Partisanship in the House and Senate," in *The Postreform Congress,* ed. Roger H. Davidson (New York: St. Martin's, 1992), esp. 34–40.

32. Helmut Norpoth, "Explaining Party Cohesion in Congress: The Case of Shared Policy Attitudes," *American Political Science Review* 70 (December 1976): 1171.

33. Morton Kondracke, "Who's Running the House? GOP Freshmen or Newt?" *Roll Call,* Dec. 18, 1995, 5.

34. Rohde, "Electoral Forces," 28.

35. Jerrold E. Schneider, *Ideological Coalitions in Congress* (Westport, Conn.: Greenwood Press, 1979); Keith T. Poole and Howard Rosenthal, "Patterns of Congressional Voting," *American Journal of Political Science* 35 (February 1991): 228–278, and Keith T. Poole and Howard Rosenthal, *Congress: A Political-Economic History of Roll-Call Voting* (New York: Oxford University Press, 1997).

36. John F. Manley, "The Conservative Coalition in Congress," *American Behavioral Scientist* 17 (December 1973): 223–247; Barbara Sinclair, *Congressional Realignment: 1925–1978* (Austin: University of Texas Press, 1982); and Mack C. Shelley, *The Permanent Majority: The Conservative Coalition in the United States Congress* (University: University of Alabama Press, 1983).

37. Robert J. Donovan, "For America, a New Coalition?" *Los Angeles Times,* July 6, 1981, 4.

38. Stephen Gettinger, "R.I.P. to a Conservative Force," *CQ Weekly,* Jan. 9, 1999, 82–83.

39. Sarah A. Binder, "The Disappearing Political Center," *Brookings Review* 15 (fall 1996): 36–39.

40. Ibid., 37.

41. Warren B. Rudman, *Combat: Twelve Years in the U.S. Senate* (New York: Random House, 1996), 243.

42. James G. Gimpel, *Fulfilling the Contract: The First 100 Days* (Boston: Allyn and Bacon, 1996), 120.

43. R. Douglas Arnold, *The Logic of Congressional Action* (New Haven: Yale University Press, 1990), 64–65. This section draws heavily upon Arnold's work. The original reference to attentive and inattentive publics is from V. O. Key Jr., *Public Opinion and American Democracy* (New York: Knopf, 1961), 265, 282–285.

44. Arnold, *The Logic of Congressional Action,* 68.

45. Ibid., 84.

46. Mark A. Peterson, "The President and Congress," in *The Presidency and the Political System,* 5th ed., ed. Michael Nelson (Washington, D.C.: CQ Press, 1998), 486–487; recent figures are from *CQ Weekly,* Jan. 9, 1999, 86.

47. See Charles O. Jones, *The Trusteeship Presidency: Jimmy Carter and the United States Congress* (Baton Rouge: Louisiana State University Press, 1988).

48. Jon Healey, "Clinton Success Rate Declined to a Record Low in 1995," *Congressional Quarterly Weekly Report,* Jan. 27, 1996, 193.

49. Ornstein, Mann, and Malbin, *Vital Statistics,* 205–208.

50. Cleo H. Cherryholmes and Michael J. Shapiro, *Representatives and Roll Calls* (Indianapolis: Bobbs-Merrill, 1969).

51. Donald R. Matthews and James A. Stimson, *Yeas and Nays* (New York: Wiley, 1975).

52. Aage R. Clausen, *How Congressmen Decide* (New York: St. Martin's, 1973).

53. David M. Kovenock, "Influence in the U.S. House of Representatives: A Statistical Analysis of Communications," *American Politics Quarterly* 1 (October 1973): 456; see also 455, 457.

54. John W. Kingdon, *Congressmen's Voting Decisions,* 3d ed. (Ann Arbor: University of Michigan Press, 1989).

55. Quoted in John F. Bibby, ed., *Congress off the Record* (Washington, D.C.: American Enterprise Institute, 1983), 22.

56. Albert R. Hunt, "Politicians Don't Play Politics All the Time," *Wall Street Journal,* May 14, 1981, 26.

57. Roger H. Davidson, *The Role of the Congressman* (Indianapolis: Bobbs-Merrill, 1969), 22–23.

58. Robert L. Peabody, "Organization Theory and Legislative Behavior: Bargaining, Hierarchy and Change in the U.S. House of Representatives" (Paper presented at the annual meeting of the American Political Science Association, New York, Sept. 4–7, 1963).

59. Carl J. Friedrich, *Constitutional Government and Democracy,* 4th ed. (Waltham, Mass.: Blaisdell Publishing, 1967), 269–270.

60. Pat Towell, "Sam Nunn: The Careful Exercise of Power," *Congressional Quarterly Weekly Report,* June 14, 1986, 1330.

61. Jeffrey H. Birnbaum, "Progress of the Tax Bill Enhances Reputation of Sen. Bill Bradley," *Wall Street Journal,* June 4, 1986, 24.

62. Quoted in Claudia Dreifus, "Exit Reasonable Right," *New York Times Magazine,* June 2, 1996, 26.

63. Edward J. Derwinski, "The Art of Negotiation within the Congress," in *International Negotiation: Art and Science,* ed. Diane B. Bendahmane and John W. McDonald Jr. (Washington, D.C.: Foreign Service Institute, U.S. Department of State, 1984), 11.

64. Lizette Alvarez, "In Slap at GOP Leadership, House Stops Move to Deny Food Stamps to Immigrants," *New York Times,* May 23, 1998, A9. For background, see John Ferejohn, "Logrolling in an Institutional Context: A Case Study of Food Stamp Legislation," in *Congress and Policy Change,* ed. Gerald C. Wright Jr., Leroy N. Rieselbach, and Lawrence C. Dodd (New York: Agathon Press, 1986), 223–253.

65. Elliott Abrams, "Unforgettable Scoop Jackson," *Reader's Digest,* February 1985. Quotation cited in U.S. Congress, *Congressional Record,* daily ed., 99th Cong., 1st sess., Feb. 20, 1985, E478.

66. David E. Rosenbaum, "The Favors of Rostenkowski: Tax Revision's Quid pro Quo," *New York Times,* Nov. 27, 1985, B6.

67. Dale Tate, "Use of Omnibus Bills Burgeons Despite Members' Misgivings," *Congressional Quarterly Weekly Report,* Sept. 25, 1982, 2379.

68. The politics of "blame avoidance" is outlined in R. Kent Weaver, "The Politics of Blame," *Brookings Review* 5 (spring 1987): 43–47. The term "credit claiming" originated with David R. Mayhew, *Congress: The Electoral Connection* (New Haven: Yale University Press, 1974), 52–61.

69. R. Douglas Arnold, "The Local Roots of Domestic Policy," in *The New Congress,* ed. Thomas E. Mann and Norman J. Ornstein (Washington, D.C.: American Enterprise Institute, 1981), 286.

70. Steve Waldman, *The Bill* (New York: Viking, 1994), 94–95.

71. Quoted in Lindsay Sobel, "NAFTA Supporters Desert Clinton on Fast-Track," *The Hill,* Nov. 12, 1997, 8.

72. Quoted in "In Defense of Political Logrolling," editorial, *The Hill,* Nov. 12, 1997, 28.

73. See William H. Riker, *The Theory of Political Coalitions* (New Haven: Yale University Press, 1962), 32. Theorists define legislative bargaining situations formally as *n*-person, zero-sum games where side payments are permitted. That is, a sizable number of participants are involved; when some participants win, others must lose; and participants can trade items outside the substantive issues under consideration.

74. John G. Stewart, "Two Strategies of Leadership: Johnson and Mansfield," in *Congressional Behavior,* ed. Nelson W. Polsby (New York: Random House, 1971), 67.

75. Russell Hardin, "Hollow Victory: The Minimum Winning Coalition," *American Political Science Review* 79 (December 1976): 1202–1214.

76. Quoted in Dreifus, "Exit Reasonable Right," 26.

77. John B. Gilmour, *Strategic Disagreement: Stalemate in American Politics* (Pittsburgh: University of Pittsburgh Press, 1995), 4.

Chapter 10 *(pages 285–308)*

1. *CQ Monitor,* March 15, 1999, 3.

2. Paul Richter and Robyn Dixon, "Senate Votes to Deploy a 'Star Wars' Defense," *Los Angeles Times,* March 17, 1999, A1.

3. David Mayhew, *Divided We Govern* (New Haven: Yale University Press, 1991), 198.

4. See Wilfred E. Binkley, *President and Congress* (New York: Knopf, 1947); Charles O. Jones, *Separate but Equal Branches* (Chatham, N.J.: Chatham House, 1995); and Richard E. Neustadt, *Presidential Power and the Modern Presidents* (New York: Free Press, 1990).

5. See Stephen Wayne, *The Legislative Presidency* (New York: Harper and Row, 1978).

6. Leonard D. White, *The Federalists* (New York: Macmillan, 1948), 55. See also Paul C. Light, "The President's Agenda: Notes on the Timing of Domestic Choice," *Presidential Studies Quarterly* (winter 1981): 67–82.

7. Leonard D. White, *The Jeffersonians* (New York: Macmillan, 1951), 35.

8. Paul C. Light, *The President's Agenda* (Baltimore: Johns Hopkins University Press, 1982), 230–231.

9. Ann Devroy and Ruth Marcus, "Ambitious Agenda and Interruptions Frustrate Efforts to Maintain Focus," *Washington Post,* April 29, 1993, A1.

10. See "For Health Care, Time Was a Killer," *New York Times,* Aug. 29, 1994, 1.

11. Dan Balz, "Health Plan Was Albatross for Democrats," *Washington Post,* Nov. 11, 1994, A1.

12. Richard Cohen, "On the Brink," *National Journal,* Feb. 22, 1997, 369.

13. Janet Hook and Faye Fiore, "Squabbling Mars Parties' Accord on Major Issues," *Los Angeles Times,* June 11, 1997, A4.
14. Mark Peterson, "The President and Congress," in *The Presidency and the Political System,* 5th ed., ed. Michael Nelson (Washington, D.C.: CQ Press, 1998), 469.
15. Elizabeth Shogren, "President Plans Blitz of Executive Orders Soon," *Los Angeles Times,* July 5, 1998, A11.
16. Susan Page, "When a Law Is Unlikely, Often an Order Will Do," *USA Today,* Aug. 11, 1997, 7A. See also Alexis Simendinger, "The Paper Wars," *National Journal,* July 25, 1998, 1732–1739.
17. "Inside the New Congress," March 5, 1999, 5.
18. Jeanne Cummings, "New Clinton Staff Chief, Key Player on Medicare, Reflects President's Post-Scandal Shift Leftward," *Wall Street Journal,* March 17, 1999, A28.
19. Light, *The President's Agenda,* 86.
20. Richard M. Pious, *The American Presidency* (New York: Basic Books, 1979), 159. See also Larry Berman, *The Office of Management and Budget and the Presidency, 1921–1979* (Princeton: Princeton University Press, 1979); and James Pfiffner, ed., *The Managerial Presidency,* 2d ed. (College Station: Texas A&M Press, 1999).
21. William Leuchtenburg, *Franklin D. Roosevelt and the New Deal, 1932–1940* (New York: Harper and Row, 1963), 43–44.
22. Dan Balz, "Claiming the Middle Ground for Democrats," *Washington Post,* Jan. 20, 1999, A1.
23. Stephen K. Bailey, *Congress Makes a Law* (New York: Columbia University Press, 1950). On legislative delegations, see Sotirios A. Barber, *The Constitution and the Delegation of Congressional Power* (Chicago: University of Chicago Press, 1975); and Louis Fisher, "Delegating Power to the President," *Journal of Public Law* 19 (1970): 251–282.
24. Woodrow Wilson, *Congressional Government* (Boston: Houghton Mifflin, 1885), 52.
25. John F. Harris and Eric Pianin, "Clinton Accepts Hill's Defense Spending Bill," *Washington Post,* Dec. 1, 1995, A1.
26. Frank B. Cross, "The Constitutional Legitimacy and Significance of Presidential 'Signing Statements,'" *Administrative Law Review* 40 (spring 1988): 209–238.
27. Jonathan Salant, "GOP Considering Its Response to Legislative Branch Veto," *Congressional Quarterly Weekly Report,* Oct. 7, 1995, 3054.
28. *Los Angeles Times,* pt. I, March 18, 1988, 4.
29. Erika Niedowski, "GOP to Skirt Line Item Veto," *The Hill,* Feb. 12, 1997, 24.
30. Andrew Taylor, "Lawmakers File Challenge to Line-Item Veto Law," *Congressional Quarterly Weekly Report,* Jan. 4, 1997, 24.
31. John F. Harris, "Clinton Wields New Authority, Vetoing 3 Items," *Washington Post,* August 12, 1997, A1.
32. John Broder, "Clinton Vetoes Eight Projects, Two in States of Leadership," *New York Times,* Oct. 18, 1997, A10.
33. Helen Dewar and Joan Biskupic, "Line-Item Vote Struck Down; Backers Push for Alternative," *Washington Post,* June 26, 1998, A1.
34. U.S. Congress, *Congressional Record,* 106th Cong., 1st sess., Feb. 23, 1999, E265.
35. James P. Pfiffner, "The President's Legislative Agenda," *The Annals* (September 1988): 29. See also George C. Edwards III, *At the Margins* (New Haven: Yale University Press, 1989).
36. Lyndon Johnson, *The Vantage Point* (New York: Popular Library, 1971), 448.
37. Jack Valenti, "Some Advice on the Care and Feeding of Congressional Egos," *Los Angeles Times,* April 23, 1978, 3.

38. George C. Edwards III, *Presidential Influence in Congress* (San Francisco: W.H. Freeman, 1980), 129.

39. Neil MacNeil, *Dirksen: Portrait of a Public Man* (New York: World, 1970), 343. See also Stanley Kelley Jr., "Patronage and Presidential Legislative Leadership," in *The Presidency,* ed. Aaron Wildavsky (Boston: Little, Brown, 1969), 268–277.

40. Richard L. Berke, "Courting Congress Nonstop, Clinton Looks for an Alliance," *New York Times,* March 8, 1993, A1.

41. Carla Robbins, "Key Senator's Crusade to Block Anthony Lake from CIA Post Puzzles Intelligence Watchers," *Wall Street Journal,* March 7, 1997, A16. See also Walter Pincus, "Lake Quits as CIA Nominee," *Washington Post,* March 18, 1997, A1.

42. Roy P. Basler, ed., *The Collected Works of Abraham Lincoln,* vol. 3 (New Brunswick: Rutgers University Press, 1953), 27.

43. Pious, *The American Presidency,* 194. See also George C. Edwards III, *The Public Presidency* (New York: St Martin's, 1983).

44. *Wall Street Journal,* Dec. 4, 1987, 8D.

45. Tom Rosenstiel and James Gerstenzang, "Bush Team Rejects Public Relations Techniques of Reagan White House," *Los Angeles Times,* April 30, 1989, 1.

46. George Hager, "For GOP, a New Song—Same Ending," *Congressional Quarterly Weekly Report,* June 14, 1997, 1406.

47. Paul Bedard, "Living, Dying by the Polls," *Washington Times,* April 30, 1993, A1.

48. Carla Robbins, "Chemical Weapons Treaty Shapes Up as Messy Battle," *Wall Street Journal,* Feb. 14, 1997, A16; and Pat Towell, "Chemical Weapons Ban Approval in Burst of Compromise," *Congressional Quarterly Weekly Report,* April 26, 1997, 973–976.

49. John Bresnahan and Jim VandeHei, "GOP Going on the Road," *Roll Call,* March 22, 1999, 19.

50. Richard Neustadt, *Presidential Power* (New York: Wiley, 1960), 187.

51. *Wall Street Journal,* April 8, 1981, 1.

52. Ibid.

53. Johnson, *The Vantage Point,* 448.

54. *New York Times,* May 27, 1979, E4.

55. Wayne, *The Legislative Presidency,* 160.

56. Hedrick Smith, "Taking Charge of Congress," *New York Times Magazine,* Aug. 9, 1981, 14.

57. Dan Goodgame, "Rude Awakening," *Time,* March 20, 1989, 23.

58. Carla Robbins and David Rogers, "Crisis in the Balkans Throws Congress into Confusion," *Wall Street Journal,* March 23, 1999, A24.

59. Edwards, *At the Margins.*

60. See Joseph P. Harris, *The Advice and Consent of the Senate* (Berkeley: University of California Press, 1953); and G. Calvin Mackenzie, *The Politics of Presidential Appointments* (New York: Free Press, 1981).

61. James MacGregor Burns, *Presidential Government* (Boston: Houghton Mifflin, 1966), 284.

62. See, for example, Stephen J. Wayne, "Great Expectations: What People Want from Presidents," in *Rethinking the Presidency,* ed. Thomas E. Cronin (Boston: Little, Brown, 1982), 185–199.

63. *New York Times,* Sept. 9, 1985, A11.

64. E. J. Dionne Jr., " 'Leverage' on the Hill," *Washington Post,* Nov. 29, 1996, A27.

65. Arthur M. Schlesinger Jr. and Alfred De Grazia, *Congress and the Presidency: Their Role in Modern Times* (Washington, D.C.: American Enterprise Institute, 1967), 1.

66. Wilson, *Congressional Government;* and Burns, *Presidential Government.*

67. See Joseph S. Clark, *Congress: The Sapless Branch* (New York: Harper and Row, 1964); and Arthur M. Schlesinger Jr., *The Imperial Presidency* (Boston: Houghton Mifflin, 1973).

68. J. William Fulbright, "The Legislator as Educator," *Foreign Affairs* (spring 1979): 726.

Chapter 11 (pages 311–333)

1. A signal event was the 1995 bombing of the federal building in Oklahoma City, which reminded citizens of the human face of government.

2. Quoted in E. J. Dionne Jr., "Back from the Dead: Neoprogressivism in the 90s," *American Prospect,* September–October 1996, 25.

3. David Hosansky, "GOP Confounds Expectations, Expands Federal Authority," *Congressional Quarterly Weekly Report,* Nov. 2, 1996, 3117.

4. Sam Howe Verhovek, "Legislators Meet, Surprised at Limit on Shift of Powers," *New York Times,* Jan. 12, 1997, 1.

5. Eliza Newlin Carney, "Power Grab," *National Journal,* April 11, 1998, 799. See also Timothy Conlan, *From New Federalism to Devolution* (Washington, D.C.: Brookings Institution, 1998).

6. Richard E. Neustadt, "Politicians and Bureaucrats," in *The Congress and America's Future,* 2d ed., ed. David B. Truman (Englewood Cliffs, N.J.: Prentice-Hall, 1973), 199. See also Louis Fisher, *The Politics of Shared Power: Congress and the Executive,* 3d ed. (Washington, D.C.: CQ Press, 1993).

7. See Herbert Emmerich, *Essays on Federal Reorganization* (University: University of Alabama Press, 1950); Peter Szanton, ed., *Federal Reorganization: What Have We Learned?* (Chatham, N.J.: Chatham House, 1981); and Harold Seidman and Robert Gilmour, *Politics, Position, and Power,* 4th ed. (New York: Oxford University Press, 1986).

8. Harold Seidman, "Congressional Committees and Executive Organization," in *Committee Organization in the House,* House Doc. No. 94-187, 94th Cong., 1st sess., 1975, 823.

9. Paul C. Light, *The Tides of Reform: Making Government Work, 1945–1995* (New Haven: Yale University Press, 1997).

10. U.S. Congress, *Congressional Record,* daily ed., 100th Cong., 1st sess., May 1, 1987, S5848.

11. Steven V. Roberts, "In Confirmation Process, Hearings Offer a Stage," *New York Times,* Feb. 8, 1989, B7.

12. Kirk Victor, "Executive Branch End Run," *National Journal,* May 16, 1998, 1112. See also David Byrd, "Affirmatively Acting," *National Journal,* March 6, 1999, 612–616.

13. William Schneider, "New Rules for the Game of Politics," *National Journal,* April 1, 1989, 830.

14. See Dennis Thompson, *Ethics in Congress* (Washington, D.C.: Brookings Institution, 1995).

15. Walter Pincus, "Lake Quits as CIA Nominee Citing 'Nasty' Process," *Washington Post,* March 18, 1997, A1.

16. Doyle McManus and Robert Shogun, "Acrid Tone Reflects Long-Term Trend for Nominations," *Los Angeles Times,* March 19, 1997, A6.

17. Peter Grier, "Why Senate Roughs Up Some Cabinet Nominees," *Christian Science Monitor,* March 19, 1997, 3. See also *Obstacle Course: The Report of the Twentieth*

Century Fund Task Force on the Presidential Appointment Process (New York: Twentieth Century Fund Press, 1996).

18. The scrutiny into Bork's nomination has even given rise to an eponymous verb: *to bork,* which means to attack nominees by launching a politically based campaign against them.

19. See, for example, Suzanne Garment, "Confirming Anita Hill?" *American Enterprise,* January–February 1993, 18–22; and Stephen L. Carter, *The Confirmation Mess* (New York: Basic Books, 1994).

20. Richard Willing, "GOP Targets President's Judicial Picks," *USA Today,* March 10, 1997, 3A; and Albert Eisele, "Senate Stalls Judges over 'Activism,'" *The Hill,* March 12, 1997, 14.

21. U.S. Congress, *Congressional Record,* daily ed., 106th Cong., 1st sess., March 2, 1999, S2092.

22. Kirk Victor, "Hatch's High-Wire Act," *National Journal,* April 4, 1998, 744.

23. David Savage, "Federal Benches Left Vacant over Utah Tug of War," *Los Angeles Times,* May 10, 1999, A1.

24. See Warren Richey, "Clinton Remaking Reagan Bench," *Christian Science Monitor,* Feb. 17, 1999, 1.

25. "Value of Ambassador's Post Hasn't Diminished over Time," *Washington Times,* May 11, 1998, A7.

26. See Joseph P. Harris, *The Advice and Consent of the Senate* (Berkeley: University of California Press, 1953); Ronald C. Moe, "Senate Confirmation of Executive Appointments," in *Congress against the President,* ed. Harvey C. Mansfield, Sr. (New York: Academy of Political Science, 1975), 141–152; and *America's Unelected Government,* ed. John W. Macy, Bruce Adams, and J. Jackson Walter (Cambridge, Mass.: Ballinger, 1983).

27. Philippe Shepnick, "Helms Says D'Amato Woos Gay Vote," *The Hill,* June 24, 1998, 6.

28. Paul C. Light, *Thickening Government* (Washington, D.C.: Brookings Institution/Governance Institute, 1995), esp. 111–116.

29. Paul C. Light, "Bill Clinton: Title King," *Government Executive,* March 1999, 12.

30. Ibid.

31. Stephen Barr, "Title Creep Reported at Agencies," *Washington Post,* March 8, 1999, A17.

32. U.S. Congress, *Congressional Record,* daily ed., 106th Cong., 1st sess., Jan. 19, 1999, S555.

33. David M. Cohen, "Amateur Government," *Journal of Public Administration Research and Theory* (October 1998): 451.

34. U.S. Congress, *Congressional Record,* daily ed., 106th Cong., 1st sess., Jan. 19, 1999, S554.

35. U.S. Congress, *Congressional Record,* daily ed., 105th Cong., 1st sess., Sept. 12, 1996, S10367.

36. *Federal Times,* Dec. 12, 1988, 6; and *Washington Post,* Aug. 6, 1987, A2.

37. *Roll Call,* March 11, 1999, 4; see also Amy Keller, "English Targets Members' COLA, Tax Break," *Roll Call,* March 11, 1999, 3.

38. Juliet Eilperin, "House Studies Cost-of-Living Pay Increase," *Washington Post,* March 19, 1999, A27.

39. Laura Michaelis, "Judge Upholds Hill Pay Raise; Old, New Congresses Benefit," *Congressional Quarterly Weekly Report,* Dec. 19, 1992, 3880.

40. David Francis, "Government Size: Don't Buy the Hype," *Christian Science Monitor*, Feb. 8, 1999, 17; and "How Big the Government?" *Christian Science Monitor*, Feb. 5, 1998, 20.

41. Joyce Price, "Lowest Levels of Government Subject to Recent Downsizing," *Washington Times*, March 13, 1999, A4.

42. Frederick C. Mosher, *The GAO: The Quest for Accountability in American Government* (Boulder: Westview Press, 1979), 297.

43. Paul C. Light, "The True Size of Government," *Government Executive*, January 1999, 20.

44. Peter Zimmerman, "Not So Big," *Government Executive*, Feb. 1999, 39, 42.

45. U.S. Congress, *Congressional Record,* daily ed., 96th Cong., 2d sess., July 1, 1980, E3320.

46. Cornelius Kerwin, *Rulemaking: How Government Agencies Write Law and Make Policy*, 2d ed. (Washington, D.C.: CQ Press, 1999), 8–9. See also Jeffrey Lubbers, *A Guide to Federal Agency Rulemaking*, 3d ed. (Chicago: ABA Publishing, 1998).

47. U.S. Congress, *Congressional Record,* daily ed., 100th Cong., 1st sess., July 29, 1987, S10850.

48. Jennifer Bradley, "Obscure New Law Gives Hill Big Powers," *Roll Call,* March 3, 1997, 1.

49. Julie Kosterlitz, "Mom and Pop Get Even," *National Journal,* March 8, 1997, 458.

50. Matthew Wald, "Court Overturns Air Quality Rules," *New York Times,* May 15, 1999, A1.

51. *Roll Call,* Dec. 4, 1995, 15.

52. Cindy Skrzycki, "OSHA Set to Propose Ergonomics Standards," *Washington Post*, Feb. 19, 1999, A1.

53. Cindy Skrzycki, "OMB Tries to Add Up the Bill for Federal Rules," *Washington Post*, Feb. 12, 1999, E1.

54. Jonathan Rauch, "Tunnel Vision," *National Journal,* Sept. 19, 1998, 2149.

55. U.S. Congress, *Congressional Record,* daily ed., 104th Cong., 1st sess., July 11, 1995, S9705.

56. Ibid., S9697.

57. Harold Seidman, "The Quasi World of the Federal Government," *Brookings Review* (summer 1988): 24.

58. Morris P. Fiorina, *Congress: Keystone of the Washington Establishment* (New Haven: Yale University Press, 1977), 48.

59. R. Douglas Arnold, "The Local Roots of Domestic Policy," in *The New Congress,* ed. Thomas E. Mann and Norman J. Ornstein (Washington, D.C.: American Enterprise Institute, 1981), 284.

60. Robert Schlesinger, "GOPers Upset with FEMA Memo," *The Hill,* Oct. 7, 1998, 4.

61. *CQ Monitor,* July 15, 1998, 5; and Donald L. Barlett and James B. Steele, "Special Report: Corporate Welfare," *Time,* Nov. 16, 1998, 79–93.

62. Joseph S. Clark, *Congress: The Sapless Branch* (New York: Harper and Row, 1964), 63–64.

63. David B. Frohnmayer, "The Separation of Powers: An Essay on the Vitality of a Constitutional Idea," *Oregon Law Review* (spring 1973): 330.

64. David B. Truman, *The Governmental Process,* rev. ed. (New York: Knopf, 1971), 439.

65. Woodrow Wilson, *Congressional Government* (Boston: Houghton Mifflin, 1885), 297.

66. *Washington Times,* Dec. 29, 1986, A1; and David Rogers, "Sen. Lott Becomes GOP's New Standard-Bearer, but His Style Will Be Tested in the Next Congress," *Wall Street Journal,* Nov. 15, 1996, A16.

67. Jackie Koszczuk, "House GOP Is Closing the Door on an Era of Aggressive Inquiry," *CQ Weekly*, Feb. 6, 1999, 328.
68. Rochelle Stanfield, "Plotting Every Move," *National Journal*, March 26, 1988, 796.
69. *Watkins v. United States*, 354 U.S. 178 (1957). See also James Hamilton, *The Power to Probe* (New York: Vantage Books, 1976).
70. William S. Cohen and George J. Mitchell, *Men of Zeal: A Candid Inside Story of the Iran-Contra Hearings* (New York: Viking Penguin, 1988), 305.
71. *Immigration and Naturalization Service v. Chadha*, 462 U.S. 919 (1983).
72. Louis Fisher, in *Extensions*, a newsletter for the Carl Albert Congressional Research and Studies Center (spring 1984): 2.
73. John R. Johannes, "Study and Recommend: Statutory Reporting Requirements as a Technique of Legislative Initiative—A Research Note," *Western Political Quarterly* (December 1976): 589–596.
74. Guy Gugliotta, "Reporting on a Practice That's Ripe for Reform," *Washington Post*, Feb. 11, 1997, A19.
75. Cindy Skrzycki, "The Regulators," *Washington Post*, Jan. 8, 1999, F7. See also *CQ Monitor*, March 25, 1996, 7.
76. Michael W. Kirst, *Government without Passing Laws* (Chapel Hill: University of North Carolina Press, 1969).
77. Joseph A. Davis, "War Declared over Report-Language Issue," *Congressional Quarterly Weekly Report*, June 25, 1988, 1752–1753; and David Rapp, "OMB's Miller Backs Away from Report-Language Battle," *Congressional Quarterly Weekly Report*, July 9, 1988, 1928.
78. "The Inspector General Act: Twenty Years Later," Hearing before the Senate Governmental Affairs Committee, Sept. 9, 1998, 32. See also Paul Light, *Monitoring Government: Inspectors General and the Search for Accountability* (Washington, D.C.: Brookings Institution, 1993).
79. Slade Gorton and Larry Craig, "Congress's Call to Accounting," *Washington Post*, July 27, 1998, A23.
80. U.S. Congress, *Congressional Record*, daily ed., 95th Cong., 1st sess., April 30, 1975, F2080.
81. One of the three federal judges impeached during the 1980s, Alcee L. Hastings, was elected in November 1992 as a Democrat to the U.S. House of Representatives from Florida. David Huckabee, "Impeachment: Days and Dates of Consideration in the House and Senate," *Congressional Research Service Report*, Jan. 13, 1999, 1.
82. See Joel D. Aberbach, *Keeping a Watchful Eye: The Politics of Congressional Oversight* (Washington, D.C.: Brookings Institution, 1990); and James Q. Wilson, *Bureaucracy: What Governmental Agencies Do and Why They Do It* (New York: Basic Books, 1991).
83. Richard Cohen, "King of Oversight," *Government Executive*, September 1988, 17.
84. Paul Bedard, "White House Fumes at Probes," *Washington Times*, April 7, 1995, A1. See also Charles Tiefer, "Congressional Oversight of the Clinton Administration and Congressional Procedure," *Administrative Law Review* (winter 1998): 199–216; Robert Weissman, "Hearings Loss: Oversight in the Republican Congress," *American Prospect* (November–December 1998): 50–55; and William West, "Oversight Subcommittees in the House of Representatives," *Congress and the Presidency* (autumn 1998): 147–160.
85. Stephen Barr, "GOP Seeking More Control of Programs and Spending," *Washington Post*, Feb. 5, 1997, A25. See also Beryl Radin, "Searching for Performance: The Government Performance and Results Act," *PS*, Sept. 1998, 553–555.

86. Jennifer Kabbany, "Armey Targets Waste in Federal Agencies," *Washington Times*, Feb. 12, 1999, A6.

87. Joel D. Aberbach, "The Congressional Committee Intelligence System: Information, Oversight, and Change," *Congress and the Presidency* 14 (spring 1987): 51–76; and Mathew McCubbins and Thomas Schwartz, "Congressional Oversight Overlooked: Police Patrol Versus Fire Alarm," *American Journal of Political Science* (February 1984): 165–177.

88. Louis Fisher, "Micromanagement by Congress: Reality and Mythology" (paper presented at a conference sponsored by the American Enterprise Institute, Washington, D.C., April 8–9, 1988), 8. See also David S. Broder and Stephen Barr, "Hill's Micromanagement of Cabinet Blurs Separation of Powers," *Washington Post*, July 25, 1993, A1.

89. Joan Biskupic, "Rehnquist Asks Congress to Clear Judiciary Funding," *Washington Post*, March 31, 1999, A27.

90. "Rehnquist: Is Federalism Dead?" *Legal Times*, May 18, 1998, 12.

91. See Lawrence Baum, *The Supreme Court*, 6th ed. (Washington, D.C.: CQ Press, 1998).

92. Linda Greenhouse, "High Court Faces Moment of Truth in Federalism Cases," *New York Times*, March 28, 1999, 23.

93. Quoted in Louis Fisher, *American Constitutional Law*, 3d ed. (Durham, N.C.: Carolina Academic Press, 1999), 392–393.

94. See Robert A. Katzman, ed., *Judges and Legislators* (Washington, D.C.: Brookings Institution, 1988). See also Robert A. Katzman, *Courts and Congress* (Washington, D.C.: Brookings Institution, 1997).

95. *New York Times*, May 12, 1983, B8.

96. Charles Rothfeld, "Judging Law: Never Mind What Congress Meant," *New York Times*, April 14, 1989, B8.

97. Antonin Scalia, *A Matter of Interpretation* (Princeton: Princeton University Press, 1997).

98. Ruth Marcus, "Lawmakers Overrule High Court," *Washington Post*, Oct. 31, 1991, A1.

99. U.S. Congress, *Congressional Record*, daily ed., 102d Cong., 1st sess., Oct. 29, 1991, S15324–15325.

100. Joan Biskupic, "Scalia Sees No Justice in Trying to Judge Intent of Congress on a Law," *Washington Post*, May 11, 1993, A4.

101. Dan Carney, "Indicting the Courts: Congress' Feud with Judges," *CQ Weekly*, June 20, 1998, 1659–1666.

102. U.S. Congress, *Congressional Record*, daily ed., 106th Cong., 1st sess., Jan. 19, 1999, S702.

103. See Louis Fisher, "Congressional Checks on the Judiciary," Congressional Research Service Report 97-497, April 29, 1997.

104. U.S. Congress, *Congressional Record*, daily ed., 105th Cong., 1st sess., Sept. 24, 1998, S10923.

105. Naftali Bendavid and Bruce Brown, "Senators Step Up Scrutiny of Judiciary," *Legal Times*, Oct. 23, 1995, 1.

Chapter 12 (pages 335–353)

1. Stephen Labaton, "House Panel Starts Work on Bank Bill," *New York Times*, May 22, 1991, D3.

2. Francis Clines, "Among the Not So Well Heeled of Gucci Gulch," *New York Times*, June 22, 1997, A28.

3. Mary Lynn Jones, "D.C. Lobbying Is a $1.2 Billion Industry," *The Hill*, Dec. 9, 1998, 5.

4. Alexis de Tocqueville, *Democracy in America*, ed. Phillips Bradley (New York: Knopf, 1951), 119. See also Richard A. Smith, "Interest Group Influence in the U.S. Congress," *Legislative Studies Quarterly* 20 (February 1995): 89–139.

5. Robert D. Putnam, "The Strange Disappearance of Civic America," *American Prospect* (winter 1996): 35.

6. Roy Rivenburg, "There Is No Such Thing as the Odd Man Out," *Los Angeles Times*, Oct. 1, 1997, B9.

7. Janny Scott, "Medicine's Big Dose of Politics," *Los Angeles Times*, Sept. 25, 1991, A15.

8. Andrea Petersen, "Episodic Illnesses: How Rare Ailments Get on Prime Time," *Wall Street Journal*, April 14, 1998, A1.

9. Putnam, "The Strange Disappearance of Civic America."

10. Suzi Parker, "Civic Clubs: Elks, Lions May Go Way of the Dodo," *Christian Science Monitor*, Aug. 24, 1998, 1.

11. Everett Carll Ladd, "The American Way—Civic Engagement—Thrives," *Christian Science Monitor*, March 1, 1999, 9.

12. Sidney Verba, Kay Lehman Schlozman, and Henry Brady, "The Big Tilt: Participatory Inequality in America," *American Prospect* (May–June 1997): 78.

13. Elise D. Garcia, "Money in Politics," *Common Cause*, February 1981, 11.

14. Jeffrey H. Birnbaum, "Lobbyists: Why the Bad Rap?" *American Enterprise*, November–December 1992, 74. See also Jeffrey H. Birnbaum, *The Lobbyists* (New York: Times Books, 1992).

15. Norman J. Ornstein and Shirley Elder, *Interest Groups, Lobbying and Policymaking* (Washington, D.C.: Congressional Quarterly, 1978), 224.

16. Jeffrey Birnbaum, "The Thursday Group," *Time*, March 27, 1995, 30–31.

17. Jim VandeHei, "DeLay Trying to Protect Majority," *Roll Call*, March 25, 1999, 1.

18. Hedrick Smith, *The Power Game* (New York: Random House, 1988), 232.

19. See, for example, David Ottaway and Dan Morgan, "Former Top U.S. Aides Seek Caspian Gusher," *Washington Post*, July 6, 1997, A1.

20. Ronald J. Hrebenar and Ruth K. Scott, *Interest Group Politics in America* (Englewood Cliffs, N.J.: Prentice-Hall, 1982), 63.

21. Janet Hook, "Ex-Members Have Access, but Not Always Clout," *Congressional Quarterly Weekly Report*, June 18, 1988, 1651–1653.

22. *Wall Street Journal*, Oct. 5, 1987, 54.

23. Thomas Hale Boggs, Jr., "All Interests Are Special," *New York Times*, Feb. 16, 1993, A17.

24. Sam Walker, "Who's In and Who's Out among Capitol Lobbyists," *Christian Science Monitor*, Nov. 8, 1995, 3.

25. *New York Times*, Jan. 20, 1981, B3.

26. Sam Walker, "Gift Ban Shows New Ethics on Hill," *Christian Science Monitor*, Sept. 19, 1995, 1.

27. Bill McAllister, "Free Liquor Still Flows on Capitol Hill," *Washington Post*, Jan. 17, 1999, A6.

28. Carol Matlack, "Getting around the Rules," *National Journal*, May 12, 1990, 1139.

29. Juliet Eilperin, "Paris? Florida? Beijing? Lobbyists Pay the Way," *Roll Call*, Feb. 16, 1998, 1. See also Donna Cassata, "Corporations Pick Up the Tab for Globe-Hopping Members," *Congressional Quarterly Weekly Report*, Dec. 6, 1997, 3032–3035.

30. Sandra Torry, "Tobacco's Influence Takes Flight in GOP," *Washington Post*, July 20, 1998, A1.

31. Jim Drinkard, "Lobbying at 30,000 Feet," *USA Today*, April 16, 1998, 2A.

32. Nancy E. Roman, "Who Should Pick Up Travel Tab?" *Washington Times*, March 31, 1997, A10. See also Tyler Marshall, "As 'Junket' Becomes Dirty Word, Congress Loses Overseas Interest," *Los Angeles Times*, Feb. 10, 1997, A8.

33. Leslie Wayne, "A Special Deal for Lobbyists: A Getaway with Lawmakers," *New York Times*, Jan. 26, 1997, 1.

34. Al Kamen, "PAC-ed on the Slippery Slopes," *Washington Post*, Jan. 17, 1997, A19.

35. Ernest Wittenberg, "How Lobbying Helps Make Democracy Work," *Vital Speeches of the Day*, Nov. 1, 1982, 47.

36. Jacob Schlesinger, "Kasich Prepares Attack on 'Corporate Welfare,' " *Wall Street Journal*, Jan. 17, 1997, A14.

37. Eric Schmitt, "How a Fierce Backlash Saved the 'Made in U.S.A.' Label," *New York Times*, Dec. 6, 1997, A1.

38. *Washington Star*, Dec. 31, 1980, C2.

39. John T. Tierney and Kay Lehman Schlozman, "Congress and Organized Interests," in *Congressional Politics*, ed. Christopher J. Deering (Chicago: Dorsey, 1989), 212.

40. Scott Shepard, "'Grass-roots' or 'Astroturf'?" *Washington Times*, Dec. 20, 1994, A2.

41. Juliet Eilperin, "Police Track Down Telecom Telegraphs," *Roll Call*, Aug. 7, 1995, 1.

42. Alison Mitchell, "A New Form of Lobbying Puts Public Face on Private Interest," *New York Times*, Sept. 30, 1998, A14. See also Ken Kollman, *Outside Lobbying: Public Opinion and Interest Group Strategies* (Princeton: Princeton University Press, 1998).

43. Sara Fritz and Dan Morain, "Stealth Lobby Drives Fuel-Additive War," *Los Angeles Times*, June 16, 1997, A6.

44. *New York Times*, Jan. 24, 1980, A16.

45. *The Economist*, June 17, 1995, 22.

46. Mitchell, "A New Form of Lobbying."

47. Craig Karmin, " 'Third Wave' Lobbyists Battle On-line over Smut Ban Proposal," *The Hill*, Dec. 20, 1995, 7.

48. "Trends in Grassroots Lobbying: Consultant Q&A," *Campaigns and Elections*, February 1999, 22.

49. Mary Lynn Jones, "How to Lobby from Home or Office," *The Hill*, Jan. 7, 1998, 7, and " 'Billion Byte March' Trips over E-mail Surge from Trial," *CQ Monitor*, Jan. 20, 1999, 1.

50. U.S. Congress, *Congressional Record*, daily ed., 105th Cong., 2d sess., March 16, 1998, S2000. See also Mary Lynn Jones, "On K Street, It's Increasingly WWW. Lobbyist.Com," *The Hill*, May 13, 1998, 11.

51. Ethan Wallison, "Jackson Spins Web to Make His Point," *Roll Call*, March 25, 1999, 1.

52. Alice Love, "Small Business Group Helps Grow Its Own Grassroots Candidates at Meeting Next Week," *Roll Call*, Oct. 16, 1995, 22.

53. Philip M. Stern, "The Tin Cup Congress," *Washington Monthly*, May 1988, 24.

54. U.S. Congress, *Congressional Record*, daily ed., 100th Cong., 1st sess., Aug. 5, 1987, S11292.

55. "Fundamentals of Fund-raising," *Washington Post*, Dec. 5, 1990, A23.
56. *Inside the New Congress*, newsletter, Washington, D.C., Feb. 26, 1999, 8.
57. Jeanne Cummings, "Candidates Learn to Defuse Outside Groups' Attack Ads," *Wall Street Journal*, July 20, 1998, A20.
58. Sarah Pekkanen, "How Lobbyists Are Changing the Lobbying Game," *The Hill*, Feb. 12, 1997, 21.
59. "Congress Daily/P.M.," *National Journal*, May 30, 1997, 6.
60. Eric Pianin, "How Business Found Benefits in Wage Bill," *Washington Post*, Feb. 11, 1997, A8.
61. Leslie Wayne, "Lobbyists' Gift to Politicians Reap Benefits, Study Shows," *New York Times*, Jan. 23, 1997, B11.
62. Jim Drinkard, "Report: Interests are Running Congress," *USA Today*, Sept. 10, 1998, 7A.
63. Kirk Victor, "Making a Leap in Logic," *National Journal*, July 16, 1988, 1904.
64. Claudia Dreifus, "And Then There Was Frank," *New York Times Magazine*, Feb. 4, 1996, 25.
65. Don Van Natta Jr., "$250,000 Buys Donors 'Best Access to Congress,' " *New York Times*, Jan. 27, 1997, A1.
66. *Roll Call*, June 19, 1988, 12. See also Brooks Jackson, *Honest Graft: Big Money and the American Political Process* (New York: Knopf, 1988).
67. John Brinkley, "Members of Congress Perform under Judging Eyes of Lobbyists," *Washington Times*, March 16, 1994, A16.
68. Bill Whalen, "Rating Lawmakers' Politics by Looking into Their Eyes," *Insight*, Oct. 20, 1986, 21.
69. *New York Times*, May 13, 1986, A24.
70. *CQ Monitor*, April 13, 1998, 4.
71. U.S. Congress, *Oversight of the 1946 Federal Regulation of Lobbying Act*, Hearings before the Senate Committee on Governmental Affairs, 98th Cong., 1st sess., Nov. 15 and 16, 1983, 228.
72. Kirk Victor, "New Kids on the Block," *National Journal*, Oct. 31, 1987, 2727.
73. Mary Lynn Jones, "Survey Says Lobbyists Find Information Rules the Hill," *The Hill*, Nov. 18, 1998, 8. See also Allan J. Cigler and Burdett Loomis, *Interest Group Politics*, 5th ed. (Washington, D.C.: CQ Press, 1998.)
74. Mary Lynn Jones, "Panel Assignments Bring Respect, Dollars," *The Hill*, Feb. 10, 1999, 10.
75. Scott, "Medicine's Big Dose of Politics," A12.
76. Bob Pool, "Survivors Take Stock of Gains against Cancer," *Los Angeles Times*, May 30, 1997, B1.
77. *New York Times*, May 31, 1985, D16.
78. *Roll Call*, March 19, 1998, 1.
79. Nina Bernstein, "Deletion of Word in Welfare Bill Opens Foster Care to Big Business," *New York Times*, May 4, 1997, 1.
80. *CQ Monitor*, Jan. 26, 1998, 3.
81. Elizabeth Drew, "A Reporter at Large, Jesse Helms," *New Yorker*, July 20, 1981, 80.
82. For a detailed listing of the informal congressional groups active in the 105th Congress, see *Congressional Yellow Book*, spring 1997 (Washington, D.C.: Leadership Directories, 1997), sect. VI.
83. *Washington Star*, May 22, 1978, A1.
84. U.S. Congress, *Congressional Record*, daily ed., 96th Cong., 1st sess., April 3, 1979, 7065.

85. JoAnn Kelly, "Rural Members Lead Internet Drive," *The Hill*, Feb. 3, 1999, 10.

86. U.S. Congress, *Organization of the Congress*, House Rept. 1675, 79th Cong., 2d sess., 1946, 26.

87. Francesca Contiguaglia, "GAO Finds That Lobbyist Registration Has Soared," *Roll Call*, May 14, 1998, 14.

88. Sam Fulwood, "Lobbying Reform Passes House on Unanimous Vote," *Los Angeles Times*, Nov. 30, 1995, A9.

89. Eierdre Shesgreen, "Shining a Dim Light," *Legal Times*, Dec. 21 and 28, 1998, 26, 27.

90. Robert Schlesinger, "Foreign Interests Spent $43M Lobbying U.S.," *The Hill*, April 22, 1998, 4.

91. Steven Erlanger, "For Forty-Seven Years, a Lobby with Muscle Has Tirelessly Tended U.S.-Israeli Ties," *New York Times*, April 26, 1998, 6.

92. Katharine Seelye, "National Rifle Association Is Turning to World Stage to Fight Gun Control," *New York Times*, April 2, 1997, A12.

93. See Adam Hochschild, "Into the Light from the Heart of Darkness," *Los Angeles Times*, Dec. 6, 1998, M1.

94. Steven Pearlstein and John Mintz, "Too Big to Fly?" *Washington Post*, May 4, 1997, H7.

95. Sara Fritz, "Big Firms Plant Seeds of 'Grass-roots' China Lobby," *Los Angeles Times*, May 12, 1997, A8.

96. Edgar Lane, *Lobbying and the Law* (Berkeley: University of California Press, 1964), 18.

Chapter 13 (pages 355–379)

1. Susan Page and William Welch, "Departure of the Deficit Heralds Politics of Plenty," *USA Today*, Jan. 21, 1999, 2A.

2. Lawrence Goodrich, "A Season of Stalemate on Hill," *Christian Science Monitor*, June 30, 1998, 10.

3. See David Easton, *The Political System* (New York: Knopf, 1963); Harold D. Lasswell, *Politics: Who Gets What, When, How* (New York: Meridian Books, 1958); and Randall B. Ripley and Grace A. Franklin, *Congress, the Bureaucracy, and Public Policy*, 5th ed. (Pacific Grove, Calif.: Brooks/Cole, 1991).

4. Theodore R. Marmor, *The Politics of Medicare* (Chicago: Aldine Publishing, 1973).

5. John W. Kingdon, *Agendas, Alternatives, and Public Policies* (Boston: Little, Brown, 1984), 3.

6. Ibid., 17–19.

7. Ibid., chap. 2.

8. Nelson W. Polsby, "Strengthening Congress in National Policymaking," *Yale Review* (summer 1970): 481–497.

9. James L. Sundquist, *Politics and Policy: The Eisenhower, Kennedy, and Johnson Years* (Washington, D.C.: Brookings Institution, 1968).

10. Elizabeth Wehr, "Numerous Factors Favoring Good Relationship between Reagan and New Congress," *Congressional Quarterly Weekly Report*, Jan. 24, 1981, 173.

11. Kingdon, *Agendas*, 148–149.

12. American Enterprise Institute, *The State of the Congress: Tomorrow's Challenges?* (Washington, D.C.: AEI, 1981), 8.

13. Theodore Lowi, "American Business, Public Policy, Case Studies, and Political Theory," *World Politics* (July 1964): 677–715; Lowi, "Four Systems of Policy, Pol-

itics and Choice," *Public Administration Review* (July-August 1972): 298–310; Samuel P. Huntington, *The Common Defense* (New York: Columbia University Press, 1961); and Ripley and Franklin, *Congress, the Bureaucracy, and Public Policy.*

14. *Wall Street Journal*, May 13, 1988, 17R.

15. Mary Russell, " 'Park-Barrel Bill' Clears House Panel," *Washington Post,* June 22, 1978, A3.

16. Ben Wildavsky, "Pigging Out," *National Journal,* April 19, 1997, 755.

17. Lewis Lord, "Grand Old Pork," *U.S. News and World Report,* March 23, 1998, 7.

18. Edwin Chen, "Senate Fattens Its 'Ice Tea' with Porky Politics," *Los Angeles Times,* March 10, 1998, A6.

19. Ricardo Alonso-Zaldivar, "Frustrated Air Travelers May Get 'Bill of Rights,' " *Los Angeles Times,* March 11, 1999, A3.

20. See, for example, Margaret Kriz, "Heavy Breathing," *National Journal,* Jan. 4, 1997, 8–12.

21. Joby Warrick, "White House Taking a Hands-on Role in Writing New Clean Air Standards," *Washington Post,* May 22, 1997, A10.

22. Brad Knickerbocker, "Why the GOP Changed Little in Environment," *Christian Science Monitor,* Jan. 2, 1996, 18.

23. Marmor, *The Politics of Medicare,* 108–109.

24. Lewis A. Froman Jr., *Congressmen and Their Constituencies* (Chicago: Rand McNally, 1963).

25. Benjamin I. Page, "Cooling the Legislative Tea," in *American Politics and Public Policy,* ed. Walter Dean Burnham and Martha Wagner Weinberg (Cambridge: MIT Press, 1978), 171–187.

26. Judy Sarasohn, "Money for Lat. 40 N, Long. 73 W," *Congressional Quarterly Weekly Report,* May 12, 1979, 916.

27. Paula Drummond, "Unfunded Mandates Bill Becomes Law," *Kansas Government Journal,* May 1995, 122.

28. Judy Keen, "States a Testing Ground for Campaign Finance Reform," *USA Today,* May 2, 1997, 1A.

29. "Don't Just Do Something, Sit There," *Economist,* Dec. 23, 1995–Jan. 5, 1996, 11–12.

30. Barber Conable, "Government Is Working," *Roll Call,* April 19, 1984, 3. To be sure, there are many instances when Congress has initiated change. A classic example is the 37th Congress (1861–1863), which drafted "the blueprint for modern America" by enacting measures to finance the Civil War, build the transcontinental railroad, eradicate slavery, promote the land-grant college movement, provide settlers with homesteaded land, and create the Department of Agriculture. See James M. McPherson, *Battle Cry of Freedom: The Civil War Era* (New York: Ballantine, 1988), 452.

31. Robert Luce, *Legislative Problems* (Boston: Houghton Mifflin, 1935), 426. See also Louis Fisher, "The Authorization-Appropriation Process in Congress: Formal Rules and Informal Practices," *Catholic University Law Review* (fall 1979): 51–105; and Richard F. Fenno Jr., *The Power of the Purse* (Boston: Little, Brown, 1966).

32. See Louis Fisher, "Annual Authorizations: Durable Roadblocks to Biennial Budgeting," *Public Budgeting and Finance* (spring 1983): 23–40.

33. William Schneider, "A New GOP Track: Bang, Bang, Kiss, Kiss," *National Journal,* Feb. 15, 1997, 356.

34. Janet Hook, "Political Fight Endangers Disaster Aid," *Los Angeles Times,* May 1, 1997, A4.

35. Erik Eckholm, "Payments to the Retired Loom Ever Larger," *New York Times*, Aug. 30, 1992, E1, E4.
36. Jason DeParle, "U.S. Welfare System Dies as State Programs Emerge," *New York Times*, June 30, 1997, A1.
37. Robert Rosenblatt, "Medicare Panel Fails to Adopt Plan to Rescue System," *Los Angeles Times*, March 17, 1999, A1.
38. John W. Ellwood, "Budget Control in a Redistributive Environment," in *Making Economic Policy in Congress*, ed. Allen Schick (Washington, D.C.: American Enterprise Institute, 1983), 93.
39. George Hager, "A Process Packed with Power," *Congressional Quarterly Weekly Report*, June 5, 1993, 1414.
40. Richard Sammon, "1998: The Year the Budget Resolution Died?" *CQ Weekly*, Oct. 29, 1998, 21.
41. Quoted in Jonathan Rauch, "The Politics of Joy," *National Journal*, Jan. 17, 1987, 130. See also Jonathan Rauch, "Is the Deficit Really So Bad?" *Atlantic Monthly*, February 1989, 36–42.
42. *CQ's Congressional Monitor*, Jan. 8, 1996, 1.
43. Ann Devroy, "Bills Signed to Fully Reopen Government," *Washington Post*, Jan. 7, 1996, A6.
44. Eric Pianin and John F. Harris, "President, GOP Agree on Balanced Budget Plan," *Washington Post*, May 3, 1997, A1.
45. David Sanger, "A Booming Economy Made It All Much Easier," *New York Times*, May 2, 1997, A21. See also Jackie Calmes and Greg Hitt, "As Deficit Shrinks, Clinton and GOP Make Plans to Spend Budget Surpluses," *Wall Street Journal*, July 10, 1997, A2.
46. U.S. Congress, *Congressional Record*, daily ed., 105th Cong., 2d sess., Oct. 2, 1998, S11321.
47. Alexis Simendinger and David Bauman, "Let the Good Times Roll," *National Journal*, Jan. 30, 1999, 248.
48. Elizabeth Shogren and Janet Hook, "Clinton Hails First Fiscal Year in Surplus in Three Decades," *Los Angeles Times*, Oct. 1, 1998, A1.
49. Stephen Moore, "Supply Side Not 'Voodoo' after All," *Los Angeles Times*, Oct. 1, 1998, A11.
50. Shogren and Hook, "Clinton Hails First Fiscal Year Surplus," A7.
51. U.S. Congress, *Congressional Record*, daily ed., 105th Cong., 2d sess., Sept. 2, 1998, S9888.
52. Andrew Taylor, "Members Struggle with the Nuances of Social Security and the Surplus," *CQ Weekly*, Feb. 6, 1999, 294.
53. Richard Stevenson, "Red Ink No More," *New York Times*, Oct. 1, 1998, C23.
54. Matthew Miller, "It's Party Time," *U.S. News and World Report*, Jan. 12, 1998, 20.
55. See, for example, Andrew Taylor, "Clinton's Strength Portends a Tough Season for GOP," *CQ Weekly*, Feb. 6, 1999, 290–295; Richard Stevenson, "The Surplus," *New York Times*, Jan. 21, 1999, A19; and Eric Pianin and George Hager, "With Black Ink, Clinton Draws a Line," *Washington Post*, Jan. 21, 1999, A6.
56. William Welch, "GOP Budget Outline Promises Big Tax Cuts," *USA Today*, March 24, 1999, 12A.
57. Alexis Simendinger and David Baumann, "Tax Cut Conundrum," *National Journal*, April 10, 1999, 931.
58. Richard Stevenson, "Spending on Balkans Opens Door to Other Tests of Budget's Limits," *New York Times*, April 24, 1999, A14.

59. National Journal's *Congress Daily*, April 20, 1999, 3.
60. Alison Mitchell, "Republicans Seize the Banner on Social Security," *New York Times*, April 16, 1999, A18.
61. George Hager, "GOP Budget Plan, Spending Caps to Collide, Panel Chairmen Warn," *Washington Post*, March 10, 1999, A4.
62. Ibid.
63. National Journal's *Congress Daily*, Dec. 8, 1998, 5.
64. Sen. Bob Graham, "We Must Stop 'Emergency' Raids on Budget Surplus," *Roll Call*, Jan. 18, 1999, A4.
65. John Godfrey, "Lawmakers Plan to Pay for War Tab as an Emergency," *Washington Times*, April 16, 1999, A8.
66. Jacob Schlesinger, "Senate Leaders Call for Easing of Rules Limiting Tax Cuts and Spending Increases," *Wall Street Journal*, Dec. 7, 1998, A3.
67. U.S. Congress, *Congressional Record*, daily ed., 106th Cong., 1st sess., Feb. 11, 1999, S1439.
68. U.S. Congress, *Congressional Record*, daily ed., 106th Cong., 1st sess., March 24, 1999, S3165.
69. *New York Times*, Feb. 11, 1988, A20.

Chapter 14 (pages 381–404)

1. E. J. Dionne Jr., "No Rush to Judgment for the Uncommitted," *Washington Post*, Jan. 11, 1991, A22.
2. Stephen Earl Bennett, "The Persian Gulf War's Impact on Americans' Political Information" (paper presented at the National Election Study's Conference on the Political Consequences of War, Washington, D.C., Feb. 28, 1992), cited in Stephen Earl Bennett and Linda L. M. Bennett, "Out of Sight, Out of Mind: Americans' Knowledge of Party Control of the House of Representatives, 1960–1984," *Political Research Quarterly* 46 (March 1993): 69.
3. Edward S. Corwin, *The President: Office and Powers, 1787–1957*, 4th ed. (New York: New York University Press, 1957), 171. See also Cecil V. Crabb Jr. and Pat M. Holt, *Invitation to Struggle: Congress, the President, and Foreign Policy*, 4th ed. (Washington, D.C.: CQ Press, 1992).
4. Corwin, *The President*, 171.
5. U.S. Congress, *Annals of Congress*, 6th Cong., 1800, 613.
6. *United States v. Curtiss-Wright Export Corp.*, 299 U.S. 304 (1936).
7. *Youngstown Sheet and Tube Co. v. Sawyer*, 343 U.S. 636 (1952).
8. John Jay, *The Federalist*, No. 64, ed. Edward Mead Earle (New York: Modern Library, n.d.), 420.
9. Quoted in David Baumann, "A Spending Bonanza, Thanks to Kosovo," *National Journal*, April 24, 1999, 1110.
10. Tim Smart, "Getting the F-22 Off the Ground," *Washington Post*, April 20, 1998, 12.
11. Melissa Healy, "The Stubborn Osprey Flies On," *Los Angeles Times*, Nov. 29, 1990, A1.
12. "Military 'Pork Barrel' Wastes Billions a Year, Official Says," *New York Times*, April 1, 1985, A17.
13. Quoted in Kevin Sack, "For the South, GOP Secures Defense Bounty," *New York Times*, Nov. 18, 1997, A1.
14. Helen Dewar and Kevin Merida, "When Defense Cuts Hit Home," *Washington Post*, March 22, 1993, A1.

15. Karl Viox, "It's Closing Time for Base Commission," *Washington Post,* Dec. 29, 1995, A21. Scholars regard this as an intriguing example of blame-avoidance politics. See, for example, Christopher J. Deering, "Congress, the President, and Automatic Government: The Case of Military Base Closures," in *Rivals for Power: Presidential-Congressional Relations,* ed. James A. Thurber (Washington, D.C.: CQ Press, 1996).

16. Rep. Joel Hefley, "Base Closings? 'Over My Dead Body,' " *The Hill,* May 2, 1997, 24.

17. Quoted in Robert Schlesinger, "Defense Downsizing Also Impacts Hill Committees," *The Hill,* May 21, 1997, 17.

18. I. M. Destler, *Making Foreign Economic Policy* (Washington, D.C.: Brookings Institution, 1980), 204ff.

19. Vladimir Pregelj, *Fast-Track Implementation of Trade Agreements: History, Status, and Other Options,* Congressional Research Service Report, No. 97-41E, Dec. 27, 1996.

20. Quoted in David E. Sanger, "Trade Fight Was Battle of Perception against Analysis," *New York Times,* Nov. 16, 1997, 26.

21. U.S. Congress, *Congressional Record,* daily ed., 102d Cong., 2d sess., Aug. 6, 1992, H7701–7703.

22. Keith Bradsher, "NAFTA: Something to Offend Everyone," *New York Times,* Nov. 14, 1993. See also I. M. Destler, "Protecting Congress or Protecting Trade?" *Foreign Policy* 62 (spring 1986): 96–107.

23. Charles McC. Mathias Jr., "Ethnic Groups and Foreign Policy," *Foreign Affairs* 59 (summer 1981): 975–998.

24. Christopher J. Deering, "Congress, the President, and Military Policy," *Annals of the American Academy of Political and Social Science* 499 (September 1988): 143ff.

25. Deborah Shapley, "A Few Too Many Men," *Washington Post,* March 7, 1993, C1.

26. Thomas W. Lippman and Peter Baker, "Bipartisanship, but at a Price," *Washington Post,* April 25, 1997, A1.

27. Loch Johnson and James M. McCormick, "Foreign Policy by Executive Fiat," *Foreign Policy* 28 (fall 1977): 118–124.

28. Peter Grier, "Why 48 Treaties Languish in the Senate," *Christian Science Monitor,* March 20, 1997, 3.

29. Ellen C. Collier, *Congress and Foreign Policymaking,* Congressional Research Service Report, No. 90-627F, Dec. 12, 1990, 3.

30. This section draws upon the invaluable summary of congressional policy initiation in Ellen C. Collier, *Foreign Policy Roles of the President and Congress,* Congressional Research Service Report, No. 93-20F, Jan. 6, 1993, 11–17.

31. The classic account of this incident is Chalmers M. Roberts, "The Day We Didn't Go to War," *The Reporter,* Sept. 14, 1954, 31–35.

32. Alison Mitchell, "In Vote Clinton Sought to Avoid, House Backs a Force for Kosovo," *New York Times,* March 12, 1999, A1.

33. Ellen C. Collier, "Foreign Policy by Reporting Requirement," *Washington Quarterly* 11 (winter 1988): 75.

34. James M. Lindsay, "Congress, Foreign Policy, and the New Institutionalism," *International Studies Quarterly* 38 (June 1994): 281–304.

35. Steven Lee Myers, "State Dept. Set for Reshaping, Pleasing Helms," *New York Times,* April 18, 1997, A1.

36. An early, influential analysis of this phenomenon is John E. Mueller, *War, Presidents, and Public Opinion* (New York: Wiley, 1973), 208–213.

37. Richard F. Grimmett, *Instances of Use of United States Armed Forces Abroad*, Congressional Research Service Report, No. 98-881F, Oct. 27, 1998.

38. Harold M. Hyman, *Quiet Past and Stormy Present: War Powers in American History* (Washington, D.C.: American Historical Association Bicentennial Essays on the Constitution, 1986).

39. Quotes from Helen Dewar, "Congress's Reaction to TV Coverage Shows Ambivalence on Foreign Policy," *Washington Post*, Oct. 9, 1993, A14; and Dewar, "Clinton, Congress at Brink of Foreign Policy Dispute," *Washington Post*, May 16, 1994, A1.

40. Richard F. Grimmett, *War Powers Resolution: Presidential Compliance*, Congressional Research Service Issue Brief 81050, April 12, 1999.

41. Ellen C. Collier, *The War Powers Resolution: Twenty Years of Experience*, Congressional Research Service Report, No. 94-42F, Jan. 1, 1994, 31.

42. Jane Perlez, "Step by Step: How the U.S. Decided to Attack, and Why the Move Came So Fast," *New York Times*, March 26, 1999, A9.

43. Quoted in Alison Mitchell, "Deadlocked House Denies Support for Air Campaign," *New York Times*, April 30, 1999, A1.

44. Quotes from Gabriel Kahn, "House Saves Its War Power," *Roll Call*, June 8, 1995, 21.

45. Christopher J. Deering and Steven S. Smith, *Committees in Congress*, 3d ed. (Washington, D.C.: CQ Press, 1997), 92.

46. Quoted in Dewar, "Clinton, Congress at Brink," A10.

47. Holbert N. Carroll, *The House of Representatives and Foreign Affairs*, rev. ed. (Boston: Little, Brown, 1966), 20.

48. Quoted in *Washington Post*, Jan. 11, 1989, A19.

49. *Miller Center Reports*, Newsletter of the White Burkett Miller Center of Public Affairs, University of Virginia, Winter 1986, 1.

50. Frans R. Bax, "The Legislative-Executive Relationship in Foreign Policy. New Partnership or New Competition?" *Orbis* 20 (winter 1977): 881–904.

51. Aaron Wildavsky, "The Two Presidencies," in *The Presidency*, ed. Aaron Wildavsky (Boston: Little, Brown, 1969), 230.

52. I. M. Destler, "Dateline Washington: Congress as Boss?" *Foreign Policy* 42 (spring 1981): 167–180.

53. U.S. Congress, *Report of the Congressional Committees Investigating the Iran-Contra Affair*, 100th Cong., 1st sess., 1987, 59.

54. John E. Reilly, *Public Opinion and Foreign Policy* (Chicago: Chicago Council on Foreign Relations, April 25, 1999).

55. Steven Kull and I. M. Destler, *Misreading the Public: The Myth of a New Isolationism* (Washington, D.C.: Brookings Institution, 1999), 204.

56. James M. Lindsay, "Congress and Foreign Policy: Why the Hill Matters," *Political Science Quarterly* 107 (winter 1992–1993): 626–627.

57. Quotes from Lindsay Sobel, "Hill Profile: Sen. Bob Kerrey," *The Hill*, Oct. 29, 1997, 24; and Helen Dewar, "Farming Locally, Thinking Globally," *Washington Post*, April 21, 1998, A1.

Chapter 15 (pages 407–420)

1. Benjamin Ginsberg and Martin Shefter, *Politics by Other Means: The Declining Importance of Elections in America* (New York: Basic Books, 1990).

2. See Charles O. Jones, *The Presidency in a Separated System* (Washington, D.C.: Brookings Institution, 1994).

3. U.S. Congress, *Congressional Record,* daily ed., 105th Cong., 1st sess., May 21, 1997, H3072.
4. Glenn R. Parker and Roger H. Davidson, "Why Do Americans Love Their Congressmen So Much More Than Their Congress?" *Legislative Studies Quarterly* 4 (February 1979): 53–61.
5. Dan Barry, "An Icon Goes to Washington," *New York Times Magazine,* June 22, 1997, 22.
6. Thomas E. Mann, *Unsafe at Any Margin: Interpreting Congressional Elections* (Washington, D.C.: American Enterprise Institute, 1978).
7. Sandy Hume, "Rep. Myers Calls It Quits," *The Hill,* Jan. 10, 1996, 11.
8. William S. Cohen, "Why I Am Leaving," *Washington Post,* Jan. 21, 1996, C7.
9. Richard E. Cohen, "Chaos Still Prevailing over Civility," *National Journal,* July 5, 1997, 1382.
10. Adam Clymer, "Politics and the Dead Art of Compromise," *New York Times,* Oct. 22, 1995, E3.
11. Bob Benenson, "Savvy 'Stars' Making Local TV a Potent Tool," *Congressional Quarterly Weekly Report,* July 18, 1987, 1551–1555.
12. Timothy Cook, *Making Laws and Making News: Media Strategies in the U.S. House of Representatives* (Washington, D.C.: Brookings Institution, 1989), 82–83.
13. Norman J. Ornstein, "Prosecutors Must End Their Big Game Hunt of Politicians," *Roll Call,* April 26, 1993, 16.
14. Quoted in T. R. Goldman, "The Influence Industry's Senior Class," *Legal Times,* June 16, 1997, 4.
15. Ornstein, "Prosecutors," 16.
16. For background on the House "bank," see the debate on H. Res. 393, U.S. Congress, *Congressional Record,* daily ed., 102d Cong., 2nd sess., March 12, 1992, HI225–H1263.
17. Cass R. Sunstein, "Unchecked and Unbalanced," *American Prospect* 38 (May–June 1998): 23.
18. Glenn R. Parker, "Some Themes in Congressional Unpopularity," *American Journal of Political Science* 21 (February 1977): 93–109; Roger H. Davidson, David M. Kovenock, and Michael K. O'Leary, *Congress in Crisis* (North Scituate, Mass.: Duxbury Press, 1966), 59–62.
19. Diane Hollern Harvey, "Who Should Govern? Public Preferences for Congressional and Presidential Power" (Ph.D. diss., University of Maryland, 1998).
20. S. Robert Lichter and David R. Amundson, "Less News Is Worse News," in *Congress, the Press, and the Public,* ed. Thomas E. Mann and Norman J. Ornstein (Washington, D.C.: Brookings Institution, 1994), 131–140.
21. Kimberly Coursen Parker, "How the Press Views Congress," in *Congress, the Press, and the Public,* 161–166.
22. Quoted in Bernard Aronson, "Tired of 'Gotcha' Journalism," *Washington Post,* March 6, 1997, A21.
23. Parker and Davidson, "Why Do Americans Love Their Congressmen So Much More Than Their Congress?"
24. John R. Hibbing and Elizabeth Theiss-Morse, *Congress as Public Enemy* (Cambridge: Cambridge University Press, 1995), 147.
25. Ibid., 158.
26. Thomas Hargrove and Guido Stempel, "Poll Says Americans Suspect Worst of Their Government," *Washington Times,* July 5, 1997, A2.

27. Dan Baltz and Ceci Connolly, "Voters Feeling Remote from Issues in Capital," *Washington Post*, July 10, 1997, A1.
28. Alvin Toffler, "Congress in the Year 2000," *GAO Review*, Fall 1980, 44.
29. "Disappearing Taxes," *Economist*, May 31, 1997, 21.
30. E. J. Dionne, Jr., "All Politics Is Now Global," *Washington Post*, July 13, 1993, A15.
31. "Lessons on Opposition," interview with Barney Frank, *Working Papers Magazine*, May–June 1982, 43.
32. Quoted in Francis X. Clines, "Weary of Political Noise, a Senator Sees a Peaceful Farm in Her Future," *New York Times*, Dec. 3, 1995, 30.
33. Robert J. Samuelson, "Cultural Salami," *National Journal*, Jan. 28, 1984, 175.
34. Jack L. Walker, "The Origins and Maintenance of Interest Groups in America," *American Political Science Review* 77 (June 1983): 390–406. For a more recent review of empirical findings, see Everett C. Ladd, "The Data Just Don't Show Erosion of America's 'Social Capital,'" *Public Perspective* 7 (June–July 1996): 1–22.
35. Toffler, "Congress in the Year 2000," 44.
36. Alan Ehrenhalt, "The Increasing Irrelevance of Congress," American Political Science Association, *Legislative Studies Section Newsletter*, January 1998, 15.
37. Benjamin R. Barber, *Strong Democracy: Participatory Politics for a New Age* (Berkeley: University of California Press, 1984). See also Jane J. Mansbridge, *Beyond Adversary Democracy* (Chicago: University of Chicago Press, 1983).
38. U.S. Congress, Joint Committee on the Organization of Congress, *Hearing*, July 1, 1993 S. Hrg., 103-148. 103d Cong., 1st sess. (Washington, D.C.: U.S. Government Printing Office, 1993), 33.
39. Woodrow Wilson, *Constitutional Government in the United States* (New York: Columbia University Press, 1908), 79–80.

Suggested Readings

This list of suggested readings is not intended to be exhaustive. Journal articles, papers delivered at meetings, doctoral dissertations, and individual essays in books are not included. We have listed those books we feel are most useful and accessible to students. In addition, we have listed Internet addresses that are good sources of information about Congress.

Reference Works

Bacon, Donald C., Roger H. Davidson, and Morton Keller, eds. *Encyclopedia of the United States Congress*. 4 vols. New York: Simon and Schuster, 1995.

Barone, Michael, and Grant Ujifusa, with Richard E. Cohen. *The Almanac of American Politics, 2000*. Washington, D.C.: National Journal, 1999.

Byrd, Robert C. *The Senate, 1789–1989*. 4 vols. Washington, D.C.: U.S. Government Printing Office, 1988–1993.

Congressional Quarterly's Politics in America, 2000. Washington, D.C.: CQ Press, 1999.

Ornstein, Norman J., Thomas E. Mann, and Michael J. Malbin. *Vital Statistics on Congress, 1998–2000*. Washington, D.C.: American Enterprise, 1999.

Internet Addresses

Architect of the Capitol: http://www.aoc.gov
Campaigns and Elections: http://www.camelect.com
Center for Legislative Archives (National Archives): http://www.nara.gov/nara/legislative
Center for Responsive Politics: http://www.crp.org
CNN/*Time* Allpolitics: http://www.allpolitics.com
Congressional Quarterly: http://www.cq.com
C-SPAN: http://www.c-span.org
Democratic National Committee: http://www.democrats.org
Dirksen Center's Congresslink: http://www.congresslink.org
Federal Election Commission: http://www.fec.gov
Federal judiciary: http://www.uscourts.gov *or* http://www.fjc.gov
Federal statistics: http://www.fedstats.gov
Government Printing Office: http://www.access.gpo.gov
Library of Congress: http://www.lcweb.loc.gov *or* http://www.thomas.loc.gov
New York Times: http://www.nytimes.com
Project Vote Smart: http://www.vote-smart.org
Republican National Committee: http://www.rnc.org
Roll Call: http://www.rollcall.com

U.S. House of Representatives: http://www.house.gov *or* http://www.clerkweb.
house.gov
U.S. Senate: http://www.senate.gov
Washington Post: http://www.washingtonpost.com
White House: http://www.whitehouse.gov

Chapter 1   The Two Congresses

Hibbing, John R., and Elizabeth Theiss-Morse. *Congress as Public Enemy.* Cambridge: Cambridge University Press, 1995.

Mayhew, David R. *Congress: The Electoral Connection.* New Haven: Yale University Press, 1974.

Parker, Glenn R. *Characteristics of Congress: Patterns in Congressional Behavior.* Englewood Cliffs, N.J.: Prentice Hall, 1989.

Chapter 2   Evolution of the Modern Congress

Binder, Sarah A. *Minority Rights, Majority Rule. Partisanship and the Development of Congress.* Cambridge: Cambridge University Press, 1997.

Currie, David P. *The Constitution Congress: The Federalist Period, 1789–1801.* Chicago. University of Chicago Press, 1997.

Galloway, George B. *History of the House of Representatives.* Rev ed. Edited by Sidney Wise. New York: Crowell, 1976.

Haynes, George H. *The Senate of the United States: Its History and Practice.* 2 vols. Boston: Houghton Mifflin, 1938.

Josephy, Alvin M., Jr. *On the Hill: A History of the American Congress.* New York: Simon and Schuster, 1980

MacNeil, Neil. *Forge of Democracy: The House of Representatives.* New York: McKay, 1963.

Miller, William Lee *Arguing about Slavery: John Quincy Adams and the Great Battle in the United States Congress.* New York: Vintage, 1998.

Rakove, Jack N. *Original Meanings: Politics and Ideas in the Making of the Constitution.* New York: Vintage, 1997.

Swift, Elaine K. *The Making of an American Senate: Reconstitutive Change in Congress, 1787–1841.* Ann Arbor: University of Michigan Press, 1996.

Young, James S. *The Washington Community, 1800–1828.* New York: Columbia University Press, 1966.

Chapter 3   Going for It: Recruitment Roulette

Ehrenhalt, Alan. *The United States of Ambition.* New York: Random House, 1991.

Fowler, Linda L., and Robert D. McClure. *Political Ambition: Who Decides to Run for Congress.* New Haven: Yale University Press, 1989.

Jacobson, Gary C., and Samuel Kernell. *Strategy and Choice in Congressional Elections.* New Haven: Yale University Press, 1981.

Kazee, Thomas A., ed. *Who Runs for Congress? Ambition, Context, and Candidate Emergence.* Washington, D.C.: Congressional Quarterly, 1994.

Loomis, Burdett. *The New American Politician.* New York: Basic Books, 1988.

Lublin, David. *The Paradox of Representation: Racial Gerrymandering and Minority Interests in Congress*. Princeton: Princeton University Press, 1997.

Magleby, David B., and Candice J. Nelson. *The Money Chase: Congressional Campaign Finance Reform*. Washington, D.C.: Brookings Institution, 1990.

Chapter 4   Making It: The Electoral Game

Alexander, Herbert E. *Financing Politics: Money, Elections, and Political Reform*. 4th ed. Washington, D.C.: CQ Press, 1992.

Cain, Bruce, John Ferejohn, and Morris Fiorina. *The Personal Vote: Constituency Service and Electoral Independence*. Cambridge: Harvard University Press, 1987.

Fenno, Richard F., Jr. *Senators on the Campaign Trail: The Politics of Representation*. Norman: University of Oklahoma Press, 1996.

Herrnson, Paul S. *Congressional Elections: Campaigning at Home and in Washington*. 2d ed. Washington, D.C.: CQ Press, 1998.

Jacobson, Gary C. *The Politics of Congressional Elections*. 4th ed. New York: Longman, 1996.

King, Anthony. *Running Scared: Why Politicians Spend More Time Campaigning than Governing*. New York: Free Press, 1997.

Krasno, Jonathan S. *Challengers, Competition, and Reelection*. New Haven: Yale University Press, 1994.

Thurber, James A., and Candice J. Nelson, eds. *Campaigns and Elections, American Style*. Boulder: Westview Press, 1995.

Westlye, Mark C. *Senate Elections and Campaign Intensity*. Baltimore: Johns Hopkins University Press, 1991.

Chapter 5   Being There: Hill Styles and Home Styles

Baker, Ross K. *Friend and Foe in the U.S. Senate*. New York: Free Press, 1980.

_____. *House and Senate*. 2d ed. New York: Norton, 1995.

Davidson, Roger H. *The Role of the Congressman*. Indianapolis: Bobbs-Merrill, 1969.

Fenno, Richard F., Jr. *Home Style: House Members in Their Districts*. Boston: Little, Brown, 1978.

Fiorina, Morris P. *Congress: Keystone of the Washington Establishment*. 2d ed. New Haven: Yale University Press, 1989.

Hibbing, John R. *Congressional Careers: Contours of Life in the U.S. House of Representatives*. Chapel Hill: University of North Carolina Press, 1991.

Parker, Glenn R. *Homeward Bound: Exploring Changes in Congressional Behavior*. Pittsburgh: University of Pittsburgh Press, 1986.

Price, David E. *The Congressional Experience: A View from the Hill*. Boulder: Westview Press, 1992.

Chapter 6   Leaders and Parties in Congress

Aldrich, John H. *Why Parties? The Origins and Transformation of Party Politics in America*. Chicago: University of Chicago Press, 1995.

Bader, John B. *Taking the Initiative: Leadership Agendas in Congress and the "Contract with America."* Washington, D.C.: Georgetown University Press, 1996.

Baker, Richard A., and Roger H. Davidson, eds. *First Among Equals: Outstanding Senate Leaders of the Twentieth Century*. Washington, D.C.: Congressional Quarterly, 1991.

Cox, Gary W., and Mathew D. McCubbins. *Legislative Leviathan: Party Government in the House*. Berkeley: University of California Press, 1993.

Davidson, Roger H., Susan Webb Hammond, and Raymond W. Smock, eds., *Masters of the House: Congressional Leaders over Two Centuries*. Boulder: Westview Press, 1998.

Peters, Ronald M., Jr. *The American Speakership: The Office in Historical Perspective*. 2d ed. Baltimore: Johns Hopkins University Press, 1997.

Rohde, David W. *Parties and Leaders in the Postreform House*. Chicago: University of Chicago Press, 1991.

Sinclair, Barbara. *Legislators, Leaders, and Lawmaking: The U.S. House of Representatives in the Postreform Era*. Baltimore: Johns Hopkins University Press, 1995.

_____. *Majority Leadership in the U.S. House*. Baltimore: Johns Hopkins University Press, 1983.

_____. *The Transformation of the U.S. Senate*. Baltimore: Johns Hopkins University Press, 1989.

Chapter 7   Committees: Workshops of Congress

Deering, Christopher J., and Steven S. Smith. *Committees in Congress*. 3d ed. Washington, D.C.: CQ Press, 1997.

Evans, C. Lawrence. *Leadership in Committee: A Comparative Analysis of Leadership Behavior in the U.S. Senate*. Ann Arbor: University of Michigan Press, 1991.

Fenno, Richard F., Jr. *Congressmen in Committees*. Boston: Little, Brown, 1973.

Hall, Richard L. *Participation in Congress*. New Haven: Yale University Press, 1996.

King, David C. *Turf Wars: How Congressional Committees Claim Jurisdiction*. Chicago: University of Chicago Press, 1997.

Krehbiel, Keith. *Information and Legislative Organization*. Ann Arbor: University of Michigan Press, 1991.

Maltzman, Forrest. *Competing Principals: Committees, Parties, and the Organization of Congress*. Ann Arbor: University of Michigan Press, 1997.

Wilson, Woodrow. *Congressional Government*. Reprint of 1885 ed. Baltimore: Johns Hopkins University Press, 1981.

Chapter 8   Congressional Rules and Procedures

Binder, Sarah A., and Steven S. Smith. *Politics or Principle? Filibustering in the United States Senate*. Washington, D.C.: Brookings Institution, 1997.

Campbell, Colton C., and Nicol C. Rae, eds. *New Majority or Old Minority? The Impact of the Republicans on Congress*. Lanham, Md.: Rowman and Littlefield, 1999.

Evans, C. Lawrence, and Walter J. Oleszek. *Congress under Fire: Reform Politics and the Republican Majority*. Boston: Houghton Mifflin, 1997.

Krehbiel, Keith. *Pivotal Politics: A Theory of U.S. Lawmaking.* Chicago: University of Chicago Press, 1998.

Longley, Lawrence D., and Walter J. Oleszek. *Bicameral Politics: Conference Committees in Congress.* New Haven: Yale University Press, 1989.

Oleszek, Walter J. *Congressional Procedures and the Policy Process.* 4th ed. Washington, D.C.: CQ Press, 1996.

Sinclair, Barbara. *Unorthodox Lawmaking: New Legislative Processes in the U.S. Congress.* Washington, D.C.: CQ Press, 1997.

Smith, Steven S. *Call to Order: Floor Politics in the House and Senate.* Washington, D.C.: Brookings Institution, 1989.

Chapter 9   Decision Making in Congress

Arnold, R. Douglas. *The Logic of Congressional Action.* New Haven: Yale University Press, 1990.

Baumgartner, Frank, and Bryan D. Jones. *Agendas and Instability in American Politics.* Chicago: University of Chicago Press, 1993.

Edwards, George C. *At the Margins: Presidential Leadership of Congress.* New Haven: Yale University Press, 1989.

Kingdon, John W. *Congressmen's Voting Decisions.* 3d ed. Ann Arbor: University of Michigan Press, 1989.

Poole, Keith T., and Howard Rosenthal. *Congress: A Political-Economic History of Roll Call Voting.* New York: Oxford University Press, 1996.

Chapter 10   Congress and the President

Binkley, Wilfred. *President and Congress.* New York: Knopf, 1947.

Fisher, Louis. *Constitutional Conflicts between Congress and the President.* 4th ed. Lawrence: University Press of Kansas, 1997.

Gilmour, John B. *Strategic Disagreement: Stalemate in American Politics.* Pittsburgh: University of Pittsburgh Press, 1995.

Jones, Charles O. *The Presidency in a Separated System.* Washington, D.C.: Brookings Institution, 1994.

LeLoup, Lance T., and Steven A. Shull. *The President and Congress: Collaboration and Combat in National Policymaking.* Boston: Allyn and Bacon, 1999.

Mayhew, David R. *Divided We Govern: Party Control, Lawmaking, and Investigating, 1946–1990.* New Haven: Yale University Press, 1991.

Peterson, Mark A. *Legislating Together: The White House and Capitol Hill from Eisenhower to Reagan.* Cambridge: Harvard University Press, 1990.

Thurber, James A., ed. *Rivals for Power: Presidential-Congressional Relations.* Washington, D.C.: CQ Press, 1996.

Wayne, Stephen J. *The Legislative Presidency.* New York: Harper, 1978.

Chapter 11   Congress, the Bureaucracy, and the Courts

Aberbach, Joel D. *Keeping a Watchful Eye: The Politics of Congressional Oversight.* Washington, D.C.: Brookings Institution, 1990.

Arnold, R. Douglas. *Congress and the Bureaucracy: A Theory of Influence.* New Haven: Yale University Press, 1979.

Foreman, Christopher J., Jr. *Signals from the Hill: Congressional Oversight and the Challenge of Social Regulation*. New Haven: Yale University Press, 1988.

Katzmann, Robert A. *Courts and Congress*. Washington, D.C.: Brookings Institution, 1997.

Light, Paul C. *The Tides of Reform: Making Government Work, 1945–1995*. New Haven: Yale University Press, 1997.

_____. *The True Size of Government*. Washington, D.C.: Brookings Institution, 1999.

Obstacle Course: The Report of the Twentieth Century Fund Task Force on the Presidential Appointment Process. New York: Twentieth Century Fund, 1996.

Ogul, Morris S. *Congress Oversees the Bureaucracy*. Pittsburgh: University of Pittsburgh Press, 1976.

Chapter 12   Congress and Organized Interests

Biersack, Robert, et al. *After the Revolution: PACs, Lobbies, and the Republican Congress*. Boston: Allyn and Bacon, 1999.

Birnbaum, Jeffrey H., and Alan S. Murray. *Showdown at Gucci Gulch: Lawmakers, Lobbyists, and the Unlikely Triumph of Tax Reform*. New York: Random House, 1987.

Cigler, Allan J., and Burdett A. Loomis, eds. *Interest Group Politics*. 5th ed. Washington, D.C.: CQ Press, 1998.

Rauch, Jonathan. *Demosclerosis: The Silent Killer of American Government*. New York: Times Books, 1994.

Truman, David B. *The Governmental Process, Political Interests, and Public Opinion*. 2d ed. New York: Knopf, 1971.

Chapter 13   Congress, Budgets, and Domestic Policy Making

Cohen, Richard E. *Washington at Work: Back Rooms and Clean Air*. New York: Macmillan, 1992.

Elving, Ronald D. *Conflict and Compromise: How Congress Makes the Law*. New York: Simon and Schuster, 1995.

Kerwin, Cornelius M. *Rulemaking: How Government Agencies Write Laws and Make Policy*. 2d ed. Washington, D.C.: CQ Press, 1999.

Kingdon, John W. *Agendas, Alternatives, and Public Policies*. Boston: Little, Brown, 1984.

Mann, Thomas E., and Norman J. Ornstein, eds. *Intensive Care: How Congress Shapes Health Policy*. Washington, D.C.: Brookings Institution, 1995.

Meyers, Roy T. *Strategic Budgeting*. Ann Arbor: University of Michigan Press, 1996.

Palazzolo, Daniel J. *Done Deal? The Politics of the 1997 Budget Agreement*. Chatham, N.J.: Chatham House, 1999.

Schick, Allen. *The Federal Budget: Politics, Policy, Process*. Washington, D.C.: Brookings Institution, 1995.

Chapter 14   Congress and National Security Policies

Crabb, Cecil V., Jr., and Pat M. Holt. *Invitation to Struggle: Congress, the President, and Foreign Policy*. 4th ed. Washington, D.C.: CQ Press, 1992.

Fisher, Louis. *Presidential War Powers*. Lawrence: University Press of Kansas, 1995.

Hinckley, Barbara. *Less Than Meets the Eye: Foreign Policy Making and the Myth of the Assertive Congress*. Chicago: University of Chicago Press, 1994.

Lindsay, James. *Congress and the Politics of U.S. Foreign Policy*. Baltimore: Johns Hopkins University Press, 1994.

Mann, Thomas E., ed. *A Question of Balance: The President, the Congress, and Foreign Policy*. Washington, D.C.: Brookings Institution, 1990.

Chapter 15   The Two Congresses and the American People

Bessette, Joseph M. *The Mild Voice of Reason: Deliberative Democracy and American National Government*. Chicago: University of Chicago Press, 1994.

Cook, Timothy E. *Making Laws and Making News: Media Strategies in the U.S. House of Representatives*. Washington, D.C.: Brookings Institution, 1989.

Mann, Thomas E., and Norman J. Ornstein, eds. *Congress, the Press, and the Public*. Washington, D.C.: Brookings Institution, 1994.

Thurber, James A., and Roger H. Davidson, eds. *Remaking Congress: Change and Stability in the 1990s*. Washington, D.C.: Congressional Quarterly, 1995.

Index

Index

Congressional Time Line: Nineteenth Century

	1790	1800	1810	1820	1830
Size of House of Representatives	65	142	186	213	242
Size of Senate	26	34	36	48	48

Parties

Federalist Era (1789–1800) — Jeffersonian Era (1800–1828) — Jacksonian Era (1828–1856)

- 1st Congress Antifederalists (1792)
- Congressional Nominating Caucus (1804–1828)
- J. Q. Adams elected (1824)
- Presidential nominating conventions (1832)

Internal

- Congress convenes; Ways and Means Committee (1789)
- Jefferson's *Manual* (1801)
- Procedural rules, standing committees (1790s)
- Speaker Henry Clay (1811)
- Committees control legislation (1820s)
- Unlimited debate in Senate (1828)

Major Court Cases

- Alien and Sedition Acts (1798)
- Judicial review *Marbury v. Madison* (1803)
- *McCulloch v. Maryland* (1819)
- Marshall Court (1801–1835)

Major Laws/ Investigations

- St. Clair Investigation (1792)
- Bill of Rights (1791)
- Slave importation halted (1807)
- Louisiana Purchase (1803)
- Rivers and Harbors Act (1823)
- Missouri Compromise (1820)

Science/ Technology/ Communications

- "National Road" (Wheeling–Cumberland) (1806)
- Lewis and Clark Expedition (1803–1806)
- Rotary printing press (1814)
- Commercial railroads (1830s)
- Telegraph demonstrated (1838)

Wars/ World Events

- Barbary pirates (1801–1805)
- War of 1812 (1812–1814)
- Monroe Doctrine (1823)

Presidents

- Washington (1789–1797)
- Jefferson (1801–1809)
- "Jeffersonians" (Madison; Monroe) (1809–1825)
- Jackson (1829–1837)

1790	1800	1810	1820	1830